DEFINING DOCUMENTS
IN AMERICAN HISTORY

The 1930s (1930-1939)

Editor

Michael Shally-Jensen, PhD

SALEM PRESS
A Division of EBSCO Information Services
Ipswich, Massachusetts

GREY HOUSE PUBLISHING

Copyright ©2014, by Salem Press, A Division of EBSCO Information Services, Inc. and Grey House Publishing, Inc.

All rights reserved. No part of this work may be used or reproduced in any manner whatsoever or transmitted in any form or by any means, electronic or mechanical, including photocopy, recording, or any information storage and retrieval system, without written permission from the copyright owner. For information contact Grey House Publishing/Salem Press, 4919 Route 22, PO Box 56, Amenia, NY 12501

∞ The paper used in these volumes conforms to the American National Standard for Permanence of Paper for Printed Library Materials, Z39.48 1992 (R1997).

Library of Congress Cataloging-in-Publication Data

The 1930s (1930-1939) / editor, Michael Shally-Jensen, PhD. -- [First edition].

   pages ; cm. -- (Defining documents in American history)

Includes bibliographical references and index.
ISBN: 978-1-61925-495-4

   1. United States--History--1919-1933--Sources. 2. United States--History--1933-1945--Sources. 3. United States--Politics and government--1929-1933--Sources. 4. United States--Politics and government--1933-1945--Sources. 5. United States--Social conditions--1918-1932--Sources. 6. United States--Social conditions--1933-1945--Sources. 7. United States--Economic conditions--1918-1945--Sources. 8. Nineteen thirties. I. Shally-Jensen, Michael. II. Title: Nineteen thirties (1930-1939)

E806 .A19 2014
973.91

FIRST PRINTING
PRINTED IN THE UNITED STATES OF AMERICA

DEFINING DOCUMENTS IN AMERICAN HISTORY

The 1930s (1930-1939)

Table of Contents

Publisher's Note ix
Editor's Introduction xi
Contributors xv

SETTING UP THE NEW DEAL

President Roosevelt: Fireside Chat on "The Forgotten Man" 1
FDR on Government's Role in the Economy 5
Herbert Hoover Speaks Against the New Deal 15
Letter From Herbert Hoover to Franklin D. Roosevelt 27
President Roosevelt: Fireside Chat Outlining the New Deal 31
John Maynard Keynes: An Open Letter to President Roosevelt 38
Letter-Report Concerning the Tennessee Valley 45
FDR on Social Security 51
Speech Against the President's "Court Packing" Plan 57
President Roosevelt: Fireside Chat on the Current Recession 66
The Hatch Act 75

UNEMPLOYMENT AND RELIEF

Bumming in California 83
United We Eat—The Phenomenon of Unemployed Leagues 88
Letter From a Dust Bowl Survivor 97
Letter Regarding Assistance to the Poor 100
Memories of the Flint Sit-Down Strike 104
It's a Great Life in the CCC 109
I'd Rather Not Be on Relief 113
What REA Service Means to Our Farm Home 117
My Hopes for the CCC 121

WOMEN, MINORITIES, AND YOUTH

Women on the Breadlines 131
Eleanor Roosevelt: What Ten MiIllion Women Want 134

v

Eleanor Roosevelt on Women and the Vote 140

The Repatriation of Mexicans and Mexican Americans 146

The Hurricane of 1932 in Puerto Rico 149

A New Deal for American Indians. 156

Indians at Work 160

A Negro in the CCC. 170

Letter Regarding the Needs of Puerto Ricans in New York 176

Plea from a Scottsboro Boy 179

Dear Mrs. Roosevelt 182

Our Jobless Youth: A Warning 186

What Does American Democracy Mean to Me?. 194

THE BONUS ARMY

Herbert Hoover to Reed Smoot Regarding the Bonus Loan Bill. 201

Attack on the Bonus Army. 205

Veterans March to Washington 209

FOREIGN POLICY

Henry Stimson to Senator Borah Regarding the Nine-Power Treaty. 217

Criticism of the Neutrality Act 223

Neutrality Act of 1935. 227

Defense of the Neutrality Act 233

Address Delivered by the Secretary of State. 239

Winston Churchill: The Lights are Going Out in Europe 248

Winston Churchill: A Hush Over Europe 254

Charles Lindbergh: Neutrality and War 259

CULTURE, CRIME, AND MORE

The National Anthem Established: The Star Spangled Banner 265

What I Knew About John Dillinger 269

The *Hindenburg* Disaster 275

From the Federal Writers' Project: *Cape Cod Pilot* 278

On *The War of the Worlds* Radio Broadcast 286
Lou Gehrig: Farewell to Baseball 294

APPENDIXES

Chronological List 299
Web Resources 301
Bibliography 303
Index 309

Publisher's Note

Defining Documents in American History series, produced by Salem Press, consists of a collection of essays on important historical documents by a diverse range of writers on a broad range of subjects in American history. *Defining Documents in American History: 1930s* surveys key documents produced from 1930-1939, organized under six broad categories:

- Setting Up the New Deal
- Unemployment and Relief
- Women, Minorities, and Youth
- The Bonus Army
- Foreign Policy
- Culture, Crime, and More

Historical documents provide a compelling view of this unique period of American history. Designed for high school and college students, the aim of the series is to advance historical document studies as an important activity in learning about history.

Essay Format
1930s contains 50 primary source documents – many in their entirety. Each document is supported by a critical essay, written by historians and teachers, that includes a Summary Overview, Defining Moment, Author Biography, Document Analysis, and Essential Themes. Readers will appreciate the diversity of the collected texts, including journals, letters, speeches, political sermons, laws, government reports, and court cases, among other genres. An important feature of each essay is a close reading of the primary source that develops evidence of broader themes, such as author's rhetorical purpose, social or class position, point of view, and other relevant issues. In addition, essays are organized by section themes, listed above, highlighting major issues of the period, many of which extend across eras and continue to shape American life. Each section begins with a brief introduction that defines questions and problems underlying the subjects in the historical documents. A brief glossary included at the end of each document highlights keywords important in the study of the primary source. Each essay also includes a Bibliography and Additional Reading section for further research.

Appendixes
- **Chronological List** arranges all documents by year.
- **Web Resources** is an annotated list of web sites that offer valuable supplemental resources.
- **Bibliography** lists helpful articles and books for further study.

Contributors
Salem Press would like to extend its appreciation to all involved in the development and production of this work. The essays have been written and signed by scholars of history, humanities, and other disciplines related to the essay's topics. Without these expert contributions, a project of this nature would not be possible. A full list of contributor's names and affiliations appears in the front matter of this volume.

Editor's Introduction

The 1930s are forever associated with two things: the Great Depression and the New Deal. That Franklin D. Roosevelt led the nation for most of the decade (and beyond) makes him a good candidate for being counted as a third major force or icon of the era.

The decade began, however, with Herbert Hoover in the White House. While the disastrous crash of the stock market in 1929 was not the result of any one party's or individual's policies or actions, Hoover became the fall guy for the crash and all that came after it. Hoover and his Republican predecessor in the White House, Calvin Coolidge, strongly believed in keeping government out of the way of business, so that when the crash did come Hoover's response was to regard it as a transient phenomenon that the next business cycle would correct. All that was needed, he felt, was to make some adjustments involving foreign credits and to get the wheels of volunteerism going in order to provide relief at the local level. Together with Congress, the administration set up the Reconstruction Finance Corporation in January 1932 to make government loans to financial institutions, large industries, railroads, and public works projects. Given the scale of the problem, and its human dimension, the response was clearly inadequate, and Hoover was seen as being blind to the plight of millions of suffering Americans.

Adding to Hoover's woes was another matter he inherited from the decade before. Veterans of World War I had advocated for, and received promises regarding, the payment of war bonuses. Although technically the payments had been authorized to begin in 1945, tens of thousands of unemployed veterans saw the matter differently and demanded the immediate payment of their bonuses. Thus, in the summer of 1932, a presidential election year, some 12,000 veterans and their families marched and set up make-shift camps in the capital. Under pressure to pay, but fearing its effects on the US Treasury, Congress moved a Bonus Bill through the House of Representatives but failed to get it past the Senate. Many of the former soldiers in the ragtag "Bonus Army," as the protesters were called, departed on news of the bill's demise, but many others stayed behind. In July, Hoover authorized Army troops under General Douglas MacArthur to clear the camps and restore order. The scene played badly in newspapers and on the radio and did nothing to endear Hoover to voters in the upcoming election. He was easily defeated in the fall by his Democratic opponent, New York governor Franklin D. Roosevelt.

A New Deal for Americans

The New Deal of the Roosevelt era was a massive, complicated reform effort designed to save the nation from near collapse. Parts of the enterprise were reasonably successful, while other parts generally were not. It helped put people to work and provided a sense of recovery, but never was there anything like the prosperity that had been enjoyed in the previous decade. Virtually everything about the New Deal was controversial, beginning with the very idea that the government should be responsible for economic salvation and social welfare. In the United States, these had traditionally been left to the individual states or to the private sector—or so critics of the New Deal proclaimed. Roosevelt and his "Brain Trust" of New Dealers (i.e., a group of bright minds who advised the president and carried out the administration's policies) countered that government had long been involved in creating programs, regulating the economy, and seeing to the health and welfare of the nation's citizens. They argued that it was the 1920s, with its *laissez-faire* attitude, that had got the country into the mess it was now in, and there was no reason to go back and repeat the calamity.

Looked at from a distance, the New Deal reflects the traditional American balance between government involvement and independent initiative, albeit with the scales tilted in the direction of the political left. It was anything but the wholesale Soviet-style social engineering experiment that its harshest critics claimed it to be. It sought to tackle the problem of the Depression by a variety of means, focusing on the delivery of immediate relief to individuals, the provision of financial supports for business groups and farmers, the stimulation of the economy overall, and the establishment of a basis for the long-term security of all citizens.

The New Deal is also remembered for having created an "alphabet soup" of new government agencies and programs, each with its own abbreviation or acronym. Here is a partial listing:

Federal Emergency Relief Administration (FERA)
Created in May 1933 based on an earlier program under the Hoover administration, FERA disbursed federal funds to states and localities in the form of grants and

loans. The monies were to be used for relief programs and job creation. FERA ceased operating in 1935, replaced by the Works Progress Administration (WPA) and the Social Security Administration (SSA).

National Recovery Administration (NRA)

Established in June 1933, the NRA set up specialized codes, or regulations, meant to ensure fair competition in industry. The codes specified wages, prices, and production levels, chiefly with respect the operations of large firms. Small-business owners, farmers, and labor leaders complained that the codes were harmful to their interests, and consumers didn't much appreciate the NRA pricing system. Neither were many people put to work or the economy improved as a result of NRA activities. In 1935 the US Supreme Court ruled, in *Schechter Poultry Corp. v. United States*, that the NRA was unconstitutional; it was shut down in January 1936.

Civilian Conservation Corps (CCC)

The CCC, which was created around the same time as FERA and NRA, employed millions of young men in conservation projects such as park creation, reforestation, land reclamation, forest management, fire fighting, and erosion control. The workers lived in camps and were paid wages, most of which were expected to go to their families. The CCC closed operations in 1942.

Public Works Administration (PWA)

Not to be confused with the Works Progress Administration (WPA), the PWA built large-scale public works such as dams, tunnels, bridges, schools, hospitals, public buildings, and sewer systems. It was headed by Interior Secretary Harold Ickes and operated between 1933 and 1943.

Civil Works Administration (CWA)

The CWA, headed by top Roosevelt advisor Harry Hopkins, operated between 1933 and 1934, during which time it put men to work improving or erecting buildings and grounds, laying roads, building schools, and constructing airports.

Agricultural Adjustment Administration (AAA)

Between 1933 and 1935 the AAA sought to regulate farm production, mainly by paying farmers not to grow certain crops and destroy them if they had grown them. The idea was to reduce production levels in order to force a rise in prices and help restart the agricultural sector. Subsidies were also provided for key commodities. The scheme was declared unconstitutional by the US Supreme Court in 1935.

Tennessee Valley Authority (TVA)

The TVA, created in May 1933, was a regional development project designed to bring hydroelectric power to seven southern states and improve river navigation, introduce modern flood control, optimize land usage, and stimulate economic development. Thousands of people were put to work as a result. TVA still exists today, although there is more private-sector involvement. The original experiment was never replicated owing to opposition by private power companies.

Securities and Exchange Commission (SEC)

Established in 1934 and remaining in operation today, the SEC was charged with policing the market in stocks and bonds (i.e., securities) to end misleading practices and price manipulations. The intent was to restore investor confidence in a damaged institution and get the financial markets moving again. Its first chairman was Joseph P. Kennedy, Sr., father of John F. Kennedy. The *Glass-Steagall Act of 1933* imposed a barrier between commercial lending banks and investment firms. The act was repealed in 1999, and some commentators have argued that the repeal contributed to the financial collapse of 2007-2009.

Works Progress Administration (WPA)

Headed by Harry Hopkins, the WPA operated between 1935 and 1943. (It was renamed the Work Projects Administration in 1939.) Like the CWA, the WPA was focused on small- and medium-scale construction projects such as roads, bridges, parks, schools, libraries, sporting grounds, swimming pools, gyms, city halls, courthouses, post offices, sidewalks, and waterworks. As many as 8 million people worked for the WPA, 3 million at any given time. Besides planners, project managers, and laborers, the program employed artists and writers under the auspices of the Federal Arts Project.

National Labor Relations Board (NLRB)

Created in 1935 and still operating today, the NLRB was charged with ensuring workers' right to organize, bargain collectively, and go on strike. It basically monitors employers' labor practices to make sure they are fair according to the National Labor Relations Act (Wagner Act) of 1935 and the Fair Labor Standards Act of 1938, among other laws.

Social Security Administration (SSA)

Originally the Social Security Board, this agency was created as part of the Social Security Act of 1935. The act set up an old-age pension system and a temporary unemployment benefits program. Later, it was expanded to include dependents and the disabled. Since its inception, Social Security has become a mainstay of American society and has served hundreds of millions of citizens, most of whom contribute to it through paycheck withholdings.

National Youth Administration (NYA)

Existing between 1935 and 1943, the NYA distributed funds to high schools and colleges for the employment of youth on a part-time basis. Young people not attending school were provided with vocational training.

Government, Politics, and World Affairs

The types of actions taken by the Roosevelt administration in the 1930s defined the role of government in American society for much of the rest of the century—and beyond. The New Dealers strove to stimulate and regulate the economy, keep the job market going, provide welfare for those in need, undertake public works and infrastructure projects, oversee consumer affairs, monitor financial institutions, guard the interests of workers, and facilitate prosperity overall. Not that they always were successful or satisfied all parties involved, but they did change the nature of the dialogue. No longer was it a question, after the New Deal, *whether* government should play a role in managing the economy and promoting social good, but rather *how* it should achieve those goals. (One exception here is the 1980s, when, under President Ronald Reagan, there was a great pullback by government from social and economic affairs.)

Politically, the era increased divisions between the Republican and Democratic parties, as Democrats increasingly became the party of Roosevelt—with all that that meant—and Republicans increasingly became the party of Conservatism and anti-Communism. Roosevelt was swept into power in 1932, enjoyed a landslide victory in 1936, and was reelected for a third time in 1940, all the while bringing along more Democrats to fill Congress and state legislatures. In that respect, the New Deal was immensely popular and the Democratic Party came to be seen as upholding the interests of the "common man." Somewhat surprisingly, however, the party also found support among business groups associated with mass consumption, such as retailers, investment firms, building contractors, and various service industries (including legal services). These groups, along with labor unions and farmers, formed the backbone of the Democratic party. Southern Democrats supported the New Deal on the condition that it not delve into the areas of race relations and civil rights.

Republicans, meanwhile, opposed the Administration's progressive legislation at every turn. The greatest evidence of this was at the Supreme Court, where conservative justices blocked several key measures. So frustrated was the president after these reversals that he launched a misguided effort to rewrite the rules and "pack" the Court with liberal justices—an effort that blew up and turned some within his own circle against him. Republicans in Congress were also on the attack. In the House of Representatives, the House Un-American Activities Committee (HUAC) investigated alleged disloyalty and subversive activities among government employees and private citizens, particularly those with supposed communist ties. The Works Progress Administration (WPA) and the Federal Arts Project were among the main targets. The committee uncovered little if anything of substance but did manage to damage the reputations of many of the people it looked at.

The 1930s also saw a shift in foreign policy away from internationalism and toward isolationism. Early in his tenure as president, Roosevelt announced a retreat from intervention as a policy and the beginning of a "Good Neighbor Policy" toward Latin America. Fueling the dislike for him among conservatives, he also recognized the Soviet Union and removed trade barriers between the United States and a number of other nations. By the time Japan invaded China in 1937, the mood in the United States was one of "wait and see." The response was repeated when Hitler invaded Poland in 1939, launching World War II. Not until the bombing of Pearl Harbor in 1941did attitudes finally change and the United States entered the war against Germany and Japan. With that, a new era began—even while the legacy of the New Deal lived on.

Michael Shally-Jensen, PhD

Bibliography and Additional Reading

Collins, Sheila D., and Gertrude Schaffner Goldberg, eds. *When Government Helped: Learning from the Successes and Failures of the New Deal.* New York: Oxford UP, 2014.

Katznelson, Ira. *Fear Itself: The New Deal and the Origins of Our Time.* New York: Liveright, 2014.

Leuchtenburg, William E. *Franklin D. Roosevelt and the New Deal, 1932-1940.* New York: Harper Perennial, 2009.

Shlaes, Amity. *The Forgotten Man: A New History of the Great Depression.* New York: Harper Perennial: 2008.

Contributors

Anna Accettola, MA
Stockton, CA

Michael P. Auerbach, MA
Marblehead, MA

Adam J. Berger, PhD
Princeton, NJ

William E. Burns, PhD
George Washington University

Steven L. Danver, PhD
Mesa Verde Publishing
Washougal, Washington

K.P. Dawes, MA
Chicago, IL

Tracey DiLascio, Esq., JD
Framingham, Massachusetts

Kevin E. Grimm, PhD
Beloit College

Bethany Groff, MA
Historic New England

Jennifer L. Henderson Crane, PgDip
Fife, Scotland

Laurence W. Mazzeno, PhD
Alvernia University

Michael Shally-Jensen, PhD
Amherst, MA

Donald A. Watt, PhD
Middleton, ID

DEFINING DOCUMENTS
IN AMERICAN HISTORY

The 1930s
(1930-1939)

Setting Up the New Deal

Key elements of the New Deal were set up early on in Roosevelt's presidency—much of it, in fact, within the first one hundred days. It was then that such programs and agencies as the Federal Emergency Relief Administration (FERA), the Civilian Conservation Corps (CCC), the Public Works Administration (PWA), the Agricultural Adjustment Administration (AAA), and the Tennessee Valley Authority (TVA) were established. Each of these agencies was designed to bring relief to millions of unemployed or needy Americans and, it was hoped, to shore up the economy. Roosevelt laid out the basics of his plans in various speeches and policy statements, including through so-called fireside chats listened to on the radio by citizens across the nation. By and large, the public was receptive to both the message and the man.

At the same time, there were legions of critics—many of them from the business community—who felt that Roosevelt had overstepped his bounds. Roosevelt's predecessor, Herbert Hoover, for instance, while allowing that government must play an active role in turning around a broken economy, questioned the nature and scope of government intervention under the New Deal. Roosevelt's own Treasury Secretary, Henry Morgenthau, pushed for a different direction in the Administration, one more responsive to the needs of the private sector; but he lost the battle to reformers. The great British economist John Maynard Keynes wrote an open letter to the American president in the *New York Times* asking him to proceed with his reform efforts, but to do so in a way less hostile to business interests and more respectful of economic fundamentals. (In particular, Keynes warned that forcing a rise in prices in order to stimulate output and employment was the wrong way to go about things.)

A second phase of the New Deal kicked in in 1935, when yet more agencies and programs were launched. By then some pieces of the government reform effort had been declared unconstitutional by the US Supreme Court, or were soon going to be. The AAA, for example, which set production quotas in the farming industry and subsidized certain commodities, fell under the Court's scrutiny and was abolished. A similar fate was suffered by the National Recovery Administration (NRA), which established codes of fair competition in the marketplace, including codes for production levels, prices, and wages. The Court stated that such government centralization rode roughshod over the interests of private commerce and could not be tolerated. In the face of such reversals, Roosevelt sought, in 1937, to rewrite the rules of the Supreme Court in order to bring in justices who were favorable to his viewpoint. (The attempt was labeled his "court-packing scheme.") This effort, too, fell by the wayside when the public failed to respond to it positively and when further legal and legislative roadblocks were thrown up by enemies of the New Deal.

President Roosevelt: Fireside Chat on "The Forgotten Man"

Date: April 7, 1932
Author: Franklin D. Roosevelt
Genre: speech

Summary Overview

In 1932, New York governor and presidential candidate Franklin D. Roosevelt delivered a radio address to the American people regarding the economic crisis. Following the stock market crash in 1929, the Great Depression hit the United States, leading to widespread unemployment, home and farm foreclosures, and financial loss. In his address, Roosevelt stated that any permanent solution must be built from the "bottom up," and he outlined three steps he believed were necessary to secure economic recovery: first, purchasing power had to be restored to American farmers; second, the federal government had to provide financial relief to small banks in order to prevent further foreclosures; and third, tariff policies had to be revised to ensure that the United States could sell its excess consumer goods on the global market.

Defining Moment

The United States experienced an economic boom during the 1920s. Europe had suffered significant infrastructure damage during World War I, placing the United States in a relatively strong financial position with its abundant raw materials and available investment funds. Technological developments such as mass-production assembly lines allowed more goods to be manufactured quickly and cheaply. Newly imposed import tariffs encouraged citizens to buy American-made goods, and favorable tax laws encouraged businessmen to invest in the manufacturing sector.

This changed abruptly on October 24, 1929, when the US stock market began a rapid, steady decline. By the following week, panic was in full swing as stock prices across all economic sectors plummeted. Banks of all sizes were in danger of closing their doors, and many demanded immediate repayment of loans and mortgages in an attempt to save their businesses. However, few borrowers—either personal or corporate—had cash available for immediate repayment. By November 1929, the value of the stock market decreased by $30 billion; many companies closed, leading to widespread unemployment.

By the end of the 1920s, numerous countries around the world with free-market economies experienced similar financial decline. Some were hit harder than others, and the situation was especially dire in the United States. By 1932, the stock market had dropped to about 20 percent of its 1929 value. By the time the Great Depression reached its official peak in 1933, 25 percent of workers were unemployed, and thousands of US banks had collapsed. The increased unemployment led to decreased spending and lower demand for consumer goods, which led to fewer manufacturing jobs and ultimately even more unemployment. The failure of so many banks—including many large ones—led to further foreclosures and restricted access to the credit many believed was necessary to boost the depressed economy.

In the immediate aftermath of the 1929 crash, President Herbert Hoover and his administration established or expanded several government programs designed to help destitute Americans. However, the public criticized his approach as spending too heavily on corporate subsidies while ordinary Americans literally starved. For example, Hoover established the Reconstruction Finance Corporation, which lent $2 billion in government funds to banks, insurance companies, building and loan associations, agricultural credit organizations, and railroads. By contrast, Hoover declined to support a bill that would have provided additional payments to World War I veterans for their time in the service, claiming the $4 billion price tag was too high.

By 1932, Roosevelt, then the New York state governor, was campaigning in earnest to become the next president of the United States. His platform focused on establishing federal programs designed to provide immediate relief to the starving and homeless and to put Americans back to work through government-funded works projects such as environmental conservation initiatives and improvements to government buildings and other public infrastructure.

Author Biography
Franklin D. Roosevelt was born on January 30, 1882, in Hyde Park, New York. He attended Groton School in Massachusetts and received his bachelor's degree in history from Harvard University. He studied law at Columbia University in New York, but, upon passing the bar examination, left school without completing his degree in 1907. He practiced law in New York City for three years, before being elected to the New York State Senate in 1910.

President Woodrow Wilson appointed Roosevelt assistant secretary of the Navy from 1913 until 1920. Following an unsuccessful run for US vice president as the running mate of James M. Cox, Roosevelt briefly withdrew from politics. After a partial recovery from polio he contracted in 1921, Roosevelt was elected governor of New York State in 1928. In 1932, Roosevelt was elected president of the United States. He was inaugurated during the height of the Great Depression and saw the country through World War II. He died while still in office on April 12, 1945.

HISTORICAL DOCUMENT

Although I understand that I am talking under the auspices of the Democratic National Committee, I do not want to limit myself to politics. I do not want to feel that I am addressing an audience of Democrats or that I speak merely as a Democrat myself. The present condition of our national affairs is too serious to be viewed through partisan eyes for partisan purposes.

Fifteen years ago my public duty called me to an active part in a great national emergency, the World War. Success then was due to a leadership whose vision carried beyond the timorous and futile gesture of sending a tiny army of 150,000 trained soldiers and the regular navy to the aid of our allies. The generalship of that moment conceived of a whole Nation mobilized for war, economic, industrial, social and military resources gathered into a vast unit capable of and actually in the process of throwing into the scales ten million men equipped with physical needs and sustained by the realization that behind them were the united efforts of 110,000,000 human beings. It was a great plan because it was built from bottom to top and not from top to bottom.

In my calm judgment, the Nation faces today a more grave emergency than in 1917.

It is said that Napoleon lost the battle of Waterloo because he forgot his infantry—he staked too much upon the more spectacular but less substantial cavalry.

The present administration in Washington provides a close parallel. It has either forgotten or it does not want to remember the infantry of our economic army.

These unhappy times call for the building of plans that rest upon the forgotten, the unorganized but the indispensable units of economic power, for plans like those of 1917 that build from the bottom up and not from the top down, that put their faith once more in the forgotten man at the bottom of the economic pyramid.

Obviously, these few minutes tonight permit no opportunity to lay down the ten or a dozen closely related objectives of a plan to meet our present emergency, but I can draw a few essentials, a beginning in fact, of a planned program.

It is the habit of the unthinking to turn in times like this to the illusions of economic magic. People suggest that a huge expenditure of public funds by the Federal Government and by State and local governments will completely solve the unemployment problem. But it is clear that even if we could raise many billions of dollars and find definitely useful public works to spend these billions on, even all that money would not give employment to the seven million or ten million people who are out of work. Let us admit frankly that it would be only a stopgap. A real economic cure must go to the killing of the bacteria in the system rather than to the treatment of external symptoms.

How much do the shallow thinkers realize, for example, that approximately one-half of our whole population, fifty or sixty million people, earn their living by farming or in small towns whose existence immediately depends on farms. They have today lost their purchasing power. Why? They are receiving for farm products less than the cost to them of growing these farm products. The result of this loss of purchasing power is that many other millions of people engaged in industry in the cities cannot sell industrial products to the farming half of the Nation. This brings home to every city worker that his own employment is directly tied up with the farmer's dollar. No Nation can long endure half bankrupt. Main Street, Broadway, the mills, the mines will close if half the buyers are broke.

I cannot escape the conclusion that one of the essential parts of a national program of restoration must be to restore purchasing power to the farming half of the country. Without this the wheels of railroads and of factories will not turn.

Closely associated with this first objective is the problem of keeping the home-owner and the farm-owner where he is, without being dispossessed through the foreclosure of his mortgage. His relationship to the great banks of Chicago and New York is pretty remote. The two billion dollar fund which President Hoover and the Congress have put at the disposal of the big banks, the railroads and the corporations of the Nation is not for him.

His is a relationship to his little local bank or local loan company. It is a sad fact that even though the local lender in many cases does not want to evict the farmer or home-owner by foreclosure proceedings, he is forced to do so in order to keep his bank or company solvent. Here should be an objective of Government itself, to provide at least as much assistance to the little fellow as it is now giving to the large banks and corporations. That is another example of building from the bottom up.

One other objective closely related to the problem of selling American products is to provide a tariff policy based upon economic common sense rather than upon politics, hot-air, and pull. This country during the past few years, culminating with the Hawley-Smoot Tariff in 1929, has compelled the world to build tariff fences so high that world trade is decreasing to the vanishing point. The value of goods internationally exchanged is today less than half of what it was three or four years ago.

Every man and woman who gives any thought to the subject knows that if our factories run even 80 percent of capacity, they will turn out more products than we as a Nation can possibly use ourselves. The answer is that if they run on 80 percent of capacity, we must sell some goods abroad. How can we do that if the outside Nations cannot pay us in cash? And we know by sad experience that they cannot do that. The only way they can pay us is in their own goods or raw materials, but this foolish tariff of ours makes that impossible.

What we must do is this: revise our tariff on the basis of a reciprocal exchange of goods, allowing other Nations to buy and to pay for our goods by sending us such of their goods as will not seriously throw any of our industries out of balance, and incidentally making impossible in this country the continuance of pure monopolies which cause us to pay excessive prices for many of the necessities of life.

Such objectives as these three, restoring farmers' buying power, relief to the small banks and home-owners and a reconstructed tariff policy, are only a part of ten or a dozen vital factors. But they seem to be beyond the concern of a national administration which can think in terms only of the top of the social and economic structure. It has sought temporary relief from the top down rather than permanent relief from the bottom up. It has totally failed to plan ahead in a comprehensive way. It has waited until something has cracked and then at the last moment has sought to prevent total collapse.

It is high time to get back to fundamentals. It is high time to admit with courage that we are in the midst of an emergency at least equal to that of war. Let us mobilize to meet it.

Document Analysis
Roosevelt begins his radio address by recounting the Allied forces' success in World War I. He observes that success came from a "bottom-up" approach that rallied support, from not only trained military personnel, but also from more than 100 million ordinary people across the globe. He offers this story to demonstrate his position that building from the "bottom up" is the best approach to resolving the economic crisis.

Many factors contributed to the Great Depression, but Roosevelt says the main cause is relatively straightforward: Farmers—nearly half of the country's population—lost a significant amount of purchasing power when prices dropped because of overproduction. Because of this loss, families could no longer afford to purchase manufactured goods, which led to job loss in the industrial sectors. In turn, this further eroded the purchasing power of the American public and created a cycle of economic loss.

Roosevelt believes that the country must once again use a bottom-up approach in order to improve the economy. He says that large expenditures of public funds for creating government works-related jobs are only a stopgap measure, and it is necessary to address the root of the problem. The federal government must provide financial assistance to smaller banks to help them maintain solvency and prevent them from foreclosing on houses and farms. Additionally, the 1930 Hawley-Smoot Tariff Act compounds the overproduction problem: with the decline of the American consumer's purchasing power, too many excess goods exist in the domestic market, thus driving down prices. But with the high tariff rates and the prohibition on international exchange of goods in favor of cash-only transactions, companies have no viable way of selling these excesses on the global market.

Roosevelt concludes by identifying three steps necessary to bring the economy back into balance: farmers' purchasing power must be restored; the federal government must provide financial relief to small banks and homeowners; and the tariff policy must be revised to give American goods an outlet in the global market. Roosevelt closes by saying that "it is high time to get back to fundamentals," and encourages the American public to mobilize to meet the challenges presented by the state of the economy.

Essential Themes
A significant theme throughout Roosevelt's campaign and presidency was his attention to the plight of everyday Americans. Many believe that his bottom-up approach to economic recovery was a major contributing factor to his victory over Herbert Hoover in the 1932 election. Contrary to Hoover's approach, Roosevelt believed that first restoring financial security to the farmers and workers would lead to increased spending and ultimately strengthen corporate financial positions.

Additionally, Roosevelt frequently addressed the impact of global trade barriers on the domestic economy. He explained how the European and US economies were interconnected, especially in light of American investments in Europe's post–World War I rebuilding efforts. As economies softened across the globe in the early 1930s, the United States and many other countries enacted or raised tariffs to protect their domestic production from global competition. But the combination of overproduction and high export barriers created a surplus of goods that drove down prices across the manufacturing sector, thus decreasing the purchasing power of both industrial workers and farmers. Restoring a proper balance of international trade, Roosevelt believed, was another key factor to economic recovery.

Despite Roosevelt's new ideas and significant financial investment from the federal government, recovery from the Great Depression was slow. The economy showed signs of improving in 1933, but it stalled during 1934 and 1935 before picking up again between 1935 and 1937. A second wave of economic depression hit in 1937, however, from which the United States did not fully recover until entering World War II in 1941.

—*Tracey M. DiLascio, JD*

Bibliography and Additional Reading
"The Great Depression (1929–1939)." *Eleanor Roosevelt Papers Project*. George Washington U, n.d. Web. 18 May 2014.

McElvaine, Robert S. *The Great Depression: America, 1929–1941*. 25th anniversary ed. New York: Three Rivers, 2009. Print.

Smith, Jean Edward. *FDR*. New York: Random, 2007. Print.

■ FDR on Government's Role in the Economy

Date: September 23, 1932
Author: Franklin D. Roosevelt
Genre: speech

Summary Overview
In this speech, given during his 1932 presidential campaign, Franklin D. Roosevelt laid out his reasons for believing that a new relationship or "social contract" between the American people and its government was needed. As economic conditions worsened during the Great Depression, Roosevelt proposed that the government needed to be involved in a new way to protect individual rights, this time not against political tyranny, but against the economic power of corporations. Roosevelt argued that this new relationship between individual Americans and their government could preserve the core values of democracy—such as the ability of individuals to succeed through hard work—against the threat of industries that had a stranglehold on labor, resources, and finances. This new relationship became the basis for Roosevelt's New Deal policies and programs after he won the 1932 election. New Deal programs were designed to reform the financial system, stabilize the economy, and provide employment using unprecedented government regulation and intervention. The philosophical basis for Roosevelt's activist agenda was articulated clearly in this speech.

Defining Moment
On October 29, 1929, a day that came to be known as Black Tuesday, the United States stock market crashed, sending the nation into the worst economic depression it had ever seen. The 1920s had seen unprecedented growth in finance and industry, as politicians loosened regulations and unapologetically pursued pro-business policies. There was no federal deposit insurance system for banks and no unemployment insurance. Labor unions, which traditionally offered a measure of protection for working people, were weakened by anti-immigrant and anti-Socialist sentiment, internal divisions, and economic prosperity, which lessened public support for labor activism. In the fallout from the stock market crash, corporations went bankrupt, banks failed, and by 1932, approximately one-quarter of the nation's workforce was unemployed. In industrial cities and major ports, unemployment rates reached even higher than the national average. Farm prices fell by more than 50 percent. President Herbert Hoover and many others in government saw the crash as part of a recession that would quickly right itself, and Hoover urged patience and private charitable assistance to the poor, believing that it was not the government's job to interfere with business and the economy.

By the election of 1932, many Americans were destitute, and it was clear that the Great Depression was not a short-lived economic downturn. The election pitted the incumbent Hoover, a Republican, against the popular Democratic governor of New York, Franklin Delano Roosevelt. Hoover argued that Roosevelt's belief in an activist, interventionist government might help in the short term, but would ultimately lead to Socialism. Hoover opposed direct government aid to individuals, believing it to be against the spirit of American individualism. Hoover failed to see that the nation had lost all faith in the ability of corporations and industry to help put the economy right, and people in bread lines were no longer interested in the philosophical underpinnings of the Hoover administration's refusal to intervene. Roosevelt spoke of the government's responsibility to protect the individual and blamed Hoover and the Republicans for the disastrous economic situation.

Roosevelt won the 1932 election by a landslide, extending Democratic control over the House and Senate as well. An era of Republican leadership ended, as Republicans had largely dominated the presidency since 1860, with the exception of Grover Cleveland and Woodrow Wilson. Roosevelt's election signaled the beginning of twenty years of Democratic leadership in the White House.

When Roosevelt took office in March 1933, he acted quickly to bring relief to the poor and unemployed and to stabilize the economy. In the first months of his administration, he closed banks that were insolvent and reorganized those that remained, urging the American people to return their money to savings and promising to protect their investments. Roosevelt oversaw the repeal of Prohibition, initiated several major public works projects, and supported subsidies for farmers. Roosevelt encouraged organized labor, as he saw unions as a way to protect workers. In his first one hundred days in office, Roosevelt made major regulatory and domestic reforms and had clearly kept his promise to offer a "New Deal" to the American people.

Author Biography
Franklin Delano Roosevelt was born on January 30, 1882, in Hyde Park, New York, to a wealthy family. He was a distant cousin of President Theodore Roosevelt. Roosevelt attended the prestigious Groton School and then Harvard University, where he graduated with a degree in history. Roosevelt met his fifth cousin and future wife, Eleanor, in 1902, and they married in 1905. Roosevelt passed the New York State bar exam in 1907 and worked as a corporate lawyer. Roosevelt won election to the New York state senate in 1910, and he worked to end the control of the Tammany Hall branch of the Democratic Party in New York. He was appointed assistant secretary of the Navy by President Woodrow Wilson in 1913, serving until he was selected as the vice presidential running mate of James M. Cox for the 1920 presidential election. Cox was ultimately defeated by Warren G. Harding.

Roosevelt was stricken with polio in 1921 and lost the use of his legs. Roosevelt served as the governor of New York from 1929 until 1932, when he ran for and won the presidency of the United States. His first term as president coincided with the lowest point of the Great Depression, and he immediately turned his attention to the relief of the unemployed. Roosevelt implemented the New Deal, a series of domestic programs designed to return the nation to prosperity. He was reelected by a wide margin in 1936 and then won an unprecedented third term in 1940 during World War II. He was elected to a fourth term in 1944, but he died in office on April 12, 1945. He was buried in Hyde Park, New York.

HISTORICAL DOCUMENT

My Friends:

I count it a privilege to be invited to address the Commonwealth Club. It has stood in the life of this city and State, and it is perhaps accurate to add, the Nation, as a group of citizen leaders interested in fundamental problems of Government, and chiefly concerned with achievement of progress in Government through non-partisan means. The privilege of addressing you, therefore, in the heat of a political campaign, is great. I want to respond to your courtesy in terms consistent with your policy.

I want to speak not of politics but of Government. I want to speak not of parties, but of universal principles. They are not political, except in that larger sense in which a great American once expressed a definition of politics, that nothing in all of human life is foreign to the science of politics.

I do want to give you, however, a recollection of a long life spent for a large part in public office. Some of my conclusions and observations have been deeply accentuated in these past few weeks. I have traveled far—from Albany to the Golden Gate. I have seen many people, and heard many things, and today, when in a sense my journey has reached the half-way mark, I am glad of the opportunity to discuss with you what it all means to me.

Sometimes, my friends, particularly in years such as these, the hand of discouragement falls upon us. It seems that things are in a rut, fixed, settled, that the world has grown old and tired and very much out of joint. This is the mood of depression, of dire and weary depression.

But then we look around us in America, and everything tells us that we are wrong. America is new. It is in the process of change and development. It has the great potentialities of youth, and particularly is this true of the great West, and of this coast, and of California.

I would not have you feel that I regard this as in any sense a new community. I have traveled in many parts of the world, but never have I felt the arresting thought of the change and development more than here, where the old, mystic East would seem to be near to us, where the currents of life and thought and commerce of the whole world meet us. This factor alone is sufficient to cause man to stop and think of the deeper meaning of things, when he stands in this community.

But more than that, I appreciate that the membership of this club consists of men who are thinking in terms beyond the immediate present, beyond their own immediate tasks, beyond their own individual interests. I want to invite you, therefore, to consider with me in the large, some of the relationships of government and economic life that go deeply into our daily lives, our happiness, our future and our security.

The issue of Government has always been whether individual men and women will have to serve some system of Government or economics, or whether a system of Government and economics exists to serve individual men and women. This question has persistently dominated the discussion of government for many generations. On questions relating to these things men have differed, and for time immemorial it is probable that honest men will continue to differ.

The final word belongs to no man; yet we can still believe in change and in progress. Democracy, as a dear old friend of mine in Indiana, Meredith Nicholson, has called it, is a quest, a never-ending seeking for better things, and in the seeking for these things and the striving for them, there are many roads to follow. But, if we map the course of these roads, we find that there are only two general directions.

When we look about us, we are likely to forget how hard people have worked to win the privilege of government. The growth of the national Governments of Europe was a struggle for the development of a centralized force in the Nation, strong enough to impose peace upon ruling barons. In many instances the victory of the central Government, the creation of a strong central Government, was a haven of refuge to the individual. The people preferred the master far away to the exploitation and cruelty of the smaller master near at hand.

But the creators of national Government were perforce ruthless men. They were often cruel in their methods, but they did strive steadily toward something that society needed and very much wanted, a strong central State able to keep the peace, to stamp out civil war, to put the unruly nobleman in his place, and to permit the bulk of individuals to live safely. The man of ruthless force had his place in developing a pioneer country, just as he did in fixing the power of the central Government in the development of Nations. Society paid him well for his services and its development. When the development among the Nations of Europe, however, had been completed, ambition and ruthlessness, having served their term, tended to overstep their mark.

There came a growing feeling that Government was conducted for the benefit of a few who thrived unduly at the expense of all. The people sought a balancing—a limiting force. There came gradually, through town councils, trade guilds, national parliaments, by constitution and by popular participation and control, limitations on arbitrary power.

Another factor that tended to limit the power of those who ruled, was the rise of the ethical conception that a ruler bore a responsibility for the welfare of his subjects.

The American colonies were born in this struggle. The American Revolution was a turning point in it. After the Revolution the struggle continued and shaped itself in the public life of the country. There were those who because they had seen the confusion which attended the years of war for American independence surrendered to the belief that popular Government was essentially dangerous and essentially unworkable. They were honest people, my friends, and we cannot deny that their experience had warranted some measure of fear. The most brilliant, honest and able exponent of this point of view was Hamilton. He was too impatient of slow-moving methods. Fundamentally he believed that the safety of the republic lay in the autocratic strength of its Government, that the destiny of individuals was to serve that Government, and that fundamentally a great and strong group of central institutions, guided by a small group of able and public spirited citizens, could best direct all Government.

But Mr. Jefferson, in the summer of 1776, after drafting the Declaration of Independence turned his mind to the same problem and took a different view. He did not deceive himself with outward forms. Government to him was a means to an end, not an end in itself; it might be either a refuge and a help or a threat and a danger, depending on the circumstances. We find him carefully analyzing the society for which he was to organize a Government. "We have no paupers. The great mass of our population is of laborers, our rich who cannot live without labor, either manual or professional, being few and of moderate wealth. Most of the laboring class possess property, cultivate their own lands, have families and from the demand for their labor, are enabled to exact from the rich and the competent such prices as enable them to feed abundantly, clothe above mere decency, to labor moderately and raise their families."

These people, he considered, had two sets of rights, those of "personal competency" and those involved in acquiring and possessing property. By "personal competency" he meant the right of free thinking, freedom of forming and expressing opinions, and freedom of personal living, each man according to his own Rights. To insure the first set of rights, a Government must so order its functions as not to interfere with the individual. But even Jefferson realized that the exercise of the property rights might so interfere with the rights of the individual that the Government, without whose assistance the property rights could not exist, must intervene, not to destroy individualism, but to protect it.

You are familiar with the great political duel which followed; and how Hamilton, and his friends, building toward a dominant centralized power were at length defeated in the great election of 1800, by Mr. Jefferson's party. Out of that duel came the two parties, Republican and Democratic, as we know them today.

So began, in American political life, the new day, the day of the individual against the system, the day in which individualism was made the great watchword of American life. The happiest of economic conditions made that day long and splendid. On the Western frontier, land was substantially free. No one, who did not shirk the task of earning a living, was entirely without opportunity to do so. Depressions could, and did, come and go; but they could not alter the fundamental fact that most of the people lived partly by selling their labor and partly by extracting their livelihood from the soil, so that starvation and dislocation were practically impossible. At the very worst there was always the possibility of climbing into a covered wagon and moving west where the untilled prairies afforded a haven for men to whom the East did not provide a place. So great were our natural resources that we could offer this relief not only to our own people, but to the distressed of all the world; we could invite immigration from Europe, and welcome it with open arms. Traditionally, when a depression came a new section of land was opened in the West; and even our temporary misfortune served our manifest destiny.

It was in the middle of the nineteenth century that a new force was released and a new dream created. The force was what is called the industrial revolution, the advance of steam and machinery and the rise of the forerunners of the modern industrial plant. The dream was the dream of an economic machine, able to raise the standard of living for everyone; to bring luxury within the reach of the humblest; to annihilate distance by steam power and later by electricity, and to release everyone from the drudgery of the heaviest manual toil. It was to be expected that this would necessarily affect Government. Heretofore, Government had merely been called upon to produce conditions within which people could live happily, labor peacefully, and rest secure. Now it was called upon to aid in the consummation of this new dream. There was, however, a shadow over the dream. To be made real, it required use of the talents of men of tremendous will and tremendous ambition, since by no other force could the problems of financing and engineering and new developments be brought to a consummation.

So manifest were the advantages of the machine age, however, that the United States fearlessly, cheerfully, and, I think, rightly, accepted the bitter with the sweet. It was thought that no price was too high to pay for the advantages which we could draw from a finished industrial system. This history of the last half century is accordingly in large measure a history of a group of financial Titans, whose methods were not scrutinized with too much care and who were honored in proportion as they produced the results, irrespective of the means they used. The financiers who pushed the railroads to the Pacific were always ruthless, often wasteful, and frequently corrupt; but they did build railroads, and we have them today. It has been estimated that the American investor paid for the American railway system more than three times over in the process; but despite this fact the net advantage was to the United States. As long as we had free land; as long as population was growing by leaps and bounds; as long as our industrial plants were insufficient to supply our own needs, society chose to give the ambitious man free play and unlimited reward provided only that he produced the economic plant so much desired.

During this period of expansion, there was equal opportunity for all and the business of Government was not to interfere but to assist in the development of industry. This was done at the request of business men themselves. The tariff was originally imposed for the purpose of "fostering our infant industry," a phrase I think the older among you will remember as a political issue not so long ago. The railroads were subsidized, sometimes by grants of money, oftener by grants of land; some of the most valuable oil lands in the United States were granted to assist the financing of the railroad which pushed through the Southwest. A nascent merchant marine was assisted by grants of money, or by mail subsidies, so that our steam shipping might ply the seven seas. Some of my friends tell me that they do not want the Government in business. With this I agree; but I wonder whether they realize the implications of the past. For while it has been American doctrine that the Government must not go into business in competition with private enterprises, still it has been traditional, particularly in Republican administrations, for business urgently to ask the Government to put at private disposal all kinds of Government assistance. The same man who tells you that he does not want to see the Government interfere in business — and he means it, and has plenty of good reasons for saying so—is the first to go to Washington and ask the Government for a prohibitory tariff on his product. When things get just bad enough as they did two years ago, he will go with equal speed to the United States Government and ask for a loan; and the Reconstruction Finance Corporation is the outcome of it. Each group has sought protection from the Government for its own special interests, without realizing that the function of Government must be to favor no small group at the expense of its duty to protect the rights of personal freedom and of private property of all its citizens.

In retrospect we can now see that the turn of the tide came with the turn of the century. We were reaching our last frontier; there was no more free land and our industrial combinations had become great uncontrolled and irresponsible units of power within the State. Clearsighted men saw with fear the danger that opportunity would no longer be equal; that the growing corporation, like the feudal baron of old, might threaten the economic freedom of individuals to earn a living. In that hour, our antitrust laws were born. The cry was raised against the great corporations. Theodore Roosevelt, the first great Republican Progressive, fought a Presidential campaign on the issue of "trust busting" and talked freely about malefactors of great wealth. If the government had a policy it was rather to turn the clock back, to destroy the large combinations and to return to the time when every man owned his individual small business.

This was impossible; Theodore Roosevelt, abandoning the idea of "trust busting," was forced to work out a difference between "good" trusts and "bad" trusts. The Supreme Court set forth the famous "rule of reason" by which it seems to have meant that a concentration of industrial power was permissible if the method by which it got its power, and the use it made of that power, were reasonable.

Woodrow Wilson, elected in 1912, saw the situation more clearly. Where Jefferson had feared the encroachment of political power on the lives of individuals, Wilson knew that the new power was financial. He saw, in the highly centralized economic system, the despot of the twentieth century, on whom great masses of individuals relied for their safety and their livelihood, and whose irresponsibility and greed (if they were not controlled) would reduce them to starvation and penury. The concentration of financial power had not proceeded so far in 1912 as it has today; but it had grown far enough for Mr. Wilson to realize fully its implications. It is interesting, now, to read his speeches. What is called "radical" today (and I have reason to know whereof I speak) is mild compared to the campaign of Mr. Wilson. "No man can deny," he said, "that the lines of endeavor have more and more narrowed and stiffened; no man who knows anything about the development of industry in this country can have failed to observe that the larger kinds of credit are more and more difficult to obtain unless you obtain them upon terms of uniting your efforts with those who already control the industry of the country, and nobody can fail to observe that every man who tries to set himself up in competition with any process of manufacture which has taken place under the control of large combinations of capital will presently find himself either squeezed out or obliged to sell and allow himself to be absorbed." Had there been no World War—had Mr. Wilson been able to devote eight years to domestic instead of to international affairs—we might have had a wholly different situation at the present time. However, the then distant roar of European cannon, growing ever louder, forced him to abandon the study of this issue. The problem he saw so clearly is left with us as a legacy; and no one of us on either side of the political controversy can deny that it is a matter of grave concern to the Government.

A glance at the situation today only too clearly indicates that equality of opportunity as we have known it no longer exists. Our industrial plant is built; the problem just now is whether under existing conditions it is not overbuilt. Our last frontier has long since been reached, and there is practically no more free land. More than half of our people do not live on the farms or on lands and cannot derive a living by cultivating their own property. There is no safety valve in the form of a Western prairie to which those thrown out of work by the Eastern economic machines can go for a new start. We are not able to invite the immigration from Europe to share our endless plenty. We are now providing a drab living for our own people.

Our system of constantly rising tariffs has at last reacted against us to the point of closing our Canadian frontier on the north, our European markets on the east, many of our Latin-American markets to the south, and a goodly proportion of our Pacific markets on the west, through the retaliatory tariffs of those countries. It has forced many of our great industrial institutions which exported their surplus production to such countries, to establish plants in such countries, within the tariff walls. This has resulted in the reduction of the operation of their American plants, and opportunity for employment.

Just as freedom to farm has ceased, so also the opportunity in business has narrowed. It still is true that men can start small enterprises, trusting to native shrewdness and ability to keep abreast of competitors; but area after area has been pre-empted altogether by the great corporations, and even in the fields which still have no great concerns, the small man starts under a handicap. The unfeeling statistics of the past three decades show that the independent business man is running a losing race. Perhaps he is forced to the wall; perhaps he cannot command credit; perhaps he is "squeezed out," in Mr. Wilson's words, by highly organized corporate competitors, as your corner grocery man can tell you. Recently a careful study was made of the concentration of business in the United States. It showed that our economic life was dominated by some six hundred odd corporations who controlled two-thirds of American industry. Ten million small business men divided the other third. More striking still, it appeared that if the process of concentration goes on at the same rate, at the end of another century we shall have all American industry controlled by a dozen corporations, and run by perhaps a hundred men. Put plainly, we are steering a steady course toward economic oligarchy, if we are not there already.

Clearly, all this calls for a re-appraisal of values. A mere builder of more industrial plants, a creator of more railroad systems, an organizer of more corporations, is as likely to be a danger as a help. The day of the great promoter or the financial Titan, to whom we granted anything if only he would build, or develop, is over. Our task now is not discovery or exploitation of natural resources, or necessarily producing more goods. It is the soberer, less dramatic business of administering resources and plants already in hand, of seeking to reestablish foreign markets for our surplus production, of meeting the problem of underconsumption, of adjusting production to consumption, of distributing wealth and products more equitably, of adapting existing economic organizations to the service of the people. The day of enlightened administration has come.

Just as in older times the central Government was first a haven of refuge, and then a threat, so now in a closer economic system the central and ambitious financial unit is no longer a servant of national desire, but a danger. I would draw the parallel one step farther. We did not think because national Government had become a threat in the 18th century that therefore we should abandon the principle of national Government. Nor today should we abandon the principle of strong economic units called corporations, merely because their power is susceptible of easy abuse. In other times we dealt with the problem of an unduly ambitious central Government by modifying it gradually into a constitutional democratic Government. So today we are modifying and controlling our economic units.

As I see it, the task of Government in its relation to business is to assist the development of an economic declaration of rights, an economic constitutional order. This is the common task of statesman and business man. It is the minimum requirement of a more permanently safe order of things.

Happily, the times indicate that to create such an order not only is the proper policy of Government, but it is the only line of safety for our economic structures as well. We know, now, that these economic units cannot exist unless prosperity is uniform, that is, unless purchasing power is well distributed throughout every group in the Nation. That is why even the most selfish of corporations for its own interest would be glad to see wages restored and unemployment ended and to bring the Western farmer back to his accustomed level of prosperity and to assure a permanent safety to both groups. That is why some enlightened industries themselves endeavor to limit the freedom of action of each man and business group within the industry in the common interest of all; why business men everywhere are asking a form of organization which will bring the scheme into balance, even though it may in some measure qualify the freedom of action of individual units within the business.

The exposition need not further be elaborated. It is brief and incomplete, but you will be able to expand it in terms of your own business or occupation without difficulty. I think everyone who has actually entered the economic struggle — which means everyone who was not born to safe wealth — knows in his own experience and his own life that we have now to apply the earlier concepts of American Government to the conditions of today.

The Declaration of Independence discusses the problem of Government in terms of a contract. Government is a relation of give and take, a contract, perforce, if we would follow the thinking out of which it grew. Under such a contract rulers were accorded power, and the people consented to that power on consideration that they be accorded certain rights. The task of statesmanship has always been the re-definition of these rights in terms of a changing and growing social order. New conditions impose new requirements upon Government and those who conduct Government.

I held, for example, in proceedings before me as Governor, the purpose of which was the removal of the Sheriff of New York, that under modern conditions it was not enough for a public official merely to evade the legal terms of official wrongdoing. He owned a positive duty as well. I said in substance that if he had acquired large sums of money, he was when accused required to explain the sources of such wealth. To that extent this wealth was colored with a public interest. I said that in financial matters, public servants should, even beyond private citizens, be held to a stern and uncompromising rectitude.

I feel that we are coming to a view through the drift of our legislation and our public thinking in the past quarter century that private economic power is, to enlarge an old phrase, a public trust as well. I hold that continued enjoyment of that power by any individual or group must depend upon the fulfillment of that trust. The men who have reached the summit of American business life know this best; happily, many of these urge the binding quality of this greater social contract.

The terms of that contract are as old as the Republic, and as new as the new economic order.

Every man has a right to life; and this means that he has also a right to make a comfortable living. He may by sloth or crime decline to exercise that right; but it may not be denied him. We have no actual famine or dearth; our industrial and agricultural mechanism can produce enough and to spare. Our Government formal and informal, political and economic, owes to everyone an avenue to possess himself of a portion of that plenty sufficient for his needs, through his own work.

Every man has a right to his own property; which means a right to be assured, to the fullest extent attainable, in the safety of his savings. By no other means can men carry the burdens of those parts of life which, in the nature of things, afford no chance of labor; childhood, sickness, old age. In all thought of property, this right is paramount; all other property rights must yield to it. If, in accord with this principle, we must restrict the operations of the speculator, the manipulator, even the financier, I believe we must accept the restriction as needful, not to hamper individualism but to protect it.

These two requirements must be satisfied, in the main, by the individuals who claim and hold control of the great industrial and financial combinations which dominate so large a part of our industrial life. They have undertaken to be, not business men, but princes of property. I am not prepared to say that the system which produces them is wrong. I am very clear that they must fearlessly and competently assume the responsibility which goes with the power. So many enlightened business men know this that the statement would be little more than a platitude, were it not for an added implication.

This implication is, briefly, that the responsible heads of finance and industry instead of acting each for himself, must work together to achieve the common end. They must, where necessary, sacrifice this or that private advantage; and in reciprocal self-denial must seek a general advantage. It is here that formal Government—political Government, if you choose—comes in. Whenever in the pursuit of this objective the lone wolf, the unethical competitor, the reckless promoter, the Ishmael or Insull whose hand is against every man's, declines to join in achieving an end recognized as being for the public welfare, and threatens to drag the industry back to a state of anarchy, the Government may properly be asked to apply restraint. Likewise, should the group ever use its collective power contrary to the public welfare, the Government must be swift to enter and protect the public interest.

The Government should assume the function of economic regulation only as a last resort, to be tried only when private initiative, inspired by high responsibility, with such assistance and balance as Government can give, has finally failed. As yet there has been no final failure, because there has been no attempt; and I decline to assume that this Nation is unable to meet the situation.

The final term of the high contract was for liberty and the pursuit of happiness. We have learned a great deal of both in the past century. We know that individual liberty and individual happiness mean nothing unless both are ordered in the sense that one man's meat is not another man's poison. We know that the old "rights of personal competency," the right to read, to think, to speak, to choose and live a mode of life, must be respected at all hazards. We know that liberty to do anything which deprives others of those elemental rights is outside the protection of any compact; and that Government in this regard is the maintenance of a balance, within which every individual may have a place if he will take it; in which every individual may find safety if he wishes it; in which every individual may attain such power as his ability permits, consistent with his assuming the accompanying responsibility.

All this is a long, slow talk. Nothing is more striking than the simple innocence of the men who insist, whenever an objective is present, on the prompt production of a patent scheme guaranteed to produce a result. Human endeavor is not so simple as that. Government includes the art of formulating a policy, and using the political technique to attain so much of that policy as will receive general support; persuading, leading, sacrificing, teaching always, because the greatest duty of the a statesman is to educate. But in the matters of which I have spoken, we are learning rapidly, in a severe school. The lessons so learned must not be forgotten, even in the mental lethargy of a speculative upturn. We must build toward the time when a major depression cannot occur again; and if this means sacrificing the easy profits of inflationist booms, then let them go; and good riddance.

Faith in America, faith in our tradition of personal responsibility, faith in our institutions, faith in ourselves demand that we recognize the new terms of the old social contract. We shall fulfill them, as we fulfilled the obligation of the apparent Utopia which Jefferson imagined for us in 1776, and which Jefferson, Roosevelt and Wilson sought to bring to realization. We must do so, lest a rising tide of misery, engendered by our common failure, engulf us all. But failure is not an American habit; and in the strength of great hope we must all shoulder our common load.

Document Analysis

Roosevelt begins this speech by providing some historical background from before the American Revolution. Throughout history, he argues, people have formed centralized governments in order to limit the power of the aristocracy and to protect the interests of the general public. When these centralized governments became too powerful, Roosevelt asserts, "popular participation and control" have coordinated to establish "limitations on arbitrary power." Roosevelt compares American statesmen Alexander Hamilton and Thomas Jefferson and their differing visions of the role of government. Hamilton "believed that the safety of the republic lay in the autocratic strength of its Government, that the destiny of individuals was to serve that Government." Jefferson, on the other hand, saw government as "a means to an end, not an end in itself" and believed that the government was created to serve the people and to protect their individual rights. Roosevelt argues that the protection of individual rights is not ensured by a total absence of regulation but rather through government policies that enable individuals to thrive and prosper. This idea is fundamental to Roosevelt's theory of government. Since its founding, he argues, the US government has understood that it "must intervene, not to destroy individualism, but to protect it."

Most Americans prospered with minimal interference from the government in the first century following the country's founding. "So began, in American political life, the new day, the day of the individual against the system, the day in which individualism was made the great watchword of American life. The happiest of economic conditions made that day long and splendid." In other words, while there were abundant natural resources, free land in the West, and nearly limitless opportunities for expansion, individual Americans could be left alone to make their way. People who worked hard were rewarded with success without the government's help.

Roosevelt draws a hard line between the preindustrial and postindustrial United States. He describes the Industrial Revolution as a "dream of an economic machine, able to raise the standard of living for everyone . . . to release everyone from the drudgery of the heaviest manual toil," and he describes how the government, long accustomed to leaving individuals alone to make their way, found itself called upon to support industry so all Americans could benefit from the advances of the industrial age. Throughout the unprecedented industrial and financial growth of the nineteenth century, "the business of Government was not to interfere but to assist in the development of industry," and government policies protected industries, such as railroads and shipping with tariffs, land grants, and other regulatory protections. Roosevelt describes this as a circumstantial shift from a government whose purpose was the protection of the individual to one whose primary goal was the support of business, with the theory that this would benefit all.

Roosevelt concludes with a call for a new role for the government, a return to Jeffersonian principles of the protection of individual rights and government in service to the people. Unfettered industry has failed to protect these rights, Roosevelt asserts, and "equality of opportunity as we have known it no longer exists." It is time for the "soberer, less dramatic business of administering resources . . . of distributing wealth and products more equitably, of adapting existing economic organizations to the service of the people." Roosevelt asserts that if he is elected, he will provide "enlightened administration" and will use government resources to help individuals protect their rights to a fair chance of success and security.

Essential Themes

This speech was a call to consider a new, activist role for government. Roosevelt wished to convince his listeners that the protection of individual rights, a foundational belief of American democracy, now required government intervention in a way that was not needed in a preindustrial society. Roosevelt positions himself as the candidate who will protect these rights by intervening and regulating private industry, and he introduces terms that indicated a radical departure from the free-market capitalism of his predecessor. The idea that the government had a role in limiting corporate power so that wealth could be more fairly distributed set the stage for the New Deal policies and programs of his presidency.

—*Bethany Groff, MA*

Bibliography and Additional Reading

Katznelson, Ira. *Fear Itself: The New Deal and the Origins of Our Time*. New York: Liveright, 2013. Print.

Parrish, Michael E. *Anxious Decades: American in Prosperity and Depression 1920–1941*. New York: Norton, 1992. Print.

Shlaes, Amity. *The Forgotten Man: A New History of the Great Depression*. New York: HarperCollins, 2007. Print.

■ Herbert Hoover Speaks Against the New Deal

Date: October 31, 1932
Authors: Herbert Hoover
Genre: speech

Summary Overview

In one of his last campaign speeches during the 1932 presidential election, incumbent Herbert Hoover offered an analysis of the New Deal proposed by his opponent, Democratic New York governor Franklin Delano Roosevelt. Hoover cautioned his audience to see the benefits of the proposed New Deal as little more than rhetorical. He also warned that the New Deal would represent a dramatic shift away from the traditional social and governmental mechanisms that had been in place for generations. Hoover said that the government's current infrastructure was already proving effective in addressing the Depression's impact; Roosevelt's proposals were, therefore, not only ineffective, but obsolete when compared to the activity of the federal government to date. The government, Hoover determined, must remain ready to intervene when needed, but keep its distance from fostering a new "family."

Defining Moment

In 1929, the "Roaring Twenties"—distinctive because of the tremendous economic boom that occurred in the United States during this period—came to a dramatic halt. Stock markets crashed, banks folded, industries faltered, and countless jobs disappeared in what would come to be called the Great Depression.

Economists, social scientists, and other scholars have not come to a firm agreement on the specific causes of the Depression. Generally, however, experts point to citizens' inability to repay loans and credit debt, a lack of government regulation of businesses and markets, and a lack of sustainability in the country's leading industries as some of the leading causes of this event. Many scholars point to the sharp divide between the nation's wealthy and poor (including the large percentage of immigrants, who came to the country during the early twentieth century to work in the energy and manufacturing industries) as a contributing factor as well, as the latter group represented a majority of the population that would be adversely affected by any fluctuations in the economy.

Herbert Hoover, the incumbent president in 1929, had only been in office for nine months when the stock market crashed in October of that year. Hoover believed that government's role in private, economic affairs should be minimal, and he argued repeatedly that the nation's economic infrastructure was still solid and healthy despite the tumult of the Black Thursday stock market crash and other events leading to the Depression's onset. After Black Thursday, Hoover did not look to implement any major reforms or pass emergency legislation. Rather, he convened a meeting of leaders in finance, construction, labor, the Federal Reserve, and other relevant economic interest groups. As the Depression continued, he eventually acceded to ongoing pressure for federal relief and signed the Emergency Relief Construction Act, providing $2 billion for public works and $300 million for state-level direct relief programs.

Despite these actions, Hoover largely clung to his philosophy that the economy would right itself through the actions of private business and the altruism of the citizens (upon whom Hoover called to help the people most affected by the Depression). Congress, which largely disagreed with Hoover on this point, was more proactive in its efforts to pass reforms and aid packages, although few of these initiatives passed and fewer still proved effective; indeed, some (such as the Smoot-Hawley Tariff Act, which raised import and export taxes) may have aggravated the situation.

Hoover, whom many historians suggest would have

enjoyed a second term if not for the Depression, found his presidency in jeopardy during the 1932 campaign. The Democratic Party, held down by Republicans throughout the 1920s, found new life because of the Depression and Hoover's perceived inaction. They nominated New York governor Franklin Delano Roosevelt as their candidate. Roosevelt called for a New Deal for Americans, a campaign promise that included major regulatory reforms, direct aid packages, and new initiatives designed to help bring the country out of the economic doldrums for good. Hoover spoke against the program in Madison Square Garden, New York City, on October 31, 1932.

Author Biography
Herbert Clark Hoover was born on August 10, 1874, in West Branch, Iowa. Orphaned at the age of nine, he worked for a while on an uncle's farm in Oregon and, in 1891, attended the newly opened Stanford University, from which he graduated four years later with a degree in geology. During World War I, Hoover established the Committee for Relief of Belgium, an organization dedicated to providing food and other forms of aid for civilians trapped in Belgian war zones. Based on his work in this arena, President Woodrow Wilson tapped Hoover to be his food administrator. Hoover later declared his affiliation with the Republican Party and became Warren Harding's secretary of commerce. He would continue to hold this post during Calvin Coolidge's administration. In 1928, Hoover successfully sought the Republican nomination for president and easily won the election. Victimized politically by the onset of the Great Depression, Hoover lost the 1932 election to Franklin Delano Roosevelt. He remained active in public service after his presidency, including helping President Harry Truman with the post–World War II reconstruction effort. He died on October 20, 1964, while living in Iowa.

HISTORICAL DOCUMENT

My fellow citizens: …

This campaign is more than a contest between two men. It is more than a contest between two parties. It is a contest between two philosophies of government.

We are told by the opposition that we must have a change, that we must have a new deal. It is not the change that comes from normal development of national life to which I object or you object, but the proposal to alter the whole foundations of our national life which have been builded through generations of testing and struggle, and of the principles upon which we have made this Nation. The expressions of our opponents must refer to important changes in our economic and social system and our system of government; otherwise they would be nothing but vacuous words. And I realize that in this time of distress many of our people are asking whether our social and economic system is incapable of that great primary function of providing security and comfort of life to all of the firesides of 25 million homes in America, whether our social system provides for the fundamental development and progress of our people, and whether our form of government is capable of originating and sustaining that security and progress.

This question is the basis upon which our opponents are appealing to the people in their fear and their distress. They are proposing changes and so-called new deals which would destroy the very foundations of the American system of life.

Our people should consider the primary facts before they come to the judgment—not merely through political agitation, the glitter of promise, and the discouragement of temporary hardships—whether they will support changes which radically affect the whole system which has been builded during these six generations of the toil of our fathers. They should not approach the question in the despair with which our opponents would clothe it.

Our economic system has received abnormal shocks during the last three years which have temporarily dislocated its normal functioning. These shocks have in a large sense come from without our borders, and I say to you that our system of government has enabled us to take such strong action as to prevent the disaster which would otherwise have come to this Nation. It has enabled us further to develop measures and programs which are now demonstrating their ability to bring about restoration and progress.

We must go deeper than platitudes and emotional appeals of the public platform in the campaign if we will penetrate to the full significance of the changes which our opponents are attempting to float upon the wave of distress and discontent from the difficulties through which we have passed. We can find what our opponents would do after searching the record of their appeals to discontent, to group and sectional interest. To find that, we must search for them in the legislative acts which they sponsored and passed in the Democratic-controlled House of Representatives in the last session of Congress. We must look into both the measures for which they voted and in which they were defeated. We must inquire whether or not the Presidential and Vice-Presidential candidates have disavowed those acts. If they have not, we must conclude that they form a portion and are a substantial indication of the profound changes in the new deal which is proposed.

And we must look still further than this as to what revolutionary changes have been proposed by the candidates themselves.

We must look into the type of leaders who are campaigning for the Democratic ticket, whose philosophies have been well known all their lives and whose demands for a change in the American system are frank and forceful. I can respect the sincerity of these men in their desire to change our form of government and our social and our economic system, though I shall do my best tonight to prove they are wrong. I refer particularly to Senator Norris, Senator La Follette, Senator Cutting, Senator Huey Long, Senator Wheeler, William Randolph Hearst, and other exponents of a social philosophy different from the traditional philosophies of the American people. Unless these men have felt assurance of support to their ideas they certainly would not be supporting these candidates and the Democratic Party. The zeal of these men indicates that they must have some sure confidence that they will have a voice in the administration of this Government.

I may say at once that the changes proposed from all these Democratic principals and their allies are of the most profound and penetrating character. If they are brought about, this will not be the America which we have known in the past.

Now, I may pause for a moment and examine the American system of government and of social and economic life which it is now proposed that we should alter. Our system is the product of our race and of our experience in building a Nation to heights unparalleled in the whole history of the world. It is a system peculiar to the American people. It differs essentially from all others in the world. It is an American system. It is rounded on the conception that only through ordered liberty, through freedom to the individual, and equal opportunity to the individual will his initiative and enterprise be summoned to spur the march of national progress.

It is by the maintenance of an equality of opportunity and therefore of a society absolutely fluid in the movement of its human particles that our individualism departs from the individualism of Europe. We resent class distinction because there can be no rise for the individual through the frozen strata of classes, and no stratification of classes can take place in a mass that is livened by the free rise of its human particles. Thus in our ideals the able and ambitious are able to rise constantly from the bottom to leadership in the community. We denounce any attempt to stir class feeling or class antagonisms in the United States.

This freedom of the individual creates of itself the necessity and the cheerful willingness of men to act cooperatively in a thousand ways and for every purpose as the occasion requires, and it permits such voluntary cooperations to be dissolved as soon as it has served its purpose and to be replaced by new voluntary associations for new purposes.

There has thus grown within us, to gigantic importance, a new conception. That is the conception of voluntary cooperation within the community; cooperation to perfect the social organizations; cooperation for the care of those in distress; cooperation for the advancement of knowledge, of scientific research, of education; cooperative action in a thousand directions for the advancement of economic life. This is self-government by the people outside of the Government. It is the most powerful development of individual freedom and equality of opportunity that has taken place in the century and a half since our fundamental institutions were founded.

It is in the further development of this cooperation

and in a sense of its responsibility that we should find solution for many of the complex problems, and not by the extension of the Government into our economic and social life. The greatest function a government can perform is to build up that cooperation, and its most resolute action should be to deny the extension of bureaucracy. We have developed great agencies of cooperation by the assistance of the Government which do promote and protect the interests of individuals and the smaller units of business: the Federal Reserve System, in its strengthening and support of the smaller banks; the Farm Board, in its strengthening and support of the farm cooperatives; the home loan banks, in the mobilizing of building and loan associations and savings banks; the Federal land banks, in giving independence and strength to land mortgage associations; the great mobilization of relief to distress, the mobilization of business and industry in measures of recovery from this depression, and a score of other activities that are not socialism, and they are not the Government in business. They are the essence of protection to the development of free men. I wish to explore this point a little further. The primary conception of this whole American system is not the ordering of men but the cooperation of free men. It is rounded upon the conception of responsibility of the individual to the community, of the responsibility of local government to the State, of the State to the National Government.

I am exploring these questions because I propose to take up definite proposals of the opposition and test them with these realities in a few moments.

Now, our American system is rounded on a peculiar conception of self-government designed to maintain an equality of opportunity to the individual, and through decentralization it brings about and maintains these responsibilities. The centralization of government will undermine these responsibilities and will destroy the system itself.

Our Government differs from all previous conceptions, not only in the decentralization but also in the independence of the judicial arm of the Government.

Our Government is rounded on a conception that in times of great emergency, when forces are running beyond the control of individuals or cooperative action, beyond the control of local communities or the States, then the great reserve powers of the Federal Government should be brought into action to protect the people. But when these forces have ceased there must be a return to State, local, and individual responsibility.

The implacable march of scientific discovery with its train of new inventions presents every year new problems to government and new problems to the social order. Questions often arise whether, in the face of the growth of these new and gigantic tools, democracy can remain master in its own house and can preserve the fundamentals of our American system. I contend that it can, and I contend that this American system of ours has demonstrated its validity and superiority over any system yet invented by human mind. It has demonstrated it in the face of the greatest test of peacetime history—that is the emergency which we have passed in the last three years.

When the political and economic weakness of many nations of Europe, the result of the World War and its aftermath, finally culminated in the collapse of their institutions, the delicate adjustments of our economic and social and governmental life received a shock unparalleled in our history. No one knows that better than you of New York. No one knows its causes better than you. That the crisis was so great that many of the leading banks sought directly or indirectly to convert their assets into gold or its equivalent with the result that they practically ceased to function as credit institutions is known to you; that many of our citizens sought flight for their capital to other countries; that many of them attempted to hoard gold in large amounts you know. These were but superficial indications of the flight of confidence and the belief that our Government could not overcome these forces.

Yet these forces were overcome—perhaps by narrow margins—and this demonstrates that our form of government has the capacity. It demonstrates what the courage of a nation can accomplish under the resolute leadership of the Republican Party. And I say the Republican Party because our opponents, before and during the crisis, proposed no constructive program, though some of their members patriotically supported ours for which they deserve on every occasion the applause of patriotism. Later on in the critical period, the Democratic House of Representatives did develop the real thought and ideas of the Democratic Party. They were so destructive that they had to be defeated. They did delay the healing of our wounds for months.

Now, in spite of all these obstructions we did succeed. Our form of government did prove itself equal to the task. We saved this Nation from a generation of chaos and degeneration; we preserved the savings, the insurance policies, gave a fighting chance to men to hold their homes. We saved the integrity of our Government and the honesty of the American dollar. And we installed measures which today are bringing back recovery. Employment, agriculture, and business—all of these show the steady, if slow, healing of an enormous wound.

As I left Washington, our Government departments communicated to me the fact that the October statistics on employment show that since the first day of July, the men returned to work in the United States exceed one million.

I therefore contend that the problem of today is to continue these measures and policies to restore the American system to its normal functioning, to repair the wounds it has received, to correct the weaknesses and evils which would defeat that system. To enter upon a series of deep changes now, to embark upon this inchoate new deal which has been propounded in this campaign would not only undermine and destroy our American system but it will delay for months and years the possibility of recovery. …

Now, to go back to my major thesis—the thesis of the longer view. Before we enter into courses of deep-seated change and of the new deal, I would like you to consider what the results of this American system have been during the last 30 years—that is, a single generation. For if it can be demonstrated that by this means, our unequaled political, social, and economic system, we have secured a lift in the standards of living and the diffusion of comfort and hope to men and women, the growth of equality of opportunity, the widening of all opportunity such as had never been seen in the history of the world, then we should not tamper with it and destroy it, but on the contrary we should restore it and, by its gradual improvement and perfection, foster it into new performance for our country and for our children.

Now, if we look back over the last generation we find that the number of our families and, therefore, our homes, has increased from about 16 to about 25 million, or 62 percent. In that time we have builded for them 15 million new and better homes. We have equipped 20 million out of these 25 million homes with electricity; thereby we have lifted infinite drudgery from women and men. The barriers of time and space have been swept away in this single generation. Life has been made freer, the intellectual vision of every individual has been expanded by the installation of 20 million telephones, 12 million radios, and the service of 20 million automobiles. Our cities have been made magnificent with beautiful buildings, parks, and playgrounds. Our countryside has been knit together with splendid roads. We have increased by 12 times the use of electrical power and thereby taken sweat from the backs of men. In the broad sweep real wages and purchasing power of men and women have steadily increased. New comforts have steadily come to them. The hours of labor have decreased, the 12-hour day has disappeared, even the 9-hour day has almost gone. We are now advocating the 5-day week. During this generation the portals of opportunity to our children have ever widened. While our population grew by but 62 percent, yet we have increased the number of children in high schools by 700 percent, and those in institutions of higher learning by 300 percent. With all our spending, we multiplied by six times the savings in our banks and in our building and loan associations. We multiplied by 1,200 percent the amount of our life insurance. With the enlargement of our leisure we have come to a fuller life; we have gained new visions of hope; we are more nearly realizing our national aspirations and giving increased scope to the creative power of every individual and expansion of every man's mind.

Now, our people in these 30 years have grown in the sense of social responsibility. There is profound progress in the relation of the employer to the employed. We have more nearly met with a full hand the most sacred obligation of man, that is, the responsibility of a man to his neighbor. Support to our schools, hospitals, and institutions for the care of the afflicted surpassed in totals by billions the proportionate service in any period in any nation in the history of the world.

Now, three years ago there came a break in this progress. A break of the same type we have met 15 times in a century and yet have recovered from. But 18 months later came a further blow by the shocks transmitted to us from earthquakes of the collapse of nations throughout the world as the aftermath of the World War. The workings of this system of ours were dislocated. Businessmen and farmers suffered, and millions of men and women are out of jobs. Their distress is bitter. I do not seek to minimize it, but we may thank God that in view of the storm that we have met that 30 million still have jobs, and yet this does not distract our thoughts from the suffering of the 10 million.

But I ask you what has happened. This 30 years of incomparable improvement in the scale of living, of advance of comfort and intellectual life, of security, of inspiration, and ideals did not arise without right principles animating the American system which produced them. Shall that system be discarded because vote-seeking men appeal to distress and say that the machinery is all wrong and that it must be abandoned or tampered with? Is it not more sensible to realize the simple fact that some extraordinary force has been thrown into the mechanism which has temporarily deranged its operation? Is it not wiser to believe that the difficulty is not with the principles upon which our American system is founded and designed through all these generations of inheritance? Should not our purpose be to restore the normal working of that system which has brought to us such immeasurable gifts, and not to destroy it?

Now, in order to indicate to you that the proposals of our opponents will endanger or destroy our system, I propose to analyze a few of them in their relation to these fundamentals which I have stated.

First: A proposal of our opponents that would break down the American system is the expansion of governmental expenditure by yielding to sectional and group raids on the Public Treasury. The extension of governmental expenditures beyond the minimum limit necessary to conduct the proper functions of the Government enslaves men to work for the Government. If we combine the whole governmental expenditures—national, State, and municipal—we will find that before the World War each citizen worked, theoretically, 25 days out of each year for the Government. In 1924, he worked 46 days out of the year for the Government. Today he works, theoretically, for the support of all forms of Government 61 days out of the year.

No nation can conscript its citizens for this proportion of men's and women's time without national impoverishment and without the destruction of their liberties. Our Nation cannot do it without destruction to our whole conception of the American system. The Federal Government has been forced in this emergency to unusual expenditure, but in partial alleviation of these extraordinary and unusual expenditures the Republican administration has made a successful effort to reduce the ordinary running expenses of the Government....

Second: Another proposal of our opponents which would destroy the American system is that of inflation of the currency. The bill which passed the last session of the Democratic House called upon the Treasury of the United States to issue $2,300 million in paper currency that would be unconvertible into solid values. Call it what you will, greenbacks or fiat money. It was the same nightmare which overhung our own country for years after the Civil War....

The use of this expedient by nations in difficulty since the war in Europe has been one of the most tragic disasters to equality of opportunity and the independence of man.

I quote from a revealing speech by Mr. Owen D. Young upon the return of the Dawes Commission from Europe. He stated:

"The currency of Germany was depreciating so rapidly that the industries paid their wages daily, and sometimes indeed twice a day. Standing with the lines of employees was another line of wives and mothers waiting for these marks. The wife grabbed the paper from her husband's hand and rushed to the nearest provision store to spend it quickly before the rapid depreciation had cut its purchasing power in two."...

Third: In the last session of the Congress, under the personal leadership of the Democratic Vice-Presidential candidate, and their allies in the Senate, they enacted a law to extend the Government into personal banking business. I know it is always difficult to discuss banks. There seems to be much prejudice against some of them, but I was compelled to veto that bill out of fidelity to the whole American system of life and government. I may repeat a part of that veto message, and it remains unchallenged by any Democratic leader. I quote now from that veto message because that statement was not made in the heat of any political campaign. I said:

"It would mean loans against security for any conceivable purpose on any conceivable security to anybody who wants money. It would place the Government in private business in such fashion as to violate the very principle of public relations upon which we have builded our Nation, and renders insecure its very foundations. Such action would make the Reconstruction Corporation the greatest banking and money-lending institution of all history. It would constitute a gigantic centralization of banking and finance to which the American people have been properly opposed over a hundred years. The purpose of the expansion is no longer in the spirit of solving a great major emergency but to establish a privilege whether it serves a great national end or not."

I further said:

"It would require the setting up of a huge bureaucracy, to establish branches in every county and town in the United States. Every political pressure would be assembled for particular persons. It would be within the power of these agencies to dictate the welfare of millions of people, to discriminate between competitive business at will, and to deal favor and disaster among them. The organization would be constantly subjected to conspiracies and raids of predatory interests, individuals, and private corporations. Huge losses and great scandals must inevitably result. It would mean the squandering of public credit to be ultimately borne by the taxpayer."

I stated further that:

"This proposal violates every sound principle of public finance and of our Government. Never before has so dangerous a suggestion been made to our country. Never before has so much power for evil been placed at the unlimited discretion of seven individuals."

They failed to pass this bill over my veto. But you must not be deceived. This is still in their purposes as a part of the new deal, and no responsible candidate has yet disavowed it.

Fourth: Another proposal of our opponents which would wholly alter our American system of life is to reduce the protective tariff to a competitive tariff for revenue....

Fifth: Another proposal is that the Government go into the power business....

I have stated unceasingly that I am opposed to the Federal Government going into the power business. I have insisted upon rigid regulation. The Democratic candidate has declared that under the same conditions which may make local action of this character desirable, he is prepared to put the Federal Government into the power business. He is being actively supported by a score of Senators in this campaign, many of whose expenses are being paid by the Democratic National Committee, who are pledged to Federal Government development and operation of electrical power.

I find in the instructions to the campaign speakers issued by the Democratic National Committee that they are instructed to criticize my action in the veto of the bill which would have put the Government permanently into the operation of power at Muscle Shoals.... In that bill was the flat issue of the Federal Government permanently in competitive business. I vetoed it because of principle and not because it was especially applied to electrical power. In that veto I stated that I was firmly opposed to the Federal Government entering into any business, the major purpose of which is competition with our citizens except in major national emergencies. In that veto message, written long before the emergence of the exigencies of political campaigning, I stated:

"There are national emergencies which require that the Government should temporarily enter the field of business but that they must be emergency actions and in matters where the cost of the project is secondary to much higher consideration. There are many localities where the Federal Government is justified in the construction of great dams and reservoirs, where navigation, flood control, reclamation, or stream regulation are of dominant importance, and where they are beyond the capacity or purpose of private or local government capital to construct. In these cases, power is often a byproduct and should be disposed of by contract or lease. But for the Federal Government to deliberately go out to build up and expand such an occasion to the major purpose of a power and manufacturing business is to break down the initiative and enterprise of the American people; it is destruction of equality of opportunity among our people; it is the negation of the ideals upon which our civilization has been based....

"This bill would launch the Federal Government on a policy of ownership of power utilities upon a basis of competition instead of by the proper Government function of regulation for the protection of all the people. I hesitate to contemplate the future of our institutions, of our Government, and of our country, if the preoccupation of its officials is to be no longer the promotion of justice and equality of opportunity but is to be devoted to barter in the markets. That is not liberalism; it is degeneration."

From their utterances in this campaign and elsewhere, it appears to me that we are justified in the conclusion that our opponents propose to put Federal Government extensively into business.

Sixth: I may cite another instance of absolutely destructive proposals to our American system by our opponents, and I am talking about fundamentals and not superficialities.

Recently there was circulated through the unemployed in this city and other cities, a letter from the Democratic candidate in which he stated that he would support measures for the inauguration of self-liquidating public works such as the utilization of water resources, flood control, land reclamation, to provide employment for all surplus labor at all times.

I especially emphasize that promise to promote "employment for all surplus labor at all times"—by the Government. I at first could not believe that anyone would be so cruel as to hold out a hope so absolutely impossible of realization to those 10 million who are unemployed and suffering. But the authenticity of that promise has been verified. And I protest against such frivolous promises being held out to a suffering people. It is easy to demonstrate that no such employment can be found. But the point that I wish to make here and now is the mental attitude and spirit of the Democratic Party that would lead them to attempt this or to make a promise to attempt it. That is another mark of the character of the new deal and the destructive changes which mean the total abandonment of every principle upon which this Government and this American system are rounded. If it were possible to give this employment to 10 million people by the Government—at the expense of the rest of the people—it would cost upwards of $9 billion a year.

The stages of this destruction would be first the destruction of Government credit, then the destruction of the value of Government securities, the destruction of every fiduciary trust in our country, insurance policies and all. It would pull down the employment of those who are still at work by the high taxes and the demoralization of credit upon which their employment is dependent. It would mean the pulling and hauling of politics for projects and measures, the favoring of localities and sections and groups. It would mean the growth of a fearful bureaucracy which, once established, could never be dislodged. If it were possible, it would mean one-third of the electorate would have Government jobs, earnest to maintain this bureaucracy and to control the political destinies of the country....

I have said before, and I want to repeat on this occasion, that the only method by which we can stop the suffering and unemployment is by returning our people to their normal jobs in their normal homes, carrying on their normal functions of living. This can be done only by sound processes of protecting and stimulating recovery of the existing system upon which we have builded our progress thus far—preventing distress and giving such sound employment as we can find in the meantime.

Seventh: Recently, at Indianapolis, I called attention to the statement made by Governor Roosevelt in his address on October 25 with respect to the Supreme Court of the United States. He said:

"After March 4, 1929, the Republican Party was in complete control of all branches of the Government—Executive, Senate, and House, and I may add, for good measure, in order to make it complete, the Supreme Court as well."

Now, I am not called upon to defend the Supreme Court of the United States from that slurring reflection. Fortunately for the American people that Court has jealously maintained over the years its high standard of integrity, impartiality, and freedom from influence of either the Executive or Congress, so that the confidence of the people in the Court is sound and unshaken.

But is the Democratic candidate really proposing his conception of the relation of the Executive with the Supreme Court? If that is his idea, he is proposing the most revolutionary new deal, the most stupendous breaking of precedent, the most destructive undermining of the very safeguard of our form of government yet proposed by any Presidential candidate.

Eighth: In order that we may get at the philosophical background of the mind which pronounces the necessity for profound change in our economic system and a new deal, I would call your attention to an address delivered by the Democratic candidate in San Francisco early in October.

He said:

"Our industrial plant is built. The problem just now is whether under existing conditions it is not overbuilt. Our last frontier has long since been reached. There is practically no more free land. There is no safety valve in the Western prairies where we can go for a new start.... The mere building of more industrial plants, the organization of more corporations is as likely to be as much a danger as a help.... Our task now is not the discovery of natural resources or necessarily the production of more goods, it is the sober, less dramatic business of administering the resources and plants already in hand ... establishing markets for surplus production, of meeting the problem of under-consumption, distributing the wealth and products more equitably and adopting the economic organization to the service of the people...."

Now, there are many of these expressions with which no one would quarrel. But I do challenge the whole idea that we have ended the advance of America, that this country has reached the zenith of its power and the height of its development. That is the counsel of despair for the future of America. That is not the spirit by which we shall emerge from this depression. That is not the spirit which has made this country. If it is true, every American must abandon the road of countless progress and countless hopes and unlimited opportunity. I deny that the promise of American life has been fulfilled, for that means we have begun the decline and the fall. No nation can cease to move forward without degeneration of spirit.

I could quote from gentlemen who have emitted this same note of profound pessimism in each economic depression going back for 100 years. What the Governor has overlooked is the fact that we are yet but on the frontiers of development of science and of invention. I have only to remind you that discoveries in electricity, the internal-combustion engine, the radio—all of which have sprung into being since our land was settled—have in themselves represented the greatest advances made in America. This philosophy upon which the Governor of New York proposes to conduct the Presidency of the United States is the philosophy of stagnation and of despair. It is the end of hope. The destinies of this country cannot be dominated by that spirit in action. It would be the end of the American system.

I have recited to you some of the items in the progress of this last generation. Progress in that generation was not due to the opening up of new agricultural land; it was due to the scientific research, the opening of new invention, new flashes of light from the intelligence of our people. These brought the improvements in agriculture and in industry. There are a thousand inventions for comfort and the expansion of life yet in the lockers of science that have not yet come to light. We are only upon their frontiers. As for myself, I am confident that if we do not destroy our American system, if we continue to stimulate scientific research, if we continue to give it the impulse of initiative and enterprise, if we continue to build voluntary cooperation instead of financial concentration, if we continue to build into a system of free men, my children will enjoy the same opportunity that has come to me and to the whole 120 million of my countrymen. I wish to see American Government conducted in that faith and hope.

Now, if these sample measures and promises, which I have discussed, or these failures to disavow these projects, this attitude of mind, mean anything, they mean the enormous expansion of the Federal Government; they mean the growth of bureaucracy such as we have never seen in our history. No man who has not occupied my position in Washington can fully realize the constant battle which must be carried on against incompetence, corruption, tyranny of government expanded into business activities. If we first examine the effect on our form of government of such a program, we come at once to the effect of the most gigantic increase in expenditure ever known in history. That alone would break down the savings, the wages, the equality of opportunity among our people. These measures would transfer vast responsibilities to the Federal Government from the States, the local governments, and the individuals. But that is not all; they would break down our form of government. It will crack the timbers of our Constitution. Our legislative bodies cannot delegate their authority to any dictator, but without such delegation every member of these bodies is impelled in representation of the interest of his constituents constantly to seek privilege and demand service in the use of such agencies. Every time the Federal Government extends its arm, 531 Senators and Congressmen become actual boards of directors of that business.

Capable men cannot be chosen by politics for all the various talents that business requires. Even if they were supermen, if there were no politics in the selection of a Government official, if there were no constant pressure for this and for that, so large a number of men would be incapable as a board of directors of any institution. At once when these extensions take place by the Federal Government, the authority and responsibility of State governments and institutions are undermined. Every enterprise of private business is at once halted to know what Federal action is going to be. It destroys initiative and courage....

Now, we have heard a great deal in this campaign about reactionaries, conservatives, progressives, liberals, and radicals. I think I belong to every group. I have not yet heard an attempt by any one of the orators who mouth these phrases to define the principles upon which they base these classifications. There is one thing I can say without any question of doubt—that is, that the spirit of liberalism is to create free men; it is not the regimentation of men under government. It is not the extension of bureaucracy. I have said in this city before now that you cannot extend the mastery of government over the daily life of a people without somewhere making it master of people's souls and thoughts. Expansion of government in business and otherwise means that the government, in order to protect itself from the political consequences of its errors or even its successes, is driven irresistibly without peace to greater and greater control of the Nation's press and platform. Free speech does not live many hours after free industry and free commerce die. It is a false liberalism that interprets itself into Government operation of business. Every step in that direction poisons the very roots of liberalism. It poisons political equality, free speech, free press, and equality of opportunity. It is the road not to liberty but to less liberty. True liberalism is found not in striving to spread bureaucracy, but in striving to set bounds of it. It is found in an endeavor to extend cooperation between men. True liberalism seeks all legitimate freedom first in the confident belief that without such freedom the pursuit of other blessings is vain. Liberalism is a force truly of the spirit proceeding from the deep realization that economic freedom cannot be sacrificed if political freedom is to be preserved.

Even if the Government conduct of business could give us the maximum of efficiency instead of least efficiency, it would be purchased at the cost of freedom. It would increase rather than decrease abuse and corruption, stifle initiative and invention, undermine development of leadership, cripple mental and spiritual energies of our people, extinguish equality of opportunity, and dry up the spirit of liberty and progress. Men who are going about this country announcing that they are liberals because of their promises to extend the Government are not liberals; they are the reactionaries of the United States.

Now, I do not wish to be misquoted or misunderstood. I do not mean that our Government is to part with one iota of its national resources without complete protection to the public interest. I have already stated that democracy must remain master in its own house. I have stated that it is, at times, vitally necessary for the Government to protect the people when forces run against them which they cannot control. I have stated that abuse and wrongdoing must be punished and controlled. Nor do I wish to be interpreted as stating that the United States is a free-for-all and devil-take-the-hindermost society.

The very essence of equality of opportunity in our American system is that there shall be no monopoly or domination by anybody—whether it be a group or section of the country, or whether it be business, or whether it be group interest. On the contrary, our American system demands economic justice as well as political and social justice; it is no system of *laissez faire*.

I am not setting up the contention that our American system is perfect. No human ideal has ever been perfectly attained, since humanity itself is not perfect. But the wisdom of our forefathers and the wisdom of the 30 men who have preceded me in this office hold to the conception that progress can be attained only as the sum of the accomplishments of free individuals, and they have held unalterably to these principles....

My countrymen, the proposals of our opponents represent a profound change in American life—less in concrete proposal, bad as that may be, than by implication and by evasion. Dominantly in their spirit they represent a radical departure from the foundations of 150 years which have made this the greatest Nation in the world. This election is not a mere shift from the ins to the outs. It means the determining of the course of our Nation over a century to come.

Now, my conception of America is a land where men and women may walk in ordered liberty, where they may enjoy the advantages of wealth not concentrated in the hands of a few but diffused through the opportunity of all, where they build and safeguard their homes, give to their children the full opportunities of American life, where every man shall be respected in the faith that his conscience and his heart direct him to follow, and where people secure in their liberty shall have leisure and impulse to seek a fuller life. That leads to the release of the energies of men and women, to the wider vision and higher hope. It leads to opportunity for greater and greater service not alone of man to man in our country but from our country to the world. It leads to health in body and a spirit unfettered, youthful, eager with a vision stretching beyond the farthest horizons with a mind open and sympathetic and generous. But that must be builded upon our experience with the past, upon the foundations which have made this country great. It must be the product of the development of our truly American system.

Document Analysis

President Hoover's speech makes the statement that the country, while certainly under major duress from the Depression, is not at a point at which it needs fundamental changes to its government and financial systems. He cautions citizens that then-candidate Roosevelt's "New Deal" amounts to little more than rhetoric, a series of proposals stemming from panic rather than reason. The country, he says, is not in need of revolutionary changes that would transform traditional American ideals; rather, it needs Americans and the myriad agencies and organizations to cooperate with one another. Reviewing the evidence of the previous three decades, Hoover says that this approach has delivered proven results on many fronts. The principles of the New Deal, he warns, represent a dramatic (and unnecessary) shift away from this proven approach.

Roosevelt's New Deal, Hoover says, is born of panic and reactive rhetoric, when in fact, for decades, the American political and economic system has experienced periods of flux, all of which have been rectified through patience and deliberation. Certainly, the country is understandably anxious at the Depression's impact and length. The Democrats, however, are seizing upon this anxiety and calling for a major overhaul of the American system. Hoover advises his audience—and indeed all Americans—to refrain from embracing such rhetoric.

The alternative, according to Hoover, is to allow traditional American institutions and principles to remedy the economy. Business, finance and political leaders should work together in a spirit of cooperation to rejuvenate the national economy. Meanwhile, private citizens should work together to help those Americans most adversely affected by the Depression. Hoover cites the tumultuous period following the Great War as an example—in this situation, he says, all aspects of American society came together to reinvigorate the economy and withstand the hardships associated with this period.

Hoover continues by giving his analysis of what would occur if the New Deal provisions became law: government would see an added layer of bureaucracy the likes of which Americans have never before seen. Additionally, the federal government would, in the spirit of a tyranny and not a democratic republic, be free to intrude in business, without any safeguards from state and local government. He argues that the New Deal would impinge on Americans' pursuit of individual liberty, threatening to destroy citizens' "initiative and courage."

To be sure, Hoover says, there are steps to be taken to improve the existing system so that those forces accountable for the Depression cannot continue to operate unchecked; his philosophy is not that the country should be a "free-for-all." Still, he believes the best method for America to successfully reemerge from the Depression is to look to the fundamental systems that have proven effective repeatedly throughout modern American history instead of embracing the un-American proposals offered by Roosevelt and the Democrats.

Essential Themes

This speech illustrated Hoover's political philosophy regarding the handling of the Great Depression. He insisted that the very political, social, and economic institutions that helped the United States survive World War I, an economic downturn in the early 1920s, and other crises would again prove effective in reversing the Great Depression. Throughout this speech, Hoover cited his belief that, with the cooperation of business and industry as well as private citizens, the Depression would not last long.

Hoover also took the opportunity to criticize the New Deal proposed by Democratic presidential candidate Franklin Delano Roosevelt. On one level, Hoover simply dismissed the New Deal concept as mere rhetoric and argued that the Democrats were simply using the fear and anxiety prevalent throughout the country to attempt to give new life to their previously unsuccessful agenda. On another level, however, Hoover viewed the New Deal as a major threat to the liberal, democratic principles on which the United States was founded. In this light, the New Deal was not simply the product of reactionary policy, Hoover said—if made law, the New Deal would move the American political and economic system closer to a tyranny than a democratic republic.

Hoover made an effort, however, to project to his audience an understanding that the nation did indeed face a crisis that warranted action. His approach to the myriad issues arising from the Depression's onset, he argued, was neither to allow business to operate without rules nor to simply allow the issue to resolve itself. He instead advocated a response that suited the American idiom, such as the meetings he had held when the Depression first began. This series of meetings, he said, inspired the participants to strike out and reverse the Depression's effects. He also acknowledged that there were almost certainly reforms to be made to the country's infrastructure in order to both reverse the Depression and prevent such events in the future. However, he saw no cause for changing the very nature of the federal government in such a way that it would potentially endanger the personal liberties of its citizens.

—*Michael P. Auerbach, MA*

Bibliography and Additional Reading

"American President: Herbert Hoover (1874–1964)." *Miller Center*. U of Virginia, n.d. Web. 17 June 2014.

Carroll, Sarah. "Causes of the Great Depression". *OK Economics*. Boston U, 2002. Web. 17 June 2014.

Edsforth, Ronald. *The New Deal: America's Response to the Great Depression*. Hoboken: Wiley, 2000. Print.

"The Great Depression (1929–1939)." *Eleanor Roosevelt Papers Project*. George Washington U, n.d. Web. 17 June 2014.

"Herbert Clark Hoover: A Biographical Sketch." *Herbert Hoover Presidential Library and Museum*. National Archives, n.d. Web. 17 June 2014.

McElvaine, Robert S. *The Great Depression: America, 1929–1941*. 25th anniv. ed. New York: Three Rivers, 2009. Print.

Whisenhunt, Donald W. *President Herbert Hoover*. Hauppauge, NY: Nova, 2007. Print.

■ Letter From Herbert Hoover to Franklin D. Roosevelt

Date: February 18, 1933
Author: Herbert Hoover
Genre: letter

Summary Overview

February 1933 was an uncertain time for the United States as Franklin Delano Roosevelt (FDR) prepared to take office as president in March, and Herbert Hoover, who had been voted out of office by a substantial majority, was still trying to ward off what seemed to be an imminent banking collapse. In this letter, sent less than three weeks before Roosevelt's inauguration, Hoover asks the president-elect to reassure the American people that he would not inflate currency and would balance the budget. Roosevelt had his own plans, however, and he had no wish to be seen publically or privately taking Hoover's advice. The nation waited anxiously for Roosevelt to unveil his plans, which he did immediately upon taking office. Though it was denied by the Roosevelt administration for years, the president's first major move to stabilize the banks, a four-day holiday when all banks and the Federal Reserve were closed, was based on a plan drafted by the Treasury during Hoover's administration. The Emergency Banking Act, signed on March 9, was also drafted while Hoover was in office. Though Roosevelt sought to distance himself from the Republican administration of his predecessor, which he and the nation blamed for the economic crisis, several of Hoover's ideas were implemented in some measure during Roosevelt's first days in office.

Defining Moment

In 1929, the United States stock market crashed, sending the nation into the worst economic depression it had ever seen. Under Republican leadership, the 1920s had experienced unprecedented financial and industrial growth as presidents with free-market ideals loosened regulations and unapologetically pursued pro-business policies. Deposit insurance did not exist, nor did unemployment assistance, and in the fallout from the stock market crash, corporations went bankrupt, banks failed, and by 1932, over a quarter of the nation's workforce was unemployed and many more were working part-time for low wages. In some industrial cities, unemployment reached 80 or 90 percent. President Herbert Hoover and many others in government saw the crash as part of a recession that would quickly right itself. He preached "rugged individualism," and he urged patience and private assistance to the poor, believing that it was not the government's job to interfere with business and the economy.

By 1932, however, even Hoover could see that the Great Depression was not a short-lived economic correction. The election that year pitted Hoover, a Republican, against the popular governor of New York, Democrat Franklin Delano Roosevelt. Hoover was blamed for the economic crisis, and his popularity had fallen precipitously. Roosevelt won the 1932 election by a landslide, extending Democratic control over the House and Senate as well.

Hoover had taken some steps to respond to the looming crisis by imposing high tariffs on imports, raising taxes for the very wealthy, and by initiating public works projects. He was unable to turn the economic tide, however, and after Roosevelt won the election, Hoover repeatedly asked for meetings so they could work jointly on slowing the downward economic plunge and reassuring jittery investors. Roosevelt refused, arguing that it would associate him with the administration many perceived as having caused the problem. He also had a plan of his own.

The national banking system was teetering on the edge of total collapse when Roosevelt was sworn in on March 4, 1933. By that evening, thirty-two states had shut down their banks. Roosevelt blamed greedy bankers and selfish businessmen for the crisis, and he immediately took the reins of the national banking system. The day after his inauguration, Roosevelt called a special session of Congress and declared a four-day bank holiday when all of the nation's banks would be closed and then reopened when they were declared to be financially stable. On March 9, Congress passed the Emergency Banking Act, which allowed the Federal Reserve Banks to issue additional currency and gave the president broad regulatory power. In the first of his many "fireside chats," Roosevelt asked the American people to return their money to banks, and many did just that when solvent banks reopened on March 13.

Author Biography
Herbert Clark Hoover was born in Iowa in 1874 to a Quaker farming family. He was orphaned by age nine and was raised by his uncle. He entered Stanford University in 1891, its first year of operation, and graduated with a degree in geology. Following graduation, he labored in a California gold mine for two years and then, in 1897, moved to Australia, where he worked for a mining company as a geologist and mining engineer, eventually being promoted to mine manager. In 1899, he went to China to work as chief engineer for the Chinese Bureau of Mines, working for various mining companies and arranging for Chinese labor to work in mines abroad. By 1908, he was an independent mining consultant with investments all over the world. He lectured at Columbia and Stanford Universities and was a multimillionaire by 1914.

At the outbreak of World War I, Hoover helped to organize the evacuation of 120,000 Americans stranded in Europe. He also worked with the Commission for Relief in Belgium, a public–private partnership that supplied food relief to occupied Belgium and France, eventually feeding over ten million civilians daily. When the United States entered the war in 1917, Woodrow Wilson appointed Hoover to head the US Food Administration, which oversaw rationing and the food supply chain. After the war ended, Hoover was a household name, and in 1920, he unsuccessfully pursued the Republican nomination for the presidency. Warren Harding, who won the election, named Hoover to his cabinet as secretary of commerce. In 1927, when then-president Calvin Coolidge announced he would not run again for office, Hoover ran successfully and was elected president the following year, taking office just months before the stock market crashed in October 1929. Hoover was voted out of office in 1932 in the midst of precipitous economic decline. He continued to write and lecture after his retirement and was appointed to various commissions by subsequent presidents, though Roosevelt never engaged him in public service during his administration. Hoover died in 1964 at age ninety in New York City.

HISTORICAL DOCUMENT

A most critical situation has arisen in the country of which I feel it my duty to advise you confidentially. I am therefore taking this course of writing you myself and sending it to you through the Secret Service for your hand direct as obviously its misplacement would only feed the fire and increase the dangers.

The major difficulty is the state of the public mind, for there is a steadily degenerating confidence in the future which has reached the height of general alarm. I am convinced that a very early statement by you upon two or three policies of your administration would serve greatly to restore confidence and cause a resumption of the march of recovery.

The large part which fear and apprehension play in the situation can be well demonstrated by repeated experience in the past few years and the tremendous lift which has come at times by the removal of fear can be easily demonstrated.

One of the major underlying elements in the broad problem of recovery is the re-expansion of credit so critically and abruptly deflated by the shocks from Europe during the last half of 1931. The visible results were public fear, hoarding, bank failures, withdrawal of gold, flight of capital, falling prices, increased unemployment, etc. Early in 1932 we created the agencies which have steadily expanded available credit ever since that time and continue to expand it today, but confidence must run parallel with expanding credit and the instances where confidence has been injured run precisely with the lagging or halting of recovery.

With the election, there came the natural and inevitable hesitation all along the economic line pending the demonstration of the policies of the new administration. But a number of very discouraging things have happened on top of this natural hesitation. The breakdown in balancing the budget by the House of Representatives; the proposals for inflation of the currency and the wide spread discussion of it; the publication of R.F.C. loans and the bank runs, hoarding and bank failures from this cause; increase in unemployment due to imports from depreciated currency countries; failure of the Congress to enact banking, bankruptcy and other vital legislation; unwillingness of the Congress to face reduction in expenditures; proposals to abrogate constitutional responsibility by the Congress with all the chatter about dictatorship, and other discouraging effects upon the public mind. They have now culminated to a state of alarm which is rapidly reaching the dimensions of a crisis. Hoarding has risen to a new high level; the bank structure is weakened as witness Detroit and increased failures in other localities. There are evidences of flight of capital and foreign withdrawals of gold. In other words we are confronted with precisely the same phenomena we experienced late in 1931 and again in the spring of 1932. The whole has its final expression in the increase of unemployment, suffering and general alarm.

I therefore return to my suggestion at the beginning as to the desirability of clarifying the public mind on certain essentials which will give renewed confidence. It is obvious that as you will shortly be in position to make whatever policies you wish effective, you are the only one who can give these assurances. Both the nature of the cause of public alarm and experience give such an action the prospect of success in turning the tide. I do not refer to action on all the causes of alarm but it would steady the country greatly if there could be prompt assurance that there will be no tampering or inflation of the currency; that the budget will be unquestionably balanced even if further taxation is necessary; that the government credit will be maintained by refusal to exhaust it in issue of securities. The course you have adopted in inquiring into the problems of world stabilization are already known and helpful. It would be of further help if the leaders were advised to cease publication of R.F.C. business.

I am taking the liberty of addressing you both because of my anxiety over the situation and my confidence that from four years of experience that such tides as are now running can be moderated and the processes of regeneration which are always running can be released.

GLOSSARY

R.F.C.: Reconstruction Finance Corporation, a government corporation that provided loans and other financial assistance to state and local governments, banks, utilities, etc.

Document Analysis

Hoover's letter begins with a statement of urgency. He wishes to inform Roosevelt personally of a "most critical situation" and so has sent a private letter through the Secret Service so as not to inflame the hopes or fears of skittish investors; a letter concerning monetary policy would feed the "steadily degenerating confidence in the future which has reached the height of general alarm." Hoover is gravely concerned that public uncertainty about the future in the critical months between presidencies could cause a total collapse of the financial system. If Roosevelt would reveal some of his plans, it would soothe the fearful public. "I am convinced that a very early statement by you upon two or three policies of your administration would serve greatly to restore confidence and cause a resumption of the march of recovery."

Hoover goes on to describe how Congress has inflated the public distrust of the financial system. He lays out what he sees as the causes and ensuing result of this mistrust: "The breakdown in balancing the budget by the House of Representatives; the proposals for inflation of the currency and the wide spread discussion of it; . . . failure of the Congress to enact banking, bankruptcy and other vital legislation; unwillingness of the Congress to face reduction in expenditures; proposals to abrogate constitutional responsibility by the Congress with all the chatter about dictatorship, and other discouraging effects upon the public mind." The frightened public was hoarding their money, collecting gold, and threatening the stability of the entire system.

Hoover acknowledges that as president, Roosevelt will do as he pleases, but Hoover asks that Roosevelt share his plans with the public. "It is obvious that as you will shortly be in position to make whatever policies you wish effective, you are the only one who can give these assurances. Both the nature of the cause of public alarm and experience give such an action the prospect of success in turning the tide." In particular, Hoover feels that investors and the public need "prompt assurance that there will be no tampering or inflation of the currency; that the budget will be unquestionably balanced even if further taxation is necessary; that the government credit will be maintained." In the end, Roosevelt does not respond to this plea. He does, however, enact legislation initially crafted during Hoover's administration.

Essential Themes

Hoover's letter conveys a sense of urgency about the state of the nation in 1933 as he prepared to leave office and Roosevelt to enter it. Hoover believes that his experience will be of use to the incoming president, who seems, however, to have disagreed. Hoover identified fear as the primary cause of the economic instability in the country, and he begged Roosevelt to reassure the American people by giving them some insight into his plans for balancing the budget, maintaining credit, and not inflating the country's currency. Although publically and privately, Roosevelt dismissed Hoover as overreaching, he did incorporate some of Hoover's ideas into his own policy upon taking office.

—*Bethany Groff, MA*

Bibliography and Additional Reading

Fuller, Robert Lynn. *Phantom of Fear: The Banking Panic of 1933*. Jefferson: McFarland, 2012. Print.

Hamby, Alonzo L. *For the Survival of Democracy: Franklin Roosevelt and the World Crisis of the 1930s*. New York: Free, 2004. Print.

Parrish, Michael E. *Anxious Decades: American in Prosperity and Depression 1920–1941*. New York: Norton, 1994. Print.

Shlaes, Amity. *The Forgotten Man: A New History of the Great Depression*. New York: Harper Perennial, 2008. Print.

■ President Roosevelt: Fireside Chat Outlining the New Deal

Date: May 7, 1933
Author: Franklin D. Roosevelt
Genre: speech

Summary Overview

When President Franklin Delano Roosevelt took office in March 1933, the United States was in the midst of the worst financial crisis the country had ever experienced. During Roosevelt's first one hundred days in office, he worked with the Congress to create social and economic programs, collectively known as the New Deal, which were designed to stabilize the economy and provide work for the unemployed. The New Deal also included efforts to guarantee bank deposits and prevent future bank runs, to slow the rate of farm foreclosures by providing farmers with lower interest rates on their mortgages, and to provide employment to millions of Americans. In this radio address, Roosevelt outlined the main provisions of the New Deal to the American people and explained the causes of the economic crisis. He called for cooperation between individuals, private companies, government bodies, and global leaders to reverse the crisis and rebuild the economy.

Defining Moment

The United States economy boomed throughout most of the 1920s, in part due to the country's strong position relative to European countries still recovering from the financial and infrastructural damage of World War I. Abundant raw materials and technological advances in manufacturing gave US bankers investment funds, which they used to help finance some of Europe's postwar recovery efforts.

However, many European economies remained weak for years after the war, and most of Europe's financial progress during the 1920s came from trade and investments outside the continent. Furthermore, US stock values were much higher relative to the actual health of the economy. As the US economy softened toward the end of the 1920s, its investments in Europe slowed, further weakening the European economies and jeopardizing their ability to repay their loans to US creditors. On October 29, 1929, following a slight drop in stock values, investors rapidly lost confidence and the US stock market crashed. The value of publicly-traded US companies fell by $30 billion in less than one month, marking the onset of the Great Depression.

Additionally, overproduction in the agricultural and manufacturing sectors had led to a surplus of goods on the domestic US market. With supply exceeding demand, the cost of goods declined significantly, leaving farmers and manufacturers unable to recover costs or make a profit. Farmers faced foreclosure of their property, and factories laid off industrial workers in droves.

By the time Franklin Delano Roosevelt began his presidential campaign in 1932, nearly one-quarter of Americans were out of work, and many were losing their homes and even starving. The stock market had declined to about 20 percent of its 1929 value, and more than one-third of US banks had collapsed, evaporating the savings of millions of Americans. Farmers and industrial workers were frustrated by the federal government's actions under President Herbert Hoover, believing that his efforts focused too strongly on using public funds to subsidize large companies, rather than helping the people directly. As a result of the public's discontent, Roosevelt won the election by a large margin, and he immediately set out to reverse the downward economic spiral.

Within his first one hundred days in office, Roosevelt declared a multiday bank holiday, which kept the nation's banks closed (and thus in business), while he worked with the legislature to develop a plan to maintain their solvency and prevent bank runs. Once the immediate crisis passed, he worked again with Congress to establish a series of government programs designed to provide immediate relief and federally-funded jobs that would put people back to work on public-works initiatives. These programs became collectively known as the New Deal and formed the cornerstone of Roosevelt's domestic policy during his years in office.

Author Biography

Franklin Delano Roosevelt was born on January 30, 1882, in Hyde Park, New York. He was a distant cousin of President Theodore Roosevelt. He attended the prestigious Groton School in Massachusetts and received his bachelor's degree in history from Harvard University in 1903. He studied law at Columbia Law School in New York but left the school without completing his degree after he passed the state bar examination in 1907. He practiced law in New York City before being elected to the New York State Senate in 1910.

President Woodrow Wilson appointed Roosevelt assistant secretary of the Navy in 1913, a position he held until 1920. Following an unsuccessful campaign for US vice president under Democratic candidate James M. Cox in 1920, Roosevelt briefly withdrew from politics. After making a partial recovery from polio, which he contracted in 1921, Roosevelt was elected governor of New York in 1928. In 1932, Roosevelt was elected president of the United States. He was inaugurated during the nadir of the Great Depression and saw the country through World War II. Roosevelt died in office on April 12, 1945.

HISTORICAL DOCUMENT

On a Sunday night a week after my Inauguration I used the radio to tell you about the banking crisis and the measures we were taking to meet it. I think that in that way I made clear to the country various facts that might otherwise have been misunderstood and in general provided a means of understanding which did much to restore confidence.

Tonight, eight weeks later, I come for the second time to give you my report—in the same spirit and by the same means to tell you about what we have been doing and what we are planning to do.

Two months ago we were facing serious problems. The country was dying by inches. It was dying because trade and commerce had declined to dangerously low levels; prices for basic commodities were such as to destroy the value of the assets of national institutions such as banks, savings banks, insurance companies, and others. These institutions, because of their great needs, were foreclosing mortgages, calling loans, refusing credit. Thus there was actually in process of destruction the property of millions of people who had borrowed money on that property in terms of dollars which had had an entirely different value from the level of March, 1933. That situation in that crisis did not call for any complicated consideration of economic panaceas or fancy plans. We were faced by a condition and not a theory.

There were just two alternatives: The first was to allow the foreclosures to continue, credit to be withheld and money to go into hiding, and thus forcing liquidation and bankruptcy of banks, railroads and insurance companies and a re-capitalizing of all business and all property on a lower level. This alternative meant a continuation of what is loosely called "deflation", the net result of which would have been extraordinary hardship on all property owners and, incidentally, extraordinary hardships on all persons working for wages through an increase in unemployment and a further reduction of the wage scale.

It is easy to see that the result of this course would have not only economic effects of a very serious nature but social results that might bring incalculable harm. Even before I was inaugurated I came to the conclusion that such a policy was too much to ask the American people to bear. It involved not only a further loss of homes, farms, savings and wages but also a loss of spiritual values—the loss of that sense of security for the present and the future so necessary to the peace and contentment of the individual and of his family. When you destroy these things you will find it difficult to establish confidence of any sort in the future. It was clear that mere appeals from Washington for confidence and the mere lending of more money to shaky institutions could not stop this downward course. A prompt program applied as quickly as possible seemed to me not only justified but imperative to our national security. The Congress, and when I say

Congress I mean the members of both political parties, fully understood this and gave me generous and intelligent support. The members of Congress realized that the methods of normal times had to be replaced in the emergency by measures which were suited to the serious and pressing requirements of the moment. There was no actual surrender of power, Congress still retained its constitutional authority and no one has the slightest desire to change the balance of these powers. The function of Congress is to decide what has to be done and to select the appropriate agency to carry out its will. This policy it has strictly adhered to. The only thing that has been happening has been to designate the President as the agency to carry out certain of the purposes of the Congress. This was constitutional and in keeping with the past American tradition.

The legislation which has been passed or in the process of enactment can properly be considered as part of a well-grounded plan.

First, we are giving opportunity of employment to one-quarter of a million of the unemployed, especially the young men who have dependents, to go into the forestry and flood prevention work. This is a big task because it means feeding, clothing and caring for nearly twice as many men as we have in the regular army itself. In creating this civilian conservation corps we are killing two birds with one stone. We are clearly enhancing the value of our natural resources and second, we are relieving an appreciable amount of actual distress. This great group of men have entered upon their work on a purely voluntary basis, no military training is involved and we are conserving not only our natural resources but our human resources. One of the great values to this work is the fact that it is direct and requires the intervention of very little machinery.

Second, I have requested the Congress and have secured action upon a proposal to put the great properties owned by our Government at Muscle Shoals to work after long years of wasteful inaction, and with this a broad plan for the improvement of a vast area in the Tennessee Valley. It will add to the comfort and happiness of hundreds of thousands of people and the incident benefits will reach the entire nation.

Next, the Congress is about to pass legislation that will greatly ease the mortgage distress among the farmers and the home owners of the nation, by providing for the easing of the burden of debt now bearing so heavily upon millions of our people.

Our next step in seeking immediate relief is a grant of half a billion dollars to help the states, counties and municipalities in their duty to care for those who need direct and Immediate relief.

In addition to all this, the Congress also passed legislation authorizing the sale of beer in such states as desired. This has already resulted in considerable reemployment and, incidentally, has provided much needed tax revenue.

Now as to the future.

We are planning to ask the Congress for legislation to enable the Government to undertake public works, thus stimulating directly and indirectly the employment of many others in well-considered projects.

Further legislation has been taken up which goes much more fundamentally into our economic problems. The Farm Relief Bill seeks by the use of several methods, alone or together, to bring about an increased return to farmers for their major farm products, seeking at the same time to prevent in the days to come disastrous over-production which so often in the past has kept farm commodity prices far below a reasonable return. This measure provides wide powers for emergencies. The extent of its use will depend entirely upon what the future has in store.

Well-considered and conservative measures will likewise be proposed which will attempt to give to the industrial workers of the country a more fair wage return, prevent cut-throat competition and unduly long hours for labor, and at the same time to encourage each industry to prevent over-production.

One of our bills falls into the same class, the Railroad Bill. It seeks to provide and make certain definite planning by the railroads themselves, with the assistance of the Government, to eliminate the duplication and waste that is now results in railroad receiverships and in continuing operating deficits.

I feel very certain that the people of this country understand and approve the broad purposes behind these new governmental policies relating to agriculture and industry and transportation. We found ourselves faced with more agricultural products than we could possibly consume ourselves and surpluses which other nations did not have the cash to buy from us except at prices ruinously low. We found our factories able to turn out more goods than we could possibly consume, and at the same time we have been faced with a falling export demand. We have found ourselves with more facilities to transport goods and crops than there were goods and crops to be transported. All of this has been caused in large part by a complete failure to understand the danger signals that have been flying ever since the close of the World War. The people of this country have been erroneously encouraged to believe that they could keep on increasing the output of farm and factory indefinitely and that some magician would find ways and means for that increased output to be consumed with reasonable profit to the producer.

But today we have reason to believe that things are a little better than they were two months ago. Industry has picked up, railroads are carrying more freight, farm prices are better, but I am not going to indulge in issuing proclamations of over-enthusiastic assurance. We cannot ballyhoo ourselves back to prosperity. I am going to be honest at all times with the people of the country. I do not want the people of this country to take the foolish course of letting this improvement come back on another speculative wave. I do not want the people to believe that because of unjustified optimism we can resume the ruinous practice of increasing our crop output and our factory output in the hope that a kind providence will find buyers at high prices. Such a course may bring us immediate and false prosperity but it will be the kind of prosperity that will lead us into another tailspin.

It is wholly wrong to call the measure that we have taken Government control of farming, control of industry, and control of transportation. It is rather a partnership between Government and farming and industry and transportation, not partnership in profits, for the profits would still go to the citizens, but rather a partnership in planning and partnership to see that the plans are carried out.

Let me illustrate with an example. Take the cotton goods industry. It is probably true that ninety per cent of the cotton manufacturers would agree to eliminate starvation wages, would agree to stop long hours of employment, would agree to stop child labor, would agree to prevent an overproduction that would result in unsalable surpluses. But, what good is such an agreement if the other ten per cent of cotton manufacturers pay starvation wages, require long hours, employ children in their mills and turn out burdensome surpluses? The unfair ten per cent could produce goods so cheaply that the fair ninety per cent would be compelled to meet the unfair conditions. Here is where government comes in. Government ought to have the right and will have the right, after surveying and planning for an industry to prevent, with the assistance of the overwhelming majority of that industry, unfair practice and to enforce this agreement by the authority of government. The so-called anti-trust laws were intended to prevent the creation of monopolies and to forbid unreasonable profits to those monopolies. That purpose of the anti-trust laws must be continued, but these laws were never intended to encourage the kind of unfair competition that results in long hours, starvation wages and overproduction.

And my friends, the same principle that is illustrated by that example applies to farm products and to transportation and every other field of organized private industry.

We are working toward a definite goal, which is to prevent the return of conditions which came very close to destroying what we call modern civilization. The actual accomplishment of our purpose cannot be attained in a day. Our policies are wholly within purposes for which our American Constitutional Government was established 150 years ago.

I know that the people of this country will understand this and will also understand the spirit in which we are undertaking this policy. I do not deny that we may make mistakes of procedure as we carry out the policy. I have no expectation of making a hit every time I come to bat. What I seek is the highest possible batting average, not only for myself but for the team. Theodore Roosevelt once said to me: "If I can be right 75 per cent of the time I shall come up to the fullest measure of my hopes."

Much has been said of late about Federal finances and inflation, the gold standard, etc. Let me make the facts very simple and my policy very clear. In the first place, government credit and government currency are really one and the same thing. Behind government bonds there is only a promise to pay. Behind government currency we have, in addition to the promise to pay, a reserve of gold and a small reserve of silver. In this connection it is worth while remembering that in the past the government has agreed to redeem nearly thirty billions of its debts and its currency in gold, and private corporations in this country have agreed to redeem another sixty or seventy billions of securities and mortgages in gold. The government and private corporations were making these agreements when they knew full well that all of the gold in the United States amounted to only between three and four billion and that all of the gold in all of the world amounted to only about eleven billion.

If the holders of these promises to pay started in to demand gold the first comers would get gold for a few days and they would amount to about one twenty-fifth of the holders of the securities and the currency. The other twenty-four people out of twenty-five, who did not happen to be at the top of the line, would be told politely that there was no more gold left. We have decided to treat all twenty-five in the same way in the interest of justice and the exercise of the constitutional powers of this government. We have placed every one on the same basis in order that the general good may be preserved.

Nevertheless, gold, and to a partial extent silver, are perfectly good bases for currency and that is why I decided not to let any of the gold now in the country go out of it.

A series of conditions arose three weeks ago which very readily might have meant, first, a drain on our gold by foreign countries, and secondly, as a result of that, a flight of American capital, in the form of gold, out of our country. It is not exaggerating the possibility to tell you that such an occurrence might well have taken from us the major part of our gold reserve and resulted in such a further weakening of our government and private credit as to bring on actual panic conditions and the complete stoppage of the wheels of industry.

The Administration has the definite objective of raising commodity prices to such an extent that those who have borrowed money will, on the average, be able to repay that money in the same kind of dollar which they borrowed. We do not seek to let them get such a cheap dollar that they will be able to pay back a great deal less than they borrowed. In other words, we seek to correct a wrong and not to create another wrong in the opposite direction. That is why powers are being given to the Administration to provide, if necessary, for an enlargement of credit, in order to correct the existing wrong. These powers will be used when, as, and if it may be necessary to accomplish the purpose.

Hand in hand with the domestic situation which, of course, is our first concern, is the world situation, and I want to emphasize to you that the domestic situation is inevitably and deeply tied in with the conditions in all of the other nations of the world. In other words, we can get, in all probability, a fair measure of prosperity return in the United States, but it will not be permanent unless we get a return to prosperity all over the world.

In the conferences which we have held and are holding with the leaders of other nations, we are seeking four great objectives. First, a general reduction of armaments and through this the removal of the fear of invasion and armed attack, and, at the same time, a reduction in armament costs, in order to help in the balancing of government budgets and the reduction of taxation. Secondly, a cutting down of the trade barriers, in order to re-start the flow of exchange of crops and goods between nations. Third, the setting up of a stabilization of currencies, in order that trade can make contracts ahead. Fourth, the reestablishment of friendly relations and greater confidence between all nations.

Our foreign visitors these past three weeks have responded to these purposes in a very helpful way. All of the Nations have suffered alike in this great depression. They have all reached the conclusion that each can best be helped by the common action of all. It is in this spirit that our visitors have met with us and discussed our common problems. The international conference that lies before us must succeed. The future of the world demands it and we have each of us pledged ourselves to the best joint efforts to that end.

To you, the people of this country, all of us, the Members of the Congress and the members of this Administration owe a profound debt of gratitude. Throughout the depression you have been patient. You have granted us wide powers, you have encouraged us with a widespread approval of our purposes. Every ounce of strength and every resource at our command we have devoted to the end of justifying your confidence. We are encouraged to believe that a wise and sensible beginning has been made. In the present spirit of mutual confidence and mutual encouragement we go forward.

And in conclusion, my friends, may I express to the National Broadcasting Company and to the Columbia Broadcasting System my thanks for the facilities which they have made available to me tonight.

Document Analysis

Roosevelt begins his radio address by reminding the audience of the message he delivered eight weeks prior about the ongoing economic crisis. He observes that overproduction in both the agricultural and manufacturing sectors had led to greatly diminished prices for basic commodities, and as a result, businesses were unable to turn a profit and financial institutions began foreclosing on mortgages, recalling loans, and restricting credit access. Roosevelt notes that the federal government has only two possible courses of action under the circumstances: to allow the foreclosures and credit freezes to continue, thus causing the value of property, raw materials, manufactured goods, and commodities to continue to deflate, or to intervene with a plan to support these institutions while the private sector rights itself.

Roosevelt emphasizes that the social consequences of allowing deflation to continue unchecked could bring "incalculable harm" to American society, arguing that such a course of action would permanently damage people's confidence in the US economy and further hamper economic recovery. He argues that it is better for the federal government to intervene on the people's behalf and emphasizes that the plan he is about to outline received bipartisan support in the legislature.

The remainder of Roosevelt's address gives a rough outline of the social and economic programs to be established and funded by the federal government, which collectively became known as the New Deal. These initiatives include establishing the Civilian Conservation Corps to employ young men in public environmental projects, funding additional development in the Tennessee Valley region, providing federal subsidies to small banks to ease the burden of mortgage debt on farmers and homeowners, offering funds to states and counties to spend on immediate relief for their residents in need, and authorizing the sale of beer in the midst of Prohibition in order to create jobs and generate revenue through the sale and taxation of alcohol.

For the longer-term future, Roosevelt notes that it is necessary to improve farmers' returns on crops and to control the problem of overproduction in both farming and industrial manufacturing. He believes that a significant cause of the current economic crisis is that overproduction eroded the value of goods, and he criticizes the false notion that there will be an infinite demand for the increasing amount of food and manufactured goods produced in the United States. He addresses concerns that the government is seizing control over farming and business and says the New Deal and its programs are meant to be a partnership designed to ensure fair competition and promote a quick economic recovery. He asserts that it is well within the US government's rightful authority to prevent unfair businesses practices when the government has the support and assistance of the majority of that industry.

On the global front, Roosevelt says that he is working with other nations' leaders on four objectives: to reduce military armaments, remove trade barriers, stabilize currency, and reestablish friendly relations between nations. He is hopeful that these other nations recognize the interconnectedness of their economies and that they will be able to work together to bring an end to their collective economic difficulties as swiftly as possible.

Essential Themes

A significant theme throughout Roosevelt's campaign and presidency was his attention to the plight of everyday Americans. His bottom-up approach to economic recovery is considered to be a major factor in his sweeping victory over Herbert Hoover in the 1932 election. Contrary to Hoover's less interventionist approach at the onset of the Great Depression, Roosevelt believed that restoring financial security to farmers and workers first would increase spending and ultimately strengthen corporate financial positions. To this end, he proposed significant government spending on programs that put people back to work, and many Americans took government-sponsored jobs working on environmental conservation and other projects to improve public infrastructure. But Roosevelt acknowledged that government intervention alone could not provide lasting improvement to the economy; he believed that permanent change required the participation and cooperation of private companies as well, and he hoped that the New Deal programs would provide the push needed to jump-start that process.

Additionally, as a result of weakening economies across the globe, many countries tried to protect domestic production by raising tariffs on imported goods. This had the unintended effect of reducing the total value of world trade by more than half by 1932, and the increased restrictions only led to a deepening of the economic crisis. Without viable external markets, the overproduction of farm products and manufactured goods in the United States created domestic surpluses that dramatically drove down prices, harming profits and leading to reductions in the workforce and wages. Roosevelt sought to work with foreign governments to reopen international trade, hoping this would raise overseas demand for US products and ultimately put people back to work.

Roosevelt's New Deal programs brought many changes to American society and seemed to ease the burdens of the Great Depression. However, despite the new programs and financial investment from the federal government, the economic recovery was slow. The employment rate and the stock market steadily improved from 1933 through 1937. But an economic recession hit in 1937, resulting in rising unemployment, and the US economy did not fully recover from the Great Depression until the country entered World War II in December 1941.

—*Tracey M. DiLascio, JD*

Bibliography and Additional Reading

Katznelson, Ira. *Fear Itself: The New Deal and the Origins of Our Time*. New York: Liveright, 2013. Print.

McElvaine, Robert S. *The Great Depression: America, 1929–1941*. 25th anniv. ed. New York: Three Rivers, 2009. Print.

Smith, Jean Edward. *FDR*. New York: Random, 2008. Print.

"Timeline of the Great Depression." *American Experience*. WGBH Educational Foundation, n.d. Web. 11 June 2014.

■ John Maynard Keynes: An Open Letter to President Roosevelt

Date: December 16, 1933
Author: John Maynard Keynes
Genre: letter

Summary Overview
In 1933, the *New York Times* invited British economist John Maynard Keynes to give economic advice to President Franklin D. Roosevelt, then nearing the end of his dramatic first year in office. Keynes considered the president to be the greatest champion of the new type of thinking needed to bring the United States—and the world—out of the Great Depression. He suggested that conventional economic thinking that emphasized the importance of balanced budgets and a stable currency needed to be abandoned in favor of a program of debt-financed government spending to revive the US economy. Keynes also favored giving the economy more liquidity by holding down interest rates. Keynes's opinions were considered of such importance that the president's emissary Felix Frankfurter sent a copy to the president directly, so that he could see it before it appeared in the newspaper.

Defining Moment
President Roosevelt took power at the height of the Great Depression, a crisis of economic contraction and mass unemployment affecting much of the world and particularly the United States. In the 1932 election, Roosevelt defeated incumbent president Herbert Hoover, who had been discredited by his failure to solve the problems of mass unemployment. In order for Roosevelt's presidency to be considered a success, he had to get people back to work, and with the desperation of the times, he had considerable leeway to do so. The package of reforms his administration instituted was known collectively as the New Deal, representing a seismic shock in American political life. Among the many dramatic and controversial reforms of the early New Deal was Roosevelt's decision to take the United States off the gold standard. The National Industrial Recovery Act (NIRA) guaranteed the rights of organized labor, allowed for government regulation of prices, and set up codes regulating business competition, bringing the government into the day-to-day life of business like never before. Generally, the New Deal was associated with government action to rescue the economy, as opposed to the *laissez-faire* approach of minimal government interference with business that had dominated Republican administrations in the 1920s and was backed by much of the economic establishment.

Many, including Keynes, believed that the masses of unemployed could pose a radical threat to the American political system if the New Deal failed to put them back to work. The serious difficulties of capitalism were causing many to turn to the Soviet Union and Communism as a model, although this was less true in the United States than in many European countries. Another possible danger presented itself on the extreme right. Around the time of Roosevelt's inauguration, Germany had turned to Nazi leader Adolf Hitler, whose appeal was largely based on taking vigorous action to end mass unemployment. The recovery of the American economy, the largest in the world, was central to the recovery of the world economy and to avoiding the toppling of the liberal democratic order to the benefit of fascism or Communism.

Author Biography
Born June 5, 1883, in Cambridge, England, John Maynard Keynes is considered by many to be the greatest economist of the twentieth century, although many of his ideas also remain controversial. He is generally associated with the notion that governments should counteract the business cycle by cutting spending when times are good and increasing spending, financed by debt, when times are bad, in order to promote economic recovery. Keynes was a believer in a liberal capitalist approach to economics, but he was dubious about

the conventional wisdom of the dominant school of "classical" economists that supported balanced budgets and the gold standard. He was an activist who engaged with the political elite of the day on a range of issues, not an isolated academic writing principally for other scholars. The classic statement of his ideas is his book *The General Theory of Employment, Interest and Money* (1936). He died April 21, 1946, in Firle, England.

HISTORICAL DOCUMENT

In response to the *New York Times'* request for his views on the American outlook, Keynes has written "An Open Letter to President Roosevelt," which is scheduled to appear in the Sunday issue of December 31st and is to be syndicated in other parts of the United States.

So that you may see what he has to say before it is published, Keynes this morning sent me the enclosed copy of his article, which I hasten to get off directly to you through Miss LeHand (without forwarding it through the pouch) in the hope that it may catch the Bremen, which leaves tonight.

Yesterday's Times carried illuminating extracts from Wallace's Annual Report. What a good Secretary of Agriculture you have!

With warm regards,
Faithfully yours,
Felix Frankfurter

* * *

Hon. Franklin D. Roosevelt
Enc.

AN OPEN LETTER TO PRESIDENT ROOSEVELT

By John Maynard Keynes.

Dear Mr President,

You have made yourself the Trustee for those in every country who seek to mend the evils of our condition by reasoned experiment within the framework of the existing social system. If you fail, rational change will be gravely prejudiced throughout the world, leaving orthodoxy and revolution to fight it out. But if you succeed, new and bolder methods will be tried everywhere, and we may date the first chapter of a new economic era from your accession to office. This is a sufficient reason why I should venture to lay my reflections before you, though under the disadvantages of distance and partial knowledge.

At the moment your sympathisers in England are nervous and sometimes despondent. We wonder whether the order of different urgencies is rightly understood, whether there is a confusion of aim, and whether some of the advice you get is not crack-brained and queer. If we are disconcerted when we defend you, this may be partly due to the influence of our environment in London. For almost everyone here has a wildly distorted view of what is happening in the United States. The average City man believes that you are engaged on a hare-brained expedition in face of competent advice, that the best hope lies in your ridding yourself of your present advisers to return to the old ways, and that otherwise the United States is heading for some ghastly breakdown. That is what they say they smell. There is a recrudescence of wise head-waging by those who believe that the nose is a nobler organ than the brain. London is convinced that we only have to sit back and wait, in order to see what we shall see. May I crave your attention, whilst I put my own view?

You are engaged on a double task, Recovery and Reform;—recovery from the slump and the passage of those business and social reforms which are long overdue. For the first, speed and quick results are essential. The second may be urgent too; but haste will be injurious, and wisdom of long-range purpose is more necessary than immediate achievement. It will be through raising high the prestige of your administration by success in short-range Recovery, that you will have the driving force to accomplish long-range Reform. On the other hand, even wise and necessary Reform may, in some respects, impede and complicate Recovery. For it will upset the confidence of the business world and weaken their existing motives to action, before you have had time to put other motives in their place. It may over-task your bureaucratic machine, which the traditional individualism of the United States and the old "spoils system" have left none too strong. And it will confuse the thought and aim of yourself and your administration by giving you too much to think about all at once.

Now I am not clear, looking back over the last nine months, that the order of urgency between measures of Recovery and measures of Reform has been duly observed, or that the latter has not sometimes been mistaken for the former. In particular, I cannot detect any material aid to recovery in N.I.R.A., though its social gains have been large. The driving force which has been put behind the vast administrative task set by this Act has seemed to represent a wrong choice in the order of urgencies. The Act is on the Statute Book; a considerable amount has been done towards implementing it; but it might be better for the present to allow experience to accumulate before trying to force through all its details. That is my first reflection—that N.I.R.A., which is essentially Reform and probably impedes Recovery, has been put across too hastily, in the false guise of being part of the technique of Recovery.

My second reflection relates to the technique of Recovery itself. The object of recovery is to increase the national output and put more men to work. In the economic system of the modern world, output is primarily produced for sale; and the volume of output depends on the amount of purchasing power, compared with the prime cost of production, which is expected to come on the market. Broadly speaking, therefore, an increase of output depends on the amount of purchasing power, compared with the prime cost of production, which is expected to come on the market. Broadly speaking, therefore, an increase of output cannot occur unless by the operation of one or other of three factors. Individuals must be induced to spend more out of their existing incomes; or the business world must be induced, either by increased confidence in the prospects or by a lower rate of interest, to create additional current incomes in the hands of their employees, which is what happens when either the working or the fixed capital of the country is being increased; or public authority must be called in aid to create additional current incomes through the expenditure of borrowed or printed money. In bad times the first factor cannot be expected to work on a sufficient scale. The second factor will come in as the second wave of attack on the slump after the tide has been turned by the expenditures of public authority. It is, therefore, only from the third factor that we can expect the initial major impulse.

Now there are indications that two technical fallacies may have affected the policy of your administration. The first relates to the part played in recovery by rising prices. Rising prices are to be welcomed because they are usually a symptom of rising output and employment. When more purchasing power is spent, one expects rising output at rising prices. Since there cannot be rising output without rising prices, it is essential to ensure that the recovery shall not be held back by the insufficiency of the supply of money to support the increased monetary turn-over. But there is much less to be said in favour of rising prices, if they are brought about at the expense of rising output. Some debtors may be helped, but the national recovery as a whole will be retarded. Thus rising prices caused by deliberately increasing prime costs or by restricting output have a vastly inferior value to rising prices which are the natural result of an increase in the nation's purchasing power.

I do not mean to impugn the social justice and social expediency of the redistribution of incomes aimed at by N.I.R.A. and by the various schemes for agricultural restriction. The latter, in particular, I should strongly support in principle. But too much emphasis on the remedial value of a higher price-level as an object in itself may lead to serious misapprehension as to the part which prices can play in the technique of recovery. The stimulation of output by increasing aggregate purchasing power is the right way to get prices up; and not the other way round.

Thus as the prime mover in the first stage of the technique of recovery I lay overwhelming emphasis on the increase of national purchasing power resulting from governmental expenditure which is financed by Loans and not by taxing present incomes. Nothing else counts in comparison with this. In a boom inflation can be caused by allowing unlimited credit to support the excited enthusiasm of business speculators. But in a slump governmental Loan expenditure is the only sure means of securing quickly a rising output at rising prices.

That is why a war has always caused intense industrial activity. In the past orthodox finance has regarded a war as the only legitimate excuse for creating employment by governmental expenditure. You, Mr President, having cast off such fetters, are free to engage in the interests of peace and prosperity the technique which hitherto has only been allowed to serve the purposes of war and destruction.

The set-back which American recovery experienced this autumn was the predictable consequence of the failure of your administration to organise any material increase in new Loan expenditure during your first six months of office. The position six months hence will entirely depend on whether you have been laying the foundations for larger expenditures in the near future.

I am not surprised that so little has been spent up-to-date. Our own experience has shown how difficult it is to improvise useful Loan-expenditures at short notice. There are many obstacles to be patiently overcome, if waste, inefficiency and corruption are to be avoided. There are many factors, which I need not stop to enumerate, which render especially difficult in the United States the rapid improvisation of a vast programme of public works. I do not blame Mr Ickes for being cautious and careful. But the risks of less speed must be weighed against those of more haste. He must get across the crevasses before it is dark.

The other set of fallacies, of which I fear the influence, arises out of a crude economic doctrine commonly known as the Quantity Theory of Money. Rising output and rising incomes will suffer a set-back sooner or later if the quantity of money is rigidly fixed. Some people seem to infer from this that output and income can be raised by increasing the quantity of money. But this is like trying to get fat by buying a larger belt. In the United States to-day your belt is plenty big enough for your belly. It is a most misleading thing to stress the quantity of money, which is only a limiting factor, rather than the volume of expenditure, which is the operative factor.

It is an even more foolish application of the same ideas to believe that there is a mathematical relation between the price of gold and the prices of other things. It is true that the value of the dollar in terms of foreign currencies will affect the prices of those goods which enter into international trade. In so far as an over-valuation of the dollar was impeding the freedom of domestic price-raising policies or disturbing the balance of payments with foreign countries, it was advisable to depreciate it. But exchange depreciation should follow the success of your domestic price-raising policy as its natural consequence, and should not be allowed to disturb the whole world by preceding its justification at an entirely arbitrary pace. This is another example of trying to put on flesh by letting out the belt.

These criticisms do not mean that I have weakened in my advocacy of a managed currency or in preferring stable prices to stable exchanges. The currency and exchange policy of a country should be entirely subservient to the aim of raising output and employment to the right level. But the recent gyrations of the dollar have looked to me more like a gold standard on the booze than the ideal managed currency of my dreams.

You may be feeling by now, Mr President, that my criticism is more obvious than my sympathy. Yet truly that is not so. You remain for me the ruler whose general outlook and attitude to the tasks of government are the most sympathetic in the world. You are the only one who sees the necessity of a profound change of methods and is attempting it without intolerance, tyranny or destruction. You are feeling your way by trial and error, and are felt to be, as you should be, entirely uncommitted in your own person to the details of a particular technique. In my country, as in your own, your position remains singularly untouched by criticism of this or the other detail. Our hope and our faith are based on broader considerations.

If you were to ask me what I would suggest in concrete terms for the immediate future, I would reply thus.

In the field of gold-devaluation and exchange policy the time has come when uncertainty should be ended. This game of blind man's bluff with exchange speculators serves no useful purpose and is extremely undignified. It upsets confidence, hinders business decisions, occupies the public attention in a measure far exceeding its real importance, and is responsible both for the irritation and for a certain lack of respect which exists abroad. You have three alternatives. You can devalue the dollar in terms of gold, returning to the gold standard at a new fixed ratio. This would be inconsistent with your declarations in favour of a long-range policy of stable prices, and I hope you will reject it. You can seek some common policy of exchange stabilisation with Great Britain aimed at stable price-levels. This would be the best ultimate solution; but it is not practical politics at the moment unless you are prepared to talk in terms of an initial value of sterling well below $5 pending the realisation of a marked rise in your domestic price-level. Lastly you can announce that you will definitely control the dollar exchange by buying and selling gold and foreign currencies so as to avoid wide or meaningless fluctuations, with a right to shift the parities at any time but with a declared intention only so to do either to correct a serious want of balance in America's international receipts and payments or to meet a shift in your domestic price level relatively to price-levels abroad. This appears to me to be your best policy during the transitional period. In other respects you would regain your liberty to make your exchange policy subservient to the needs of your domestic policy—free to let out your belt in proportion as you put on flesh.

In the field of domestic policy, I put in the forefront, for the reasons given above, a large volume of Loan-expenditures under Government auspices. It is beyond my province to choose particular objects of expenditure. But preference should be given to those which can be made to mature quickly on a large scale, as for example the rehabilitation of the physical condition of the railroads. The object is to start the ball rolling. The United States is ready to roll towards prosperity, if a good hard shove can be given in the next six months. Could not the energy and enthusiasm, which launched the N.I.R.A. in its early days, be put behind a campaign for accelerating capital expenditures, as wisely chosen as the pressure of circumstances permits? You can at least feel sure that the country will be better enriched by such projects than by the involuntary idleness of millions.

I put in the second place the maintenance of cheap and abundant credit and in particular the reduction of the long-term rates of interest. The turn of the tide in great Britain is largely attributable to the reduction in the long-term rate of interest which ensued on the success of the conversion of the War Loan. This was deliberately engineered by means of the open-market policy of the Bank of England. I see no reason why you should not reduce the rate of interest on your long-term Government Bonds to 2½ per cent or less with favourable repercussions on the whole bond market, if only the Federal Reserve System would replace its present holdings of short-dated Treasury issues by purchasing long-dated issues in exchange. Such a policy might become effective in the course of a few months, and I attach great importance to it.

With these adaptations or enlargements of your existing policies, I should expect a successful outcome with great confidence. How much that would mean, not only to the material prosperity of the United States and the whole World, but in comfort to men's minds through a restoration of their faith in the wisdom and the power of Government!

With great respect,
Your obedient servant
J M Keynes

GLOSSARY

bond: a certificate of debt issued by a government guaranteeing repayment plus interest in the future

City man: a denizen of London's financial district; a banker

depreciate: to lower the value of

Ickes: Harold Ickes, secretary of the Interior

recrudescence: a break out anew (of something) following a period of quiet

Treasury issues: government bills, notes, bonds, etc.

Document Analysis

Keynes views economic recovery as the central priority of political leadership during the Depression. Although he agrees with many New Deal reforms, he cautions that long-term structural reforms, however praiseworthy in themselves, should not be allowed to interfere with the immediate goal of economic recovery. (Keynes is frequently associated with the quotation "In the long run we are all dead," which endorses putting priority on short-term crises.) He uses the NIRA, which allowed the government to set prices, as an example of a reform that interfered with recovery, although he did not oppose the act itself.

The short-run solution to the challenge of the Depression was an increase in government spending, which Keynes and his followers viewed as the most efficient way to get a stalled economy back into recovery. Keynes cautions that new government spending will not significantly help the economy if it is financed primarily by taxes, which would take more money out of the economy and diminish purchasing power. Instead, spending should be financed principally by government borrowing, he believes. Keynes views himself as a revolutionary in the field of economic thought, and his line of reasoning goes against the orthodoxy of classical economists, who valued balanced budgets and *laissez-faire* policies. The power of "orthodox" economics was not restricted to academia; conservative beliefs were also held by financiers and bankers—the "City men" (with "City" referring to London, the financial center of Britain and the British Empire), whom Keynes describes as skeptical of Roosevelt's policies. Even government officials and leaders of Britain's nominally socialist Labour Party were believers in economic orthodoxy; therefore, Keynes—and, he believes, Roosevelt—face formidable foes. Keynes also recommends lowering interest rates, a policy he believes has already been successful in Great Britain.

Keynes points out that a program of economic reform that lifts economies out of the Depression is one way to stave off political revolution. The Soviet Union seemingly avoided the worst of the Great Depression, and many Western intellectuals unaware or unconcerned with the massive scale of Stalinist repression became Communists or Communist sympathizers. However, Keynes was not one of them. He accepted liberal democracy and free-market capitalism, and, like Roosevelt and his advisers, he hoped that economic experimentation would take place within "the framework of the existing social system." Keynes believes that, by providing an example of how an economy can recover without Communist revolution or fascist dictatorship, American recovery could also inspire the world in a positive direction. Keynes's letter ends on a note of optimism for both the United States and the world.

Essential Themes

President Roosevelt's New Deal, as Keynes advised, incorporated deficit-financed spending, although the degree to which this was a result of Keynes's advice is debated among historians. This deficit financing went against Roosevelt's own predilection for working with a balanced budget. Historians generally believe the New Deal successfully promoted economic recovery, although some economists and political conservatives argue that it did not. Nonetheless, the New Deal brought political stability, as the US political system was not seriously challenged by either the extreme right (fascism) or the extreme left (Communism). However, the United States fully emerged from the Depression only with the tremendous stimulus applied to the economy by World War II. Although the New Deal did have some international influence, the American example of stimulating the economy through democratic government action did not spread as widely as Keynes had hoped. In 1933, Hitler came to power in Germany, another depression-racked country, and revived the economy in a militarized fashion, providing an alternative authoritarian model of recovery to the democratic one favored by Roosevelt and Keynes.

Keynes's advocacy of deficit spending during recessions and depressions as a way of stimulating the economy remains controversial. Conservative economists remain suspicious of any form of government interference in the business cycle, and to many people, the idea that government should cut spending or "tighten its belt" during an economic downturn seems intuitively obvious. (The other half of the Keynesian idea, that the government should cut spending during good times, also seems counterintuitive.) The debate over Keynesian economic policy remains controversial, as seen in the disagreement among American policy makers during and after the economic downturn that began in 2008.

—*William E. Burns, PhD*

Bibliography and Further Reading

Backhouse, Roger, and Bradley W. Bateman. *Capitalist Revolutionary: John Maynard Keynes*. Cambridge: Harvard UP, 2011. Print.

Clark, P. F. *Keynes: The Rise, Fall and Return of the Twentieth Century's Most Influential Economist*. New York: Bloomsbury, 2009. Print.

Hiltzik, Michael. *The New Deal: A Modern History*. New York: Free, 2011. Print.

Letter-Report Concerning the Tennessee Valley

Date: June 11, 1934
Authors: Lorena Hickok
Genre: report; letter

Summary Overview

In 1933, Lorena Hickok, chief investigator of the Federal Emergency Relief Administration (FERA), began a nationwide tour to examine the effects of the Great Depression and whether New Deal programs were helping to mitigate them. In this report to FERA chief Harry Hopkins, she summarized her observations while traveling through the Tennessee Valley, including stops in Memphis, Tupelo, and parts of Arkansas. Hickok described public sentiment toward the New Deal, President Franklin D. Roosevelt, and the Depression. She also offered criticism on the areas in which Roosevelt's policies and actions fell short. Hickok's tour gave the president and his administration a firsthand view of conditions and attitudes during a key period in the first two years of Roosevelt's presidency.

Defining Moment

When Franklin Delano Roosevelt won the 1932 presidential election, he promised that Americans would be cut a "new deal" in a sweeping set of policy measures aimed at combating the worst of the Great Depression's fallout. At the time, Roosevelt's plan represented a radical re-envisioning of the role of the federal government. In the face of backlash from major actors in business and other sectors, Roosevelt stressed the urgency of the situation—with a quarter of the population out of work and banks closing at an alarming rate, the circumstances called for swift and drastic action.

Roosevelt and his congressional supporters introduced a wide range of bills designed to bring relief to those hardest hit by the Depression. Among these initiatives were direct financial aid, social services, work programs—including the landmark Civilian Conservation Corps—and grants to offset the effects of the Dust Bowl. Roosevelt's approach was a major departure from the activities of the previous three administrations—all Republican—which had advocated for a much smaller and less interventionist federal government.

Programs like the Civilian Conservation Corps—a program designed to provide environmental and conservation jobs to able-bodied young men and veterans—were illustrative of the New Deal philosophy: unemployed Americans would be given an opportunity to work for the federal government rather than simply receive an unemployment check. The Federal Emergency Relief Administration (FERA)—legislation for which was enacted in May of 1933—was a prime example of this approach. Headed by longtime Roosevelt advisor Harry Hopkins, FERA was launched as a two-year program divided into three areas: social service, public works, and rural rehabilitation. Initially, $500 million was to be issued to state agencies as grants (the states did not need to repay these funds). While a portion of FERA funds would be used in part to provide emergency food and shelter to the most impacted citizens, the main focus of state programs was to get Americans back to work.

In an effort to assess the efficacy of the New Deal programs on a human level, Hopkins turned to Lorena Hickok. Hickok was charged with traveling throughout the United States and documenting conditions and public attitudes as well as critiquing FERA program operations. Hickok's tour gave Hopkins and Roosevelt a firsthand view of the New Deal's effectiveness against the Great Depression's impacts.

Author Biography

Lorena Alice Hickok was born in East Troy, Wisconsin, on March 7, 1893. She attended, but did not graduate from Lawrence College in Appleton, leaving after her freshman year and becoming a writer for a Battle

Creek, Michigan, newspaper. She worked on a number of newspapers thereafter, eventually being hired as a feature writer by the Associated Press in 1928. In 1932, she met and befriended Eleanor Roosevelt. In 1933, she was hired by Harry Hopkins to be the chief investigator for FERA. She would later work closely with Eleanor Roosevelt during her husband's administration. In 1940, Hickok was tapped to be the executive secretary of the Women's Division of the Democratic National Committee. Following Roosevelt's presidency, she moved to New York, collaborating with Eleanor Roosevelt on a book, *Women of Courage*, and later writing a biography of Mrs. Roosevelt. Hickok died in 1968.

HISTORICAL DOCUMENT

From Lorena Hickok
To Harry L. Hopkins
Enroute, Memphis to Denver, June 11, 1934

Dear Mr. Hopkins:

As you can see, I've finished my trip through the Tennessee Valley and adjacent territory and am on my way to Colorado and the sugar beets.

I wound up this last weekend in Memphis, where I saw several kinds of people, including: One wealthy cotton man and banker who gives the impression that he thinks all tenants are lazy beggars and should be treated as serfs and would rather see the price of cotton stay down at 5 cents a pound forever than be boosted with Government control and Government insistence on any sort of fair play for share-croppers and laborers.

The local political boss, who assured me that everything was just too hunky dory, but who wasn't at all enthusiastic about the possibility of 3,000 transients now in Memphis remaining there forever.

A flock of social workers, who would like to see Tennessee have a good, strong public welfare department and are, they said, working toward that end, but whose approach to the relief problem is so typical of the old line social worker, supported by private philanthropy and looking down his—only usually it was HER—nose at God's patient poor, that it made me gag a little.

The conservative editor of the conservative *Memphis Commercial-Appeal*, who thinks we've got a big rural relief load that will stay on our hands forever, if we don't drop 'em pretty soon, and who wonders if the people down in Tupelo, Mississippi, who are now getting their electricity for one third of what it used to cost them, aren't going to have to make up for it later on in higher taxes.

And the liberal editor of the *Scripps-Howard* newspaper, who thinks the New Dealers aren't aggressive enough—don't do enough propagandizing.

One thing I've noticed particularly. That is that people outside the relief business aren't thinking much about it. They are more like they used to be last summer, when things were booming and, if they were conscious of relief at all, they were bored by it—not critical, just bored. CWA apparently aroused public interest in relief for a time. Now that's gone, and they've lapsed back into indifference. The comment you usually hear is, "You've got a lot of people on relief who are there to stay as long as you'll let 'em." And that's all they have to say. No criticism. No commendation. They're just indifferent.

On this trip I've tried not to be too preoccupied with relief. I've tried to find out what the people as a whole are thinking about—people who are at work. I carry away the impression that all over the area, from Knoxville, Tennessee, to Tupelo, Mississippi, and on up to Memphis and Nashville, people are in a pretty contented, optimistic frame of mind. They just aren't thinking about the Depression any more. They feel that we are on our way out and toward any problems that have to be solved before we get out their attitude seems to be, "Let Roosevelt do it."

They are strong for the President. They seem to have absolute confidence in him. Their attitude toward the rest of the New Dealers seems to be one of good natured tolerance—so long as they themselves are not hampered by any of the New Dealers' policies. They didn't take Dr. Wirt seriously at all. When I asked the political boss in Memphis what people thought about the Brains Trust, he grinned and replied:

"Oh, just a necessary evil, I guess."

Outside of one town, there isn't any particularly militant labor leadership in Tennessee, apparently. So Toledo, the threatened steel strike, the labor difficulties elsewhere in the textile industry, and troubles down around Birmingham seem to make little impression in Tennessee. You don't see much evidence of restlessness.

There apparently isn't much among the people on relief, either. That may be due to the fact that in Tennessee the number of skilled workmen and white collar people on relief is relatively small. The load is largely rural, of a class of people whose incomes normally and whose standards of living are so low that relief does not seem inadequate to them at all. They are quite satisfied with it. The problem is going to be getting them off.

Everywhere, even though the relief loads remain large, you hear the same story. Business has picked up. Retail sales and advertising in Memphis, for instance. I was told that no city in the South has received greater benefits from the cotton program than has Memphis, a shipping and trading center. Down in Tupelo everybody seems to be feeling grand. Garment factories and a textile mill are going peacefully along under the code, the Chamber of Commerce is getting inquiries from industries attracted there by the low power rate, and the proprietor of a 38-room hotel relates with satisfaction how she operates her hotel, with lights, fans in all rooms, two vacuum cleaners, two electric irons, refrigerator, and radio with an electric bill of around $20 a month.

Incidentally there are now in Tupelo six companies selling electric equipment, including both the expensive kinds and the new, cheaper models put out by the manufacturers in agreement with TVA. They say that in 17 days, after the new models were brought in, 137 refrigerators were sold and 17 ranges—that one dealer sold in one week 21 units, i.e., stoves or refrigerators.

Differences in prices between the regular equipment and the new models, not quite so deluxe, run something like this: electric refrigerators, top standard price $137, new price $80; hot water heaters, top standard price around $95, new top price $60; ranges, top standard price $137, new top price $80.

When I was in Tupelo they had no figures to show just how much electric equipment had been sold, but I was impressed with the figures of one dealer, who handles only the high priced stuff. In less than a month he had sold ten refrigerators and five ranges. And Tupelo is only a small town, about 6,000 population.

It is still a little early to see what the new electric rate is going to do for householders and farmers in and around Corinth and Tupelo. I went down there thinking perhaps I could see some urban housewives and farm wives actually using the electric refrigerators and stoves that they'd never have had in their lives if it hadn't been for TVA. But it hasn't reached that class yet. New wiring is just being begun—10 miles of it in Tupelo! But it's going along. Dealers say they are taking orders from farmers right along. One thing they are doing is to cut down greatly the cost of wiring a house. For instance, in Tupelo it used to cost as high as $60 to have an electric stove installed in your house. It now costs $5

Even though I was disappointed in not being able to find in Tupelo and the surrounding country housewives using electric equipment that they had never expected to have, I felt that my trip was not in vain. Private industry, to a large extent, in Tupelo has actually tried out the subsistence homestead idea! And it seems to work!

It began back in 1923 with one garment factory, the management of which adopted a policy of hiring only workers who lived out in the country, on their own little farms. The movement spread. There are in Tupelo two garment factories and a textile mill that employ a total of around 2,000 people, and of these, I was told, only 700 or 800 live in town. Busses collect the workers from their farms, averaging around 15 acres each, every morning and bring them to work. And each evening take them home. As a matter of fact, they are school busses. They bring the workers into town first, then take the children to school, and in the afternoon they take the children home and then come after the workers.

People generally around Tupelo are pretty keen about the idea after having seen it in operation for several years. Relief workers told me that very, very few of the workers who lived that way had appeared on the relief rolls. One young man, a clerical worker in one of the garment factories, told me how it works out for him. He has a 10-acre farm, about three miles from town. Has a cow, some pigs and chickens, garden, some pasturage, a good comfortable house. Raises practically everything he eats.

"As a matter of fact," he said, "except for what I pay out for clothes and the upkeep of my car, the salary I earn here in the factory is just about all net profit! And I've got the place, all clear of debt, to go to if anything happens to my job."

They are setting up near Tupelo a subsistence homestead unit to which no one will be admitted who hasn't a job. Most of them are employed in the garment factories. Well, at least those people have a reasonably good chance of being able to pay their way out....

I think perhaps the most interesting person I've met this last week was the *Scripps-Howard* editor in Memphis. He's sold, heart and soul, on the Roosevelt program. But he's worried.

The thing that bothers him most is the ignorance, the lack of understanding, on the part of the general public of what we're up against and what we're trying to do.

To begin with, he thinks, most people still don't understand that this is no ordinary depression. The part that technological development plays in it just hasn't sunk in on people generally at all, he thinks. And I'm inclined to agree with him

Now, he says, with business picking up due largely to heroic effort on the part of the New Dealers, the businessmen who aren't actually fighting the New Deal have settled back into a comfortable complacency, lulled off to sleep by improvement in their own particular situations. People ARE so damned lazy mentally. They WON'T think.

"Take our cotton planters and our merchants here in Memphis," he said. "They are a lot better off than they were a year ago. So, aside from kicking a little about Government expense, they're perfectly contented as long as they aren't interfered with. They have no conception at all of the problem or of what Roosevelt is trying to do.

"Now all really thoughtful people realize that things are never going to be the same again. They've got to change—they ARE changing—whether we like it or not. And if Roosevelt isn't able to bring about that change in an orderly fashion, it's going to happen the other way, with a lot of disorder and suffering.

I feel that the Administration is falling down, badly, in not getting this over to the public. We've got to sell the public the idea that this change is coming—that it's bound to come—and that Roosevelt is the boy who is going to put it over with the least amount of suffering for everybody."

"Well, how are you going to propagandize with most of the newspapers of the country agin you?" I demanded.

"It will have to be clever propaganda, concealed propaganda—propaganda in 'made news,'" he said. "This is a democracy. Our government can't put over propaganda the way they do in Russia and in Germany. It can't suppress news. We don't want any censorship. But you can put propaganda over in the news. What's happened to Charley Michelson, by the way? He did exactly that thing all through the Hoover administration, didn't he? That was destructive propaganda, tearing the Hoover administration to pieces. Now we want the same thing, only constructive instead of destructive. I don't care how anti-administration the newspapers are, they're going to print news and don't you forget it. What we've got to do is to give 'em the right kind of news."

And, with 20 years' background in the newspaper business myself, may I add that we must slip over this propaganda sugar-coated with news, so they don't realize it's propaganda they're getting. That is what Charley Michelson did during the Hoover administration as a matter of fact.

You certainly don't hear much about the drouth down here. We are now traveling through Arkansas, and the country looks grand. They're harvesting, winter wheat apparently. Cornfields look good, and the stock is fat.

Well, despite drouth and pig-headed capitalists and labor leaders, people who don't have to be on relief but want to, and people who have to be on relief and hate it, the machine that takes jobs away from men, stupidity and indifference on the part of the public toward what we are trying to do, and all the other things there are to worry about—it's funny, but I believe that probably in many large areas of the United States right now go percent of the people are perfectly happy and contented, working along, thinking, as Rex Tugwell says, "mostly about baseball and the races!"

That's probably true in much of the territory I covered in my last trip before this one. Only I stuck too close to the relief picture, I guess, and couldn't see anything else.

GLOSSARY

agin: against

Brains Trust: a nickname for a group of advisers surrounding President Franklin D. Roosevelt

code: the: rules governing labor relations

drouth: drought

subsistence homestead: part of a federal housing project designed to provide homes and garden plots for "subsistence" farming

Tugwell, Rex(ford): head of the federal subsistence homestead division

TVA: Tennessee Valley Authority, a federally owned regional power utility

Document Analysis

Lorena Hickok's June 11, 1934, report to Harry Hopkins covers her travels in the Tennessee Valley from the major cities of Tennessee, south to Tupelo, Mississippi, and west to Arkansas. During this trip, she met a wide range of political leaders, media representatives, and private citizens. In these locales, Hickok reports, citizens were generally pleased with President Roosevelt's New Deal programs, particularly the establishment of the Tennessee Valley Authority. She also saw an improvement in citizen morale with regard to the economy—although businesses were still slow to recover, she said, they were nonetheless improving.

The South was an area particularly hard hit by both the Depression and the Dust Bowl drought of the early 1930s. Hickok says that many of the programs implemented through the New Deal appeared to be improving conditions, however. The Tennessee Valley Authority (TVA) was bringing electricity to some of the region's most rural and isolated communities. Crops were starting to return in great numbers, including staples like cotton. Attitudes were also starting to improve with regard to the Depression, Hickok reports. Although many were still out of work and living in poverty, they were receiving steady streams of aid from the government to sustain them. Certainly, there were incidents she observed that would warrant improvement, such as social workers who seemed to have a condescending attitude toward aid recipients. Those citizens who were not optimistic at least had come to accept and adjust to the hardships that had been placed upon them by the collapsed economy.

Hickok also observed the political landscape of these areas. Political bosses and leaders alike were energized by the New Deal and its impact on their respective constituents, Hickok reports. Some businesses expressed disdain for the principles of the New Deal and the increased activity of the federal government, she writes, but most of the same people who protested the government's activities were seeing improved business—their protests, therefore, rang hollow.

One important trend Hickok reports is the fact that many citizens in the Tennessee Valley region were "ignorant" of the Depression's scope and impact, as well as what the federal government was attempting to do to reverse this economic trend. Part of the blame for this ignorance, she writes, rests on the shoulders of the citizens themselves. Although their businesses suffered and then started to improve again, she says, they were too "lazy mentally" to understand what had occurred.

Within her report, Hickok recounts a conversation she had with the editor of the Memphis *Scripps-Howard* newspaper. In their talk, the editor placed some of the blame for the public's ignorance on the Roosevelt administration and alluded to the role the press might play in better propagandizing on behalf of New Deal programs and goals. It is important for the government, Hickok writes, to take stock of the Depression's effects, disseminate information about the programs it offered to address these issues, and even take credit when those programs were successful. People were slowly becoming more optimistic about the economy, Hickok says, and such optimism was generated by the New Deal's programs.

Essential Themes

As a former journalist, Lorena Hickok was deemed by the Roosevelt administration to be the ideal individual to travel the United States and report on the Depression as well as the effectiveness of the New Deal. Hickok reported that the New Deal was indeed having a positive effect on the areas of the Tennessee Valley that were hardest hit by the Depression. There remained work to be done, both in terms of the economy and in terms of how the federal government informed the public. Nevertheless, she said, public sentiment was improving, a trend that warranted optimism about economic recovery.

Hickok met with a wide range of individuals and groups during her visits in Memphis, Knoxville, Nashville, Tupelo, and elsewhere. In general, she said, people were either optimistic that the economy was turning around, or had adjusted to the Depression's effects. What she did not see was desperation, nor did she see the devastation of the Dust Bowl drought. People were appreciative of the president's efforts, she reported, as Roosevelt's programs were having a positive impact.

One of the largest issues she observed in this report, however, was that of ignorance. Those who philosophically objected to the New Deal, she argued, had but to look around them to see their businesses showing signs of improvement as a direct result of New Deal policies. Far too many people other than partisans, however, also did not take stock of what had occurred during the Depression and what the government was doing to reverse the trend. These residents, she concluded, were the victims of their own laziness—they had but to look around themselves for evidence of improvement, but could not be made to do so.

Besides the willfully ignorant, Hickok said, there were those who sought, but could not find, the best possible information. In this arena, she stated, the federal government was well-advised to do more to communicate with the citizenry. But Hickok advised that Washington should "sugar-coat" its propaganda with news, so as to communicate information without coming off as blatantly propagandizing. The New Deal's success was a story worth telling the people, she suggested.

—*Michael P. Auerbach, MA*

Bibliography and Additional Reading

Deeben, John P. "Family Experiences and New Deal Relief: The Correspondence Files of the Federal Emergency Relief Administration, 1933–1936." *Prologue*. National Archives, 2012. Web. 25 June 2014.

"Federal Emergency Relief Administration." *Gilder Lehrman Institute of American History*. Gilder Lehrman Institute, 2014. Web. 25 June 2014.

Hickok, Lorena A., Richard Lowitt, & Maurine Hoffman Beasley. *One Third of a Nation: Lorena Hickok Reports on the Great Depression*. Urbana: U of Illinois P, 1981. Print.

"Lorena Alice Hickok (1893–1968)." *The Eleanor Roosevelt Papers Project*. George Washington University, 2014. Web. 25 June 2014.

Rose, Nancy Ellen. *Put to Work: Relief Programs in the Great Depression*. New York: Monthly Rev., 1994. Print.

■ FDR on Social Security

Date: January 17, 1935 and August 14, 1935
Author: Franklin Delano Roosevelt
Genre: address; speech

Summary Overview

As President Franklin Roosevelt entered the third year of his presidency, he and his advisors faced an economy still in the midst of the deepest recession of the twentieth century, the Great Depression. Compounding this were unusually dry conditions, the Dust Bowl, which destroyed many Midwestern farms, adding many thousands more to those in poverty. The mixture of urban and rural unemployment created a situation in which many older individuals no longer had the ability to support themselves, and their families did not have the resources to assist them. The proposed national Social Security system, which would pay retirement benefits based upon contributions made while working, would be a major step toward ending poverty among senior citizens. This revolutionized the concept of retirement in America. In addition, Roosevelt proposed a standardized unemployment compensation system to be administered by the states, as well as grants to states for the assistance of children in need. Although this assistance was targeted at just these three areas, the overall social and political impact of the legislation proposed by Roosevelt, and passed by Congress, cannot be overstated.

Defining Moment

Although an economic slump had begun during the summer of 1929, the stock market crash of October 1929 focused everyone's attention on the economy and destroyed the optimistic outlook that had prevailed during most of the 1920s. President Hoover incorrectly believed that this would be a short-lived downturn. With rising unemployment and a slumping economy, Hoover lost the 1932 presidential election to Franklin Roosevelt, who campaigned on a promise that he would give a New Deal to Americans. The 25 percent unemployment rate was a major focus of Roosevelt's early legislative efforts. His programs, as well as a slowly recovering economy, caused a major reduction in unemployment. However, one significant demographic sector remained in serious trouble. The poverty rate for older Americans was about 50 percent. Between urban economic problems in the manufacturing sector and poor agricultural prospects because of the Dust Bowl, it was unlikely that older people could re-enter the labor market. The stock market and financial crisis of the past few years had wiped out the savings of many. In Roosevelt's view, a program to raise older Americans out of poverty, at that time and in the future, was needed.

He proposed the creation of the Social Security program, initially funded by the government, with future beneficiaries' benefits paid by their own contributions. This was to be a radically new program for the United States, changing the old pattern of individual or family support for those who were no longer able to work. Having been elected in 1932, and with the Democratic Party also getting a large majority in both houses of Congress in both the 1932 and 1934 elections, Roosevelt could get virtually all of his legislation passed without significant problems. This included the Social Security program. The system, along with funding for those who were already at retirement age, was authorized and signed into law in August 1935. While slightly increasing the national debt to meet the needs of the first recipients, the program, in its initial years, dramatically reduced the number of older Americans living in poverty. The unemployment compensation program that was part of the legislation also helped insure that workers losing a job would have a minimum level of support, as would children in need. While passage of the law was part of Roosevelt's plan to stimulate the economy, he and the program's backers hoped that old-age security and unemployment benefits would help keep such depressions from recurring in the future.

Normally, it is only under unusual circumstances that landmark legislation like the Social Security Act can pass into law and be accepted. The year 1935 allowed for such momentous legislation because of the single-party majority and the will of political leaders to address not only current problems, but likely future problems as well.

Author Biography

Franklin Delano Roosevelt (1882–1945) from Hyde Park, New York, was the thirty-second president of the United States. He married Anna Eleanor Roosevelt in 1905, and they had six children. Franklin began his political career in 1910 as a New York state senator, later serving as assistant secretary of the Navy and governor of New York prior to his being elected president in 1932. The early 1920s brought two low points in his life: being the losing vice presidential candidate in 1920 and being stricken by polio in 1921. He was the first person with a major disability to be elected president. (He never regained full use of his legs.) His economic policies, as governor, were the foundation for his presidential campaign. Roosevelt transformed the nation through his aggressive agenda to restore the economy. In addition to the Social Security and unemployment programs, Roosevelt transformed the laws regulating the banking system, stock trading, farm price supports, and the mortgage process and devised a temporary means to employ idle workers through the Civilian Conservation Corp (CCC) and Works Progress Administration (WPA). He supported the nations fighting Germany in World War II and, once the United States entered the war in 1941, was very active in overseeing military operations.

HISTORICAL DOCUMENT

[President's Message to Congress on Social Security, January 17, 1935]

In addressing you on June eighth, 1934, I summarized the main objectives of our American program. Among these was, and is, the security of the men, women, and children of the Nation against certain hazards and vicissitudes of life. This purpose is an essential part of our task. In my annual message to you I promised to submit a definite program of action. This I do in the form of a report to me by a Committee on Economic Security, appointed by me for the purpose of surveying the field and of recommending the basis of legislation.

I am gratified with the work of this Committee and of those who have helped it: The Technical Board on Economic Security drawn from various departments of the Government, the Advisory Council on Economic Security, consisting of informed and public spirited private citizens and a number of other advisory groups, including a committee on actuarial consultants, a medical advisory board, a dental advisory committee, a hospital advisory committee, a public health advisory committee, a child welfare committee and an advisory committee on employment relief. All of those who participated in this notable task of planning this major legislative proposal are ready and willing, at any time, to consult with and assist in any way the appropriate Congressional committees and members, with respect to detailed aspects.

It is my best judgment that this legislation should be brought forward with a minimum of delay. Federal action is necessary to, and conditioned upon, the action of States. Forty-four legislatures are meeting or will meet soon. In order that the necessary State action may be taken promptly it is important that the Federal Government proceed speedily.

The detailed report of the Committee sets forth a series of proposals that will appeal to the sound sense of the American people. It has not attempted the impossible, nor has it failed to exercise sound caution and consideration of all of the factors concerned: the national credit, the rights and responsibilities of States, the capacity of industry to assume financial responsibilities and the fundamental necessity of proceeding in a manner that will merit the enthusiastic support of citizens of all sorts.

It is overwhelmingly important to avoid any danger of permanently discrediting the sound and necessary policy of Federal legislation for economic security by attempting to apply it on too ambitious a scale before actual experience has provided guidance for the permanently safe direction of such efforts. The place of such a fundamental in our future civilization is too precious to be jeopardized now by extravagant action. It is a sound idea—a sound ideal. Most of the other advanced countries of the world have already adopted it and their experience affords the knowledge that social insurance can be made a sound and workable project.

Three principles should be observed in legislation on this subject. First, the system adopted, except for the money necessary to initiate it, should be self-sustaining in the sense that funds for the payment of insurance benefits should not come from the proceeds of general taxation. Second, excepting in old-age insurance, actual management should be left to the States subject to standards established by the Federal Government. Third, sound financial management of the funds and the reserves, and protection of the credit structure of the Nation should be assured by retaining Federal control over all funds through trustees in the Treasury of the United States.

At this time, I recommend the following types of legislation looking to economic security:

1. Unemployment compensation.
2. Old-age benefits, including compulsory and voluntary annuities.
3. Federal aid to dependent children through grants to States for the support of existing mothers' pension systems and for services for the protection and care of homeless, neglected, dependent, and crippled children.
4. Additional Federal aid to State and local public health agencies and the strengthening of the Federal Public Health Service. I am not at this time recommending the adoption of so called "health insurance," although groups representing the medical profession are cooperating with the Federal Government in the further study of the subject and definite progress is being made.

With respect to unemployment compensation, I have concluded that the most practical proposal is the levy of a uniform Federal payroll tax, ninety per cent of which should be allowed as an offset to employers contributing under a compulsory State unemployment compensation act. The purpose of this is to afford a requirement of a reasonably uniform character for all States cooperating with the Federal Government and to promote and encourage the passage of unemployment compensation laws in the States. The ten per cent not thus offset should be used to cover the costs of Federal and State administration of this broad system. Thus, States will largely administer unemployment compensation, assisted and guided by the Federal Government. An unemployment compensation system should be constructed in such a way as to afford every practicable aid and incentive toward the larger purpose of employment stabilization. This can be helped by the intelligent planning of both public and private employment. It also can be helped by correlating the system with public employment so that a person who has exhausted his benefits may be eligible for some form of public work as is recommended in this report. Moreover, in order to encourage the stabilization of private employment, Federal legislation should not foreclose the States from establishing means for inducing industries to afford an even greater stabilization of employment.

In the important field of security for our old people, it seems necessary to adopt three principles: First, non-contributory old-age pensions for those who are now too old to build up their own insurance. It is, of course, clear that for perhaps thirty years to come funds will have to be provided by the States and the Federal Government to meet these pensions. Second, compulsory contributory annuities that in time will establish a self-supporting system for those now young and for future generations. Third, voluntary contributory annuities by which individual initiative can increase the annual amounts received in old age. It is proposed that the Federal Government assume one-half of the cost of the old-age pension plan, which ought ultimately to be supplanted by self-supporting annuity plans.

The amount necessary at this time for the initiation of unemployment compensation, old-age security, children's aid, and the promotion of public health, as outlined in the report of the Committee on Economic Security, is approximately one hundred million dollars.

The establishment of sound means toward a greater future economic security of the American people is dictated by a prudent consideration of the hazards involved in our national life. No one can guarantee this country against the dangers of future depressions but we can reduce these dangers. We can eliminate many of the factors that cause economic depressions, and we can provide the means of mitigating their results. This plan for economic security is at once a measure of prevention and a method of alleviation.

We pay now for the dreadful consequence of economic insecurity—and dearly. This plan presents a more equitable and infinitely less expensive means of meeting these costs. We cannot afford to neglect the plain duty before us. I strongly recommend action to attain the objectives sought in this report.

* * *

[*President's Statement upon Signing the Social Security Act, August 14, 1935*]

Today a hope of many years' standing is in large part fulfilled. The civilization of the past hundred years, with its startling industrial changes, has tended more and more to make life insecure. Young people have come to wonder what would be their lot when they came to old age. The man with a job has wondered how long the job would last.

This social security measure gives at least some protection to thirty millions of our citizens who will reap direct benefits through unemployment compensation, through old-age pensions and through increased services for the protection of children and the prevention of ill health.

We can never insure one hundred percent of the population against one hundred percent of the hazards and vicissitudes of life, but we have tried to frame a law that will give some measure of protection to the average citizen and to his family against the loss of a job and against poverty-ridden old age.

This law, too, represents a cornerstone in a structure that is being built but is by no means complete. It is a structure intended to lessen the force of possible future depressions. It will act as a protection to future Administrations against the necessity of going deeply into debt to furnish relief to the needy. The law will flatten out the peaks and valleys of deflation and of inflation. It is, in short, a law that will take care of human needs and at the same time provide the United States an economic structure of vastly greater soundness.

I congratulate all of you ladies and gentlemen, all of you in the Congress, in the executive departments and all of you who come from private life, and I thank you for your splendid efforts in behalf of this sound, needed and patriotic legislation.

If the Senate and the House of Representatives in this long and arduous session had done nothing more than pass this Bill, the session would be regarded as historic for all time.

GLOSSARY

offset: in this case, reducing one's federal unemployment tax payment by substituting (offsetting) payments to one's state for unemployment compensation

vicissitudes: changes in life, for better or worse

Document Analysis

The legislation proposed by Franklin D. Roosevelt was one of the most important pieces of legislation in the modern history of American government. Since its inception in 1935, the Social Security system has affected virtually every American citizen. While not touching as many lives directly as Social Security, the strengthening of the system for unemployment compensation and federal aid to children in difficult circumstances have also been important down through the decades. Together, these provisions served to create a safety net upon which many people have depended on in the past and continue to depend on today.

In June of 1934, Roosevelt began the process of developing what would become the Social Security system when he announced the appointment of five cabinet members to be the Committee on Economic Security, charged with developing plans for the system. With wide-ranging input, including a study of the world's first public pension system in Germany, the Committee drew up a proposal that Roosevelt then forwarded to Congress with the first message reproduced here (Jan. 17). As stated in his third paragraph, Roosevelt pressed for prompt passage.

Although resistance to federal deficit spending was not as strong in 1935 as it has been in some eras, a substantial deficit had been created during the first years of the Great Depression owing, in part, to the implementation of programs designed to stimulate the economy. Thus, Roosevelt emphasized that this new retirement program would be self-supporting. The principal regarding self-support limited what could be accomplished because Roosevelt did not want to have future government actions "jeopardized by extravagant action" in the present. Thus, the new "old-age benefits" would be funded by "compulsory" contributions by workers (in the form of paycheck withholdings). In the minds of those who developed the basic plan, this was a key provision for public acceptance of the program and long-term stability.

However, in order to meet the needs of poverty-stricken older Americans in 1935, a second program had to be included in the proposal. This was the "noncontributory old-age pensions" given to those already sixty-five or older. The legislation established a temporary state-administered program, with money given to the states by the federal government for the welfare of senior citizens. This money is included in the "one hundred million dollars" mentioned in the speech. Most of the money not needed for old-age benefits was slated for "children's aid" and health initiatives. The unemployment compensation plan, like Social Security, was an insurance-style program with a "payroll tax" collected to fund much of its cost. Although it would not help individuals who had previously lost their jobs, a system for assisting those who became unemployed in the future was seen as a major step toward reducing "the dangers of future depressions."

The second statement here (Aug. 14), written seven months after the first, was made when Roosevelt signed the bill into law. This brief statement encompasses Roosevelt's hopes that this legislation might assist the "average citizen" to cope with unfortunate circumstances in the future. As he recognized, the law did not achieve everything that might have been desired, but it did create a strong economic foundation on which people could and have relied.

Essential Themes

When Roosevelt set out this proposal, it was a means to address the economic situation for the nation and for individual citizens. The input given him by his advisors (the Committee on Economic Security) supplied the basis for a plan to relieve some of the economic worries faced by people as the country went through the Great Depression and gradually shifted from a predominantly rural to a predominantly urban citizenry. Historically, that is, individuals with economic problems were commonly assisted by the extended family, the members of which often lived on the same farm or in the same rural community. With the shift to an increasingly urban population, the traditional form of assistance was no longer available to everyone. The proposal, therefore, was intended to help persons in need and to bolster the national economy at the same time. Children too young to fend for themselves, people who became unemployed through no fault of their own, and older Americans not able to participate in the workforce were the subjects of this legislation. State programs for the first two categories were to be strengthened through the addition of federal funds and regulations. The first two (for children and unemployed) used general tax dollars, while the third (for retirees) would be an insurance-style program with charges made to working individuals and their employers. The latter premiums or contributions would give the system a solid foundation without adding to the federal budget deficit, even in times of an economic downturn. While there have been times of greater and lesser support for both of these programs, neither has been repealed.

It is the retirement portion of the legislation that has most benefitted the general population. Although certain categories of workers (farm workers, state teachers) have long been exempt, the vast majority of working Americans have been covered by the retirement system that started collecting contributions in 1937. The success of the Social Security system as a whole has been remarkable. While many changes have been made to the system, and many others have been proposed since it was implemented, there has never been a widespread movement to totally abolish the Social Security system (though libertarians and Tea Party activists have begun to question its workings). Although Social Security alone has not allowed most people to keep their pre-retirement standard of living, it has provided a basic monthly income for most retirees. Thus, this section of the law has allowed workers and their families to continue to have an acceptable standard of living in retirement while not unduly burdening others.

—Donald A. Watt, PhD

Bibliography and Additional Reading

"Biography of Franklin D. Roosevelt." *Franklin D. Roosevelt Presidential Library and Museum*. National Archives and Records Administration, n.d. Web. 18 August 2014.

Brinkley, Alan. *Franklin Delano Roosevelt*. Oxford: Oxford University Press, 2009. Print.

DeWitt, Larry, Daniel Beland, & Edward D. Berkowitz. *Social Security: a Documentary History*. Washington, DC: CQ Press, 2007. Print.

"FDR's Greatest Hits." *Franklin D. Roosevelt Presidential Library and Museum*. National Archives and Records Administration, n.d. Web. 18 August 2014.

Freidel, Frank, & Hugh Sidey. "The Presidents of the United States of America: Franklin D. Roosevelt," *The Whitehouse: The Presidents*. The White House Historical Association, 2006. Web. 18 August 2014.

■ Speech Against the President's "Court Packing" Plan

Date: July 9, 1937
Authors: Burton K. Wheeler
Genre: speech

Summary Overview

In 1937, President Franklin D. Roosevelt proposed a series of measures that would dramatically alter the face of the Supreme Court. Sen. Burton K. Wheeler of Montana, one of the leading opponents of Roosevelt's proposals, argued vehemently that the president's efforts amounted to "packing the courts" with his supporters and changing the country's political landscape without the input of the people. Wheeler also criticized the initiatives' proponents for not supporting a constitutional amendment rather than allowing the president to drive legislative changes to the judiciary. Citing the power-consolidating efforts of Hitler and Mussolini, he further criticized those who would support the measures because these bills reflected "the needs of the times."

Defining Moment

When Franklin Delano Roosevelt won the 1932 presidential election, he did so with the promise that a "new deal" was coming for Americans who suffered under the stagnation of the Great Depression. Not only would the federal government take a far more visible role in aiding citizens and businesses back to financially solid ground, he offered, it would work to create safeguards to prevent another recession. The New Deal would require a different perspective on the role of the federal government, a departure that threatened decades of standard business practices. Still, Roosevelt stressed the urgency of the situation—25 percent of the population was out of work, banks were closed, and businesses were failing across the country.

Roosevelt famously put a large chunk of his New Deal's many components into action during the first one hundred days of his presidency. The speed with which the New Deal was introduced, and the sweeping nature of its reforms, led to severe backlash from certain organizations, including states-rights and small-government advocates, the press, and business and finance groups. Many opponents of the New Deal filed suit, some getting their cases heard by the Supreme Court. In such instances, Roosevelt often came out on the losing end, as the court's justices held to the traditional philosophy of a federal government with limited powers. The Supreme Court was also known to be less receptive to the complaints of organized labor as well as interest groups representing the poor.

Stymied by the judiciary, Roosevelt began to take dramatic and controversial steps. He proposed a comprehensive court reorganization measure known as the Judicial Procedures Reform Bill of 1937. Among the bill's initiatives was a provision that allowed the president to appoint an additional judge for any sitting judge who had ten years of experience on the bench and had reached the age of seventy. Under this plan, Roosevelt could appoint as many as six additional Supreme Court justices. The plan was framed as a measure that could alleviate an overburdened judiciary. However, many saw the initiative as little more than an effort by Roosevelt to pack the courts with policymaking judges who shared Roosevelt's governmental vision.

Roosevelt had been swept into power with the full support of his own Democratic Party. However, this particular bill significantly divided the Democratic members of Congress, while Republicans were unified against it. Despite the president's best efforts, even some of his usual supporters in Congress bristled at the proposals. After all, the Senate was the legislative body charged with approving the president's nominees for federal courts. One Senator, Montana Democrat Burton K. Wheeler, encouraged the president to pursue a constitutional amendment to achieve his goals, a suggestion that proponents of the court-packing bill claimed would take too much time.

Author Biography
Burton Kendall Wheeler was born in Hudson, Massachusetts, on February 27, 1882. In 1905, he graduated from law school at the University of Michigan and moved to Butte, Montana, to start practicing law. In 1909, he began career in politics, winning a seat in the Montana state legislature and later holding the post of US district attorney for Montana. In 1922, Wheeler was elected to the US Senate, a position he would hold for four terms, through 1947. In 1924, he was tapped by Wisconsin senator and presidential candidate Robert La Follette to be the Independent Progressive Party's candidate for vice president. Although the bid was unsuccessful, Wheeler gained a national reputation as an independent-minded leader. In 1940, President Roosevelt asked Wheeler to serve as his running mate, despite their differences over the former's court reorganization plan, but Wheeler declined. He returned to practicing law in Washington, DC, after leaving the Senate. He died on January 6, 1975, in Washington.

HISTORICAL DOCUMENT

Never before in the history of the Senate of the United States, at least during the 14 or 15 years I have been a member of it, have I seen such appeals to the prejudices of the people, to the uninformed, as have been made with reference to this piece of proposed legislation. Never before have I seen on both sides such deep feeling aroused. The reason for it, of course, is that this is a fundamental issue which everyone who has any feeling at all and who knows anything about the proposal realizes goes to the very foundation of our Government.

When the bill was first introduced the Attorney General of the United States in a radio speech used this language:

> Ladies and gentlemen, only nine short days have passed since the President sent to the Congress recommendations for the reorganization of the Federal judiciary. Yet in that brief time unfriendly voices have filled the air with lamentations and have vexed our ears with insensate clamor calculated to divert attention from the merits of his proposal.

Why was it that immediately there was aroused such feeling that protests came from the masses of the people of the country against the proposal? It was because they felt that the bill was an attempt on the part of the administration to do by indirection what it did not want to do by direction.

Again, Mr. President, after the appeal was made to the drought-stricken farmers in the "dust-bowl" that we must pack the Supreme Court and must do it now in order to afford relief to those farmers, after an appeal was made to the widows and orphans, and after an appeal was made to the flood victims along the Ohio River in order to get them stirred up in favor of the proposal and to cause them to send protests to their Senators who were opposed to it, we found another kind of appeal being made. We found an appeal being made by the Postmaster General of the United States on the ground of party loyalty, that every Democrat ought to support the bill because of party loyalty regardless, of its effect upon the Constitution of the United States and regardless of its violation of the spirit of the Constitution.

We heard Mr. Farley saying, "It is in the bag." In another place and at another time he said, "We will *let* the Senate talk and then we will let the House talk. Then we will call the roll. We have the votes." The press of the country after the last election pronounced Mr. Farley one of the greatest prognosticators the country had ever seen. Think of it, Mr. President, here in the United States.

Postmaster General has said, "We will let the Senate talk." Certainly, our constituents ought to feel very grateful to Postmaster General for permitting the Members of the Senate of the United States, whom they have elected to office to speak their minds in the Senate.

As to the present controversy there is not the slightest difference in principle between this bill and the Court bill so far as the objectives sought to be attained by the proponents of the bills are concerned. The only difference is the one that was urged in the case of the girl who came before the judge charged with delinquency. When the judge said to her, "Mary, I shall have to send you to the house of correction, because you have had an illegitimate child," Mary spoke up and said, "Oh, but, Judge, it is only a little baby." So this is "only a little baby," and it is only a small packing of the Supreme Court; but the results that are sought to be obtained are exactly identical with the results sought to be obtained in the first instance.

The distinguished Senator from Pennsylvania [Mr. Guffey] rose in the Senate the other day and in a violent attack upon the Chief Justice of the United States said, "He is a terrible politician".

I submit that this attack upon Chief Justice Hughes is ill-becoming a Member of the Senate. He has practically charged Chief Justice Hughes with being a cheap politician. I voted against the confirmation of Mr. Hughes; but let us see who were those who voted for him. Some Democrats who are in this body at the present time voted for him.

The Senator from Arizona, Mr. Ashurst, the original proponent of this bill, voted for the confirmation of Mr. Hughes.

The Senator from Kentucky, Mr. Barkley, voted for the confirmation of Mr. Hughes.

The Senator from Mississippi, Mr. Harrison, voted for the confirmation of Mr. Hughes.

The present Secretary of the Navy, Secretary Swanson, then a Senator from Virginia, not only voted for the confirmation of Mr. Hughes but he worked incessantly in this body to secure his confirmation.

So, if Mr. Hughes was such a terribly bad man then, if he was a known politician, and a cheap politician at that, why did these distinguished leaders of the Democratic Party vote for his confirmation and urge his confirmation upon the floor of the Senate of the United States? It should be remembered that Mr. Hughes was actively engaged in politics prior to the date of his confirmation. Mr. Hughes had "economic royalists" for clients whom he had actively served just before his nomination by President Hoover. And who "packed" Mr. Hughes upon the Supreme Court?

Let us take the case of Mr. Justice Roberts. I think every Democrat and every Liberal and every Progressive and every Republican voted for his confirmation. If Mr. Justice Roberts was "packed" on the Supreme Court, then the Senate of the United States was responsible, and violated its duty and its oath of office, when it voted to confirm his nomination and to put him upon the Supreme Court.

Who led the fight in this body for the confirmation of Mr. Justice Butler?

It was not a Republican, not a reactionary, not a Tory, but one of the great liberals of his time, my late colleague, Thomas J. Walsh. He led the fight for Justice Butler. Was he seeking to pack the Court when he led that fight?

Then there is Justice Sutherland. The Senate confirmed him. When, in the opinion of the Senator from Pennsylvania, did Mr. Hughes and every other Republican in this country become such bad men? Who are these bad men with whom I am lined up, that the Senator should feel so sorry for me and sympathize with me so greatly? Let me say to the Senator for his information that I do not need his sympathy. Sometime ago a Republican lawyer was speaking to a colored audience in my home town, and he said, "I am going to see to it that the colored people of this town get justice. "An old colored lady sitting beside her husband nudged him and said, "I am not for that man." He said, "Why are you not for him? He said he was going to give us justice." She replied, "It's not justice us colored folks want; it's sympathy."

I do not want sympathy. I have never had the sympathy of many people in this country and I do not want the sympathy of Senators now; they would only be wasting it upon me. I will take care of myself.

I say now that if a spirit of intolerance is to pervade the Senate, if there is to be an attempt to try to drive this bill through, if the proponents of the bill are going to try to put pressure on us, if they are going to try to get rough with us, others can get rough just as well as they can.

I do not propose to be intimidated, and the rest of us do not propose to be intimidated, by name callers, or by anyone else, and our opponents might just as well make up their minds to that fact first as last. We are going to have a legitimate debate upon this question before the Senate, regardless of whether Mr. Farley wants us to or whether anybody else wants us to. The country is entitled to it.

Mr. President, threats have been made against Senators by Mr. Farley, who stated that the Senator from Wyoming and the Senator from Nevada probably would not get what they were seeking from the administration if they did not go along with the bill.

Speeches that were made over the radio have been censored, some of the radio stations cut off time after they had promised it to us. Thus far in the Senate debate on this bill, the proponents have not argued the provisions or the effect of the bill.

Oh, the Senator from Indiana said, "I want my President to look toward the shrine of George Washington at Mount Vernon." I want him to look there, and I want him to remember the words of George Washington, for this is what George Washington said:

> The basis of our political systems is the right of the people to make and to alter their constitutions of government.

We say that we want a constitutional amendment submitted. The Senator from Arkansas said, "You cannot deny the right of the Members of the Senate, the representatives of the people, to vote upon this pending bill." We are saying that the Constitution does not belong to the Congress of the United States, it does not belong to the President of the United States. The Constitution belongs to the people. We are asking that the people of the United States shall have an opportunity to voice their opinion and to say whether or not they want the Constitution amended. This Court bill seeks to amend the Constitution by interpretative processes.

Oh, but it is said that it will take 15 years to amend the Constitution. Nonsense! Ratification of the "lame duck" amendment came in 11 months. Ratification of the prohibition and the repealing amendment came within 14 months. Someone told me that a Senator stated that for $50,000 they could stop a constitutional amendment in his State. If they can, his State is far more corrupt than any other State of the Union of which I know.

Take 15 years? We all know that under the Constitution of the United States a proposal to amend that instrument can be submitted, and I assure the Senate that Senators on this side who are opposed to the bill will vote to submit any reasonable constitutional amendment.

It can be provided in the proposed amendment that it must be voted on within 1 year or 2 years, and it can be provided that it must be submitted, not to the legislatures, but to conventions in the various States.

We are told that there is great opposition to 5–4 decisions. Let us examine that matter for a moment. There is no longer any need for the passage of this bill because of 5-to-4 decisions. There is a vacancy on the Supreme Court. Why has not that vacancy been filled? We all know the reason, and it is not necessary for me to state it at this time.

We do not need to fear 5-to-4 decisions, because we will no longer have them. If the judge to be appointed does not disappoint the proponents of the bill, they can have 6-to-3 decisions, or they can have at least 5-to-4 decisions. The administration can be sure of such decisions on any reasonable proposition. They can be sure of 5-to-4 decisions in their favor. There is no longer any "no man's land." There is no longer any "Mr. Justice Roberts' land." Think what happened when Mr. Justice Van Devanter resigned. Proponents of the bill have been wanting resignations, but when he resigned just think of the statement that was made! "One down and five to go" was the comment made by the Secretary to the President of the United States.

There is a word in use in New England with which many are familiar which describes the sort of discussion that has been taking place on the part of the proponents of the bill, a word that describes it better than any other expression I can think of. That is the word "cheap." It was "cheap" for the Secretary to the President of the United States to say "One down and five to go," "One down and four to go." It was cheap, Mr. President, for the Postmaster General to say, "We have it in the bag." It was cheap for him to say that he would let the Senate talk.

After all, speaking of 5-to-4 decisions, do we want a Supreme Court that simply will agree entirely with our viewpoint? Is that what we want? Let me call attention to the fact that it is out of the clash of opinions that the truth comes. The worst thing that could happen to Congress, the worst thing that could happen to the country, would be to have but one strong political party. We get better legislation in this body because we have a clash of opinions as to proposed legislation. We get better bills out of committees when we have a clash of opinions. The

American form of government depends upon the clash of opinions of its people, and not upon a subservient people who are voting as they are told to vote because they are getting hand-outs from the Treasury of the United States.

We are told that all the farmers of the country are for this measure. Let me say that I was out in Montana not long ago. Many farmers came to see me and said, "I am with the President. I do not know anything about this bill, but I am for it because I think the President wants it." Labor leaders came to me and said to me, "I am for the bill because I think the President wants it. I do not know anything about it." W.P.A. workers came to me and said, "I am on the public payroll, and I want the bill because the President wants it. That is the reason." I say to the members of the Senate, however, that practically every man with whom I have come in contact, from one end of the country to the other, who has given the question any serious thought or who knows anything about our problems or our constitution is opposed to this measure

Mr. President, I say there is nothing liberal about the proposal before us; there is nothing progressive about it. It has been dressed up in gaudy clothes for the purpose of attracting the fancy of some of the younger generation, who have not given it any serious thought and do not know that the liberties which have become commonplace to us were earned only by the lifeblood of our forefathers. Our liberties are so commonplace that few people give any serious consideration to them.

Why should we be zealous about this cause? When we look at world affairs we realize that in Germany there is a dictator, under whose iron heel are 70,000,000 people. How did he come into power? On what plea did he come into office? He came in under the constitution of Germany. Every step that was taken by him at first was taken in a constitutional way. Mr. Hitler acted "to meet the needs of the times."

Mussolini came into office upon the plea that he would improve economic conditions and he assumed the power of a dictator and abolished the legislative body of Italy and set up his own court, in order that he might "meet the needs of the times" in that country. In every place where a dictatorship has been set up it has been done "in order to meet the needs of the times."

Let me quote Mr. Justice Brandeis. He said:

Experience should teach us to be most on guard to protect our liberty when purposes of government are beneficent. Men born to freedom are naturally alert to repel invasion of their liberty by evil-minded persons. The greatest dangers to liberty lurk in insidious encroachment by men of zeal, well-meaning, but without understanding.

The Attorney General of the United States said if the Justices do not like this law, let them get off. What is the object of passing the proposed legislation? There is just one reason behind it. Its proponents may camouflage it just as much as they desire, but the Attorney General said that they want a court to meet the needs of the times. What does that mean? What are the needs of the time? Who is to judge what are the needs of the time?

I think I stated before upon this floor that the needs of the times are like the shifting sands upon the beach. What may be the needs of the times today may not be the needs of the times tomorrow. If a President comes into office with a great majority behind him, is he going to say, "I have 11,000,000 majority, I have a Congress which is subservient to me, so I am going to increase the membership of the Court, because I want men there who are going to decide in accord with the needs of the times"?

There are courts in Germany, there are courts in Italy, there are courts in Russia, and men are placed on them to meet the needs of the times as the dictators see the needs, and those judges do what the dictators want them to do. Can the Democratic Party afford to be placed in the position of saying to the people of this country, "We are going to put men on the Supreme Bench to meet the needs of the times as we see them"?

The State of Nebraska passed a law to the effect that the German language should not be taught in the schools of Nebraska. The State of Nebraska thought that was in accordance with the needs of the time.

That occurred during the Great War hysteria, when people were seeing bogeymen, and when they wanted every man who had a German name to be sent to the penitentiary because of his name. But the Supreme Court of the United States, bad as its members may be, and having great politicians among its members, as some distinguished Senators have pointed them out to be, said that law was contrary to the Constitution of the United States.

Then a case arose concerning one Angelo Herndon down in Georgia who was a Communist, and was found with Communist literature in his pocket. He was arrested under an old statute in the State of Georgia duly enacted by the legislature of that State. The Georgia Supreme Court upheld his conviction, and sentence of 18 years imprisonment for "having incited to insurrection." The Supreme Court of the United States, removed as it was from mob hysteria, freed him. Of course, the Court disagreed with his political philosophy, but notwithstanding that fact it turned him loose because it said his arrest, prosecution, and trial were contrary to the Constitution of the United States of America.

What were the needs of the times during the reconstruction era following the Civil War? Senators from the South will find that at some time a man will come here as President of the United States who will say to southern Senators and to their States that the needs of the times require action which is going seriously to affect the economic life of their States and their people. Make no mistake about it.

So, my friends, the needs of the times, I repeat, are like shifting pebbles upon the beach. The needs of the times are one thing today and something else tomorrow. When men are appointed upon the Supreme Court Bench to interpret the Constitution to meet the needs of the times, I say that a step is being taken which is reactionary. A step is being taken which, while it is within the letter of the Constitution, is against the spirit of the Constitution, and I defy anyone who knows the difference between the spirit of the law and the letter of the law to deny that statement.

I think I have once before quoted to this body a statement made by the President of the United States on the question of increasing the Supreme Court of the United States to meet the needs of the times. Why should I be accused of breaking the heart of the President, why should I be accused of being in bad company, when I agree now with the statement which the President of the United States made a few years ago? This is what he said in 1933:

In the face of this congestion the remedy commonly proposed is to add new judges or new courts, but it will readily be seen that if the problem is what I have stated it to be, such a so-called remedy merely aggravates the complaint. There are, of course, legitimate demands for additional judicial manpower in sections where the population has grown rapidly. But it is easy to see that to apply this remedy in all cases is to add to the ravages of the disease, to contribute to the confusion, and, what is profoundly important at this time, to burden still further an already seriously embarrassed taxpayer.

Senators were told that they rode in on the coattails of the President of the United States and that they ought to support him for that reason; that they ought to support the measure because of party loyalty; that they ought to support the bill because some economic royalist disagrees with the President; that they ought to support the measure because some newspaper or some Republican says it is wrong; that they ought to be intimidated and afraid to vote their own convictions. Yes; but who first said that which we who oppose the measure are now saying? The President of the United States, in 1933. When Senators vote against this bill to increase the Supreme Court to "meet the needs of the times," to make it subservient, they are only doing what the President of the United States in 1933 said was the right thing to do. He said it before the Republicans said it. He said it before any of the newspapers he is now criticizing said it. He said it before those now opposed to him in this matter said it. Am I attacking the President of the United States because I am agreeing with what he said in 1933?

Mr. President, in closing I say that we cannot afford to set such a precedent as the enactment of the pending measure would set. We cannot afford to denounce the members of the Supreme Court and hold them up to ridicule when they are carrying on and voting their honest convictions, whether we agree with them or whether we do not.

The distinguished Senator from Indiana said the members of the Supreme Court are themselves packing the Supreme Court. Well, they were appointed for life. Can the Senator look into their innermost souls and say they are only staying on the Supreme Court in order to pack it? Can the Senator look into the soul and read the mind of Justice Brandeis and say he is staying on the Court because he wants to pack it in favor of the President, and that Justice Hughes wants to stay on the Court in order to pack it in favor of or against the President? I should like to have the Senator tell me how he knows that Justice Sutherland is staying on the Court just to vote against the President. I should like to have him tell me how he knows any one of the present Justices are remaining on the Court in order to pack the Court against the President of the United States. Let the Senator write that down in his notebook and tell me how he knows it when his time comes.

Mr. President, one by one the arguments with reference to the six-men bill were demolished until there was an overwhelming majority in the Senate against that bill, and nobody at heart was for it. Everyone knows that what I am saying is true. So, no one at heart is for the pending bill, because, as everyone knows, it merely provides a slow packing process. As a matter of fact, if I had to choose between packing the Court with six Justices and the method proposed by this bill, I would prefer to pack it with the six at once rather than to pack it in the way which is now proposed. To pack the Court is the reason for the pending bill; and, if we are going do it, let us put on the six men at once.

We were told there would be no compromise; that we would have to vote it up or vote it down; that no compromise suggestion would be listened to, and that it was "in the bag."

We are now told that the proponents of the measure have got the votes and they are going to try to jam it through. They are going to shut off debate. They have invoked an old rule that I have never before seen invoked in this body during the first 2 or 3 days of debate on a measure, a rule that is violated all the time by every member of the Senate with impunity. Yet we are told that the proponents of the measure are going to try to force us, pound us, knock the bill down our throats, if you please, in order to put it through. Well, those who are opposed to it will not be the losers if the supporters of the bill should succeed in passing it. The only man who can lose in a fight of that kind is the President of the United States himself.

As I have previously said, I give the President all credit for the great things he has accomplished during the last 4 years for the people of this nation. We have given him more power than any President of the United States has ever had in peacetime or in war. He has powers that no other President ever had. We delegated to him the power to issue currency and to fix and regulate the value thereof.

He can raise or lower the gold content of the dollar. He can issue $3,000,000,000 of currency. He can demonetize silver up to 16 to 1. He has $2,000,000,000 with which he can buy German marks, British bonds, French francs, or Japanese yen, or take any other course he may desire for the purpose of stabilizing our currency. He can raise or lower the tariff on practically everything that is produced in the United States. He can close the stock markets for a period of 30 days. We have just given him $1,500,000,000 for relief purposes, and he has wide discretionary power in its distribution. We have given him the power to say to the farmers of the country, "We will give you money for not producing crops," and $500,000,000 has been provided for that purpose. He can say to them, "Let this piece of land lie fallow and we will pay you for not planting it." We have given him the power over the economic life and destiny of the American people. He has a substantially subservient Congress. No man in the history of the United States, not even the Father of his Country, ever had reposed in him such vast and extraordinary power. We have given him the power to declare war. We have given him a power over treaties never given to any other President of the United States. He can say to one community, Denver for instance, "I will give you money for a project in your city," or he can say, "I will deny a project to your city." He has the power to say, "I will build a project in Houston, Tex., but I will deny a project to some other place in Texas."

He has a right to say to the people of the State of Illinois or the people of the city of Chicago, "I will build that parkway in your State or that subway in the city of Chicago at the behest of the political bosses of your city, or I will deny it at their behest." He has the right to say the same thing to the city of New York. I am not complaining. Conditions in the country were such that we had to give him that power and I am not complaining about the way he has used it.

But with a subservient Congress, with such tremendous power in the Executive, has not the time come in this nation when we should say there is a line beyond which no man should pass? Has not the time come when we should say, "No matter how beloved you may be, no matter how profound and wonderful you may be, no matter how much your sympathies are with the masses of the people of the United States, no matter what you want to do, the time has come when we should say there is a line beyond which, under this American Government of ours and under our Constitution, no man shall pass."

Document Analysis

Burton K. Wheeler's July 9, 1937, speech on the floor of the Senate was a strong criticism of President Roosevelt's Judicial Procedures Reform Bill, as well as those who supported it. The Montana Senator sharply criticized the measure as unconstitutional, arguing that the president should seek a constitutional amendment rather than attempting to change the courts through legislation. Furthermore, he spoke out against efforts to force the bill through Congress, including alleged attempts to threaten and intimidate legislators into supporting Roosevelt's agenda.

Wheeler stated that there was a tremendous public backlash against Roosevelt's proposals. This outcry, Wheeler said, underscored the fact that the public, like Wheeler's congressional colleagues, saw through Roosevelt's rhetoric. Whereas the president was arguing that this bill would quickly bring help to Depression-stricken Americans, Wheeler argued, it was clear that Roosevelt's actual intent was to pack the courts with his own judges.

Wheeler also took issue with the manner by which the president and other leaders outside of Congress were attempting to push through the bill. Postmaster general and Democratic Party chair James Farley acted as though the legislative process was but a formality—that the Senate and House would have an opportunity to speak on the measure, but that the president would easily prevail, Wheeler said. He added that other officials attempted to intimidate and coerce senators to fall in line with the president, threats to which Wheeler said he would not bow.

The public backlash against the president's bill also underscored Wheeler's position that the only means by which Roosevelt's proposed changes could be found acceptable was through the Constitution. This course of action was certainly brought to the attention of the president, Wheeler said, but Roosevelt and his supporters felt that it would take years to ratify such an amendment. Wheeler criticized this point of view, citing the fact that some amendments took less than a year to be ratified. The administration's argument was, therefore, inaccurate.

Wheeler said the real problem facing Roosevelt was not the length of time it would take to approve the measure via constitutional amendment, but with public sentiment. Americans simply were not as up in arms over "5–4 decisions" in the Supreme Court as Roosevelt was, Wheeler said. The Supreme Court, he said, was comprised of many justices, for whom Wheeler's Senate colleagues—many of whom were now supporting Roosevelt's bill—had voted to approve their nominations to the court. The Supreme Court might be divided at times over key legal issues, Wheeler concluded, but the justices were honorable men, who were performing their jobs properly and within constitutional guidelines. Wheeler said he saw no need to interfere in the court's affairs, even if time was of the essence in obtaining a favorable ruling on the New Deal's provisions and programs.

Essential Themes

Although a member of the Democratic Party, Senator Burton Wheeler was known as an independent-minded leader who was not afraid to question the actions of his party or his president. Wheeler's speech on July 9, 1937, served as a reminder of this characteristic. Wheeler understood the fact that the president was frustrated with the country's legal system. However, he could not condone the president's actions—namely, attempting to correct the ongoing issue by adding his own hand-picked judges to the judiciary.

Furthermore, Wheeler could not accept the manner in which the bill was being pushed through Congress. The Senate, he argued, had long been responsible for approving the president's nominees. This measure, therefore, did not just undermine the judiciary's constitutional authority; it undermined the Senate's as well. The bill's advocates, Wheeler added, arrogantly presumed that the Democrats would simply fall in line behind Roosevelt. Those who did not support the bill were threatened, intimidated, and otherwise coerced until they agreed. Wheeler spoke for those who refused to yield to such behavior.

In reality, Wheeler said, the reason for such tactics (and for that matter, the bill itself) was that the public was simply not in agreement that such a major change was necessary. If there was sentiment to advance such a controversial matter, Wheeler continued, the only acceptable vehicle for this matter would be a constitutional amendment. It did not take nearly as long to ratify an amendment as the president claimed, Wheeler continued—all that was necessary was the public will, a concept disregarded by the president and his supporters.

The president enjoys a wide range of constitutionally acceptable exertions of power, Wheeler said. The Senate and the House take full advantage of the parameters of their own power, as does the judiciary, he added. In this case, however, the president was asking the legislature to use its powers to undermine the judiciary. Wheeler, citing these examples, could not stand idly by while the very framework he swore to protect was threatened for the purposes of advancing the president's agenda.

—*Michael P. Auerbach, MA*

Bibliography and Additional Reading

Holt, Daniel S. *Debates on the Federal Judiciary: A Documentary History, Volume II: 1875–1939*. Washington: Federal Judicial History Office, 2013. Print.

McKenna, Marian Cecilia. *Franklin Roosevelt and the Great Constitutional War: The Court-Packing Crisis of 1937*. New York: Fordham UP, 2002. Print.

Menaker, Richard G. "FDR's Court-Packing Plan: A Study in Irony." *Gilder Lehrman Institute of American History*. Gilder Lehrman Institute, 2014. Web. 23 June 2014.

Sanburn, Josh. "FDR vs. The Supreme Court." *Time*. Time, Inc., 2011. Web. 23 June 2014.

Wheeler Azqueta, Robin. "Biography, Burton Kendall Wheeler." *Wheelercenter.org*. Burton K. Wheeler Center, 2013. Web. 23 June 2014.

President Roosevelt: Fireside Chat on the Current Recession

Date: April 14, 1938
Author: Franklin D. Roosevelt
Genre: speech

Summary Overview

After five years of slow but steady recovery, the US economy once again faced major difficulties in 1938. President Franklin Delano Roosevelt delivered this radio address as many Americans experienced another round of layoffs and foreclosures, reassuring them that the federal government would continue to invest in the social and economic programs necessary to restore balance. He explained that overproduction had once again caused a decline in purchasing power and that the joint efforts of individuals, businesses, and the government were required to bring the situation under control. He told the public not to be alarmed by the rising national debt because the money would return to the Treasury in the form of tax payments once workers were employed and total wages returned to previous levels. He concluded by assuring the public that, while his efforts might not always be perfect, he had their best interests at heart and would strive to understand the difficulties they face so the government could help facilitate a lasting solution to the economic crisis.

Defining Moment

In the United States, the economic boom of the 1920s abruptly gave way to the Great Depression, led by the stock market crash of October 1929. In the years that followed, millions of workers lost their jobs, farmers lost their land, companies went out of business, and banks became insolvent. By the time the Depression reached its height in 1933, the United States was experiencing its worst financial crisis since the Civil War. The stock market plummeted to about 20 percent of its pre-crash value, one in four American workers was unemployed, and thousands of US banks had collapsed.

Franklin Delano Roosevelt was elected president in 1932, and within weeks of taking office in early 1933, he was working closely with the legislature to stem the immediate financial crisis and prevent a further downward spiral. The result of these efforts was a series of programs known as the New Deal. Key components included establishing the Civilian Conservation Corps to help put people back to work, providing federal subsidies to small banks to ease the burden of mortgage and credit debt, and lending or granting money to states and counties to spend on immediate relief for their hungry and homeless residents. Later, the Emergency Relief Appropriation Act of 1935 established the Works Progress Administration (WPA) to administer relief programs and create additional public sector and infrastructure improvement jobs. Before its dissolution in 1943, the WPA provided more than eight million jobs to American workers, but it was never intended to be a permanent solution.

Initially, the New Deal seemed to be working—the economy showed small but immediate signs of improvement in 1933 as people went back to work and the foreclosure rate slowed—but progress stalled the following year. A new injection of funds from the Emergency Relief Appropriation Act sparked another upward shift in 1935, but by 1937, many areas of the United States experienced a resurgence of unemployment and foreclosures.

By the time Roosevelt made his radio address in 1938, Americans were exhausted by the struggles caused by the Depression. Financial analysts, businessmen, and workers worried that the New Deal programs were insufficient to reverse the downward trend and feared that the huge price tag—and the accompanying national debt—would make the situation worse in the long term. Roosevelt's address was primarily designed to reassure the public that he would continue working with the legislature both to provide necessary immediate relief to those in need, and to find a long-term solution to the crisis.

Author Biography

Franklin Delano Roosevelt was born on January 30, 1882, in Hyde Park, New York. He attended Groton School in Massachusetts and received his bachelor's degree in history from Harvard University in 1903. He studied law at Columbia University in New York, but, upon passing the bar examination, left school without completing his degree in 1907. He practiced law in New York City for three years, before being elected to the New York State Senate in 1910.

President Woodrow Wilson appointed Roosevelt assistant secretary of the Navy from 1913 until 1920. Following an unsuccessful campaign to become US vice president with running mate James M. Cox, Roosevelt briefly withdrew from politics. After a partial recovery from polio that he contracted in 1921, he was elected governor of New York State in 1928. In 1932, Roosevelt was elected president of the United States. He was inaugurated during the height of the Depression and saw the country through World War II. Roosevelt died in office on April 12, 1945.

HISTORICAL DOCUMENT

MY FRIENDS:

Five months have gone by since I last spoke to the people of the Nation about the state of the Nation.

I had hoped to be able to defer this talk until next week because, as we all know, this is Holy Week. But what I want to say to you, the people of the country, is of such immediate need and relates so closely to the lives of human beings and the prevention of human suffering that I have felt that there should be no delay. In this decision I have been strengthened by the thought that by speaking tonight there may be greater peace of mind and that the hope of Easter may be more real at firesides everywhere, and therefore that it is not inappropriate to encourage peace when so many of us are thinking of the Prince of Peace.

Five years ago we faced a very serious problem of economic and social recovery. For four and a half years that recovery proceeded apace. It is only in the past seven months that it has received a visible setback.

And it is only within the past two months, as we have waited patiently to see whether the forces of business itself would counteract it, that it has become apparent that government itself can no longer safely fail to take aggressive government steps to meet it.

This recession has not returned us to the disasters and suffering of the beginning of 1933. Your money in the bank is safe; farmers are no longer in deep distress and have greater purchasing power; dangers of security speculation have been minimized; national income is almost 50 percent higher than it was in 1932; and government has an established and accepted responsibility for relief.

But I know that many of you have lost your jobs or have seen your friends or members of your families lose their jobs, and I do not propose that the Government shall pretend not to see these things. I know that the effect of our present difficulties has been uneven; that they have affected some groups and some localities seriously but that they have been scarcely felt in others. But I conceive the first duty of government is to protect the economic welfare of all the people in all sections and in all groups. I said in my Message opening the last session of the Congress that if private enterprise did not provide jobs this spring, government would take up the slack—that I would not let the people down. We have all learned the lesson that government cannot afford to wait until it has lost the power to act.

Therefore, my friends, I have sent a Message of far-reaching importance to the Congress. I want to read to you tonight certain passages from that Message, and to talk with you about them.

In that Message I analyzed the causes of the collapse of 1929 in these words: "over-speculation in and over-production of practically every article or instrument used by man.... millions of people, to be sure, had been put to work, but the products of their hands had exceeded the purchasing power of their pocketbooks... Under the inexorable law of supply and demand, supplies so overran demand that production was compelled to stop.

Unemployment and closed factories resulted. Hence the tragic years from 1929 to 1933."

Today I pointed out to the Congress that the national income—not the Government's income but the total of the income of all the individual citizens and families of the United States—every farmer, every worker, every banker, every professional man and every person who lived on income derived from investments—that national income had amounted, in the year 1929, to eighty-one billion dollars. By 1932 this had fallen to thirty-eight billion dollars. Gradually, and up to a few months ago, it had risen to a total, an annual total; of sixty-eight billion dollars—a pretty good come-back from the low point.

I then said this to the Congress:

> But the very vigor of the recovery in both durable goods and consumers' goods brought into the picture early in 1937, a year ago, certain highly undesirable practices, which were in large part responsible for the economic decline which began in the later months of that year. Again production had (outran) outrun the ability to buy.
>
> There were many reasons for this overproduction. One of them was fear—fear of war abroad, fear of inflation, fear of nation-wide strikes. None of these fears have been borne out.
>
> .... Production in many important lines of goods outran the ability of the public to purchase them, as I have said. For example, through the winter and spring of 1937 cotton factories in hundreds of cases were running on a three-shift basis, piling up cotton goods in the factory, (and) goods in the hands of middle men and retailers. For example, also, automobile manufacturers not only turned out a normal increase of finished cars, but encouraged the normal increase to run into abnormal figures, using every known method to push their sales. This meant, of course, that the steel mills of the Nation ran on a twenty-four hour basis, and the tire companies and cotton factories and glass factories and others speeded up to meet the same type of abnormally stimulated demand. Yes, the buying power of the Nation lagged behind.
>
> Thus by the autumn of 1937, last autumn, the Nation again had stocks on hand which the consuming public could not buy because the purchasing power of the consuming public had not kept pace with the production.
>
> During the same period... the prices of many vital products had risen faster than was warranted.... For example, copper—which undoubtedly can be produced at a profit in this country for from ten to twelve cents a pound—was pushed up and up to seventeen cents a pound. The price of steel products of many kinds was increased far more than was justified by the increased wages of steel workers. In the case of many commodities the price to the consumer was raised well above the inflationary boom prices of 1929. In many lines of goods and materials, prices got so high in the summer of 1937 that buyers and builders ceased to buy or to build.
>
> ...the economic process of getting out the raw materials, putting them through the manufacturing and finishing processes, selling them to the retailers, selling them to the consumer, and finally using them, got completely out of balance.
>
> ...The laying off of workers came upon us last autumn and has been continuing at such a pace ever since that all of us, Government and banking and business and workers, and those faced with destitution, recognize the need for action.

All of this I said to the Congress today and I repeat it to you, the people of the country tonight.

I went on to point out to the Senate and the House of Representatives that all the energies of government and business must be directed to increasing the national income, to putting more people into private jobs, to giving security and a feeling of security to all people in all walks of life.

I am constantly thinking of all our people—unemployed and employed alike—of their human problems, their human problems of food and clothing and homes and education and health and old age. You and I agree that security is our greatest need—the chance to work, the opportunity of making a reasonable profit in our business—whether it be a very small business or a larger one—the possibility of selling our farm products for enough money for our families to live on decently. I know these are the things that decide the well-being of all our people.

Therefore, I am determined to do all in my power to help you attain that security and because I know that the people themselves have a deep conviction that secure prosperity of that kind cannot be a lasting one except on a basis of (business) fair business dealing and a basis where all from the top to the bottom share in the prosperity. I repeated to the Congress today that neither it nor the Chief Executive can afford

> to weaken or destroy great reforms which, during the past five years, have been effected on behalf of the American people. In our rehabilitation of the banking structure and of agriculture, in our provisions for adequate and cheaper credit for all types of business, in our acceptance of national responsibility for unemployment relief, in our strengthening of the credit of state and local government, in our encouragement of housing, and slum clearance and home ownership, in our supervision of stock exchanges and public utility holding companies and the issuance of new securities, in our provision for social security itself, the electorate of America wants no backward steps taken.

We have recognized the right of labor to free organization, to collective bargaining; and machinery for the handling of labor relations is now in existence. The principles are established even though we can all admit that, through the evolution of time, administration and practices can be improved. Such improvement can come about most quickly and most peacefully through sincere efforts to understand and assist on the part of labor leaders and employers alike.

The never-ceasing evolution of human society will doubtless bring forth new problems which will require new adjustments. Our immediate task is to consolidate and maintain the gains we have achieved.

In this situation there is no reason and no occasion for any American to allow his fears to be aroused or his energy and enterprise to be paralyzed by doubt or uncertainty.

I came to the conclusion that the present-day problem calls for action both by the Government and by the people, that we suffer primarily from a failure of consumer demand because of lack of buying power. Therefore it is up to us to create an economic upturn...

I went on in my Message today to propose three groups of measures and I will summarize my recommendations.

First, I asked for certain appropriations which are intended to keep the Government expenditures for work relief and similar purposes during the coming fiscal year that begins on the first of July, keep that going at the same rate of expenditure as at present. That includes additional money for the Works Progress Administration; additional funds for the Farm Security Administration; additional allotments for the National Youth Administration, and more money for the Civilian Conservation Corps, in order that it can maintain the existing number of camps now in operation.

These appropriations, made necessary by increased

unemployment, will cost about a billion and a quarter dollars more than the estimates which I sent to the Congress on the third of January last.

Second, I told the Congress that the Administration proposes to make additional bank reserves available for the credit needs of the country. About one billion four hundred million dollars of gold now in the Treasury will be used to pay these additional expenses of the Government, and three-quarters of a billion dollars of additional credit will be made available to the banks by reducing the reserves now required by the Federal Reserve Board.

These two steps taking care of relief needs and adding to bank credits are in our best judgment insufficient by themselves to start the Nation on a sustained upward movement.

Therefore, I came to the third kind of Government action which I consider to be vital. I said to the Congress:

> You and I cannot afford to equip ourselves with two rounds of ammunition where three rounds are necessary. If we stop at relief and credit, we may find ourselves without ammunition before the enemy is routed. If we are fully equipped with the third round of ammunition, we stand to win the battle against adversity.

This third proposal is to make definite additions to the purchasing power of the Nation by providing new work over and above the continuing of the old work. First, to enable the United States Housing Authority to undertake the immediate construction of about three hundred million dollars worth of additional slum clearance projects.

Second, to renew a public works program by starting as quickly as possible about one billion dollars worth of needed permanent public improvements in our states, and their counties and cities.

Third, to add one hundred million dollars to the estimate for Federal aid highways in excess of the amount that I recommended in January.

Fourth, to add thirty-seven million dollars over and above the former estimate of sixty-three million for flood control and reclamation.

Fifth, to add twenty-five million dollars additional for Federal buildings in various parts of the country.

In recommending this program I am thinking not only of the immediate economic needs of the people of the Nation, but also of their personal liberties—the most precious possession of all Americans. I am thinking of our democracy. I am thinking of the recent trend in other parts of the world away from the democratic ideal.

Democracy has disappeared in several other great nations—disappeared not because the people of those nations disliked democracy, but because they had grown tired of unemployment and insecurity, of seeing their children hungry while they sat helpless in the face of government confusion, government weakness,—weakness through lack of leadership in government. Finally, in desperation, they chose to sacrifice liberty in the hope of getting something to eat. We in America know that our own democratic institutions can be preserved and made to work. But in order to preserve them we need to act together, to meet the problems of the Nation boldly, and to prove that the practical operation of democratic government is equal to the task of protecting the security of the people.

Not only our future economic soundness but the very soundness of our democratic institutions depends on the determination of our Government to give employment to idle men. The people of America are in agreement in defending their liberties at any cost, and the first line of that defense lies in the protection of economic security. Your Government, seeking to protect democracy, must prove that Government is stronger than the forces of business depression.

History proves that dictatorships do not grow out of strong and successful governments but out of weak and helpless governments. If by democratic methods people get a government strong enough to protect them from fear and starvation, their democracy succeeds, but if they do not, they grow impatient. Therefore, the only sure bulwark of continuing liberty is a government strong enough to protect the interests of the people, and a people strong enough and well enough informed to maintain its sovereign control over its government.

We are a rich Nation; we can afford to pay for security and prosperity without having to sacrifice our liberties into the bargain.

In the first century of our republic we were short of

capital, short of workers and short of industrial production, but we were rich, very rich in free land, and free timber and free mineral wealth. The Federal Government of those days rightly assumed the duty of promoting business and relieving depression by giving subsidies of land and other resources.

Thus, from our earliest days we have had a tradition of substantial government help to our system of private enterprise. But today the Government no longer has vast tracts of rich land to give away and we have discovered, too, that we must spend large sums of money to conserve our land from further erosion and our forests from further depletion. The situation is also very different from the old days, because now we have plenty of capital, banks and insurance companies loaded with idle money; plenty of industrial productive capacity and many millions of workers looking for jobs. It is following tradition as well as necessity, if Government strives to put idle money and idle men to work, to increase our public wealth and to build up the health and strength of the people—to help our system of private enterprise to function again.

It is going to cost something to get out of this recession this way but the profit of getting out of it will pay for the cost several times over. Lost working time is lost money. Every day that a workman is unemployed, or a machine is unused, or a business organization is marking time, it is a loss to the Nation. Because of idle men and idle machines this Nation lost one hundred billion dollars between 1929 and the Spring of 1933, in less than four years. This year you, the people of this country, are making about twelve billion dollars less than you were last year.

If you think back to the experiences of the early years of this Administration you will remember the doubts and fears expressed about the rising expenses of Government. But to the surprise of the doubters, as we proceeded to carry on the program which included Public Works and Work Relief, the country grew richer instead of poorer.

It is worthwhile to remember that the annual national people's income was thirty billion dollars more last year in 1937 than it was in 1932. It is true that the national debt increased sixteen billion dollars, but remember that in that increase must be included several billion dollars worth of assets which eventually will reduce that debt and that many billion dollars of permanent public improvements—schools, roads, bridges, tunnels, public buildings, parks and a host of other things meet your eye in every one of the thirty-one hundred counties in the United States.

No doubt you will be told that the Government spending program of the past five years did not cause the increase in our national income. They will tell you that business revived because of private spending and investment. That is true in part, for the Government spent only a small part of the total. But that Government spending acted as a trigger, a trigger to set off private activity. That is why the total addition to our national production and national income has been so much greater than the contribution of the Government itself.

In pursuance of that thought I said to the Congress today:

> I want to make it clear that we do not believe that we can get an adequate rise in national income merely by investing, and lending or spending public funds. It is essential in our economy that private funds must be put to work and all of us recognize that such funds are entitled to a fair profit.

As national income rises, "let us not forget that Government expenditures will go down and Government tax receipts will go up."

The Government contribution of land that we once made to business was the land of all the people. And the Government contribution of money which we now make to business ultimately comes out of the labor of all the people. It is, therefore, only sound morality, as well as a sound distribution of buying power, that the benefits of the prosperity coming from this use of the money of all the people ought to be distributed among all the people—the people at the bottom as well as the people at the top. Consequently, I am again expressing my hope that the Congress will enact at this session a wage and hour bill putting a floor under industrial wages and a limit on working hours—to ensure a better distribution of our prosperity, a better distribution of available work, and a sounder distribution of buying power.

You may get all kinds of impressions in regard to the total cost of this new program, or in regard to the amount that will be added to the net national debt. It is a big program. Last autumn in a sincere effort to bring Government expenditures and Government income into closer balance, the Budget I worked out called for sharp de creases in Government spending during the coming year. But, in the light of present conditions, conditions of today, those estimates turned out to have been far too low. This new program adds two billion and sixty-two million dollars to direct Treasury expenditures and another nine hundred and fifty million dollars to Government loans—the latter sum, because they are loans, will come back to the Treasury in the future.

The net effect on the debt of the Government is this—between now and July 1, 1939—fifteen months away—the Treasury will have to raise less than a billion and a half dollars of new money.

Such an addition to the net debt of the United States need not give concern to any citizen, for it will return to the people of the United States many times over in increased buying power and eventually in much greater Government tax receipts because of the increase in the citizen income.

What I said to the Congress today in the close of my message I repeat to you now.

> Let us unanimously recognize the fact that the Federal debt, whether it be twenty-five billions or forty billions, can only be paid if the Nation obtains a vastly increased citizen income. I repeat that if this citizen income can be raised to eighty billion dollars a year the national Government and the overwhelming majority of state and local governments will be definitely 'out of the red.' The higher the national income goes the faster will we be able to reduce the total of Federal and state and local debts. Viewed from every angle, today's purchasing power—the citizens' income of today—is not at this time sufficient to drive the economic system of America at higher speed. Responsibility of Government requires us at this time to supplement the normal processes and in so supplementing them to make sure that the addition is adequate. We must start again on a long steady upward incline in national income.

...And in that process, which I believe is ready to start, let us avoid the pitfalls of the past—the overproduction, the over-speculation, and indeed all the extremes which we did not succeed in avoiding in 1929. In all of this, Government cannot and should not act alone. Business must help. And I am sure business will help.

We need more than the materials of recovery. We need a united national will.

We need to recognize nationally that the demands of no group, however just, can be satisfied unless that group is prepared to share in finding a way to produce the income from which they and all other groups can be paid.... You, as the Congress, I, as the President, must by virtue of our offices, seek the national good by preserving the balance between all groups and all sections.

We have at our disposal the national resources, the money, the skill of hand and head to raise our economic level—our citizens' income. Our capacity is limited only by our ability to work together. What is needed is the will.

The time has come to bring that will into action with every driving force at our command. And I am determined to do my share. "... Certain positive requirements seem to me to accompany the will—if we have that will.

There is placed on all of us the duty of self-restraint. That is the discipline of a democracy. Every patriotic citizen must say to himself or herself, that immoderate statement, appeals to prejudice, the creation of unkindness, are offenses not against an individual or individuals, but offenses against the whole population of the United States

...Use of power by any group, however situated, to force its interest or to use its strategic position in order to receive more from the common fund than its contribution to the common fund justifies, is an attack against and not an aid to our national life.

Self-restraint implies restraint by articulate public opinion, trained to distinguish fact from falsehood, trained to believe that bitterness is never a useful instrument in public affairs. There can be no dictatorship by an individual or by a group in this Nation, save through division fostered by hate. Such division there must never be.

And finally I should like to say a personal word to you.

I never forget that I live in a house owned by all the American people and that I have been given their trust.

I try always to remember that their deepest problems are human. I constantly talk with those who come to tell me their own points of view—with those who manage the great industries and financial institutions of the country—with those who represent the farmer and the worker—and often, very often with average citizens without high position who come to this house. And constantly I seek to look beyond the doors of the White House, beyond the officialdom of the National Capital, into the hopes and fears of men and women in their homes. I have travelled the country over many times. My friends, my enemies, my daily mail bring to me reports of what you are thinking and hoping. I want to be sure that neither battles nor burdens of office shall ever blind me to an intimate knowledge of the way the American people want to live and the simple purposes for which they put me here.

In these great problems of government I try not to forget that what really counts at the bottom of it all is that the men and women willing to work can have a decent job,—a decent job to take care of themselves and their homes and their children adequately; that the farmer, the factory worker, toe storekeeper, the gas station man, the manufacturer, the merchant—big and small—the banker who takes pride in the help that he can give to the building of his community—that all of these can be sure of a reasonable profit and safety for the earnings that they make—not for today nor tomorrow alone, but as far ahead as they can see. I can hear your unspoken wonder as to where we are headed in this troubled world. I cannot expect all of the people to understand all of the people's problems; but it is my job to try to understand all of the problems.

I always try to remember that reconciling differences cannot satisfy everyone completely. Because I do not expect too much, I am not disappointed. But I know that I must never give up—that I must never let the greater interest of all the people down, merely because that might be for the moment the easiest personal way out.

I believe that we have been right in the course we have charted. To abandon our purpose of building a greater, a more stable and a more tolerant America would be to miss the tide and perhaps to miss the port. I propose to sail ahead. I feel sure that your hopes and I feel sure that your help are with me. For to reach a port, we must sail—sail, not lie at anchor, sail, not drift.

Document Analysis

Roosevelt opens his radio address by apologizing for his timing: it is Easter week, and while he wanted to postpone political talk, he felt it was important to address the public to provide some peace of mind going into the holidays. He explains that, while the nation had recovered significantly from the Great Depression of five years prior, the economy had recently experienced another downturn. While not as widespread or severe, people in some areas had been, once again, hit hard by layoffs and foreclosures, and he wants to provide information about how the federal government plans to assist recovery.

Roosevelt explains that the downturn is the result of overproduction, largely in the manufacturing sector, and cites cotton goods and automobiles as some of the items with significant surplus. He notes that again the purchasing power of the American public had failed to keep pace with production, and the price inflation of raw materials is further increasing the cost of finished goods at a time when Americans are already struggling to afford them.

Roosevelt emphasizes that his primary objective is to restore security to the American people. He proposes additional funding and expansion of the work projects and infrastructure improvement programs under the New Deal. He addresses concerns about the growing national debt by assuring the public that the money will be made back in tax revenue once wages have been restored to their usual levels, and he tries to rally support by reminding Americans that gainful employment is the key to protecting American democracy, especially at a time when democracies around the world are falling to dictators as citizens grow tired of being hungry. He says, "We are a rich nation; we can afford to pay for security and prosperity without having to sacrifice our liberties into the bargain."

Regarding the improvements of the previous years, Roosevelt admits that the economic gains and increase in overall wages were not only the result of the federal government pumping cash into the system. Instead, he says, the government funding was the trigger for the economy to right itself, as it helped American households regain purchasing power. As people used this money to purchase food and manufactured goods, companies, in turn, were able to hire more workers, thus creating a positive financial cycle.

Roosevelt concludes by emphasizing that it will require the effort of individuals, businesses, and government to finish turning the economy around. He ends on a personal note, explaining that he takes seriously the stories he hears, whether from bankers, farmers, or ordinary citizens and tries to understand the difficulties each person faces within his or her different circumstances. He admits that his proposed measures under the New Deal might not be perfect, but insists that he always has the best interest of the American people in mind.

Essential Themes

As the economy started slipping again, Roosevelt's New Deal programs came under fire because of their significant cost. Critics argued that private industry, not the federal programs, caused the economic recovery during the mid-1930s. Roosevelt did not deny this. He maintained that the plan all along was to establish "partnerships" between the federal government and private industry, and that federal money was necessary to kick-start this process—not that federal dollars were meant to single-handedly save the economy.

Financial analysts and the general public worried about rising national debt during this period as well. The New Deal was expensive—the national debt nearly doubled during Roosevelt's first two terms in office—and in some cases, the government borrowed money to finance the programs. Despite the growing criticism, Roosevelt expanded the New Deal programs anyway, emphasizing the need to maintain Americans' personal security and trust in democracy—an important prospect as many European countries adopted socialism, Communism, and even dictatorships because their citizens were tired of starvation and unemployment. But the federal government could not continue borrowing money to feed the American people indefinitely, and the enormous bureaucracy created by the New Deal, as the number of government employees jumped from 600,000 in 1932 to nearly 1,000,000 by the end of the decade, could not sustain itself forever.

The United States was still recovering from this second wave of economic depression when it entered World War II in December 1941. The demand for food, transportation, raw materials, ammunition, and other goods brought about by the war helped lift the United States out of its economic slump, as factories and farms suddenly needed employees at unprecedented levels to feed, transport, and supply troops for the war effort.

—*Tracey M. DiLascio, JD*

Bibliography and Additional Reading

"Biography of Franklin D. Roosevelt." *Franklin D. Roosevelt Presidential Library and Museum*. National Archives, n.d. Web. 6 June 2014.

"The Great Depression (1929–1939)." *Eleanor Roosevelt Papers Project*. George Washington U, n.d. Web. 6 June 2014.

"Great Depression and World War II, 1929–1945." *American History*. Library of Congress, n.d. Web. 6 June 2014.

McElvaine, Robert S. *The Great Depression: America, 1929–1941*. New York: Times, 1993. Print.

Smiley, Gene. "Great Depression." *Library of Economics and Liberty*. Liberty Fund, n.d. Web. 6 June 2014.

Smith, Jean Edwards. *FDR*. New York: Random, 2007. Print.

"Timeline of the Great Depression." *American Experience*. PBS, n.d. Web. 6 June 2014.

■ The Hatch Act

Date: August 2, 1939
Author: US Congress
Genre: legislation

Summary Overview

The Hatch Act was an attempt by Congress to take an additional step in de-politicizing the non-elective positions in the American government. The act outlawed partisan political activity by federal government employees or any actions on their part that would interfere with open, fair, and honest elections. While the national government had grown rapidly prior to the Great Depression, throughout the 1930s millions of individuals had been added to the government payroll through the Civilian Conservation Corps (CCC) and the larger Works Progress Administration (WPA). Fearful that President Franklin Roosevelt might somehow use these individuals to assist in his re-election campaign and amid accusations that some Democratic congressional candidates had already done so in the 1938 elections, the Hatch Act was passed to limit political participation by virtually all (non-elected) federal employees. Named for the primary Senate sponsor, Senator Carl Hatch (Democrat from New Mexico), Congress passed the bill to regulate the activities of government employees, in order to preserve the integrity of elections and protect those same employees from potential political abuse. This law has continued to serve as an effective buffer between partisan politics and those seeking to focus their efforts on providing efficient government services.

Defining Moment

The government of the United States was established, under the Constitution, to serve all the people of the nation. Elected members of the government were chosen by the citizens, based upon the policies and ideology espoused by the candidates. Although individuals already holding office could point to their accomplishments, it was not anticipated that these individuals working for the government would use the powers of their office to coerce voters into giving the incumbents their votes. The small size of the national government, for the first several decades of the history of the United States, limited its potential influence on voters, but even President Jefferson felt compelled to address the issue, warning federal employees not to use their positions to try to influence elections. Although the "spoils system," in which federal employees were hired or fired at the discretion of the president, tended to fill government posts with politically active individuals, restraint was expected of most while working for the government. The passage of the Pendleton Act of 1883 was a major step toward ending the "spoils system," by making the hiring merit based for many federal jobs. President Theodore Roosevelt issued an executive order making the separation between federal employment and partisan politics clearer. With the passage of the Hatch Act in 1939, this separation became established by law, protecting employees from being forced to assist, under the threat of losing their jobs, in electoral politics. Conversely, it also kept government officials from interfering with electoral activities on their own initiative.

President Franklin Roosevelt's second term (1937–1941) was the most difficult for him, in terms of domestic politics. Having lost a key advisor, Roosevelt ineptly tried to change the law regarding membership on the Supreme Court and was defeated, even though Democrats controlled both houses of Congress. This defeat of a Roosevelt proposal seemed to give Democrats who disagreed with him the strength to oppose him on other issues. Republican gains in the midterm elections of 1938 strengthened the anti-Roosevelt forces considerably. Although no investigation conclusively proved that Roosevelt or other Democrats used WPA workers to help election efforts in 1938, enough charges had been made that many observers were worried over the upcoming 1940 elections. (Because WPA jobs were not permanent, people believed these workers could be coerced to work on partisan politics more easily than regular federal workers.) As a result, a coalition of Congressional members (conservative Democrats, Republicans, and anti-patronage Democrats) passed the Hatch Act as a precaution against possible future electoral tinkering. Although he had not supported its passage, Roosevelt signed the legislation with a strong statement of support for its goals.

Author Biography
The Hatch Act, ("Hatch Political Activity Act: An Act to Prevent Pernicious Political Activities") was passed by the Seventy-sixth Congress of the United States on August 2, 1939. At that time, both houses were firmly under the control of the Democratic Party, although that party was divided between the more liberal, Roosevelt faction and conservative Democrats, who tended to be from Southern states. Of the ninety-six senators, sixty-eight were Democrats; and in the House of Representatives, 256 of the 435 members were Democrats. Senator Carl Hatch was a conservative Democrat from New Mexico and was the primary author of the legislation. A senator since 1933, he had previously served as a tax collector, state judge, and an examiner for the New Mexico bar. After his retirement from the Senate in 1949, he was appointed a US district judge.

HISTORICAL DOCUMENT

An Act To Prevent Pernicious Political Activities
[August 2, 1939]

Be it enacted, That it shall be unlawful for any person to intimidate, threaten, or coerce, or to attempt to intimidate, threaten, or coerce, any other person for the purpose of interfering with the right of such other person to vote or to vote as he may choose, or of causing such other person to vote for, or not to vote for, any candidate for the office of President, Vice President, Presidential elector, Member of the Senate, or Member of the House of Representatives at any election....

SEC. 2. It shall be unlawful for any person employed in any administrative position by the United States, or by any department, independent agency, or other agency of the United States (including any corporation controlled by the United States or any agency thereof, and any corporation all of the capital stock of which is owned by the United States or any agency thereof), to use his official authority for the purpose of interfering with, or affecting the election or the nomination of any candidate for the office of President, Vice President, Presidential electors Member of the Senate, or Member of the House of Representatives, Delegates or Commissioners from the Territories and insular possessions.

SEC. 3. It shall be unlawful for any person, directly or indirectly, to promise any employment, position, work, compensation, or other benefit, provided for or made possible in whole or in part by any Act of Congress, to give consideration, favor, or reward for any political activity or for the support of or opposition to any candidate or any political party in any election.

SEC. 4. Except as may be required by the provisions of subsection (b), section 9 of this Act, it shall be unlawful for any persons to deprive, attempt to deprive, or threaten to deprive, by any means, any person of any employment, position, work, compensation, or other benefit provided for or made possible by any Act of Congress appropriating funds for work relief or relief purposes, on account of race, creed, color, or any political activity, support of, or opposition to any candidate or any political party in any election.

SEC. 5. It shall be unlawful for any person to solicit or receive or be in any manner concerned in soliciting or receiving any assessment, subscription, or contribution for any political purpose whatever from any person known by him to be entitled to or receiving compensation, employment, or other benefit provided for or made possible by any Act of Congress appropriating funds for work relief or relief purposes.

SEC. 6. It shall be unlawful for any person I for political purposes to furnish or to disclose, or to aid or assist in furnishing or disclosing, any list or names of persons receiving compensation, employment, or benefits provided for or made possible by any Act of Congress appropriating, or authorizing the appropriation of, funds for work relief or relief purposes, to a political candidate, committee, campaign manager, or to any person for delivery to a political candidate, committee, or campaign manager, and it shall be unlawful for any person to receive any such list or names for political purposes.

SEC. 7. No part of any appropriation made by any Act, heretofore or hereafter enacted making appropriations for work relief, relief, or otherwise to increase employment by providing loans and grants for public-works projects, shall be used for the purpose of, and no authority conferred by any such Act upon any person shall be exercised or administered for the purpose of, interfering with, restraining, or coercing any individual in the exercise of his right to vote at any election.

SEC. 8. Any person who violates any of the foregoing provisions of this Act upon conviction thereof shall be fined not more than $1,000 or imprisoned for not more than one year, or both.

SEC. 9. (a) It shall be unlawful for any person employed in the executive branch of the Federal Government, or any agency or department thereof, to use his official authority or influence for the purpose of interfering with an election or affecting the result thereof. No officer or employee in the executive branch of the Federal Government, or any agency or department thereof, shall take any active part in political management or in political campaigns. All such persons shall retain the right to vote as they may choose and to express their opinions on all political subjects. For the purposes of this section the term "officer" or "employee" shall not be construe to include (1) the President and the Vice President of the United States; (2) persons whose compensation is paid from the appropriation for the office of the President; (3) heads and assistant heads of executive departments; (4) officers who are appointed by the President, by and with the advice and consent of the Senate, and who determine policies to be pursued by the United States in its relations with foreign powers or in the Nation-wide administration of Federal laws.

(b) Any person violating the provisions of this section shall be immediately removed from the position or office held by him, and thereafter no part of the funds appropriated by any Act of Congress for such position or office shall be used to pay the compensation of such person.

SEC. 9A. (1) It shall be unlawful for any person employed in any capacity by any agency of the Federal Government, whose compensation, or any part thereof, is paid from funds authorized or appropriated by any Act of Congress, to have membership in any political party or organization that advocates the overthrow of our constitutional form of government in the United States.

(2) Any person violating the provisions of this section shall be immediately removed from the position or office held by him, and thereafter no part of the funds appropriated by any Act of Congress for such position or office shall be used to pay the compensation of such person.

SEC. 10. All provisions of this Act shall be in addition to, not in substitution for, of existing law.

SEC. 11. If any provision of this Act, or the application of such provision to any person or circumstance, is held invalid, the remainder of the Act, and the application of such provision to other persons or circumstances, shall not be affected thereby.

GLOSSARY

his: at this time, the male pronoun was used to stand for people in general

pernicious: malicious; causing great harm

Document Analysis

Although it has been amended several times since 1939, the Hatch Act (Public Law 76–252) has been a basic policy of the federal government since it was signed into law. The dual protections that were written into the law, for employees and for those active in the electoral process, have strengthened the ability of the government to serve the citizens and strengthened democracy in the United States. While some have complained about the limitations the law has placed on government employees' political activities, most have seen it as an important step toward insuring good and fair government. By and large, patronage positions were clearly outlawed under the act, except for high-level positions reporting to the president. Similarly, federal employees could not be active in party politics in activities ranging from speaking for mainstream candidates up to and including assisting groups that advocated violent revolution.

The Pendleton Act and later presidential orders had made most of the positions in the US government's executive branch into civil service positions, with hiring based on merit. However, there were individuals who did not follow the intention of the law, even if they did not blatantly break it. The merit system was strengthened through the Hatch Act, by its outlawing of promises regarding "employment, position, work, compensation, or other benefit" (including the *denial* of such benefits) to those in or seeking government employment. This was especially important for temporary programs, such as the WPA. Because the issue had arisen in connection with WPA increases before the 1938 elections, "public-works projects" were specifically mentioned in the text of the law as an area in which it was illegal to use public funds to coerce individuals in their vote. Thus, with the implementation of the Hatch Act, federal employees gained specific protection from anyone who might want to force them to participate in the political process.

At the same time, the law limited an employee's *voluntary* participation in partisan politics. Erring on the side of caution, the law's drafters strictly limited federal employees' political activities. Donations to political causes, or other visible support of politicians, were not allowed. The prohibition against taking part "in political campaigns" was interpreted broadly by law enforcement officials. One of the most extreme consequences, dismissal, was reserved for employees found to belong to political groups seeking the overthrow of the US government; at the time, this was understood to mean the Communist Party and certain fascist organizations. However, few people held such extreme views; therefore, for most employees, the law limited only their overt participation in partisan politics.

The other impact of the law was to limit the direct use of one's position to attempt to affect the outcome of elections. Anyone who tried to "use his official authority for the purpose of interfering with, or affecting the election or nomination" of individuals for federal position was in violation of the Hatch Act. In 1940, this was expanded to state elections as well. Sharing lists of people active in federally funded programs was also prohibited, as this information might be used by political operatives to coerce the participants in the programs. Section 9 of the act lists high-level administrators in the executive branch who are exempt from the law. Overall, the law attempts to balance the needs of the nation with those of individual employees, yet it does so by tilting slightly in the direction of electoral fairness over the capacity of individuals (i.e., employees) to act freely in the political arena.

Essential Themes

Although in American politics incumbents win re-election a very high percentage of the time, one intention of the Hatch Act was to keep that tendency from becoming a virtual certainty. If government officials could use their employees as workers in their re-election campaigns, whether the workers wanted this or not, it would give such officials an overwhelming advantage at the ballot box. In addition, there could be situations, without the law, where government officials could coerce average citizens into supporting the officials because of their position, or because of information from government files, which the campaign could use against the average citizen. The Hatch Act was a bold attempt to keep both of these situations from occurring. It was an effort to keep coercion out of politics. The amendments of 1940, 1993, and 2012, did not result in any major changes to the law. By accepting a position in the federal government, or taking federal funding for one's program, the individual gives up certain First Amendment rights. The Supreme Court has upheld the constitutionality of the Hatch Act, asserting that the tradeoff of limiting employee rights in order "to protect a democratic society" is justified as a necessary component of good government—particularly since the employee retains the right to vote.

Thus, the bill has survived as the law of the land in the United States for several decades. The political fortunes of the Republican and Democratic parties have risen and fallen during that time, but neither has sought to change the essence of the law. The most recent amendments were attempts to bring the law up to date, reflecting the fact that federal funding had become pervasive throughout society and that a wider range of potential punishments should reflect the wider range of potential violations. With the advent of social media, for example, the potential for government employees to inadvertently violate the Hatch Act has become a much greater possibility. It is not easy to balance the need for fair electoral politics, including keeping possible coercive practices by government officials in check, with the rights of individuals who serve the public by working in government positions. The Hatch Act has been an attempt to do this in a manner beneficial to the majority. While not everyone has accepted this approach, it has had the support of both major political parties since it was signed into law.

—Donald A. Watt, PhD

Bibliography and Additional Reading

Dunn, Susan. *Roosevelt's Purge: How FDR Fought to Change the Democratic Party*. Cambridge, MA: Belknap Press, 2010. Print.

McElhatton, Jim. "Hatch Act Probe Nets Hundreds; Few Penalized." *Federal Times*. Springfield, VA: Gannett Government Media Site, 2014. Web. 20 August 2014.

Office of Special Counsel. "Overview." *Hatch Act*. Office of Special Counsel, n.d. Web. 20 August 2014.

Office of Special Counsel. *Political Activity and the Federal Employee*. Office of Special Counsel, 2005. Web. 20 August 2014.

Smith, Jason Scott. *A Concise History of the New Deal*. Cambridge: Cambridge University Press, 2014. Print.

Unemployment and Relief

Today, most American communities having any age to them can be shown to have been beneficiaries of Roosevelt's "New Deal for the American people," as the president referred to his program in his inaugural speech of March 1933. In attacking the great problem of unemployment in the 1930s, the New Deal took hungry, desperate men (for the most part) and put them to work. Through programs like the Civilian Conservation Corps and the Works Progress Administration, roads were built, buildings were erected, National Parks were improved, the electrical grid was extended, and towns, cities, and neighborhoods everywhere were transformed. Many of the young men (and women) who worked on these projects would later form the core of the US military in its battle against aggression in Europe and Asia.

Many other long-term benefits derived from the New Deal, as well. Social Security, for example, was launched under the Roosevelt Administration. It provided for the basic economic welfare of retirees and those unable to contribute directly to the economy. New Deal banking legislation guaranteed deposits up to $100,000 in FDIC (Federal Deposit Insurance Corporation) banks—a valuable measure in light of the bank closures that took place after the 1929 stock market crash. Not only were entire communities built (under the Resettlement Administration), but hundreds of existing communities were beautified or otherwise exposed to the arts (through the Federal Arts Project). Murals were painted, theatrical productions were mounted, oral histories were recorded, valuable documentary photographs were taken, and so on.

Above all, people were able to obtain food, clothing, and housing to meet their immediate needs. In other words, people's lives were transformed along with their communities under the New Deal.

■ Bumming in California

Date: 1931 (published 1937)
Author: Eluard Luchell McDaniel
Genre: memoir

Summary Overview

By 1931, the Great Depression was entering its low point. The male unemployment rate, already over 15 percent, would climb to nearly 25 percent within the next two years. As people lost their jobs, factories closed, and farms faced foreclosure, an increasing number of men became transient—part of a great migratory army of homeless vagabonds roaming the continent. Homeless and penniless, they took to the roads and the rails, looking for work and opportunity. These bums, and hobos, as they became known, lived daily with the struggle against hunger, while facing little more than hostility from local authorities concerned about the safety of their towns and cities. The author of the firsthand account included here, Eluard Luchell McDaniel, was one such bum, making his way around California, living each day just hoping to survive to the next. In a brief memoir, he recalls his journey around the state. It is emblematic of the hardships of the time, but also of the optimism that would eventually lead the United States back to prosperity.

Defining Moment

There is a lot of debate among historians for the specific cause of the Great Depression. Certainly, the 1929 stock market crash had a big impact on the collapse of the economy, but scholars point to a host of other factors at play throughout the late 1920s and early 1930s. Some of the theories include a poor banking structure with little federal oversight, a declining farm market, a monetary policy built on the gold standard, and the instability of the European economy. Whatever the cause, beginning in 1929 and reigning throughout the decade until the start of World War II, the Great Depression affected every facet of life. Hundreds of banks failed, family farms were foreclosed on and liquidated, factories closed, and people lost their jobs by the tens of thousands. The first to be affected were the young and old, but soon, Americans of all ages began to feel the pains of economic uncertainty.

As unemployment steadily climbed into the double digits, a great number of Americans found themselves not only without work but also without homes. Ramshackle towns made out of tents, cardboard boxes, and sheds sprang up across the nation. Dubbed "Hoovervilles" in (mocking) honor of President Herbert Hoover, these camps, along with men standing in long lines at soup kitchens, became among the starkest symbols of the country's financial collapse.

While the political winds began to shift toward the more populist policies of President Franklin D. Roosevelt and his New Deal, many men began to crisscross the country in search of work. Tens of thousands of homeless and desperate men, known as bums or hobos, hitched onto freight trains or simply walked, doing whatever odd jobs they could find along the way or, more often, relying on the charity of strangers. It wasn't an easy life. Travel by freight train was dangerous. Men died or were injured while trying to board trains, or through exposure to the elements. Local police and train security workers, nicknamed "bulls," were known to use violence as a means to dissuade trespassers.

Although grim and difficult, the stories of the men who rode the rails during the Great Depression became an essential part of American mythology. The notion of opportunity out West helped to strengthen American optimism even at the nation's worst moments. As the Depression gradually ended and World War II began, many of the men who lived off the charity of others, who rode the rails in search of work, would rise to defend the country from the armies of Imperial Japan and Nazi Germany.

Author Biography

Eluard Luchell McDaniel was born in Mississippi in 1912. Having left home at an early age and unable to make ends meet in the first years of the Depression, he rode the rails to California at the age of fourteen. In San Francisco, he met the noted female photographer Consuelo Kanaga, who would later become famous for her photographs of African Americans. Kanaga employed McDaniel as a handyman and chauffer and helped him finish high school and, eventually, college. McDaniel became a union organizer, founding, among others, the Alabama Sharecroppers' Union. He wrote stories for the Federal Writer's Project, a WPA program. In 1937, McDaniel volunteered to fight the fascist forces of Francisco Franco in Spain, becoming first a driver and later an infantryman. He distinguished himself in several engagements, earning the nickname "El Fantastico" from the Loyalist troops he served with. Wounded in battle, he returned to the United States in 1938 and joined the Merchant Marine. Eventually, forced out of the maritime service for his Communist ties in the 1950s, McDaniel found work in a factory in San Francisco, where he remained until he retired. McDaniel died in 1985.

HISTORICAL DOCUMENT

In the winter of 1931, three Bums and myself began to see California by a I-O-U. About twenty-five cents among the four of us. Sleeping in the most comfortable box-cars in the Southern Pacific Railroad yard. There were no hotels in the city of Los Angeles, for the price we had to pay. Twenty-five cents would only pay for one in a common flop-house.

At that time hitch-hiking was not so good. People were afraid to trust strangers in their automobiles. The people that would give anyone a ride, did not want their car dirtyed up by Bums like us. We done most of our traveling by train. In the railroad yard floaters were from all parts of America.

The railroad Bulls were plentyful. They stayed busy trying to keep Bums from riding the trains. Policemen were busy ordering floaters out of towns throughout California.

Some of the guys was from California, most came from the North, South, and East. There was no trouble to find gangs from everywhere. Some floaters could tell you every railroad stop from the Atlantic to the Pacific.

There were four in our group: Luchell McDaniel, B. Jay Hubert, Asti Butt Slim, and Mulligan Joe. The railroad Bull put us off the trains from Los Angeles. Walking taken place. We seen a milepost it showed six miles from Los Angeles city limit, on the road no ride and no stops.

Not one had enough money to buy food for the group. We were saving the twenty-five cents for ferry fare into San Francisco. Every one of us had something different to say about food. Not one was in humor to say much about anything. We were expecting to land in Oakland off some highspeed Limited from the Valley Line. It was harder to hobo the Coast Line. The talk were something to eat.

When we were three miles pass San Bernardino, Asti Butt Slim spied some farmer's ranch. We taken to the ranch as if it were our own. Eating taken place. That ranch was the best friend we had on our journey over California, by a I-OU. We had been boasting about the wholesale terminal, but the policemen had made it so hot, Los Angeles was not the place for anymore Bums.

That ranch had peaches, grapes, and apricots, we made ourselves at home. We had our pockets full. That satisfied us a full stomach, without bumming anything.

We were on the ranch three hours and twenty minutes. Mulligan Joe called us by name, let's go guys; not me, answered Asti Butt Slim. I ain't thinking about going nowhere. Then B. Jay Hubert spoke up: Man, as long as we went without eating, you guys should never talk about leaving this kingdom. Mulligan Joe said, well, you know that my home ain't here. It don't make me no different now if you guys never leave this farmer's ranch.

Mulligan Joe was long and tall, he was seven feet tall and weight one hundred and ninety pounds. He had allways been call Joe but when we found him to be the biggest Mulligan eats that where he get the name of Mulligan Joe. Joking taken place. Us Floaters had America and the World to talk about. The ranch owner name were never mentioned. We never forget the peaches, grapes, and apricots we had taken from the ranch. We heard trains blowing the whistles but there were not a one in that group cared anything about trains or whistles anymore.

By the time we were to leave the ranch, six more floaters from Los Angeles came walking in to make their selves at home. Not one of that gang asked who own the ranch. What's your name? one of the other Bums ask me. Luchell McDaniel. Whose those other guys with you? One answered I am Mulligan Joe, another I am B. Jay Hubert, I am Asti Butt Slim. Rocking Chair Buddy told the names of his gang. These guys is: Long Coat Lizy, Sugar Butt Sam, Candy Dodging Dayboy, High Cap Swanginggate, Slicker Fastblack, and Didy Waw Didy. We waited until they were full from peach ranch and began looking for a train.

Not a passenger train in sight. Bums were walking around the little station, like soldiers on the army ground. Loud talking. No place to go, we were in such hurry. What's rush? ask Mulligan Joe. No rush, I just want to be doing something, answered Asti Butt Slim. B. Jay Hubert never said a word. Another: Deal me out this time. Our gang had the peach and apricot blues.

We rode the Fireball Special for three hours and twenty minutes. Another unhappy stop. Most of the fruit from the ranch had almost petered out. Not so much high talking and laughing. No one cared about how large New York was, or how small the next town. The talk were food. Some said that nothing could worrie they mind but the lack of food was worrying all of our stomachs.

Only two hours before daytime. We never had sleeping to worrie about. The train stop about three miles of town. All of us taken a little headache. No bad off sick. The idea of having to walk three miles on an empty stomach. In Fresno, California, a train of sugarbeets was couple to a dead engine. Not even a watchman nor a Bull in sight. We had been kind of choice about our food, especially after we left the peach, grape, and apricot ranch.

That morning it wasn't a bad choice about anything we ate. We found that sugar-beet train to be a friend. We made a breakfast of raw sugar-beets. The Fireball Special standing in the yard at Fresno, California. Floaters were walking up and down the sugarbeet train like ants on a meat skin. Eating beets wherever we wanted. We fill the empty spots in our stomachs, and began to talk about traveling. Some wanted to gamble. We had cards and dice. About twenty-five of us in one box-car. Us twenty-five had one dollar and thirty cents. Mulligan Joe had a deck of black-jack cards and banking his own game with twenty-five cents. Only thirty-five cents around Mulligan box table, including his own twenty-five cents. We known that Mulligan Joe was the biggest game runner-on that train.

B. Jay Hubert and Asti Butt Slim were playing across the log, with Rocking Chair Buddy and High Cap Swanginggate. Luchell McDaniel, Candy Dodging Dayboy, Seal Goodstuff, Cantie Catchen, Long Broadway, and Slicker Fastblack were playing the Georgia Skin. In the lefthand side of that box-car, was Long Coat Lizy and Didy Waw Didy, playing Kune Can. We gambled until the sugar-beets began to wear out.

We never stop walking. Some singing the blues, some telling stories while other talking about railroads. Not a policeman on our mind. Who's that man, ask Asti Butt Slim? Another Bum like you, answered Long Coat Lizy. It is two of them guys, said Mulligan Joe. If it twenty policemen we don't give a dog, some answered. A well dress man and his son walk to us and ask if we would like to work. Don't talk like that, said Didy Waw Didy, you known that we want something. Well, I have a lot of hay to get in before it get wet and if you boys will hall it for me I will pay you well.

Bums began to whisple from one to the other. Boys, if we take this job, everything will be allright. Yes, answered Didy Waw Didy. Didy Waw Didy was known more than any hobo. He had cross the country more than any floater in America. He could dot in and out a town more than any hobo, that why he was known Didy Waw Didy.

We stayed on that ranch for two days. That farmer paid us six dollars for the two days. We went some distance from that ranch and began our usual oldtime game. Gambling on everything but the time of day and with six dollars each, we had something to gamble with.

We gambling like we had a income. We made agreement not to break each other all of us had been broke once. No one could lose anymore than three dollars of his money on that train.

Before the Fireball Special got to Oakland we stop in another one horse town. That town was not large enough to worrie us about policemen. After we had been there for only a short time the chief of police came down and ordered us out town. Long Coat Lizy began to show the officer where he was wrong about calling us Bums. We got money, answered some of the other boes. The chief never cared what we had.

We Bums had too much money in our pocket for any man to talk that way to us. Didy Waw Didy said: Officer, if you give me five or ten minutes, I will leave this one man town. He ask us again: who's going to jail or whose going to leave this town. Sugar Butt Sam was allways too smart anyway. He made the officer angry. Mulligan Joe, who had such kind way of talking, never had a chance. Sie Boleg, the Bum that could never be satisfied playing cards except he was in jail, keep his self trying to get everybody arrested.

Asti Butt Slim was round shouldered from getting in and out of patrol wagons, stayed in different jails more than he lived in anybody home, did everything to have all of us put in the can. The chief taken us before the desk sargent: book these fellows. Where about? How is we going to keep all this many guys in that small jail. Well, answered the chief, in a angry way; if the jail won't whole these birds, we will put all over in the post-office. We may have to put some of these birds in the Western Warehouse for safe keep.

You seven guys that begging so hard may go. No you: slim one. You are going to the workhouse. You ten birds, standing by the fence beat it. You eight guys here will serve a plenty time. What your names? I am Luchell McDaniel, I am B. Jay Hubert, I am Asti Butt Slim, I am Mulligan Joe, I am Long Coat Lizy, I am Sugar Butt Sam, I am Sie Boleg, I am Cantie Catchen, and that guy over there is Didy Waw Didy. It is good thing that I didn't have to take the names of that whole group, said the chief. You know that some time ago, we got the news from South that a gang of floaters coming to San Francisco did a lot of harm in San Bernidena and Fresno, I hope you are not the one's. What was the harm? All just a bunch of unthoughtful Bums wreks some Farmer ranch. Beside that, the police in Northern California is on the lookout for that worthless gang of hobos.

We hobos could not afford to speak. That chief was talking about us and we knew it. Not one in our bunch knew anything about that town or what happen. We knew that he was talking about us. Mulligan Joe were all upset about having to go and serve the thirty days, that he lost his head. Well, officer, why tell us what happen in the South? That ain't going to fill our stomach. Didy Waw Didy never had anything to say while the officer were talking but he went to whispleing the black snake blues.

How old is you guys? I am 15 — I am 14 — I am 16 — I am 17 — I am 16 — I am 17 — I am 15 — I am 14. You boys is just kids, ain't you? Yes sir. Still you are old enough to do a lot of harm. I never got your age, McDaniel. I am 14 years old. What did you say and how old? I am 14 years old. The officer was silent for two or three minutes. I was fixing to turn you boys aluce but he had to liar. No liar, officer. Well, I just know, that it ain't no way in hell for you to get that big, fat, and ugly in 14 years.

He let us go without having to serve anytime in prison. We promise that officer that we would never try it again. That was the last time we Bums were arested for trying to travel on the I-O-U over California.

Document Analysis

Eluard Luchell McDaniel recounts his time bumming across California. A fourteen-year-old boy travelling with a small "gang" of other boys, he and his friends ride in boxcars, eating whatever food they can find along the way. Their journey is not an easy one, their anxiety nearly constant. Where will they find their next meal? Where can they find work? It ends with them narrowly avoiding prison and McDaniel deciding that his time bumming was at an end. McDaniel's story is representative of a large segment of the male population during the Great Depression, a time when tens of thousands of Americans became itinerant, migratory workers, dreaming not of riches, but simply the chance to survive.

McDaniel writes as an uneducated bum, riding the rails, would. His intent, through recollection, is to impart the hardships of being poor, homeless, and without support. He and his fellow "floaters" represented every corner of the nation. They travelled in search of food, work, and new opportunities. They were willing to work, but, at times, they were not above taking what they needed. People didn't help much then. Police made life difficult. Railroad security could be dangerous.

They picked clean a fruit ranch. They gorged themselves on raw sugar beets on a train. They gambled. They talked. Eventually they came upon a farmer willing to pay them six dollars each for two days' work. The experience that McDaniel writes about is alien to that of most people living in America today. It was a time when groups of young men might travel for days on the rumor of work. When a significant portion of the citizenry was destitute.

Eventually, McDaniel and his gang stop in a town outside of Oakland. The local police chief tells the group to clear out. Their kind is not welcome in the town. Despite the boys having money from their job, the policeman insists that they leave and threatens them with jail time if they stay. All of them have had bad experiences with the authorities in the past, McDaniel informs us, not because they were bad people, but because of the times in which they live.

When the chief of police informs the boys that they might be wanted in connection with food theft at a fruit ranch, each member of the group pleads for their lives. When they reveal their ages, the police take pity on them and let them go. These are not hardened criminals on a spree through the state, they are just kids trying to survive, searching for the American dream. In exchange for being set free, McDaniels and his friends agree to stop bumming and play it straight.

Essential Themes
McDaniel's account offers us a unique insight into the lives of the people most affected by the Great Depression. Little more than a teenager, without any form of support and seemingly without any prospects, McDaniel faces a daily struggle against hunger. Trying to survive the worst economic downturn in the nation's history, McDaniel and his friends are under threat of near constant harassment by the very authorities who should be helping them. Going from town to town, travelling wherever the train takes them, groups of boys and men live in a constant state of stress. And yet, there's a shared comradery and optimism among McDaniels and his group. Their lives are hard and uncertain from one day to the next, but one gets the sense that they believe that things might get better. The very act of travelling west is indicative of this optimism. At no point does McDaniels wallow in pessimism, but continues on, hoping against hope. This is fairly typical of the American experience of the Great Depression. While countries like Italy, Germany, and Spain descended into dictatorship and authoritarianism, in 1932, the United States elected a populist president and, despite legal and political challenges, invested fully in his ideas of shared responsibility. While citizens in other countries blamed their governments for the Great Depression, overthrowing one after another, Americans largely blamed themselves, resolving to do whatever was necessary to pull themselves back up again. McDaniels was soon rewarded for his optimism, with work under FDR's New Deal. Although the Depression continued on for the rest of the decade and the ranks of bums would swell, that belief in a brighter future would help the United States not just survive, but thrive.

—KP Dawes, MA

Bibliography and Additional Reading
McElvaine, Robert S. *The Great Depression: America, 1929-1941*. New York: Three Rivers Press, 2009.
Shlaes, Amity. *The Forgotten Man: A New History of the Great Depression*. New York: HarperCollins, 2007.
Terkel, Studs. *Hard Times: An Oral History of the Great Depression*. New York: The New Press, 2005.

United We Eat—The Phenomenon of Unemployed Leagues

Date: August, 1934
Authors: John S. Gambs
Genre: article

Summary Overview

In 1934, journalist and author John S. Gambs published an article that described the rise and impacts of so-called unemployed leagues. These organizations were involved not only in providing limited forms of local aid during the Great Depression, but also in active protests—which were sometimes violent—against the local, state, and federal governments over perceived inaction on behalf of the poor. As they grew in number and strength, Gambs reported, their activities expanded to include forming labor networks and affiliating with leftist organizations. Gambs speculated on the future of these organizations: either they would wither away once economic recovery occurred, or they would be forcibly disbanded by police action.

Defining Moment

In 1929, the "Roaring Twenties"—distinctive because of the tremendous economic boom that occurred in the United States during this period—came to a dramatic halt. Stock markets crashed, banks folded, industries faltered, and countless jobs disappeared in what would come to be called the Great Depression.

Economists, social scientists, and other scholars have not come to a firm agreement on the specific causes of the Depression. Generally, however, experts point to citizens' inability to repay loans and credit debt, a lack of government regulation of businesses and markets, and a lack of sustainability in the country's leading industries as some of the leading causes of this event. Many scholars point to the sharp divide between the nation's wealthy and poor—including the large percentage of immigrants, who came to the country during the early twentieth century to work in the energy and manufacturing industries—as a contributing factor as well, as the latter group represented a majority of the population that would be adversely affected by any fluctuations in the economy.

Herbert Hoover, the incumbent president in 1929, had only been in office for nine months when the stock market crashed. Hoover believed that government's role in private economic affairs should be minimal and argued repeatedly that the nation's economic infrastructure was still solid and healthy despite the tumult of Black Thursday in October 1929 and other events leading to the Depression's onset. After Black Thursday, Hoover did not look to implement any major reforms or pass emergency legislation that would give direct aid to the poor. Instead, Hoover called upon citizens to cooperate with one another through a spirit of volunteerism. Because of his perceived *laissez-faire* approach to the crisis, Hoover and the federal government were increasingly seen by the public as distant and unwilling to help. His successor, Franklin D. Roosevelt, was more open to instituting federal aid programs, but Roosevelt's early attempts to address the growing crisis by creating jobs through the Federal Emergency Relief Administration were not sufficient to aid the millions of unemployed Americans, and unrest continued.

Protests against federal, state, and local governments' perceived indifference to the plight of the poor and unemployed gave rise to organizations known as "unemployed leagues." The first of these organizations was launched in 1931 in Seattle, when labor leader Carl Branin of the Seattle Labor College established the Unemployed Citizens' League, which raised money to purchase a wide range of goods and food to redistribute to the poor. As more leagues organized, they seized on public discontent with government aid programs and launched their own programs (including short-lived "scrip" programs—replacing unavailable legal currency with substitute money to purchase food and services) to both help the poor and widen the protest against the government. Protests ranged from direct verbal confrontations with government employees to violence and strikes. Over time, leagues began to compete in many ways with organized labor as they sought new members.

Adding to the growing controversy over unemployed leagues was the specter of Communism. Communists were active in the country's major cities, actively recruiting members who had grown disenchanted with their local, state, and federal government. Many government officials and business leaders saw unemployed leagues as willing partners with Communists, if not Communists themselves. This perceived connection only added to the animosity between the government and the leagues, inciting more confrontations and protests as the Depression continued through the 1930s.

Author Biography

Little has been written about the life and career of John S. Gambs. Around the time of publication of the article reprinted here, Gambs was a junior faculty member at Columbia University, specializing in institutional economics. He had studied as a student at Columbia with the noted economist Wesley C. Mitchell. Later, he served as a labor economist at the US War Labor Board and went on to write many books on economics. In 1982, he was awarded the Veblen-Commons Award for distinguished work in institutional economics. He died in 1986.

HISTORICAL DOCUMENT

In a district relief office in Pittsburgh, three men are sitting along one side of a table. They represent five hundred unemployed families. Opposite them sits a woman, the district supervisor. There has been excited talk. Suddenly one of the men gets up, his face white. He puts his head close to the woman's; his eyes blaze at her:

> "Damn you! You don't care what happens to the unemployed. God! how I hate you. I could tear your foul body to shreds, cut it up into strips—you don't know what it means to be evicted. You live in a steam-heated apartment. I hate you. I could break every bone in your dirty carcass."

The scene changes. A delegation of an unemployed league is in Harry L. Hopkins' office. The spokesman begins by saying something like this:

> "Before we submit our complaint, Mr. Hopkins, we want you to know that we have no faith in you. We are well aware that your policy is not to relieve the unemployed, but to stretch out relief thinly enough to save the incomes of the rich, at the same time that you give enough to prevent an uprising of the workers."

Last January, when the Colorado legislature met to consider the desperate relief situation, the galleries were packed with members of an unemployed league. They sang while the assembly was trying to deliberate; whenever a legislator rose and started to leave the chamber—as legislators usually do—the crowd shouted, "Sit down." He sat down. One senator was so exasperated at the tactics of the unemployed that he said: "If this is the kind of people relief agencies are feeding, let them starve."

I talked with a man in Allegheny County, Pennsylvania. He was the leader of an organization of the unemployed. "Unless I win the appeal, which I won't, I go to jail for two or three years, I guess. They charged me with resisting an officer and inciting to riot. All I did was to try to stop the forced sale of the man's house." He talked casually about two or three years in prison—like a scholar or businessman who is about to leave for China or Asia, to study or open a branch office.

A similar incident but with a different outcome is described in *Labor Action*, a paper published by the American Workers' Party:

> "This constable is for sale. How much is the bid? Sold for 8 cents." The Pennsyl-

vania Unemployed League at Pittsburgh sold the constable at an eviction fight. The eviction was stopped by a mass demonstration. When leaving an "accident" occurred to the constable and the landlord. They went to the hospital. "Who threw the bricks?" Shrugged shoulders was the reply. No more evictions for six months. (*Labor Action*, May 1, 1934, p. 3.)

In the daily press we see such headlines as: 200 Cops Guard Relief Parley, or, 600 Rioters Here Battle 100 Police at Relief Bureau. In the labor press: Police Slug Jobless as 500 Demonstrate for Relief in Los Angeles; 55 Jailed in Ohio as State Acts to Curb FERA Strike; FERA Strikes Worry Relief Heads in Ohio; Ohio State Jobless Vote Relief Strike for August First.

In this fashion, carrying on their banners the device used by men in the Continental Navy—the coiled rattlesnake and the militant words, Don't Tread on Me—thousands of men and women are protesting the inadequacies of unemployment relief. They sing songs like this, to the tune of the chorus of My Bonnie Lies Over the Ocean:

Soo-oop, soo-oop,

They gave us a bo-ole of soo-oop,

Soo-oop, soo-oop

They gave us a bo-ole of soup.

Their slogans and catch phrases are: "Empty guts are real guts"; "United we eat, divided we starve." A speaker says to an audience of three thousand: "The unemployed are either yellow or red—and we're not yellow." There is prolonged applause.

So much for one side of the picture. Here is the other.

"We're sorry, Miss Jones, but orders is orders. We got to demonstrate in front of your district office at ten next Saturday. The County Council of the Unemployed voted a mass demonstration. There won't be many of us—we'll just sort of march past and stop awhile and maybe sing a song. We'll have banners. Don't worry none about us. You're OK." That happened in Pittsburgh.

Members of unemployed leagues, sitting around a table in some abandoned warehouse, are busily going through papers, sorting, typing, filing. The men—and women—comment:

"Can't do anything about the Smith case—they're getting what they deserve.... See if we can get some coal for Mrs. Rettchik; she shared her last order with Mrs. Rubinow.... Type that complaint over and make a carbon; it looks lousy—can't hand in a thing that looks like that. . . . What's this? That Chiesa guy again! He's always bellyaching. Throw it out; he'd ask for a Rolls Royce if we let him, and crab because they didn't send a chauffeur along."

In Chicago, leagues of unemployed citizens bring complaints to a central bureau, through their representatives. A case submitted is calmly considered on its merits. The relief officer in charge has the confidence of the delegates. There is no audience of other persons on relief before whom the representatives of the unemployed may dramatize a complaint.

Last January relief agencies in Denver fostered organizations among the unemployed—organizations that succeeded in having a tax bill and a relief-bond bill enacted. The clients called on members of the legislature to explain their predicament, tried to still the violent opposition of the newspapers, and worked quietly but effectively at the polls on election-day.

There are probably 100,000 persons in unemployed leagues, in every part of the United States. They are tolerably well organized; they have their own newspapers; they meet in national and regional conventions. Precisely what do they want? What is their program? If, as many social workers have asked, they are granted certain demands today, will they come back tomorrow with an entirely new list of demands? Are members of leagues

Communists? Are the leaders of unemployed organizations mere psychopathic troublemakers, who seize on the desperate problems of the hour to feed their megalomania? These questions have, all of them, two sides, and should be understood genetically rather than answered categorically. We will be in a better position to venture an opinion if we go back to the beginnings of unemployed protest during this depression. tar

In the fall of 1931 we began to hear rumblings of protest against inadequate relief. There were hunger marches, to be sure, but most of us took notice of another movement of protest. This movement tended, in typically American fashion, to concern itself with monetary schemes and self-reliance. I refer, of course, to the so-called barter movement [see "Making Money," by Jacob Baker, *Survey Graphic*, February 1933; *Producers' Exchanges*, by E. Wight Bakke, July 1933].

At first this movement (which was not barter at all, but a "production-exchange system," to use Joanna C. Colcord's phrase) sought to bring relief to the destitute without calling into aid the offices of local or federal government. Scrip was expected to perform miracles; or economic ventures were to be undertaken which would bring to self-help leagues an adequate supply of commodities.

Very soon, however, the limitations of scrip were seen, and the boundaries of self-help discovered. It was then that to leagues began to exert pressure on public officials. In February 1933 thousands of former barterers took forcible possession of the county-city building in Seattle. In Denver, a large production-exchange association became a league of protest. "Next winter," I was told a year ago by a member of the Denver barter association, "we won't dicker with farmers and harvest their crops on shares. What we'll do, we'll drive our trucks up to the wholesale places and take what we need." Pat May, a leader in the self-help leagues of Los Angeles, is as good at grumbling as at organizing production-exchange systems. In July of 1933, the charming Mormon gentlemen who had established the Natural Development Association (a self-help league) spent their time demonstrating, protesting and making speeches against the evils of the present social order. The once-thriving store of the Association was all but deserted.

These leagues soon fell under the leadership of three left-wing groups: Communists, members of the American Workers' Party, and members of the Socialist Party. It is difficult to say at the moment which party has the strongest leagues. It may be ventured, however, that the Socialist Party has the one with largest organizations, but the least militant ones. Although each party dominates leagues in most sections of the United States, some are stronger in one area than in another. The American Workers' Party, for example, seems to have cornered the market in Ohio.

It should be clearly understood that, in the three types of organizations mentioned—Socialist, Communist and American Workers' Party—the rank and file of the membership may be Republican, Democrat, Catholic, Jewish or pro-Aryan. The leagues are nonpartisan. What happens is that the unemployed, responding to some gregarious impulse during these difficult years of stress, form an inchoate organization. Neither our relief programs, nor any other sort of program, has a plan for canalizing the stream of this impulse, or the deep pools of incipient unrest. The only people today who have seemed in any degree willing to execute a plan or submit a program are the three groups mentioned. Their purposeful 5 to 10 percent an organization will capture it. The only competition is among themselves—and sometimes that is enough to wreak a large, powerful league.

One must not infer from the foregoing that all unemployed leagues have as leaders Communists, Socialists or members of the American Workers' Party. Some leagues are independent in every sense. Some are Technocratic in bias, others anarchistic. The Utah League mentioned above is a curious combination of naturalism, technocracy, Mormonism and 100 percent Americanism. Other leagues, no doubt, would be found to be just as difficult to analyze.

First, then, we have barter leagues and other spontaneous organizations of the unemployed which were captured by left-wing leadership. Hunger marches and other demonstrations, in the pre-FERA era, supersede barter. The next phase seems to be marked by direct dealing with local relief agencies soon after the establishment of the FERA. In these negotiations, the keynote seems to be that Mr. Roosevelt an Mr. Hopkins are friends of the unemployed—perhaps even the state relief director is all right—but the local director of relief finds his greatest pleasure in seeing numbers of people starve to death.

This attitude came about quite naturally. The President promised that nobody should starve; if, then, relief was inadequate, it was probably the fault of the county relief board, or of the nearest district supervisor. Because—at least partly because—of the difference between the fine statements which came from federal officials, and the relatively low standard of living that was actually meted out by state and local officials, leagues made district relief offices bear the brunt of their complaints, demonstrations, riots and abuse.

At this time, the following attitude was (and is) characteristic: unemployment relief should be something quite different from "welfare." Persons willing and able to work, but being honestly incapable of finding employment, should not be urged or forced to exhaust completely their resources, give up their homes, live with relatives, take a major portion of a grown son's or daughter's wages, receive no medical attention unless there is a critical illness, and so on. The unemployed should be able to register the fact of their unemployment; and, upon verification of this fact, relief should begin. It is by such preconceptions that conferences with relief agencies are dominated.

More specifically, the following demands have been made by unemployed leagues: greater promptness in getting various forms of relief, especially in emergencies; briefer waiting periods in reception rooms; less humiliating "case work" and abolition of the "pauper's oath"; more sympathetic and better-trained social workers; continued opportunity to present complaints, at regular times, to the principal relief officers of the area; general improvement of relief among Negroes, and no discrimination against them; provision of toilets in waiting-rooms; issue of a type of order permitting its use in several stores; cash relief; better relief for single persons; fewer changes and less confusion in regulations having to do with the giving of relief; inspection of stores that honor relief orders, to see that they do not profiteer; payment of rent and no evictions.

The leagues are still protesting against these things, and still laying the blame for inadequacies on local officers. There seems, however, to be a growing tendency to put the blame on Washington or the state Capital, and a decreased tendency to lay the entire blame for all shortcomings at the feet of local administrators.

Recently something rather dramatic has happened. The leagues have taken on a new function, logical enough in view of their history, but unrelated to protest against inadequate relief. There has been a generally rising distrust of the National Recovery Program. It has expressed itself, so far as concerns our inquiry, by a wave of strikes and threatened strikes on the part of employed labor. Now, unemployed leagues have, in their short life, shown a remarkable solidarity with employed labor. Those on work relief, for example, have demanded rates equal to those of ordinary labor in order that current wage-rates should not be threatened; and there have been severe demonstrations in which this matter was an issue. They feel that the unemployed may be transformed into a substrate of the working classes. Even more, they fear that such a substratum, if created, will challenge the security of the labor force employed by business enterprise. There has also been solidarity in ordinary strikes. Unemployed leagues have tried to prevent their members, and other unemployed, from taking the jobs created by a labor dispute. They have picketed as assiduously as have the strikers themselves; and, in some cases, as in the recent Toledo strike, the leaders of the unemployed have played prominent roles in the labor conflict.

While this is being written, the leagues are girding themselves for the impending steel strike. At a convention of the Pennsylvania Unemployed League in Allentown resolutions were voted to support the threatening strike. They offered their services, their leadership and their press. They promised not to scab, and to prevent others among the unemployed—so far as is possible—from scabbing.

From barter and protest to planned participation major labor disputes—that, in a few words, summarizes the history of unemployed activity. What has happened is not much that the leagues are becoming bolder and border, but that the background against which they have operated constantly changing. It must also be remembered that the present administration is making the first national experiment in the giving of poor relief; it is not to be wondered if the guinea pigs squeal and twist as the experiment progresses.

How much of the activity described above is sound

and fury, and how much is intelligent pursuit of goals? Is a man like the police commissioner of New York City right when says that the unemployed "injure their cause by resorting to unlawful action. . . . The result [of taking part in demonstrations] is that those of the unemployed who lend themselves to this exploitation only add to their own difficulties."

The goals of unemployment leagues are of two sorts, expressed and unexpressed. The expressed range from getting a ton of coal for Mrs. O'Connor who, somehow, has been neglected by a social worker, to demands for a state patterned after the Soviet Union. The unexpressed goals are the desire for companionship, engaging in activities that absorb ones (typing complaints or taking part in riots), being of service to one's fellows, competing for recognition and so on.

Both goals have been advanced by organizations of the unemployed. Demonstrations have, without doubt, been followed by better relief. Riots work—at least up to a certain point. In the last century a hunger march in London resulted in the trebling of the relief fund within a few hours; in Minneapolis, a few months ago, a similar demonstration had similar results. In 1922 the British Unemployed attacked the Islington Guards; the dole was continued. In Pittsburgh, members of a militant organization of war veterans swoop on the district offices because, in their opinion, they are being unjustly treated; they usually get what they ask for. One could repeat instance after instance.

As to the ventures of the unemployed in national strikes, they have not yet had an opportunity to demonstrate their strength. It is certainly true, however, that no group of strikers can hope to win important concessions unless the unemployed, through their own organization, undertake to spoil the market for strike-breakers.

As to the second goal, the unexpressed goal of finding a way to manifest competitive, altruistic and gregarious impulses—that, too, has been achieved in part by unemployed leagues.

Through "chiseling"—to use their term—and cooperative begging, leagues may secure a dozen branch offices; the quarters are furnished with tables, chairs, typewriters and filing cases. These branch offices fulfill useful recreational and social functions. Members come in to smoke, chat or read. Sometimes a puppy or a cat is mascot—a spoiled animal, receiving the tender care of rough hands. In winter, branch offices are warmer than some of the homes. Lunches are served to the regular office staff. Sometimes a dormitory is established for a group of unmarried workers. At the central office out of two or three old cars owned, one, somehow, is kept in operating order. It is used, of course, only on official business. There are also dances to raise money and large mass meetings. Public opinion has been sufficiently favorable to allow the leagues, rather generally, to meet in schoolhouses or the halls of public libraries.

Some members of leagues serve their fellows directly by being members of "service committees." The functions of these committees are to turn on the gas after it has been turned off by the company; ditto electricity. As for water, the committees will sometimes pour cement over the valve when it is open; when the cement hardens, it is troublesome, not to say expensive, to shut off the water. Probably most of the leagues are equipped to give convincing work references to members who have no recommendations from former employers. And it is also likely that an evicted citizen could get, from his league, forged rent receipts covering the past six months, to present to a prospective landlord.

What next? Will the leagues grow and extend their influence? Estimates will vary, but it seems clear that, including women and older adolescents, ten million persons are candidates for membership. Will the leagues grow from their present 100,000 (an unreliable figure, of course) to—say—five millions? That would give the unemployed an organization rivaling in numbers the AFL at its peak, and would constitute an organization fifty times larger than the IWW in its best days.

Hardly. Internal and external forces militate against such growth. The internal forces revolve around the recurrent factional struggles of left-wing unionism in the United States. In Pittsburgh, where I made an intensive study of unemployed unions, the customary process of karyokinesis was going on unabated. Each group had split off from some other group, and the remaining groups were riven by cliques. Last summer, the self-help movement in California—where it was strongest—was a bundle of animosities, personal hatreds, petty jealousies [see "Whither Self-Help?" Paul S. Taylor and Clark Kerr, *Survey Graphic*, July].

It seems, moreover, to be characteristic of unionism that, as it grows in numbers, it goes further from unemployment leagues first, as relief policies are more lightened, and include in their ambit such measures as unemployment insurance, housing and the like. In similar fashion, a generously conceived public-works program will attract the unemployed away from their unions. Complementing this force will be increasing sagacity of the social worker. Workers and their superiors will learn how to meet delegations of the unemployed with candor, sympathy and tact. I know a district supervisor who been brought up in such refinement that she shudders visibly every time a member of an unemployed delegation spits into her waste basket. Such things get around; and probably five times as much spitting goes on in her office as would go on had she never drawn attention to it. Persons on relief are people. They resent the superciliousness of some social workers; they respond with loyalty to the friendliness of others. If it be socially desirable that unemployed leagues should decrease in size or in militancy, then relief workers, by their conduct, have a real responsibility to the community.

Finally, it must be remembered that there may be days of prosperity again. Recovery will probably deal a severe blow to unemployed unions.

The second sort of external force tending to break up the leagues will be the probable withdrawal of civil liberties, the use of police, and the creation of a public opinion unfavorable to leagues. These techniques are already being used. Leaders of the unemployed report more severe treatment by the constabulary recent months. The leagues are being described as revolutionary, in order to alienate the toleration of the middle classes. The *New York Times* of June 12 says that the police commissioner of New York has announced his intention of being less lenient hereafter towards demonstrations of the unemployed. No doubt other municipal officials are similarly modifying their policies.

The use of force against organizations of the submerged tenth has worked very well in the past. It broke the backbone of IWW in 1918. The good old way may be tried again—but with this caution: the years in which sallies were made against the militant IWW were, taken on the whole, years of plentiful jobs and there were months of high prosperity; clubbing and jailing may not go so well when the workers of the United States have nothing to lose but their skins.

GLOSSARY

AFL: American Federation of Labor, a labor union

barter: to trade with or engage in commerce using goods and services as the medium of exchange (instead of money)

canalize: to provide an outlet for; channel

constable: officer or agent of the law

FERA: Federal Emergency Relief Administration, a New Deal assistance program

Hopkins, Harry: secretary of the Interior and head of relief programs

IWW: Industrial Workers of the World, a radical (largely Communist) labor union

karyokinesis: splitting or dividing

scrip: legal tender, in either coin or paper form, issued during a temporary emergency; it usually could not be exchanged for cash

technocratic: of or relating to a technocracy, or government control by technicians and scientists

Document Analysis

John S. Gambs's article, published in the August 1934 edition of the progressive magazine *Survey Graphic*, provides an illustration of the extent to which unemployed leagues grew in influence and hostility toward the government. Gambs describes the anger and frustration that fueled the leagues as they increasingly launched protests, strikes, and violent confrontations. Furthermore, Gambs examines the validity of the prevailing theory that behind the success of the leagues was the shadowy hand of international Communism.

In his article, Gambs recalls a number of incidents in which league organizers and leaders, overtly angry with the perceived inaction and indifference of government officials at aid departments, lashed out verbally and even physically against employed individuals. Gambs describes an environment in which there are two distinct and adversarial groups of Americans: the employed and the unemployed. The latter group's members are empowered by the leagues, as these citizens border on starvation and lack any viable options to return to financial and nutritional health. On the other end of the spectrum are those who are gainfully employed (in the cases Gambs describes, these individuals are representatives of the government), who show little to no interest in helping the most destitute.

Gambs attempts to describe how the leagues were able to generate such support by exploring their roots. These groups began in 1931 as simple aid networks, providing scrip and barter programs to help the poor find food and other necessities. Over time, however, the efforts of these leagues fell short, as "the limitations of scrip were seen and the boundaries of self-help discovered" due to the growing volume of unemployed people in the United States. The leagues turned their attention to the government, seeing a target for the collective frustration and ire of those they claimed to represent. This anger is focused mainly on local government agencies, which Gambs argues is due to "the difference between the fine statements which came from federal officials and the relatively low standard of living that was actually meted out by state and local officials." Leagues became involved in illegal protests, labor strikes, and other activities. Their activity, Gambs says, can be sorted into two categories: expressed and unexpressed. In the former, leagues work on specific goals, such as finding supplies for a member or protesting the government. In the latter category, the leagues seek members and partners to help maintain their strength and grow their numbers.

Gambs also explores the question of whether the leagues' growth is facilitated by Communists, suggesting that, almost certainly, some leagues are influenced by them. Then again, other leagues are connected to socialists, while others are completely independent. An argument could be made that the leagues are heavily influenced by such groups, Gambs says, but there is no singular influence, such as the Communists, that can be linked to every league. Furthermore, although the leadership of the groups may tend to be affiliated with leftist organizations, the "rank and file of the membership" has a much greater diversity of political opinion.

Gambs concludes that the leagues will meet their eventual end in one of two possible ways. First, the Depression could end, bringing new jobs and relief for the poor—such a turnaround would mean the removal of a driving motivation behind the leagues. The second is that the government could forcibly dismantle the leagues while the Depression persists, which Gambs suggests it is already attempting to do. However, he cautions that, while violent tactics have succeeded in the past against organizations such as the International Workers of the World, they may be less effective under the current economic conditions, "when the workers of the United States have nothing to lose but their skins."

Essential Themes

Gambs's article looked critically at some of the furor surrounding the unemployed leagues, examining the real reasons behind their formation and growing popularity: not Communist agitation, but a dire economic situation and the failure of the government to aid those affected by it. Without condoning the leagues' more radical actions, Gambs discouraged the use of force against them and suggested that the most effective way to disband the leagues was to address the conditions that had led to their creation.

Indeed, as Roosevelt's welfare reforms and job creation efforts continued, the leagues' membership fell and their power diminished. By 1936, many of the leagues had shut down or merged into other, more general radical labor groups, and many of the former leaders of the movement had left. Though the Depression did not end until the United States entered World War II, the anger of the unemployed was, as Gambs predicted, significantly lessened once they felt the government was listening to their concerns.

—*Michael P. Auerbach, MA*

Bibliography and Additional Reading

Edsforth, Ronald. *The New Deal: America's Response to the Great Depression*. Hoboken, NJ: Wiley, 2000. Print.

"The Great Depression (1929–1939)." *Eleanor Roosevelt Papers Project*. George Washington U, n.d. Web. 17 June 2014.

McElvaine, Robert S. *The Great Depression: America, 1929–1941*. 25th anniv. ed. New York: Three Rivers, 2009. Print.

Olson, James Stuart, ed. *Historical Dictionary of the Great Depression, 1929–1940*. Westport: Greenwood, 2001. Print.

Whisenhunt, Donald W. *President Herbert Hoover*. Hauppauge, NY: Nova, 2007. Print.

■ Letter from a Dust Bowl Survivor

Date: March 24, 1935
Author: Grace
Genre: letter

Summary Overview
In March of 1935, a Kansan named Grace wrote to relatives, sharing the recent difficulties in her hometown of McCracken during the Dust Bowl, a period of severe drought and dust storms that afflicted the Great Plains region in the 1930s. She opens with a tongue-in-cheek quip that what her readers thought was a dust storm was actually her beating out carpets and linens. When Grace penned her letter, the Great Depression was in its sixth year and the Dust Bowl in its fourth (by government counts). Both crises ended roughly by 1939. Grace's letter is a strikingly clear example of one family's dealings with the daily struggles created by the Dust Bowl, and it describes, with resignation, how even things as simple and basic as a sneeze were utterly changed.

Defining Moment
The Dust Bowl affected the Great Plains of the United States roughly from 1931 until 1939, unfortunately coinciding with the years of the Great Depression. Five states were primarily affected: Texas, Oklahoma, Kansas, New Mexico, and Colorado. The conditions at the beginning—a parching drought—set the stage for the winds to pick up and carry the dried dirt that lay on the land. One result of this was seen in the deaths of the livestock that were part and parcel of the agricultural life along the Plains. These animals, often found dead on the ground and covered with residual dirt, had inhaled the dust and succumbed to it. It was also not uncommon for men, women, and children to cough up lumps of earth, and the inhalation of dust led to a condition known as "dirt pneumonia" or "dust pneumonia." Grace notes that common sneezes and spit produced mud, and she is aware that pneumonia was prevalent.

The Dust Bowl has been examined not only by historians, but also by economists, meteorologists, and agriculturalists, all in an effort to understand how it happened and why it lasted for as long as it did. One theory, espoused by Donald Worster, is that the Great Plains as a whole had suffered from protracted farming, and the lands, in contrast to the perception of them as expansive, golden wheat fields, were, in actuality, often too changeable—too unpredictable for such industrialized, heavy farming. According to this theory, the droughts and high winds inevitably produced the conditions for what transpired. However, a geographical and meteorological analysis by Geoff Cunfer suggests a more complex interplay between nature and mankind. Cunfar's data points to the Plains having had more localized climate patterns, with some areas, which had not been farmed extensively, experiencing dust storms prior to the 1930s and others where soil erosion was clearly implicated in the development of such storms. Moreover, older analyses described smaller-scale, but similar events going back to the mid-nineteenth century. Computer simulations from NASA scientists indicate that abnormal surface temperature shifts in the Atlantic and Pacific Oceans may have weakened jet stream winds and moved them south, reducing precipitation levels in the Plains. Regardless of the extent to which human activity or climatic shifts may be responsible for causing the Dust Bowl, its effects are undeniable.

Grace's letter stands as one example of daily life during the Dust Bowl, exhibiting the pleasures and hardships of ordinary men and women in the midst of harsh economic times. For instance, she describes their "frenzied time of cleaning, anticipating the comfort of a clean feeling once more," which was, for them, a purely sensual pleasure worth the physical effort to produce, despite its momentary nature. To the historian and researcher, Grace's letter holds greater significance, due in part to the fact that she wrote for family, without thought of future notoriety, and thus expressed her circumstances perhaps far more honestly.

Author Biography
Grace's letter indicates little in the way of specifics about her background. Although she mentions that "there has not been much school" the week of her writing, it is unclear why Grace notes this—whether as a student or an adult, perhaps a mother or teacher. Given her use of proper grammar and opening witticism, she may have been a teenager or adult at the time.

Grace's town of McCracken lies near the center of Kansas and, at the time of Grace's birth, still was a relatively young community, having been founded around 1886 along the Missouri Pacific Railroad. There is no way to determine what kind financial situation Grace's family was in at the time of her writing, nor how large her family was. Her letter indicates that her family had, or at least had had, "gardens," but it is unclear whether they were farmers by profession. It is equally unknown what became of Grace and her relatives after the Dust Bowl ended.

HISTORICAL DOCUMENT

March 24, 1935

Dear Family,
Did some of you think that you had a dust storm? I'll tell you what it was. It was us shaking our bedding, carpets, etc. For over a week we have been having troublesome times. The dust is something fierce. Sometimes it lets up enough so we can see around; even the sun may shine for a little time, then we have a frenzied time of cleaning, anticipating the comfort of a clean feeling once more.

We keep the doors and windows all shut tight, with wet papers on the sills. The tiny particles of dirt sift right through the walls. Two different times it has been an inch thick on my kitchen floor.

Our faces look like coal miners', our hair is gray and stiff with dirt and we grind dirt in our teeth. We have to wash everything just before we eat it and make it as snappy as possible. Sometimes there is a fog all through the house and all we can do about it is sit on our dusty chairs and see that fog settle slowly and silently over everything. When we open the door, swirling whirlwinds of soil beat against us unmercifully, and we are glad to go back inside and sit choking in the dirt. We couldn't see the streetlight just in front of the house. One morning, early, I went out during a lull, and when I started to return I couldn't see the house. I knew the direction, so I kept on coming, and was quite close before I could even see the outline. It sure made me feel funny.

There has not been much school this week. It let up a little yesterday and Fred went with the janitor and they carried dirt out of the church by the scoopful. Four of them worked all afternoon. We were able to have church this morning, but I think many stayed home to clean. A lot of dirt is blowing now, but it's not dangerous to be out in it. This dirt is all loose, any little wind will stir it, and there will be no relief until we get rain. If it doesn't come soon there will be lots of suffering. If we spit or blow our noses we get mud. We have quite a little trouble with our chests. I understand a good many have pneumonia.

As for gardens, we had ours plowed, but now we do not know whether we have more or less soil. It's useless to plant anything.

Grace

Document Analysis
Grace opens her letter with a general address to family. While this may appear odd to the modern reader, it reveals that she probably intended the letter's distribution to a wide family network, rather than to anyone specifically. Just as it was common for Civil War soldiers' letters to be circulated throughout their home communities, and vice versa, Grace may have wished her missive to reach as many of her relatives as possible. It is possible that the relatives to whom she addresses her letter may not have been experiencing the Dust Bowl themselves, as Grace goes into such detail about her and her immediate family's daily struggle with the dust and dirt. Had they lived in an area affected by it, Grace would not have needed to include such detail; they, too, would have dealt with the same matters as often as she.

Her writing is simple and to the point; having her hair matted with dirt and the same gritty particles between her teeth was the norm. Although it had been the better part of four years since the beginning of the droughts and dust storms, and the preceding year had seen the worst droughts ever recorded, there is no sense of complaint in her letter, even when she describes washing right before meals and having to ensure that it was done "snappy." In one incident, she left her house during what she terms "a lull," but quickly found that the murkiness returned: "I knew the direction, so I kept on coming, and was quite close before I could even see the outline [of the house]. It sure made me feel funny." Her behavior and nonchalance in describing such an episode displays how much she had grown used to this way of life. Grace is also fairly matter-of-fact in reporting the rising numbers plagued by the dirt pneumonia that resulted from breathing in all the dust. She herself was not immune to health worries related to this, as she confides that they all have "trouble with our chests."

While Grace and her family took up a rare opportunity to attend church, many others within the community did not do likewise; she presumes they "stayed home to clean." Given her earlier mention of the temporary joy in having things tidy, it was a very understandable choice, and her words convey a nonjudgmental attitude about this.

There is one note of despondency near the close of her letter. She notes that they have made efforts to perform gardening and plowing tasks; however, with the winds and the dust and dirt sweeping along, the family has been left unable to determine whether their soil quantities have lessen or increased. She concludes with the acknowledgment that "it's useless to plant anything."

Essential Themes
Although little information is available about Grace, her age, and the dynamics of her family, and how both major crises of the 1930s—the Depression and the Dust Bowl—affected them personally in the ensuing years, Grace's casual letter serves as a window into the day-to-day realities of surviving those crises. The experiences she describes showcase the challenges of her time and place, from the mundane difficulties of maintaining household cleanliness to the larger issues of poor health, social isolation (inability to hold school or attend church), and economic and/or nutritional impacts (the uselessness of raising crops in their garden).

At the writing of this letter, one of the worst days in Dust Bowl history, Black Sunday, was yet to come. On April 14, 1935, an enormous dust storm, with winds up to sixty miles per hour, ravaged Oklahoma and parts of Texas. Government-mandated soil conservation efforts would begin to show definitive results—a 65 percent reduction in soil loss—by 1937, and the drought finally abated another two years thereafter, in 1939. But by then, about 2.5 million Plains inhabitants had given up hope and packed up, bound for places like Southern California, where unemployment, migrant labor on corporate-run farms, and shantytowns awaited.

—*Jennifer Henderson Crane, PgDip*

Bibliography and Additional Reading
Duncan, Dayton, & Ken Burns. *The Dust Bowl: An Illustrated History*. San Francisco: Chronicle, 2012. Print.
Mulvey, Deb, ed. *We Had Everything but Money*. Greendale: Reiman, 1992. Print.
Sleight, Kenneth. "America's Exodus: The 1930s and the Dust Bowl." *Bright Hub*. Bright Hub, 11 Mar. 2014. Web. 5 June 2014.
"Surviving the Dust Bowl." *American Experience*. WGBH Educational Foundation, n.d. Web. 5 June 2014.

Letter Regarding Assistance to the Poor

Date: September 26, 1935
Author: Fenimore E. Cooper
Genre: letter

Summary Overview

Writing in response to a letter sent by President Franklin D. Roosevelt to more than 120,000 members of the American clergy, the Reverend Fenimore E. Cooper asked the president to take a more careful look at assistance programs for the country's poor. In a letter dated September 26, 1935, he suggested that Roosevelt continue such programs, particularly those that kept senior citizens and disabled Americans out of poverty. However, he also asked the president to keep in mind that some Americans might prefer to receive government funds indefinitely instead of finding work. Finally, Cooper advised the president not to create too much national debt or increase the federal government's power through his New Deal proposals.

Defining Moment

In 1929, the fantastic economic boom the United States enjoyed throughout the 1920s came to an equally fantastic collapse. Stock markets crashed, banks folded, industries faltered, and countless jobs disappeared, sending the United States into what would come to be called the Great Depression. In the decades after the stock market crashed in 1929, economists, social scientists, and other scholars have attempted to understand the specific causes that ushered in this tumultuous period. Generally, experts point to the inability of citizens to repay loans, a lack of business and market regulation by government, and a lack of sustainability in the country's leading industries as some of the major causes of this event. Many scholars also indicate the sharp divide between the nation's wealthy and poor as a contributing factor, as the latter group represented a majority of the population and was adversely impacted by any fluctuations in the economy.

Although the debate over the exact formula of causes that set off this financial meltdown continues, two important facts about the Depression cannot be refuted. The first is that the collapse sent millions of Americans into unemployment and poverty, shut down hundreds of banks and businesses, and caused a financial malaise that persisted for a decade. The second is that, although many political leaders and economic experts espoused theories on how to halt this trend, initial efforts to turn the economy around proved fruitless.

In 1932, the Democratic Party, buoyed by the inability of Republican president Herbert Hoover to end the crisis, nominated Roosevelt, the governor of New York, as its candidate for president. In his acceptance speech for the nomination, Roosevelt pledged to give Americans a "new deal," in which the economic and social conditions that languished during the Depression would be remedied. When Roosevelt won in a landslide victory in November, he immediately set about his agenda. Chief among his goals were generating jobs, restoring the markets, and rejuvenating the American economy over the long term. A defining element of Roosevelt's New Deal was its departure from the *laissez-faire* approach to the economy employed by his predecessors; Roosevelt's platform called for a much larger role for the federal government, which would address the crisis through regulatory reform, major financial investments, and the creation of new federal agencies to service the public's needs.

As part of Roosevelt's efforts to halt the Depression, the president looked to the public for input. In September of 1935, Roosevelt sent a letter to more than 120,000 members of the clergy, requesting their suggestions and comments on how to ensure the New Deal's success. The Reverend Fenimore E. Cooper, rector of the All Saints' Church in Syracuse, New York, and a self-professed supporter of President Roosevelt, responded with a series of suggestions that focused mainly on the government's financial aid programs.

HISTORICAL DOCUMENT

Honorable and Dear Sir:

It was with great pleasure that your friendly letter reached me two days ago, and after some reflection I am undertaking a reply in the same spirit. I am pleased to have been one of your supporters in the last election, and have continually been friendly to your aims in helping the American people out of the morass in which they were entangled three years ago. Your courage all along has been an inspiration to them.

Since you ask for a statement of conditions in our community, and how we feel the government can better serve the people, I shall answer frankly, and to the best of my ability.

First of all, the care of the indigent aged and crippled children and those unemployed through no fault of their own, is a most worthy objective. It would seem to me, however, that time is granted the old should be just above subsistence level, for the reason that otherwise savings and preparation for that time is discouraged, and thrift is indirectly penalized. There is already appearing and growing stronger a wide-spread tendency to depend upon the government, which where it appears tends to replace the older American spirit of independence. This may be unavoidable, but in any case it is a sign of decadence and most alarming. It goes along with the failure of personal initiative.

Secondly, most of us feel that government spending, while necessary during the past few years, has reached a point where it is creating a mountainous debt which future tax-payers will have to shoulder, to their grief. The budget, we believe, should be balanced with all possible dispatch.

Thirdly, there seems to have been created, as a result of necessary relief, a large group of people who had much rather "get along" on what they receive from the dole, than to perform much-needed (but possibly more disagreeable) tasks for which they would receive remuneration. Farmers and housewives are finding it difficult to secure needed assistance. People on relief, once they accept the lower standard, find security, and a complete command of their own time preferable to work. Much-needed zeal for work is thus being killed off in this class, which becomes more difficult to satisfy, and to deal with because of its strength at the polls. Its birth rate tends to rise, we are told in Syracuse. This should be a source of great alarm to yourself, honorable Sir.

Personally, I believe any further concentration of power in the central government is undesirable and menacing to the hard-won liberties of democracy, which our own nation with England, France and the Scandinavian countries, seems to be preserving in the face of a decadent world. Anything approaching dictatorship is most violently abhorred by the people of this section.

With this, we are happy to note an improvement of economic conditions in this city. What I do not note, is an improvement of moral fibre: there is an increasing tendency to exalt the mass man as he is. The ant-hill ideal of society will continue to make inroads in American, unless our moral degeneration can be checked.

Respectfully yours,

Rev. Fenimore E. Cooper, Rector

All Saints' Church
South Salina Street at McLennan Avenue
Syracuse, NY
September 26, 1935

Document Analysis
Cooper's response to Roosevelt's letter encourages the president to be mindful of the financial investments the government was making in aiding those most affected by the Depression. He advises the president to avoid inadvertently creating a population that is overly reliant on financial aid and urges him to spend money with care, as too much spending would only add to the government's mounting debt. Finally, Cooper calls upon Roosevelt to provide financial support to the country's most needy at a rate that keeps them out of poverty, but does not impede their desire to pursue employment and become active participants in American society.

Cooper, by his own admission, believed strongly that Americans should not become dependent on the government. Likewise, he writes in his letter, the government should not become too involved in Americans' lives. His message to the president, therefore, calls for a measured approach to aiding the country's most needy citizens. For example, Cooper encourages the president to continue to provide the needy with financial support until they could take advantage of employment opportunities once the economy recovered. Disabled and elderly citizens should be adequately cared for, Cooper argues, but Americans should nonetheless be encouraged to save in preparation for old age rather than be allowed to rely completely on government aid. Cooper is particularly concerned that some Americans could grow dependent on the government. Many individuals, he argues, might move away from their own individual pursuits of financial stability and instead embrace a lifestyle based on receiving and depositing unemployment benefits. He cautions that many of these individuals would likely pass this government-dependent perspective on to their children, creating long-term populations that knew only government aid instead of what Cooper calls a "zeal for work."

Cooper further cautions Roosevelt to be mindful of the government's limited financial resources. The Depression had taken its toll on virtually every sector of the American economy, and the government was not immune. Cooper advocates targeting expenditures of aid programs in order to protect the most vulnerable. However, he advises Roosevelt not to spend more than revenues permitted. Debt, he argues, was already a problem, and implementing new government spending programs threatened to add significantly to it. This attitude coincided with Cooper's belief that the government should be careful not to intervene in every issue facing US citizens. If the federal government did so, Cooper writes, it would run the risk of resembling a dictatorship rather than the democracy Cooper preferred.

Cooper concludes with an optimistic note, mentioning that the economy was showing signs of improving. He, therefore, suggests that the pressure to move along a more interventionist governmental path was lessening. Still, he writes, the "moral fibre" of the United States was not, in his estimation, showing a concurrent trend toward improvement. On this front, at least, the country still had a great deal of work to do as it toiled to recover from the Depression.

Essential Themes
Responding to President Roosevelt's letter asking members of the clergy to share their thoughts on his New Deal programs, Cooper took the opportunity to express his opinion, focusing on several main areas of concern. First, he expressed his support for financial aid for the needy, a perhaps predictable stance considering his profession. Cooper told Roosevelt that aid was critical during the Depression, especially for the country's vulnerable citizens. However, he warned that aid programs ran the risk of creating a class of people who simply took the government's money instead of pursuing employment. Despite this risk, Cooper noted that Roosevelt's aid programs would be most beneficial to disabled and elderly Americans, whom he suggested would otherwise be employed or pursuing work if physical limitations had not impeded them from doing so.

Cooper was also particularly concerned about the effects that Roosevelt's aid programs might have on the nation's financial position. Although there were signs that the economy was improving, Cooper argued that the government was not in a position to overspend its resources. If the country continued to spend beyond its means, the United States' debt would continue to worsen, and the nation's recovery from the Depression would be slowed. Furthermore, he believed that while limited and targeted aid for the neediest citizens was important, the government should respect the private pursuits of Americans and avoid involving itself greatly in their lives. Finally, Cooper expressed his concern about the moral character of the American people, noting that while economic conditions were improving, morals were not. As a member of the clergy, Cooper was particularly disturbed by this trend. He warned Roosevelt that the United States would not truly recover unless steps were taken to end the "moral degeneration" of American society.

—*Michael P. Auerbach, MA*

Bibliography and Additional Reading

Edsforth, Ronald. *The New Deal: America's Response to the Great Depression*. Malden: Blackwell, 2000. Print.

"The Great Depression." *The Eleanor Roosevelt Papers Project*. George Washington University, n.d. Web. 13 June 2014.

McElvaine, Robert S. *The Great Depression: America, 1929–1941*. 25th anniv. ed. New York: Three Rivers, 2009. Print.

"President Franklin Delano Roosevelt and the New Deal, 1933–1945." *American Memory Timeline: Great Depression/WWII, 1929–1945*. Lib. of Congress, n.d. Web. 13 June 2014.

Memories of the Flint Sit-Down Strike

Date: 1936–1937 (recorded later)
Author: Genora Johnson Dollinger
Genre: memoir; oral history

Summary Overview

The struggle between labor and industry was long and often bloody in the United States. After the abuses of the Gilded Age, suffering through court battles and attempts by industrialists to prevent collectivization, American workers began to organize the first unions at the end of the nineteenth century. After major declines in the labor movement during the 1920s, mainly due to anti-labor sentiment in both industry and government, the Great Depression brought about a new age for unions. Beginning in 1932, and gaining urgency under President Franklin D. Roosevelt, government passed a series of acts greatly expanding the power of organized labor. Through the passage of the National Industrial Recovery Act, in particular, labor unions saw massive gains in power and membership. Unions organized protests and strikes to improve working conditions and negotiate higher wages, most often employing techniques of passive resistance, such as work stoppages and sit-downs. Between 1936 and 1937, the United Auto Workers (UAW) union in Flint, Michigan, initiated just such a strike. As the men occupied the General Motors plant, calling for a redress of grievances, women, such as Genora Dollinger, found new forms of empowerment.

Defining Moment

As the Industrial Age ramped up, working conditions in American factories became insufferable. Basic safety prevention, such as fire escapes, were often ignored, wages were extremely low, and workers were often forced to work long hours without any sort of overtime. As journalists began to call attention to the deaths of factory workers and the prevalence of child labor, reformers and organizers began to build the first-ever unions. Starting with the National Labor Union (NLU), the Knights of Labor, the American Federation of Labor (AFL), and eventually the Industrial Workers of the World (IWW), unions were first organized in major industries, such as railroads and textiles, but soon extended to all labor fields. As the Progressive Movement took hold at the turn of the century, major strikes were called across the nation. Between 1900 and 1920, unions managed to negotiate higher wages and better working conditions in the railroad, steel, and coal industries, among others.

With the economic boom of the Roaring Twenties, and the pro-business policies of several Republican administrations leading the federal agenda, labor unions suffered losses between 1920 and 1929. Lack of strong leadership, anti-union propaganda during the Red Scare, and general hostility from the courts, all led to major declines in union membership. This was reversed, however, with the 1929 stock market crash and the advent of the Great Depression.

As an increasing number of Americans lost their jobs, unions were able to step in to help and protect workers. With the election of Franklin D. Roosevelt and the passage of pro-union legislation, organized labor became the centerpiece for the New Deal's plan for economic recovery. Suddenly, new, more powerful umbrella unions began to organize, among them the Congress of Industrial Organizations (CIO) and the United Auto Workers (UAW), the formation of which was largely helped by the high-profile Flint sit-down strike. Throughout the 1930s, unions—with strong backing from both the government and the public at large—led several successful campaigns to improve the working lives of not just union members, but all American workers. Although unions would eventually decline in membership and power in the second half of the twentieth century, the strategies they employed would serve as inspiration for the civil rights and feminist movements to follow. In fact, one can argue, it was through the struggle of women such as Genora Dollinger that an entire generation of disenfranchised Americans first found their political voice.

Author Biography
Genora Johnson Dollinger was only twenty-three when she organized the Women's Auxiliary of the United Auto Workers during the Flint sit-down strike. Wife to a UAW committee member, Dollinger led the Women's Emergency Brigade, which not only fed and sheltered the more than 2,000 striking General Motors workers, but also shielded them from security agents hired by the auto manufacturer to physically attack workers.

The strike, with no small help from Dollinger and her Women's Auxiliary, crippled GM, forcing the auto company to come to the negotiating table after just over a month of work stoppage. Owing to her part in the strike, Dollinger was blacklisted by GM and moved to Detroit, where she became the leader of a radical group within the UAW. In 1937, Dollinger was severely beaten in a Mafia-organized lead-pipe attack, part of a wave of violence targeting UAW leaders. A life-long Socialist and a Socialist Workers Party candidate for the Senate in 1952, Dollinger went on to organize against the Vietnam War and several other causes. In 1994, a year before her death at the age of 82, she was inducted into the Hall of Fame of the Michigan Women's Historical Center in the state's capital, Lansing.

HISTORICAL DOCUMENT

Sit Down!

The first sit-down was on December 30 in the small Fisher Body Plant 2 over a particularly big grievance that had occurred. The workers were at the point where they had just had enough, and under a militant leadership, they sat down. When the UAW leaders in the big Fisher Body Plant 1 heard about the sit-down in Fisher 2, they sat down, also. That took real guts, and it took political leadership. The leaders of the political parties knew what they had to do because they'd studied labor history and the ruthlessness of the corporations.

Picket lines were established and also a big kitchen in the south end of Flint, across from the large Fisher 1 plant. Every day, gallons and gallons of food were prepared, and anybody who was on the picket lines would get a ticket with notification that they had served on the line so they'd be able to get a good hot meal.

The strike kitchen was primarily organized by the Communist Party women. They brought a restaurant man from Detroit to help organize this huge kitchen. They were the ones who made all of those good meals.

We also had what we called scavengers, groups of people who would go to the local farmers and ask for donations of food for the strikers. Many people in these small towns surrounding Flint were factory workers who would also raise potatoes, cabbages, tomatoes, corn or whatever. So great quantities of food were sent down to be made into dishes for the strikers. People were very generous.

John L. Lewis and the United Mine Workers helped us financially so that if there was somebody in serious difficulty we could help them out a little bit. Later on, the garment workers sent money. But with thousands of workers, you couldn't help everybody, so many families were taken care of by committees forming in plants, whether they were on strike or not. Committees in Buick, Chevrolet, and Fisher Body took care of some of the urgent cases so nobody starved or got into really major medical difficulties.

After the first sit-down started, I went down to see what I could do to help. I was either on the picket lines or up at the Pengelly Building all the time, but some of the strike leaders didn't know who I was and didn't know that I had been teaching classes in unionism and so on. So they said, "Go to the kitchen. We need a lot of help out there." They didn't know what else to tell a woman to do. I said, "You've got a lot of little, skinny men around here who can't stand to be out on the cold picket lines for very long. They can peel potatoes as well as women can." I turned down the idea of kitchen duty.

Instead, I organized a children's picket line. I got Bristol board and paints, and I was painting signs for this children's picket line. One of my socialist comrades came up and said, "Hey, Genora, what are you doing here?" I said, "I'm doing your job". Since he was a professional sign painter, I turned the sign-painting project over to him and that was the beginning of the sign-painting department.

We could only do the children's picket line once because it was too dangerous, but we got an awful lot of favorable publicity from it, much of it international. The picture of my two-year-old son, Jarvis, holding a picket sign saying, "My daddy strikes for us little tykes," went all over the nation, and people sent me articles from French newspapers and from Germany and from other European countries. I thought it was remarkable that the news traveled so far.

Women Come Forward

I should tell you how the Women's Auxiliary was formed. The last days of December 1936 were when the sit-downs began. Following that came New Year's Eve. Among working class families, everybody celebrates New Year's Eve. I was amazed at the number of wives that came down to the picket line and threatened their husbands, "If you don't cut out this foolishness and get out of that plant right now, you'll be a divorced man!" They threatened divorce loudly and openly, yelling and shouting at their husbands. I knew I couldn't go and grab each one of them to talk to them privately. So I could only watch as some of the men climbed out of the plant window up on the second floor, down the ladder to go home with their wives. These were good union members, but they were hooted and hollered at by their comrades in the plant who were holding the fort in the sit-down. This was a very dangerous turn of events because I knew how few men were inside holding that plant, and it worried many of us.

The next day, we decided to organize the women. We thought that if women can be that effective in breaking a strike, they could be just as effective in helping to win it. So we organized the Women's Auxiliary and we laid out what we were going to do.

Now remember, the UAW was still in the process of getting organized. It didn't have elected officers or by-laws or any of the rest of it. So we were free to organize our Women's Auxiliary, to elect our president, vice-president, recording secretary and heads of committees, all on our own.

We couldn't have women sitting down in the plants because the newspapers were antagonizing the wives at home by saying that women were sleeping over in the plant. In fact, GM sent anonymous messages to the wives of some of the strikers alleging that there were prostitutes in those embattled plants. But we knew we could get women on the picket lines.

So we organized a child-care center at the union headquarters, so children would have some place to go when their mothers marched on the picket line. Wilma McCartney, who had nine children and was going to have her tenth, took charge of that. At first, the women were scared to death to come down to the union, and some may have been against the union for taking away their pay check so they couldn't feed their children who were hungry or crying for milk. Then this wonderful woman, this mother of nine children who was pregnant with another, would talk to them about how it would benefit them for their husbands to participate actively. And if they won the strike, it would make all the difference in the world in their living conditions. We recruited a lot of women just through the child-care center.

We also set up a first aid station with a registered nurse in a white uniform and red union arm-band. She was a member of the Women's Auxiliary. The women in the Auxiliary also made house calls to make sure every family had enough to eat, and they gave advice on how to deal with creditors.

But that wasn't enough as far as I was concerned. Women had more to offer than just these services. So we set up public speaking classes for women. Most of the women had never even been to a union meeting. In those days, many of the men would go to union meetings and say to the women, "It's none of your damn business. Don't you mix into our affairs." So the women didn't express any of their ideas about what could be done to better their conditions.

One of our Socialist Party women, Tekla Roy, took over the public speaking classes and was very popular. She was a very tall woman with a low and resonant voice. She seemed like a person who could handle any man or any opposition. She also taught labor history: what had happened in America in the early days when child labor was eliminated, and how the women garment workers in New York were the first to organize unions in the United States. Women came out of those classes thinking, "Well, women did play a role in the unions. We have got a right to say something." We trained them in how to get up in union meetings and what appeals to make. We gave them an outline of a speech and they practiced in the classes.

Some of the men were very opposed to having their wives at the union headquarters and a few of them never gave up their sexist attitudes. But most of the men encouraged their wives. They thought we were doing a wonderful job, making things better for them at home because their wives understood why their husbands had to be on the picket line all day long and do a lot of extra things for the union. They could talk and work together as companions. And the children were learning from their parents' discussions about the strike.

A few men still opposed women becoming active or walking the picket lines. I was often called a "dyke." Some men said that women who came down to the picket line were prostitutes or loose women looking for men. But as more married men with families became active in the strike, they kept those elements quiet. We eventually won respect and were praised highly by the leaders of the strike after victory was declared.

Organizing the women in the strike was the most wonderful experience of my whole life. I was not as tall as Tekla but I had experience organizing. I was interested in building the Socialist Party and in building a socialist society, so I had a great deal of influence with these women.

Document Analysis

Mainly a simple retelling of her memories, Genora Dollinger's account of the Flint sit-down strike and, specifically, her role in organizing the Women's Auxiliary of the UAW, is a powerful reminder of the importance of organized labor in American history. Through her account, we see the future of American protest. By organizing women, we see the foundations for the later feminist movement; and through Dollinger's tactics, we see much of the inspiration for civil rights. It is hard not to gain an appreciation for the slow building of the liberal movement, beginning in the shadow of FDR's New Deal and extending to the social and political struggles of today.

Genora Dollinger is a proud Socialist and repeatedly mentions the contributions of Socialism and the Communist Party in building organized labor and helping in the early stages of the strike, while workers occupied the plant. At first, one of the largest challenges for the union was simply helping the families of striking workers with food and shelter and making ends meet in the absence of pay. Other unions and organizations, most notably the United Mine Workers (UMW), helped as they could, but it was not enough. Learning from the women of the Communist Party, Dollinger begins to organize the wives of the UAW, despite the protests of some of their husbands, as a means to not only bolster the power of the UAW, but also to unify the workers against General Motors. It is dangerous work. The company uses whatever means it can to discredit both the workers and the women. The strikers are under near constant attack. Women's sexuality is used against them, they're denounced as "whores" and "prostitutes." No "decent" woman would take part in such an act. But for every tactic used against them, Dollinger comes up with a plan to strike back.

The Women's Auxiliary organizes a medical unit and public speaking and labor history classes for its women members. Women serve as a buffer against the attacks on the strikers and go door-to-door checking in on families, providing whatever assistance and reassurance they can. Throughout the document, we gain an appreciation for Dollinger's awakening as a political organizer. She is empowered by the Flint sit-down strike, and, perhaps even more so, she is empowering other women. Thanks in large part to her actions and that of the Women's Auxiliary, the strike is a success. For Dollinger, it remained the best experience of her life.

Essential Themes

Genora Dollinger is a firm believer in the power of socialism to change society. As a union member and organizer, she strongly believes that only through a shared commitment can society truly provide for all of its members. The story that Dollinger presents is very much David and Goliath, with the union struggling to provide for families in the face of great opposition. One gets the sense that capitalism is inherently uneven, and that only through organization can ordinary people hope to get ahead. Although we never gain insight into her politics when it comes to social issues, we can definitely see that she is committed to economic fairness. It is no wonder that so many of the political movements to follow would gain so much inspiration from the activities of unions in the 1930s, in terms not only of best practices, but also of organizational philosophy. Most related to this document is the eventual development of the feminist movement of the 1970s. One can see the beginnings of women's empowerment in the work of Dollinger and others to educate women, encouraging wives and husbands to speak as equals.

Interestingly, Dollinger repeatedly draws the reader's attention to the use of female sexuality as a weapon. Detractors call the UAW women "whores," "dykes," and "prostitutes," while the Women's Auxiliary uses men's perceptions of women as the "weaker sex" to help the strikers in ways men could not. It would be this type of coded language, the difference in standard between the sexes that would eventually lead to a revolution in the ways in which women are perceived in American society. Dollinger may never have achieved her ideal socialist vision, but as an organizer, union leader, and especially as a woman, she helped shift the conversation and transform the way people perceive themselves and others. In the end, it was these social changes that remained as the enduring legacy of Dollinger and other women who worked in the labor movement, for in the decades to come, the unions would begin to become partly corrupt and fall increasingly out of favor.

—KP Dawes, MA

Bibliography and Additional Reading

Bernstein, Irving. *The Turbulent Years: A History of the American Worker, 1933–1941*. Boston: Houghton-Mifflin, 1970. Print.

Dollinger, Sol, & Genora Dollinger. *Not Automatic: Women and the Left in the Forging of the Auto Workers' Union*. New York: Monthly Review P, 2000. Print.

Dray, Philip. *There Is Power in a Union: The Epic Story of Labor in America*. New York: Anchor Books, 2011. Print.

Jackson, Carleton. *Child of the Sit-Downs: The Revolutionary Life of Genora Dollinger. Kent*, OH: Kent State UP, 2008. Print.

Morris, Bob. *Built in Detroit: A Story of the UAW, a Company and a Gangster*. Bloomington, IN: iUniverse, 2013. Print.

■ It's a Great Life in the CCC

Date: 1937
Author: Robert L. Miller
Genre: article

Summary Overview
In October 1933, Robert L. Miller, unemployed and living in near poverty in California, joined the Civilian Conservation Corps (CCC). In a 1937 article, he chronicled his experience working at camps in the Sierra Nevada Mountains and Hayward, California. In addition to discussing the financial and health benefits of working for the corps, Miller emphasized the effects his participation had on his personal character. Although he was lacking in confidence and personal drive when he enlisted, as a direct result of his experience, he said he developed leadership skills and deep friendships that allowed him to regain his self-esteem. Thanks to President Franklin D. Roosevelt's CCC initiative, Miller argued, he had transformed from a physically and emotionally underdeveloped child into a man.

Defining Moment
In 1929, the Roaring Twenties came to an abrupt and devastating end. Stock markets crashed, banks folded, and industries faltered as the United States entered a severe economic downturn that would become known as the Great Depression. One of the most visible impacts of the Depression was the tremendous loss of jobs it caused, with the unemployment rate in the United States peaking at more than 20 percent. Crime rates also soared, a trend that many linked to the lack of job opportunities. Meanwhile, President Roosevelt, who was inaugurated in 1933, began working on his New Deal, which would involve comprehensive reforms intended to restore both the American economy and American society. Many of the New Deal's key components were passed by Congress in the first hundred days of Roosevelt's first term.

Only weeks after Roosevelt's inauguration, Congress passed the Emergency Conservation Work Act, which created the CCC, an organization that would recruit able-bodied and willing young men and veterans of World War I to develop and maintain the country's state parks and other land. Headed by labor leader Robert Fechner, the CCC operated with the assistance of three major agencies: the Department of Labor, tasked with recruiting participants; the War Department, which helped transport the workers; and the Department of Agriculture, which planned and managed a wide range of projects in parks and forests. Roughly 250,000 men joined the CCC in the first few months of its existence, and millions more joined the corps during the following decade.

Roosevelt's focus on environmental and natural resource concerns was not arbitrary. During the Depression, a major drought hit the nation's heartland. In 1933, the same region experienced numerous severe dust storms, all of which tore up the topsoil needed for crops and replaced it with worthless dust. Hundreds of thousands of Americans were displaced as a result of these storms, which devastated millions of acres of farmland. Many of the farmers who were displaced by these storms returned to the Midwest as part of the CCC, building natural park roadways, establishing soil conservation programs, and working to rebuild the nation's forests and natural resources.

HISTORICAL DOCUMENT

There is no need to mention much of my life before I enrolled in the Civilian Conservation Corps. It is sufficient to say that the six months previous to my enlistment were most unsatisfactory, from both a financial and mental standpoint. I was often hungry, and almost constantly broke.

When I finally enrolled in this great enterprise at Sacramento, California, in October, 1933, I was conscious of just one thing—I would be fed, clothed and sheltered during the coming winter. Also I would receive enough actual cash each month to provide the few luxuries I desired.

The two weeks I had to wait between the time I enrolled and the day we were to leave for camp were given over to much thinking. I began to wonder what kind of a life I was going to live for the next six months. Several questions flashed through my mind. Would I make friends with my fellow members? What kind of work would I be doing? Would I be able to "take it"? This last question was by far the most important to me.

Let me pause for a moment to give you a short character analysis of myself. For years I had been conscious of an inferiority complex that had a firm grip on me. I had tried to hide this complex beneath an outer coating of egotism. To a certain extent I had been successful— I had fooled nearly everyone but myself. Try as I may, I could not overcome the feeling that I was just a little inferior to my fellow men. I did not credit myself with the quality of a leader among men, but how I longed for that virtue. I had always been content to sit back and let someone else get ahead while I wished I were in his boots. It was in this frame of mind that I joined seventy other young men on the morning of October 26, to leave for our camp in the Sierra Nevada Mountains.

Our arrival at camp that same evening was an event that I shall never forget. I was pleasantly surprised at the feeling of genuine hospitality and good cheer that existed among the older members of the company, and reached out to greet we new comers. I had expected a much different atmosphere, and I am ashamed to admit I arrived in camp with a chip on my shoulder. This feeling was soon lost in my pleasant surrounding.

Some of my self-imposed questions were answered in the first two weeks of camp life. Yes, I could make friends with my fellows, and quite easily too. Most of the friendships that I made early in my enlistment have lasted to this day. Some of those friends have left the company, others are with me now. And for those who remain, time has only strengthened the bond between us.

The second question to be answered early in the game was, could I take it? I found that I could and liked it I could work with these boys, play with them, argue with them and hold up my end. They seemed to like me, and I knew I was fond of them.

This new life had a grip on me, and for the first time in months I was really happy. Good food, plenty of sleep, interesting work and genial companions had created quite a change—my mind was at peace.

Early in November we moved to our winter camp near Hayward, California. During the period of camp construction that followed our move, I was put in charge of several small jobs. They were insignificant in their nature, but it did me a lot of good Just to think that I was considered reliable enough to boss even a small project. These appointments started me thinking, if I could boss a small job satisfactorily, why couldn't I manage a large one? Then that old feeling would return. I would crawl in my shell and let someone else get the Job I wanted and the raise in pay I coveted.

On December fifteenth several new leaders and assistant leaders were appointed. I held my breath, secretly hoping and praying I would be among the chosen ones. But as usual I was left out, just one of the many, a small cog in a large machine.

One night I went to bed rather early, belay rather tired after a hard days work. Something was wrong, and I didn't fall asleep right away as was my usual custom. I lay awake and thought of many things, finally dwelling on my present situation. My thoughts, when simmered down, were something like this—Here is my big chance to see if I'm going to go ahead in this world, or be just one of the crowd the rest of my life. I'm just one man in a group of two hundred young fellows, and I have just as good a chance as any of the others. So here goes, from now on I'm going to try for advancement—and I'm going to succeed. Such were my thoughts that night, for the first time I realized I had the same chance as the rest to make good.

Next morning in the light of day, things did not look so promising as I had pictured them during the night. But I now had the determination, all I needed was a starting point. In a few days I was to have my start, but it was a queer beginning.

At various times in my life I had done a bit of wrestling, and once or twice had engaged in bouts at camp. I was asked to wrestle a boy in our camp, the bout to be a preliminary to a boxing match between our camp and a neighboring camp. I agreed, not knowing who my opponent was to be. He was not selected until the day of the fight, and when I heard his name I wanted to back out. Pride alone kept me from calling off the bout. My opponent was a huge fellow, weighing twenty-two pounds more than I, and a good three inches taller. No matter how I looked at it, I could picture only a massacre with myself on the losing end. It wasn't fear that made me want to back out, but I dreaded the thought of defeat in front of three or four hundred people.

I climbed into the ring that nite a very doubtful, but determined young man. At least I would put up a good fight. When the bout was over and I emerged the victor, I knew immediately that I had made my start. I was terribly stiff and sore, but very proud and happy. Sleep did not come easily that nite. I was too excited. I kept saying to myself, "I've done it, I'm on my way." Why a physical victory should put me mentally at ease I do not know, but it did.

Then things began to happen rapidly, and soon I became convinced that I was on the right track. A group of sixteen of the most popular boys in camp were forming a club, and I was asked to become a charter member. I was only too glad to Join as most of the boys in the club were either leaders or assistant leaders, and by associating with them I might learn a lot. Election of officers of the club was a prolonged affair but when it was completed, I was the president. For several days I was so excited I had a hard time controlling myself.

At sometime or other, most of us have a friend that has enough interest in our well-being to try to bring us back on the right path after we have gone astray. So it was in my case. There resides in Oakland a young lady whom I have known for several years. As it was only a short distance from camp to Oakland, I was frequently a weekend visitor at her home.

One Sunday afternoon, about a month after my election as president of the club, this young lady and I sat talking in the living room of her home. As we had always been very outspoken with each other, I was not surprised when she said she was going to tell me a few things. I may not have been surprised when she started, but by the time she had finished I'm afraid my face was a trifle red. She told me that in the last month I had changed from a quiet, unassuming young man to a conceited, self-centered prude. She topped it off by saying she could get along very nicely without my company until I recovered from my attack of pig-headedness. That night I slept very little spending most of the nite trying to get things straight in my mind. Out of the chaos of thoughts that came to me I realized two things. First, the young lady was indeed a friend and she had spoken harshly to try to bring me to my senses. Secondly, I realized that my new-found success had gone to my head, and I was making a perfect fool of myself.

For several days I pondered over my problem with no tangible result. It appeared to me that my job was to strike a happy medium between my old self and this new person that had taken possession of me. I didn't want to go back to the old way, and it was evident that I couldn't continue as I had been doing. The only solution was for me to find an average.

Unconsciously I must have succeeded. Three weeks later when I again visited the young lady for the weekend, she complimented me on my success. She claimed that I was an entirely new person, and she was very very pleased. That Sunday night I returned to camp a very happy young man.

A short time later news came to camp that an Educational Advisor was coming to camp to direct the boys in their pursuit of education. Also we heard that some man in camp was to be appointed to the newly created position of Assistant Educational Advisor. This new position was to carry an assistant leaders rating, which meant a raise in pay for the man lucky enough to get the job. It wasn't long before a rumor spread through camp that three men were being considered for the new position. Imagine my surprise when I learned from a reliable source that I was one of the three.

On April 6, our Educational Advisor arrived in camp, and that evening I was told I had been appointed his assistant. My goal had been reached. I was at last one of the chosen few. Out of a group of two hundred young men I had been chosen for a position of real importance. Why, I did not know, but I felt sure there must be a reason.

Everything was made clear to me about two weeks later. One evening I was talking to our first lieutenant, he told me how it all came about. It seems the captain was aware of the year and a half I had been to college. He knew I was president of a club that had as its members most of respected men in camp. He had studied my actions and character when I was not aware I was being watched, and he had decided I was the man for the Job. All this the lieutenant told me, much to my surprise.

In a little less than six months I had literally found myself. For twenty-two years I had doubted my right to call myself a man. My fight had been a long one, and here, in sir short months I had proved to myself that I was really a man. A great deal of my success I owe to this certain young lady who brought me back on the right path. But if I had not joined the Civilian Conservation Corps I never would have made a start.

I shall try to convey to you just what the Civilian Conservation Corps has meant to me. There are a great many things of which I could tell, but I shall write of only the most important. The rest I shall keep, deep down in my heart.

First of all, by enrolling in President Roosevelt's peace time army! I managed to retain my self respect. I did not have to become either a parasite, living off my relatives, or a professional bum. In other words, it gave me a chance to stand on my own two feet and make my own way in the world.

Then it gave me the opportunity to make friendships that will live forever. Nine months of living in close contact with young men of my own age could hardly pass without at least a few lasting friendships. They are fine young men, those chaps who go into the forests of our country to do their bit to preserve our woods, and they are worthy of anyone's friendship. I'm very proud of the friends I've made, and if we should never meet again I can truthfully say they shall never be forgotten.

By living in close contact with these young men I learned the value of appreciating the other fellow's rights. To take one's place among his fellow men and be accepted as a friend is a fine thing for any man.

I had an excellent chance to develop myself physically. Many months of work in the sun have put layers of muscle on my body and turned my skin a dark tan.

But my memories, those golden thoughts that I shall keep forever, are my most valued and treasured keepsake. My album is full of pictures, each one serving as only a starting point for a long Journey into the land of happy days. Days of work in the woods, nights around the fire in the barracks, a trick played on an innocent chap, an all day hike with some of my friends, a fishing trip with one of my pals, the rush for the mess hall when the gong sounds, all of these thoughts are dear to me, and I feel sure that the next few months will bring countless more treasures with each passing day.

These things I have mentioned are benefits derived by every young man who has been a member of the Civilian Conservation Corps. But my personal achievement is the one glorious gift I have received from my association with the young men of the Civilian Conservation Corps.

I enrolled as a boy, unsteady, groping, unsure. I wanted something, but could not describe it or discover a means for attaining it. Then I discovered what it was I was seeking—it was the right to call myself a man. My life at camp has given me that right, and I shall be ever grateful to President Roosevelt and the C.C.C. Now that I am a man, with my feet firmly planted on the steps of life, I feel sure of a reasonable amount of success.

If, in my humble way I have made you realize what the Civilian Conservation Corps has done for me, I am very happy. I do not claim any honor for the change that occurred in me, it just had to be. I'm only deeply thankful that I had the change to get acquainted with the real me.

So in parting I say "Thank God for President Roosevelt and his C.C.C. I shall never forget you."

A true statement of actual facts by,

Robert L. Miller
Company 999 C.C.C.
Pine Grove, California.

■ I'd Rather Not Be on Relief

Date: 1938
Authors: Lester Hunter
Genre: song

Summary Overview

This song, penned at the Farm Security Administration's Shafter Camp in California, describes life as a migrant worker during the Dust Bowl drought in the 1930s. In the song, migrant workers arrive at the camp in droves, seeking work on farms, but finding limited employment with minimal pay. Lester Hunter sang about the workers' preference to work on a farm instead of living on federal government programs, like the Works Progress Administration (WPA). Meanwhile, the song's lyrics read, the migrants lived in shanties, wearing ragged clothes and suffering from hunger while they searched for work.

Defining Moment

Beginning in 1929 and lasting through the early 1940s, the Great Depression was one of the most tumultuous periods in modern American history. One of the major contributors to its longevity was the severe drought in the American South and the Great Plains, creating what would be known as the "Dust Bowl." The devastation caused by this event sent migrant farmers into exile as they searched for employment and lived in abject poverty.

The causes of the Dust Bowl date back several decades before the Depression. During the 1860s, Americans, enabled by the passage of the Homestead Act (1862), moved westward, establishing farms in the semi-arid Plains as well as the Midwest and South. Quickly, the region's grasslands were cleared by overgrazing. Adding to the depletion of the area's natural ground cover was the demand for wheat. Wheat requires a deep plough, and during periods of adequate rainfall, this deep ploughing would pay off with a rich bounty of wheat, one of the most sought-after crops of the nineteenth and twentieth centuries. When there wasn't sufficient rainfall, however, the soil quickly became unusable.

The lack of grass (caused by decades of overgrazing), unusable topsoil, and drought conditions converged to create the Dust Bowl—so named because high winds would kick up huge amounts of dry topsoil, creating dust storms that darkened the skies for days and made life unbearable for residents. Farms across this vast region went out of business, and farmers began a mass exodus westward in search of new employment.

A major destination for these millions of migrant farmers was California, drawn by word of that state's wide range of fruit, cotton, and vegetable farms. These migrant workers arrived in California with nothing but their families and whatever they could pack in their vehicles. They built shanties and even tents alongside the road during their journey and continued to live in such conditions when they arrived. When President Roosevelt's New Deal became law, these workers were given opportunities to work for the government, migrant camps in which to live, and direct monetary aid.

Although the area affected by the Dust Bowl spanned from the Plains states through the South, many migrant farm workers that evacuated for California were from Oklahoma and Arkansas. "Okies" and "Arkies"—called so by the locals, regardless of where they actually came from—arrived in tremendous numbers, settling in federal Farm Security Administration camps and searching for employment on the nearby farms. Here, they lived alongside Mexican and Filipino immigrants, who had long worked at these farms before the Dust Bowl migrants arrived. Their wages were low, even when the federal government provided struggling states with relief grants to aid the needy migrants.

Life in the camps was difficult, as workers lived in cramped, decrepit shelters, eating little and wearing shabby clothes. To pass the time while they either worked or looked for work, many of these migrants wrote songs about their experiences on the road to California, the hardships they endured, and the conditions in which they lived.

HISTORICAL DOCUMENT

I'd Rather Not Be on Relief

We go around all dressed in rags
While the rest of the world goes neat,
And we have to be satisfied
With half enough to eat.
We have to live in lean-tos,
Or else we live in a tent,
For when we buy our bread and beans
There's nothing left for rent.

I'd rather not be on the rolls of relief,
Or work on the W. P. A.,
We'd rather work for the farmer
If the farmer could raise the pay;
Then the farmer could plant more cotton
And he'd get more money for spuds,
Instead of wearing patches,
We'd dress up in new duds.

From the east and west and north and south
Like a swarm of bees we come;
The migratory workers
Are worse off than a bum.
We go to Mr. Farmer
And ask him what he'll pay;
He says, "You gypsy workers
Can live on a buck a day."

I'd rather not be on the rolls of relief,
Or work on the W. P. A.,
We'd rather work for the farmer
If the farmer could raise the pay;
Then the farmer could plant more cotton
And he'd get more money for spuds,
Instead of wearing patches,

We'd dress up in new duds.
We don't ask for luxuries
Or even a feather bed.
But we're bound to raise the dickens
While our families are underfed.
Now the winter is on us
And the cotton picking is done,
What are we going to live on
While we're waiting for spuds to come?

Now if you will excuse me
I'll bring my song to an end.
I've got to go and chuck a crack
Where the howling wind comes in.
The times are going to better
And I guess you'd like to know
I'll tell you all about it,
I've joined the C. I. O.

Document Analysis

Written by a migrant farm worker named Lester Hunter, "I'd Rather Not Be on Relief" is a song about the migrant worker experience during the Depression. The lyrics describe the conditions in which the migrants lived, even while receiving direct benefits from the federal government. Hunter also describes the simple desires of these workers—to find a job that pays them a reasonable wage for their work and to not be obliged to live off government support.

Hunter—who had arrived at central California's Shafter Farm Labor Camp—uses his song to tell the story of migrant workers, who, "like a swarm of bees," came in droves from all over the country looking for work. These people, "worse off than a bum," had little more than tattered and worn clothing, lived in "lean-tos" (three-walled, roofed houses usually used as temporary shelters), and barely ate enough to live. Their haggard appearance, along with their impoverished way of life, led would-be employers and the federal government officials on site at Shafter to treat them with little respect. Employers only offer workers a dollar per day, Hunter writes, in light of the workers' status as "gypsies."

According to Hunter's lyrics, the migrant workers simply want gainful employment, not federal government handouts. They would prefer not to live in the camps or to earn meager wages, but the stark reality is that they will take whatever money they can get to feed their families. These workers live in shanties and tents that become cold at night. Some don't even have a lean-to in which to live when the workday is over.

"I'd Rather Not Be on Relief" is an acknowledgement of the hardships migrant workers faced, having left their homes and moved more than a thousand miles away. While they hoped to one day get a more lucrative job, they settled for whatever work they could find. Still, as the song goes, the workers were given assurances that work and better wages would come, especially if they joined the labor unions—the last line of the song cites the Congress of Industrial Organizations (CIO). Although there was little promise for better jobs until the Depression came to an end, the unions—by advocating on their behalf in negotiations with employers—at least gave the disenfranchised migrant workers some hope their work conditions might improve.

Essential Themes

Like many of the songs written by migrant workers during the Great Depression, Lester Hunter's "I'd Rather Not Be on Relief" paints a grim picture of the lives of migrant workers in federal camps. The song describes the conditions in which migrant workers lived, the treatment they received, and their outlook on the future.

As the song demonstrates, migrant workers and their families arrived at camps, like the one at Shafter with little more than the ragged clothes they wore. Many of these workers lived in lean-tos and other temporary shelters. Food supplies were, as the song's lyrics read, half of what was needed to feed a family. There was some work available on the nearby farms, but the migrants competed with others for those jobs, which paid meager salaries for a hard day's work.

These conditions, Hunter's song reads, made the workers feel less like qualified laborers and more like "bums" and "gypsy workers." There was an obvious social stratification that occurred between those with steady jobs and the migrants. Migrant workers did not embrace their lesser status. The song suggests they knew that the quality of work they were offered might, under normal economic conditions, enable them to earn enough to feed their families, not to mention buy a home and new clothing.

Because the migrant workers of the song arrived with skills and abilities, along with a personal desire to find gainful employment, they were reluctant to accept federal assistance. They accepted their positions, living conditions, and government aid out of an obligation to support their families. However, as the song's title suggests, the migrant workers' ideal situation was to simply find gainful employment without turning to the government for assistance.

Even as they lived as impoverished outcasts in California, the migrant workers continued to show optimism about the future. The song's lyrics suggest that the Depression would one day come to an end. In the meantime, however, organized labor offered some promise that some of the wage issues with which the workers were grappling would be addressed. "The times are going to better," the song concludes, reminding the listener that even under these conditions, the "Okies" and "Arkies" would not fold under the weight of the Depression.

—*Michael P. Auerbach, MA*

Bibliography and Additional Reading

Babb, Sanora. *On the Dirty Plate Trail: Remembering the Dust Bowl Refugee Camps.* Austin: U of Texas P,

2007. Print.

"Dust Bowl Exodus: How Drought and the Depression Took Their Toll." *Bill of Rights in Action*. Constitutional Rights Foundation, 2005. Web. 24 June 2014.

Fanslow, Robin A. "The Migrant Experience." *Library of Congress*. Library of Congress, 6 Apr. 1998. Web. 24 June 2014.

"Farm Labor in the 1930s." *Rural Migration News* 9.4 (October 2003). Web. 12 Sept. 2014.

"Great Depression and World War II: The Dust Bowl." *Library of Congress*. Library of Congress, n.d. Web. 24 June 2014.

Worster, Donald. Dust Bowl: *The Southern Plains in the 1930s*. New York: Oxford UP, 2012. Print.

What REA Service Means to Our Farm Home

Date: March 1939
Author: Rose Dudley Scearce
Genre: article

Summary Overview

Rose Dudley Scearce, a resident of rural Kentucky, wrote this article for the magazine *Rural Electrification News*, the public information arm of the Rural Electrification Administration (REA), to extol the benefits of electricity in her farm home. By the 1930s, the vast majority of urban areas in the United States had access to electricity, but early distribution systems were primitive and could only carry a charge over short distances. Electrical companies claimed that the cost of bringing electricity to sparsely populated rural areas was prohibitive, as it required a much higher voltage transmitter to carry electricity across long distances. The REA was established in 1935 as part of President Franklin D. Roosevelt's New Deal, a series of domestic programs established to fight unemployment and reinvigorate the US economy during the Great Depression. The REA provided low-cost federal loans to local electrical cooperatives that organized teams of electricians and laborers to wire rural homes and barns in their area. In the first four years of its existence, the REA helped to bring electricity to more than two hundred thousand rural homes.

Defining Moment

By the 1920s, electricity was common in urban areas across the United States. Approximately 90 percent of American city dwellers had access to electrical service by 1930. In rural areas, however, the cost of running lines to remote homes and farms was considered prohibitive, and only about 11 percent of farmers had electricity, many from small wind-powered plants. Charged batteries, used for limited lighting and appliances, were unreliable and sometimes dangerous. Gas-powered machines were also prohibitively expensive to purchase and fuel. In addition to the cost of running distribution lines to remote areas, the amount of power that could be delivered dropped significantly over long distances, and the voltage distribution system had to be more than doubled in order to maintain sufficient strength. Electrical utilities companies were, therefore, unwilling to provide power to rural areas unless farmers agreed to build the distribution lines themselves at great cost and then turn over ownership of the distribution network to the electric companies.

In 1923, with the support of the University of Minnesota and the Northern States Power Company, the Red Wing Project was established to demonstrate the feasibility of providing electricity to rural farms. The Red Wing Project worked to electrify nine farms in rural Minnesota using high-voltage lines and then analyzed the methods and use of rural electricity over several years. Engineers worked to adapt hand- or horse-powered machines to run on electricity. By 1926, Minnesota farmers were using electric motors to simplify and speed up a wide variety of agricultural tasks, including grinding grain, separating cream from milk, refrigerating farm products, pumping water, and mixing concrete. However, the onset of the Great Depression in 1929 hampered any further interest in rural electrification.

In 1935, the Rural Electrification Administration (REA) drew on the success of the Red Wing Project as a model for its own success. President Roosevelt set up the REA by executive order on May 11, 1935, with the dual mission of bringing electrical distribution systems to rural America and providing desperately needed jobs for electricians, laborers, and engineers during the Great Depression. REA teams canvassed the countryside, distributing information about the benefits of electricity for farmers. The REA provided low-cost federal loans to local cooperatives that established electrical distribution networks in their area and then purchased power on a wholesale basis. As more farms became electrified, the demand for power helped to offset the significant cost of bringing power to these remote areas, as the average farm utilized more power than the average urban household. The government also developed a low-cost loan program to help farmers purchase electrical appliances and equipment. Furthermore, despite the initial costs, electricity significantly increased the productivity of rural farms and helped to decrease their operating costs. Many utility companies objected to government interference in their business and saw the rural cooperatives as unfair competition. Some politicians argued that it was a step closer to socialism. Many farmers were initially skeptical about the reliability and usefulness of electricity. Still, by 1939, the REA had overseen the establishment of more than four hundred rural electric cooperatives that provided approximately 288,000 farms with electricity, a jump from 11 to 25 percent. By 1960, 97 percent of all American farms had been electrified. The REA became part of the US Department of Agriculture in 1939. In 1949, the Rural Electrification Act was extended to allow telephone companies to use the same organizational structure to bring telephone service to rural areas across the United States.

Author Biography

Rose W. Dudley Scearce was born on January 4, 1887, in Fayette, Kentucky. Little is known about her life, but she was one of seven children and is listed on census records as having graduated from college. Her marriage date is unknown, but she had her first child with her husband, Ralph Scearce, in 1920 at the age of thirty-three. Rose Dudley Scearce died of cirrhosis of the liver on October 8, 1947, at the age of sixty and is buried in Shelbyville, Kentucky.

HISTORICAL DOCUMENT

The first benefit we received from the REA service was lights, and aren't lights grand? My little boy expressed my sentiments when he said, "Mother, I didn't realize how dark our house was until we got electric lights." We had been reading by an Aladdin lamp and thought it was good, but it didn't compare with our I. E. S. reading lamp. Are all of you reading by an I. E. S. lamp? If you are not, get one tomorrow. When you compare how much easier on your eyes an I. E. S. lamp is than an ordinary electric lamp, you will not hesitate, especially when you find they do not cost any more than an ordinary lamp. The I. E. S. lamps are not made by just one company but are lamps approved by the Illuminating Engineering Society.

Recently I read in the *Rural Electrification NEWS* that the radio was the most popular appliance that had been bought. So, like the rest of the people, we changed our storage-battery radio into an electric radio. This was our next benefit.

Next we bought an electric refrigerator. Of course, next after a refrigerator comes making ice cream in the trays. We changed our washing machine from a machine driven by gasoline to one driven by the electric current as our next improvement. The machine was all right with gasoline, but, my, the noise it made! It is such a blessed relief to do the laundry in peace and quiet. We changed our pump for the pressure tank in our bathroom and water system from a hand pump to an electric pump. I did not buy an electric iron at first, as I do not do my own ironing. I was impressed, when I did, at how much improved irons were since I moved to the country. I can turn my dial on the iron to any fabric I may be ironing and the iron will stay the temperature needed for the fabric until I move the dial. The next benefit we received from the current was our electric stove. We were so anxious for the current that we wired our house many months before the current was turned on, and we wired our kitchen for an electric range.

If you follow the directions in the cook book given you with your range, that is, use very little water in cooking, use a covered pan as big as your heating unit, and use your "free heat," you will be surprised at how little electricity you will burn.

Before the current was turned on, when anyone asked me what appliance I wanted most I always said that I wanted a vacuum cleaner. I do not know what kind of a person you are, but I expect that you are a nice, neat person and that when it rains you put on your overshoes on the porch before you go out and take the muddy overshoes off on the porch before you come into the house. We don't do that way at our house. We rush out when it rains without overshoes, and when we come in we wipe half the mud on the mat at the door and the other half we wipe on my living-room carpet. I have an old-fashioned body Brussells carpet on my living-room floor, and when I swept it I raised as much dust as if I had been sweeping the dusty pike. When I finished I was choking with the dust, the carpet was not clean, and I was in a bad humor. Now with the vacuum cleaner, I can even dust the furniture before I clean the carpet, the carpet gets clean, and I stay in a good humor.

So you see I am thoroughly enjoying the many things that electricity had made possible, and I am enjoying life more because I have more time to spend visiting my friends, studying and reading, and doing the things that make life richer and fuller.

GLOSSARY

Body Brussells carpet: a type of thick carpet

dusty pike: dirt road

I.E.S.: Illuminating Engineering Society, a professional association for lighting engineers

Document Analysis

Rose Dudley Scearce's testimonial to the joys of rural electricity was published in a magazine distributed by the REA and is, therefore, designed to appeal to rural Americans who were considering electrification of their farms, perhaps reluctantly. Scearce does not address the farm work that is made easier with electricity, but she speaks of the domestic improvements to her home. She appeals to mothers and homemakers, arguing that their lives will be made far easier with the introduction of electricity.

Scearce opens her article by expounding on the joys of electric lighting, calling on her role as a mother to help make the case that this is a necessary change. "My little boy expressed my sentiments when he said, 'Mother, I didn't realize how dark our house was until we got electric lights.'" She encourages her readers to get a lamp approved by the Illuminating Engineering Society (IES), which she touts as being of higher quality than regular electric lamps.

Scearce explains that her family then purchased an electric radio, and she refers to her own readership of the *Rural Electrification News* as her motivation for its purchase: "The radio was the most popular appliance that had been bought. So, like the rest of the people, we changed our storage-battery radio into an electric radio." Next, her family purchased a refrigerator and washing machine. Scearce describes how she had made use of a gasoline-powered washing machine, but is grateful for the great reduction in noise. "It is such a blessed relief to do the laundry in peace and quiet," she writes. Indoor plumbing is also made much easier with the use of electric rather than manual water pumps, and she is particularly impressed with the electric iron, as she had not done her own ironing before. She exclaims "I can turn my dial on the iron to any fabric I may be ironing and the iron will stay the temperature needed for the fabric until I move the dial."

Scearce's description of her cooking stove is particularly illuminating. Many homemakers saw the electrical stove as the answer to many hours of drudgery as coal and wood stoves required constant maintenance and close supervision to maintain the correct temperature. Scearce describes how she was so eager to use an electric stove that "many months before the current was turned on . . . we wired our kitchen for an electric range."

The vacuum cleaner is the one item that Scearce most wanted, and she waxes nearly poetic about it. On a dusty, dirty farm, it is nearly impossible to keep her house clean, she says. Without electricity, she explains, "When I finished [sweeping the carpet] I was choking with the dust, the carpet was not clean, and I was in a bad humor." This is the primary thrust of Scearce's argument in favor of electrification. Electricity does not just enable cooking and cleaning and ironing to be completed quickly, but they also open up the possibility of leisure time. In Scearce's mind, electricity is not just a technological improvement, but the key to happiness. Scearce concludes, "I am enjoying life more because I have more time to spend visiting my friends, studying and reading, and doing the things that make life richer and fuller."

Essential Themes
The electrification of rural America profoundly changed the lives of millions of Americans. In this article, Scearce urges rural homemakers to take full advantage of electrification by offering her own home and her experience as an example. While the benefits of electricity in facilitating farm work had been demonstrated by the Red Wing Project, Scearce focuses on describing the domestic benefits of electricity. She addresses the hesitation that many felt at the introduction of electrical appliances, which represented not only a new technology but a new way of life, by providing examples of how the changes in her home have been a great benefit to herself and her family. She also argues that, with the help of electricity in the home, the quality of life of rural homemakers will improve.

—*Bethany Groff, MA*

Bibliography and Additional Reading

Campbell, Dan. "When the Lights Came On." Rural Cooperatives 67.4 (2000): 6–9. Print.

Katznelson, Ira. Fear Itself: The New Deal and the Origins of Our Time. New York: Liveright, 2013. Print.

Shlaes, Amity. *The Forgotten Man: A New History* of the Great Depression. New York: Harper, 2007. Print.

United States. Rural Electrification Administration. Rural Lines, USA: The Story of the Rural Electrification Administration's First Twenty-Five Years. Washington: GPO, 1960. Print.

■ My Hopes for the CCC

Date: January 1939
Authors: Robert Fechner
Genre: article; editorial

Summary Overview

In January 1939, Robert Fechner, director of the Civilian Conservation Corps (CCC), offered his assessment of the CCC's accomplishments to date. Fechner also gave an overview of his improvement goals for the program, including improving the educational and vocational training programs the CCC offered. Fechner did not recommend a significant expansion of the CCC's main focus—forestry—although he did suggest that the CCC look at increasing efforts to offset erosion, expand the number of recreational sites, and plant new trees in previously bare spaces.

Defining Moment

In 1929, the fantastic economic boom the United States enjoyed throughout the previous decade suffered an equally fantastic collapse. Stock markets crashed, banks folded, industries faltered, and countless jobs disappeared in what would come to be called the Great Depression. More than eight decades after the Wall Street crash of October 1929, when the US stock market experienced its greatest losses, signifying for many the official start of the Depression, economists, social scientists, and other scholars are still seeking to understand the specific causes that, in aggregate, ushered in this decade of economic turmoil. Experts point to citizens' inability to repay loans and credit debt, a lack of government regulation of businesses and markets, and a lack of sustainability in the country's leading industries as some of the leading causes of this event. Many scholars cite the sharp divide between the nation's wealthy and poor—including the large percentage of immigrants who came to the country during the early twentieth century to work in the energy and manufacturing industries—as a contributing factor.

One of the most visible impacts of the Depression was widespread unemployment. In the first few years of the Depression, the country's unemployment rate had reached 25 percent. Meanwhile, President Franklin Roosevelt, who was inaugurated in 1933, began working on his "New Deal," which would involve comprehensive moves to restore both the American economy and society.

Only weeks after his inauguration, Roosevelt introduced to Congress the Emergency Conservation Work Act. The proposal, which was quickly passed into law, created the Civilian Conservation Corps (CCC). The CCC would recruit able-bodied and willing young men to develop and maintain the country's state parks. Headed by Robert Fechner (a longtime Democratic supporter), the CCC would utilize four major agencies: the Department of Labor would recruit these men, the War Department would train them in camps for two weeks, and the Departments of Agriculture and the Interior would administer the wide range of projects in parks and forests.

Roosevelt's focus on environmental and natural resource concerns was not arbitrary. When the Depression began, a major drought hit the nation's heartland. In 1933, the same region experienced crippling dust storms known as the Dust Bowl, which tore up the topsoil needed for crops and replaced it with worthless dust. Hundreds of thousands of Americans were displaced as a result of these storms, which devastated millions of acres of farmland. Many of the farmers who were displaced returned to the Midwest as part of the CCC, building natural park roadways, establishing soil conservation programs, and working to rebuild the nation's forests and natural resources.

In the January 1939 edition of the American Forestry Association's publication *American Forests*, Fechner outlined the CCC's accomplishments to date and presented a few of the goals he hoped to achieve in the near future.

Author Biography
Robert Fechner was born on March 22, 1876, in Chattanooga, Tennessee. He received training as a machinist in Georgia and, during the course of his work in this arena, rose through the ranks of organized labor, ultimately becoming a board member of the International Association of Machinists. From 1914 to 1933, Fechner was based in Boston and lectured on labor relations at the Harvard Graduate School of Business Administration before being tapped by President Roosevelt to head the CCC. Roosevelt had previously worked with Fechner to negotiate the end of two New England machinist strikes. Under Fechner, the CCC saw the nearly 2.5 million men enrolled in the program develop the country's national, state, and local parks while also working to fight soil erosion, forest fires, and intrusive insects. He died in Washington, DC, on December 31, 1939.

HISTORICAL DOCUMENT

For five and a half years, a Legion of Youth, the Civilian Conservation Corps, has been charting a new conservation course for Uncle Sam, a course that provides for the gradual upbuilding of our natural resources of timber and soil. As a result, the nation is moving toward an admittedly distant goal of a balanced natural resources budget.

Under the competent supervision of trained foresters and technicians of federal and state departments and agencies dealing with conservation matters, some two million young men, together with a sprinkling of war veterans and Indians, have been laboring since the spring of 1933 on a wide variety of conservation projects. They have planted new forests on unproductive lands, strengthened forest and park protection systems to reduce forest devastation by forest fires, insects and disease, built new recreational facilities to improve the civic usefulness of our parks and forests and initiated and advanced a huge scale program for demonstrating practical erosion control measures to farmers.

Altogether, some 4,500 CCC camps of 200 men each have been established in national, state and private forests, on the public domain and on wildlife refuges in various parts of the country. At the present time more than 1,500 camps, including those on Indian reservations and in Alaska, Puerto Rico, the Virgin Islands and Hawaii, are in operation. Out of these camps each day go some 300,000 enrollees to plant trees, build truck trails, erect fire detection towers, lay telephone lines, improve grazing conditions in national forests and on the public domain, rehabilitate reclamation projects in the west and drainage ditches on farm lands, build check dams and plant quick growing trees and vegetation to protect private farm lands from soil wastage, to conserve water and prevent floods, to conduct campaigns against the white pine blister rust, the gypsy moth, bark beetles and rodents, to improve living conditions for wildlife and to do a host of other jobs related in a greater or lesser degree to the national task of conserving and rebuilding America's natural resources wealth.

The records in my office indicate that the 2,300,000 enrollees who have left their homes to work for from a few months to two years in the healthful outdoor atmosphere of the CCC camps have labored on some 150 different types of work. Operating under regulations and policies initiated or approved by the office of the director, the War Department has enrolled the men after they had been selected by the Department of Labor and the Veterans' Administration, constructed the camps, transported the men to and from projects, paid enrollees, clothed and fed them and looked after their welfare. The cost of maintaining a boy in a CCC camp this year, with all costs charged against the enrollee, is about $1,000. Next year it will be a little larger, as new camps will have to be built. Altogether about two billion dollars has been expended on the CCC program, about twenty-three per cent going home to the parents of enrollees in the form of relief.

No attempt has been made to turn the camps into formal schools. We do everything we can to fit enrollees for a useful life but the CCC is a work centered organization and not a substitute for high schools and colleges. It is, however, a practical school where young men in their teens and early twenties are taught how to work, how to live and how to get ahead. In the camps enrollees learn the fundamentals of good citizenship while acquiring work experience and practical skills. One of the fundamentals of the CCC program is that enrollees put in a full five day, forty hour week whenever climatic conditions permit. This is done in the belief that the work discipline and training acquired by enrollees on the job and through the normal routine of orderly camp living represents the best training and preparation for useful citizenship that we can offer. Every effort is made to improve the physical condition of enrollees so that they will leave the camp with sound physiques. Good food, medical care, comfortable clothing and instruction in sanitation and personal hygiene are furnished all enrollees.

In camp enrollees follow a daily regime which includes regular hours for sleeping, eating, working, recreation, as well as a reasonable time for study and personal advancement. Academic courses and vocational training in a more limited degree are provided in all camps. Illiterates are taught to read and write. Backward enrollees are grounded in the three "r's."

So much for the broad outline of the CCC program to date. It is my opinion that sufficient time has now elapsed for the average citizen to pass judgment upon the usefulness of the Corps, both as a force for conserving our natural resources and as a builder of vigorous young manhood.

As director of the Corps, I have watched it grow from an experimental question mark into a sound, well-knit operating organization which takes pride in the fact that it gives the taxpayer a full return for every cent spent. There is no doubt but that the four cooperating departments--War, Interior, Agriculture and Labor—have done a splendid job.

But notwithstanding the fact that the Corps has been and continues to be popular with the general public, the question arises as to whether steps cannot be taken which will improve our work output and the service rendered youth and the nation. Some students of the CCC program have suggested that more time be devoted to enrollee education and training. Some have felt that the Corps costs too much. The question also has arisen as to whether the Corps was not departing too much from its original work objectives.

Before discussing possible changes in future work programs, I want to go on record as stating that in my opinion no phase of the CCC program is more important than our relationship with youth. I am hopeful that as time passes we can do even more than we are doing today to assist youth to become self-supporting. I am not a believer in coddling youngsters and so long as I am director I intend to do everything I can to help young men develop self-reliance and pride in their ability to make their own way in the world. I want enrollees to have every possible educational and training opportunity that can be given them without sacrificing the CCC work program. I have never been in favor of shortening the work week of forty hours to provide additional time for schooling, as I believe young men obtaining their first work experience should learn at the beginning that they must do an honest day's work and do it every day when they are employed if they are to be worth their salt. I take genuine pride in the fact that employers uniformly report that former enrollees have the right attitude toward work.

We have been making a thorough study of the CCC educational system this last year. We are improving the education and training set-up from the top down, developing improved training and instructional courses, closely scrutinizing the results being obtained and developing a system which will make certain that education and training facilities in each camp are used to the utmost. I am hopeful that at the end of this year I can report that each enrollee received ten hours of general and vocational instruction each week.

Our records show we have spent about two billion dollars on the CCC. Although I do not consider CCC costs have been high when viewed in the light of the Corps' accomplishments, pressure is being exerted at every point to reduce CCC expenditures. I hope it will be possible through consolidation of motor repair units, the operation of salvage and reclamation depots similar to the one operated by the Army at Columbus, Ohio, and a general tightening up of the CCC administrative and operating machine, to reduce costs still lower. A reduction in enrollee turnover between enrollment periods, except when men leave to accept employment, would help. In this connection it is interesting to know that some 450,000 enrollees have left to accept jobs prior to completing their terms of enrollment.

On one point, however, the CCC cannot afford to

economize too far. I refer to the expenditure of funds for careful supervision and guidance of camp work projects. The fact that all CCC work has been carefully supervised has added to CCC costs, but it has been worth it. The Corps seeks to give enrollees the best possible leadership and the best technical direction. High class, experienced reserve officers in charge of camps mean better leadership for the enrollees, better camp morale, better food, fewer desertions and disciplinary discharges and a better all around camp atmosphere. Carefully trained and experienced project superintendents and foremen mean carefully planned work programs, a higher work output and better trained enrollees. Seasoned and able camp educational advisers mean that camp educational programs will be simple and practical and well organized.

The CCC's health program has been outstandingly successful. Without exception, Corps area commanding officers have acted vigorously to safeguard the health of enrollees and build them up physically. In some Corps areas, physical training has been made a regular rather than an optional feature of daily camp life. While undoubtedly enrollees get plenty of exercise, the physical drills have been helpful in improving posture and in developing coordination of mind and muscle. Perhaps it would be a good thing if physical training were provided in all camps.

Adoption of a first class distinctive uniform which enrollees could wear when not at work would be a good thing for the Corps. It would undoubtedly build up morale and improve the appearance of the enrollees. I hope it will be possible to give the CCC a uniform before a not too distant date.

Before expressing my hopes for the future in the field of conservation, let me present a few figures on work accomplishments. Our records compiled from camp figures by the Bureau of the Census show that the national reforestation program has been advanced by the planting of more than 1,501,662,800 forest tree seedlings on 1,501,663 acres of bare, barren or unproductive land; by improving forest stands on 3,115,534 acres and by campaigns against tree diseases, such as the white pine blister rust, and tree-attacking insects on 17,279,975 acres.

Forest fire protection systems have been strengthened in public forests and parks and adjacent areas by the construction of 98,444 miles of truck trails and minor roads, the building of 66,161 miles of telephone lines, reduction of fire hazards along 65,576 miles of roads and trails, the erection of more than 3,459 fire lookout houses and towers, and the construction of 41,303 bridges and 45,350 buildings of various types.

The presence of enrollees in the forests has furnished the nation a first class forest fire-fighting patrol during fire seasons with the result that millions of acres of forest and park land have been saved from fire damage. Civilian Conservation Corps enrollees have expended 7,930,912 man-days on forest fire-fighting duty or on fire prevention or fire pre-suppression work.

It has furnished men and material for the initiation and advancement of a nation-wide erosion control program. Since the spring of 1934 the Corps has constructed 4,132,660 check dams and planted 175,886,495 quick-growing type trees on eroded farm areas.

It has opened up recreational opportunities in the nation's forests and parks for millions by stimulating new state park development projects, by improving and developing recreational facilities in national and state parks, and in other areas.

It has aroused national interest in wildlife conservation by furnishing men and funds for acquisition and development of a chain of wildlife refuges, by improving conditions for fishing and by stimulating federal and state agencies to greater wildlife conservation activity. In this connection, the CCC has built 4,105 fish-rearing pools, expanded national and state fish hatchery facilities, improved more than 6,207 miles of streams, stocked lakes, ponds and streams with 636,447,728 fingerlings and young fish and conducted rodent control operations over 30,774,049 acres.

In reviewing the past five years of the Corps, and looking into its future, it is well to recall its original purpose and scope. The original CCC Act of March 31, 1933, sets up pretty clearly the two main purposes of the Corps, unemployment relief and "restoration of the country's depleted natural resources." Later wording amplifies the first statement and refers to "forestation" of federal and state "lands suitable for timber production, protection or prevention of forest fires, floods and soil erosion, insect and fungous attacks, and the construction, maintenance and repair of paths, trails and fire lanes within national forests and parks."

The Act of June 28, 1937, sets up three objectives of great importance—to provide employment, to provide vocational training and to perform "useful public work in connection with the conservation and development of the natural resources of the United States."

First, let me emphasize that the providing of jobs for unemployed youth is equally but no more important than the doing of needed conservation work. Secondly, that the two CCC Acts both emphasize that the work program is to be conservation of natural resources.

But back of these Congressional Acts, before even the original Act was passed on March 31, 1933, President Franklin D. Roosevelt expressed himself very clearly on what he had in mind as to the CCC, its purpose, scope and work. In his message of March 21, 1933, to the Congress, he said in part:

"I propose to create a civilian conservation corps to be used in simple work, not interfering with normal employment, and confining itself to forestry, the prevention of soil erosion, flood control and similar projects."

Since the first camps were established on national forests and national parks, we have departed in some measure from that original program of objectives—"forestry, the prevention of soil erosion, flood control and similar projects." In addition to forestation and erosion work, the Corps has done a vast amount of recreational work. It has developed parks in states, counties, municipalities and other areas set aside by federal or local agencies for recreational use. It is not too much to say that the CCC put the now flourishing state park system on its feet.

But has it done enough of tree planting? Has it concentrated enough on work which will conserve water and soil and prevent floods? Have enough men been assigned to blister rust control and on campaigns to reduce damages caused by insects such as the bark beetle? I believe that the work we have done to develop our national parks and state parks and related areas has been more than justified by the avenues of outdoor enjoyment which we have made available to the public and that we should continue our recreational work on a scale commensurate with public need. At the same time, I think the time has come when it would be well to give consideration to the placing of even greater emphasis than we have in the past upon the planting of trees and other reforestation work, the control of erosion, upstream engineering and the protection and improvement of national parks and monuments.

Projects for which adult unemployed labor is available or for which adult labor is better suited normally should not be done with CCC labor. This means that the use of the CCC in or near towns or cities, or on large engineering structures where either the adult unemployed or contract labor can be properly used, should not ordinarily be undertaken by the Corps. The CCC is a young, unskilled, mobile force which can be employed to advantage in regions remote from cities or labor centers. There have been complaints on the ground that the CCC youths have deprived locally available adult labor of jobs in different parts of the country. Greater care should be taken to avoid approval of projects requiring a large amount of annual maintenance to keep them usable. In this connection, state and local organizations should refrain from recommending work projects which they are unprepared to maintain in a usable condition after the CCC camp completes its work.

Before listing some of the types of conservation work which I believe should be stressed in the future, I venture the hope that both federal and state conservation organizations will concentrate on the working out of long-range programs for the conservation and use of natural resource wealth so that the CCC work programs can be maintained at their present high standard. I hope that state and federal officials will work out comprehensive programs for development work in each state so that every bit of work done by the CCC will be of maximum value to the state and to the general public. I would like to see a national program, with major types of project shown, covering conservation work that should be done over the nest five or ten years. If such a master plan is available, I have not seen it. In my own opinion, major types of work upon which the CCC should concentrate, are:

(1) Forest Protection. Forests in federal, state and private ownership and federal and state parks must continue to be protected from fire, insects and fungi.

(2) Reforestation. There are some 138 millions of acres of barren, denuded, aban-

doned forest and sub-marginal lands in this country. These should be made productive by growing forests, whether in national park or forest or in state forest or park. The CCC has not done enough tree planting. A program calling for the planting each year of 500,000,000 trees would not be too ambitious.

(3) Flood Control. The "upstream engineering" part of the national flood control job entrusted to Army engineers and the Department of Agriculture by Congress under the Flood Control Act of 1936 is admirably suited for the CCC to perform. This work is not suited for contract labor, as it consists of many small jobs and is in remote or isolated locations where the Corps can function to good advantage. The CCC should be definitely in this program.

(4) Soil Conservation. The saving of our fertile soils and the building up of depleted soils are basic to our future as a nation wherever these lands lie. Here is a splendid job for the Corps to continue.

(5) Development of Recreation Resources. The population of the country is growing and public appreciation of outdoor recreational facilities is mounting. I feel this work should be continued where needed. As public use and enjoyment of our wooded areas increases, public interest in our conservation stake will rise.

(6) Wildlife Restoration. Many years of restoration work yet remains to be done on federal forests and parks and in federal and state game refuges and sanctuaries.

Document Analysis
Robert Fechner takes the opportunity given to him by the American Forestry Association to discuss two themes. The first is to review the many accomplishments of the Civilian Conservation Corps as of 1939, including the program's significant expansion over its relatively brief existence, and the fact that the federal government's money was utilized responsibly and with positive returns. The second is to outline his aspirations for the continued expansion of the CCC's operations, including programs to plant trees, prevent flooding, and restore wildlife populations.

Fechner first describes what he sees as the CCC's most notable accomplishments. In only its first few years, Fechner writes, the program provided work opportunities for about 2.3 million people at approximately 4,500 different camps across the country. The cost to the government for these young men to be trained and work at these camps was about $1,000 per person, Fechner says. He concedes that there is room for economizing the myriad programs involved, but stresses that his agency is spending the monies appropriated by the federal government efficiently and in line with the provisions of the law that created it.

The returns on the government's $2 billion investment, Fechner continues, spoke for themselves. CCC laborers, working under the collective supervision of the Departments of the Interior, Agriculture, Labor, and War, had successfully built fire watch towers, ran telephone lines, restored grazing lands, improved water flow and drainage systems, and planted trees. These activities remained true to the legislative intent of the Emergency Conservation Work Act, linking available workers to restoring and protecting the country's natural resources and, thereby, helping prevent future natural disasters, like the Dust Bowl.

An added bonus to the CCC program, Fechner writes, is that it provides an experienced-based education for the workers. While he is careful not to suggest that the CCC was providing a replacement for school—which would be beyond the scope of its legislative mandate—Fechner writes that the workers, many of whom lacked even a basic education, were, through their duties, learning the fundamentals of good citizenship, including developing the desire and tools to pursue a career once the Depression came to an end. Furthermore, CCC camp residents were given clean facilities and healthy meals so that they would be in the best possible physical condition when their stay at the camps came to a close.

In light of these successes, Fechner says, the CCC was in a good position to move forward. He next presents a few areas in which the CCC could be improved. For all the success the CCC has had in developing the country's parks, Fechner writes, the agency would do well to invest more energy in its tree-planting, water conservation, soil conservation, wildlife restoration, and flood mitigation programs. Fechner writes of his hope that the federal and state governments will work together more effectively to develop and implement more projects, as the broad framework in which the CCC was constructed has relevance to countless potential projects and programs.

Essential Themes
In the mind of CCC founding director Robert Fechner, the Civilian Conservation Corps by 1939 was an unmitigated success. Millions of unemployed young laborers were being put to work protecting the country's natural resources. Fechner—who had been tapped by President Roosevelt to lead the CCC because of Fechner's well-known leadership and organizational skills—said in an article featured in *American Forests* that the program functioned well within its operational and budgetary parameters. Moreover, the CCC was successfully engaging in projects that protected and restored the country's grazing land, forests, soil, and water resources.

Fechner also commented on the fact that the CCC was providing an education of sorts to its workers as they labored at camps across the country. This education gave workers the psychological tools to pursue a meaningful career as well as continue to be positive contributors to American society even after they left the CCC camps. Although the CCC achieved almost immediate success—in terms of its recruitment, organization and completion of projects—Fechner did see areas in which the CCC's activities could be improved. He suggested that the CCC could continue to streamline budgets, for example, but he also said that there were many other activities in which the CCC could become engaged. The objective of the Emergency Conservation Work Act was not just to give millions of American workers short-term employment, he suggested. It was to protect the country's natural resources. As long as the CCC stayed within its legislative parameters—and the economy continued to keep the CCC's participants out of long-term work—Fechner said, there were a great many other projects in which the CCC could invest.

—Michael P. Auerbach, MA

Bibliography and Additional Reading
Edsforth, Ronald. *The New Deal: America's Response to the Great Depression*. Oxford: Blackwell, 2000. Print.

Maher, Neil M. *Nature's New Deal: The Civilian Conservation Corps and the Roots of the American Environmental Movement*. Oxford: Oxford UP, 2008. Print.

McElvaine, Robert S. *The Great Depression: America, 1929–1941*. 25th anniv. ed. New York: Three Rivers, 2009. Print.

Roach, Edward J. "Fechner, Robert." *American National Biography*. Ed. Mark C. Carnes. New York: Oxford UP, 2005. 166–77. Print.

Salmond, John A. *The Civilian Conservation Corps, 1933–1942: A New Deal Case* Study. Durham: Duke UP, 1967. Print.

Sommer, Barbara W. *Hard Work and a Good Deal: The Civilian Conservation Corps in Minnesota*. St. Paul: Minnesota Historical Society, 2008. Print.

Women, Minorities, and Youth

During the Great Depression, women bore as much as or, arguably, more of the brunt of the era's ravages than men did. Yet women were not dealt with programmatically under New Deal relief legislation. Rather, they found jobs where they could find them, struggled to make ends meet at home, and voted their conscience at the polls. Advocate-in-chief of American women and, indeed, of all downtrodden souls was First Lady Eleanor Roosevelt, who wrote, spoke, toured, and engaged in policy debates on women's behalf. She was largely successful in being a feminist activist while not fully appearing to be so, in light of her more conventional role at the White House. Other officials who contributed to the advance of women were Labor Secretary Frances Perkins—the first ever female US cabinet member—and Molly Dewson, head of the women's division of the Democratic National Committee. Generally speaking, though, women did what they always have done: work, learn, manage families, and serve as citizens.

As with women's rights, minority rights were not systematically advanced under the New Deal. Only slight inroads were made in selective areas. Roosevelt, for example, failed to authorize anti-lynching legislation in order to secure the allegiance of southern Democrats. He did, on the other hand, put blacks to work in the Civilian Conservation Corps and other agencies—albeit often in separate African American units. It was largely left-wing political groups that helped organize southern black sharecroppers, not government relief programs. (In fact, farm workers were excluded from the new Social Security legislation.) The educator and activist Mary McLeod Bethune helped organize a number of black organizations, including the National Council of Negro Women. With Eleanor Roosevelt's blessing, Bethune also served as an African American youth advocate inside the government.

Meanwhile, Latinos faced challenges and met them largely on their own. During the previous decade, many Mexicans migrated to California and parts of the southwest to become agricultural laborers or urban workers. They were initially welcomed as a source of cheap labor, but when the Depression set in they encountered hostility over the matter of jobs and their place in the economy. A program of "repatriation" was instituted under which they were deported en masse to Mexico. In the northeast, Puerto Ricans were becoming more populace as they too worked the fields and manned the factories. Here, there was no systematic deportation in reaction to Depression-era joblessness, but there was a concerted effort, even among some Puerto Rican leaders, to "mainstream" members of the community and have them speak English first and generally conform to the ways of the white majority.

For American Indians, the 1930s brought one notable improvement. John Collier, an anthropologist and social reformer, appointed by Roosevelt as head of the Bureau of Indian Affairs, ushered in a series of laws culminating in the Indian Reorganization Act of 1934. The law gave Native Americans greater responsibility for self-government on the reservations and permitted increased cultural and educational freedoms. Increasingly, too, Indians were brought into the workforce, particularly in the areas of building construction, logging, and fisheries.

■ Women on the Breadlines

Date: 1932
Author: Meridel Le Sueur
Genre: essay

Summary Overview
This selection from "Women on the Breadlines" is excerpted from a longer essay, originally published in the magazine the *New Masses*, in which Meridel Le Sueur considers the plight of poor women during the Great Depression, particularly single mothers and the unemployed. It is noteworthy that the year in which Le Sueur published this piece, 1932, was considered the worst year of the Depression. Millions of Americans were out of work, with the national unemployment rate reaching nearly 25 percent. While the financial troubles of the Depression affected men as well as women, Le Sueur focused her essay on the particular plight of American women, who faced unique challenges, such as shouldering the primary responsibility for child care and lacking access to opportunities and resources that were more readily available to men.

Defining Moment
On October 29, 1929, on a day known as Black Tuesday, the United States stock market crashed, sending the nation into the worst economic depression in US history. The Great Depression, which lasted for nearly a decade into the late 1930s, was a national financial disaster. A series of banking panics in the early 1930s resulted in the insolvency and collapse of nearly one-third of all US banks, causing many Americans to lose their entire savings, as bank deposits were not yet federally insured. Unemployment soared, peaking at 25 percent in 1933, and families across the country faced uncertainty over how to provide for their children and their futures. Le Sueur was interested in reporting the real stories of individual Americans and how they were coping with the changes and troubles brought on by the economic collapse.

Her piece, "Women on the Breadlines," takes a close look at the struggles of individual women in the midst of the Great Depression. Le Sueur seemed particularly concerned for those women who had been left to fend for themselves, either because they had been abandoned by their husbands and children or because they had chosen to eschew marriage and motherhood. What is most defining about "Women on the Breadlines," and many of her other works, is that Le Sueur aimed to be a voice for the marginalized. All too often, historical accounts of the Great Depression are told by way of economic and financial statistics. While such data provide important insight into these events, much can be learned from reading the actual struggles of individuals whose stories were recorded by reporters, such as Le Sueur.

Author Biography
Meridel Le Sueur was born on February 22, 1900, to William and Marian Wharton in Murray, Iowa. In 1910, her parents separated, and she moved with her mother and two brothers to Oklahoma. Her mother supported herself and her three children by lecturing on education and women's issues for the Chautauqua circuit. After her mother married Arthur Le Sueur in 1917, Meridel Le Sueur adopted his surname. She contributed stories and reports to several popular publications, including the *Daily Worker* and the *New Masses*. Le Sueur's legacy to American history has been grounded in her gripping and compassionate writings, particularly on social issues, and she published fiction and nonfiction throughout her lifetime. Le Sueur died on November 14, 1996, in Hudson, Wisconsin.

HISTORICAL DOCUMENT

It's one of the great mysteries of the city where women go when they are out of work and hungry. There are not many women in the bread line. There are no flop houses for women as there are for men, where a bed can be had for a quarter or less. You don't see women lying on the floor at the mission in the free flops... Yet there must be as many women out of jobs in cities and suffering extreme poverty as there are men. What happens to them? Where do they go? Try to get into the Y.W. without any money or looking down at heel. Charities take care of very few and only those that are called "deserving." The lone girl is under suspicion by the virgin women who dispense charity... A woman will shut herself up in a room until it is taken away from her, and eat a cracker a day and be as quiet as a mouse so there are no social statistics concerning her. I don't know why it is... In the afternoon the young girls, to forget the hunger and the deathly torture and fear of being jobless, try to pick up a man to take them to a ten-cent show. They never go to more expensive ones, but they can always find a man willing to spend a dime to have the company of a girl for the afternoon... It's no wonder these young girls refuse to marry, refuse to rear children. They are like certain savage tribes, who, when they have been conquered refuse to breed. Mrs. Grey, sitting across from me is a living spokesman for the futility of labour. She is a warning. Her hands are scarred with labour. Her body is a great puckered scar. She has given birth to six children, buried three, supported them all alive and dead, bearing them, burying them, feeding them. Bred in hunger they have been spare, susceptible to disease. For seven years she tried to save her boy's arm from amputation, diseased from tuberculosis of the bone. It is almost too suffocating to think of that long close horror of years of child bearing, child feeding, rearing, with the bare suffering of providing a meal and shelter. Now she is fifty. Her children, economically insecure, are drifters. She never hears of them. She doesn't know if they are alive. She doesn't know if she is alive. Such subtleties of suffering are not for her. For her the brutality of hunger and cold, the bare bone of life. That is enough. These will occupy a life. Not until these are done away with can those subtle feelings that make a human being be indulged... Her face is not the face of a human being. She has born more than it is possible for a human being to bear. She is reduced to the least possible denominator of human feelings. It is terrible to see her little bloodshot eyes like a beaten hound's, fearful in terror.

GLOSSARY

down at heel: disheveled or shabby

YW: YWCA, or Young Women's Christian Association

Document Analysis

This except from Le Sueur's "Women on the Breadlines" opens with the author questioning the scarcity of the women along the breadlines. Le Sueur relates this to the lack of "flophouses" for women, which were available only to men. Flophouses were cheap forms of lodging for the poor and destitute. It is a provoking thought: if flophouses existed for men, surely there would be a counterpart for women. However, it is important to consider the status of women at this time. By 1932, American women had held the right to vote for less than fifteen years, and a woman's place was still widely considered to be within the family home. There remained a pervasive expectation at this time that women would be cared and provided for by their fathers or husbands, even as Le Sueur's account exposes the breakdown of the American family during the Great Depression.

Le Sueur recounts her impression of several women who are waiting in the employment bureau with her, many of whom had been abandoned by their husbands or their children in the wake of the economic collapse. Furthermore, Le Sueur describes the young, pretty girls who try "to pick up a man to take them to a ten-cent show" in order to distract themselves, if only for a short while, from the "deathly torture and fear of being jobless." For many of these women, the young men who were interested in enjoying their company represented their only reprieve from the crushing poverty they faced, and Le Sueur remarks, "It's no wonder these young girls refuse to marry, refuse to rear children." Le Sueur's account gives the impression that motherhood, which was once considered to be the ultimate achievement for American women, was increasingly being seen as an unreasonable burden by poor young women during the Depression.

Le Sueur also describes the deep embarrassment and shame that the majority of these women felt when seeking assistance. She explains that many women prefer to withdraw rather than seek aid. "A woman will shut herself up in a room until it is taken away from her, and eat a cracker a day and be as quiet as a mouse so there are no social statistics concerning her," Le Sueur writes. Although there were charitable organizations established to dispense aid to the poor, Le Sueur explains that many women were reluctant to seek their assistance for fear of judgment. Contrasting the average impoverished woman in need of aid with the older women who managed these predominantly religious charities, Le Sueur explains, "the lone girl is under suspicion by the virgin women who dispense charity."

Finally, Le Sueur's account speaks to the deep disappointment and disillusionment of many of these women. She describes one older woman in the employment office, Mrs. Grey, as the "living spokesman for the futility of labour." Despite Mrs. Grey's efforts and sacrifices to raise and support her family, she has been abandoned by her husband and ignored by her impoverished children, leaving her bereft of the support and security that husbands and children were expected to provide to their wives and mothers at the time. Le Sueur describes Mrs. Grey as "a warning" to other women of the insecurity of family and the empty promise of hard work in the midst of the Great Depression.

Essential Themes

"Women on the Breadlines" was an endorsement for those individuals who had fallen by the wayside of society when they were most in need. Le Sueur depicted the great social and economic changes brought on by the Great Depression by describing the stories of individual women. The social turmoil of this time is particularly exemplified by the case study of Mrs. Grey, who had given birth to six children, buried three, and tired herself to the bone to be a mother to them. At the time of Le Sueur's writing, however, Mrs. Grey did not know of the whereabouts of her surviving children or her husband, and she was left impoverished and alone in late middle age. Most of the women described by Le Sueur had had their lives and expectations completely upended by the Great Depression, and they were forced to adapt their attitudes, their lifestyles, and even their morals to survive in the new social and economic environment. Those women who could not adapt, such as Mrs. Grey, were likened to "a person drowning, doomed." Le Sueur presented a sympathetic portrayal of the poor, the unemployed, and the homeless in much of her writings and, with "Women on the Breadlines," she attempted to elucidate the reasons behind the behavior and attitudes of women whose lives had changed completely in the Great Depression.

—*Jennifer Henderson Crane, PgDip*

Bibliography and Additional Reading

Broner, E. M. "Meridel LeSueur, 1900–1996." *Nation* (17 Feb. 1997): 33–35. Print.

Hedges, Elaine, ed. *Ripening: Selected Work*. 2nd ed. New York: Feminist, 1990. Print.

Pratt, Linda Ray. "Women Writers in the CP: The Case of Meridel LeSueur." *Women's Studies* 14.3 (1988): 247–64. Print.

Raymond, Mary. "Reflections of Meridel Le Sueur." *Hurricane Alice* 5.3 (1988): 4. Print.

Eleanor Roosevelt: What Ten Million Women Want

Date: March 1932
Author: Eleanor Roosevelt
Genre: article; essay

Summary Overview

Eleanor Roosevelt, niece of Theodore Roosevelt and wife of Franklin Delano Roosevelt, was closely involved in the social reforms that took place at the beginning of the twentieth century. She was a lifelong progressive activist and a popular commentator on social issues. "What Ten Million Women Want" was published in the March 1932 issue of the *Home Magazine*, a publication with a middle-class female readership. It was one of many pieces she wrote about contemporary political concerns.

The article examines the roles that women could play in American politics at the time. In it, Roosevelt demonstrated a number of ways in which women could be ideal candidates for some political offices and addressed political issues that she considered important to women. Writing just twelve years after American women had won the right to vote, she admonished them to become just as involved in political life as men had traditionally been, to become active and informed voters, and to use their new political power wisely.

Defining Moment

Eleanor Roosevelt has become an icon of American history. Understanding her enduring appeal requires an appreciation of the social and historical context in which she lived. She was born into a privileged New York family at a time when it was fashionable for the wealthy to devote their time and resources to improving conditions for those less fortunate. Moreover, she was a Roosevelt, part of a family that had long been famed for its philanthropic generosity and eventually produced two American presidents known for their reformist zeal. From the 1920s onward, Eleanor Roosevelt enjoyed widespread fame for her articles, speeches, and radio addresses, in which she candidly voiced political views that many considered quite radical.

The United States had gone through major demographic shifts in the nineteenth century. The Industrial Revolution in the first part of the century led to a mass migration of laborers from rural settings to urban centers where factories were concentrated. People also came in record numbers from overseas to pursue work in US cities. This process of urbanization created serious social problems. Many cities became notorious for their high rates of poverty, crime, and disease, and the end of the nineteenth century saw a growing awareness of the widespread economic inequality between the rich and the poor. Wealthier concerned citizens helped form numerous charitable organizations to provide assistance to those in need. The Progressive Era, as this period in American history has come to be called, can be roughly dated to between 1890 and 1920.

Women gained a more significant role in the American political system when the Nineteenth Amendment to the Constitution was ratified in 1920, removing gender barriers to suffrage. While women now had the vote, Americans, both male and female, were uncertain about what role women should play in politics. When the Great Depression began in 1929, families everywhere faced severe economic hardship, and people became increasingly desperate for real systemic change. Many women started to question traditional gender norms, including those around political leadership.

"What Ten Million Women Want" was a response to questions about how women could help improve the political system. Published in 1932—the year of a heated presidential race between Franklin Delano Roosevelt, campaigning as a reformer, and Herbert Hoover, blamed by many for the Great Depression—the article was also a practical effort to mobilize women voters. Indeed, women's votes helped deliver the election to

Franklin Delano Roosevelt. His presidency focused on a series of social programs known as the New Deal, which addressed areas of social inequality that had first gained widespread attention in the Progressive Era, thanks in part to activists such as his wife, Eleanor Roosevelt.

Author Biography

Anna Eleanor Roosevelt was born in New York City on October 11, 1884. She was the eldest child of socialites Anna Rebecca Hall Roosevelt and Elliot Bulloch Roosevelt. Her father's older brother was Theodore Roosevelt, who became governor of New York, then vice president, and then president of the United States.

Eleanor Roosevelt had an unhappy childhood. By the time she was ten years old, her mother had died of diphtheria and her father had died of complications related to alcoholism. As a teenager, Eleanor was sent to study at Allenswood Academy, a private all-girls school in London. When she returned to New York in 1902, she became involved in a number of progressive philanthropies, influenced in part by her uncle's reformist policies. In 1905, she married Franklin Delano Roosevelt, her fifth cousin, and his rapidly advancing political career as a reformer made her one of the most influential women in American progressive politics. The couple became centrally involved in American politics. Roosevelt supported her husband's political career as he became a New York state senator, assistant secretary of the Navy, governor of New York, and finally president.

Eleanor Roosevelt was an outspoken advocate for social reform, writing numerous articles and giving many speeches outlining her beliefs. After her husband's death in 1945, she remained active in politics, serving as a delegate to the United Nations, an organizer for the Democratic Party, and an adviser to presidents. By the time of her death on November 7, 1962, Eleanor Roosevelt had established an enduring reputation as one of the most influential women in American political culture.

HISTORICAL DOCUMENT

What do ten million women want in public life? That question could be answered in ten million different ways. For every woman, like every man, has some aspirations or desires exclusively her own.

We women are callow fledglings as compared with the wise old birds who manipulate the political machinery, and we still hesitate to believe that a woman can fill certain positions in public life as competently and adequately as a man.

For instance, it is certain that women do not want a woman for President. Nor would they have the slightest confidence in her ability to fulfill the functions of that office.

Every woman who fails in a public position confirms this, but every woman who succeeds creates confidence.

Judge Florence Allen on the Supreme Court Bench in Ohio, Frances Perkins as Labor Commissioner in New York, have done much to make women feel that a really fine woman, well trained in her work, can give as good an account of her stewardship as any man, and eventually women, and perhaps even men, may come to feel that sex should not enter into the question of fitness for office.

When it comes to the matter of having a woman as a member of the President's Cabinet, there are I think, many women who feel that the time has come to recognize the fact that women have practically just as many votes as men and deserve at least a certain amount of recognition.

Take the Department of Labor for instance. Why should not the Secretary of Labor be a woman, and would not a woman's point of view be valuable in the President's Council? There are many other places to which women may aspire, and the time will come when there will be new departments, some of which will undoubtedly need women at their heads.

When we come to finances we realize that after all, all government, whether it is that of village, city, state or nation, is simply glorified housekeeping.

Little by little we are getting budget systems into our public housekeeping and budgets are something all women understand.

Every woman knows that dire results happen when she exceeds her own budget, and it is only a short step from this to understanding what happens in the city, the state or the nation when finances are not carefully administered and watched. Every woman demands that her government be economically managed, but she knows, far better perhaps than the average man, that there are two kinds of economy. There is such a thing as parsimonious spending which in the end costs more than a wise study of the needs of the future, and the spending which takes into account the social side of life.

For instance, it may be wise to spend fifty thousand dollars this year in buying space for parks, first because the land will increase in value, secondly because we are beginning to recognize that for the youth growing up in the cities, play space in the city and play space in the country beyond, is most important for healthful development. Perhaps we could save this sum today, but it would cost us far more in physical and spiritual value twenty years from now, as well as in actual cash.

Women are detail minded, they have had to be for generations, therefore, they are much more apt to watch in detail what is done by their public officials in the case of finances than does the average man.

Ten million women may not at the moment be quite awake to their opportunities along this line, still I think we can safely say that this is one of the wants that lies back in the mind of every woman.

Do women want to take an active part in framing our laws? I think the answer to that is decidedly yes. There are more and more women elected to Legislative Bodies every year. This session of Congress has six Congresswomen on its roll, three Democrats and three Republicans.

The names of Ruth Bryan Owen and Mrs. McCormick are far better known than those of many male Congressmen. We have in this new Congress for a time at least, the first active woman United States Senator in Mrs. Caraway. She was elected this January for the full term and she will be, from all indications, a real power in the Upper House, and very far from a rubber stamp.

Welfare legislation touches very closely the home life of every woman, and therefore demands her interest and careful criticism both in the provisions of the laws, and in the administration of those laws when they actually become effective. Because these laws are interpreted and enforced by our courts, I think women feel they are entitled to places on the bench.

Women judges are no longer a novelty, and in some classes of courts, particularly those dealing with juvenile offenders, the women have proven themselves decidedly superior to the men.

I do not think women would approve of having women heads of police departments. I do think they feel policewomen and matrons a necessity for the proper care of girl and women offenders. As for a national police commissioner, male or female, I think women are decidedly opposed to it.

It is our conviction that crime to be dealt with successfully, must be dealt with locally with a thorough understanding of local conditions. Every woman is, of course, deeply interested in the crime situation.

But I think because of her education and knowledge of the home, she realizes that it is through better education and better living conditions in our crowded cities that the prevention of crime, which is the ultimate aim of all criminology, must be achieved.

While I do not believe in a national police commissioner, or a national police commission, I think women approve the recommendation that there should be available at Washington a national department where data relating to criminals, and statistics relating to crime should be available for the use of all the state and local police departments of the country.

I think that those women who have given this question of crime most serious consideration are generally in agreement that the first and most practical step to its eradication would be in the wiping out of certain tenement house localities in our big cities and the raising of educational standards generally.

Women to whom, after all, the education of the child is largely entrusted by the men, understand far better than the average man the need of education and improvement in teaching.

Too often, the father's actual knowledge of how his child is being educated is gleaned from a hasty scanning of the report card once a month, but the mother knows all the virtues of the successful teacher and the faults of the poor one. She understands the defects of our system which produces, I am sorry to say, so many who have not the heaven-sent gift of instructing the young successfully.

There is much research work that a Department of Education might be doing. What actual education possibilities does each state offer? Are all children furnished with standard textbooks? Are libraries accessible for all children? Do we need, for a great majority of children more specialized and vocational training?

All these questions should be made the subject of research on a national scale, but there is a great division of opinion as to what authority should be vested in a national department of education.

The women who travel over this country realize that standards of education are woefully low in certain places, and there is no doubt it would be most useful for the public at large to know that the actual standards vary greatly in different parts of the United States. But this is a very different thing from placing absolute control over the various state departments of education in a "Department of National Education," such as has been proposed by some.

What do women want to do about prohibition? Women generally consider prohibition as social legislation, not from the economic standpoint as the men do as a rule, but when you ask "what do women want to do about prohibition?," the answer is the same as it would be if we asked "what do men want to do about prohibition?"

Not only are political parties split, but there is no uniform answer to this in the case of either sex. No one can say what the women want to do about prohibition.

We can say this, however, that few women are completely satisfied with the present-day conditions, and many are not satisfied with any of the remedies which have been as yet set forth. Only a few fortunate people feel they have found the answer to this problem and not enough people agree with them as yet to settle it.

The matter of proper laws dealing with marriage has been one much considered by all women in every state in the union interested in social conditions. Everyone feels it should be harder to get married and more solemnity and sense of permanence should accompany the ceremony. Uniform divorce laws might help to this end.

My fourth point is the woman's desire to see government lighten her burdens. The first of these burdens is the taxes. On the whole when women see that taxes which they pay bring direct returns in benefits to the community, I do not think that they are averse to paying them, but I do think that our ten million women want much more careful accounting for how their taxes are expended in the local, state or national government. They want to see the actual good which comes to them from these expenditures.

They feel very strongly that governments should not add to their burdens but should lighten them. They are gradually coming to grasp the relation of legislation to the lightening of these burdens, for instance, in such questions as the regulation of public utilities and the development of the water power of our nation. They realize now that cheaper electricity means less work in the home, more time to give to their children, more time for recreation and greater educational opportunities.

In Canada, across the border from Buffalo, where so much power is generated, there are proportionately many more electric washing machines and ironers and electric stoves and vacuum cleaners and hot water heaters in use because of the cheaper cost of electricity, than we have on this side of the line, although we have the same possibilities before us, and the women are beginning to ask why they are not within our grasp. Hence their interest is growing daily in the aspects of the whole public utilities question.

Then we come to the fifth point, which after all while it is entirely in the hands of the national government, still comes back to the home of every individual woman. She may wake up someday to find that her nation is at war and her boys and even her girls in one war or another, are drafted into service a service from which they may not return, or they may return with mangled bodies, but if they do return to her with physical bodies unchanged, there may be some kind of mental and spiritual change which will alter their characters and their outlook on life.

It may do them good, but the reading of history does not lead us to hope for great benefits for the younger generation from any war. Therefore, every woman's interest in the amicable relations of her country is very great and she has come to realize that this is not merely a question of polite phrases between diplomats.

The only danger that women will not get what they want lies in the fact that there are still a goodly number who do not know how to use their influence and how to make known their ideas.

I heard a teacher not long ago discussing a referendum with her class; she suggested that in New York State such a referendum had been taken in the last election when the people voted on certain amendments. One of the children looked up brightly and said, "Oh, yes, my mother knew nothing about any of those so she voted 'no' on all of them!" This is a dangerous attitude for any woman to allow herself if she hopes to get what she wants from her government.

If ten million women really want security, real representation, honesty, wise and just legislation, happier and more comfortable conditions of living, and a future with the horrors of war removed from the horizon, then these ten million women must bestir themselves.

They can be active factors in the life of their communities and shape the future, or they can drift along and hide behind the men. Today is a challenge to women. Tomorrow will see how they answer the challenge!

GLOSSARY

callow fledgling: a young bird

parsimonious: frugal or stingy

prohibition: the banning of alcohol

referendum: submission of an issue for direct vote by the public

Document Analysis

"What Ten Million Women Want" begins by asking what role women should play in public life. Roosevelt immediately notes that there is no single answer to this question and that individual women, like men, have their own ideas. She states that women are "callow fledglings" compared to the "wise old birds who manipulate the political machinery," a metaphor that would have appealed to the growing numbers of women discontented with the political establishment as the economic effects of the Great Depression began to be felt by ordinary people.

In the article, Roosevelt claims that women are not ready to elect women to certain political roles, such as the presidency. Her own husband, Franklin Delano Roosevelt, was a contender for the presidency in 1932, and this remark can be read as a tacit endorsement of his campaign, supporting a man for president while maintaining the article's pro-woman message. Yet to demonstrate that talented women can be successful in political office, she then goes on to say that women are nevertheless ready for other political jobs and gives examples of women who have already excelled in political office, such as an Ohio Supreme Court judge, a New York labor commissioner, and six congresswomen.

Roosevelt argues that women have skills that make them ideal candidates for certain political roles. For example, she believes that because women are typically in charge of household budgets, they may be more careful with public finances and better at balancing budgets than men. "After all," she claims, "all government, whether it is that of village, city, state or nation, is simply glorified housekeeping." She also asserts that women should be more involved in making laws, since much social welfare legislation concerns the domestic sphere, typically considered a female domain; and that women should head a proposed Department of Education, since women are more involved in the education of children than men are. In addition, she favors more female judges and police officers because women are naturally concerned about the social impacts of crime and its effects on their families, and because "policewomen and matrons [are] a necessity for the proper care of girl and women offenders."

Roosevelt then notes some other ways in which women are dissatisfied with the contemporary political reality. She says that marriage laws must be reformed to create uniform divorce rights throughout the country and that American women want the government to take steps to make utilities, such as water and electricity, cheaper, as is already the case in many Canadian cities because "cheaper electricity means less work in the home, more time to give to their children, more time for recreation and greater educational opportunities." She then raises the issue of international relations, stating that this is a topic women should pay better attention to because their children might be victims of future wars if the United States is not able to maintain "amicable relations" with other countries.

The main hurdle that women must overcome in asserting more control over government decisions, Roosevelt plainly states, is that "there are still a goodly number who do not know how to use their influence and how to make known their ideas." She recounts a story, in which a woman voted against a series of proposed amendments in a referendum simply because she did not understand them—a cautionary example of what can happen when women remain ignorant of political issues. Women must become as politically active as men are, Roosevelt concludes, if they are to help the United States achieve a better future.

Essential Themes

"What Ten Million Women Want" appeared in 1932, the same year that Eleanor Roosevelt's husband, Franklin Delano Roosevelt, was running for president. Over a decade had passed since American women had gained the right to vote. In the 1932 election cycle, there was much debate in American society about what role women should play in political life. This article was Eleanor Roosevelt's response. It also addresses several concerns American women had in 1932, such as laws surrounding marriage and divorce.

The ultimate message that Roosevelt sought to send to her female audience was that they had an unprecedented potential to effect political change, but they needed to learn how to use this power. She argued that women must develop the same level of interest in political activities as men and that voting without understanding the issues of the day was a harmful waste of the right. Only through ongoing and active participation in political life could women help build a stronger American government.

—Adam J. Berger, PhD

Bibliography and Additional Reading

Buhle, Mari Jo, & Paul Buhle, eds. *The Concise History of Woman Suffrage: Selections from History of Woman Suffrage*. Urbana: U of Illinois P, 2005. Print.

Jaycox, Faith. *The Progressive Era*. New York: Facts on File, 2005. Print.

Kearney, James R. *Anna Eleanor Roosevelt: The Evolution of a Reformer*. Boston: Houghton, 1968. Print.

Roosevelt, Eleanor. *The Autobiography of Eleanor Roosevelt*. New York: Harper, 1961. Print.

Eleanor Roosevelt on Women and the Vote

Date: 1933
Author: Eleanor Roosevelt
Genre: essay

Summary Overview

Eleanor Roosevelt, wife of President Franklin Delano Roosevelt, was First Lady of the United States from 1933 to 1945. She is remembered as one of the most active women to ever hold that position. "Women and the Vote" is an essay in a book entitled *It's Up to the Women*, which Eleanor Roosevelt authored in 1933, the first year of her husband's presidency.

This essay is a celebration of the passage of the Nineteenth Amendment, which gave American women the right to vote. It is also an acknowledgement of the great responsibilities and opportunities this new right afforded them. Perhaps most importantly, this piece is a call to women to help turn the crisis of the Great Depression into an opportunity to build a new American society on stronger egalitarian and democratic values.

Defining Moment

In order to understand how and why the essay reflected important contemporary issues, it is necessary to fully appreciate the changes going on in American culture at the time. Doing so involves taking a somewhat broader view of the historical moment.

In the early nineteenth century, America was by and large an agrarian society, with most people earning their livings through farming and animal husbandry. As that century unfolded, manufacturing took on new importance to the economy. The Industrial Revolution, as this process of economic change has come to be called, increased the importance of cities. As factories opened in America's cities, people flocked to them from the countryside and from abroad, dramatically increasing the nation's urban population.

American cities, including Roosevelt's native New York, became centers of both concentrated poverty and wealth. For members of the working class, life in cities was difficult and dangerous. Overcrowding, disease, crime, and exploitative working conditions were common features of life for America's working poor. At the same time, industrial capitalism allowed a minority of people to become quite wealthy.

Some wealthier members of society began to address the negative aspects of life in America's cities, supporting philanthropic channels designed to help the urban poor. At the same time, many people began to ask important questions about America's political culture, such as what the role of race was, how to help ensure the safety of workers, and how women should be involved in American politics. The Progressive Era, as this broad trend of activism is called, is typically dated from the 1890s to the 1920s. Eleanor Roosevelt was both a product of and a central figure in this wider movement.

Women's rights became a major issue of the Progressive Era. The right to vote, in particular, gained significant support. In 1918, the Nineteenth Amendment to Constitution was introduced, removing gender barriers to participation in democratic elections. It was eventually ratified in 1920.

In the years after the Nineteenth Amendment's ratification, there was much controversy about how exactly women should use their new right. Many people still considered women incapable of making important decisions about the public sphere or of understanding nuanced political issues. Eleanor Roosevelt published many pieces about this topic, taking the view that women should strive to be just as informed about and involved in politics as their male counterparts. As she began her new role as first lady, Eleanor Roosevelt was keenly aware of the potential political power of women voters. This essay expresses her views on the matter at the time.

Author Biography

Born on October 11, 1884, Eleanor Roosevelt was the oldest child of New York socialites. Her parents both died before she was ten years old, and her relatives took over responsibility for her care. The Roosevelts were an old, wealthy, and powerful New York family, in the political spotlight because of Theodore Roosevelt, Eleanor's paternal uncle.

Eleanor Roosevelt was sent to study at the Allenswood Girls Academy in London, where she worked under headmistress Marie Souvestre, known in educational circles for her pioneering work in girls' education. When Roosevelt returned to New York in 1902, she was expected to enter the city's elite social scene as a debutante. Instead, she got involved in philanthropic work, joining thousands of middle-class women in trend of popular social activism.

In 1905, she married her fifth cousin, Franklin Delano Roosevelt, with whom she had kept up a friendly correspondence for years. His political career took him from the New York State Senate to New York's governor's mansion and then to the White House after the 1932 elections. Meanwhile, Eleanor Roosevelt developed a successful career as a political commentator. She voiced her progressive opinions in newspaper articles, in essays, in speeches, and on the radio.

As first lady, she helped her husband develop the social service programs of the New Deal designed to pull America out of the Great Depression. She always rejected the idea of running for political office herself, despite her immense popularity. However, even after her husband's death in 1945, she remained an important organizer within the Democratic Party and the United Nations.

When Eleanor Roosevelt died, on November 7, 1962, she was eulogized as having been the world's most influential woman, an honor supported by several international polls. She was always a prolific and outspoken critic of the political status quo, taking on such issues as women's rights, racial equality, and class bias at a time in American history when women were not expected to discuss such controversial matters. Her progressive views were lambasted as radical by some. However, she was a great personal hero to many other Americans, especially women, as they struggled to make sense of life in a rapidly modernizing United States.

HISTORICAL DOCUMENT

There is one new activity which entered the life of women with the passage of the Nineteenth Amendment in 1918. With the right to vote, a whole new field of responsibility and direct power came into the hands of the women of the country. A few of our states had already given women the right to vote and in some communities they were allowed to vote in school elections, but they did not enjoy the full privileges of citizenship as the equals of men throughout the whole country until 1918.

Many fine men and women had worked for this change for many years and the stories of Elizabeth Cady Stanton, Dr. Anna Shaw, Susan B. Anthony and Carrie Chapman Catt are inspiring reading, because of the unselfish devotion they brought to this cause, which they felt meant a just recognition of the rights of a big group of people. Looking even beyond the justice of the cause they felt this power given to women would herald great changes for the good of mankind.

Fourteen years have now gone by and everywhere people are asking, "What have the women done with the vote?" I often wonder why they don't ask the men the same question, but I realize that it is a high compliment to women that evidently they were expected to bring about some marked change in political conditions and so I would like to look into the question of women as citizens and see just what we have done and are doing and then perhaps dream a little about what we may do in the future.

The vast majority of women, like the vast majority of men, have little time to give to anything but the earning of their daily bread either by actually working themselves or by caring for home and children and making other people's earnings go as far as possible. Their good citizenship consists in leading their lives so as to make them as productive of good for all around them as they can be, and their public duty is expressed by using their vote as intelligently as possible.

A vote is never an intelligent vote when it is cast without knowledge. Just doing what someone else tells you to do without any effort to find out what the facts are for yourself is being a poor citizen. When women first had the vote, many of them did not know how to get information on questions of government. Others had seen the men for years go and vote, had heard them talk a little during the weeks just before election about this or that candidate or this or that party, but had never gathered that there was much concern for the things the parties stood for. You were a democrat or a republican because your family belonged to one or to the other party, because your people had been in the north or in the south at the time of the war between the states, or because it was easier to get advancement in business in your locality if you belonged to one or the other party. These reasons and some others like them did not greatly stir the patriotism of the women. A few women formed the League of Women Voters, a non-partisan organization which tries, as far as human agencies can do so, to control the prejudices of its members and have them look at both sides of political questions and to furnish unbiased information to any women asking to know about candidates or measures proposed by any political party. Other organizations sprang up for political study and long-established women's clubs added departments of citizenship where their politically minded members could study such questions as interested them. The vast majority of women, however, remain as indifferent to the vote and how they use it as are the vast majority of men.

If we look about us in the world today or read past history, we will find that benevolent monarchs and good dictators have as a rule had contented, well-governed people. The reason, I fear, is that we are all glad to let someone do our thinking for us as long as we go on fairly comfortably and happily. It is only when bad rulers oppress their people for a long time that those people begin to think for themselves and eventually overthrow their rulers.

Those of us who live in democracies have known of such occurrences in the past but if our leaders have led us through fairly still waters we are as content as other peoples under other forms of government to let some people do our thinking for us, and it takes stern times to shake us out of our apathy.

Women are no different from men in this and though certain subjects may be of greater interest to them, they have been slow as a group to act because political thought and action were new and following women leaders was new. How many times have I heard older women say, "Well, I really feel safer with a man doctor and I take a man's advice on certain questions because he's been at it so much longer than we women!" The sex is still the basis of judgment; they don't just say, "I like Henry as a doctor better than Susie," or "I think James' opinion on that question is more sensible than Jenny's." That day is just beginning to arrive and, strange coincidence, it is arriving just when stern necessity is driving many people in our country to think about questions which for years they have been willing to leave to their leaders.

For a number of years I, with many other women, have traveled our various states trying to arouse women to an interest in government, pointing out how it affected their homes, building and working conditions, the water they drank, the food they ate, their children, the schools, the public health, the recreations. We have used the World War to show how much, as women, we are concerned with governments in other lands and our relations with them. We have showed the necessity for women of different lands, whose fundamental interests are the same, to know and understand each other. We have tried to dramatize some of the lessons learned between 1914 and 1920 as to the waste and futility of war and frequently found a polite response, a temporary burst of interest and then the old apathy creeping back as the sense of present security and comfort spread around our women.

Now, there is for many people no sense of security and no comfort and no ease and no luxury, and even the right to work, not always looked upon as a blessing, has become a precious and sought-after right. Now you do not, either in men or women, have to arouse interest in their government; it is the one hope they have and they look to it for salvation. Political news in papers has become interesting; books on economics and on government are eagerly read; there is a revolution in thinking and that always presages a revolution in action. One can have a bloodless revolution if one can count on leaders of sufficient vision to grasp the goal for which the mass of people is often unconsciously striving, and courage enough in the nation as a whole to accept the necessary changes to achieve the desired ends.

Some women have been educating themselves in the past fourteen years; the mass of their sisters is now awake. Are there women ready to lead in these new paths? Will other women follow them? We do not know, but one thing is sure, the attitude of women towards changes in society is going to determine to a great extent our future in this country. Women in the past have never realized their political strength. Will they wake up to it now? Will they realize that politics in the old sense, a game played for selfish ends by a few politicians, is of no concern any longer to anyone and that recognition in the sense of receiving a political job is perhaps necessary but only important because of the opportunity it affords a woman or a man to show what they conceive to be the duty of a government servant? If our government offices are not held in the next few years by men and women with new conceptions of public service, then our revolution may not continue to be bloodless and changes may not come gradually as they are coming now, but violently and suddenly as they have come in the past in France and in Russia and we will go back before we gather up the pieces and move forward again.

So in reviewing the past fourteen years let us acknowledge that women have made a few changes in politics. It is quite safe for them to be at polling places on election day and very gradually the men are accepting them as part of the party machinery and today if a woman wants to work and can prove her ability and is not too anxious and insistent upon recognition and tangible reward, she can be part of almost any party activity except the inner circle where the really important decisions in city, county and state politics are made! She can get into this inner circle in national politics more easily than in state, county and city and I wonder if the reason might be that men in Washington are a little more formal with each other and therefore the presence of a woman does not "cramp their style" to the same degree that it would in the other conferences? Women have made no great changes in politics or government and that is all that can be said of the past and now for the present.

Women are thinking and that is the first step toward an increased and more intelligent use of the ballot. Then they will demand of their political parties clear statements of principles and they will scrutinize their party's candidates, watch their records, listen to their promises and expect them to live up to them and to have their party's backing, and occasionally when the need arises, women will reject their party and its candidates. This will not be disloyalty but will show that as members of a party they are loyal first to the fine things for which the party stands and when it rejects those things or forgets the legitimate objects for which political parties exist, then as a party it cannot command the honest loyalty of its members.

Next, I believe women will run for office and accept victory or defeat in a sporting spirit. The proportion of women holding elective office is small. There are two reasons for this: one is that many women have dreaded the give and take of a campaign, they have dreaded the public criticism, they have not learned to discount the attacks of the opposition; but business and professional life is paving the way and this reason will not deter them much longer.

The second reason is that as a rule nominations which are given women by any of the political parties are in districts where it is almost impossible for one holding their political beliefs to win; in other words, a woman who is willing to make a well-nigh hopeless fight is welcomed by a local leader trying to fill out his ticket. The changing attitude towards women in general may bring a change in this. We have good women in political office today and much depends on their success. They are blazing the new paths and what is far more important they are exemplifying what we mean by the new type of public servant. When Frances Perkins says, "I can't go away because under the new industrial bill we have a chance to achieve for the workers of this country better conditions for which I have worked all my life," she is not staying because she will gain anything materially, for herself or her friends, but because she sees an opportunity for government to render a permanent service to the general happiness of the working man and woman and their families. This is what we mean as I see it by the "new deal." Look carefully, O people, at the record of some of your public servants in the past few years! Does this attitude strike you as new? If so, the women are in part responsible for it, and I think at present we can count on a more active interest from them and a constantly increasing willingness to bear their proper share of the burdens of government.

Now for the dreams of the future:

If women are really going to awake to their civic

duties, if they are going to accept changes in social living and try to make of this country a real democracy, in which the best of opportunity is available to every child and where the compensations of life are not purely material ones, then we may indeed be seeing the realization of a really new deal for the people. If this is to come true, it seems to me that the women have got to learn to work together even before they work with men, and they have got to be realistic in facing the social problems that have to be solved. They cannot accept certain doctrines simply because they sound well. I have often thought that it sounded so well to talk about women being on an equal footing with men and sometimes when I have listened to the arguments of the National Woman's Party and they have complained that they could not compete in the labor market because restrictions were laid upon women's work which were not laid upon men's, I have been almost inclined to agree with them that such restrictions were unjust, until I came to realize that when all is said and done women are different from men. They are equals in many ways, but they cannot refuse to acknowledge their differences. Not to acknowledge them weakens the case. Their physical functions in life are different and perhaps in the same way the contributions which they are to bring to the spiritual side of life are different. It may be that certain questions are waiting to be solved until women can bring their views to bear upon those questions.

I have a friend who wrote me the other day saying that because she and her husband lost all of their money, they have been obliged to go and live in a rural community in a small farmhouse. She and her daughters are doing all their own work and they have chosen the community in which they are living not because they found a house which they liked, but because they found a school for the children that they felt would give a real education. After the school was found, they found the house. She adds, "I do not regret the money—it has been a marvelous experience, giving my children a true sense of values, and I have learned what real people my country neighbors are. Because we have struggled together we know each other far better than do the average people who live in far easier circumstances."

There are many people who may make this same discovery and it is not always necessary to lose everything in order to make it, but it is necessary to attain the vision of a new and different life.

I was reading lately a book which Ramsay MacDonald wrote about his wife who died in 1911 and who seems today to be alive as one reads the pages of the book. She was far ahead of her time in many ways, but her most striking characteristic, from youth up, was the feeling of not being able to live in comfort when so many others suffered. She felt that all human beings were her brothers and sisters and her work has lived after her. Many women in this country have been carrying on similar work and perhaps we are going to see evolved in the next few years not only a social order built by the ability and brains of our men, but a social order which also represents the understanding heart of the women.

Document Analysis

"Women and the Vote" begins by noting that the Nineteenth Amendment opened up a "new field of responsibility and direct power" for American women. Roosevelt then pays homage to some of heroes of the women's suffrage movement, who had worked for years to secure equal voting rights for women. Such champions of women's suffrage, Roosevelt explains, showed "unselfish devotion" to the struggle because they believed giving women the vote would "herald great changes for the good of mankind." Roosevelt seeks to take stock of what women have done and are doing over a decade after the achievement of the right to vote.

She notes that most people, women and men, are too busy earning a living to pay much attention to political issues, and says women in particular may not know where to find information upon which to base their voting decisions. Roosevelt mentions that groups have been formed to help with this, and names the League of Women Voters, founded in 1920, as a resource for securing unbiased candidate information.

Roosevelt then posits that the involvement of women in American politics is particularly important in 1933, as the Great Depression undermines the financial security of families throughout the country. She believes that there has been "a revolution in thinking" as women seek the government's help to survive the economic upheaval. She predicts a future in which women are thoughtfully engaged in political decisions, involve themselves in the organization of political parties, and win political offices in large numbers.

She mentions Frances Perkins (1880–1965), United States secretary of labor from 1933 to 1945, as an example of the new kind of female civil servant who can help put America back to work. Roosevelt goes on to argue that further labor law reforms are needed to improve economic opportunities for women. She mentions some reforms suggested by the National Woman's Party as being partially reasonable. This group was considered to be a radical women's rights organization in 1933. In agreeing with some of its positions, Roosevelt takes a bold stand in favor of continued equal rights reforms.

Roosevelt then mentions she is reading a book by former British prime minister Ramsay MacDonald (1866–1937). In it, MacDonald describes the charitable nature of his late wife, saying that she believed in the brotherhood and sisterhood of all human beings. Roosevelt hopes this realization will help to inform a new social order informed by both "the brains of our men" and "the understanding heart of the women."

Essential Themes

The first theme Roosevelt sought to communicate in this essay was that it was appropriate to celebrate the ratification of the Nineteenth Amendment as a major accomplishment afforded by decades of struggle. She recommended that women make an effort to inform themselves so that they could vote with confidence in their decisions, become involved in political parties, and even win elected offices.

The economic reality of the Great Depression and the disruption it caused in the lives of many American families were also important parts of Roosevelt's message in this essay. She contended that people were looking to the government to help lead the country out of the economic crisis and, therefore, were becoming more avid and savvy consumers of political information. She envisioned a possible future in which women could lead social and labor reforms that would result in improved opportunities for all Americans.

Roosevelt also struck an idealistic note in this essay. She postulated that the crisis of the Great Depression could be an opportunity to reform values and to build a more equal and democratic America. She spoke of the potential evolution of a society informed by the acknowledgement that all men and women are brothers and sisters and of a social order reflecting the compassion of women as well as the intelligence of men.

—*Adam J. Berger, PhD*

Bibliography and Additional Reading

Beasley, Maurine, & Holly Shulman. *The Eleanor Roosevelt Encyclopedia*. Westport: Greenwood, 2001. Print.

Buhle, Mari Jo, & Paul Buhle. *The Concise History of Woman Suffrage*. Urbana: U of Illinois P, 2005. Print.

Jaycox, Faith. *The Progressive Era*. New York: Facts on File, 2005. Print.

Roosevelt, Eleanor. *The Autobiography of Eleanor Roosevelt*. Cambridge: Da Capo, 2000. Print.

The Repatriation of Mexicans and Mexican Americans

Date: August 1932
Author: Armando C. Amador
Genre: letter

Summary Overview

The early years of the Great Depression saw a massive exodus, as hundreds of thousands of Mexicans and Mexican Americans were compelled to leave the United States for Mexico, allegedly to reduce economic pressure on the government and create job openings for those who remained. In August 1932, the Mexican consulate in San Diego, California, distributed a letter to residents of San Diego County who faced deportation, offering free transportation for them and their belongings from the city to one of six Mexican states. Recipients were strongly encouraged to take advantage of the offer and were assured that the Mexican government would provide them with farmland in whichever of the six states they chose.

Defining Moment

The repatriation of Mexicans and Mexican Americans during the Great Depression is an often-overlooked chapter in US history. Even American-born citizens of Mexican descent were subjected to this treatment; their rightful citizenship was not enough to shield them. The government body behind the repatriation was the Bureau of Immigration, which operated under the auspices of the Department of Commerce and Labor from 1903 to 1933, at which time it became the Immigration and Naturalization Service (INS) and was transferred to the Department of Justice.

Immigration from Mexico to the United States had increased significantly in the years following the Mexican Revolution, which started in 1910 and continued for at least the next decade. While work was plentiful throughout the 1910s and 1920s (except during a brief recession at the beginning of the latter decade), calls for repatriation of immigrants had begun even before the stock market crash of 1929. The ensuing years saw unemployment levels reach as high as 25 percent, leaving many men and women unable to support themselves or their families. With the scarcity of jobs came distrust of immigrants, or even those citizens perceived as such, and a heightened sense that they were stealing jobs from rightful citizens. In 1930, the San Diego County Board of Supervisors barred all "aliens" from working on public projects, objecting to the fact that, according to Supervisor Edgar F. Hastings, many county road workers were Mexican citizens. Throughout the country, many other state and local governments introduced similar legislation.

A bill proposed by Senator William J. Harris of Georgia would have instituted a strict quota for Mexican immigrants; it was approved by the Senate in 1930, but failed to pass the House of Representatives. Nevertheless, government agencies continued to seek ways to deport Mexicans living in the United States, with no particular distinction made between immigrants and American-born citizens. Secretary of Labor William N. Doak, appointed in 1930, argued that this removal would reduce unemployment levels by freeing jobs for native-born citizens. Doak instituted sweeping raids of public places and private residences in search of illegal immigrants to deport. The raids were also a psychological tactic, intended to coerce immigrants to leave the country voluntarily. Many "voluntary" *repatriados* had been born in the United States, but left to remain with their families or as the result of fear instilled by the raids and the increasing anti-immigrant sentiment that was sweeping the nation. Between 1929 and 1939, an estimated one to two million people left the United States through either deportation or voluntary repatriation, approximately 60 percent of whom were native-born US citizens.

Author Biography

Armando Cuitláhuac Amador Sandoval was born in 1897 in Zacatecas, Mexico. He served in various Mexican consulates throughout the United States in the late 1920s and early 1930s, including the one in New Orleans, Louisiana, where he held the post of consul from September 1931 until his move to San Diego in March 1932. Following his tenure in San Diego, Amador headed the Mexican consulate in Yokohama, Japan, from 1933 to 1935, after which he was stationed in Nanjing, China, and then Shanghai. He later held various posts in the Mexican government, including a stint in the Secretariat of Foreign Affairs, and represented Mexico in the Organization of American States from 1954 to 1960.

In addition to his work as a statesman, Amador published several works of fiction, including the novel *Bajo la marquesina* (*Beneath the Marquee*, 1925) and the short-story collection *Tres cuentos mexicanos* (*Three Mexican Tales*, 1944), as well as a book of poetry called *Tierra mojada* (*Wet Soil*, 1925). He died in 1970.

HISTORICAL DOCUMENT

The Government of Mexico, with the cooperation and aid of the Welfare Committee of this County, will effect the repatriation of all Mexicans who currently reside in this County and who might wish to return to their country.... Those persons who are repatriated will be able to choose among the States of Sonora, Sinaloa, Nayarit, Jalisco, Michoacán, and Guanajuato as the place of their final destination, with the understanding that the Government of Mexico will provide them with lands for agricultural cultivation... and will aid them in the best manner possible so that they might settle in the country.

Those persons who take part in this movement of repatriation may count on free transportation from San Diego to the place where they are going to settle, and they will be permitted to bring with them their furniture, household utensils, agricultural implements, and whatever other objects for personal use they might possess.

Since the organization and execution of a movement of repatriation of this nature implies great expenditures, this Consulate encourages you... to take advantage of this special opportunity being offered to you for returning to Mexico at no cost whatever and so that... you might dedicate all your energies to your personal improvement, that of your family, and that of our country.

If you wish to take advantage of this opportunity, please return this letter... with the understanding that, barring notice to the contrary from this Consulate, you should present yourself with your family and your luggage on the municipal dock of this port on the 23rd of this month before noon.

Document Analysis

This letter, written by Mexican consul Armando C. Amador on behalf of the Mexican government, begins by establishing that the offer of repatriation assistance is being made primarily by "the Government of Mexico," and San Diego's Welfare Committee is simply lending its "cooperation and aid." As increasing numbers of Mexicans chose to leave the United States voluntarily, whether out of fear or financial hardship, the Mexican government began to offer repatriation assistance, motivated partly by the desire to reclaim the immigrant population lost to the United States.

Amador's letter offers free transportation for "all Mexicans who currently reside in this County and who might wish to return to their country," emphasizing both Mexico's desire to receive and welcome repatriates and the Mexican government's policy that US residents of Mexican descent are still considered Mexican nationals, regardless of their place of birth. The letter also promises free agricultural land for repatriates, implying that their residence in Mexico is intended to be permanent, as such land requires a lengthy period of time to cultivate.

In addition to free transportation for repatriates and their families from San Diego to their choice of six destinations—the states of Sonora, Sinaloa, Nayarit, Jalisco, Michoacán, and Guanajuato—the letter also promises transportation for "their furniture, household utensils, agricultural implements, and whatever other objects for personal use they might possess" as well. This offer may have served to preempt protests from some that they did not have the financial means to relocate. By encouraging repatriates to take their work tools, it also allows them to begin work immediately upon reaching Mexico.

Amador implores the recipients of this letter to accept the offer, counseling that they are encouraged "to take advantage of this special opportunity being offered to you for returning to Mexico at no cost whatever," so that once there, all their energy could be devoted to the "personal improvement" of themselves, their families, and their country. This, again, implies the intended permanence of the relocation. Because most of the repatriates were young families, typically headed by the father or another male relative, the repatriation plan would ensure that the children of these families, many of whom were rightful American citizens by birth, would nonetheless grow up in Mexico and feel a sense of belonging there, as well as one of obligation.

Essential Themes
This letter from the Mexican consulate in San Diego provides assurances of the full backing and support of the Mexican government. While perhaps made in good faith, these promises were not fulfilled; instead, repatriates faced discrimination from many native-born Mexicans, while the government did not have the financial or bureaucratic resources to live up to its guarantees.

One charge leveled against Mexicans and Mexican Americans in the United States was that they were receiving disproportionate amounts of government aid, making them a burden on the state. Ironically, while this was untrue, widespread efforts to scare employed immigrants out of their jobs caused them to seek aid that they would not otherwise have needed. Unfortunately, this cycle—the threat of deportation, abuse, and loss of employment—left these same people susceptible to further coercion to repatriate. Numerous newspapers and political figures assured the public that once Mexican immigrants were removed, unemployment numbers would drop, and the crisis would be all but over.

What this document displays is the instability of the supposed rights granted by US citizenship for those individuals whose ethnic background is considered insufficiently white. Like the Japanese Americans forced into internment camps during World War II, Mexican Americans faced exclusion from the land of their birth based on nothing more than their family's country of origin.

—*Jennifer Henderson Crane, PgDip*

Bibliography and Additional Reading
Frame, Craig Steven. "History." *Mexican Repatriation: A Generation between Two Borders*. California State U San Marcos, 2009. Web. 6 June 2014.

Guerin-Gonzales, Camille. *Mexican Workers and American Dreams: Immigration, Repatriation, and California Farm Labor, 1900–1939*. New Brunswick: Rutgers UP, 1994. Print.

Hoffman, Abraham. *Unwanted Mexican Americans in the Great Depression: Repatriation Pressures, 1929–1939*. Tucson: U of Arizona P, 1974. Print.

McKay, Robert R. "Mexican Americans and Repatriation." *Texas State Historical Association*. Texas State Hist. Assn., 15 June 2010. Web. 6 June 2014.

"What Happened during the Repatriation of Mexicans from San Diego?" *San Diego Mexican & Chicano History*. San Diego State U, 7 Nov. 2011. Web. 6 June 2014.

The Hurricane of 1932 in Puerto Rico

Date: July 1, 1933
Author: James Rumsey Beverley
Genre: report

Summary Overview
In September 1932, a massive hurricane, also known as the San Ciprián hurricane, struck the coast of Puerto Rico. Ten months later, the governor of Puerto Rico, James R. Beverley (1894–1967), issued an official report of the course of events, damage, and numbers reflecting the cost of the hurricane, including loss of life, agriculture, and livestock as well as costs related to property damage. This report, which was addressed to Secretary of War George Henry Dern (1872–1936), served as a thorough breakdown of how the crisis was handled, what offices became involved, and the extent of Governor Beverley's dedication to the island of Puerto Rico.

Defining Moment
The hurricane of 1932 ravaged a third of Puerto Rico during what many historians consider the worst year of the Great Depression. In his report, Governor Beverley estimated that the storm caused more than $35.5 million worth of damage to the island and affected nearly 77,000 families. Fatalities at the time of the report held at 257, but the report notes that number did not include individuals who died later as a result of injuries sustained during the storm.

Governor Beverley's report is thorough in its description of the groups that organized to provide relief for families. The 1932 storm came on the heels of another devastating hurricane that tore through the island in September 1928. That storm carried more intense winds and affected a much wider area of Puerto Rico, but it incurred less damage than the 1932 hurricane.

Beverley outlined the agencies that were enlisted to assist in preparing the island for the storm, stating that a flag system was in place in the capital city of San Juan and in local areas in order to notify the residents of the approaching storm. Beverley proudly affirmed that he believed "every inhabitant of the Island knew of the hurricane's approach. . . . No one was caught without ample time to make adequate preparations." There were procedures in place to reach and warn as many residents as possible, thereby reducing the amount of damage done to the island and the loss of life. Such early prevention and awareness led to positive results, which were continued in his relief and rebuilding efforts following the storm.

Author Biography
Governor James Rumsey Beverley was born on June 15, 1894, in Amarillo, Texas. He served in the Army during World War I and began his political career as assistant attorney general of Puerto Rico in 1925, an office he held for two years. In 1927, he became attorney general of Puerto Rico and remained in that position until he was named acting governor in January 1932, the same year the hurricane would test his governing abilities.

Of the fifteen non-native Puerto Rican governors between 1900 and 1952, Beverley was the only one fluent in Spanish. During his relatively short term in office, which ended in July 1933, he not only faced the devastation brought by the San Ciprián hurricane, but he also dealt with the end of Prohibition on the island and was embroiled in a dispute over his support of birth control, a controversial issue for the primarily Roman Catholic Puerto Rican population.

Beverley's term as acting governor ended July 1, 1933. He chose to stay on the island to practice law and was involved with several local committees. He returned to his native Texas in the 1960s, settling in Austin, where he lived until his death in 1967 at the age of seventy-three.

HISTORICAL DOCUMENT

The most important event during the year under consideration, from the standpoint of the welfare of the People of Puerto Rico was the terrific hurricane which ripped its way across the northern half of the Island during the night of September 26–27, 1932, laying waste approximately one-half of the Island. This hurricane is known locally as "San Ciprián", from the saint's day upon which it occurred; and while the area covered was not so wide as that covered by the hurricane of September 13, 1928, nor was the estimated wind velocity as high, nevertheless the damage done in the area covered was much more severe than in 1928. The center of the storm entered Puerto Rico between Ceiba and Fajardo and passed in a generally western direction veering slightly north and left the Island somewhere between Dorado and Arecibo, and then continued practically along the coast of the Island past Aguadilla.

Warnings of the approach of the storm were received early on the morning of September 26, and all mayors of municipalities and police stations throughout the Island were notified at once in order that preliminary arrangements might he made to safeguard lives and property. A further warning was sent to all police stations and municipalities at four o'clock in the afternoon. At the beginning of the hurricane season the Governor had instructed the mayors to organize emergency committees in each municipality, and to give wide publicity to a plan whereby official information from the Governor's office as to any hurricane warnings would be communicated to the people by signal flags to be flown from the Cathedral and City Hall in each town. This plan functioned perfectly. I believe it is safe to say that every inhabitant of the Island knew of the hurricane's approach before noon; certainly no one was caught without ample time to make adequate preparations.

During the day, the Governor called a meeting of the Chief of Insular Police, the Adjutant General of the National Guard, the Commissioner of Health, the Commissioner of the Interior, the President of the Senate, the Manager of the Puerto Rican Chapter of the American Red Cross, and a few other prominent citizens, to take preliminary steps for handling any situation which might arise. The National Guard was instructed to be in readiness, the Commissioner of the Interior was directed to mobilize road overseers and workmen in order to reestablish communications immediately after the passage of the storm, and the police were given instructions to centralize people in the strongest buildings wherever it was thought necessary. The headquarters for all activities were maintained in the Governor's office.

By 11 o'clock at night telephone and telegraph communication to San Juan from the eastern end of the Island was out entirely and the storm was raging in full fury. The climax of the storm reached San Juan shortly after midnight, and by three o'clock in the morning the force of the wind at San Juan had died down considerably. The force of the wind was tremendous, and impossible to describe.

At daylight I drove out through San Juan, Hato Rey and Rio Piedras and along the road toward Caguas, as far as it was opened. The work of the Department of the Interior and of the police in opening roads and restoring communications cannot be praised too highly. Many of these men left their own homes in ruins, their families shelterless, to report for work before daylight and get the lines open. The police were active all during the storm and it is no exaggeration to say that the loss of life would have been much heavier had it not been for their splendid work. The activity of the Department of the Interior can be judged from the fact that shortly after dawn the main road from San Juan toward Caguas was passable to about one kilometer beyond Rio Piedras. At that time, of course, San Juan was completely isolated; it was not known whether the storm had swept the entire Island or not, and the spectacle presented in San Juan, Hato Rey and Rio Piedras was extremely disheartening. Hundreds of houses were blown away entirely, roads and streets were a mass of debris, all light and telephone poles and wires were down, trees were uprooted everywhere and even strong houses had suffered severely through losing roofs and doorways and windows.

The National Guard was ordered into immediate service and distributed over the storm-stricken area. In all of the towns prisoners and volunteer workers went to work clearing streets. As the day wore on, the injured began to be brought in from the country and reports of the death toll and of the injuries mounted. The Red Cross immediately established feeding stations and within twenty-four hours supplies, both medical and food, had either arrived at the principal towns in the storm-covered area, or were on the road.

During the day of September 27, the Governor's Secretary, Mr. Woodfin L. Butte, was directed to take advantage of the offer of the Pan-American Airways and to make a flight over the eastern part of the Island in an attempt to delimit the storm area and determine the approximate percentage of damage to houses and buildings. On the following day the Governor, with his Military Aide Lieut. William G. Caldwell, made another flight from San Juan westward as far as Mayagüez in order to determine the damage and limits of the storm in that area. By these two flights the entire northern half of the Island was covered and information as to the relative situation of the different municipalities was available much more quickly than would it have been possible had we waited for reports brought overland. We were also thus enabled to check up on exaggerated reports which came in from some towns which had been only lightly hit.

On September 27, a preliminary citizens' meeting was called for the purpose of forming a Hurricane Relief and Rehabilitation Commission to cooperate with the Red Cross and to take such other steps as might be considered necessary. At this meeting, Dr. Jose Padín, Commissioner of Education, was selected Chairman of the Executive Committee, Hon. Pablo Berga, Judge District Court of San Juan, Secretary, and Mr. Frederick King, Treasurer. The other members of the Executive Committee were: Colonel George L. Byroade, 65th Infantry, and Chief Justice Emilio del Toro of the Supreme Court of Puerto Rico.

Two sub-committees were formed, one on Price Control, the chairmanship of which was given to Hon. Ira K. Wells, Judge of the United States District Court for the District of Puerto Rico, with whom were appointed Mr. Antonio Vicens Ríos and Hon. Jose Ramón Quiñones, Special Prosecuting Attorney at Large of the Insular Government. The other Sub-Committee was on Finance. The members of this sub-committee were: Hon. Luis Sanchez Morales, Chairman, Mr. Manuel González, Mr. Frederick King, Mr. Victor Braegger, Mr. Fred. Holmes, Mr. Emilio S. Jiménez, Mr. Diego Carrión, Hon. R. H. Todd, Mr. William H. Ferguson, Mr. P. J. Rosaly, Mr. Jaime Annexy, Hon. R. Sancho Bonet, Hon. R. Arjona Siaca, Mr. Enrique Calimano and Col. Raúl Esteves.

The Executive Committee and both of these sub-committees did excellent work. Prices of necessities were prevented from rising by the vigorous work of the Committee on Price Control and by the threat of the Governor to publish in every newspaper in the Island the names of every merchant who raised prices during the period of the emergency. The Finance Committee collected the sum of $74,998.09 to aid hurricane sufferers.

The Red Cross was designated as the agency in charge of food and shelter relief for the Committee, and the Department of Health was given charge of the care and hospitalization of the injured. All members of the committees and all officers of the Insular Government worked in the closest harmony and with the finest spirit of cooperation. The National Red Cross sent field representatives by air who aided greatly in the immediate emergency. So many persons aided so generously in the disaster relief work that it is impossible to call attention to each one by name.

As soon as radio station WKAQ was in shape to operate, the Governor broadcast an appeal to the people in general to make common cause in each municipality for the reconstruction of homes and for the clearing away of debris. Embodied in the radio address was the thought that due to the difficult economic situation in the continental United States, we must not and could not expect to receive such generous aid as we had received after the disaster in 1928. To say that the people of Puerto Rico in general responded to this appeal is to put it mildly, since as a matter of fact they demonstrated a splendid spirit from the very moment the storm ceased. Scarcely had the wind died down when throughout the storm stricken area people were at work everywhere with hammer and saw repairing, so far as they could, the damage caused by the hurricane. Naturally, the poor suffered most in the hurricane due to the flimsy construction of their houses and to the fact that the poor have no reserves against disaster. The Commanding Officer of the United States troops in Puerto Rico was especially active in relief work and placed all of the army supplies in the Island at the disposal of the relief committee and the Red Cross.

Dr. Jose Padín was instructed to use the teachers

of the Island in a survey to determine the property loss exclusive of damage to crops, and the Commissioner of Agriculture and Commerce, Hon. Edmundo D. Colón, was instructed to make a survey of the monetary damage to crops. The Insular police took care of reporting the number of persons killed and injured. As a result of the careful estimates made by the Department of Education, it was found that the total value of property loss through the storm, exclusive of damages to school houses and government buildings, and also exclusive of damages to crops, reached the total of $14,975,850. 06. The Commissioner of Agriculture and Commerce estimated damages to crops at approximately $20,000,000, while the estimated value of public-school property destroyed was $395,745 and the destruction of rented-school property amounted to $196,750; the total estimated damage to the Island of Puerto Rico through the storm thus reaching $35,568,345.06. The dead as an immediate result of the hurricane numbered 257 and over 4,820 persons were injured, many of them seriously. The number of injured who died later as a result of their injuries has not been determined.

Forty-nine municipalities were affected in a more or less serious way and according to the report of the Red Cross, 76,925 families were in actual distress for a greater or less period as a result.

All money collected by the Relief Committee was turned over to the Red Cross, except a small part used for immediate purchases of relief material. The emergency fund of the Insular Government, created by Act No. 33, approved April 28, 1932, proved its wisdom and worth. On the second day after the hurricane the Emergency Committee voted $40,000 to be spent by the Red Cross in immediate relief work and later from time to time other sums were appropriated for relief work as they were needed. The establishment of this fund was a wise measure and it may be said here in passing that the administration should resist any attempts to dissipate the moneys in this fund or to use the same for any purpose other than emergencies. The total amount used from the emergency fund as a result of the hurricane of September 26–27, 1932, was $164,285.12, including a loan of $50,000 to the Fruit Growers Cooperative Credit Association, which was used for straightening and re-setting citrus trees and for the purchase of fertilizer urgently needed as a result of the storm, and without which it is generally conceded the 1933 citrus fruit crop could never have been properly matured. This $50,000 was a loan and is believed to be amply secured.

The final report of the American Red Cross, Puerto Rico Chapter, is attached hereto as Appendix "A". Some details as to property loss will be found in the tables.

This severe hurricane, striking an Island just beginning to recover from the 1928 storm and during a time of world-wide depression had far-reaching effects upon agriculture, banking and government finance, and especially upon the condition of the laboring classes.

Statistics on Hurricane

Municipalities affected—49
Number of dwellings totally destroyed—45,554
Number of dwellings partially destroyed—47,876

Number of animals killed:
Horses—777
Cows—3,402
Goats—5,054
Pigs—13,282
Poultry—446,890
Total—496,405

Number of stores totally destroyed—1,256
Number of stores partially destroyed—1,533
Number of farm buildings totally destroyed—10,000
Number of farm buildings partially destroyed—1,992

Total value of property destroyed excluding schools and equipment:
Dwellings totally destroyed—$5,095,387.76
Dwellings partially destroyed—3,546,979.94
Furnishings destroyed—1,543,648.51
Personal effects destroyed—872,383.44
Value of animals killed—470,837.59
Stores totally destroyed—379,303.30
Stores partially destroyed—268,226.49
Farm building totally destroyed—1,650,105.48
Farm buildings partially destroyed—188,263.65
Miscellaneous property destroyed—960,713.90
Total value of property destroyed—$14,975,850.06

Summary of Approximate Agricultural losses on Account of the Storm of San Ciprián of September 26–27, 1932, on the Basis of the Information Received by the Department of Agriculture and Commerce to Date.

1. Sugar Cane:	**Tons of Sugar**	**Value**
Damage to cane based on an average price of $3.00 per quintal of sugar and an allowance of 50 cents for harvesting, shipping and selling expenses	142,850	$7,142,500
1% reduction in sugar yield on remaining crop	40,000	2,000,000
Extraordinary field expenses on 168,000 acres at $400 per acre		672,000
Estimated total of claims on insurance companies for damage to factories, outlying buildings, railroads, and laborers' houses		1,739,032
Total		$11,553,332
2. Coffee:	**Quintals**	**Value**
Crop loss (20.57%) at $20.00 per quintal, less cost of harvesting and processing, $5.00 per quintal	30,401	$456,015
Coffee trees at 20 cents per tree		1,485,965
Shade trees at $1.00 each		962,349
Temporary shade (bananas) 50% of value at 30 cents per stool		838,508
Total		$3,742,837
3. Citrus and Pineapples:	**No. of Boxes**	**Value**
Loss of packed boxes of U S. Nos. 1 and 2 fruit at about $1.00 per box (approximate production cost)	800,000	$800,000
Loss of boxes of cull fruit good for canning at 20 cents a box	250,000	50,000
Profit loss (an estimate) per crate shipped	800,000	400,000
Clearing of wreckage at $10.00 per acre		60,000
Loss of 6% of 300,000 trees, or 18,000 trees, at $10.00 per tree		180,000
Packing house, residences and other outlying buildings very approximately estimated at		195,000
Direct loss to crop of pines		55,000
New plantings		500
Crop retardation		165,000
Loss to laborers' houses not available		
Total		$1,905,500
4. Coconuts:	**Number**	**Value**
Zone A, palms destroyed at $4.00 each (41%)	101,295	$405, 180
Nuts lost (100%-15% salvaged) at $10.00 per thousand less $5.00 cost of harvesting	5,100,000	26,775
Total		$784,760
Zone B, palms destroyed (25%) at $4.00 each	83,710	334,840
Nuts lost (75%)	3,402,000	17,965
Zone C, loss negligible		
Total		$11,553,332
5.Tobacco:		**Value**
Barns destroyed		$738,500
Seed beds destroyed		13,250
Total		$751,750
6.Bees:		**Value**
Loss of 1,000 gallons honey		$2,085

Loss of 1,734 hives		5,194
Total		$7,279
7. Livestock:	**Value**	
Heads (cattle, horses, hogs)		
Total	$29,501	
8. Minor Fruits:		
Losses to dairy establishments have been heavy; but not reliable data fixing them are yet at hand		
Total	$1,666,627	

NOTE: The losses to coffee industrial plants and other establishments are negligible, for which reason no report is made on them. Those on laborers' houses are not reported upon for lack of reliable information.

Document Analysis
Governor Beverley explains in a preface to his report to Secretary of War George Henry Dern that, although he is no longer acting governor of Puerto Rico (he had been succeeded by Robert Haynes Gore), he nonetheless wishes to compile the Annual Report of the Governor, since "the most important event during the year" occurred while he was in office. It is unclear whether Beverley is obligated to submit the report, or if he feels it is his responsibility to do so. What is evident, however, is Beverley's dedication to the island and to the people of Puerto Rico. He says he utilized every agency and resource available to him as governor in order to prepare residents and businesses for the storm. His commitment to effectively monitor all official organizations in the cleanup and relief efforts is clear, and his description of the storm's aftermath shows how deeply the devastation affected him.

Beverley begins his official report noting that the storm is locally referred to as San Ciprián, "the saint's day upon which it occurred." He provides a general overview of the hurricane's intensity as compared to the more powerful, yet less devastating 1928 hurricane, and he notes the path that San Ciprián took across the island.

The next portion of the report is a detailed outline of the pre-storm preparations Beverley orchestrated, as well as the specific groups and government bodies that were charged with storm-related tasks. He notes that his office began hurricane safety preparation at the start of the hurricane season and that his instructions to municipal mayors to establish a hurricane warning system utilizing signal flags worked flawlessly during the September storm. He then explains that on the day the hurricane was due to make landfall, he called a meeting with local and national officials, and each organization head was given specific tasks geared toward protecting the safety of residents and property before, during, and after the storm. The governor's office was the official headquarters for all such activities.

Beverley recounts that by 11:00 pm on September 26, all telephone and telegraph communication was out, and "the storm was raging in full fury" with tremendous winds "impossible to describe." The following day he toured as much of the area as was accessible and remarks that "hundreds of houses were blown away entirely, roads and streets were a mass of debris . . . [and] light and telephone poles and wires were down." It is clear that he is shocked by the damage, yet he praises the efforts of the island's police and believes the death toll would have been much higher without their work.

Cleanup and rebuilding efforts were led by the National Guard and the Department of the Interior, which Beverley praises for "opening roads and restoring communication." The Red Cross was charged with providing food, shelter, and medicine. The Department of Health oversaw the care and hospitalization of the injured. Pan-American Airways transported Beverley and a member of his staff on two separate occasions to fly over the island, which allowed the governor to assess the damage much more quickly than if he had waited for reports to be brought overland.

The day after the hurricane hit, Beverley formed commissions, committees, and subcommittees comprised of citizens and members of the military as well as relief groups in order to begin to formulate ways that

Puerto Ricans could be helped and their island rebuilt. Also addressed was the matter of ensuring that the prices of what he terms "necessities" were fixed and not allowed to rise following the storm.

Throughout the report, Governor Beverley showers praise on every member of the local and national organizations that aided in relief efforts. It is evident, however, that without his commitment and dedication to his office and to the people of Puerto Rico and without his leadership abilities as governor, the short- and long-term effects of the hurricane would have been much more devastating.

Essential Themes
Beverley's report indicates that the systems put in place by both officials and civilians in 1932 were effective in mitigating the impact of the storm on the inhabitants of the island. In his report, Beverley wrote of the people of Puerto Rico who, before the hurricane subsided, already came together trying to repair what damage they could find. Once communication lines were restored, the local radio station served as a tool for communicating with everyone on the island.

With memories of the 1928 hurricane undoubtedly still fresh in the minds of many residents, compounded by the stress and worry the Depression elicited, the push to prepare and to assist were resonant themes at this time. Of particular concern were the individuals living in remote areas. The previous storm had brought with it several thousand cases of dysentery. However, because of the medical supplies and medical aid available, the hurricane of 1932 saw very few deaths from tetanus and only a single case of dysentery.

Hurricane San Ciprián led to significant loss of life and occurred in desperate times close on the heels of a previously devastating storm. However, government and community bodies, the military, and civilians alike did their best to prepare for the storm and came together to rebuild afterward, reducing the effects to the best of their ability.

—*Jennifer Henderson Crane, PgDip*

Bibliography and Additional Reading
Palm, Risa, & Michael E. Hodgson. "Natural Hazards in Puerto Rico." *Geographical Review* 83.3 (1993): 280–89. Print.
"The Public Health Aspects of the Hurricane of San Ciprián, September 26–27, 1932." *Libraria*, n.d. Web. 16 June 2014. PDF file.
Robles, Michelle. "Hardships in the Land of Enchantment: The Economic Effects of the Great Depression on the United States Territory of Puerto Rico." *University of South Florida Sarasota-Manatee*. Michelle Robles, 2010. PDF file.
Rodríguez, Havidán. "A Socioeconomic Analysis of Hurricanes in Puerto Rico: An Overview of Disaster Mitigation and Preparedness." *Hurricanes*. Ed. Henry F. Diaz & Roger Pulwarty. New York: Springer, 1997. 121–43. Print.

■ A New Deal for American Indians

Date: November 30, 1934
Author: John Collier
Genre: report

Summary Overview

With the passage of one act on June 18, 1934, US government policy toward American Indians underwent one of the most fundamental changes in the history of Indian-white relations. Though it did not come close to solving all of the issues faced by American Indian peoples, the Indian Reorganization Act changed the entire goal of American Indian policy. Commissioner of Indian Affairs John Collier proposed a thorough reform of federal Indian policy, ending the allotment of tribal lands into individual parcels, consolidating Indian land holdings, creating tribal governments, and instituting Indian courts. Collier believed strongly in cultural pluralism rather than assimilation of American Indians into white society, and personally lobbied the act (also called the Wheeler-Howard Act) through Congress. In his portion of the Department of the Interior's annual report, Collier outlined the changes contained in the act and the intended effects of the act.

Defining Moment

For most of the 1920s, federal American Indian policy continued as it had since the Civil War, namely, the forced conversion, relocation, and assimilation of American Indians, as well as the acquisition of their lands. However, events began to occur during the 1920s that would be the beginning of massive changes in the way American Indians were viewed by the federal government. Business interests wanted to have unhindered access to mineral and petroleum resources on Indian lands and reservations and sought to force Indians to assimilate into white American society and break up the reservation system. But there were some new reform voices during the 1920s, among which John Collier's was perhaps the loudest. The influence of this reformist approach to American Indian policy can be seen in a 1928 report titled *The Problem of Indian Administration*, also known as the Meriam Report, which outlined the directions federal Indian policy would eventually take under Collier, whom President Franklin D. Roosevelt appointed commissioner of Indian affairs when he took office in 1933.

Under Collier, the role of the Bureau of Indian Affairs (BIA) changed. The BIA now tried to help Indians retain their culture, and further, even commercialize it so that they could earn money through jewelry, pottery, baskets, blankets, and other items. Opposition to Collier's proposals was swift, vocal, and aggressive. Conservative white assimilationists said that the only future for the Indians was Christian assimilation into American life. Business interests that had leasing rights on the reservations opposed the land consolidation provisions. Some Indians themselves saw the tribal council system of government as another imposition from Washington that would displace traditional leaders and give an advantage to English-speaking, Christian Indians. Others saw Collier's concepts of cultural pluralism as naive and elitist. As a result of these discordant voices, the legislation that eventually passed, called the Indian Reorganization Act, was not the bill originally drafted. The Indian Reorganization Act did not fundamentally change the relationship between American Indians and larger American society, although it did curb some of the worst abuses. Its greater influence was the creation of Indian tribal governments with rights and responsibilities like the federal government.

The act gave tribes one year to hold a vote to decide if they wanted to adopt a constitution and set up tribal councils. Collier, sure of his goals and the means to achieve them, was confident that many tribes would see the benefits of the tribal council form of government. He concentrated on getting key reservations to approve the act, in an attempt to create a bandwagon effect. The report filed in November 1934, almost six months after the passage of the act, reflects Collier's ideal vision of the act and its ramifications for Indian country.

Author Biography

John Collier was born in Atlanta, Georgia, in 1884. He had a long history of social reform activity by the time he was appointed commissioner of Indian affairs under President Franklin D. Roosevelt in 1933. Collier, in reaction to a tragic childhood and home life—his mother died of drug addiction and his father committed suicide before he was sixteen—rejected material pursuits and became a social reformer, working to improve the lives of immigrants in New York City during the early 1900s. He became civic secretary of the People's Institute, an organization set up to foster a sense of community among the city's immigrant population. Upon a visit to Taos, New Mexico, in 1920, Collier became aware of both the beauty of and problems facing American Indian cultures. He immediately became an advocate for the Pueblo tribes, who were facing legislation that would deprive them of much of their land. In 1923, he founded the American Indian Defense Association and was instrumental in the promotion of the findings of the Meriam Report, which brought Indian issues to public attention. He served as commissioner of Indian affairs from 1933 until 1945.

HISTORICAL DOCUMENT

The Wheeler-Howard Act, the most important piece of Indian legislation since the eighties, not only ends the long, painful, futile effort to speed up the normal rate of Indian assimilation by individualizing tribal land and other capital assets, but it also endeavors to provide the means, statutory and financial, to repair as far as possible, the incalculable damage done by the allotment policy and its corollaries....

The repair work authorized by Congress... aims at both the economic and spiritual rehabilitation of the Indian race. Congress and the President recognized that the cumulative loss of land brought about by the allotment system, a loss reaching 90,000,000 acres—two-thirds of the land heritage of the Indian race in 1887—has robbed the Indians in large part of the necessary basis for self-support. They clearly saw that this loss and the companion effort to break up all Indian tribal relations had condemned large numbers of Indians to become chronic recipients of charity; that the system of leasing individualized holdings had created many thousands of petty landlords unfitted to support themselves when their rental income vanished; that a major proportion of the red race was, therefore, ruined economically and pauperized spiritually....

Through 50 years of "individualization," coupled with an ever-increasing supervision over the affairs of individuals and tribes so long as these individuals and tribes had any assets left, the Indians have been robbed of initiative, their spirit has been broken, their health undermined, and their native pride ground into the dust. The efforts at economic rehabilitation cannot and will not be more than partially successful unless they are accompanied by a determined simultaneous effort to rebuild the shattered morale of a subjugated people that has been taught to believe in its racial inferiority.

The Wheeler-Howard Act provides the means of destroying this inferiority complex, through those features which authorize and legalize tribal organization and incorporation, which give these tribal organizations and corporations limited but real power, and authority over their own affairs, which broaden the educational opportunities for Indians, and which give Indians a better chance to enter the Indian Service.

Document Analysis

In his commissioner's report for the fiscal year 1934, John Collier sought to describe the situation in Indian country and what his signature piece of legislation, the Indian Reorganization Act, would do to improve the lives of American Indian people across the nation. Even before the IRA was passed, Collier was working to reform the BIA and federal Indian policy as a whole. He abolished the Board of Indian Commissioners, which sought to assimilate Indians into mainstream American life. He convinced Interior Secretary Harold Ickes to temporarily end the policy of allotting tribal land to individual Indians, which had resulted in the passage of two-thirds of tribal land into non-Indian hands, until he could get the IRA passed. He also cancelled the debts owed by many tribes to the federal government, a necessary precondition for any degree of tribal government autonomy.

Finally, in June 1934, the Wheeler-Howard Act was passed by Congress and signed by President Roosevelt. Though many BIA officials, attached to the agency's long-held goal of assimilation of American Indians, disagreed with Collier's reforms, Collier put the end of allotment and assimilation front-and-center in his description of the act. Not only was the policy of assimilation going to end, but means of repairing the damage to the Indian land base also became a priority. Cultural pluralism replaced assimilation as the aim of the BIA. Whereas individual land parcels encouraged assimilation, consolidating tribal land encouraged the revival of Indian cultures, as well as—it was hoped—providing the tribes with a means of self-support. Thanks to the policy of assimilation, Collier argues, "the Indians have been robbed of initiative, their spirit has been broken, their health undermined, and their native pride ground into the dust." Collier asserts that the act provides the means not only to provide for the tribes financially through giving them a degree of sovereignty and restoring as much land as possible, but even more importantly, that the act, by encouraging cultural pluralism, will restore the Indians' spirit and empower them to oversee their own affairs.

Essential Themes

After the IRA was passed, Collier worked to convince key reservations to approve the act. By the completion of the one-year voting period, 181 tribes had accepted the IRA and set up tribal councils, and seventy-seven tribes had rejected it, most notably the Navajo, who had the largest reservation in the country. A few tribes, such as the Hopi, divided into factions over IRA reforms. Those Hopis who did go along with the IRA were led largely by progressive factions of the tribe, whereas many traditionalists opposed the IRA. This struggle between accepting a federally proposed government that gives a degree of sovereignty and holding to traditional tribal government forms continues in some tribes still.

In the end, the Indian Reorganization Act has had relatively positive effects, restoring lands that tribes had lost in 1920s, giving the tribes greater autonomy and authority, and ending assimilationist policies in place since the 1890s. In assessing the relative success or failure of the IRA, some have noted that the act failed to attain some of Collier's idealistic goals, which he set out in his commissioner's report. Perhaps this is understandable, considering the fact that some of the more controversial, sweeping aspects of Collier's reform platform were stricken from the proposed bill before it was passed by Congress.

But perhaps the most trenchant criticism is that it did not end the poverty many tribes experienced as a part of reservation life. The IRA's goals of economic development and the restoration of tribal self-determination were not met by the IRA itself. Economic development proceeded at a pace that was glacial at best, as Congress allocated little money to the effort. Collier's goal of self-determination for the tribes was short circuited as soon as he left office, as a new group of "reformers" sought once again to force assimilation of Indians into American society, this time by the disastrous "termination" policy. It was not until the late 1960s and early 1970s, and the advent of the Red Power movement, that Indian self-determination would become a priority for the federal government. But none of these reforms dealt with one of the basic problems pointed out in the Meriam Report: the failure of the federal government to honor the treaties it had signed with the tribes.

—Steven L. Danver, PhD

Bibliography and Additional Reading

Collier, John. *From Every Zenith: A Memoir; and Some Essays on Life and Thought*. Denver: Sage, 1963. Print.

Deloria, Vine, Jr., & Clifford M. Lytle. *The Nations Within: The Past and Future of American Indian Sovereignty*. New York: Pantheon, 1984. Print.

Hauptman, Lawrence M. "The Indian Reorganization Act." *The Aggressions of Civilization: Federal Indian*

Policy since the 1980s. Ed. Sandra L. Cadwalader & Vine Deloria, Jr. Philadelphia: Temple UP, 1984. 131–48. Print.

Kelly, Lawrence C. *The Assault on Assimilation: John Collier and the Origins of Indian Policy Reform.* Albuquerque: U of New Mexico P, 1983. Print.

Philp, Kenneth R. *John Collier's Crusade for Indian Reform, 1920–1954.* Tucson: U of Arizona P, 1977. Print.

■ Indians at Work

Date: June 1934
Author: John Collier
Genre: editorial; article

Summary Overview

Much of what Commissioner of Indian Affairs John Collier did in 1933 and early 1934 set the stage for broader reforms of the federal government's relationship with American Indian nations. Collier wanted to see a radical change in the focus and goals of the Bureau of Indian Affairs (BIA)—from doing everything it could to assimilate American Indians into mainstream society, to preserving and celebrating the cultural diversity represented by American Indian peoples. This change, which took the form of the Indian Reorganization Act (IRA), was not easily accomplished, and many people opposed Collier's tactics as well as his overall aims. One way that Collier sought to convince people of the morality of his cause was to write articles that appeared in national periodicals, outlining his reform agenda. His June 1934 article in *Survey Graphic* was published just as the congressional debates over the IRA were coming to a head.

Defining Moment

Collier used the case of the Navajo to illustrate his point about the need for more effective tribal governments. Though he used them as a positive example of a tribal government cooperating with a federal livestock reduction program, he truth was a bit more complex. By the time Collier took office, the number of livestock held by the Navajo, combined with the natural erosion and drought cycles of the region, had taken a heavy toll on the rangelands. The government feared that overgrazing and trampling hooves broke down the soils needed to support the grasses and that accumulations of silt from the reservation's runoff threatened the functioning of Boulder Dam, farther down the Colorado River. Regardless of the economic and environmental arguments behind the ensuing livestock reduction, the program's cultural effects on the Navajo had a dramatic impact on the relationship between the Navajo and the federal government.

Navajo viewed sheep and goat herds as extensions of their family in addition to being symbols of wealth, success, and social prestige. Though Collier portrayed great cooperation between the Navajo Council and the government, the way that collaboration was obtained was by tying their cooperation with stock reduction to the success of pending legislation regarding the extension of reservation boundaries, the availability of relief programs needed during the Great Depression, and improvements to reservation infrastructure. In the end, the Navajo Council was forced to pass the stock reduction requests even though they were fully aware of the social and economic impact the program would have on tribal members. The number of stock owned by poorer Navajo was reduced to the point that their subsistence was threatened. Further, the cultural function of the herds in Navajo society was not considered, and many Navajo reacted emotionally for many years to what they saw as a unilateral federal action.

The role of the BIA changed with the IRA (also called the Wheeler-Howard Act), as the agency began working to help Indians retain their culture rather than actively suppressing it. Collier needed to convince people of the efficacy of his cause because opposition to his plan was vocal. Assimilationists strongly believed that the only future for the Indians was assimilation into American life. Business interests that had leasing rights on the reservations feared strengthened tribal governments with greater control over Indian land. Some Indians also opposed the tribal council system of government proposed by the IRA because it would displace traditional leaders and governmental systems.

Author Biography

John Collier was born in Atlanta, Georgia, in 1884. He had a long history of social reform activity by the time he was appointed commissioner of Indian affairs under President Franklin D. Roosevelt in 1933. Collier, in reaction to a tragic childhood and home life—his mother died of drug addiction and his father committed suicide before he was sixteen—rejected material pursuits and became a social reformer, working to improve the lives of immigrants in New York City during the early 1900s. He became civic secretary of the People's Institute, an organization set up to foster a sense of community among the city's immigrant population. Upon a visit to Taos, New Mexico, in 1920, Collier became aware of both the beauty of and problems facing American Indian cultures. He immediately became an advocate for the Pueblo tribes, who were facing legislation that would deprive them of much of their land. In 1923, he founded the American Indian Defense Association and was instrumental in the promotion of the findings of the Meriam Report, which brought Indian issues to public attention. He served as commissioner of Indian affairs from 1933 until 1945.

HISTORICAL DOCUMENT

Is it too late for Indian tribes, wards of the government, to demonstrate statesmanship? Have the Indians still a race to run?

The twelve months behind, even the five years behind, have supplied, for the Indians as a whole, merely the beginnings of a possible answer. Whether (ignoring the question of their capacity) the Indians shall be allowed to try to run their race at all, is still an unanswered question. It is discussed below. But let us start at the point of clearest evidence and greatest hope.

That point is the Navajo tribe and the Navajo regional plan. Forty-five thousand Indians, pure bloods and mostly non-English-speaking; in their religion, pre-Columbian; a nomad desert tribe, occupying nearly twenty-five thousand square miles of desert land of wild, somber and splendid beauty. They have multiplied nearly fourfold in seventy years. Their flocks have multiplied faster. They overpopulate and congest their barren range, and their sheep and goats desperately overgraze it. Their material standard of living very low indeed, their psychical standard is high, their *elan vital* is irrepressible. They are esthetes, adventurers, gamblers, sportsmen and nature-mystics. They have not the peasant's submissiveness to work, nor the bourgeois's idolatry toward it.

And suddenly the Navajos have been faced with a crisis which in some aspects is nothing less than a head-on collision between immediate advantages, sentiments, beliefs, affections and previously accepted preachments, as one colliding mass, and physical and statistical facts as the other.

The crisis consists in the fact that the soil of the Navajo reservation is hurriedly being washed away into the Colorado river. The collision consists in the fact that the entire complex and momentum of Navajo life must be radically and swiftly changed to a new direction and in part must be totally reversed.

And the changes must be made—if made at all—through the choice of the Navajos themselves; a choice requiring to be renewed through months and years, with increasing sacrifices for necessarily remote and hypothetical returns, and with a hundred difficult technical applications.

Nor is the burden of sacrifice an equal one; indeed, those Navajos, individuals and families, who have the greatest power to prevent the collective sacrifice from being made are the ones whose uncompensated individual sacrifice must be greatest.

It is the Navajos' past which has made their virtues. Their past still is, psychologically, their present. These virtues, aggressive and yet attractive and appealing, must not die from the new order which has suddenly become a matter of life or death. Yet can they live on? For human qualities are institutional products. The question is intense with sociological as well as with human interest.

About ten months ago, a joint committee of the Departments of Agriculture and Interior described the crisis and charted the emergency program. Soil erosion, they found, due to extreme overgrazing, had totally destroyed several hundred thousand acres of the Navajo range. It had seriously damaged millions of acres more. It was advancing not in arithmetical but in geometrical progression, and in fifteen, perhaps twenty years the Navajo reservation would be changed to a divinely painted desert and the Navajos would be homeless on the earth.

Whereupon, last July, the Navajo tribal council and two thousand other Navajos were brought together at Fort Wingate, New Mexico. With technical detail, through interpreters and endless hours of discussion the facts were supplied them. And the condition precedent to an ultimate saving of the soil was stated with no sparing of words That condition was a sacrifice of hundreds of thousands of their sheep and goats. But in addition there must be a planning of economic use for the whole reservation; range control, with redistribution of range privileges; an intensive revival of subsistence farming, irrigated and dry; a recasting and diminution of the road-building program; the fencing of areas of the range for soil experimentation, with total removal of stock from these areas; and erosion engineering and re-vegetative operations, under time pressure, throughout the wide region.

Nor could government funds pay for all the needed innovations. The Navajos themselves must pay, in labor and money.

The Navajo reservation is being washed into the Boulder Dam reservoir. That reservoir's rate of silting has been computed upon a static erosion rate which is but a fraction of the present and speeding-up rate. Hence; Southern California, as well as New Mexico and Arizona, is involved with the Navajos in their crisis. Actually, two thirds of the silt being fed to Boulder Dam is washed from the Navajo lands.

Mandatory sheep and goat reduction, mandatory range control, federal dominance over the Navajos' present and future program, are already possible in law and might be justified from the standpoint of national necessity.

But the Navajos were expressly and formally told that compulsion would not be used. This problem was their own and they, not the government, must do the things necessary to its solution. Profound recasting of the economic and social life of a people must be sought through knowing consent of the people and must be forced through their own will, or it must fail.

How did the Navajos respond? The tribal council adopt the program, with the proviso that it must go by referendum to the whole Navajo people through those local "chapters" which are the ultimate units of Navajo government. The tribe adopted the program at this referendum.

Again, after four months, a more drastic and more fast-moving program went before the council, was by it submitted to the people and was adopted. The Navajos through this decision surrendered ninety thousand of their sheep.

And again, after four months, a yet more drastic program was submitted. It called for the immediate sacrifice of 50,000 Navajo goats, and for coordinate adjustments that will cut the total of Navajo flocks by much more than one third. The cost of this latest stock reduction will be $225,000; the government does not undertake to pay the bill and the Navajos themselves are proposing to pay it, dependent on a government loan to the tribe. This latest sacrifice was adopted by referendum and confirmed by the tribal council in early April.

Meantime, the positive tasks of erosion control are well under way. The technical direction is being supplied by the Soil Erosion Service of the Department of the Interior. The Navajos are themselves carrying out the projects. In February, at Washington, the Carnegie Institute presented a photographic display showing erosion as a menacing condition threatening many parts of the United States. The exhibit climaxed with photographs of model erosion-control operations. The pictures bore no local designations, but they were photographs of the engineering works not merely built with Navajo hands but planned, practically in their entirety, by the Navajos. Four hundred Navajos had worked at the projects, assisted by only two white men.

I do not believe that any white community in the United States would have met a complicated and profound, urgent challenge, entailing the upset of widely distributed but unequal vested property interests, with the spirit, the audacity and the resourcefulness which the Navajo tribe has shown. Be it remembered that the Navajos are illiterates, in the main, and speak only the Navajo language, in the main And that the women are in most cases the owners of the goats and sheep; and that goats and sheep are viewed by the Navajos emotionally, all but as human children.

Let me quickly sketch the social program, going beyond erosion and range control, now being put into effect by the Navajos and by the government as their partner. First comes the drastic decentralization of Indian Service administration. The new Navajo capital (called Nee Alneeng, which means Center of the Navajo World) will be the Indian Service office for the whole reservation. Into it, whatever Washington authority can be legally transplanted will be transplanted. Under the pending Wheeler-Howard bill, discussed below, that will be substantially the whole authority of the federal government.

Here, likewise, will be the capitol of the tribe—the headquarters of the tribal council.

But beyond this headquarters, decentralization will be carried to the more than twenty-five sub-agencies, each the center of the locally organized Navajos and the administrative office for the school work, health work, agricultural extension, erosion, law-enforcement and other services of the government. These sub-agencies will be people's houses, and into them the formal schooling of the Navajos will be merged; indeed, if hopes are fulfilled there will be no formal schooling of the cloistrated or standardized order. All educational work will start from, and end in, the community group. The Navajo language will be used coordinately with English; Navajos and the government's workers with the Navajos will be bilingual in the future. The employee at these sub-agencies, and at the capital, will increasingly be (again, subject to the enactment of the Wheeler-Howard bill) Navajo Indians.

I have begun with this happy and inspiring example, and I will give one bright instance more because it testifies to what qualities there are in all Indians; and then I will pass to the gloomy side. For it will become evident that the Indians, now as before, are shrouded in gloom.

Last May, President Roosevelt decided that 14,000 Indians in all parts of the Indian country should be admitted to emergency conservation camps, to work on reforestation, on water development and erosion control. We were glad, but we were frightened. For the permission extended beyond the Pueblos, Pimas, Papagos and Navajos, famed for their sobriety and their industry. It reached to the Oklahoma, Dakota, Montana and Pacific Coast tribes—to those Indians reputedly not willing to work and reputedly demoralized. Would the camps become centers of drink, of debauchery? Would the Indians respond to their opportunity, and after they responded, would they work?

The sequel has been, I believe, the most impressive event in Indian affairs in these "lonesome latter years" of Indian life. The Indians thronged to the camps and projects. The camps became and have uniformly remained (there has not arisen even one exception) models of orderly, happy living. The work-projects, involving every kind of technical operation connected with forestry and with land conservation and use, have been pursued with better than mere industry—rather, with joyous ardor. Of all the technical and supervisory positions, more than 60 percent are now being efficiently filled by Indians, and the rank-and-file of the workers is 100 percent Indian. But the main significance is here: that the southwestern tribes have in no degree, in no particular, excelled those of the other regions.

These Indians of the allotted areas have been, at the camps, like creatures released from prisons and dungeons. Once more they have been allowed to live in groups, to work in groups and to work for a common good. They have furnished the solution of the so-called problem of the American Indian. Just in such a way, the Mexican peons of yesterday, now members of the recreated pueblos or *ejidos* of Old Mexico, have furnished the solution of the problem of the Indians south of the Rio Grande.

Because this article has space limits I shall now deal with only one other matter, the Wheeler-Howard Indian land and home-rule bill and, in conclusion, with the objection raised against this bill, namely that it tends toward an unfortunate segregation of the Indians.

Though this article will be published too late to have persuasive weight with the out-going Congress, a description of the Wheeler-Howard bill will serve to give a perspective of the Indian situation as a whole, and will tell what it is that the present administration seeks to do. President Roosevelt has thus summarized the intent of the bill:

In offering the Indian these natural rights of man, we will more nearly discharge the federal responsibility for his welfare than through compulsory guardianship that has destroyed initiative and the liberty to develop his own culture.

The bill primarily drives against two states of fact—an Indian landholding system fatal, sinister and dishonest, and a system of law which makes of the executive an unreviewable czar over Indian life.

The present system of land tenure was ushered in fifty-seven years ago with the passage of the General Allotment Act. Previous to this time the soil of the various Indian reservations was owned in common, title resting in the tribe. Every member of a tribe had the right to occupy as much land as he could beneficially use; his house and other improvements passed on to his heirs, but he could not alienate and dispose of a square foot of tribal soil. Those reservations which escaped allotment have today as much and frequently more land than they contained sixty years ago.

Through the General Allotment Act the government proceeded to break up the reservations, to attach to each Indian then living a tract of land as his individual property and throw the part of the reservations not used in this individual land distribution open to white settlement. Thus the Indian was to become an individualized farmer and assume all the white man's burden after a comparatively short "trust" period during which the privilege of mortgaging and selling his land was denied him.

After allotment the individualized land began to slip out of the Indian owners' hands at high speed. When the trust period expired or the Indian was declared "competent," he disposed of his land in short order, spent the proceeds and went to live with his relatives. And when an allotted Indian died, the usual impossibility to make an equitable partition of the land forced its sale not to Indians, but to those who had the money to buy, to the waiting white people. Thus allotment dissipated, continues to dissipate the Indian estate.

In 1887, the Indians were owners of 136,340,950 acres of the best land. In 1933 they were owners of 47,311,099 acres, of which a full 20,000,000 acres were desert or semi-desert. The surface value of the Indian-owned lands had shrunk 90 percent in these forty-six years. Of the residual lands, 7,032,237 acres (the most covetable of the remnant) were awaiting "knock-down sale" to whites—sale conducted by the government itself, usually without reference to Indian choice. And of the usable land still owned by the allotted Indians, a full three fourths was already possessed and used by whites under the allotment leasing system. Such land is tax-exempt, and the white lessees (cattlemen, sheep-men, farmers and grain corporations) reap the benefit of tax exemption. Since 1887, one hundred and fifty thousand Indians have been rendered totally landless; and existing law—the practices mandatory or administratively inescapable under it—insured the dispossession of the remaining allotted Indians within the present generation.

What the Indians themselves have done or have left undone has been a negligible factor in the above-stated record. The allotment law and system intends and compels the transfer of Indian title to whites. Less swift than treaty-breaking with Indians or than outright rape of Indian lands, but surer and cheaper, bloodless and silent, the allotment law has fulfilled the "civilizing" intentions of the government of 1887.

The facts of 1933 are the facts of today. I give some other facts of the workings and consequences of Indian land allotment.

The Indian lives in an ever-narrowing prison-pen of allotment until his last acre is gone, and then he is summarily cast out from federal responsibility. But the Indian service, hardly less than the Indian, lives, and endeavors to work, in a prison-pen of land allotment. Governmental appropriations into the millions each year, sorely needed for health service to Indians, for education, for relief, and for the economic rehabilitation of Indians, are of necessity diverted to the real-estate operations connected with the still-shrinking allotted lands. *Pari passu* with the swindling of the lands, the costs of administration rise. And there is no escape from these results under existing law.

I refer, of course, to the allotted areas, but these are all of the Indian country of Oklahoma and nearly all of the Indian country of Wisconsin, Minnesota, the Dakotas, Montana, Nebraska and Kansas, Wyoming, Oregon, Washington and California.

The allotment system fights against all the human services attempted for Indians. Two Oklahoma cases will serve as examples, chosen because the bitterest of the embittered opposition to the Wheeler-Howard bill comes from whites.

At the Kiowa and Comanche agency, the total government expenditure, school costs aside, is $80,000 a year. Of this total, only $15,000 can be used for health, relief, reimbursable loans, agricultural extension and all the other human services. Sixty-five thousand is required for the real-estate operations of the allotted lands. Meantime the lands inexorably pass to whites by government sale. About sixty of every hundred Indians in this jurisdiction are totally landless, all but a few are in poverty, and their needs for service are extreme. At most allotted jurisdictions, the proportion of the landless Indians is greater than at this one.

On its work other than schools, the Five Civilized Tribes agency of Oklahoma spends $300,000 a year. All except $60,000 of this total is devoured by the real-estate operations of the allotted lands. Of the 100,000 Five Tribes Indians, 72,000 are totally landless; the remaining lands are swiftly being forced into white ownership; and the per capita income of the Five Tribes, omitting oil and mineral royalties paid to a few individuals, is forty-seven dollars a year. These Five Tribes possessed, twenty-five years ago, 15 million acres of the best Oklahoma land; they now possess 1 1/2 million acres.

Subdivision of inherited allotments, on a hundred reservations, has proceeded to that point where an individual equity is fixed by subdividing, for example, the sum 5200 into the sum 114,307,200, and the government solemnly pays each heir the value of a postage stamp once a month. The heir possesses an equity in ten, thirty, or fifty separate allotments. Administration costs more than the total rental, even the total value of the lands. Not merely farming lands, but grazing properties and even forests have been fractionated to these vanishing dimensions, making impossible the working of their own assets by the allotees; and the fading Indian lands are dots within the sea of white ownership. Twenty-five years ago the areas were solidly Indian.

The Wheeler-Howard Bill centers in the land problem. The bill's forty-eight pages are their own explanation, but the principles can be stated in a few words. Under the bill, individual allotted titles may be exchanged for equitable rights in a community title. Use of the land, ownership of the improvements, ownership of the rental value of the land, and the right to use an equal area or value of land within the community estate, is safeguarded and made into an inheritable vested right. The physical allotments may be inherited so long as their subdivision does not reach the point of destroying their economic use.

Under the bill, reservation areas are to be marked out for ultimate consolidation into unbroken Indian holdings. The new land procedures will apply only inside these consolidated areas. To buy the white-owned tracts, and to purchase the Indian heirship lands for the communities, the bill authorizes $2 million a year. This grant will be used likewise for buying land on which homeless Indians will be colonized. In addition, submarginal lands, now being purchased by the government, will be furnished the Indian communities, and funds from the subsistence homestead appropriation will be used for experimental colonies.

Financial credits which is now practically denied the Indians, is essential to the Wheeler-Howard plan, and the bill establishes a revolving fund of $10 million, which will be a federal grant, allocated to the Indian communities to be used by them as a revolving loan fund, capitalizing the individual and group enterprises.

The bill forbids any and all allotment of lands hereafter, and forbids the sale of Indian lands to whites, and through many devices seeks to enable the Indians to repossess their lands now rented to whites and to become their own operators.

The so-called home-rule provisions of the Wheeler-Howard Bill are "geared" with the land provisions, but their application is more general than that of the land provisions. Under existing law the secretary of the interior and Indian commissioner practically are forced to stand as absolutists over the Indians. Usually their actions are exempt from court review. But they, in turn, are victims of the mandatory allotment system and of an appropriation and budgeting system which conceals facts and which freezes government moneys into out-moded and sometimes even fictitious uses, leaving Congress itself helpless to control the expenditures, while the Indian office is no less helpless and the Indian is kept in the dark.

The total effect of these above conditions has been to impose on the Indian service an extreme centralization at the Washington Office. The free movement of ideas, of experimentation and of local adjustment is impeded everywhere, and in the allotted areas is all but prohibited. There has been a wealth of bold effort and of truly creative initiative within the Indian Service during the last four or five years, and by "main strength and awkwardness," as it were, some of this innovation has been pushed through to the Indians' actual life in the two hundred reservations. But the autocratic and centralized system practically defies the human effort, and the best administration, whether from the headquarters or from the field, is as water poured into the labyrinthine sands of bureaucracy which is forbidden by law to reorganize itself.

The Wheeler-Howard Bill cuts through the tangle of legal compulsions and inhibitions and provides for a radical decentralization of the Indian Service. Indians may organize and become chartered for any of the tasks or interests of their own lives; their organization may be geographical or functional, according to their wishes or requirements. When organized, the chartered Indian communities become instrumentalities of the federal government. Doing less or more according to the facts of the innumerable variable cases, these communities in their fullest development may become wholly self-governing, subject only to Congress and the Constitution. Any function of Indian Service, with the appurtenant federal moneys, may be transferred to these communities. The communities in turn may enter into contract with states, counties and any other local institutions.

A special Indian civil service is created by the bill, and communities may appoint their qualified members for any position of local Indian service, and power of recall over local government employees is given to the communities.

The bill in its Title 2 broadens the authority for Indian educational work, and through a system of loans and scholarship grants opens the colleges and the professional and technical schools to Indian youth.

Title 4 of the bill sets up a Court of Indian Affairs, with functions ministerial as well as judicial, and brings the Indian Service and the Indian communities under the review of this court. Through this court the constitutional rights will be insured, including minority rights, religious rights and the due process of law in matters of life and property which are necessarily withheld from Indians under the present system.

I conclude with some necessary remarks directed to the only reasoned criticism which has been brought against the Wheeler-Howard Bill and the Roosevelt-Ickes Indian policy. The bill and policy, it is contended, make for racial segregation and would wall the Indians off from civilization and from modern opportunity. To meet the contention is to bring the Indian situation under a sociological searchlight.

Where the trend or drift of a race has gone in one direction—in the case of most of the Indians, downhill—for a hundred years more or less, there cannot be any sudden or easy reversal of the trend. Subtle and deep readjustments, sociological, psychological and even biological, take place within peoples; human beings make structural adaptations to the life-limiting environment. The prison psychosis would furnish an illustration.

Space limits forbid the pursuit of this analysis, but as a practical matter, the Indian Service task has to be visioned in relation to such facts as the following.

The extreme poverty of the Indians, which was recognized as a controlling factor by the Institute for Government Research in 1928, continues unrelieved. Indeed, with data greatly enriched, the fact of Indian poverty has become more impressive. The shrinkage of landholdings, due to allotment, actually is smaller than the shrinkage of capital funds. These have disappeared altogether, in the cases of scores of tribes.

Earned income and subsistence production have continued at an almost unbelievably low level. Only when the land system is examined do the facts become credible, especially in the light of the proved readiness of Indians to work, and their ability to work efficiently, as displayed in emergency activities during the past year.

The incomplete returns have now been tabulated from ten allotted areas in the six states of South Dakota, North Dakota, California, Kansas, Montana and Oklahoma. The studies were remade by competent investigators employed under a Civil Works grant. Case records were made for families containing 38,772 individuals. The per capita per year income was found to be $47.78, after excluding the oil and mineral royalties paid to a handful of individuals in these ten areas.

This per capita income—$47.78—represents the earned income and the lease money and the market value of goods produced or consumed. These Indians have consumed no more than $47.78 worth of goods in the year. The ascertained figure is higher, not lower, than it would be in an average year, because federal emergency expenditures, on works projects in the Indian country, were rising toward their peak during the time of the survey.

The poverty of the Indians contributes to their continuing morbidity and deathrates. The deathrate, taking the Indians as a whole, continues at twice the deathrate of the general population including the Negroes. Tuberculosis, with an Indian deathrate more than seven times the white, is not yet being controlled. Trachoma is uncontrolled although clinical treatment has been multiplied tenfold since 1925.

Less tangible, but no less important, are the registrations of economic inferiority in the mental and social reactions of the Indians. Between the elder and younger generations, suppressed or open conflict rages. Between the pure bloods and the mixed bloods, conflict rages. Between the allotted Indians and the government, conflict rages. Rarely, where these conflicts go on, are the causes understood by the Indians. The causes are objective and imminent, residing as they do in the allotment system, in the dictatorial and centralized Bureau management and in the segregation forced upon the Indians by their poverty and their under-equipment. But the conflicts, psychologically analyzed, are essentially neurotic conflicts—compensations, escapes, and rationalizations of misery. And in the allotted areas, it is largely out of the question to recapture and harness these neurotic energies for practical social tasks, because the tasks are forbidden by the law and the system.

The total effect of these and related conditions is to degrade the Indian social level, and the degradation goes steadily forward. The real "values" of the Indian are driven inward, insulated from world intact, and compelled to face toward remembered glory, remembered plenty and power. And assimilation, whether biological or social, becomes for Indians, with each passing year, an assimilation into still inferior levels of the white life.

The Indian Rights Association, in company with some of the Missionaries' fears the policies of Secretary Ickes' administration, and looks with doubt on the Wheeler-Howard Bill, on the ground, stated above, that the policies and the bill are working toward the segregation of Indians. I have stated the facts of Indian poverty because from any point of view they are controlling in the appraisal of the Indian situation, but also because they dispose, I believe, of the segregation argument. The Indians today are segregated by factors all-penetrating, infinitely more potent than mere geographical segregations could ever be. Their extreme poverty segregates them. Their inferiority status in law intensifies their segregation. Their infectious diseases segregate them. Their inferiority sentiment, elaborately planted at the center of their consciousness by deliberate governmental policy as well as by the unintended action of poverty, effectually segregates them.

Their ancient interests and loyalties, which are far from being extinct, are by these same conditions imprisoned, and denied the chance to partake in social action, to salvage themselves through development and change.

And the Indian, in his profounder psyche, is condemned to that which could be termed a social-psychic infantilism, a dream-escape to the social mother—that social mother who, to the Indian, is always his own tribe. Yet even this escape takes with it a conflict into the very heart of the Indian's life. Due to the rendering of the ancient values powerless by social segregation, insecurity and inferiority haunt even this inmost refuge or shrine.

The mechanisms and policies of the Wheeler-Howard Bill are, first and last, a prescription for bringing this Indian segregation to an end.

GLOSSARY

bourgeois: middle-class person

cloistrated: cloistered

ejido: an area of communal land

élan vital: life spirit or creative force

pari passu: hand-in-hand with

Document Analysis

Looking to convince skeptics that his plan to reform and create a sustainable future for American Indian tribes was the right way to go, John Collier took to writing articles in national publications. The article in the June 1934 issue of *Survey Graphic* contains a number of arguments, all leading to the conclusion that the Indian Reorganization Act is a much-needed reform that would create sustainable tribal nations through ending assimilation, reinforcing the land base of the tribes, and giving the tribes a working governmental system through the formation of tribal councils. Though Collier spends much of the article addressing cases that are seemingly unrelated to his main point, he attempts to convey to the American public that the Indians are not merely the remnants of a nomadic race, living in obscurity and not contributing to society. On the contrary, Collier asserts, they are already active partners in his reform efforts and would benefit even more if the IRA were passed by Congress and signed into law.

Collier begins by talking about the Navajo and how they have cooperated with federal efforts to deal with the soil erosion caused by an overabundance of livestock. Collier conveniently omits any discussion of the devastating toll that the livestock reduction program had on the Navajo, concentrating instead on the functioning of the Navajo Tribal Council in cooperating with the federal government. The argument seems to follow that, if a functioning government on the largest Indian reservation in the nation could cooperatively work with the federal government on the livestock problem, then such a government would be capable of handling much larger matters. Collier goes on to praise the spirited participation of American Indians in federal conservation work programs. If the American Indian people were capable of working in Great Depression–era work programs, he argues, they could be just as successful as whites when prosperity returned.

After the Navajo case study, Collier shows the negative impact of American Indian policy since the Civil War. The General Allotment Act of 1887 apportioned tribally-held lands to individual Indian landowners, selling the "surplus" lands to whites and reducing the total land owned by Indians by about two-thirds, he notes. The policy of allotment, instituted in 1887, worked to deprive Indians of their land base and, thus, their means of attaining economic prosperity. Collier argues that the IRA will address these land problems by ending allotment and seeking to augment the Indian land base. Further, Indians would benefit psychologically, by having an opportunity for prosperity that they had not had since their first contact with Euro-Americans.

Essential Themes

The Navajo case study and the IRA as a whole both had important legacies after the June 1934 article appeared and after Congress passed the IRA that same month. The IRA meant true reform to the goals of federal Indian policy. It ended the allotment program, it replaced the goal of assimilation with the goal of cultural diversity, and it created a tribal council system of government that could be instituted by any tribe that was willing to do so. By those counts it was a success, but it is ironic that Collier uses the Navajo as his primary example of the tribal cooperation that could be expected after the passage of the IRA.

The ill will the Navajo felt toward the government— a direct result of the stock reduction program—manifested as firm opposition to the IRA. Although the tribal council supported many of Collier's reforms, a large number of Navajo held Collier personally responsible for the stock reduction program. This resistance came to a head when the time came for the Navajo to vote on whether or not to accept the provisions of the Wheeler-Howard Act. When the referendum was held in June 1935, 98 percent of eligible Navajo voted to firmly reject the act. The Navajo were among the seventy-seven tribes that rejected the IRA, whereas 181 tribes accepted it.

—Steven L. Danver, PhD

Bibliography and Additional Reading

Collier, John. *From Every Zenith: A Memoir; and Some Essays on Life and Thought*. Denver: Sage, 1963. Print.

Deloria, Vine, Jr., & Clifford M. Lytle. *The Nations Within: The Past and Future of American Indian Sovereignty*. New York: Pantheon, 1984. Print.

Hauptman, Lawrence M. "The Indian Reorganization Act." *The Aggressions of Civilization: Federal Indian Policy since the 1980s*. Ed. Sandra L. Cadwalader & Vine Deloria, Jr. Philadelphia: Temple UP, 1984. 131–48. Print.

Iverson, Peter. Diné: *A History of the Navajo*. Albuquerque: U of New Mexico P, 2002. Print.

Kelly, Lawrence C. *The Assault on Assimilation: John Collier and the Origins of Indian Policy Reform*. Albuquerque: U of New Mexico P, 1983. Print.

McPherson, Robert S. "Navajo Livestock Reduction in Southeastern Utah, 1933–46: History Repeats Itself." *American Indian Quarterly* 22.1/2 (1998): 1–18. Print.

Philp, Kenneth R. *John Collier's Crusade for Indian Reform, 1920–1954*. Tucson: U of Arizona P, 1977. Print.

White, Richard. *The Roots of Dependency: Subsistence, Environment, and Social Change among the Choctaws, Pawnees, and Navajos*. Lincoln: U of Nebraska P, 1983. Print.

■ A Negro in the CCC

Date: August 1935
Author: Luther C. Wandall
Genre: article; memoir

Summary Overview

The Civilian Conservation Corps, or CCC, was a public-works program that employed unmarried, unemployed men from 1933 to 1942, during the worst years of the Great Depression. These men, who had to be between eighteen and twenty-five to qualify, were sent to perform unskilled manual labor jobs related to natural resources on federal and state land. More than three million young men were involved in this program over the course of its nine years, with its highest enrollment level at any given time around 300,000. Volunteers planted trees, cleared parks, built roadways and park buildings, and worked to mitigate soil loss and erosion. African American men were eligible to serve, and according to various estimates, from 200,000 to 350,000 enrolled in the CCC in its nine years. Facilities were initially integrated, then segregated, but for many young African American men, it was the only chance of having food, shelter, and a wage during the Depression, and the CCC also employed African American directors and staff. The CCC ran much like the military, with fines for poor work or bad behavior, but it was a desirable posting for young men and gave them valuable work experience and skills. In 1935, the African American periodical *The Crisis* published an account by New Yorker Luther C. Wandall, about whom no other information is available, detailing his experience working with the CCC.

Defining Moment

Public-works programs, such as the CCC, were part of President Franklin D. Roosevelt's New Deal. This term encompassed initiatives that provided individuals with work and support during the severe economic crisis of the Great Depression. Roosevelt had founded a similar organization while governor of New York and sent a proposal in March 1933 to create a national program for young men that would focus on "forestry, the prevention of soil erosion, flood control and similar projects." The CCC was jointly supervised by the federal Departments of War, Agriculture, Interior, and Labor, with special programs for veterans and American Indians. Officers from the Army Reserves supervised camps in military fashion, but there was no formal military training and no expectation of military service. Enrollees worked for a minimum of six months and could serve up to two years if they were not able to find outside employment.

CCC work camps were independent, often mobile units, able to feed, house, and entertain hundreds of young men. Since the greatest concentration of projects was in the West and South, while the greatest number of workers was in the East, they also required a network of enrollment camps near urban Northeast cities. As manpower moved West, the CCC was able to make real progress in conservation work, and it is credited with constructing nearly 3,500 fire lookout towers, laying 97,000 miles of fire roads, logging more than four million man-days fighting fires, and planting more than three billion trees.

African American participation in the CCC grew from 3 percent of total enrollment at the program's outset to nearly 11 percent, though it had been capped at 10 percent, roughly the same as the African American proportion of the population overall. Initially, CCC camps were integrated, though African Americans often had the least desirable facilities and jobs. As the CCC camps traveled through the country, including the deeply racially-divided South, these camps faced local hostility. In July 1935, the CCC became thoroughly segregated, despite the protestations of the National Association for the Advancement of Colored People (NAACP) and other civil rights groups. The CCC remained segregated for the rest of its existence, and there were 150 CCC companies of African American men.

In June 1942, in the face of another world war, funding was cut for the CCC, effectively abolishing it. Its legacy included the completion of countless projects for public benefit and the enrichment of the lives of millions of men, who were reasonably well fed and healthy, had gained work experience, and had traveled across the country in unprecedented numbers.

HISTORICAL DOCUMENT

During the two years of its previous existence I had heard many conflicting reports concerning the Civilian Conservation Corps, President Roosevelt's pet project. One boy told me that he almost froze to death one night out in Washington. Some said that the colored got all the leftovers. Others said that everything was all right. But my brother, who is a World War veteran, advised me emphatically: "I wouldn't be in anything connected with the Army."

So it was with some apprehension that I surveyed the postal card instructing me to see Miss A. at the Home Relief Bureau the following Friday. At this Bureau I signed a paper, of which I kept two copies, and the Bureau one. This paper asserted that I was "accepted for enrollment," and should report the following Monday "to U.S. Army authorities for further registration."

One thing I saw at the Bureau increased my apprehension. So many of the boys who appeared in answer to cards were excused because they had been "dishonorably discharged" in a previous enlistment. It was impossible to tell whether they were disappointed or not, but they were not always discreditable-looking persons.

According to instructions, I went Monday morning at 8 o'clock to Pier I, North River. There were, I suppose, more than 1,000 boys standing about the pier. And here I got another shock. Many of the boys carried suitcases. I had not been instructed that we would leave that day. But still, I reasoned, we would be given time to go home and tell our folks goodbye.

The colored boys were a goodly sprinkling of the whole. A few middle-aged men were in evidence. These, it turned out, were going as cooks. A good many Spaniards and Italians were about. A good-natured, lively, crowd, typical of New York.

At eight o'clock we were rapidly admitted to the pier, given papers and herded into the warehouse, out on the water. And here the "fun" began. A few boys were being admitted from time to time to a lower platform through a small gate in the center. And of course, everyone in that mob was anxious to get there.

At first there was a semblance of order. The men in charge of us formed us into companies of fifty as we came up. But suddenly a U.S. Army officer in full uniform entered the door. A mighty roar went up from the boys, who surged forward, evidently thinking that they could follow him. But the officer, a tall handsome fellow, moving with easy grace, completely ignored them, and passed on through.

With some effort we were finally forced back into a so-called line. But a newspaper photographer appeared. The line broke again, and after that confusion reigned for the most part.

There were no seats where we were. So I stood about until two o'clock before I finally got through that little gate. We answered questions, and signed papers, and then a group of us marched over to U.S. Army headquarters on Whitehall Street in charge of an Army officer.

Here we stripped for a complete physical examination. Then we were grouped into busloads. Each busload of 35 ate a meal at South Ferry before boarding the bus. This meal consisted of beans, pickles, bread, coffee and butter, and was eaten out of Army mess-kits.

So there I was, on a bus bound for Camp Dix, New Jersey, without having prepared or told anyone goodbye. Our bus was comfortable, and equipped with a radio, so the ride was a very enjoyable one.

Jim Crow at Camp Dix

We reached Camp Dix about 7:30 that evening. As we rolled up in front of headquarters an officer came out to the bus and told us: "You will double-time as you leave this bus, remove your hat when you hit the door, and when you are asked questions, answer 'Yes, sir,' and 'No, sir.'"

And here it was that Mr. James Crow first definitely put in his appearance. When my record was taken at Pier I, a "C" was placed on it. When the busloads were made up at Whitehall street an officer reported as follows: "35, 8 colored." But until now there had been no distinction made.

But before we left the bus the officer shouted emphatically: "Colored boys fall out in the rear. The colored from several buses were herded together, and stood in line until after the white boys had been registered and taken to their tents. This seemed to be the established order of procedure at Camp Dix.

This separation of the colored from the whites was completely and rigidly maintained at this camp. One Puerto Rican, who was darker than I, and who preferred to be with the colored, was regarded as pitifully uninformed by the officers.

While we stood in line there, as well as afterwards, I was interested to observe these officers. They were contradictory, and by no means simple or uniform in type. Many of them were southerners, how many I could not tell. Out of their official character they were usually courteous, kindly, refined, and even intimate. They offered extra money to any of us who could sing or dance. On the other hand, some were vicious and ill-tempered, and apparently restrained only by fear.

Southerners at West Point! Emotional, aristocratic, with refined features and soft blue eyes. And paradoxically they choose the Army for a career. Slaves to traditions and fetishes....

We were finally led away to our tents. And such tents! They were the worst in Camp Dix. Old, patched, without floors or electric lights. It was dark already, so we went to bed immediately, by candlelight. And since it was cold, we slept in most, and in some cases all, of our clothes.

The bedding was quite ample: four blankets, two sheets, and a pillowcase. But Camp Dix is a cold place, and the condition of our tents didn't help. Then, too, it was raining.

Next day we rose at 6:15; There was roll call and "mess." A few minutes later we were shocked to see snow falling, on April 16! The boys built a fire, so we were able to keep somewhat warm. Then there was another questionnaire, and more papers to sign.

Southerners Plentiful

By now only one thought occupied my mind: When do I leave this place? I understood that Camp Dix was only a replacement camp, and that we would be leaving, probably within a week. So you can imagine my feelings when an officer, a small quiet fellow, obviously a southerner, asked me how I would like to stay in Camp Dix permanently as his clerk! This officer was very courteous, and seemed to be used to colored people, and liked them. I declined his offer.

We slept six in a tent. And right here I might attempt to describe the class of young men I found myself with. Two things surprised me: that out of the whole crowd, I had known not one in New York, and that almost without exception they were of a very low order of culture. Such low ideals. Of course many were plainly ignorant and underprivileged, while others were really criminal. They cursed with every breath, stole everything they could lay hands on, and fought over their food, or over nothing at all.

That same day we got another complete physical examination, two vaccinations and one "shot." They were for typhoid fever, parathyroid and smallpox.

The following day, which was a Wednesday, we got our first clothes, a complete outfit. They were Army clothes, and fitted as well as could be expected. That afternoon we worked. I was on a truck hauling lumber. The next two days we sampled several different kinds of work, none of it very hard. We also heard a very edifying health lecture, chiefly on venereal diseases.

Food at Camp Dix was poor in quality and variety, and barely sufficient in quantity. A typical breakfast: boiled eggs, corn flakes, milk, bread, coffee, butter. Lunch: frankfurters, sauerkraut, potatoes, gravy, bread, apple-butter, coffee. Dinner: bologna, applesauce, potato salad, bread, coffee, cake.

We stayed at Camp Dix eight days. We were never told officially where we were going. Just before we boarded the train we were split into two companies. I was placed in Company Y.

The Ride was quite enjoyable. On through Jersey,

with the sun setting like a ball of fire on golden Delaware. Maryland, with night falling like a shroud.

We were taken to permanent camp on a site rich in Colonial and Revolutionary history, in the upper South. This camp was a dream compared with Camp Dix. There was plenty to eat, and we slept in barracks instead of tents. An excellent recreation hall, playground, and other facilities.

I am still in this camp. At the "rec" we have a radio, a piano, a store called a "canteen," a rack of the leading New York papers, white and colored, as well as some from elsewhere. There is a little library with a variety of books and magazines. All sports are encouraged. We have a baseball team, boxing squad etc. An orchestra has been formed, and classes in various arts and crafts.

Colored People Unfriendly

In fact, the setup is quite ideal. The rest is left with the officers and the men. But the final result leaves much to be desired. Things are not always run efficiently, food is often poorly cooked.

During the first week we did no work outside camp, but only hiked, drilled, and exercised. Since then we have worked five days a week, eight hours a day. Our bosses are local men, southerners, but on the whole I have found nothing to complain of. The work varies, but is always healthy, outdoor labor. As the saying goes, it's a great life, if only you don't weaken!

There are colored people living on farms on all sides of this camp. But they are not very friendly toward CCC boys in general, and toward the northerners in particular. (There are four companies here: two of southerners, one of veterans, and our own.) So that, socially, the place is "beat."

Our officers, who, of course, are white, are a captain, a first lieutenant, a doctor, and several sergeants. Our athletic director is colored, as is our vocational teacher. Discipline is maintained by imposing extra duty and fines on offenders. The fines are taken only from the $5 a month which the men receive directly.

On the whole, I was gratified rather than disappointed with the CCC. I had expected the worst. Of course it reflects, to some extent, all the practices and prejudices of the U. S. Army. But as a job and an experience, for a man who has no work, I can heartily recommend it.

Document Analysis

Luther Wandall begins the article on his experience in the CCC by outlining the reasons for his initial trepidation about joining. He had heard that African Americans were mistreated and given the worst of everything, a rumor that was often true, as even when camps were integrated overall, they were often internally segregated. Furthermore, Wandall's brother, a veteran, warned him to avoid "anything connected with the Army." Still, like many men of his age and station, Wandall was unable to find other work, and so he reported to register for duty and was sent to a pier to await further instructions. Wandall describes how his apprehension was increased by the number of men who showed up with registration cards and were then turned away for previous bad behavior, but when he got to the pier, he was surrounded by a familiar scene: "The colored boys were a goodly sprinkling of the whole. . . . A good many Spaniards and Italians were about. A good-natured, lively, crowd, typical of New York."

A chaotic scene ensued as men jostled for position in a disorganized line, and finally Wandall, who was expecting only to register, was given a physical and placed "on a bus bound for Camp Dix, New Jersey, without having prepared or told anyone goodbye." It was a disorienting start to Wandall's tenure with the CCC, and his next encounter was a shock as well, as he encountered segregation for the first time at Fort Dix, where "separation of the colored from the whites was completely and rigidly maintained." Wandall noted that the officers, all white, and many from the South, varied in temperament from kind to cruel. He was offered a position at Camp Dix, but was eager to leave, particularly after his warning that they would get the worst of everything proved to be true, at least in the case of their tents. When Wandall was shipped out to a site somewhere in the "Upper South," the conditions were much better: "There [is] plenty to eat, and we [sleep] in barracks instead of tents. An excellent recreation hall, playground, and other facilities."

Wandall's primary complaints seem to be that the other African Americans he finds himself with are unsavory characters. Though he does acknowledge that there are some officers at Fort Dix that were petty and cruel, he had generally positive comments on the white men he encounters, but describes the African Americans he is with at Fort Dix as "of a very low order of culture. . . . many were plainly ignorant and underprivileged, while others were really criminal. They cursed with every breath, stole everything they could lay hands on, and fought over their food, or over nothing at all." He is surprised to find that the African Americans in the South seem unfriendly to Northern black men.

Still, in the end, Wandall found much to recommend about the CCC, though of course it "reflects, to some extent, all the practices and prejudices of the US Army. But as a job and an experience, for a man who has no work, I can heartily recommend it."

Essential Themes
Wandall's article is intended to give a clear picture of the Civilian Conservation Corps to any African American men considering joining the organization. He seems to present a balanced picture, describing the food, camp arrangements, and people that pleased or displeased him. In the end, he feels that the balance tips in favor of the CCC, as he has been able to work and have experiences he would not have had otherwise. Unclear is whether his opinion would have changed had he joined the CCC later, when units were fully segregated and resistance to African American workers in the South was more pronounced.

—*Bethany Groff, MA*

Bibliography and Additional Reading
Cole, Olen, Jr. *The African-American Experience in the Civilian Conservation Corps*. Gainesville: UP of Florida, 1999. Print.
Parrish, Michael E. *Anxious Decades: America in Prosperity and Depression 1920–1941*. New York: Norton, 1992. Print.
Shlaes, Amity. *The Forgotten Man: A New History of the Great Depression*. New York: Harper, 2007. Print.
Woolner, David. "African Americans and the New Deal:

A Look Back in History." *Roosevelt Institute*. Roosevelt Institute, n.d. Web. 10 June 2013.

■ Letter Regarding the Needs of Puerto Ricans in New York

Date: October 11, 1935
Author: Alberto B. Baez
Genre: letter

Summary Overview

In response to a letter sent by President Franklin D. Roosevelt to more than 120,000 American clergymen during the Great Depression, Alberto B. Baez of the First Spanish Methodist Church in Brooklyn, New York, asked for the president's help in addressing the needs of the growing Latino community—specifically, the Puerto Ricans with whom he lived in Brooklyn. Baez says that, in addition to jobs, Puerto Ricans needed English language skills, better health practices, and recreational activities outside their isolated slums.

Defining Moment

In 1929, the stunning economic boom the United States had enjoyed throughout the 1920s came to an equally stunning end. Starting in late October, stock markets crashed, banks folded, industries faltered, and countless jobs disappeared in what would come to be called the Great Depression. Economists, social scientists, and other scholars have attempted to understand the specific causes that, in the aggregate, ushered in this tumultuous decade in US and world history. Generally, experts point to citizens' inability to repay loans and credit debt, a lack of government regulation of businesses and markets, and a lack of sustainability in the country's leading industries as some of the leading causes of this event. Many scholars also point to the sharp divide between the nation's rich and poor (including the large percentage of immigrants, who came to the country in the early twentieth century to work in the energy and manufacturing industries) as a contributing factor, as the latter group represented a large proportion of the population that would be adversely impacted by fluctuations in the economy.

In any case, although many political leaders and economic experts, including President Herbert Hoover, advanced theories on how to halt the downturn, efforts to turn around the economy proved fruitless. In 1932, the Democratic Party, buoyed by Hoover's inability to right the financial ship, nominated New York governor Franklin D. Roosevelt as its candidate to replace Hoover in the White House. In his acceptance speech for the Democratic presidential nomination, Roosevelt pledged a "new deal" for Americans in which the economic and social ills of the Depression would be remedied. When Roosevelt won in a landslide victory in November, he immediately set about implementing his agenda. He envisioned several areas that needed addressing, chief among them were generating jobs, restoring the markets, and rejuvenating the American economy over the long term. A defining feature of Roosevelt's New Deal was its departure from the *laissez-faire* approach to the economy employed by his predecessors—Roosevelt's platform called for a much larger role for the federal government in addressing the crisis, including regulatory reform, major financial investments, and a much larger set of federal agencies to service the public's needs.

As part of his effort to halt the Depression, Roosevelt looked to the public for input. In September of 1935, for example, Roosevelt sent a letter to over one hundred thousand members of the clergy. In the letter, he requested suggestions and comments on how to ensure the New Deal's success. A month later, the pastor of Brooklyn's First Spanish Methodist Church, Alberto B. Baez, responded with the suggestion that the president consider addressing the country's Latino immigrant experience.

HISTORICAL DOCUMENT

Dear Sir:

I have read your letter with the greatest of interest and delight, because I have been waiting for an opportunity like this to express my opinion about the condition of the community where I have been working for almost 20 years.

The problem in this community is unique. The people are Puerto Ricans, American citizens, who never have the privileges of citizens, because they do not speak the language, and do not understand American living. They have been terribly hit by the depression, helped by the Home Relief and unfortunately greatly spoiled by it also.

Their needs? Jobs, in the first place, of course. But strange as it might seem this is not the most important thing. They need to be convinced that they must learn to speak the English language. The older generation will not go to public Schools. They must have a teacher who can talk to them in their own language, because their knowledge of it is very, very limited. They need almost to be forced to give more attention to their health. They need sane recreation to take them away from their slums. All this taking into consideration that a great majority do not speak English and are utterly foreign. The people selected to work for them, must understand them and must speak both languages, and one who has the American as well as the Spanish point of view.

If anything is ever going to be done for the Puerto Ricans in Brooklyn, and I can be of any help, I will be more than happy to do all in my power, to help better their condition in general.

Very respectfully yours,

Alberto B. Baez, Pastor

First Spanish Methodist Church
305 Warren Street
Brooklyn, NY
October 11, 1935

Document Analysis

When President Roosevelt called upon the country's religious leaders for input regarding the efficacy of his New Deal, Pastor Baez—whose parish was located in the immigrant-heavy New York borough of Brooklyn—offered an atypical response. While jobs were essential to restarting the economy, Baez argued, immigrants (particularly the Puerto Rican community, which had grown rapidly in Brooklyn since the beginning of the century) were in need of social programs that would help them better integrate into American society.

Puerto Rican immigrants began arriving in Brooklyn in large numbers during the early twentieth century. Although Brooklyn lacked many economic opportunities, arriving Puerto Ricans saw more potential there than they did on their home island. Puerto Ricans quickly established barrios (Spanish-speaking neighborhoods) and a strong network in this borough, but theirs was a relatively separate existence from the rest of American society. They lacked English language skills, for example, as well as occupational training (since life in Puerto Rico was largely agrarian in nature).

In his letter to the president, Baez suggests that this group of immigrants is in danger of becoming entrenched in poverty even if the Great Depression were to come to an end, as they are uninspired to learn English or pursue the training they needed to find a job. Baez, therefore, suggests that, in addition to generating jobs, the New Deal will greatly serve Puerto Ricans by helping them learn English and the skills they need to succeed in the United States. Baez says Puerto Ricans living in impoverished Brooklyn "need to be convinced that they must learn to speak the English language." Employable older Puerto Rican immigrants, Baez said, refuse to go to public schools, especially since the teachers do not speak to them in their native tongue. The schools, he continued, were the optimal vehicle for inspiring Puerto Ricans to pursue jobs: in addition to learning the country's primary language of English, these immigrants would also learn better hygiene and health practices. "They need almost to be forced to give more attention to their health," he says.

Baez's suggestion is that the New Deal should include an investment in education for the country's large population of immigrants. A teacher who understands the Puerto Rican perspective, he said, would prove invaluable in inspiring students to become more actively involved in the community through work and activities. The goal of such an investment program would be to draw Puerto Ricans out of their slums and impoverished state. Instead of inactive and socially isolated, these people would become engaged and productive members of society, willing and ready to work when employment opportunities finally became available.

Essential Themes
When President Roosevelt promised Americans a "new deal," he focused on more than reversing the economic course manifest in the Great Depression: Roosevelt wanted to restore the social fabric of American society. In this arena, Roosevelt looked for input not only from political leaders and advisors but from community leaders as well. He sent a letter to the clergy, asking for their opinions on how to revitalize the United States. Baez's response was reflective of his own local experiences in Brooklyn, although its themes had broader geographic and social applications.

Baez attempted to help Roosevelt understand the plight of Brooklyn's growing Puerto Rican population. Puerto Ricans, he said, had become entrenched in the barrios they created for themselves since the early twentieth century. In this environment, they did not see the need to learn English or obtain occupational training, Baez argued. As a result, Brooklyn's Puerto Ricans continued to live in poverty and isolation from the rest of American society, he said.

Reverend Baez urged the president to work to reverse this trend. Puerto Ricans needed to learn English, he said. Spanish-speaking teachers who could teach them English and inspire them to pursue meaningful employment opportunities, Baez said, would be the most effective vehicles for drawing Puerto Ricans out of the barrio. Baez suggested that a useful part of the New Deal could be investment in training Puerto Ricans themselves to become teachers. Even older members of the Puerto Rican community, with exposure to such educators, would likely take advantage of such training, Baez said.

Baez's response to the president's letter did not offer specific policy suggestions to train Puerto Ricans in these two areas. However, it did provide a glimpse into a community of immigrants that had become isolated from the rest of American society (as was the case with many other immigrant groups). Their condition was certainly exacerbated by the Great Depression, Baez argued, but their isolation and poverty had existed long before the stock market crash of 1929. The key to reversing Puerto Ricans' entrenched way of life, Baez said, was to inspire them to change their social and economic course in their own way.

—Michael P. Auerbach, MA

Bibliography and Additional Reading
Edsforth, Ronald. *The New Deal: America's Response to the Great Depression*. Hoboken: Wiley, 2000. Print.
McElvaine, Robert S. *The Great Depression: America, 1929–1941*. 25th anniv. ed. New York: Three Rivers, 2009. Print.
"President Franklin Delano Roosevelt and the New Deal, 1933–1945." *American Memory Timeline: Great Depression/WWII, 1929–1945*. Lib. of Congress, n.d. Web. 13 June 2014.
"Puerto Rican New York during the Inter-War Years." *Hunter College: Center for Puerto Rican Studies*. City U of New York, 2010. Web. 12 June 2014.

■ Plea from a Scottsboro Boy

Date: July 24, 1937
Author: Andy Wright
Genre: letter

Summary Overview

During the Great Depression, thousands of men and women rode freight trains across the country looking for work or adventure or escaping intolerable circumstances at home. On a freight train in Alabama in 1931, a fight broke out between a group of white men and African American youths. When two women were found to be on board the train, the black men were accused of rape. Andy Wright was one of the so-called Scottsboro Boys, a group of nine African American teenagers convicted of raping the two young white women. The case polarized the nation, as threatened lynching, numerous court maneuvers, celebrity lawyers, and dramatic reversals revealed a justice system in the American South that routinely denied African Americans the right to a fair trial by a jury of their peers and with a competent defense. In this letter, written six years after his initial arrest and published in *The Nation*, Wright pleads with the nation to consider his case.

Defining Moment

On March 25, 1931, a group of young men and women, white and African American, were riding a Southern Railroad freight train headed for Memphis, Tennessee. One of the white men allegedly stepped on the hand of a young black man named Haywood Patterson, and a fight broke out between the two groups. Eventually, all but one of the white men were forced to jump from the train, and they notified the local sheriff that they had been attacked. The sheriff wired ahead to the next station, in Paint Rock, Alabama, and a posse formed to meet the train. At the Paint Rock station, nine African American teenagers, the oldest nineteen and the youngest at most thirteen years old, were arrested, tied together, and marched off to the jail in Scottsboro, Alabama.

When two young women, Ruby Bates and Victoria Price, were also found to have been on the train, the situation took a dramatic and dangerous turn. The women claimed that they had been raped by the men in the Scottsboro jail at knife and gunpoint, and they were examined by a doctor who found physical evidence of sexual activity. The legal penalty for a black man raping a white woman in Alabama was death, although the legal process was often circumvented: African American men accused of assaulting white women were often lynched in the South, hanged by a crowd while law enforcement either participated in the killing or ignored it. The posse that met the train in Alabama in 1931 quickly turned into a lynch mob, when word of the alleged rapes began to spread. The young men barely escaped with their lives when the Scottsboro sheriff managed to hold off the attack and then called in the Alabama National Guard to protect the young men.

On March 30, a grand jury indicted all nine of the Scottsboro Boys, and the trials were set immediately because of the extremely volatile environment. Lawyers for the defendants were hastily selected and of questionable quality. Within ten days, all but one of the Scottsboro Boys had been sentenced to death. The fate of Roy Wright, the younger brother of the Andy Wright, was inconclusive, when one juror held out against the death penalty because of his age—he was thirteen. The execution date for the other eight was set for the earliest available date, July 10, 1931.

As news spread across the nation of the age of the accused, the lynch mob, the hasty trials, and the severe verdicts, the American public became polarized, with many in the North calling for new trials for the boys and many in the South defending the verdict. Progressive and civil rights organizations, primarily the National Association for the Advancement of Colored

People and the International Labor Defense (ILD), a Communist legal advocacy organization, became involved in the case. Appeals were filed, and the Alabama Supreme Court stayed the executions of the youths just seventy-two hours before they were scheduled to die. In March 1932, the Alabama Supreme Court upheld all of the convictions except one, also on account of age (thirteen).

In October 1932, the case went to the US Supreme Court, where the ILD lawyer argued persuasively that there had been no jurors of color, and rolls that showed African American names had been forged. In the high court's ruling in *Powell v. Alabama*, the convictions were overturned and sent back to Alabama for a retrial. Once again the men were convicted, though Ruby Bates now claimed that she had never been raped. In the end, after another appeal to the Supreme Court (*Patterson v. Alabama*, 1935), the men were returned to jail, though none was ultimately executed. The last of the Scottsboro Boys to leave prison was Andy Wright, who was finally freed in 1950. All of them were eventually pardoned, the last three posthumously, in 2013.

Author Biography

Andy Wright was born in 1912 in Chattanooga, Tennessee. He attended school until the sixth grade, when he left to help support his family after the death of his father. Wright drove a truck for a while, but he lost that position when the company learned of his young age. He boarded the Southern Railroad train in March of 1931, at age nineteen, with his younger brother Roy and two friends, because he had heard there were government jobs in Memphis. Wright was convicted of rape conclusively in 1937, and sentenced to ninety-nine years in prison. He was paroled in 1943, but he fled Alabama in violation of the terms of his parole. He was returned to prison and was finally released for good in 1950, after which he moved to Albany, New York. In Albany, Wright was again accused of rape, and although he was eventually acquitted, he spent another eight months in jail. Wright also lived in New York City and Cleveland, Ohio. He is believed to have spent the last years of his life in Connecticut, although his death date is not known.

HISTORICAL DOCUMENT

Dear Sirs

I am quite sure you all have read the outcome of my trial, and seen that I was given a miscarriage of justice. I feel it is my duty to write you all the facts of my case, which you perhaps overlooked, or perhaps it was not published in the papers. I was framed, cheated, and robbed of my freedom. First, beginning March 25, 26, and 27, 1931, I wasn't charged with criminal assault on either girl, and was carried through the first, second, and third degree, and even on the basis I would gain my freedom by turning state evidence against the other eight boys. Just because I didn't know nothing, nor neither would I lie on the other boys the charge of rape was framed and placed against me on the 28th day of March, 1931.

I was tried, convicted, and given the death sentence, and in November, 1932, the Supreme Court of the United States reversed the sentence and a retrial ordered. The 19th day of July, 1937, I was retried and sentenced to 99 years' imprisonment.

Now I wish to call your attention to how the judge charged the jury. He charged them in a perjury way. Out of his one hour and twenty-five minutes summation he only mentioned acquittal three times and each time he contradicted it by saying if you juries find a doubt which goes to me reconsider it. Never did he mention a single defense witness in his hour and twenty-five minutes summation to the jury.

How can I receive justice in the state of Alabama, especially of Morgan County, when perjury is used against me and my attorneys too? And I beg you, dear friends, readers, all stick together and work and struggle together and see that justice be brought to light. Let us all pull and struggle together and see that justice be done. It is not that I hate to go to prison, but I am innocent, and the slander is being thrown on our race of people and my family, is my reason of wanting to fight harder than ever.

ANDY WRIGHT

Document Analysis

Wright's 1937 letter to the editors of *The Nation* magazine begins with his statement of innocence: "I was framed, cheated, and robbed of my freedom." He is concerned that though the public may have read about his case, they do not know the facts. "I feel it is my duty to write you all the facts of my case, which you perhaps overlooked, or perhaps it was not published in the papers." Wright also mentions that he was questioned for several days without being charged with rape, in the hope that he would turn against some of the other accused. He says he was charged with rape because of his refusal to testify against his codefendants: "Just because I didn't know nothing, nor neither would I lie on the other boys the charge of rape was framed and placed against me."

Wright sent this letter just after his second conviction, after the US Supreme Court had reversed the first conviction, and Wright had been retried. He outlines the reasons why he believes the trial was unfair and based on a presupposition of guilt on the part of the judge: "Out of his one hour and twenty-five minutes summation he only mentioned acquittal three times and each time he contradicted it by saying if you juries find a doubt which goes to me reconsider it." He further mentions that the judge made no reference to any defense witnesses during his summation.

Wright sees this and his treatment over the previous six years as proof that justice is impossible in Alabama. He pleads with the readers of his letter for help. "I beg you, dear friends, readers, all stick together and work and struggle together and see that justice be brought to light."

Essential Themes

The primary theme of this letter is the author's plea with the public to believe in his innocence and help him. He lays out the reasons why his conviction is unjust and he feels that he will not receive justice in Alabama without the intervention of outsiders. He feels that he needs to fight the conviction, not only because of his innocence, but because "slander is being thrown on our race of people and my family."

—*Bethany Groff, MA*

Bibliography and Additional Reading

Aretha, David. *The Trial of the Scottsboro Boys*. Greensboro: Morgan Reynolds, 2007. Print.

Blinder, Alan. "Alabama Pardons 3 'Scottsboro Boys' after 80 Years." *New York Times*. New York Times, 21 Nov. 2013. Web. 11 June 2014.

Gates, Henry Louis, Jr., & Evelyn Brooks Higginbotham, eds. *African America Lives*. New York: Oxford UP. 2004. Print.

Shlaes, Amity. *The Forgotten Man: A New History of the Great Depression*. New York: Harper, 2007. Print.

■ Dear Mrs. Roosevelt

Date: July 27, 1938; August 2, 1938
Author: W. B.; M. L. T.
Genre: letter

Summary Overview

On July 27, 1938, late in the Great Depression, a young Connecticut woman known only as W. B. wrote a letter to First Lady Eleanor Roosevelt (1884–1962). W. B. asked Roosevelt for her assistance in finding employment for her father and financing her own room and board in Chicago so that she could attend Moody Theological College. Missives such as hers were common during the Great Depression; many children and young adults sought the help of Roosevelt, who became well known for her charitable initiatives during her husband's time in office. As a young African American woman, W. B. had even fewer opportunities for financial relief than most poverty-stricken young people, and Roosevelt, who supported civil rights for African Americans, was a symbol of hope. However, the sheer number of people requesting Roosevelt's assistance prevented the First Lady from helping most of them, and on August 2, an assistant known as M. L. T. wrote to W. B. to tell her that her requests could not be granted.

Defining Moment

Following the stock market crash of October 1929, the United States entered the Great Depression, the worst financial downturn in the nation's history. Throughout the 1930s, numerous Americans lost their jobs and were unable to find new ones, and a significant portion of the population faced extreme poverty. President Franklin D. Roosevelt, elected in 1932, introduced numerous economic initiatives in the hope of lowering unemployment, providing assistance to needy Americans, and revitalizing the American economy. His wife, Eleanor Roosevelt, likewise worked to help the American people and became widely known for her activism, particularly through the publication of her newspaper column, "My Day."

As a central figure championing the welfare of the young and impoverished, Roosevelt attracted the attention of many disadvantaged people, who saw her as accessible and easy to relate to. Over the course of the decade, young people from across the United States wrote to Roosevelt, asking for help paying for clothing, medicine, and other necessities. Despite Roosevelt's commitment to those living in poverty, the cost of granting hundreds of such requests was too high, and she was generally unable to help those who wrote to her.

In addition to her concern for the welfare of the nation's poor, Roosevelt was widely known as a supporter of African American civil rights. Racial discrimination remained prevalent during the 1930s, and financial assistance for African Americans affected by the Depression was very limited. To make matters worse, African Americans who sought to improve their lives and overcome poverty often faced challenges that their white counterparts did not. In the case of W. B., who wrote to Roosevelt in 1938, the college she hoped to attend accepted African American students, but did not allow them to live in the school's dormitories. Instead, black students were forced to find outside accommodations, the cost of which could be prohibitive. Writing to the First Lady, who was known to be friendly toward African Americans, might have been seen as the best hope an individual had of obtaining financial assistance.

Author Biography

Little is known about W. B., as she, like many of the people who wrote to Roosevelt seeking financial assistance, insisted that the First Lady keep her identity private. She was born and raised in Old Saybrook, a coastal town in southern Connecticut. W. B. graduated from Old Saybrook High School in June of 1935 and then completed an extra year, ultimately leaving school in June 1936. Those dates suggest that she was likely born around 1917 or 1918. Her letter did not note her immediate family's size; however, she mentioned that her father had sixteen years of work experience but was unable to find a job and that she had tried to find work herself but lacked the necessary experience. W. B. hoped to study theology at Moody Theological College (now the Moody Bible Institute) in Chicago, Illinois, after which she wanted to work as a missionary or a choir singer.

HISTORICAL DOCUMENT

Dear Mrs. Roosevelt:

I am a poor *colored* girl who thinks quite a lot of you and your family, and I know you have done a lot for my race and we appreciate it immensely.

Now I am going to ask you two personal favors which I hope you can do. The first is: *will you find my daddy a job* as caretaker and gardener on an estate or as a janitor of a club or theater? He can't find one and we can't afford to put an advertisement in the papers. He has sixteen years experience.

The second thing I want to ask you to do for me is a *big* favor but I do hope and pray you will do it. My situation is as follows: I am a girl who lives in this small town called Old Saybrook. I was born here and have lived here all of my life. In June of 1935, I was graduated from the Old Saybrook High School and in June of 1936, I was post graduated from the same high school. Now I desire to continue my education by studying "theology" at the "Moody Theological College" in Chicago. Upon graduation from Moody College I would like to become a foreign Missionary or professional quoir singer or teacher.

I am ambitious and determined to succeed, and because I am determined to succeed and ambitious I am writing to ask you if you *will* and *could* please finance my expenses for me. You don't know what it would mean to me if you would do it for me. You see, I couldn't bring myself to ask just any body to do this. I had to ask some one who has money and some one who is good and kind to *colored* people and does not *hate* them. You know as well as I do that a lot of the white people hate the colored people, so I couldn't ask just anybody like a white girl could. Therefore I was doomed until I thought if you. I hope you won't think I am bold in asking you to do this for me.

I would try to complete my course in about 2½ years. There is no charge for tuition. But I must pay for my room and board which would be about seven (7) dollars a week. Then I must pay for incidentals etc. I figure that if you would allow me ten (10) dollars a week I could make my ends meet. We go to school from September to the first week in August. Negros are not allowed to stay at the dormitories so I would have to room and board outside. The superintendent said that he would find me a suitable place to stay. Then I would need about eight dollars ($8) extra to have four of my teeth fixed before I can get my doctors certificate in and checked by Moody College.

I would like to go this fall in September so I wish you would let me hear from you right away. I have been out of school 2 years already and would not like to keep waiting. I tried to get a job but none of the people wanted me because I have no experience in house work. Now it is too late for me to get a job because August is here and it will soon be September. I don't feel smart enough to work my way through and keep up with my studies at the same time. Therefore, now that it's so late I am asking you for help. I want you to understand that I would be willing and glad to pay you back after I had been graduated and received a position. I would like to pay you so much at a time until I had it all paid up.

I *beg* and *implore* you please do not give my name to the newspapermen and please do not give them this letter to print. I would be very hurt and embarrassed; this is a personal matter between you and me. I do not want my name in the papers because I live in a small town and everyone knows me, and they would make fun of me, I know. So, once again I beg you do not let the newspapermen hear of this. *Thank you very much.*

Hoping you will get my daddy a job so that he can pay his bills and hoping that you will lend me the money for my schooling so that I may go in September, I am,

Yours affectionately,

W. B.

P.S. I have tried to get a loaning concern to lend me the money, but they don't want to wait, until I have been graduated, for their money. I have been trying to get work or some means to get to Moody ever since I was graduated and because my future looked black I have come to you in desperation. I hope you will lend a hand to a poor colored girl who would appreciate it and I will endeavor to make myself worthy of your extented hand and kindness. You understand that I would like to pay it back and would like about ten (10) dollars a week and eight dollars extra in advance. I want to go in September. Once more I will beg you not to give my name and this letter to the newspapermen or any officials. Thanking you for what you will do for me, I remain

Yours respectfully,

W. B.

* * *

[Reply to the letter]
August 2, 1938

My dear Miss B.:

Mrs. Roosevelt asks me to acknowledge your letter and to tell you that she is very sorry that she cannot help you financially. She receives so many requests similar to yours that she finds it impossible to comply with them, much as she would like to do so.

Mrs. Roosevelt suggests that you get in touch with the National Youth Administration, Washington, D.C., in the hope that that agency could help you, and she also suggests that your father register with the United States Employment Service under the Department of Labor.

Very sincerely yours,

Administrative Officer
Social Correspondence
(M. L. T.)

Document Analysis

W. B.'s letter to Roosevelt begins by announcing her race and that she lives in poverty, immediately establishing her financial situation and suggesting the discrimination she faced. Her first request is not for herself but for her father, who, by 1938, had been out of work for two years. Asking Roosevelt to help find her father a job, W. B. provides the information Roosevelt would need to do so, mentioning her father's lines of work and his many years of experience. This demonstrates the faith W. B. had in Roosevelt, who she seems to have believed could help if given the necessary details.

It is only after making the request for her father that W. B. begins her own plea for help. Asking for assistance in paying for college, she assures the First Lady that she has the tenacity and iron will necessary to complete a college education. She explains that although her chosen institution does not charge tuition, she must pay for housing, as African American students were not permitted to live in the school's dormitories. Unable to afford the costs herself, W. B. asks Roosevelt to lend her the necessary funds, promising to pay her back after graduating.

As in her first request, W. B. is methodical in the information she provides. All of the necessary costs, including incidentals and room and board, are itemized. She asks for the bare minimum to get by during her time at college, and her only other request is for eight dollars, to be used to fix her teeth so that she can get her "doctors certificate in and checked by Moody College" prior to attending. It is important to note that W. B. requests a loan rather than a gift. In doing so, she displayed the seriousness of her intentions, which she hoped would be taken into account by Roosevelt. In a postscript to the letter, W. B. assures the First Lady that her attempts at obtaining a loan from a bank had failed, so contacting Roosevelt was truly her only remaining option.

W. B.'s letter suggests that she had significant faith in Roosevelt's ability to help her and her family. Although the idea of asking the First Lady for money may seem unrealistic to twenty-first-century readers, the actions of W. B. and the countless young people like her speak to the desperation of many Americans during the Depression, as well as to Roosevelt's reputation as a compassionate and charitable public figure. Although Roosevelt was unable to grant either of W. B.'s requests, the letter did not go unanswered. An administrative officer known as M. L. T. (possibly Malvina Thompson, Roosevelt's assistant) responded on August 2, 1938. M. L. T.'s letter explains why Roosevelt could not help W. B. and suggests that she contact the National Youth Administration for college assistance. M. L. T. adds that W. B.'s father should register with the United States Employment Service. These suggestions are said to have come from Roosevelt herself, solidifying the First Lady's reputation as a figure eager to help those in need, even when she could not do so personally.

Essential Themes
W. B.'s letter to Roosevelt is characterized by several key themes that were common in letters sent to the First Lady during the Depression. First, W. B. sought to emphasize her need while making it clear that she was only contacting Roosevelt as a last resort, perhaps to prevent those reading the letter from considering her lazy or presumptuous. Her postscript to the letter, which discusses her attempts to secure a loan from a bank, demonstrates that she had tried to obtain the money through more traditional methods prior to contacting Roosevelt. Like many petitioners, W. B. seems to have had a strong sense of pride. She was interested not in charity but in a loan, and she insisted that she would succeed in college and pay Roosevelt back once she had finished her studies. Along with her sense of pride came a need for privacy. W. B. noted that she lived in a small town and would face humiliation and harassment if the other residents knew about her letter, so she asked that her name and letter not be published or publicized. This impassioned plea was repeated again in the letter's postscript, further underscoring her need for privacy. This desire for privacy was a common component in the letters sent to Roosevelt by young people who wanted to help their struggling families without injuring the family's pride. W. B., in doing likewise, sought to make clear that she was not looking for notoriety in seeking help. Instead, she simply wanted to better herself and help her family survive the Great Depression.

—*Jennifer Henderson Crane, PgDip*

Bibliography and Additional Reading
Cohen, Robert. "Dear Mrs. Roosevelt: Cries for Help from Depression Youth." *Social Education* 60.5 (1996): 271–76. Print.

Cohen, Robert, ed. Dear Mrs. Roosevelt: *Letters from Children of the Great Depression*. Chapel Hill: U of North Carolina P, 2002. Print.

"Dear Mrs. Roosevelt." *New Deal Network*. Franklin and Eleanor Roosevelt Inst., 2003. Web. 10 June 2014.

■ Our Jobless Youth: A Warning

Date: October 1939
Author: John Chamberlain
Genre: article; report

Summary Overview

This article was written for *Survey Graphic* magazine, a publication that largely catered to those in the social service and welfare field. The magazine was published concurrently with *Survey Midmonthly* by Survey Associates, a nonprofit organization concerned with the proper application of philanthropy to address social problems. In this article, author John Chamberlain voiced concern that American youth would turn to fascism, which was sweeping through Europe at the time, if they were unable to find meaningful jobs at a reasonable wage. Chamberlain offered sociological information from a survey of Maryland youths and from his own experience to argue that young people were cynical about the political process and believed that a strong central state should be regulating working conditions and pay. In addition, he identified heightened expectations created by education and then not borne out by experience as a dangerous factor in the anticipated "explosion" of fascism among the several million young Americans who were out of school, unemployed or underemployed, and "trapped."

Defining Moment

Young people bore a disproportionate share of the suffering and deprivation of the Great Depression. A 1933 census revealed that children under sixteen years of age accounted for 42 percent of Americans receiving relief benefits, despite making up only 31 percent of the population. Many children had to leave school early in order to try to earn money for their families, and the economic crisis quickly became an educational crisis as well. In 1934, insufficient tax revenues resulted in the closure nearly 20,000 schools in rural areas, and school terms were drastically shortened. At the nadir of the Great Depression, thousands of young men and women left home and hitched rides on freight trains, crossing the country in search of work. Politicians and social workers began referring to a "youth crisis" as traditional family relationships crumbled under the strain of chronic poverty and unemployment.

In an attempt to address this crisis, student groups and proponents of New Deal liberalism formed organizations to advocate for educational and employment opportunities and to push for federal aid to schools. The American Youth Congress and the American Student Union led the first national youth marches on Washington. President Franklin D. Roosevelt's administration supported school construction and managed to keep thousands of schools open by paying teachers from New Deal emergency funds, while the Works Progress Administration (WPA) opened nearly three thousand free nursery schools and provided free lunches for impoverished students. The National Youth Administration provided more than two million students with work-study jobs that allowed them to continue their education.

Still, by the end of the decade, between three and four million Americans under the age of twenty-four had left school and were out of work. Like the author of this article, many social scientists were concerned that decreasing opportunities for success and the European example of a strong centralized state could lead to the rise of fascism among young people in the United States. If youths no longer believed that they could control their own destiny, they argued, what was to stop them from handing over total control to a dictator?

By the time this article appeared in the October 1939 issue of *Survey Graphic*, the year had already seen an astonishing amount of political and international upheaval. In March, fascist dictator Francisco Franco took control of Spain. Benito Mussolini was firmly ensconced in a fascist dictatorship in Italy, having been in power since 1922. On September 1, 1939, Nazi Germany invaded Poland, and France and the United Kingdom declared war on Germany two days later. In the United States, despite the concerns of many youth leaders during the Great Depression, fascist organizations emerged sporadically but never gained a large following.

Author Biography

John Rensselaer Chamberlain was born in New Haven, Connecticut, on October 28, 1903. He graduated in 1925 from Yale University, where he had been on the editorial board of the *Yale Record*, the campus humor magazine. Following a brief stint as a copywriter for an advertising agency, Chamberlain began his journalism career at the *New York Times*, where he became assistant editor of the *New York Times Book Review* in 1928 and wrote a daily review column from 1933 to 1936. In 1926, the same year he started working at the *Times*, he married Margaret Sterling, with whom he had two children. Following Margaret's death in 1955, he married Ernestine Stodelle, and the two had one child, Chamberlain's third.

Chamberlain worked for numerous other newspapers and magazines during his long career, including *Life* magazine, the *Wall Street Journal*, *Scribner's*, *Barron's*, *Fortune*, and *Harper's*. He taught at various universities, including the Columbia University Graduate School of Journalism, and was dean of the journalism school at Alabama's Troy State University from 1972 to 1977. He published eight books, the last of which was *The Turnabout Years* (1991), a collection of articles and essays.

Chamberlain was an influential political theorist, leaning more toward libertarianism than his 1930s-era liberalism as he grew older. He died on April 9, 1995, in New Haven, Connecticut.

HISTORICAL DOCUMENT

I have a friend, let us say his name is Joe Cairns, who used to work in an office down the corridor from me. Two years ago Joe was an office boy, a bright one who had hopes of writing. He had been, at an incredibly youthful age, both an organizer for the CIO in eastern Pennsylvania and a communist, and as an office boy he took a deeply earnest interest in the local chapter of the American Newspaper Guild. Joe regarded me as a benighted liberal, a person with—maybe—a good heart but with just a little too much income to stay put on the radical side of the fence. I used to have fun arguing with Joe. You could actually get him on the subject of his political affiliation, for he was quite willing to admit that communists in Russia had scant regard for civil liberties, for political democracy, or for the legal traditions of those countries which Professor George Catlin has lumped together under the larger heading of "Anglo-Saxony." But Joe always returned stubbornly to the same point. "A young fellow's got to believe that his life is coming to something," he used to say. "This economic system is never going to spread out enough to take us all in. You liberals, the New Deal and all that, can give us something. But only enough to make us ask for more. If we succeed in getting a living wage by reformist political measures, why should we be content to stop there?"

Thus argued Joe Cairns for a few months after he had ceased to be an office boy. He was despairful at the time of ever making the grade as a magazine writer, although his education had been sufficient to arouse his sustained curiosity about a great number of things. But slowly the despair ebbed. Joe's new-found confidence did not alter his beliefs, but you could sense change of emphasis in his daily living. "You know," he said one day, "I've never known a big personality on the communist Left. They're all too wrapped up in the class war; they haven't time to become broad human beings." Joe had left the Communist Party; its demands on time and energy were getting in the way of both education and vocation. But he still retained all his old interest in the Newspaper Guild.

The story of Joe Cairns is not offered as typical of modern out-of-school youth; indeed, Joe is about as a-typical as he could be. To begin with, he is an intellectual and a New Yorker, which puts him in a very small minority at once. Second, he has been a communist. But Joe's story is instructive, for it dramatizes the difficulty of pinning youth down. Had a sample test interviewer caught Joe in a truthful mood two years ago he would have put him down as a radical anti-democrat who subscribed to all the rigmarole about "boring from within." Had he caught Joe last spring he would have discovered a person whose beliefs were in a state of flux. And two years from now—just where will Joe be then? It all depends on how things break for Joe in his chosen vocation.

Since Joe became a communist at a tender age, we can assume that he was badly educated in the values of democracy. But his story illustrates the weaknesses of the theory that correct education is what is necessary to bind youth firmly to the democratic scheme of things. If Joe gets the breaks, if the economic system expands in the future to give him pride of place, his youthful communism will probably be forgotten in spite of his education. On the other hand, if the economic system continues to contract, Joe will probably go back to his communism—or to some more inchoate form of anti-democratic radicalism. But the point to be made here is that other young people who have had democratic values drilled into them from birth will be with Joe, too. Education is a weak bulwark for democracy if democracy can't deliver the goods in the form of jobs, a future, or just plain hope.

The other evening I heard Phil La Follette, former governor of Wisconsin, say that a definite fault-line of character divides youth from age in the United States. Phil implied that our out-of-school youth is unstable, apathetic (but maybe preparing to move in a hurry), and unable to derive much comfort from slow parliamentary attempts at meliorism. Sidney Hillman made light of Phil's fears that a psychic "explosion," a crise des nerfs, is necessarily coming to America sometime in the Forties but Sidney Hillman was obviously thinking in terms of mature clothing workers, all of whom have certain skills—or at least a pattern of remembered daily activity upon which to build a political program. Phil's rebuttal was this: given five more years of a contracting or even a static capitalism, then young people who have no pattern of remembered activity will simply stampede. They won't go radical in a way to please socialists or neo-socialists; for they will lack the trade union discipline that is needed for old-line socialist or reformist political activity. Phil La Follette is obviously right when he says that a trapped generation will "explode." And the explosion will come, as it came in Italy and Germany, regardless of education.

(Note to readers: for "explosion" read fascism if you like.)

But suppose our economic system rocks along, with production picking up. In that case, out-of-school youth does offer a real current challenge to educators. There must be educational opportunities to take up the slack of a temporary period of unemployment; there must be education in vocational skills. Above all, there must be education to sharpen youth's faculty to see a job where no job has ever existed before. Such education does not necessarily mean putting youth back into high school or college. But it does involve the creation or expansion of night schools, vocational schools, and alert vocational guidance. And dead end jobs must be accompanied with training on the side for other jobs.

What Youth Is Doing

No census has been taken since 1930. But it is a reasonable guess that there are 20,500,000 young people in the United States between the ages of sixteen and twenty-four. Of these, some ten million are in school. Of the ten million plus that have quit school, mostly for economic reasons, some seven million have either full time or part time jobs (with a majority working full time), and some three million are just hanging around. The unemployment among out-of-school youth may be figured thus to be around 40 percent (including the time spent on the sidelines by those with only partial employment). All of which means, of course, that out-of-school youth has the highest unemployment of any age level in the country.

To know whether the schools have done their part in preparing young people to make the best of a period that offers only partial employment to some and mere hopes for employment to a good many more, we must somehow get inside the collective mind of a whole generation. But a word of caution is in order before we go exploring. Since youth is evanescent, since its problems become merged with the adult problems of a whole economy, a whole civilization, in pretty short order, the achievement of getting inside the collective mind of a generation may not be worth very much three years hence. Back in 1933, for example, we had a boy and girl tramp problem, with thousands of kids in their late 'teens and early twenties taking to the road and the hobo jungle. Had a sample test been taken at the time, we might have predicted the worst for our young people: with one in twenty growing up entirely outside the social system (as some of the more inflamed guesses had it), the dice certainly seemed loaded against our traditional democracy of opportunity. One would have been quite justified on the basis of a 1933 sample test in shaking one's head over the failure of a social system that could not keep young people in school, or even off the brake beams of the through freights.

Yet the period of the "wild children" lasted only for a brief moment. Things are better now than they were in 1933, even for young people. As we shall see, the CCC and the National Youth Administration have thrown lifelines to the most desperate cases. And what with FERA and WPA and AAA and Social Security, homes have ceased to break up. "We have bought ourselves time to think," said Mrs. Franklin D. Roosevelt. That goes for youth, too.

A Sample of American Youth

What, then, is youth thinking? When I see an eighteen-year-old listening hour after hour as the radio "entertainment" drools on, or when I watch Bobby Riggs playing one of his typically lackadaisical tennis matches, I doubt that youth is thinking at all. But this is obviously the prejudice of an old gaffer in his thirties; after all, Bobby Riggs does manage to win important tournaments against smart players. Back in 1936 and 1937 the American Youth Commission of the American Council on Education interviewed some 13,500 young people between the ages of sixteen and twenty-four in the state of Maryland. What emerges from the report of the commission, "Youth Tell Their Story," is a picture of a generation whose group personality is somewhat recessive and apathetic. But, underneath the protective coloration of diffidence, the youth of the Maryland sample have ideas that are just as well defined as Riggs' tennis game.* Two out of three are convinced that wages are generally too low, which would seem to indicate that the underconsumption theory of a faltering capitalism (the theory that has been most assiduously popularized by the New Deal) has sunk in. The youth that is least inclined to regard general wages as too low are the farm boys, but these, nevertheless, are the most inclined to consider their own wages too low. Again, this would seem to argue a high degree of receptivity to the principle of parity of purchasing power for agriculture. Twenty years ago individual youths might have grumbled about their own particular rewards, but would they have complained about wage scales as a whole? One wonders.

But how are wages to be raised from the farm boy's median weekly average of $58.44 and the city boy's average of $13.82? Again, youth's answer here is more or less the answer of the New Deal: 40 percent believe in government regulation of wages (and a surprising number of young people approved of the NRA), while 22 percent think labor unions could turn the trick. Only 10 percent believe in "individual effort," and a mere 4 percent is for a "new economic system." So much for the extremes of rugged individualism and communism.

It would be easy to argue from these figures that a fair majority of young people are for the democratic "social service" state. Well, they are—and they aren't. They share the fundamental American distrust of "isms," but they believe government should, in Leon Henderson's words, "do what it takes." On the other hand, they tend to be cynical about the suffrage. Fifty-five percent consider that candidates are elected to office for reasons of "political pull," or "money, graft and bribery." Seventeen percent answered: "Political machine." Only 5 percent believe that "personality" can elect a candidate to public office.

Is it paradoxical that this youth that is cynical about democratic processes can also believe in government regulation of wages and hours, central administration of relief (90 percent regard relief as a valid concern of Washington), and government regulation of child labor? Perhaps it is. Or perhaps it merely proves that American youth is pragmatic, willing to let the "crooked" politicians vote (under penalty of removal from office) for legislation that will benefit the masses. After all, one can regard one's ward boss as a double-dyed rascal, and one's Senator as a fathead and still prefer them to the self-chosen "elite" of a dictatorship.

"Give Us Security"

On the basis of the Maryland sample test, youth itself

considers economics to be the essence of the "youth problem." Two thirds of the sample voted "economic security" as "youth's own problem," and almost 60 percent think "economic security" is synonymous with the "youth problem in general." "Education, vocational choice" trails far behind as a chosen category; only 13 percent voted for this as "youth's own problem." In other words: "Give us jobs, and we'll let the education follow in due course."

How representative is the Maryland sample? The state itself offers a pretty good cross-section of American conditions as a whole: its westernmost tip is hill country; its northern and central counties consist largely of slightly rolling farm lands, like those of southeastern Pennsylvania or south central Ohio; its Calvert County, where tobacco is raised, has a distinct southern flavor and many Negroes; its "eastern shore" gets its living from salt water and from truck farming; its city of Baltimore is both a manufacturing center and a port; and its Prince George County is a suburb of the national capital at Washington. In all these regions people are divided pretty much as elsewhere into poor and well-to-do, unprivileged and privileged, educationally retarded and college bred. Possibly the "old American" character of most Maryland regions gives a "100 percent American" touch to the Maryland survey that would not be found, say, in an equivalent sample for New York State or Massachusetts. Generally speaking, however, the Maryland sample percentages conform to national percentages; and we can take the word of accredited statisticians that, as sample tests go, the Maryland survey is entirely trustworthy.

The Maryland sample does not prove that our "democracy of opportunity" is functioning for youth; children from the poorest families tend to get the worst jobs and, moreover, they tend to stay in the worst jobs. Class tends to perpetuate class, an American reality that clashes with traditional American theory. And the least privileged groups tend to produce the most children, meaning that there are more and more of a given helpless class to be gripped by the economic vise. To break this vicious circle of economic determinism, the American Youth Commission advocates more efficient educational, vocational and recreational programs for all youth." Certainly youth itself, on the basis of the Maryland sample, is not overly enthusiastic about existing educational, vocational and recreational opportunities. Young people who manage to stay in school until they are eighteen do discover that education helps in job-getting. But the employment and the income of a young person's father profoundly affect the amount of schooling that a given youth is likely to receive. Here, again, we find the vicious circle of economic determinism working. The selective principle behind the recruiting of high school and college students is distinctly not intellectual; it is almost entirely economic. As for vocational guidance in school, it proves helpful insofar as there is any; 70 percent of the young people who have received this guidance are grateful for it. But in most schools there is no attempt at vocational guidance; according to the Maryland report, "when all the youth including those now in school are considered, one still finds that only sixteen out of every hundred have received what they consider helpful vocational guidance from their schools." Looking beyond the Maryland sample, we discover from the studies of Carter Goodrich and other sources that vocational opportunities appear most plentifully where they are least needed, and vice versa. The Great Plains region, the coal plateaus of the southern Appalachians, the old Cotton Belt, all have an excess of births over deaths—and the fewest jobs, the poorest schooling, and the least adequate vocational guidance in the country. The richest agricultural regions tend to have the best agricultural schools; in marginal farming regions, where it takes a skilful man to get a living from the soil, the young and aspiring farmer finds the most difficulty in acquiring skills. And when the surplus population of the Ozark-Appalachian plateaus, the old Cotton Belt and the Great Plains region is drained into the cities, where there is an excess of deaths over births, it finds itself at a disadvantage in competing with urban youth that knows the way around.

Ugly Alternatives

In certain European countries youth has sold itself into state slave-service for a pittance. As Hans Kohn says, the "great personal and creative appeal of autonomous freedom and human comradeship which distinguished . . . the pre-war period" is lost. In Russia, five million young people in the Komsomols are under the strict military discipline of the Communist Party. But youth must eat, and if democracy can't provide jobs, then democratic youth may be expected to go the way of German, Italian and Russian youth.

Democracy's stop-gap answer to the challenge of unemployed out-of-school youth has been the Civilian Conservation Corps and the National Youth Administration. Ever since 1933, the CCC has been taking young men from families on the public relief rolls and placing them—an over-all number of at least 350,000 at any given time since 1935—in forestry, park, and soil erosion camps. The CCC is voluntary, but a candidate must enroll for a minimum service of six months. According to Howard Oxley, 50,000 illiterate boys learned to read and write in CCC camps between 1933 and 1937. Some 300,000 more continued elementary schooling, 200,000 studied high school subjects, and 50,000 took college subjects. Vocationally, the CCC is limited; but it has turned out young men with a useful knowledge of soil conservation, road building, forestry, automobile mechanics, carpentry, furniture-making, and cooking. Not a few youthful truck drivers in private industry owe their jobs to CCC apprenticeship. The National Youth Administration, set up in June of 1935, has not had the funds to take care of more than a mere fraction of the young people who are unemployed or unable to afford vocational school or college. But, for a few hundred thousand boys and girls, it has helped to provide work on locally sponsored projects, and its pay checks have enabled a number of young people to continue their education on at least a part time basis. Residence projects, which are really cooperative schools, have resulted in a few young people learning how to become farmers, seamstresses and stenographers.

But with three million and more out-of-school youth waiting around for something to turn up, the opportunities for temporary employment and limited vocational training offered by CCC and NYA are obviously not enough. Our mass production economic system demands higher skills from fewer people, whereas our school system has been giving better cultural training in recent years to more people. This results in a scissors, the two blades of which open to create an ever larger area of discontent in between. When more and more of the discontented find themselves with time on their hands and no way to pay for the enjoyments of the good life which school has led them to demand, we are likely to discover ourselves with an ugly and morose younger population—a population with latent potentialities for political evil. Nothing much is being done to prevent the growth of such a phenomenon; and our do-nothingism in this respect is the measure of our democratic failure.

* For the sake of brevity I will use the present tense in discussing the Maryland sample. (See "Youth Goes Round and Round;" by Martha Bensley Bruere in *Survey Graphic*, April 1938.)

GLOSSARY

AAA: Agricultural Adjustment Administration, a New Deal farm-assistance program

CCC: Civilian Conservation Corps, a New Deal forestry program

CIO: the Congress of Industrial Organizations, a labor union

crise de nerfs: hysterics

FERA: Federal Emergency Relief Administration, a program that replaced the Works Progress Administration

Komsomol: the youth division of the Communist Party of the Soviet Union

meliorism: the idea that society can be improved by human effort

NRA: National Recovery Administration, a New Deal programmed aimed at fostering cooperation among labor, industry, and government

WPA: Works Progress Administration, a New Deal jobs program

Document Analysis

John Chamberlain begins his article with an anecdote. He introduces the reader to Joe Cairns, a pseudonymous office boy whose case illustrates both the changeable nature of young people and the effect of economic opportunities on political views. When Chamberlain first meets Cairns, he is an avowed Communist who believes that "this economic system is never going to spread out enough to take us all in." After a promotion from office boy to magazine writer, Cairns leaves Communism behind, as his new profession requires his time and attention and, presumably, has given him a new direction. He is on the cusp of success, but Chamberlain argues that his ultimate beliefs will depend on his opportunities: "Had a sample test interviewer caught Joe in a truthful mood two years ago he would have put him down as a radical anti-democrat. . . . Had he caught Joe last spring he would have discovered a person whose beliefs were in a state of flux. And two years from now—just where will Joe be then? It all depends on how things break for Joe in his chosen vocation." Cairns's case proves to Chamberlain that education—which Cairns, whom he describes as "an intellectual," received to an extent "sufficient to arouse his sustained curiosity"—can only go so far; he argues, "Education is a weak bulwark for democracy if democracy can't deliver the goods in the form of jobs, a future, or just plain hope."

The length and breadth of the Great Depression is another area of concern for Chamberlain. Young people, he says, have no memory of a good economy with plentiful opportunities. They have limited opportunities for job training and no experience to fall back on when work becomes available once again. They are, Chamberlain claims, "a trapped generation [that] will 'explode.' And the explosion will come, as it came in Italy and Germany, regardless of education. (Note to readers: for 'explosion' read fascism if you like.)" This is the key issue for Chamberlain, who argues that fascism is very appealing to a generation that has never seen capitalism working well and has seen the pitfalls of socialism and communism as well. He believes that vocational training is necessary to prepare young people to work when jobs become available, saying that their success depends on the "creation or expansion of night schools, vocational schools, and alert vocational guidance. And dead end jobs must be accompanied with training on the side for other jobs."

Writing as he is for a social-science magazine, Chamberlain provides his readers with some statistics. If there are around ten million young people (defined as between the ages of sixteen and twenty-four) in the United States who are not currently in school, seven million of whom are employed either full or part time, that leaves "some three million [who] are just hanging around." Taking into account "the time spent on the sidelines by those with only partial employment," this makes the unemployment rate among out-of-school young people approximately 40 percent.

Additional statistical information is gleaned from a 1936–37 survey of 13,500 Maryland residents between sixteen and twenty-four. Chamberlain describes the result of the survey as "a picture of a generation whose group personality is somewhat recessive and apathetic." The majority of young people surveyed are "cynical about democratic processes" but still believe that the government should regulate labor and wages and provide financial relief. Limited opportunities to escape poverty and advance—Chamberlain argues that "children from the poorest families tend to get the worst jobs and . . . stay in the worst jobs" and that "class tends to perpetuate class"—mean that young people are "a population with latent potentialities for political evil." "Nothing much is being done to prevent the growth of such a phenomenon," he concludes, and "our do-nothingism in this respect is the measure of our democratic failure."

Essential Themes

In this article, Chamberlain urges his readers to consider the impact of limited vocational opportunities on young people in the United States. Since young people have never seen capitalism working and have also seen the failures of some communist and socialist ideas, fascism will appeal to them if nothing is done to address the issue. Chamberlain highlights the connection between youthful ideas, which are changeable and malleable, and economic and educational opportunities, which can set young people on a positive path.

—*Bethany Groff, MA*

Bibliography and Additional Reading

Cohen, Robert. *When the Old Left Was Young: Student Radicals and America's First Mass Student Movement, 1929–1941*. New York: Oxford UP, 1993. Print.

Modell, John. *Into One's Own: From Youth to Adulthood in the United States, 1920–1975*. Berkeley: U of California P, 1989. Print.

Reiman, Richard A. *The New Deal and American Youth: Ideas and Ideals in a Depression Decade*. Athens: U of Georgia P, 1992. Print.

Shlaes, Amity. *The Forgotten Man: A New History of the Great Depression*. New York: Harper, 2007. Print.

■ What Does American Democracy Mean to Me?

Date: November 23, 1939
Author: Mary McLeod Bethune
Genre: address; speech

Summary Overview

In 1939, the United States was still mired in the Great Depression as war began to engulf Europe once again. At such a time, civil rights for black Americans was not very high on the agenda of most white Americans. But Mary McLeod Bethune was ahead of her time in many ways. She had already seen both the best black Americans could offer their country and the worst with which America had repaid them. She had held prominent positions in civil rights organizations and in the federal government. She had the ear of both President Franklin D. Roosevelt and First Lady Eleanor Roosevelt. And in this speech to a national radio audience, she answered a very simple question: "What does American democracy mean to me?" Her response to that question would outline what she felt needed to be done in order to make the United States "a more perfect union."

Defining Moment

The Great Depression was devastating for many Americans, but doubly so for African Americans. Many, still sharecropping in the South, suffered as cotton prices plummeted. In the North, factory jobs became harder to find, and many of those that were available were controlled by labor unions, many of which excluded black workers. As jobs became more and more scarce, even positions traditionally held by black people, such as train porters, cooks, maids, and garbage men, went to unemployed whites. Unemployment among black Americans was about twice the national rate throughout the 1930s. Racial tensions increased with the economic pressure felt by many whites. Jim Crow laws and white supremacist groups like the Ku Klux Klan kept blacks in a subservient position throughout the nation.

These factors did not change suddenly when Franklin D. Roosevelt became president in 1933. Many black voters were loyal Republicans, since that was the party of the Great Emancipator, Abraham Lincoln. However, the way Roosevelt attacked the problems of the Depression impressed many African Americans. His ability to communicate and empathize with the plight of the populace made many black Americans feel a sense of belonging. However, needing the votes of Southern senators to pass his New Deal reforms, Roosevelt did little to directly benefit African Americans during his first term. However, Eleanor Roosevelt, an outspoken opponent of prejudice, pushed the president to move toward a more progressive position. The president began to speak publicly on issues important to African Americans, such as lynching. Over time, many African Americans, such as Mary McLeod Bethune, changed their party affiliation from Republican to Democrat.

Though discrimination and segregation were a part of many New Deal programs, and Roosevelt's perspective on civil rights is best described as moderate, his administration marked a shift from the national leaders that preceded him. Over the course of Roosevelt's time in office, a higher share of New Deal agency jobs went to black workers, and by the late 1930s, black income from government relief and work programs was nearly equal to black income from private employment. Roosevelt also began to bring black leaders into the White House, consulting with them on matters of civil rights.

Black leaders such as A. Philip Randolph and Mary McLeod Bethune became nationally known. Bethune's position in the National Youth Administration and as an advisor to Roosevelt made her a personality who occasionally appeared on radio programs, and it was with the history of African Americans both before and during the Great Depression in mind that she appeared on NBC's *America's Town Meeting of the Air* broadcast, along with a number of other panelists, to answer the question, "What does American democracy mean to me?"

Author Biography

Mary McLeod Bethune was one generation removed from slavery. Born in South Carolina in 1875, she grew up doing exactly what her parents had done: picking cotton. However, she did it on land that her family owned, and she had the drive to pursue the best educational opportunities available to a black girl at the time. After graduating from Scotia Seminary, she was denied a missionary posting in Africa because of her race. Instead, she began teaching in Augusta, Georgia, before marrying and eventually moving to Florida where she opened the Daytona Educational and Industrial Training School for Negro Girls in 1904. During the 1920s and 1930s, Bethune led various women's civil rights organizations, and worked as director of the Division of Negro Affairs in the National Youth Administration. In this position, she became friends with Eleanor and Franklin Roosevelt, forming the Federal Council of Negro Affairs, popularly known as the Roosevelt's "Black Cabinet." As such, she became one of the best-known and most influential black women in the nation.

HISTORICAL DOCUMENT

Democracy is for me, and for 12 million black Americans, a goal towards which our nation is marching. It is a dream and an ideal in whose ultimate realization we have a deep and abiding faith. For me, it is based on Christianity, in which we confidently entrust our destiny as a people. Under God's guidance in this great democracy, we are rising out of the darkness of slavery into the light of freedom. Here my race has been afforded [the] opportunity to advance from a people 80 percent illiterate to a people 80 percent literate; from abject poverty to the ownership and operation of a million farms and 750,000 homes; from total disfranchisement to participation in government; from the status of chattels to recognized contributors to the American culture.

As we have been extended a measure of democracy, we have brought to the nation rich gifts. We have helped to build America with our labor, strengthened it with our faith and enriched it with our song. We have given you Paul Lawrence Dunbar, Booker T. Washington, Marian Anderson and George Washington Carver. But even these are only the first fruits of a rich harvest, which will be reaped when new and wider fields are opened to us.

The democratic doors of equal opportunity have not been opened wide to Negroes. In the Deep South, Negro youth is offered only one-fifteenth of the educational opportunity of the average American child. The great masses of Negro workers are depressed and unprotected in the lowest levels of agriculture and domestic service, while the black workers in industry are barred from certain unions and generally assigned to the more laborious and poorly paid work. Their housing and living conditions are sordid and unhealthy. They live too often in terror of the lynch mob; are deprived too often of the Constitutional right of suffrage; and are humiliated too often by the denial of civil liberties. We do not believe that justice and common decency will allow these conditions to continue.

Our faith envisions a fundamental change as mutual respect and understanding between our races come in the path of spiritual awakening. Certainly there have been times when we may have delayed this mutual understanding by being slow to assume a fuller share of our national responsibility because of the denial of full equality. And yet, we have always been loyal when the ideals of American democracy have been attacked. We have given our blood in its defense—from Crispus Attucks on Boston Commons to the battlefields of France. We have fought for the democratic principles of equality under the law, equality of opportunity, equality at the ballot box, for the guarantees of life, liberty and the pursuit of happiness. We have fought to preserve one nation, conceived in liberty and dedicated to the proposition that all men are created equal. Yes, we have fought for America with all her imperfections, not so much for what she is, but for what we know she can be.

Perhaps the greatest battle is before us, the fight for a new America: fearless, free, united, morally re-armed, in which 12 million Negroes, shoulder to shoulder with their fellow Americans, will strive that this nation under God will have a new birth of freedom, and that government of the people, for the people and by the people shall not perish from the earth. This dream, this idea, this aspiration, this is what American democracy means to me.

[applause]

GLOSSARY

chattels: property; slaves

sordid: squalid; wretched

Document Analysis

In her answer to the question, "What does American democracy mean to me?," Mary McLeod Bethune takes the occasion first to praise the things American democracy has given black Americans, then to demonstrate how, even so, the promise of that democracy has not come close to being fully realized for the nation's black population. Bethune made clear what had been accomplished, the promise of what could be accomplished, and the distance between the two.

Bethune mentions her "deep and abiding faith" in the dream of full inclusion in American democracy; her belief that God's providence has led black people from slavery to freedom; from illiteracy to literacy; from poverty to ownership of property and businesses. After discussing how far African Americans have come, Bethune notes the important contributions many famous black people have made to science, literature, and the performing arts.

Despite such progress, Bethune points out, the African American story in 1939 was still one of little educational opportunity, few job prospects, extreme poverty, and fear of racial oppression at the hands of groups like the Ku Klux Klan. Bethune makes clear that America is still a work in progress, and that the founding documents of American democracy set forth ideals that have not yet been met, but toward which the nation and its people continually strive.

That is the reason for her hope and what, in the end, American democracy means to her—that, quoting Abraham Lincoln, "this nation under God will have a new birth of freedom, and that government of the people, for the people and by the people shall not perish from the earth."

Essential Themes

When viewed in the context of the decades that followed Bethune's radio address, her words seem prophetic. But Bethune wasn't the first to point out the hypocrisy of American democracy. Frederick Douglass expressed many of the same sentiments—that America had not yet lived up to its stated mission because of its treatment of blacks—in his speeches and writings. Those same sentiments infused the words of civil rights leaders during the 1950s and 1960s. Using the rhetoric of American liberty to point out that liberty was being denied to the nation's black population was effective in pricking the conscience of many Americans.

When the United States entered World War II, job discrimination in the defense industries and in the military itself was still accepted. It was only after United Brotherhood of Sleeping Car Porters union leader A. Philip Randolph threatened a massive march on Washington, DC, that Roosevelt relented and issued Executive Order 8802, which allowed anyone, regardless of race, creed, color, or national origin, to be free from discrimination by federal agencies and any companies or unions involved in the war effort.

Once the war was over, African American men returned home from the fighting with a distinct feeling that they had earned the right to be full participants in American society, which made a return to discrimination even less acceptable. It was in that context—and because of the groundwork laid by people like Mary McLeod Bethune—that the NAACP pursued the 1954 *Brown v. Board of Education* decision that outlawed segregation in public schools; that nine black students in Little Rock, Arkansas, braved hate-filled crowds in 1957 to attend the previously all-white Central High School; and that a new cadre of national leaders, such as Dr. Martin Luther King, Jr., would push for civil and

voting rights legislation in the mid-1960s.
—Steven L. Danver, PhD

Bibliography and Additional Reading

Bethune, Mary McLeod. *Building a Better World: Essays and Selected Documents*. Bloomington: Indiana UP, 1999. Print.

Egerton, John. *Speak Now against the Day: The Generation before the Civil Rights Movement in the South*. Chapel Hill: U of North Carolina P, 1994. Print.

Franklin, John Hope, & August Meier, eds. *Black Leaders of the Twentieth Century*. Urbana: U of Illinois, 1982. Print.

Kirby, John B. *Black Americans in the Roosevelt Era: Liberalism and Race*. Chattanooga: U of Tennessee P, 1992. Print.

Sitkoff, Harvard. *A New Deal for Blacks: The Emergence of Civil Rights as a National Issue, Vol. 1: The Depression Decade*. New York: Oxford UP, 1978. Print.

Sullivan, Patricia. *Days of Hope: Race and Democracy in the New Deal Era*. Chapel Hill: U of North Carolina P, 1996. Print.

Weiss, Nancy Joan. *Farewell to the Party of Lincoln: Black Politics in the Age of FDR*. Princeton: Princeton UP, 1983.

The Bonus Army

The so-called Bonus Army was made up of World War I veterans who demanded payment of war bonuses promised them through previous Congressional actions. The matter was not finalized under President Hoover owing to fears about bankrupting the US Treasury. To force the issue, in the summer of 1932 over 12,000 veterans and their families marched in the Capitol and camped in tents and shanties. Ultimately, the Bonus Bill was defeated and most of the protesters left to return home. When those staying behind became louder in their calls for assistance, Hoover sent in Army troops under General Douglas MacArthur. The camps were burned and the protesters were driven out. Press coverage of the event spurred outcries from the public and contributed to Hoover's defeat in the 1932 presidential election. A smaller group of veterans returned to protest in 1933, but again the bonuses were turned down. Finally, in 1936 Congress passed legislation authorizing about $2.5 million in veterans bonuses—a somewhat modest but not insignificant amount at the time.

Herbert Hoover to Reed Smoot Regarding the Bonus Loan Bill

Date: February 18, 1931
Author: Herbert Hoover
Genre: letter

Summary Overview
The World War Adjusted Compensation Act of 1924 authorized bonuses for veterans of World War I, to be paid in 1945. The bonuses, which were calculated based on length of service, averaged approximately $1,000 each. In February 1931, shortly after the start of the Great Depression, Congress voted on legislation that would authorize veterans to borrow up to 50 percent of the value of these bonuses. The administration of President Herbert Hoover vigorously opposed the legislation, arguing that the cost of the new loan program, approximately one billion dollars, would place the nation in even greater financial peril. After the House of Representatives passed the Emergency Adjusted Compensation Bill, commonly referred to as the bonus loan bill, President Hoover sent a letter to the Senate Finance Committee outlining his objections and urging the Senate to reject the legislation. Hoover explained why the government could not afford the expenditure and argued that it was unfair to single out veterans for special assistance when the entire population was suffering economic hardship.

Defining Moment
Almost immediately after World War I ended, groups began to lobby Washington to pay bonuses to veterans, a tradition dating back to 1776. After five years of debate, Congress passed the World War Adjusted Compensation Act, or Bonus Act for short, authorizing payment of bonuses averaging about $1,000 each. The bonuses were awarded in the form of certificates, which could not be redeemed for cash until 1945. These bonuses were intended to serve as a kind of pension for aging veterans. President Calvin Coolidge vetoed the legislation, but Congress overrode the veto, and the Bonus Act became law. The law was later amended to allow veterans to borrow up to 22.5 percent of the value of their bonus at low interest.

When the country went into a financial tailspin in 1929, Representative Wright Patman of Texas led a campaign to allow veterans covered by the Bonus Act to receive immediate cash payments of the full value of their bonus. Patman and others saw this move as a way to assist veterans suffering financial hardship in the early days of the Great Depression. Similar legislation, granting extended disability pensions to Spanish-American War veterans, was passed in 1930; President Hoover vetoed the bill, but Congress overrode the veto.

Late in 1930, support for immediate cash payment of bonuses began to grow in both houses of Congress. The American Legion and the Veterans of Foreign Wars (VFW) weighed in on the debate early, lobbying members of Congress to support the bill. The Hoover administration stood firm against the legislation, pointing out that the cost of immediate cash payments could exceed $3 billion—nearly equal to the federal government's $3.6 billion annual budget for the fiscal year.

When Senator Arthur Vandenberg of Michigan proposed a compromise that would replace immediate cash payments with a provision allowing veterans to borrow up to 50 percent of the value of their bonus, some thought the administration might change its position. However, Treasury Secretary Andrew Mellon appeared before the Senate Finance Committee on January 28, 1931, to state the administration's strong objections to any proposal that would add to the nation's debt in a time of financial crisis.

Despite the administration's efforts to kill the legislation, on February 16, the House passed the Emergency Adjusted Compensation Bill by a vote of 363–39, and the Senate seemed ready to follow suit. In an effort to sway votes, Senator Reed Smoot of Utah, chair of the Senate Finance Committee and an ally of the president, invited Hoover to send a letter to the committee outlining his reasons for opposing the legislation. The letter was released to the press, and newspapers across the country printed it over the next two days, providing Hoover a national platform for his objections.

Author Biography
Herbert C. Hoover was born August 10, 1874, in West Branch, Iowa. Orphaned at age nine, he grew up with relatives in Iowa and Oregon before entering Stanford University in 1891, the same year it opened. After graduation, Hoover worked as a mining engineer in Australia and China. In 1899, he married Lou Henry, a fellow Stanford graduate with a geology degree. By the outbreak of World War I, he was a multimillionaire. During the war, he helped establish the Commission for Relief in Belgium and later became head of the United States Food Administration, both agencies that organized relief efforts to feed millions in Europe. After hostilities ended, Hoover became head of the American Relief Administration, continuing his relief work in Europe and Russia.

From 1921 to 1928, Hoover served as secretary of commerce for Presidents Warren G. Harding and Calvin Coolidge. In 1928, he was elected president of the United States. During the next four years, as the country entered a period of severe financial crisis, Hoover held fast to his principles, believing that limited government and private-sector initiatives would lead the United States out of the Great Depression. His policies, coupled with worsening conditions in the nation that culminated in the Bonus Army incident of 1932, made him highly unpopular, and he was defeated in his reelection bid by Franklin Delano Roosevelt. Following World War II, Hoover chaired two presidential commissions and served as an adviser to several government officials. He died on October 20, 1964.

HISTORICAL DOCUMENT

I have given thought to your request that I should express to you and the Senate Finance Committee my views upon the bill passed by the House of Representatives, increasing the loans to World War veterans upon the so-called bonus certificates. In view of the short time remaining in this session for its consideration I shall comply with your request.

The proposal is to authorize loans upon these certificates up to 50% of their face value. And to avoid confusion it must be understood that the "face value" is the sum payable at the end of the 20 years period (1945) being based on the additional compensation to veterans of about $1,300,000,000 granted about six years ago, plus 25% for deferment, plus 4% compound interest for the 20 year period. As the "face value" is about $3,423,000,000, loans at 50% thus create a potential liability for the Government of about $1,172,000,000, and, less the loans made under the original Act, the total cash which might be required to be raised by the Treasury is about $1,280,000,000 if all should apply. The Administrator of Veterans' Affairs informs me by the attached letter that he estimates that if present conditions continue, then 75% of the veterans may be expected to claim the loans, or a sum of approximately $1,000,000,000 will need to be raised by the Treasury.

I will not undertake to enumerate all of the grounds for objection to this proposal. There are a number of most serious objections, some of which are matters of method and some of which are matters of fundamental principle affecting the future of our country and the service men themselves.

I have supported, and the nation should maintain, the important principle that when men have been called into jeopardy of their very lives in protection of the Nation, then the Nation as a whole incurs a special obligation beyond that to any other groups of its citizens. These obligations cannot be wholly met with dollars and cents. But good faith and gratitude require that protection be given to them when in ill health, distress and in need. Over 700,000 World War Veterans or their dependents are today receiving monthly allowances for these reasons. The country should not be called upon, however, either directly or indirectly, to support or make loans to those who can by their own efforts support themselves.

By far the largest part of the huge sum proposed in this bill is to be available to those who are not in distress.

The acute depression and unemployment create a situation of unusual economic sensitiveness, much more easily disturbed at this time than in normal times by the consequences of this legislation, and such action may quite well result in a prolongation of this period of unemployment and suffering in which veterans will themselves suffer with others.

By our expansion of public construction for assistance to unemployment and other relief measures, we have imposed upon ourselves a deficit in this fiscal year of upwards of $500,000,000 which must be obtained by issue of securities to the investing public. This bill may possibly require the securing of a further billion of money likewise from the public. Beyond this, the Government is faced with a billion dollars of early maturities of outstanding debts which must be refunded aside from constant renewals of a very large amount of temporary Treasury obligations. The additional burdens of this project cannot but have damaging effect at a time when all effort should be for the rehabilitation of employment through resumption of commerce and industry.

There seems to be a misunderstanding in the proposal that the Government securities already lodged with the Treasury to the amount of over $700,000,000 as reserve against these certificates constitute available cash to meet this potential liability. The cash required by the veterans can only be secured by the sale of these securities to the public. The legislation is defective in that this $700,000,000 of Government securities is wholly inadequate to mend either a potential liability of $1,280,000,000 or approximately $1,000,000,000 estimated as possible by the Administrator of Veterans' Affairs, and provision would need to be made at once for this deficiency.

The one appealing argument for this legislation is for veterans in distress. The welfare of the veterans as a class is inseparable from that of the country. Placing a strain on the savings needed for rehabilitation of employment by a measure which calls upon the Government for a vast sum beyond the call of distress, and so adversely affecting our general situation, will in my view not only nullify the benefits to the veteran but inflict injury to the country as a whole.

GLOSSARY

maturity (maturities): the date on which a loan is due in full

securities: stocks, bonds, etc.

Document Analysis
In his letter to Senator Smoot and members of the Senate Finance Committee, President Hoover presents a three-pronged attack on the Bonus Loan Bill before the committee: first, the legislation places an onerous financial burden on the government and, ultimately, on the American people; second, those veterans requiring special assistance are already receiving help; and third, providing special assistance to veterans at a time when the entire populace is suffering economic hardship is unfair and could be counterproductive in leading the United States out of the Great Depression.

Unlike the rhetoric employed by lobbying groups such as the American Legion and the VFW, which argued that veterans deserved a cash bonus because they had already made great sacrifices for the country, Hoover's letter is remarkably dispassionate and businesslike. A good portion of it is devoted to technical discussion of monetary policy that the senators on the committee would understand without special explanation. Most notable, however, is his repeated use of numbers as a means of calling attention to the magnitude of the issue before Congress. Perhaps aware that his letter would be printed in newspapers across the nation, Hoover carefully works through a series of calculations to spell out the cost to the country that could be incurred if the Bonus Loan Bill is passed: $1 billion. Hoover concludes his case against the bill on financial grounds with a veiled warning: since the United States is already running a budget deficit, this additional money "will need to be raised by the Treasury." Senators would realize immediately that the government would have to either raise taxes or borrow additional funds, further weakening its financial position.

Hoover goes on to argue that, besides finding the measure fiscally unsound, he has other "serious objections, some of which are . . . matters of fundamental principle." He acknowledges that the nation owes a debt of gratitude to those who served in combat, and that when they are "in ill health, distress and in need," the government has an obligation to provide help. However, he points out that 700,000 veterans are already receiving monthly assistance because of illness or disability. He follows this with a statement not of fact but of principle, one that would resonate with Americans who believed strongly in the idea of limited government: "The country should not be called upon . . . to support or make loans to those who can by their own efforts support themselves." After once again reviewing the financial burdens posed by the Bonus Loan Bill , Hoover closes with a strong emotional appeal for fairness. To provide special treatment to veterans is to unfairly burden other groups in the United States, and doing so would "inflict injury to the country as a whole."

Essential Themes

The events surrounding the eventual passage of the 1931 Bonus Loan Bill over Hoover's objections offer a lesson in the power of sentiment and effective lobbying at the national level. The president's dispassionate, reasoned argument had little effect on the Senate, which passed the bill on February 19 by a vote of 72–12. On February 26, Hoover vetoed the bill, returning it to the House of Representatives with a stinging rebuke. Unimpressed and undaunted, the House voted within an hour to override the veto, 328–79. The next day, the Senate followed suit, voting 76–17. The fact that the potential $1 billion cost of the loans was equal to one quarter of the entire federal budget for the year did not sway many in either house.

The passage of the Bonus Loan Bill also raised hopes of those in favor of immediate cash payment of the entire bonus that they might muster sufficient support for their cause in the future. Both the American Legion and the VFW continued their lobbying efforts, and individual veterans were urged to show their support as well. In the summer of 1932, a contingent of more than 40,000 veterans and their families traveled across the country to Washington, DC, to protest in favor of immediate cash payments. This group, known as the Bonus Expeditionary Force or Bonus Army, remained in the capital from late May until late July, when federal troops under the command of General Douglas MacArthur forcibly evicted them from the District of Columbia. This unusual and almost unprecedented decision to use military forces against civilian protesters became a factor in the 1932 presidential election, when Hoover was defeated by Franklin Delano Roosevelt.

—*Laurence W. Mazzeno, PhD*

Bibliography and Additional Reading

Daniels, Roger. *The Bonus March: An Episode of the Great Depression*. Westport: Greenwood, 1971. Print.

Dickson, Paul, & Thomas B. Allen. *The Bonus Army: An American Epic*. New York: Walker, 2004. Print.

Lisio, Donald J. *The President and Protest: Hoover, Conspiracy, and the Bonus Riot*. 2nd ed. New York: Fordham UP, 1994. Print.

Ortiz, Stephen R. "Rethinking the Bonus March: Federal Bonus Policy, the Veterans of Foreign Wars, and the Origins of a Protest Movement." *Journal of Policy History* 18.3 (2006): 275–303. Print.

■ Attack on the Bonus Army

Date: July 29, 1932
Author: Lee McCardell
Genre: article

Summary Overview

In the summer of 1932, nearly 20,000 military veterans, along with their families and various support groups, came to Washington, DC, from across the country to lobby for passage of legislation that would pay them an immediate cash bonus for their service during World War I. Legislation passed in 1924 had authorized bonuses payable in 1945, but financial hardships caused by the Great Depression prompted many veterans to ask for immediate disbursement. During its summer session, Congress failed to pass the legislation. In late July, the administration of President Herbert Hoover and officials of the District of Columbia decided to use military force to evict the veterans from the nation's capital. A 600-man contingent, led by US Army chief of staff General Douglas MacArthur used tear gas and a show of force to drive protesters from their temporary living quarters and out of the district.

Defining Moment

In late May 1932, a contingent of World War I veterans, led by Walter W. Waters of Portland, Oregon, arrived in Washington, DC, to lobby Congress for passage of a bill that would provide them immediate cash payments of a bonus dating from 1924. That year, the World War Adjusted Compensation Act had awarded veterans deferred bonuses in the form of certificates that could be redeemed for payment in 1945. The value of each bonus depended on the veteran's length of service, with an average payout of approximately $1,000, and veterans were allowed to borrow against this sum in certain circumstances. In 1929, shortly before the onset of the Great Depression, Representative Wright Patman of Texas introduced a bill that would allow veterans to receive immediate cash payments of their bonuses. The Hoover administration felt that such a large outlay—up to three billion dollars—would further stress the government's finances, and administration officials fought to keep the bill from passing. Patman's first bill was defeated in committee, but he continued to push for the legislation, and in 1932, a similar bill reached Congress for a vote. The House of Representatives passed the bill on June 15, 1932, but two days later, as the protesters gathered at the Capitol building, it was defeated in the Senate.

Throughout June and July, the number of veterans and their families and supporters assembling in the nation's capital swelled to over 40,000. The veterans conducted peaceful protests and demonstrations to highlight their cause. The group took as its name the Bonus Expeditionary Force (BEF), a reference to the American Expeditionary Force, the US military contingent that went to Europe during World War I. Washington's police superintendent, Pelham Glassford, managed to maintain order. A major camp was set up in the city's Anacostia neighborhood, but some veterans took up residence in unoccupied buildings close to the Capitol. Under Glassford's supervision, the protesters received some assistance from private citizens and government agencies. However, Hoover and others feared that the veterans were being controlled by Communist elements and were wary that violence would eventually erupt. After Congress adjourned on July 17, the president's administration and District of Columbia commissioners became more aggressive in their efforts to evict the BEF from Washington. Notices of eviction were issued to clear buildings downtown.

On July 28, while attempting to carry out evictions, Washington police clashed with veterans. Bricks and stones were thrown by protesters, and two veterans were shot and killed by police officers. In response, Hoover authorized the Army to move into downtown

Washington to quell the protesters. Army chief of staff MacArthur personally led a contingent of six hundred infantry, mounted cavalry, and tanks into the city, where they evicted around ten thousand bonus marchers from Capitol Hill and its immediate environs. Ignoring the president's directive to return the protesters to their camps and hold them there for identification, MacArthur instead ordered troops to drive the veterans and their families from the camps, over the Anacostia River, and out of the capital. Although no shots were fired and no direct casualties occurred, the soldiers used tear gas on the protesters, and their show of force, with loaded rifles, bayonets, swords, cavalry, and tanks rolling down streets, provoked fear among BEF members. Tents and equipment at the Anacostia camp were burned. When Hoover ordered the eviction stopped, MacArthur again ignored him. By the next morning, the bonus marchers had begun traveling away from the city. Some stopped for a time in Johnstown, Pennsylvania, mistakenly thinking they would be welcome there. Eventually, the veterans and their families returned home.

Author Biography
Lee McCardell was born in Frederick, Maryland, on June 8, 1901. After graduating from the local public high school, he enrolled at the Carnegie Institute of Technology (now part of Carnegie Mellon University) to pursue studies in engineering, but he soon transferred to the University of Virginia, where he earned a degree in liberal arts. In 1925, McCardell went to work for *The Baltimore Evening Sun* as a reporter and feature writer. On July 28, 1932, he was in Washington, DC, when federal troops evicted the Bonus Army veterans and their families from their temporary camps. His story of the event received an honorable mention by the Pulitzer Prize committee the following year. McCardell served in Europe as a war correspondent throughout World War II; afterward, he spent eighteen months as chief of the *Sun*'s London bureau before becoming city editor of the *Evening Sun*. In 1954, he was promoted to assistant managing editor. After spending three years as chief of the *Sun*'s new Rome bureau, he returned to his position as assistant managing editor, where he remained until his death on February 7, 1963.

HISTORICAL DOCUMENT

WASHINGTON, *July 29*

The bonus army was retreating today—in all directions.

The fight had begun, as far as the Regular Army was concerned, late yesterday afternoon. The troops had been called out after a veteran of the Bonus Army had been shot and killed by a Washington policeman during a skirmish to drive members of the Bonus Army out of a vacant house on Pennsylvania Avenue, two blocks from the Capitol.

The soldiers numbered between seven hundred and eight hundred men. There was a squadron of the Third Cavalry from Fort Myer, a battalion of the Twelfth Infantry from Fort Washington, and a platoon of tanks (five) from Fort Meade. Most of the police in Washington seemed to be trailing after the soldiers, and traffic was tied up in 115 knots.

The cavalry clattered down Pennsylvania Avenue with drawn sabers.

The infantry came marching along with fixed bayonets.

All Washington smelled a fight, and all Washington turned out to see it.

Streets were jammed with automobiles. Sidewalks, windows, doorsteps were crowded with people trying to see what was happening.

"Yellow! Yellow!" From around the ramshackle shelters which they had built on a vacant lot fronting on Pennsylvania Avenue, just above the Capitol, the bedraggled veterans jeered. . . .

The cavalrymen stretched out in extended order and rode spectators back on the sidewalks. The infantry started across the lot, bayonets fixed.

Veterans in the rear ranks of a mob that faced the infantry pushed forward. Those in front pushed back. The crowd stuck. An order went down the line of infantrymen. The soldiers stepped back, pulled tear-gas bombs from their belts, and hurled them into the midst of the mob.

Some of the veterans grabbed the bombs and threw them back at the infantry. The exploding tins whizzed around the smooth asphalt like devil chasers, pfutt-pfutt-pfutt. And a gentle southerly wind wafted the gas in the faces of the soldiers and the spectators across the street.

Cavalrymen and infantrymen jerked gas masks out of their haversacks. The spectators, blinded and choking with the unexpected gas attack, broke and fled. Movie photographers who had parked their sound trucks so as to catch a panorama of the skirmish ground away doggedly, tears streaming down their faces.

The police tied handkerchiefs around their faces.

"Ya-a-a-ah!" jeered the veterans.

But more gas bombs fell behind them. The veterans were caught in the back draft. They began to retreat. But before they quit their shacks they set them on fire. The dry wood and rubbish from which the huts were fashioned burned quickly. The flames shot high. Clouds of dirty brown smoke blanketed the avenue.

Document Analysis

McCardell's first-person account of the US Army's eviction of the Bonus Army protesters is an excellent example of the kind of journalism that was popular and respected in the United States during the early twentieth century. There is virtually no editorializing and no strong statements that affix blame or champion one side or another. Instead, McCardell's spare style focuses on the events as they unfolded before his eyes, recording the sights and sounds of this clash between a group of "bedraggled" veterans and a contingent of well-armed soldiers commanded personally by the Army's chief of staff.

On the surface, McCardell's narrative reads like an on-the-scene report of combat between two opposing military forces. His opening sentence, "The bonus army was retreating today," immediately sets up that scenario. Opposing this group is the "Regular Army," a force of "between seven hundred and eight hundred men," equipped with horses and tanks. The cavalry carries "drawn sabers," while the infantry is equipped with "fixed bayonets." At one point, the soldiers don their gas masks and launch an "unexpected gas attack."

Notably absent is any mention of weaponry carried by the bonus marchers—because they were unarmed. In fact, McCardell repeatedly refers to them as a "mob." Their only aggressive actions are to stand firm in the face of the advancing infantry and to grab the "tear-gas bombs" and throw them back, all the while jeering at their attackers.

Although the clash between veterans and regulars took place at several locations throughout the District of Columbia, McCardell focuses on the action along Pennsylvania Avenue just north of the Capitol building, where veterans had set up "ramshackle shelters." Keeping the focus on actions in the center of the city allows McCardell to interweave throughout his account descriptions of spectators who turn out to watch what is to them a curious spectacle, at least at first. To the residents of Washington, this potentially life-and-death encounter is little more than an afternoon's entertainment—or perhaps a terrible nuisance, since "traffic was tied up in 115 knots."

McCardell does not say directly where readers' sympathies should lie, but his careful choice of language highlights the essential disparity between the opposing forces. The Army comes off as an imperious conquering force, the veterans as heroic resistance fighters who retreat only because they are outgunned.

Essential Themes

Before the Bonus Army was forcibly evicted from Washington, national opinions over their actions were mixed. While most Americans appreciated the service these veterans had provided to the nation, many politicians and opinion leaders expressed concern that one group might receive special assistance during a time when everyone in the country was suffering. Newspapers and magazines carried editorials urging the president and Congress to resist efforts by lobby groups, such as the Veterans of Foreign Wars and the American Legion, to wrest concessions from the government and further jeopardize the nation's precarious financial status.

The contrast between the treatment of the veterans by Chief of Police Glassford and Army Chief-of-Staff MacArthur provides a lesson in public officials' management of potentially hostile crowds. Glassford won the confidence of protesters by providing them with a limited number of food and shelter items that made their stay in otherwise squalid conditions palatable; he also allowed BEF officials to police their camps. MacArthur treated the veterans as enemy combatants, and although the soldiers under his command showed some restraint, their actions were akin to those used during wartime to deal with hostile belligerents.

Initially the attack on the Bonus Army was met with approval by the press, as Hoover's insistence that the marchers were being manipulated by Communist agitators was widely believed. As facts came to light, however, public opinion turned, and the military action came to be perceived as governmental overreach, an unwarranted use of force on a group engaged in peaceful civil protest. Resentment against Hoover's actions was a contributing factor in his resounding loss to Franklin D. Roosevelt in the 1932 presidential election.

—*Laurence W. Mazzeno, PhD*

Bibliography and Additional Reading

Daniels, Roger. *The Bonus March: An Episode of the Great Depression*. Westport: Greenwood, 1971. Print.

Dickson, Paul, & Thomas B. Allen. *The Bonus Army: An American Epic*. New York: Walker, 2004. Print.

Liebovich, Louis. *Bylines in Despair: Herbert Hoover, the Great Depression, and the US News Media*. Westport: Greenwood, 1994. Print.

Lisio, Donald J. *The President and Protest: Hoover, Conspiracy, and the Bonus Riot*. 2nd ed. New York: Fordham UP, 1994. Print.

Sterne, Joseph. *Combat Correspondents: The Baltimore Sun in World War II*. Annapolis: Maryland Hist. Soc., 2009. Print.

■ Veterans March to Washington

Date: December 1932
Author: Veterans Central Rank and File Committee
Genre: broadside

Summary Overview
In December 1932 the Communist Party of the United States organized a march on Washington, DC, to protest the treatment of veterans of World War I. The march was modeled on one that had taken place the preceding summer, when as many as twenty thousand veterans and their families camped out in Washington until President Herbert Hoover ordered the army to evict them. The December 5 march, timed to coincide with the start of a new session of Congress, gave Communist leaders an opportunity to use veterans' demands for payment of a cash bonus for their service to highlight inequities between working-class Americans and the privileged few who had not been affected as seriously by the Great Depression.

Defining Moment
In 1924, Congress approved cash bonuses for veterans of World War I; however, payment was not to be made until 1945. After the US economy began spiraling downward in late 1929, many veterans urged Congress to pay those bonuses immediately. While provisions were made to allow veterans to borrow against the bonuses, veterans' groups grew more adamant that veterans should receive cash immediately.

The Communist Party, seeing the growing tension as a way to promote its political cause, formed the Workers Ex-Servicemen's League (WESL) to organize veterans who were unhappy with their treatment by the government. WESL leaders formed the Veterans Rank and File Committee to spearhead protest activities; John T. Pace, an organizer from Detroit, Michigan, was named the committee's leader. Pace went to Washington, DC, in May 1932, when veterans from across the country, calling themselves the Bonus Expeditionary Force (commonly known as the Bonus Army), descended on the capital in a mass protest aimed at securing cash payments. For weeks, Pace worked to discredit the Bonus Army's leaders and take control of the movement himself. More than 20,000 veterans and their families camped at locations in the District of Columbia until July 28, when Hoover ordered the Army to evict them.

Wishing to take advantage of the turmoil created by the government's actions, Communist leaders announced that a second march on Washington would take place in December 1932, when Congress would reconvene. The Veterans Rank and File Committee published materials outlining a list of grievances that went far beyond the failure of the government to pay the cash bonus and proposed a series of sweeping remedies that would favor veterans and other working-class Americans.

Groups of veterans began appearing in Washington in the late fall of 1932. Among the organizers present were two who had appeared before Congress in April 1932 to testify in favor of paying the bonus: James W. Ford, the Communist candidate for vice president in the 1932 election, and Samuel Stember, an organizer from New York. On December 14, representatives of the new bonus marchers went to Capitol Hill to present petitions demanding immediate payment of the bonus and censure of President Hoover for his actions that July. Stember presented the petition to Vice President Charles Curtis, who accepted it but struck out the passage calling for censure, while Ford met with Speaker of the House John Nance Garner.

Author Biography
The broadside inviting veterans to march to Washington in December 1932 was issued by the Veterans Rank and File Committee, an agency of the Workers Ex-Servicemen's League. That group was formed by

the Communist Party of the United States several years earlier to coordinate activities of veterans disaffected by the actions of the federal government. John T. Pace, a Communist organizer from Detroit, was named leader of the Rank and File Committee. Pace had previously been involved in a protest at the Ford Motor Company plant in March 1932, during which police and private security forces killed several workers. He was an important figure in the American Communist Party until 1936, when he left the party.

HISTORICAL DOCUMENT

VETERANS MARCH TO WASHINGTON
TO ARRIVE AT OPENING OF CONGRESS
DECEMBER 5th, 1932
TO DEMAND
CASH PAYMENT of BONUS

MARCH TO BE LED BY RANK AND FILE VETERANS

Again the veterans are going to march to Washington, to demand immediate full cash payment of the Bonus! This time we will have fighting leadership that won't sell us out. Why are we going to march? Let's see.

A WINTER OF HUNGER FACES THE VETERANS

Cold, brutal winter is now on us. Over a million and a half unemployed veterans are hungry; hundreds of thousands of us have no shelter. And there will be more of us in that fix by the time winter comes.

Those of us who still have some work have suffered wage cuts, and the stagger plan, and face more wage cuts.

INTEREST CHARGES WIPE OUT BONUS BY 1945

In 1945 there will be no Bonus for the rank and file veteran. The balance is now being eaten up by the compound interest charged by the government to all who borrowed the fifty percent of the Adjusted Service Certificate. In 1945 there will be only about $30 to $60 for the great majority of the veterans entitled to the Bonus. WE MUST FIGHT FOR THE BONUS NOW!

THE ENEMIES OF THE BONUS ARE UNITED AGAINST US

The Republican, Democratic and Socialist Parties are all united in the fight against the payment of the balance due the veterans on the Bonus. They get the full support of the boss press, and the liberal writers, too.

Waters, the Hoke Smiths, the Doak Carters and other former leaders of the B. E. F. are fighting the rank and file veterans who are putting up a fight for the immediate payment of the Bonus.

The newly elected commander Johnson has had recent correspondence with Hoover and will not fight for the Bonus. General Glassford and the Hoover government are again preparing to prevent the veterans from making direct demands on Congress.

These fakers are all lined up with the enemies of the Bonus to prevent the rank and file of the veterans from uniting their mass power to march to Washington and again demand the immediate payment of the Bonus and fight against cutting of the disability allowance.

RANK AND FILE VETERANS, MARCH TO WASHINGTON!

All Veterans March to Washington!

Veterans' organizations, elect Bonus Marchers. All rank and file veterans, including employed and unemployed veterans, should elect delegated Bonus Marchers. Veterans from shops, mills, mines, factories and farms should be elected. Bonus marchers should be elected from the veteran membership in labor, fraternal and social organizations.

ELECT CITY RANK AND FILE COMMITTEES

City rank and file committees representing the various groups and organizations of veterans should meet to carry out the program of Central Rank and File Committee elected by the Cleveland Conference of the Rank and File Veterans. (Sept. 23–26.)

HEROES IN 1917; THEY CALL US "CRIMINALS" NOW

In 1917 the government appealed to the masses: "Shall we be more tender with our dollars than with the lives of our sons?" (Second Liberty Bond poster, 1917.)

And now, in 1932: "The bonus marchers are criminals." (Statement of President Hoover.)

Neither then nor now did the Wall Street government care about the welfare of the soldier, "the lives of our sons."

Billions went to the billionaires who in 1917 made huge profits from the war, and today the billions go to the same crowd. The Congress that refused to give the starving veterans the bonus gave through the Reconstruction Finance Corporation four and a half billion dollars for the bankers, the railroads and other big corporations.

We got the bullets and the gas in 1917. Many of us were maimed and crippled for life. In 1932 we get the bullets and gas of the police, as we did in Washington, and of the troops, which Hoover called out against us.

Because we were demanding the Bonus so that we and our families could have something to eat, the President of the United States orders the army to gas and bayonet us, to burn our meagre belongings and to drive our wives and children out into the dark of the night.

WALL STREET GOVERNMENT GIVES BILLIONS FOR WAR AND BANKERS

We are facing starvation. But the boss government does not care about us. However, through the Reconstruction Finance Corporation the banks, the railroads and the large industries get billions. The 15 million unemployed workers, the poor and mortgaged farmers, the small shopkeeper get nothing. Bankruptcy, foreclosures, public sales of farms and starvation face the great masses of the people. And at the same time billions are being spent by the government for another world war.

UNITY OF VETERANS WILL WIN OUR DEMANDS

The coming march of the veterans will unite all the veterans. Negro and white veterans must struggle together against all attempts to divide them. All veterans, unemployed and employed, skilled and unskilled workers, starving farmers, small bankrupt shopkeepers, professional men, homeless and friendless unmarried veterans, must unite for the coming march.

From cities, towns and villages they will come.

No matter what our political beliefs are, we must unite in this fight. Foreign-born and native veterans must be united. The wives, mothers and children of the vets must support the fight for the Bonus. The rank and file of veterans' organizations, despite their boss class commanders will join the fight. It is such unity that will give us the strength to fight our enemies.

WE NEVER FORGET HUSHKA AND CARLSON

While in Washington we will commemorate the murder of Hushka and Carlson who were murdered by the Glassford police and now lie buried in Arlington Cemetery.

A fitting tribute will be paid to the veterans who were murdered by the Glassford police.

BONUS MARCH OF RANK AND FILE GIVES RELIEF TO 214,000 VETERANS

The Bonus March proved that the mass pressure of the rank and file of the veterans is the only way to win results.

The Bonus March forced Congress to remove the two year restriction clause and to give Immediate payment to over 214,000 veterans, of fifty percent of the adjusted service compensation due them. The Bonus March taught the rank and file how to organize their mass strength and exposed the enemies within our own ranks as well as those outside our ranks.

MASS SUPPORT FOR THE VETERANS

The fight of the veterans is part of the fight of all the people against hunger, wage cuts, unemployment and war. The support of the veterans who are not marching to Washington, the people as a whole, the veterans and other organizations is more necessary now than ever before. The organized opposition is stronger. Intimidation and threats will be used against us and those who support us. The full support of those who are not marching will be needed.

WINTER CLOTHES, BLANKETS, FOOD AND MONEY, NEEDED

The marchers will face cold weather. Blankets and heavy clothes will be needed for the trip. The delegates who will be elected and other veterans who will again march are carrying on the fight for all of us who cannot march to Washington. They must move forward with our support, financial as well as moral. Donate your extra blankets, heavy clothing, cooking utensils. Help collect food and money. Support the demonstrations of the veterans and the unemployed.

DEMANDS OF THE VETERANS: BONUS

Congress to pass a bill for the immediate cash payment of the Bonus with the following provisions:
1. Congress authorize the immediate payment of the balance due on the adjusted service certificates, upon demand of those entitled to it.
2. All interest charges on certificates to cease.
3. All interest deducted from loans already made including the transportation loans advanced the Bonus Marchers to be added to the balance due.
4. Funds to be raised as follows:
   a) Surtax on industries;
   b) Inheritance tax;
   c) All funds for immediate war preparations;
   d) Reconstruction Finance Corporation funds.

DISABLED

Not a cent off the disability allowances.
Negro war veterans to be admitted in all hospitals.
Jim-crowing of Negro veterans to cease. This applies to all hospitals in the South in particular.
Veterans to have right to choose their own doctors and expense to be paid by the government.

UNEMPLOYED

House and feed all unemployed unmarried veterans as well as other unmarried unemployed without police surveillance at local government and federal government expense.
Unemployment and social insurance for all unemployed at the expense of the federal government and the employers.

DETACH AND MAIL TO

VETERANS CENTRAL RANK AND FILE COMMITTEE
P. O. BOX 38
NEW YORK CITY

Comrades:

Please send me more information about what to do to make the Bonus March a success.

NAME..........ADDRESS
CITY..........STATE

• ____ I condemn the Hoover administration for using the troops against the veterans.
• ____ I support immediate payment of the Bonus.
• ____ I will support the March to Washington.

Issued by Veterans Central Rank and File Committee, P.O. Box 38, New York, N. Y.

Document Analysis

Although sometimes mistaken for an advertisement for the more famous summer gathering of the Bonus Army that camped out in Washington from May to July 1932, the broadside printed by the Veterans Rank and File Committee and encouraging veterans to assemble in Washington on December 5, 1932, alludes to the violent ending of that summer's encampment as part of the rallying cry to encourage veterans of World War I to keep up their battle for payment of the bonuses to which they were entitled. In testimony before Congress in 1949, Pace claimed to have received orders from the Communist Party to use veterans' protests as a means of encouraging dissent and discrediting the Hoover administration. The inflammatory language of the broadside is designed in part to achieve that end. Its authors constantly cite the wrongs done to veterans by the federal government and business interests. The "boss government" favors "the banks, the railroads and the large industries," the same group of "billionaires" who "made huge profits" from World War I. Meanwhile, the "unemployed workers, the poor and mortgaged farmers, the small shopkeeper[s] get nothing." The masses face "starvation."

The broadside repeatedly refers to the failed efforts of the preceding summer. Its assertion that "this time we will have fighting leadership that won't sell us out" is a rebuff of the leaders of the Bonus Army, particularly Walter Waters, who was anti-Communist and had encouraged peaceful protest during the previous summer. The document warns of the danger that the new protesters are likely to face, including "the bullets and the gas" of the police and military. The mention of the "murder of Hushka and Carlson" reminds veterans that two of their number had been killed in the summer protests. Veterans are also warned that "intimidation and threats" will once again be used against them. The only way to succeed is for all veterans—those marching and others who cannot come to Washington—to stand united in what the organizers suggest is a kind of workers' revolution.

The list of demands included in the broadsheet goes far beyond payment of the bonus. It reads instead like a Communist manifesto, calling for elimination of interest charges on loans veterans had taken out with their bonus money as security. There is a call for the rich to be taxed heavily to pay for programs to support workers and even a demand for fair and equal treatment for African Americans. Typical of Communist propaganda, the broadside alludes to threats posed to veterans, who are equated with workers being exploited by business owners and the government in a capitalist system.

Essential Themes

The broadside inviting veterans to march on Washington to demand what was due to them provides an excellent example of the way American Communists attempted to subvert the government by using the tools of democracy. Under the banner of free speech and the right to assemble, organizers sought to incite dissent among those whose grievances were being ignored by federal officials. However, the Hoover administration had learned from the summer's catastrophic experience with the Bonus Army that forcibly quelling such protests was counterproductive. This second march was allowed to proceed peacefully, and petitioners were allowed to deliver a list of their grievances and demands to high-ranking government officials. The willingness of thousands of World War I veterans to join in activities sponsored by the Communist Party reveals the level of frustration and despair many felt as a result of the economic hardships they were suffering at the time. Unquestionably, the Communists' efforts to highlight the plight of veterans and others hit hard by the Great Depression had an impact on future actions by Congress and the executive branch.

Undaunted by the failure of the December march to generate any serious action in Congress, Communist organizers planned another gathering for May 1933. That initiative was publicly denounced by many veterans' groups, including the Bonus Army, the Disabled American Veterans, and the American Legion. Most veterans sought to distance themselves from what they considered the taint of Communism. Marchers arrived in Washington in smaller numbers than anticipated, and newly inaugurated president Franklin Roosevelt blunted the initiative by offering veterans jobs in the newly created Civilian Conservation Corps. While active protests died down, interest in the issue persisted, and, in 1936, Congress voted for the immediate payment of bonuses authorized twelve years earlier.

—*Laurence W. Mazzeno, PhD*

Bibliography and Additional Reading

Daniels, Roger. *The Bonus March: An Episode of the Great Depression*. Westport: Greenwood, 1971. Print.

Dickson, Paul, & Thomas B. Allen. *The Bonus Army: An American Epic*. New York: Walker, 2004. Print.

Lisio, Donald J. *The President and Protest: Hoover, Conspiracy, and the Bonus Riot*. Columbia: U of Missouri P, 1974. Print.

Ortiz, Stephen R. "Rethinking the Bonus March: Federal Bonus Policy, the Veterans of Foreign Wars, and the Origins of a Protest Movement." *Journal of Policy History* 18.3 (2006): 275–303. Print.

Foreign Policy

Although a variety of matters in foreign policy arose in the 1930s, the overriding one was the question of neutrality versus war—or preparations for war—as Europe once again headed toward major armed conflict and tensions rose in the East between Japan and other nations. Neutrality proponents urged a policy of refusing to differentiate between aggressor nations and victims, arguing that both should be viewed as equal parties. Thus, the first Neutrality Act of 1935 authorized the president to declare an embargo on arms shipments to "belligerents" involved in war but did not prohibit trade in goods such as oil, food, and supplies. Additional neutrality acts in 1936 and 1937 extended bans to loans and credits and limited the activities of merchant ships and the trade in war materiel. Still, these strictures were meant to apply equally to belligerents and only came into play when a state of war was declared to exist. Thus, when in 1937 Japan attacked China, Roosevelt declined to label the act as one of war, thereby permitting continued open trade with both China and Japan. A 1939 neutrality act was even more lenient, just as Europe was becoming wrapped up in war and British Prime Minister Winston Churchill, among others, was pleading with the Americans to act. So rooted was neutrality as a policy that it was only when the US Naval Base at Pearl Harbor was attacked in December 1941 that portions of the earlier neutrality laws were finally stripped away and the United States was put on war footing.

Henry Stimson to Senator Borah Regarding the Nine-Power Treaty

Date: February 23, 1932
Author: Henry L. Stimson
Genre: letter

Summary Overview

In a letter to the Senate Foreign Relations Committee's Republican chairman William E. Borah of Idaho, Secretary of State Henry Stimson put forth the policy of the Herbert Hoover administration regarding Japanese interference in China, reaffirming the traditional American line of equal trade for all in China and respect for Chinese sovereignty—known as the Open Door policy. The subject of the letter is the Nine-Power Treaty between the major powers of the Pacific, including the United States, Japan, and China, concluded in 1922. Stimson regards the principles of the Nine-Power Treaty and other related treaties such as the Kellogg-Briand Pact (1928) as important to uphold. However, as a response to Japanese aggression, he offers only nonrecognition of those changes that would impair Chinese sovereignty or threaten American interests in China. He does not speak of taking economic, military, or active diplomatic measures against Japan at this point.

Defining Moment

The partial disintegration of Chinese central government following the Chinese Revolution of 1911 and the overthrow of the imperial Qing dynasty had opened up opportunities for aggression by China's neighbor Japan, such as the Twenty-One Demands Japan made on China in 1915, which, among other things, strengthened Japanese control over Manchuria. Japan was taking advantage of a time when the Western powers were involved in World War I. There was a long-standing rivalry between the United States and Japan in the Pacific, which was not significantly alleviated by the two countries being allies against Germany in World War I. The Japanese were frequent targets of American racism as well.

There had been some hope of establishing friendlier relations between the United States and Japan during the early 1920s, when both countries had been signatories to the Washington Naval Treaty (or Five-Power Treaty) and the Nine-Power Treaty governing the relations of the Pacific powers. In a related treaty signed then, Japan had even returned Shandong Province, which it had taken from the Germans in World War II, to Chinese control. However, by the late 1920s, Japanese policy had once again taken a militaristic turn. Much of postrevolutionary China was under the control of warlords, opening the door to invasion. In 1931, Japan invaded the region of Manchuria in China's northeast, the traditional homeland of the Manchu people, the founders of the Qing dynasty. Japanese influence had been growing stronger there ever since Japan's victory over Russia in the Russo-Japanese War in 1905, by which, in the Treaty of Portsmouth, Japan had solidified its control over the Korean peninsula and taken control of Manchurian railroads.

The Japanese demand for economic privileges in China and attacks on Chinese sovereignty in Manchuria conflicted with the long-standing American policy of the Open Door, which called for commercial equality and the preservation of China as an independent nation. However, American involvement in World War I had led many Americans to be wary of involvement in the affairs of foreign nations, and during the Great Depression, the focus of most Americans' interest was domestic rather than foreign affairs. President Herbert Hoover shared this domestic focus and prevented Stimson from advocating more forceful measures. On January 7, 1932, Stimson sent a letter to the Chinese and

Japanese governments, stating that the United States would not recognize any treaty or agreement between the two states that affected US rights in China, Chinese territorial changes, or the Open Door policy. However, given President Hoover's opposition to economic sanctions, the policy could not be enforced. Manchukuo, a Japanese puppet state in the territory of Manchuria, declared its independence from China on February 18, 1932, a few days before Stimson's letter to Borah.

American sympathy for the Chinese cause was not merely a matter of government policy, however, but was also rooted in American culture. Pearl S. Buck's epic about Chinese peasant life, *The Good Earth*, was the best-selling novel in the country in both 1931 and 1932. Many Americans supported the efforts of Christian missionaries in China, although Chinese immigrants in America faced much racist discrimination.

Author Biography

Henry Lewis Stimson (1867–1950) was a prominent lawyer, major American statesman, and Republican political figure for decades. Stimson was secretary of war during the William Howard Taft administration (1911–13) and later served as governor-general of the Philippines from 1927 to 1929. He became secretary of state in the administration of Republican president Herbert Hoover. Stimson became strongly identified with opposition to Japanese expansion in China, formulating the Stimson Doctrine that the United States would not recognize territorial changes that impinge on US treaty rights or are brought about by aggression. As secretary of war again in World War II, he played a major role in the American decision to drop atomic bombs on the Japanese cities of Hiroshima and Nagasaki. Stimson retired in September 1945.

HISTORICAL DOCUMENT

MY DEAR SENATOR BORAH:

You have asked my opinion whether, as has been sometimes recently suggested, present conditions in China have in any way indicated that the so-called Nine Power Treaty has become inapplicable or ineffective or rightly in need of modification, and if so, what I considered should be the policy of this Government.

This Treaty, as you of course know, forms the legal basis upon which now rests the "Open Door" policy towards China. That policy, enunciated by John Hay in 1899, brought to an end the struggle among various powers for so-called spheres of interest in China which was threatening the dismemberment of that empire. To accomplish this Mr. Hay invoked two principles (1) equality of commercial opportunity among all nations in dealing with China, and (2) as necessary to that equality the preservation of China's territorial and administrative integrity. These principles were not new in the foreign policy of America. They had been the principles upon which it rested in its dealings with other nations for many years. In the case of China they were invoked to save a situation which not only threatened the future development and sovereignty of that great Asiatic people, but also threatened to create dangerous and constantly increasing rivalries between the other nations of the world. War had already taken place between Japan and China. At the close of that war three other nations intervened to prevent Japan from obtaining some of the results of that war claimed by her. Other nations sought and had obtained spheres of interest. Partly as a result of these actions a serious uprising had broken out in China which endangered the legations of all of the powers at Peking. While the attack on those legations was in progress, Mr. Hay made an announcement in respect to this policy as the principle upon which the powers should act in the settlement of the rebellion.

He said

> The policy of the government of the United States is to seek a solution which may bring about permanent safety and peace to China, preserve Chinese territorial and administrative entity, protect all rights guaranteed to friendly powers by treaty and international law, and safeguard for the world the principle of equal and impartial trade with all parts of the Chinese Empire.

He was successful in obtaining the assent of the other

powers to the policy thus announced.

In taking these steps Mr. Hay acted with the cordial support of the British Government. In responding to Mr. Hay's announcement, above set forth, Lord Salisbury, the British Prime Minister expressed himself "most emphatically as concurring in the policy of the United States."

For twenty years thereafter the Open Door policy rested upon the informal commitments thus made by the various powers. But in the winter of 1921 to 1922, at a conference participated in by all of the principal powers which had interests in the Pacific, the policy was crystallized into the so-called Nine Power Treaty, which gave definition and precision to the principles upon which the policy rested. In the first article of that Treaty, the contracting powers, other than China, agreed

1. To respect the sovereignty, the independence and the territorial and administrative integrity of China.

2. To provide the fullest and most unembarrassed opportunity to China to develop and maintain for herself an effective and stable government.

3. To use their influence for the purpose of effectually establishing and maintaining the principle of equal opportunity for the commerce and industry of all nations throughout the territory of China.

4. To refrain from taking advantage of conditions in China in order to seek special rights or privileges which would abridge the rights of subjects or citizens of friendly states, and from countenancing action inimical to the security of such states.

This Treaty thus represents a carefully developed and matured international policy intended, on the one hand, to assure to all of the contracting parties their rights and interests in and with regard to China, and on the other hand, to assure to the people of China the fullest opportunity to develop without molestation their sovereignty and independence according to the modern and enlightened standards believed to maintain among the peoples of this earth. At the time this Treaty was signed, it was known that China was engaged in an attempt to develop the free institutions of a self-governing republic after her recent revolution from an autocratic form of government; that she would require many years of both economic and political effort to that end; and that her progress would necessarily be slow. The Treaty was thus a covenant of self-denial among the signatory powers in deliberate renunciation of any policy of aggression which might tend to interfere with that development. It was believed-and the whole history of the development of the "Open Door" policy reveals that faith—that only by such a process, under the protection of such an agreement, could the fullest interests not only of China but of all nations which have intercourse with her best be served.

In its report to the President announcing this Treaty, the American Delegation, headed by the then Secretary of State, Mr. Charles E. Hughes, said, "It is believed that through this Treaty the 'Open Door' in China has at last been made a fact."

During the course of the discussions which resulted in the Treaty, the Chairman of the British delegation, Lord Balfour, had stated that

> The British Empire delegation understood that there was no representative of any power around the table who thought that the old practice of 'spheres of interest' was either advocated by any government or would be tolerable to this conference. So far as the British Government were concerned, they had, in the most formal manner, publicly announced that they regarded this practice as utterly inappropriate to the existing situation.

At the same time the representative of Japan, Baron Shidehara announced the position of his Government as follows: "No one denies to China her sacred right to govern herself. No one stands in the way of China to work out her own great national destiny."

The Treaty was originally executed by the United States, Belgium, the British Empire, China, France, Italy, Japan, the Netherlands and Portugal. Subsequently it was also executed by Norway, Bolivia, Sweden, Denmark and Mexico. Germany has signed it but her parliament has not yet ratified it.

It must be remembered also that this Treaty was one of several treaties and agreements entered into at the Washington Conference by the various powers concerned, all of which were interrelated and interdependent. No one of these treaties can be disregarded without disturbing the general understanding and equilibrium which were intended to be accomplished and effected by the group of agreements arrived at in their entirety. The Washington Conference was essentially a disarmament conference, aimed to promote the possibility of peace in the world not only through the cessation of competition in naval armament but also by the solution of various other disturbing problems which threatened the peace of the world, particularly in the Far East. These problems were all interrelated. The willingness of the American Government to surrender its then commanding lead in battleship construction and to leave its positions at Guam and in the Philippines without further fortification, was predicated upon, among other things, the self-denying covenants contained in the Nine Power Treaty, which assured the nations of the world not only of equal opportunity for their Eastern trade but also against the military aggrandizement of any other power at the expense of China. One cannot discuss the possibility of modifying or abrogating those provisions of the Nine Power Treaty without considering at the same time the other promises upon which they were really dependent.

Six years later the policy of self-denial against aggression by a stronger against a weaker power, upon which the Nine Power Treaty had been based, received a powerful reinforcement by the execution by substantially all the nations of the world of the Pact of Paris, the so-called Kellogg Briand Pact. These two treaties represent independent but harmonious steps taken for the purpose of aligning the conscience and public opinion of the world in favor of a system of orderly development by the law of nations including the settlement of all controversies by methods of justice and peace instead of by arbitrary force. The program for the protection of China from outside aggression is an essential part of any such development. The signatories and adherents of the Nine Power Treaty rightly felt that the orderly and peaceful development of the 400,000,000 of people inhabiting China was necessary to the peaceful welfare of the entire world and that no program for the welfare of the world as a whole could afford to neglect the welfare and protection of China.

The recent events which have taken place in China, especially the hostilities which having been begun in Manchuria have latterly been extended to Shanghai, far from indicating the advisability of any modification of the treaties we have been discussing, have tended to bring home the vital importance of the faithful observance of the covenants therein to all of the nations interested in the Far East. It is not necessary in that connection to inquire into the causes of the controversy or attempt to apportion the blame between the two nations which are unhappily involved; for regardless of cause or responsibility, it is clear beyond peradventure that a situation has developed which cannot, under any circumstances, be reconciled with the obligations of the covenants of these two treaties, and that if the treaties had been faithfully observed such a situation could not have arisen. The signatories of the Nine Power Treaty and of the Kellogg-Briand Pact who are not parties to that conflict are not likely to see any reason for modifying the terms of those treaties. To them the real value of the faithful performance of the treaties has been brought sharply home by the perils and losses to which their nationals have been subjected in Shanghai.

That is the view of this Government. We see no reason for abandoning the enlightened principles which are embodied in these treaties. We believe that this situation would have been avoided had these covenants been faithfully observed, and no evidence has come to us to indicate that a due compliance with them would have interfered with the adequate protection of the legitimate rights in China of the signatories of those treaties and their nationals.

On January 7th last, upon the instruction of the President, this Government formally notified Japan and China that it would not recognize any situation, treaty or agreement entered into by those governments in violation of the covenants of these treaties, which affected the rights of our Government or its citizens in China. If a similar decision should be reached and a similar position taken by the other governments of the world, a caveat will be placed upon such action which, we believe, will effectively bar the legality hereafter of any title or right sought to be obtained by pressure or treaty violation, and which, as has been shown by history in the past, will eventually lead to the restoration to China of rights and titles of which she may have been deprived.

In the past our Government, as one of the leading powers on the Pacific Ocean, has rested its policy upon an abiding faith in the future of the people of China and upon the ultimate success in dealing with them of the principles of fair play, patience, and mutual goodwill. We appreciate the immensity of the task which lies before her statesmen in the development of her country and its government. The delays in her progress, the instability of her attempts to secure a responsible government, were foreseen by Messrs. Hay and Hughes and their contemporaries and were the very obstacles which the policy of the Open Door was designed to meet. We concur with those statesmen, representing all the nations, in the Washington Conference who decided that China was entitled to the time necessary to accomplish her development. We are prepared to make that our policy for the future.

Very sincerely yours,

[signed]

Document Analysis

The letter is a statement of administration policy in the waning days of the Hoover administration, before the presidency passed to Franklin D. Roosevelt. (Presidents were inaugurated on March 4 before the Twentieth Amendment went into effect in 1933, moving the date to January 20.) Stimson states the opposition of the United States to territorial changes achieved by force and support of the Open Door to China, the American policy by which all countries were to have equal rights to trade with China. The growing desire of Japan to exert economic hegemony over China was a threat to the Open Door and specifically to US trade with China. Although the letter is addressed specifically to Senator Borah, it was published almost immediately and Stimson likely wrote it with a public audience in mind. Borah was generally regarded as an isolationist, who had opposed American entry into the League of Nations following World War I and was wary of American involvement in European affairs. However, like many American isolationists, he was more willing for the United States to take a strong position in the Asia-Pacific region than in Europe.

Stimson first recapitulates the history of American diplomatic involvement in China, the Open Door policy, and the Nine-Power Treaty, which Stimson viewed as embodying the Open Door policy. He emphasizes that not only the United States, but the world's other preeminent maritime power, the British Empire, endorsed this policy, putting it forth as a consensus position rather than a purely American policy. The Nine-Power Treaty was part of a complex of international agreements, including the Washington Naval Treaty, which demilitarized much of the Pacific and guaranteed the independence of China. This position was reinforced and partially globalized with the adoption of the Kellogg-Briand Pact six years later, which set the face of the international community against territorial aggrandizement by force and aggression. Stimson argues that the recent threat to the treaty caused by conflict between China and Japan (and he is careful not to lay blame on one party) only means that the terms of these treaties, and the international order based on them, need further support. The difficulty was how the treaties, which contained little in the way of enforcement mechanisms, could be upheld. The possibility of enforcement through the League of Nations is not mentioned, as the United States was not a member.

What Stimson offers as a response to Japanese aggression in China is American nonrecognition of those changes that threatened Chinese sovereignty or American rights in China. However, he offers nothing beyond that in the way of either economic sanctions against Japan (which Hoover opposed), aid to China, or military action.

Essential Themes

American opposition to Japanese expansion and support of the Open Door policy in China continued into the Democratic administration of Franklin Delano Roosevelt, when the Republican Stimson was replaced by Democrat Cordell Hull as secretary of state. Despite Hull's efforts to keep peace between the United States and Japan while opposing Japanese imperialism, the conflict intensified with the actual breakout of war between Japan and China in 1937. The broader principle regarding the territorial acquisition by force was also challenged by the expansionist power of Nazi Germany and Fascist Italy. The growing power of the aggressor states and their disregard for the political order set up in the 1920s led to the adoption of more active policies to oppose them, such as the embargo that the Roosevelt administration eventually imposed on Japan. Growing hostility between the United States and Japan culminated in the Japanese attack on Pearl Harbor on December 7, 1941, and American entrance into World War II. Stimson himself, as secretary of war during World War II, was a strong advocate of using nuclear weapons on the Japanese population.

Along with the League of Nations, the United States refused to give diplomatic recognition to Manchukuo, the puppet state the Japanese had carved out of China. The policy of not recognizing territorial changes made by force is sometimes referred to as the Stimson Doctrine and remains part of US policy, although, in practice, its application has been flexible. The same doctrine applied to the US nonrecognition of the Soviet annexation of the Baltic States (Latvia, Lithuania, and Estonia) during World War II, and was a policy maintained throughout the Cold War.

—William E. Burns, PhD

Bibliography and Additional Reading
Fairbank, John K. *The United States and China*. 4th ed. Cambridge: Harvard UP, 1983. Print.
Hodgson, Geoffrey. *The Colonel: The Life and Wars of Henry Stimson, 1867–1950*. New York: Knopf, 1990. Print.
Jeansonne, Glen. *The Life of Herbert Hoover: Fighting Quaker, 1928–1933*. New York: Palgrave, 2012. Print.

Criticism of the Neutrality Act

Date: August 24, 1935
Author: Tom Connally
Genre: speech

Summary Overview

As political tensions rose throughout Europe in the mid-1930s, the United States sought to retain its neutrality. Critics believed that the United States' entry into World War I in 1917 was fueled by diplomatic mistakes and the financial interests of bankers and arms dealers, which helped sway public opinion toward isolationism by the 1930s. In 1935, the United States Congress passed the first of several Neutrality Acts, which prohibited trade of arms, ammunition, and other "implements of war" to any nation involved in a war. A majority of legislators believed the act was necessary to avoid repeating past mistakes, but a vocal minority, including Texas senator Thomas Connally, believed it placed too many restrictions on the president's ability to authorize such a trade if he deemed it to be a sound foreign policy decision or otherwise necessary to protect US commercial interests and national security.

Defining Moment

In 1935, the United States was still struggling to recover from its worst financial crisis since the Civil War. As political conflict rose again in Europe, the United States focused on bolstering its own failing economy, feeding its starving population, and stemming the tide of home and farm foreclosures, failing businesses, and collapsing financial institutions.

Additionally, opinion on US involvement in World War I had shifted over time. The United States had initially tried to remain neutral in the conflict, but in 1917, President Woodrow Wilson declared war on Germany, and Americans were swept up in a wave of patriotism. But in the years after the war, many came to suspect that the business interests of bankers and arms manufacturers had motivated the country's involvement far more than the desire to make the world, in Wilson's words, "safe for democracy."

Together, these two factors fueled the isolationist mood within the United States during the 1930s. As war in Europe came to seem imminent, public opinion broadly supported laws and policies that would maintain US neutrality in armed conflicts between other countries. Legislators believed that doing so required prohibitions on trade and financial dealings with warring nations in order to avoid the appearance of support for any country involved in conflict, thus preventing US territories and vessels from becoming targets, and to remove the financial incentive for bankers and munitions traders to encourage entry into the war.

To this end, the Seventy-fourth United States Congress passed three Neutrality Acts between 1935 and 1937. The first, the Neutrality Act of 1935, prohibited the trade of "arms, ammunition, and implements of war" with countries involved in an armed conflict. It also required any merchant dealing in these goods to register with the secretary of state and authorized the president to establish stronger restrictions as necessary to protect US interests and security. Initially, President Franklin D. Roosevelt opposed the act, but legislative influence and public opinion were strongly in favor of policies that would keep the United States out of the developing conflict in Europe, so he eventually conceded. The Neutrality Act of 1936 renewed the terms of the first act and extended them to include a prohibition on loans to belligerent nations. The Neutrality Act of 1937 extended those terms indefinitely, and added a provision that permitted the sale of supplies other than armaments to belligerent nations at the president's discretion, provided they were sold on a "cash-and-carry" basis, meaning the purchasing nation had to pay for the goods immediately and transport them on its own ships.

Congressional opinion on the first Neutrality Act was

split, although obviously most lawmakers favored its passage. Aside from suspicion about financial motives, supporters believed that allowing passenger ships and merchant vessels to carry supplies to and from warring countries would contribute to US involvement in war, and they considered the act necessary to prevent such mistakes. Critics of the law, however, believed that the blanket trade prohibition established by the Neutrality Act was not really neutral at all; because aggressor nations have the advantage in wars of their own creation, they argued, refusing to trade arms and ammunition with a country that needs to defend itself is tantamount to supporting the aggressor nation.

A fourth Neutrality Act was passed in 1939, repealing the previous acts and extending the cash-and-carry provision to cover weaponry as well as other supplies. The US policy of neutrality came to an end with the passage of the Lend-Lease Act in 1941, and many of the Neutrality Act's provisions were revoked in October and November of that year, although the provisions banning the unlicensed import or export of arms remained in effect.

Author Biography
Thomas Terry Connally was born near Hewitt, Texas, on August 19, 1877. He graduated from Baylor University in 1896 and received his law degree from the University of Texas at Austin in 1898. He was admitted to the bar the same year. Connally moved to Waco, Texas, to begin a private law practice. He served in the Texas Volunteer Infantry during the Spanish-American War and was an infantry brigade captain in the US Army during World War I. In 1904, he married Louise Clarkson, with whom he had a son. Seven years after Louise's death in 1935, he married Lucile Sanderson Sheppard, the widow of fellow Texas senator Morris Sheppard.

Connally began his political career in the Texas House of Representatives, where he served from 1901 to 1904, after which he was the prosecuting attorney for Falls County, Texas, from 1906 to 1910. As a member of the Democratic Party, he was elected to the House of Representatives six times between 1917 and 1928, then served in the Senate from 1928 until 1953. During his legislative career, Connally sat on several committees, including the Committee on Public Buildings and Grounds and the Committee on Foreign Relations. In 1946, he represented the United States at the first and second sessions of the General Assembly of the United Nations. Connally died on October 28, 1963, in Washington, DC.

HISTORICAL DOCUMENT

Is it an expression of neutrality to say to two warring nations, one of which has ambitions for territorial conquest, the other unprepared, the other weak, the other trying to pursue its own destiny—is it neutral to say to those nations, "We shall give arms to neither of you," thereby insuring the triumph of the prepared nation, the covetous nation, the ambitious nation, the nation which seeks by force of arms to impose its will on a weaker and defenseless nation?

Mr. President, that is not neutrality; that is a form of unneutrality. That is a form of declaration which announces that the United States will take the side of the strong and powerful against the weak, the unprepared, and the defenseless. Why not leave that determination to the President of the United States when and if, in his conduct of our foreign relations, it becomes a sound American policy for him to take a position in a crisis of that kind?

We cannot now put the United States into an international strait jacket and thereby keep out of war. We cannot by an act of Congress put the United States into a concrete cast internationally which will fit all future occasions and solve all future problems.

Document Analysis

In Senator Tom Connally's criticism of the Neutrality Act of 1935, he argues that when two nations are at war, with the aggressor country having "ambitions for territorial conquest" and the attacked country being "unprepared" for conflict and simply "trying to pursue its own destiny," it is not a truly neutral position to refuse to assist either party, since the practical effect of such refusal increases the likelihood of victory for the aggressor. Specifically, he claims that because of the imbalance of power between the aggressor country and the attacked country, the Neutrality Act's blanket prohibition on arms trade cannot truly be neutral. Rather, it means the United States is effectively supporting the aggressor country, which will inherently be better prepared for an armed conflict of its own creation. The United States might not want to lend its support to the aggressor, but the prohibition on arms trade with attacked countries will inevitably have this effect.

Additionally, Connally is concerned that the Neutrality Act's prohibition on arms sales to warring countries under any circumstances would prevent the president of the United States from making sound decisions about arms sales based on the facts of a particular circumstance. He points out that a time could arise when "sound American policy" would require the president to allow the United States to provide aid to a country involved in a war. He criticizes the Neutrality Act for placing the nation in an "international strait jacket" in the false belief that such a prohibition "will fit all future occasions and solve all future problems."

Essential Themes

Between the domestic economic crisis and increased cynicism regarding the United States' reasons for entering World War I, public opinion in the 1930s leaned strongly toward isolationism. In 1930, Congress had passed to the Smoot-Hawley Tariff Act, which placed high tax barriers on imported goods in an effort to protect US domestic production from foreign competition. By the mid-1930s, tensions ran high across all of Europe, and many Americans wanted the United States to stay as far away as possible from the growing conflict. They supported the Neutrality Act because they believed it would avoid the appearance of taking sides and remove the financial incentives for US companies to become involved in the war.

President Franklin D. Roosevelt did not support these isolationist tendencies. From the beginning of his term, he sought to overturn the import tariffs and restore balance to international trade. He initially opposed the Neutrality Act as well, but he ultimately relented in the face of strong public opinion and legislative support. Senator Tom Connally of Texas provided one of the few strong voices within the legislature against isolationist policies. Perhaps because of his strong interest in international relations, he advocated making decisions about wartime trade based on individual circumstances rather than a blanket mandate.

Revisions of the Neutrality Act in 1936 and 1937 further tightened the original restrictions. The 1936 renewal prohibited US financial institutions from extending loans to nations involved in armed conflicts, while the 1937 act prohibited Americans from traveling on ships that belonged to nations engaged in war. However, the Neutrality Act of 1937 also loosened restrictions somewhat, introducing the cash-and-carry provision for goods other than arms and munitions. After the Neutrality Act of 1939 expanded the cash-and-carry policy to include arms and munitions, the United States began providing military supplies directly to Allied nations in Europe. Ultimately, the United States' decision to provide support to the Allies trumped the desire for neutrality.

In the end, despite efforts to remain neutral, the United States officially joined World War II in December 1941, following the bombing of Pearl Harbor by Japanese forces. Connally maintained his interest in foreign policy throughout World War II and beyond, serving as chairman of the Senate Foreign Relations Committee from 1941 to 1947, helping devise the United Nations and create its charter, and participating in the establishment of the North Atlantic Treaty Organization (NATO).

—*Tracey M. DiLascio, JD*

Bibliography and Additional Reading

Ferraro, Vincent, comp. "Documents of the Interwar Period." *Resources for the Study of International Relations and Foreign Policy.* Mount Holyoke Coll., n.d. Web. 10 June 2014.

Kennedy, David M. "The Great Depression and World War II, 1929–1945." *Gilder Lehrman Institute of American History.* Gilder Lehrman Institute, n.d. Web. 10 June 2014.

McElvaine, Robert S. *The Great Depression: America, 1929–1941.* 25th anniv. ed. New York: Three Rivers, 2009. Print.

United States. Dept. of State. *Office of the Historian*.
   "Milestones: 1921–1936." Office of the Historian.
   US Dept. of State, n.d. Web. 10 June 2014.

■ Neutrality Act of 1935

Date: August 31, 1935
Author: Seventy-fourth US Congress
Genre: legislation

Summary Overview

Despite attempts to remain neutral during World War I, the United States was drawn into the conflict by 1917. In hope of avoiding the same fate as a second European war came to seem inevitable in the mid-1930s, the US Congress passed the Neutrality Act of 1935. The act prohibited US merchants from trading arms, munitions, and other "implements of war" with any nation involved in an armed conflict and restricted the movement of American merchant vessels carrying those types of goods. It also established a federal register to allow the US Department of State to keep records of any US merchant engaged in sale or transport of arms and munitions and authorized the president to impose additional restrictions necessary to promote peace and protect US security. But even with the neutrality acts in place, the United States eventually joined World War II in December 1941, following the bombing of Pearl Harbor.

Defining Moment

After years of attempting to remain neutral in World War I, the United States entered the conflict in 1917. President Woodrow Wilson declared that the United States must protect its interests and help make the world "safe for democracy," and a wave of patriotism swept the nation. However, in the years that followed, critics suspected that American entry into the war was primarily driven by business interests, rather than by the need to protect US security.

Following the war, the United States experienced a financial boom. But the economy spiraled quickly at the end of the 1920s, and by the early 1930s, the country was in the throes of the Great Depression. Nearly one-quarter of workers came to be unemployed, farms and homes went into foreclosure, companies went out of business, and financial institutions become insolvent. President Franklin D. Roosevelt's New Deal established federal programs to provide publicly funded jobs in public works and infrastructure projects; those seemed to help, but full recovery was a long way off.

Taken together, these circumstances inspired isolationist laws and policies to maintain US neutrality during any future wars. In the mid-to-late 1930s, the US Congress passed several neutrality acts to prohibit financial dealings and munitions trading with countries at war. The issue became pressing as political unrest in Europe and the Far East made another war appear increasingly likely. Public opinion swayed so strongly in support of isolationist policies that Roosevelt, despite private reservations, ultimately signed each of these acts.

Opinion on the first Neutrality Act was divided in Congress, although most representatives favored the restrictions. Some believed that US actions, such as allowing merchant ships to carry arms and supplies to warring European countries, had needlessly drawn the country into World War I. Neutrality Act supporters believed that prohibiting such actions would protect US passenger and merchant vessels from aggressor nations and help keep the country out of war. Others, such as H. C. Englebrecht and F. C. Hanighen, contended that US involvement was encouraged by munitions dealers and bankers, who stood to make an enormous profit supplying and financing war efforts. With the prohibition on arms trading, American businesses would have no vested interest in pressuring the United States to join a war in which it did not have a true safety or security interest.

Critics, including Roosevelt, primarily argued that refusing to trade with nations on the receiving end of aggression was not a truly neutral position. The aggressor nation would be better prepared for the armed conflict of their own creation, so refusing to provide arms, ammunition, and other supplies to countries trying to defend themselves from a hostile takeover was tantamount to supporting the aggressor nation.

Author Biography
The Seventy-fourth Congress sat in Washington, DC, from 1935 to 1937. During the 1934 elections, widespread public support for Roosevelt's New Deal plan for economic recovery increased the Democratic majority. The Seventy-fourth Congress began its session with 322 Democratic, 103 Republican, 7 Progressive, and 3 Farmer-Labor congressional representatives, as well as 13 Democratic and 1 Farmer-Labor freshman senators.

During its two-year session, the Seventy-fourth Congress passed many reform initiatives, including Social Security and regulation of public utilities, as well as several neutrality acts designed to keep the United States out of foreign wars by prohibiting arms trade and financial dealings with countries involved in armed conflicts. Some of that legislation was later declared unconstitutional by the US Supreme Court, but many of the initiatives brought significant social and economic changes to American society during the 1930s and beyond.

HISTORICAL DOCUMENT

"Neutrality Act" of August 31, 1935, Joint Resolution 49 stat. 1081; 22 U.S.C. 441

Providing for the prohibition of the export of arms, ammunition, and implements of war to belligerent countries; the prohibition of the transportation of arms, ammunition, and implements of war by vessels of the United States for the use of belligerent states; for the registration and licensing of persons engaged in the business of manufacturing, exporting, or importing arms, ammunition, or implements of war; and restricting travel by American citizens on belligerent ships during war.

RESOLVED by the Senate and House of Representatives of the United States of America in Congress assembled, That upon the outbreak or during the progress of war between, or among, two or more foreign states, the President shall proclaim such fact, and it shall thereafter be unlawful to export arms, ammunition, or implements of war from any place in the United States, or possessions of the United States, to any port of such belligerent states, or to any neutral port for transshipment to, or for the use of, a belligerent country.

The President, by proclamation, shall definitely enumerate the arms, ammunition, or implements of war, the export of which is prohibited by this Act.

The President may, from time to time, by proclamation, extend such embargo upon the export of arms, ammunition, or implements of war to other states as and when they may become involved in such war.

Whoever, in violation of any of the provisions of this section, shall export, or attempt to export, or cause to be exported, arms, ammunition, or implements of war from the United States, or any of its possessions, shall be fined not more than $10,000 or imprisoned not more than five years, or both, and the property, vessel, or vehicle containing the same shall be subject to the provisions of sections 1 to 8, inclusive, title 6, chapter 30, of the Act approved June 15, 1917 (40 Stat. 223–225; U. S. C., title 22, sees. 238–245).

In the case of the forfeiture of any arms, ammunition, or implements of war by reason of a violation of this Act, no public or private sale shall be required; but such arms, ammunition, or implements of war shall be delivered to the Secretary of War for such use or disposal thereof as shall be approved by the President.

When in the judgment of the President the conditions which have caused him to issue his proclamation have ceased to exist he shall revoke the same and the provisions hereof shall thereupon cease to apply.

Except with respect to prosecutions committed or forfeitures incurred prior to March 1, 1936, this section and all proclamations issued thereunder shall not be effective after February 29, 1936.

Sec. 2.
That for the purpose of this Act— (a) The term "Board" means the National Munitions Control Board

which is hereby established to carry out the provisions of this Act. The Board shall consist of the Secretary of State, who shall be chairman and executive officer of the Board; the Secretary of the Treasury; the Secretary of War; the Secretary of the Navy; and the Secretary of Commerce. Except as otherwise provided in this Act, or by other law, the administration of this Act is vested in the Department of State; (b) The term "United States" when used in a geographical sense, includes the several States and Territories, the insular possessions of the United States (including the Philippine Islands), the Canal Zone, and the District of Columbia; (c) The term "person" includes a partnership, company, association, or corporation, as well as a natural person.

Within ninety days after the effective date of this Act, or upon first engaging in business, every person who engages in the business of manufacturing, exporting, or importing any of the arms, ammunition, and implements of war referred to in this Act, whether as an exporter, importer, manufacturer, or dealer, shall register with the Secretary of State his name, or business name, principal place of business, and places of business in the United States, and a list of the arms, ammunition, and implements of war which he manufactures, imports, or exports.

Every person required to register under this section shall notify the Secretary of State of any change in the arms, ammunition, and implements of war which he exports, imports, or manufactures; and upon such notification the Secretary of State shall issue to such person an amended certificate of registration, free of charge, which shall remain valid until the date of expiration of the original certificate. Every person required to register under the provisions of this section shall pay a registration fee of $500, and upon receipt of such fee the Secretary of State shall issue a registration certificate valid for five years, which shall be renewable for further periods of five years upon the payment of each renewal of a fee of $500.

It shall be unlawful for any person to export, or attempt to export, from the United States any of the arms, ammunition, or implements of war referred to in this Act to any other country or to import, or attempt to import, to the United States from any other country any of the arms, ammunition, or implements of war referred to in this Act without first having obtained a license therefore.

All persons required to register under this section shall maintain, subject to the inspection of the Board, such permanent records of manufacture for export, importation, and exportation of arms, ammunition, and implements of war as the Board shall prescribe.

Licenses shall be issued to persons who have registered as provided for, except in cases of export or import licenses where exportation of arms, ammunition, or implements of war would be in violation of this Act or any other law of the United States, or of a treaty to which the United States is a party, in which cases such licenses shall not be issued.

The Board shall be called by the Chairman and shall hold at least one meeting a year.

No purchase of arms, ammunition, and implements of war shall be made on behalf of the United States by any officer, executive department, or independent establishment of the Government from any person who shall have failed to register under the provisions of this Act.

The Board shall make an annual report to Congress, copies of which shall be distributed as are other reports transmitted to Congress. Such report shall contain such information and data collected by the Board as may be considered of value in the determination of questions connected with the control of trade in arms, ammunition, and implements of war. It shall include a list of all persons required to register under the provisions of this Act, and full information concerning the licenses issued hereunder.

The Secretary of State shall promulgate such rules and regulations with regard to the enforcement of this section as he may deem necessary to carry out its provisions.

The President is hereby authorized to proclaim upon recommendation of the Board from time to time a list of articles which shall be considered arms, ammunition, and implements of war for the purposes of this section.

This section shall take effect on the ninetieth day after the date of its enactment.

Sec. 3.

Whenever the President shall issue the proclamation provided for in section 1 of this Act, thereafter it shall be unlawful for any American vessel to carry any arms, ammunition, or implements of war to any port of the belligerent countries named in such proclamation as being at war, or to any neutral port for transshipment to, or for the use of, a belligerent country.

Whoever, in violation of the provisions of this section, shall take, attempt to take, or shall authorize, hire, or solicit another to take any such vessel carrying such cargo out of port or from the jurisdiction of the United States shall be fined not more than $10,000 or imprisoned not more than five years, or both; and, in addition, such vessel, her tackle, apparel, furniture, equipment, and the arms, ammunition, and implements of war on board shall be forfeited to the United States.

When the President finds the conditions which have caused him to issue his proclamation have ceased to exist, he shall revoke his proclamation, and the provisions of this section shall thereupon cease to apply.

Sec. 4.

Whenever, during any war in which the United States is neutral, the President, or any person "hereunto authorized by him, shall have cause to believe that any vessel, domestic or foreign, whether requiring clearance or not, is about to carry out of a port of the United States, or its possession, men or fuel, arms, ammunition, implements of war, or other supplies to any warship, tender, or supply ship of a foreign belligerent nation, but the evidence is not deemed sufficient to justify forbidding the departure of the vessel as provided for by section 1, title V, chapter 30, of the Act approved June 15, 1917 (40 Stat. [221[22]]; U. S. C. title 18, sec. 31), and if, in the President's judgment, such action will serve to maintain peace between the United States and foreign nations, or to protect the commercial interests of the United States and its citizens, or to promote the security of the United States, he shall have the power and it shall be his duty to require the owner, master, or person in command thereof, before departing from a port of the United States, or any of its possessions, for a foreign port, to give a bond to the United States, with sufficient sureties, in such amount as he shall deem proper, conditioned that the vessel will not deliver the men, or the cargo, or any part thereof, to any warship, tender, or supply ship of a belligerent nation; and, if the President, or any person thereunto authorized by him, shall find that a vessel, domestic or foreign, in a port of the United States, or one of its possessions, has previously cleared from such port during such war and delivered its cargo or any part thereof to a warship, tender, or supply ship of a belligerent nation, he may prohibit the departure of such vessel during the duration of the war.

Sec. 5.

Whenever, during any war in which the United States is neutral, the President shall find that special restrictions placed on the use of the ports and territorial waters of the United States, or of its possessions, by the submarines of a foreign nation will serve to maintain peace between the United States and foreign nations, or to protect the commercial interests of the United States and its citizens, or to promote the security of the United States, and shall make proclamation thereof, it shall thereafter be unlawful for any such submarine to enter a port or the territorial waters of the United States or any of its possessions, or to depart therefrom, except under such conditions and subject to such limitations as the President may prescribe. When, in his judgment, the conditions which have caused him to issue his proclamation have ceased to exist, he shall revoke his proclamation and the provisions of this section shall thereupon cease to apply.

Sec. 6.

Whenever, during any war in which the United States is neutral, the President shall find that the maintenance of peace between the United States and foreign nations, or the protection of the lives of citizens of the United States, or the protection of the commercial interests of the United States and its citizens, or the security of the United States requires that the American citizens should refrain from traveling as passengers on the vessels of any belligerent nation, he shall so proclaim, and thereafter no citizen of the United States shall travel on any vessel of any belligerent nation except at his own risk, unless in accordance with such rules and regulations as the President shall prescribe: Provided, however, That the provisions of this section shall not apply to a citizen traveling on the vessel of a belligerent whose voyage was begun in advance of the date of the President's proclamation, and who had no opportunity to discontinue his voyage after that date: And provided further, That they shall not apply under ninety days after the date of the President's proclamation to a citizen returning from a foreign country to the United States or to any of its possessions. When, in the President's judgment, the conditions which have caused him to issue his proclamation have ceased to exist, he shall revoke his proclamation and the provisions of this section shall thereupon cease to apply.

Sec. 7.

In every case of the violation of any of the provisions of this Act where a specific penalty is not herein provided, such violator or violators, upon conviction, shall be fined not more than $10,000 or imprisoned not more than five years, or both.

Sec. 8.

If any of the provisions of this Act, or the application thereof to any person or circumstance, is held invalid, the remainder of the Act, and the application of such provision to other persons or circumstances, shall not be affected thereby.

Sec. 9.

The sum of $25,000 is hereby authorized to be appropriated, out of any money in the Treasury not otherwise appropriated, to be expended by the Secretary of State in administering this Act.

Approved, August 31, 1935.

Document Analysis

Section 1 of the Neutrality Act of 1935 establishes that, if the president proclaims that two foreign countries are engaged in a war in which the United States is neutral, it is unlawful to export "arms, ammunition, or implements of war" from any US territory to any country involved in the war. The president determines which goods fall under the prohibition and may extend the provisions to regulate the trade of any other type of goods—or name any additional "belligerent countries"—whenever necessary to protect US interests. Any violation of the act would be punishable by a fine of up to ten thousand dollars, imprisonment of up to five years, or both. Seized goods would be turned over to the secretary of war for use by the United States or disposal as directed by the president.

Section 2 establishes the National Munitions Control Board, which consists of the US secretaries of state, treasury, war, navy, and commerce. Administration of the act is vested in the Department of State. Any business that manufactures, exports, or imports any arms, ammunition, or implements of war must pay five hundred dollars and register with the secretary of state, who will issue a license for trade, without which it will be illegal to export or import arms, ammunition, or implements of war. Licenses will be renewable every five years. The board will dictate what records licensees must keep and then report data on trade activities and provide a list of licensees to Congress annually. The president may, following the recommendations of the board, proclaim additional items to be prohibited, and the secretary of state has the authority to create additional rules and regulations deemed necessary to enforce this section.

Section 3 prohibits American vessels from carrying arms, ammunition, or implements of war to the port of a country at war or to a neutral port for further transfer to a country at war. Section 4 allows the United States to demand the posting of a surety bond if a merchant or vessel is suspected of transporting troops or cargo to any "warship, tender, or supply ship of a foreign belligerent nation," but no proof is found of an actual violation. The president can restrict movement for the duration of a war of any vessel that has been found in violation of the act.

Section 5 authorizes the president to place additional restrictions on US ports and territorial waters, particularly on foreign submarine activity, if the president deems it necessary to maintain peace, protect US commercial interests, or promote US security. Sections 6 through 9 establish basic enforcement provisions, including penalties for violations not otherwise specified in the act, and the appropriation of $25,000 from the US Treasury for enforcing the act.

Essential Themes

By the mid-1930s, political tension ran high throughout Europe and between China and Japan, and the American public largely believed that isolationism was the best approach for keeping the United States out of existing or impending wars. The US Congress passed several neutrality acts between 1935 and 1939, hoping to not become targets of hostilities, to avoid the appearance of "taking sides" in the growing conflicts, and to remove financial incentives for munitions dealers and bankers to encourage involvement in war.

The Neutrality Act of 1935 addressed such concerns directly by prohibiting the sale of arms, ammunition, or any other item that could be considered an "implement of war" to any country involved in armed conflict. This was a blanket prohibition: for the purpose of the act, it did not matter whether the purchasing country was the aggressor or the defender. Public opinion favoring isolationism led to legislative support for the Neutrality Act, although some critics, including Roosevelt, worried that the act bound the president too tightly. While it appeared to give the president some decision-making and enforcement flexibility, the Neutrality Act really only provided authority to proclaim the existence of a war, set punishments for violations of the law, and establish further restrictions. Thus, the president could not lift the restrictions, even if he believed it would best serve US interests to provide support to a nation involved in an armed conflict.

Congress renewed and revised the Neutrality Act nearly every year until the United States joined World War II. The act's 1936 revision further prohibited US financial institutions from extending loans to nations at war. By 1937, the renewed act included civil wars in its definition of international conflict; Americans were prohibited from traveling on ships that belonged to belligerents, invoking a proviso in section 6 of the 1935 law; and US merchant ships could not transport arms manufactured outside the United States to nations involved in a war.

However, later Neutrality Act revisions showed the tide turning. In 1937, President Roosevelt pushed a provision called "cash-and-carry," which allowed warring countries to purchase, with cash, goods other than arms and munitions from the United States, if they transported the goods home on their own ships. That allowed the United States to provide indirect support to nations defending themselves from aggressors (namely, Britain and France) by selling them fuel and other raw materials, while still officially maintaining a neutral stance. By late 1939, the cash-and-carry provision had been expanded to include all trade goods, even arms, and the following year, the United States began to "lend" military supplies to the Allied nations, which by then were having difficulty paying in cash. In the end, despite its efforts to remain neutral, the United States officially became part of World War II in December 1941, following the bombing of Pearl Harbor, and the neutrality acts became obsolete.

—Tracey M. DiLascio, JD

Bibliography and Additional Reading

Kennedy, David M. "Great Depression & WWII, 1929–1945." *Gilder Lehrman Institute of American History*. Gilder Lehrman Institute, 2014. Web. 11 June 2014.

McElvaine, Robert S. *The Great Depression: America, 1929–1941*. New York: Times, 1993. Print.

"The Neutrality Acts, 1930s." *Milestones: 1921–1936*. US Department of State, Office of the Historian, n.d. Web. 11 June 2014.

■ Defense of the Neutrality Act

Date: December 1935
Author: Bennett Champ Clark
Genre: speech

Summary Overview
As political unrest swept across Europe in the 1930s, American public opinion overwhelmingly favored a policy of neutrality. These strong isolationist feelings resulted from cynicism about the true motives for US involvement in World War I, combined with overwhelming preoccupation with the financial effects of the Great Depression. In August 1935, Congress passed the first Neutrality Act, designed as a temporary measure to keep the United States out of any conflict while lawmakers crafted a more comprehensive plan to enforce American neutrality; three more Neutrality Acts would be passed over the following three years. Supporters of this first act, including Missouri senator Bennett Champ Clark, believed legislation preventing US sales of arms and ammunition to belligerents was necessary to keep the United States from needless involvement in foreign conflicts. However, he argued that the act was not strict enough and that it should include a prohibition on lending money to countries at war, as well as a more encompassing embargo on any goods that could possibly aid a belligerent nation during a war.

Defining Moment
After years of attempting to remain neutral during World War I, President Woodrow Wilson declared war on Germany in April 1917. Upon this change of policy, Americans who previously supported non-intervention suddenly rallied in favor of the war effort as a wave of patriotism swept the nation. But in the years that followed the costly conflict, many of those same people came to suspect that US involvement in World War I was driven more by the business interests of bankers and arms traders than by the need to preserve democracy and national security.

By the early 1930s, the United States was in the throes of the Great Depression: nearly one-quarter of workers were unemployed, banks foreclosed on numerous farms and homes, and financial institutions were failing. The combination of the domestic financial crisis and skepticism about the true motives for US involvement in World War I led to widespread isolationism: the public both wanted the United States to stay out of conflicts that did not directly affect its interests and security and supported laws and policies that would maintain neutrality in future wars.

To this end, Congress passed the Neutrality Act of 1935. By this time, political unrest in Europe made another great war seem increasingly possible, and Americans overwhelmingly favored keeping the United States out of any conflict. The Neutrality Act sought to accomplish this by prohibiting the trade of arms, munitions, and other "instruments of war" with any country involved in an armed conflict.

Most legislators supported the Neutrality Act. They shared the public's opinion that financial institutions and munitions traders influenced the United States' decision to enter World War I, and some believed that actions during the war—such as allowing passenger vessels and merchant ships to transport war materials to Europe—needlessly made the United States a target for aggression. However, the Neutrality Act had its detractors, including President Franklin D. Roosevelt. Critics argued that refusing to trade with all warring nations, including those on the receiving end of aggression, is not a truly neutral position. According to this perspective, since the aggressor nation is better prepared for an armed conflict of its own creation, refusing to trade arms and ammunition with countries trying to defend themselves is tantamount to supporting the aggressor nation, even if that is not the intent.

Congress passed the Neutrality Act in August 1935,

at the end of its first session. However, many of the act's trade embargo provisions did not take effect until the following year. While delivering his defense of the first Neutrality Act in December 1935, Senator Bennett Champ Clark cited reports that companies believed to manufacture war-related supplies were hiring workers and increasing their production rates. Although no direct proof existed, he said these reports raise the suspicion that companies were working hard to profit from the European conflicts as much as possible before the embargo took effect.

Author Biography

Joel Bennett Clark (later known as Bennett Champ Clark) was born on January 8, 1890, in Bowling Green, Missouri. His father, James Beauchamp "Champ" Clark, was a prominent Democratic congressman, so young Bennett grew up surrounded by politics.

Clark attended the University of Missouri and George Washington University School of Law. He joined the US Army in 1917, becoming the youngest person to achieve the rank of colonel in the American Expeditionary Forces during World War I. Upon his return, he and several other officers founded the American Legion. He practiced law for several years, and, in 1932, undertook an extensive campaign tour to secure his first term in the US Senate. He was reelected in 1938 and, during this second term, became the principal author and sponsor of the GI Bill. Bennett failed to win a third term in the 1944 election, and he briefly practiced law before being appointed a judge on the US Court of Appeals for the District of Columbia Circuit. Bennett served in the judiciary until his death on July 13, 1954.

HISTORICAL DOCUMENT

At the present the desire to keep the United States from becoming involved in any war between foreign nations seems practically unanimous among the rank and file of American citizens; but it must be remembered there was an almost equally strong demand to keep us out of the last war. In August, 1914, few could have conceived that America would be dragged into a European conflict in which we had no original part and the ramifications of which we did not even understand. Even as late as November, 1916, President Wilson was reelected because he "kept us out of war." Yet five months later we were fighting to "save the world for democracy" in the "war to end war."

In the light of that experience, and in the red glow of war fires burning in the old countries, it is high time we gave some thought to the hard, practical question of just how we propose to stay out of present and future international conflicts. No one who has made an honest attempt to face the issue will assert that there is an easy answer. But if we have learned anything at all, we know the inevitable and tragic end to a policy of drifting and trusting to luck. We know that however strong is the will of the American people to refrain from mixing in other people's quarrels, that will can be made effective only if we have a sound, definite policy from the beginning.

Such a policy must be built upon a program to safeguard our neutrality. No lesson of the World War is more clear than that such a policy cannot be improvised after war breaks out. It must be determined in advance, before it is too late to apply reason. I contend with all possible earnestness that if we want to avoid being drawn into this war now forming, or any other future war, we must formulate a definite, workable policy of neutral relations with belligerent nations.

Some of us in the Senate, particularly the members of the Munitions Investigation Committee, have delved rather deeply into the matter of how the United States has been drawn into past wars, and what forces are at work to frighten us again into the traps set by Mars. As a result of these studies, Senator Nye and I introduced the three proposals for neutrality legislation which were debated so vigorously in the last session of the Congress. A part of that legislative program was battered through both houses in the closing hours of the session late in August; a very vital part of it was held in abeyance.

Senator Nye and I made no claims then, and make none now, that the neutrality proposals will provide an absolute and infallible guarantee against our involvement in war. But we do believe that the United States can stay out of war if it wants to, and if its citizens understand what is necessary to preserve our neutrality. We feel that the temporary legislation already passed and the legislation we shall vigorously push at the coming session of the Congress point the only practical way…

The act is to terminate February 29, 1936. It is a stopgap only. But it is pointing the way we intend to go.

The President is empowered to enumerate definitely the arms, munitions, and implements of war, the exportation of which is prohibited by this act. On September 27th President Roosevelt made this enumeration in a proclamation, following closely the list submitted to the disarmament conference at Geneva in our government's proposals for international control of the munitions industry. A National Munitions Control Board has been established, composed of the Secretaries of State, Treasury, War, Navy, and Commerce, with the administration of the board in the Department of State. It is contemplated that by November 29th, when the Act takes effect, the manufacturers and exporters of war implements will all be listed in the office of this board. After that date such materials as are specified may not be exported without a license issued by the board to cover such shipment. This will, obviously, permit the government to prohibit shipments to belligerent nations. The act makes it unlawful for any American vessel to "carry arms, ammunition, or implements of war to any port of the belligerent countries named in such proclamation as being at war, or to any neutral port for transshipment to, or for use in, a belligerent country."

Further provisions of the act empower the President to restrict the use of American ports and waters to submarines of foreign nations in the event such use might disturb our position of neutrality, and to proclaim the conditions under which American citizens on belligerent ships during war must travel entirely at their own risk.

Two provisions from our original program failed to pass: prohibition of loans and credits to belligerent nations, and the application of strict embargoes upon contraband materials other than munitions and war implements…

I have called the present neutrality act a stop-gap. But it has not stopped the activities of our American war-munitions makers anxious for profits from imminent conflicts. Reports from centers of manufacturing and exporting of war implements all tell the same story: there is a boom in war preparations. Chambers of commerce in cities with large war-materials plants proudly report reemployment of skilled munitions makers in large numbers, the stepping up of output to as high as three hundred per cent, the rushing to completion of new additions to plants. Day-and-night shifts in the brass and copper mills, rising prices and large shipments of these metals, and the acquisition of large capital for immediate wartime scale production, all indicate that Mars has waved his magic wand in our direction.

Where are these war-implements shipments going? There is no proof that the munitions makers are trying to "beat the embargo" which will prohibit shipments to belligerents after November 29th, but it stands to reason they are making hay while the sun shines. Our Munitions Investigation Committee has not had time to look into immediate developments, but it needs no stretch of imagination to contemplate the rich profits that would flow from an Italian-Ethiopian war, with England jumping into the fray against Italy, and other European nations following suit on one side or the other.

And, of course, there's lots of war business right here at home. We have increased our expenditures on our Army and Navy in preparation for another and more dreadful war more rapidly than any European country in the period since the World War…

When the Congress meets in January, facing the expiration of the neutrality act on February 29th, the battle for a practical policy of neutrality will have to be fought all over again. We who believe that the detour around another devastating war is to be found only in new conceptions of neutrality will fight for the retention of the present legislation and for the passage of the two items left out in the cold at the adjournment of the Congress.

I firmly believe, whatever the status of the Italo-Ethiopian dispute at that time, whatever the position of other European powers as belligerents or as neutrals, that the United States of America cannot turn back to a policy of so-called neutrality that finally pulls us into conflict with one or all the belligerents. Surely it is obvious that the legislation forcing mandatory embargoes upon war materials will serve to check the growth of another vast munitions trade with warring powers and the dangers that follow a swing of our foreign trade in favor of our munitions customers and against those who cannot purchase the munitions. Why shall we contend for embargoes upon contraband articles as well, and prohibition of loans and credits to belligerents? Because it takes these two items to complete any sort of workable neutrality program. If we are in earnest about neutrality we may as well plan to be neutral...

Let us foresee that under conditions of modern warfare everything supplied to the enemy population has the same effect as supplies to the enemy army, and will become contraband. Food, clothing, lumber, leather, chemicals—everything, in fact, with the possible exception of sporting goods and luxuries (and these aid in maintaining civilian "morale")—are as important aids to winning the war as are munitions. Let us foresee also that our ships carrying contraband will be seized, bombed from the air or sunk by submarines. Let us not claim as a right what is an impossibility. The only way we can maintain our neutral rights is to fight the whole world. If we are not prepared to do that we can only pretend to enforce our rights against one side, and go to war to defend them against the other side. We might at least abandon pretense.

On the matter of loans and credits to belligerents, the train of events which pulled us into the World War is equally significant. Correspondence which our Munitions Investigation Committee discovered in the files of the State Department offers illuminating proof that there can be no true neutrality when our nation is allowed to finance one side of a foreign war. One letter, written by Secretary Robert Lansing to President Wilson, dated September 5, 1915, lucidly points out that loans for the Allies were absolutely necessary to enable them to pay for the tremendous trade in munitions, war materials generally, food stuffs, and the like, or else that trade would have to stop. He declared that the Administration's "true spirit of neutrality" must not stand in the way of the demands of commerce. About one month later the first great loan—the Anglo-French loan of $500,000,000—was floated by a syndicate headed by J. P. Morgan and Company. This company had been the purchasing agents for Allied supplies in the United States since early in 1915. Other loans to the Allied powers quickly followed...

"But, think of the profits!" cry our theorists. "America will never give up her lucrative trade in munitions and necessities of life when war starts!"...

Just who profited from the last war? Labor got some of the crumbs in the form of high wages and steady jobs. But where is labor to-day with its fourteen million unemployed? Agriculture received high prices for its products during the period of the War and has been paying the price of that brief inflation in the worst and longest agricultural depression in all history. Industry made billions in furnishing the necessities of war to the belligerents and then suffered terrific re-action like the dope addict's morning after. War and depression—ugly, misshapen inseparable twins—must be considered together. Each is a catapult for the other. The present world-wide depression is a direct result of the World War. Every war in modern history has been followed by a major depression.

Therefore I say, let the man seeking profits from war or the war-torn countries do so at his own risk...

If there are those so brave as to risk getting us into war by traveling in the war zones—if there are those so valiant that they do not care how many people are killed as a result of their traveling, let us tell them, and let us tell the world that from now on their deaths will be a misfortune to their own families alone, not to the whole nation.

The profiteers and others who oppose any rational neutrality shout: "You would sacrifice our national honor!" Some declare we are about to haul down the American flag, and in a future war the belligerents will trample on our rights and treat us with contempt. Some of these arguments are trundled out by our naval bureaucracy. The admirals, I am told, objected strenuously when the State Department suggested a new policy of neutrality somewhat along these lines.

I deny with every fiber of my being that our national honor demands that we must sacrifice the flower of our youth to safeguard the profits of a privileged few. I deny that it is necessary to turn back the hands of civilization to maintain our national honor. I repudiate any such definition of honor. Is it not time for every lover of our country to do the same thing?

Document Analysis
In his defense of the Neutrality Act of 1935, Senator Clark reiterates that Americans did not initially want the United States involved in World War I: even as late as November 1916, President Woodrow Wilson won his reelection campaign largely because of his neutrality position. Yet only five months later, the United States declared war on Germany and was fighting to "save the world for democracy." Clark observes that, once again, public opinion presently favors keeping the United States out of the conflicts unfolding across Europe. In light of the abrupt turn of events during World War I, the United States must firmly establish its neutrality policy well before any war fully breaks out.

Clark reports that the Senate Munitions Investigation Committee carefully analyzed the circumstances that led to US involvement in World War I, to learn from past mistakes and identify how the country can avoid another foreign conflict. Clark says that the Neutrality Act passed at the end of the last congressional term in August of 1935 is only temporary legislation. As written, the act expires on February 29, 1936, so the current congressional session must establish a more comprehensive plan for maintaining neutrality.

After briefly describing the terms of the Neutrality Act of 1935, Clark states that two important provisions were left out of the act: a prohibition on loans and credits to "belligerent nations" and an embargo on the sale to belligerents of relevant materials beyond weapons and ammunition. With respect to the trade embargo, Clark contends that essentially any supply sent to a warring country, including food, clothing, lumber, leather, and even luxury items that might improve morale, could be seen by one warring party as aid to its enemy, and therefore open US shipping to attack. He also says a broader prohibition is necessary to maintain true neutrality because otherwise US policy will inherently favor whichever country can afford to trade.

Regarding loans and credits, Clark says that "there can be no true neutrality when our nation is allowed to finance one side of a foreign war." Private companies reaped great profits by providing loans to European nations during World War I, and theorists believe these financial gains combined with increased agricultural and manufacturing production led to the US economic boom of the 1920s. But Clark observes that every major war was followed by an economic depression and that, for many reasons, war should not be used to provide a temporary boost to the economy. Clark concludes by asserting that the United States' "national honor" does not demand that it needlessly enter foreign wars, since such actions place the nation's youth in harm's way for the financial benefit of a few.

Essential Themes
After serving in the US Army during World War I, Senator Clark had no illusions about the glories of war. And like much of the public during the 1930s, he believed that US involvement in World War I was driven by the merchants and manufacturers who reaped the financial rewards, rather than by a greater need to preserve worldwide democracy and protect US national security.

In his defense of the Neutrality Act of 1935, Clark specifically noted that Americans opposed entering World War I for most of its duration, and in 1935, they overwhelmingly opposed US involvement in any of the conflicts brewing in Europe. Clark felt the United States had a tendency to meddle in international affairs and believed that lax trade and shipping policies during World War I needlessly made the United States a target for German hostilities. Because of this tendency, Clark argued in favor of establishing a strong, clear Neutrality Act well in advance of full-blown war in Europe. But since war seemed imminent because of the pervasive unrest across the continent, Clark willingly supported a weaker, "stop-gap" measure to establish a basic policy of US neutrality, and then he pushed in earnest for additional trade restrictions upon the act's renewal in 1936.

One of Clark's additional restrictions was a full embargo of almost any trade with nations at war, as nearly any supply sent to a warring country could be considered by another belligerent to aid the "enemy army." Full adoption of Clark's proposal would have effectively cut off all trade with any country involved in an armed conflict, but it was never enacted as he envisioned. The "cash-and-carry" provision of the 1937 Neutrality Act—promoted by President Roosevelt—limited trade to goods other than arms and munitions that countries could pay for in cash and carry home on their own vessels. While this imposed heavy trade restrictions, it implicitly permitted the trade of non-war-related goods. By 1939, the cash-and-carry provision expanded to include "instruments of war," including arms and munitions, intended to aid Britain and France. By 1940, despite the attempts at neutrality, the United States was supplying arms and munitions to European Allied forces.

While Clark initially opposed US involvement in the

increasingly global conflict, he and many Americans changed their position following the bombing of Pearl Harbor in December 1941. The United States officially entered World War II shortly thereafter.

—Tracey M. DiLascio, JD

Bibliography and Additional Reading

"Bennett Champ Clark." *The Champ Clark House*. Champ Clark House, n.d. Web. 12 June 2014.

"Great Depression & WWII, 1929–1945." *The Gilder Lehrman Institute of American History*. Gilder Lehrman Institute, n.d. Web. 12 June 2014.

McElvaine, Robert S. *The Great Depression: America, 1929–1941*. 25th anniv. ed. New York: Three Rivers, 2009. Print.

"Milestones: 1921–1936." *Office of the Historian*. US Dept. of State, n.d. Web. 12 June 2014.

Address Delivered by the Secretary of State

Date: March 12, 1938
Author: Cordell Hull
Genre: address

Summary Overview

In an address delivered to the National Press Club, Secretary of State Cordell Hull stated the position of the American government on international affairs, stressing the United States' support of peace and opposition to territorial expansion by force. He portrayed the world as being threatened by a rising tide of international lawlessness, avoiding naming the specific powers involved. Hull set forth a vision of an international community governed by law as an alternative to the "international anarchy" that would inevitably lead to the outbreak of World War II, less than twenty years after World War I.

Defining Moment

By the late 1930s, the post–World War I international order was breaking up, as rising powers—from minor members of the victorious coalition, such as Italy and Japan, to defeated powers, such as Germany—were increasingly taking an aggressive role on the international stage. For many Americans, the most worrisome international situation was in East Asia. Years of Japanese aggression against China had culminated in the outbreak of war between the two countries in 1937. American sympathies were with the Chinese, and it was the policy of the American government to oppose Japanese expansionism. Friction between the two countries was on the rise. The Japanese even attacked an American vessel in China, the *Panay*, late in 1937, although they claimed the attack had been a mistake and paid the United States an indemnity.

By 1938, Japanese aggression also fit into a larger global picture of the aggression of militaristic and fascist powers, including Nazi Germany and Fascist Italy. Under dictator Benito Mussolini, Italy had invaded and conquered Ethiopia in 1935 and 1936, and Germany and Italy together had intervened in the Spanish Civil War to support fascist leader Francisco Franco, while Western democracies had done little or nothing to support the legitimate government of the Spanish Republic. By the time of Hull's speech, the war had clearly tilted toward Franco's Nationalist forces, while the German Anschluss, or annexation of Austria, occurred on the same day as Hull's address. The liberal democratic order established at the end of World War I seemed under threat in both Asia and Europe. However, many Americans were still wary of involvement in "foreign quarrels," where aggressors did not pose a direct threat to the United States.

Author Biography

Cordell Hull holds the record as the longest-serving US secretary of state, having held the position for eleven years, from 1933 to 1944. Originally from Tennessee, he was active in Democratic politics from his late teens. As a congressman, he was an early ally of Franklin Roosevelt. As president, Roosevelt repaid Hull by appointing him secretary of state, though Hull had continual difficulties with Roosevelt's habit of entrusting foreign relations to White House agents, bypassing the secretary. In East Asia, Hull supported opposition to Japanese imperialism, but not at the risk of war. The ambitious Hull hoped to run for president in 1940, but lost the Democratic nomination to Roosevelt when Roosevelt made the unprecedented decision to run for a third term. He was a leading figure in the creation of the United Nations after the war and received the Nobel Peace Prize as a reward for his efforts. However, he has also been criticized for the State Department's reluctance to help Jews in Nazi-occupied Europe.

HISTORICAL DOCUMENT

In the course of the daily press conferences at the Department of State, I have occasion to see many of you and to touch upon day-to-day developments in our foreign relations. Such information as I am able to give you in these conferences must, of necessity, relate to specific questions and, oftentimes, to isolated events. Yet upon you, representatives of the press, rests a heavy responsibility in keeping our people currently and accurately informed on the vital issues which arise in our country's relations with other nations. I welcome, therefore, this opportunity to meet with the members of the National Press Club in the calmer atmosphere of an occasion like the present one, and to discuss with you some of the fundamental conditions and problems presented by our international relations and our foreign policy. The primary objectives of our foreign policy are the maintenance of the peace of our country and the promotion of the economic, the social, and the moral welfare of our people. Unfortunately, the means of attaining these objectives involve today so many factors of great complexity that their real significance is frequently misunderstood and misinterpreted.

By instinct and tradition our country has been, throughout its history, sincerely devoted to the cause of peace. Within the limitations imposed by time and circumstance we have earnestly sought to discharge our responsibilities as a member of the family of nations in promoting conditions essential to the maintenance of peace. We have consistently believed in the sanctity of treaty obligations and have endeavored to apply this belief in the actual practice of our foreign relations. In common with all other nations we have, since the end of the World War, assumed a solemn obligation not to resort to force as an instrument of national policy. All this gives us a moral right to express our deep concern over the rising tide of lawlessness, the growing disregard of treaties, the increasing reversion to the use of force, and the numerous other ominous tendencies which are emerging in the sphere of international relations.

On July 16, 1937, I issued a public statement setting forth the fundamental principles to which our Government adheres in the formulation of its foreign policy. On behalf of our Government I transmitted a copy of this statement to every government of the world, requesting such comment as each might see fit to offer. To our profound gratification an overwhelming majority of those governments joined in affirming their faith in these vital principles.

The most important of these principles, which are indispensable to a satisfactory international order, are as follows:

- Maintenance of peace should be constantly advocated and practiced. All nations should, through voluntary self-restraint, abstain from use of force in pursuit of policy and from interference in the internal affairs of other nations. All nations should seek to adjust problems arising in their international relations by processes of peaceful negotiation and agreement. All nations should uphold the principle of the sanctity of treaties and of faithful observance of international agreements.
- Modification of provisions of treaties, when need therefor arises, should be by orderly processes carried out in a spirit of mutual helpfulness and accommodation.
- Each nation should respect the rights of others and perform scrupulously its own established obligations; in brief, international law and the spirit which underlies it must be revitalized and strengthened.
- Steps should be taken toward promotion of economic security and stability the world over through lowering or removal of barriers to international trade according of effective equality of commercial opportunity, and application of the principle of equality of commercial treatment.
- National armaments should be limited and be progressively reduced; at the same time, realizing the necessity for maintaining armed forces adequate for national security, each nation should to that end be prepared to reduce or increase its own armed forces in proportion as reductions or increases are made by other nations.

Apart from the question of alliances with others, each nation should be prepared to engage in cooperative effort, by peaceful and practicable means, in support of these principles.

The peace and progress of every nation are just as dependent on international law and order, based upon the foregoing principles, as the welfare, stability, and progress of a community are dependent upon domestic law and order, based upon legal, moral, and other recognized standards of conduct. No government faithful to the sacred trust involved in the task of providing for the safety and well-being of its people can disregard these universal principles. Every nation, whatever its form of government, can support them. Every nation must support them, if civilization is to survive. The longer the nations delay acceptance and observance of these fundamental tenets of constructive statesmanship, the graver will be the jeopardy into which all worth-while international relationships will be plunged, and with them the welfare, the happiness, and the civilized existence of all nations.

The crucial issue today is whether these principles will be vitalized and be firmly established as the foundation of an international order or whether international anarchy based on brute force will inundate the world and ultimately sweep away the very bases of civilization and progress. That issue is universal. No more than a community or a nation, can the world base its existence in part on law and in part on lawlessness, in part on order and in part on chaos, in part on processes of peace and in part on methods of violence.

On August 23 I made another public statement reaffirming the principles which should underlie international order, peace, and justice, if the world is to avoid a relapse into another dark night of international anarchy and general retrogression. I called attention again to the fact that if these principles are to be effective they must be universal in their application. This statement was prompted by the fact that the progress and possibilities of armed conflict were becoming more alarming both in the European and the Far Eastern areas and that the basic principles to which I have just referred were being challenged and the doctrine of armed force was gaining supremacy in important regions of the world.

During the early months of the conflict in the Far East I appealed on several occasions, in the name of our Government, to both Japan and China to desist from using armed force and to resort to the well-recognized processes of peaceful settlement for the adjustment of whatever differences existed between them. I said that we would be glad to be of assistance toward facilitating, in any manner that might be practicable and mutually agreeable, resort by them to such processes.

On August 17, and with frequent reiteration thereafter, I stated that we did not intend to abandon our nationals and our interests in China.

From time immemorial it has been the practice of civilized nations to afford protection, by appropriate means and under the rule of reason, to their nationals and their rights and interests abroad. This policy has been pursued by the Government of the United States throughout the existence of our country. Methods and means of affording protection abroad vary according to the places in which and the circumstances under which protection is called for. In the case of China, where unusual local conditions were such that the protection afforded by local authorities did not suffice to give security against excited and lawless elements, there have occasionally been sent—not by this country alone but by a number of countries—armed forces, to contribute to the affording of such protection as is due under the rules of international law and the provisions of treaties. American forces thus sent to China have at no time had any mission of aggression, and it has been the practice of the American Government to withdraw such forces whenever and as soon as the local situation so develops as to warrant the view that their withdrawal can be effected without detriment to American interests and obligations in general.

In announcing our intention to afford appropriate and reasonable protection to our rights and interests in the Far East, I stated clearly that we are fully determined to avoid the extremes either of internationalism or of isolationism. Internationalism would mean undesirable political involvements; isolationism would either compel us to confine all activities of our people within our own frontiers, with incalculable injury to the standard of living and the general welfare of our people, or else expose our nationals and our legitimate interests abroad to injustice or outrage wherever lawless conditions arise. Steering a sound middle course between these two extremes, we are convinced that a policy of affording appropriate protection—under the rule of reason, in such form as may be best suited to the particular circumstances, and in accordance with the principles we advocate—is imperatively needed to serve our national interest.

Our decision in this matter is based not only on what

we firmly believe to be a specific and elementary duty of a government toward its citizens, but also on other and broader considerations. Respect by a country for the rights and interests of others is a visible test of the fulfillment of obligations assumed by virtue of acceptance of international law and of undertakings embodied in negotiated international instruments. It is, therefore, a test of the observance of those fundamental principles of civilized relations among nations, which, if firmly established, provide in themselves the best means of protection against violation and abuse of the legitimate rights and interests of every nation.

To waive rights and to permit interests to lapse in the face of their actual or threatened violation—and thereby to abandon obligations—in any important area of the world, can serve only to encourage disregard of law and of the basic principles of international order, and thus contribute to the inevitable spread of international anarchy throughout the world. For this country, as for any country, to act in such manner anywhere would be to invite disregard and violation of its rights and interests everywhere, by every nation so inclined, large or small.

To respect the rights of others and to insist that others respect our rights has been the traditional policy of our country. This policy was admirably expressed by James Monroe when, in his message to Congress on December 2, 1823, he said:

> Our policy . . . remains the same: . . . to cultivate friendly relations . . . and to preserve those relations by frank, firm, and manly policy, meeting in all instances the just claims of every power, submitting to injuries from none.

In a world in which the rule of force has not as yet been firmly and surely supplanted by the rule of law, it is the manifest duty of a great nation to maintain armed forces adequate for its national defense. Writing on this subject, which was as vital to our national life 150 years ago as it is today, James Madison said:

> The means of security can only be regulated by the means and the danger of attack. They will, in fact, be ever determined by these rules, and by no others.

It is the duty of the Federal Government to insure the safety of our country and to determine what "means of security" are, at any given moment, needed to provide against "the means and the danger of attack." The responsible heads of our naval establishment offer convincing reasons in support of the program, now before the Congress, to render adequate the means of our national defense. No policy would prove more disastrous than for an important nation to fail to arm adequately when international lawlessness is on the rampage. It is my considered judgment that, in the present state of world affairs, to do less than is now proposed would lay our country open to unpredictable hazards. It would, moreover, seriously restrict our Nation's ability to command, without purpose or occasion for resorting to arms, proper respect for its legitimate rights and interests, the surrender of which would constitute abandonment of the fundamental principles of justice and morality and peace among nations.

The maintenance of these principles that are of concern to all nations alike cannot and should not be undertaken by any one nation alone. Prudence and common sense dictate that, where this and other nations have common interests and common objectives, we should not hesitate to exchange information and to confer with the governments of such other nations and, in dealing with the problems confronting each alike, to proceed along parallel lines—this Government retaining at all times its independence of judgment and freedom of action. For nations which seek peace to assume with respect to each other attitudes of complete aloofness would serve only to encourage, and virtually invite, on the part of other nations lawlessly inclined, policies and actions most likely to endanger peace.

In the present Far Eastern emergency, we have consistently collaborated with other peace-seeking nations in the manner I have just described. I have said often, and I repeat again, that in this collaboration there is not a trace of alliance or involvement of any sort. We have scrupulously followed and we intend to follow the traditional policy of our country not to enter into entangling alliances or involvements with other countries.

When the Brussels Conference was called, this country, as one of the original signatories of the Nine Power Treaty and in accordance with its treaty obligations thus assumed, promptly accepted the invitation to the Conference. Our delegation cooperated fully with the representatives of the other Conference powers in examining the situation in the Far East and exploring methods of bringing about peace by processes of agreement. The Conference made a substantial contribution toward keeping alive principles of world order and of respect for the pledged word. Its declarations placed a new emphasis upon the deep concern of peaceful nations over any developments that threaten the preservation of peace.

In connection with the Far Eastern situation, this Government was confronted with the question of applying the existing neutrality legislation, which was designed primarily to keep our Nation out of war. After mature deliberation the conclusion was reached that in the circumstances attending the controversy in the Far East—a type of circumstances which the authors of the legislation could scarcely have visualized—application of the law would be most likely to endanger the very objectives which the law was designed to promote. Accordingly, exercising the discretion vested in him by the law itself, the President has refrained from putting the provisions of that law into operation. At the same time, in pursuance of our general policy of avoiding unnecessary risks, the President announced, on September 14, 1937, that "Merchant vessels owned by the Government of the United States will not hereafter, until further notice, be permitted to transport to China or Japan any of the arms, ammunition, or implements of war which were listed in the President's proclamation of May 1, 1937," and that "Any other merchant vessels, flying the American flag, which attempt to transport any of the listed articles to China or Japan will, until further notice, do so at their own risk."

Our Government pursues, in relation to every world area alike, a policy of noninterference, with ill will toward no nation and a sincere desire to be friendly with all. At the same time, we endeavor to afford appropriate protection to American citizens and American interests everywhere. During recent months, as throughout the past 100 years, the Government of the United States has sought to exercise moral influence and to cooperate in every practicable way with all peace—seeking nations in support of those basic principles which are indispensable to the promotion and maintenance of stable conditions of peace.

We have affirmed on every possible occasion and have urged upon all nations the supreme need for keeping alive and for practicing sound fundamental principles of relations among civilized nations. We have never entertained and we have not the slightest intention to entertain any such notion as the use of American armed forces for "policing the world." But we equally have not the slightest intention of reversing a tradition of a century and a half by abandoning our deep concern for, and our advocacy of, the establishment everywhere; of international order under law, based upon the well-recognized principles to which I have referred. It is our profound conviction that the most effective contribution which we, as a nation sincerely devoted to the cause of peace, can make—in the tragic conditions with which our people, in common with the rest of mankind, are confronted today—is to have this country respected throughout the world for integrity, justice, good will, strength, and unswerving loyalty to principles.

The foregoing is the essence of our foreign policy. The record is an open book. We spare no effort to make known the facts regarding our attitude, our objectives, and our acts. We are always ready to furnish to the members of the Congress essential information. You, gentlemen, have first-hand knowledge of our constant effort to keep the press and the public informed.

There is one thing that we cannot do; and that is, to prepare and to place before every government of the world a detailed chart of the course of policy and action which this country will or will not pursue under any particular set of circumstances. No man, no nation, can possibly foresee all the circumstances that may arise. Moreover, to attempt to make such a detailed chart of future action would merely result in impairing our effectiveness in working for the one objective toward which we constantly strive and on which, I am certain, there is not a vestige of disagreement among the people of our country—the establishment of durable peace.

So strong, indeed, is the desire of this country for peace that many measures have been suggested toward our keeping out of war—some of them in complete disregard of both experience and practicability. It has been urged that we apply the neutrality law automatically in all circumstances, without adequate consideration of the possible consequences of such action for our own peace and for the safety of our citizens. It has been urged that we withdraw precipitately from any part of the world in which violators of international decencies choose to assert themselves. It has even been urged that we change the very basis of our representative form of government in a frantic search for something which the proposers assume would make it more likely that this country avoid war.

I take it for granted that all of us alike are sincere friends of peace. This makes it all the more necessary for every one of us to scrutinize carefully every measure proposed, lest in our attempts to avoid war we imperil the chances of preserving peace.

The problem of the form of government best adapted to this country's needs was one with which the founders of our Republic came to grips in those stirring days when the structure of our independent national existence was being given form and substance. After exhaustive deliberation and discussion they decided upon the system of representative democracy in preference to that of pure democracy as the system through which the people could best safeguard their liberty and promote their national security and welfare. The wisdom of the founders of this Nation in deciding, with conspicuous unanimity, to place the conduct of foreign relations in the hands of the Federal Government has stood the test of generations as providing the most effective means that can be devised for assuring the peace, the security, and the independence of our people.

What warrant is there, in reason or in experience, for the assumption—which underlies such proposals as the plan for a popular referendum on the subject of declaring war—that the Chief Executive and the Congress will be at any time more eager and more likely to embark upon war than would be the general body of citizens to whom they are directly responsible? No President and no Congress have ever carried this country into war against the will of the people. On the other hand, there is not a vestige of doubt that the adoption of a procedure like the referendum plan would hopelessly handicap the Government in the conduct of our foreign relations in general and would thus disastrously impair its ability to safeguard the interests of the Nation, in the forefront among which is that of peace.

Likewise dangerous, from the viewpoint of the preservation of peace, is the proposal that we retire from the Far East, comprising the chief portion of the Pacific area. Unfortunately, many people in this country have wholly misunderstood the position and policy of our Government in relation to that situation. Some have visualized only our trade and investment relationships with China, or our moral and cultural interests there, symbolized by missionary, educational, medical, and similar activities. Some have concentrated their attention solely upon the incidental and exceptional facts of the existence of extraterritoriality and the maintenance of some armed forces to assist in safeguarding our nationals against possible mob violence and similar disorders—special rights which it is our policy to give up and forces which it is our policy to withdraw the moment the unusual conditions disappear.

All these are important. But the interest and concern of the United States—whether in the Far East, in any other part of the Pacific area, in Europe, or anywhere else in the world—are not measured alone by the number of American citizens residing in a particular country, or by the volume of investment and trade, or by exceptional conditions peculiar to the particular area. There is a much broader and more fundamental interest—which is, that orderly processes in international relationships based on the principles to which I have referred be maintained.

As I have already indicated, what is most of all at stake today, throughout the world, is the future of the fundamental principles which must be the foundation of international order as opposed to international anarchy. If we and others were to abandon and surrender these principles in regard to the Pacific area, which is almost one half of the world, we would have to reconcile ourselves to their certain abandonment and surrender in regard to the other half of the world.

It would be absurd and futile for us to proclaim that we stand for international law, for the sanctity of treaty obligations, for non-intervention in internal affairs of other countries, for equality of industrial and commercial rights and opportunities, for limitation and reduction of armaments—but only in one—half of the world, and among one-half of the world's population. The catastrophic developments of recent years, the startling events of the past weeks, offer a tragic demonstration of how quickly the contagious scourge of treaty breaking and armed violence spreads from one region to another.

Those who contend that we can and should abandon and surrender principles in one-half of the world clearly show that they have little or no conception of the extent to which situations and developments in any part of the world of today inevitably affect situations and conditions in other parts of the world. The triumph of this seclusionist viewpoint would inescapably carry the whole world back to the conditions of medieval chaos, conditions toward which some parts of both the eastern and the western worlds are already moving. Such is the fate to which extreme isolationists—isolationists at any price—all those who contend that we should neither protest against abuses nor cooperate with others toward keeping principles alive, those who say that under no circumstances should we insist upon any rights beyond our own territorial waters—such is the fate to which blind extremism of this type would consign this country and the world.

The momentous question—let me repeat—is whether the doctrine of force shall become enthroned once more and bring in its wake, inexorably, international anarchy and a relapse into barbarism; or whether this and other peaceful nations, fervently attached to the principles which underlie international order, shall work unceasingly—singly or in cooperation with each other, as circumstances, their traditional policies and practices, and their enlightened self-interest may dictate—to promote and preserve law, order, morality, and justice as the unshakeable bases of civilized international relations.

We might, if we could reconcile ourselves to such an attitude, turn our backs on the whole problem and decline the responsibility and labor of contributing to its solution. But let us have no illusions as to what such a course of action would involve for us as a nation.

It would mean a break with our past, both internationally and domestically. It would mean a voluntary abandonment of some of the most important things that have made us a great nation. It would mean an abject retreat before those forces which we have, throughout our whole national history, consistently opposed.

It would mean that our security would be menaced in proportion as other nations came to believe that, either through fear or through unwillingness, we did not intend to afford protection to our legitimate national interests abroad, but, on the contrary, intended to abandon them at the first sign of danger. Under such conditions the sphere of our international relationships economic, cultural, intellectual, and other—would necessarily shrink and shrivel, until we would stand practically alone among the nations, a self-constituted hermit state.

Thrown back upon our own resources, we would find it necessary to reorganize our entire social and economic structure. The process of adaptation to a more or less self-contained existence would mean less production and at higher costs; lower living standards; regimentation in every phase of life; economic distress to wage earners and farmers, and to their families; and the dole, on an ever-increasing scale.

All this we would be doing in pursuit of the notion that by so doing we would avoid war. But would these policies, while entailing such enormous sacrifices and rendering the Nation more and more decadent, really give us any such assurance?

Reason and experience definitely point to the contrary. We may seek to withdraw from participation in world affairs, but we cannot thereby withdraw from the world itself. Isolation is not a means to security; it is a fruitful source of insecurity.

We want to live in a world which is at peace; in which the forces of militarism, of territorial aggression, and of international anarchy in general will become utterly odious, revolting, and intolerable to the conscience of mankind; in which the doctrine of order under law will be firmly established; in which there will no longer be one code of morality, honor, justice, and fair play for the individual in his relations with other individuals, and an entirely different code for governments and nations in their relations with each other. We want to live in a world in which fruitful and constructive international relationships can serve as a medium for disseminating throughout the world the benefits of the material, spiritual, and moral progress of mankind.

To that end we will continue to give full and sincere adherence to the fundamental principles which underlie international order; we will continue to urge universal acceptance and observance of these principles; we will continue, wherever necessary and in every practicable and peaceful way, to cooperate with other nations which are actuated by the same desires and are pursuing the same objectives; we will persevere in appropriate efforts to safeguard our legitimate rights and interests in every part of the world; and we will, while scrupulously respecting the rights of others, insist on their respecting our rights. To that end we will continue to strive, through our reciprocal trade program and through other economic policies, to restore the normal processes and to expand the volume of mutually beneficial trade among the nations, which is indispensable to an increase of production, employment, purchasing power, and general economic well-being here and everywhere; we will continue to promote peace through economic security and prosperity; we will continue to participate in the numerous international scientific, technical, and other conferences and collaborative efforts, which have been such powerful influences in assisting the stream of new ideas, of new discoveries, of learning and culture, to flow throughout the world; and we will continue to urge other nations to give their support to such policies and efforts.

We believe that a world at peace, with law and justice prevailing, is possible, and that it can be achieved by methods to some of which I have referred. That is the cornerstone of our foreign policy–a policy graphically described by President Roosevelt when he said:

> There must be positive endeavors to preserve peace. America hates war. America hopes for peace. Therefore, America actively engages in the search for peace.

The objectives of our foreign policy are as easy to grasp as they are fundamental. The means we are using to attain these objectives are the only means approved by reason and by experience. For the sake of the best interests of our people, we must maintain our strength, our courage, our moral standards, our influence in world affairs, and our participation in efforts toward world progress and peace. Only by making our reasonable contribution to a firm establishment of a world order based on law can we keep the problem of our own security in true perspective and thus discharge our responsibility to ourselves—to America of today and to America of tomorrow. No other course would be worthy of our past or of the potentialities of this great democracy of which we are all citizens and in whose affairs we all participate

Document Analysis

Hull gives a major overview of American foreign policy, focusing on the situation in East Asia but dealing with the rise of aggressor powers in general. To avoid a diplomatic incident, Hull does not name the nations threatening the international order. Germany and Italy are not specifically mentioned at all, and Japan is only mentioned paired with China, with no explicit statement that one power is more to blame than the other. However, given the context, Hull's listeners would have had no doubt as to which countries were to blame for the rise of international chaos.

Hull places the American response to the conflict in China in the context of building an international society based on peace, the rule of law, and the carrying out of treaty obligations. He points out that many nations responded positively to a statement to that effect, which Hull had issued the previous year. By the time of Hull's address, the League of Nations, which the United States had never joined, had been discredited by its failures to effectively oppose fascist powers and could not credibly serve as the foundation for a global order based on law and treaty obligations. Hull does not even mention it. Hull does mention the dissolution of economic barriers to trade between nations, which many countries had raised to protect their economies during the Great Depression. As was common among "free trade" economists in the Anglo-American tradition, Hull believed that the lowering of trade barriers would contribute to peace. He also hints that the lack of an international order contributed to the outbreak of World War I. At the same time, he does not wish to alarm Americans who regret American involvement in World War I and fear involvement in another war. Following a common rhetorical strategy, he positions his recommended course of action as midway between the extremes of "internationalism" (too much involvement in foreign affairs) and "isolationism" (none at all).

Hull somewhat mythologizes American history, showing the United States as a disinterested power, working solely to advance peace and harmony between nations, a picture congenial to many patriotic Americans. He emphasizes the American tradition of honoring treaties. He justifies American actions in China as based not on imperialistic designs on Chinese territory or resources, but solely on the desire to protect American nationals and American interests.

Nonetheless, despite his belief in international law and the fear of the outbreak of another great war, Hull was not a pacifist. Part of the address is devoted to advocating for increased spending on the military so that the United States would be ready in the event of war.

Essential Themes
The hostile attitude taken by the American administration toward the expansionist and militarist fascist powers would continue until the outbreak of World War II, although the United States did not commit itself to military action and would not enter the war until late in 1941. In the late 1930s, US trade restrictions on Japan grew increasingly severe, culminating in the oil embargo imposed on August 1, 1941. This embargo was a profound threat to Japan, which was heavily dependent on the United States for its oil supply, and played a role in directing Japanese ambitions southward, toward the oil-rich Dutch East Indies, now known as Indonesia. This direction of Japanese policy culminated in the surprise attack on the American naval base at Pearl Harbor in Hawaii, shortly followed by the German declaration of war that brought the United States into the European conflict as well.

The hope of a new order also seemed to fail in Europe, where a few months later, Britain and France conceded to Hitler's demands in Czechoslovakia. Lack of backing from the United States was one reason for this "appeasement" policy. Hull's ambition to set up a new global order based on peace and international law materialized only after World War II in the form of the United Nations (UN). Hull won a Nobel Peace Prize in recognition of his work in setting up the UN. However, because of the conflict between the United States and the Soviet Union during the Cold War, Hull's vision of a peaceful world regulated by law and treaty remained unfulfilled. Instead, the United States took up the role Hull insisted on rejecting, that of "policing the world." The fall of the Soviet Union in 1991 led to a revival of ideas of a peaceful world order regulated by law and treaty.

—*William E. Burns, PhD*

Bibliography and Further Reading
Fairbank, John K. *The United States and China*. 4th ed. Cambridge: Harvard UP, 1983. Print.
Hull, Cordell. *The Memoirs of Cordell Hull*. New York: Macmillan, 1948. Print.
Macdonald, C. A. *The United States, Britain, and Appeasement, 1936–1939*. New York: St. Martin's, 1981. Print.

Winston Churchill: "The Lights Are Going Out" in Europe

Date: October 16, 1938
Author: Winston Churchill
Genre: address

Summary Overview

In this speech, British politician Winston Churchill gives his view of the international situation after the Munich Agreement and appeals to an American audience for solidarity against the "totalitarian" powers—particularly Nazi Germany under Adolf Hitler—in the wake of the French and British abandonment of Czechoslovakia to occupation by Germany. Although the statement is full of gloomy imagery, Churchill still holds forth hope that the dictators Hitler and Italy's Benito Mussolini can be stopped by united action, portraying himself as a lover and supporter of peace rather than a warmonger. He points out that America cannot isolate itself from this struggle, but must arm to join the other democracies, led by Britain and France, in a common fight against dictatorial aggressors.

Defining Moment

The National Socialists, or Nazis, led by Adolf Hitler took power in Germany in 1933, and—in addition to destroying German democracy—quickly began to reverse many provisions of the Versailles settlement reached at the end of World War I. The military limitations the peace treaty had placed on Germany—such as strict limits on the size of the army and navy—were repudiated, and in 1938, Hitler began an aggressive program of territorial expansion with the annexation of Austria, an act forbidden by the Versailles settlement but one in which the German dictator faced little opposition. His next major target was Czechoslovakia, a Central European state created in the Versailles settlement out of Slavic-dominated portions of the Habsburg Empire. Hitler's initial target was the Sudetenland, a German-speaking region in western Czechoslovakia that Hitler claimed was oppressed by the Slavic majority in the rest of the country. The major democratic powers of Europe—Britain and France—were reluctant to go to war after the horror of World War I, and hoped that Hitler's territorial demands would be limited and not worth opposing with force. This policy became known as "appeasement." Appeasement reached its height with the Munich Agreement in September 1938 between Germany, France, Italy, and Britain, which gave the Sudetenland to Germany. The mountainous Sudetenland was Czechoslovakia's first line of defense against Germany, and its loss rendered Czechoslovakia so vulnerable that it was regarded by many, including Churchill, as continuing to exist only at Germany's pleasure. In Britain and much of the rest of the world, the Munich Agreement was associated with British prime minister Neville Chamberlain. The agreement was initially quite popular in the United Kingdom, where it was viewed, in Chamberlain's words, as guaranteeing "peace in our time." However, the hopes of Chamberlain and other appeasers proved fruitless, as continuing German rapacity in Central Europe made another big war seem inevitable.

Germany was not the only power that seemed to present a threat to peace. Fascist and militarist aggression was also apparent in the actions of Fascist Italy, which under dictator Benito Mussolini had conquered and annexed Ethiopia, and Imperial Japan, which was fighting a bloody war of conquest and expansion in China. Fascist Italy and Nazi Germany had also intervened effectively in the Spanish Civil War in support of the Fascist general Francisco Franco. Franco and his allies had faced little or no effective opposition from Britain and France, who theoretically supported the cause of the legitimate Spanish Republic, but, in practice, did nothing to help it defend itself.

Author Biography

British statesman Winston Churchill, the son of a British politician and his American wife, was throughout his long career a firm believer in the Anglo-American alliance. He served as first lord of the admiralty, the cabinet member with responsibility for the Royal Navy, and in several other positions during World War I. In the late 1930s, Churchill, although a member of the ruling Conservative Party, was excluded from the cabinets of Conservative prime ministers Stanley Baldwin and Neville Chamberlain, although he continued to serve in Parliament. As an outsider, he vigorously critiqued British policy as failing to stand up to the aggressive demands of Hitler and was particularly scathing in his critique of the Munich Agreement. Churchill was regarded as vindicated by the outbreak of World War II and served as prime minister for most of it. He remained a popular figure in the United States for the rest of his life and after.

HISTORICAL DOCUMENT

I avail myself with relief of the opportunity of speaking to the people of the United States. I do not know how long such liberties will be allowed. The stations of uncensored expression are closing down; the lights are going out; but there is still time for those to whom freedom and parliamentary government mean something, to consult together. Let me, then, speak in truth and earnestness while time remains.

The American people have, it seems to me, formed a true judgment upon the disaster which has befallen Europe. They realise, perhaps more clearly than the French and British publics have yet done, the far-reaching consequences of the abandonment and ruin of the Czechoslovak Republic. I hold to the conviction I expressed some months ago, that if in April, May or June, Great Britain, France, and Russia had jointly declared that they would act together upon Nazi Germany if Herr Hitler committed an act of unprovoked aggression against this small State, and if they had told Poland, Yugoslavia, and Rumania what they meant to do in good time, and invited them to join the combination of peace-defending Powers, I hold that the German Dictator would have been confronted with such a formidable array that he would have been deterred from his purpose. This would also have been an opportunity for all the peace-loving and moderate forces in Germany, together with the chiefs of the German Army, to make a great effort to re-establish something like sane and civilised conditions in their own country. If the risks of war which were run by France and Britain at the last moment had been boldly faced in good time, and plain declarations made, and meant, how different would our prospects be today!

But all these backward speculations belong to history. It is no good using hard words among friends about the past, and reproaching one another for what cannot be recalled. It is the future, not the past, that demands our earnest and anxious thought. We must recognize that the Parliamentary democracies and liberal, peaceful forces have everywhere sustained a defeat which leaves them weaker, morally and physically, to cope with dangers which have vastly grown. But the cause of freedom has in it a recuperative power and virtue which can draw from misfortune new hope and new strength. If ever there was a time when men and women who cherish the ideals of the founders of the British and American Constitutions should take earnest counsel with one another, that time is now.

All the world wishes for peace and security. Have we gained it by the sacrifice of the Czechoslovak Republic? Here was the model democratic State of Central Europe, a country where minorities were treated better than anywhere else. It has been deserted, destroyed and devoured. It is now being digested. The question which is of interest to a lot of ordinary people, common people, is whether this destruction of the Czechoslovak Republic will bring upon the world a blessing or a curse.

We must all hope it will bring a blessing; that after we have averted our gaze for a while from the process of subjugation and liquidation, everyone will breathe more freely; that a load will be taken off our chests; we shall be able to say to ourselves: "Well, that's out of the way, anyhow. Now let's get on with our regular daily life." But are these hopes well founded or are we merely making the best of what we had not the force and virtue to stop? That is the question that the English-speaking peoples in all their lands must ask themselves to-day. Is this the end, or is there more to come?

There is another question which arises out of this. Can peace, goodwill, and confidence be built upon submission to wrong-doing backed by force? One may put this question in the largest form. Has any benefit or progress ever been achieved by the human race by submission to organized and calculated violence? As we look back over the long story of the nations we must see that, on the contrary, their glory has been founded upon the spirit of resistance to tyranny and injustice, especially when these evils seemed to be backed by heavier force. Since the dawn of the Christian era a certain way of life has slowly been shaping itself among the Western peoples, and certain standards of conduct and government have come to be esteemed. After many miseries and prolonged confusion, there arose into the broad light of day the conception of the right of the individual; his right to be consulted in the government of his country; his right to invoke the law even against the State itself. Independent Courts of Justice were created to affirm and inforce this hard-won custom. Thus was assured throughout the English-speaking world, and in France by the stern lessons of the Revolution, what Kipling called, "Leave to live by no man's leave underneath the law." Now in this resides all that makes existence precious to man, and all that confers honour and health upon the State.

We are confronted with another theme. It is not a new theme; it leaps out upon us from the Dark Ages' racial persecution, religious intolerance, deprivation of free speech, the conception of the citizen as a mere soulless fraction of the State. To this has been added the cult of war. Children are to be taught in their earliest schooling the delights and profits of conquest and aggression. A whole mighty community has been drawn painfully, by severe privations, into a warlike frame. They are held in this condition, which they relish no more than we do, by a party organisation, several millions strong, who derive all kinds of profits, good and bad, from the upkeep of the regime. Like the Communists, the Nazis tolerate no opinion but their own. Like the Communists, they feed on hatred. Like the Communists, they must seek, from time to time, and always at shorter intervals, a new target, a new prize, a new victim. The Dictator, in all his pride, is held in the grip of his Party machine. He can go forward; he cannot go back. He must blood his hounds and show them sport, or else, like Actaeon of old, be devoured by them. All-strong without, he is all-weak within. As Byron wrote a hundred years ago: "These Pagod things of Sabre sway, with fronts of brass and feet of clay."

No one must, however, underrate the power and efficiency of a totalitarian state. Where the whole population of a great country, amiable, good-hearted, peace-loving people are gripped by the neck and by the hair by a Communist or a Nazi tyranny—for they are the same things spelt in different ways—the rulers for the time being can exercise a power for the purposes of war and external domination before which the ordinary free parliamentary societies are at a grievous practical disadvantage. We have to recognise this.

And then, on top of all, comes this wonderful mastery of the air which our century has discovered, but of which, alas, mankind has so far shown itself unworthy. Here is this air power with its claim to torture and terrorise the women and children, the civil population of neighbouring countries. This combination of medieval passion, a party caucus, the weapons of modern science, and the blackmailing power of air-bombing, is the most monstrous menace to peace, order and fertile progress that has appeared in the world since the Mongol invasions of the thirteenth century.

The culminating question to which I have been leading is whether the world as we have known it—the great and hopeful world of before the war, the world of increasing hope and enjoyment for the common man, the world of honoured tradition and expanding science—should meet this menace by submission or by resistance. Let us see, then, whether the means of resistance remain to us today. We have sustained an immense disaster; the renown of France is dimmed. In spite of her brave, efficient army, her influence is profoundly diminished. No one has a right to say that Britain, for all her blundering, has broken her word—indeed, when it was too late, she was better than her word. Nevertheless, Europe lies at this moment abashed and distracted before the triumphant assertions of dictatorial power. In the Spanish Peninsula, a purely Spanish quarrel has been carried by the intervention, or shall I say the "non-intervention" (to quote the current Jargon) of Dictators into the region of a world cause. But it is not only in Europe that these oppressions prevail. China is being torn to pieces by a military clique in Japan; the poor, tormented Chinese people there are making a brave and stubborn defence. The ancient empire of Ethiopia has been overrun. The Ethiopians were taught to look to the sanctity of public law, to the tribunal of many nations gathered in majestic union.

But all failed; they were deceived, and now they are winning back their right to live by beginning again from the bottom a struggle on primordial lines. Even in South America the Nazi regime begins to undermine the fabric of Brazilian society.

Far away, happily protected by the Atlantic and Pacific Oceans, you, the people of the United States, to whom I now have the chance to speak, are the spectators, and I may add the increasingly involved spectators of these tragedies and crimes. We are left in no doubt where American conviction and sympathies lie; but will you wait until British freedom and independence have succumbed, and then take up the cause when it is three-quarters ruined, yourselves alone? I hear that they are saying in the United States that because England and France have failed to do their duty therefore the American people can wash their hands of the whole business. This may be the passing mood of many people, but there is no sense in it. If things have got much worse, all the more must we try to cope with them.

For, after all, survey the remaining forces of civilisation; they are overwhelming. If only they were united in a common conception of right and duty, there would be no war. On the contrary, the German people, industrious, faithful, valiant, but alas! lacking in the proper spirit of civic independence, liberated from their present nightmare, would take their honoured place in the vanguard of human society. Alexander the Great remarked that the people of Asia were slaves because they had not learned to pronounce the word "No." Let that not be the epitaph of the English-speaking peoples or of Parliamentary democracy, or of France, or of the many surviving liberal States of Europe.

There, in one single word, is the resolve which the forces of freedom and progress, of tolerance and good will, should take. It is not in the power of one nation, however formidably armed, still less is it in the power of a small group of men, violent, ruthless men, who have always to cast their eyes back over their shoulders, to cramp and fetter the forward march of human destiny. The preponderant world forces are upon our side; they have but to be combined to be obeyed.

We must arm. Britain must arm. America must arm. If, through an earnest desire for peace, we have placed ourselves at a disadvantage, we must make up for it by redoubled exertions, and, if necessary, by fortitude in suffering. We shall, no doubt, arm. Britain, casting away the habits of centuries, will decree national service upon her citizens. The British people will stand erect, and will face whatever may be coming.

But arms—instrumentalities, as President Wilson called them—are not sufficient by themselves. We must add to them the power of ideas. People say we ought not to allow ourselves to be drawn into a theoretical antagonism between Nazidom and democracy; but the antagonism is here now. It is this very conflict of spiritual and moral ideas which gives the free countries a great part of their strength. You see these dictators on their pedestals, surrounded by the bayonets of their soldiers and the truncheons of their police. On all sides they are guarded by masses of armed men, cannons, aeroplanes, fortifications, and the like—they boast and vaunt themselves before the world, yet in their hearts there is unspoken fear. They are afraid of words and thoughts; words spoken abroad, thoughts stirring at home–all the more powerful because forbidden—terrify them. A little mouse of thought appears in the room, and even the mightiest potentates are thrown into panic. They make frantic efforts to bar our thoughts and words; they are afraid of the workings of the human mind. Cannons, airplanes, they can manufacture in large quantities; but how are they to quell the natural promptings of human nature, which after all these centuries of trial and progress has inherited a whole armoury of potent and indestructible knowledge?

Dictatorship—the fetish worship of one man—is a passing phase. A state of society where men may not speak their minds, where children denounce their parents to the police, where a business man or small shopkeeper ruins his competitor by telling tales about his private opinions; such a state of society cannot long endure if brought into contact with the healthy outside world. The light of civilised progress with its tolerances and co-operation, with its dignities and joys, has often in the past been blotted out. But I hold the belief that we have now at last got far enough ahead of barbarism to control it, and to avert it, if only we realise what is afoot and make up our minds in time. We shall do it in the end. But how much harder our toil for every day's delay!

Is this a call to war? Does anyone pretend that preparation for resistance to aggression is unleashing war? I declare it to be the sole guarantee of peace. We need the swift gathering of forces to confront not only military but moral aggression; the resolute and sober acceptance of their duty by the English-speaking peoples and by all the nations, great and small, who wish to walk with them. Their faithful and zealous comradeship would almost between night and morning clear the path of progress and banish from all our lives the fear which already darkens the sunlight to hundreds of millions of men.

Document Analysis

The title of this address is a reference to the quotation attributed to British foreign secretary Sir Edward Grey at the dawn of World War I: "The lamps are going out all over Europe; we shall not see them lit again in our lifetime." Evoking this quotation lends gravity to Churchill's statement and summons the image of imminent disaster, quite possibly in the form of another European war. Churchill's address is both a lament for lost opportunities to stop Hitler and an exhortation for the future. Hitler can still be stopped, but it requires solidarity among the great and small powers of Europe in the face of German aggression, as well as American preparation for war.

In addressing Americans, Churchill had to confront the common American belief that events in Europe posed little threat to Americans—an idea reinforced by the feeling among many Americans that intervention in World War I had been a mistake. He flatters his American audience by suggesting that Americans have a better understanding of the issues at stake than did the ordinary citizens of Britain and France. He suggests that Nazi power is already reaching into the Americas.

Churchill places the struggle against Hitler in the context of the defense of liberal values and a way of life common to democratic countries. He particularly identifies the value of liberal institutions with the "English-speaking peoples" of Britain, the British dominions, and the United States, but admits the value of the tradition of the French Revolution and French democracy as well. Churchill was a Francophile in addition to feeling a kinship with America.

He says that the loss of Czechoslovakia is particularly painful, as it is the loss of a democratic multi-ethnic state. Churchill links Nazism to Communism as examples of complete one-party rule, "totalitarianism." Although Churchill mentions the Soviet Union—"Russia"—as a potential member of an anti-Nazi coalition, it is clearly not the type of ally he prefers. Churchill was a strong anti-Communist, who had supported vigorous intervention against the Russian Revolution, and it is possible that his emphasis on similarities between Nazism and Communism was designed to appeal to anti-Communist Americans.

Churchill warns that the coming war will be more terrible than previous wars because of technological advances, particularly the invention of the airplane and aerial bombing. The horror of aerial bombing was particularly effective in addressing British and American audiences, as it emphasized that their isolation from Continental Europe would not necessarily save them from the full horrors of war as it had in World War I.

Essential Themes

Czechoslovakia was unable to resist a full German military takeover in March 1939. The picture of the late 1930s given here by Churchill has dominated most popular thinking on the subject of the causes of World War II, and the British and French abandonment of Czechoslovakia to Hitler has come to be seen as the classic example of the failure of appeasement. The idea that Churchill was right about the failure of appeasement when others supported it would contribute much to his role as an iconic figure in both the United Kingdom and the United States (Churchill was made an honorary American citizen in 1963). Harkening back to Churchill's example in opposing appeasement has been a staple for Americans advocating more confrontational policies in both the Cold War against the Soviet Union and the War on Terror following the attacks of September 11, 2001. Churchill's linkage of the Nazi and Communist states as totalitarian and presenting a similar danger to Western democracy would also have a long future, particularly during the Cold War.

The war Churchill anticipated did indeed begin the following year, as a result of German aggression against Poland. And though America provided considerable aid to the Allied cause against Germany, it did not enter the war until the Japanese attack on Pearl Harbor and the German declaration of war against the United States late in 1941. Anglo-American victory in the war required a close alliance with the Soviet Union, but this would fall apart quickly after the war, and Churchill himself would popularize the term "Iron Curtain" to describe the division between Soviet-occupied and Western Europe.

Churchill also proved an accurate prophet of the terrors of aerial bombing directed at civilian populations, although the British under his leadership proved enthusiastic adopters of the technique in the war against Germany.

—William E. Burns, PhD

Bibliography and Additional Reading

Gilbert, Martin. *Churchill and America*. New York: Free, 2005. Print.

_____. *Winston Churchill: The Wilderness Years: Speaking Out against Hitler in the Prelude to War*. London: Tauris, 2011. Print.

Macdonald, C. A. *The United States, Britain and Appeasement, 1936–1939*. New York: St. Martins, 1981. Print.

■ Winston Churchill: A Hush Over Europe

Date: August 8, 1939
Author: Winston Churchill
Genre: address

Summary Overview

On the threshold of the outbreak of World War II, British statesman Winston Churchill addressed the American public, giving his analysis of the international situation and appealing for solidarity between democracies facing the threat of invasion from aggressive, militaristic dictatorships. He paints the situation in stark terms, enumerating the aggressive acts of Japan, Italy, and particularly Germany against their neighbors and pointing out that they have not been checked and are continuing their advance. Churchill mocks the claims that these dictatorships are acting in self-defense and vigorously condemns one-man, dictatorial rule. The liberal tradition of the English-speaking countries, he claims, is far superior, and he appeals to the cultural and political commonalities between the United States and Great Britain to call for solidarity in peace or in war.

Defining Moment

By August 1939, Adolf Hitler had overseen a series of successful territorial acquisitions in Europe, beginning with the takeover of Austria on March 12, 1938. By late 1938, Nazi Germany had annexed portions of Czechoslovakia following the Munich Agreement, which was signed by Germany, France, the United Kingdom, and Italy, and authorized the annexation of Czechoslovakia's predominantly German-speaking Sudetenland region. The failure of the Munich Agreement to end Nazi aggression by "appeasing" Germany was clear to all by March 1939, when Germany annexed the remainder of Czechoslovakia in violation of the agreement, and many saw that war with Germany was becoming increasingly unavoidable. The German dictator had set his sights on his next target—Poland, a country that had recently regained its independence after World War I and had acquired considerable territory from Germany in the Versailles Treaty that ended that war. German anti-Semitism had also made itself manifest in unmistakably violent terms, in the nationwide pogrom known as Kristallnacht (called, in English, the Night of Broken Glass) on November 9–10, 1938. The horror of Kristallnacht had been extensively reported and had turned British and American public opinion even more firmly against Hitler. Europe's other leading fascist dictator, Italy's Benito Mussolini, had taken over the small kingdom of Albania and was continuing the forcible "Italianization" of the German-speaking population of Italy's South Tyrol region. Japanese aggression in China, a subject of particular concern to Americans, was proceeding largely unchecked.

The British government under Prime Minister Neville Chamberlain, formerly viewed as the great champion of German appeasement, was taking diplomatic steps to stop the Nazi advance, but with little success. (There was still hope among some in Chamberlain's cabinet that Germany could be satiated at Poland's expense, in order to avoid war.) The Anglo-Polish Alliance was established in 1939, but had little in the way of military teeth. An alliance between Britain and France remained firm, but the hopes of an anti-Nazi alliance between the Western powers and the Soviet Union to stop further German aggression in Eastern Europe were fading fast. (Just two weeks after Churchill's radio address to the American public, representatives of Nazi Germany and the Soviet Union formalized the Nazi-Soviet Nonaggression Pact to establish a collective-security agreement between the two nations.) Without the aid of the Soviets, Britain and France had little hope of intervening effectively to protect Poland, and they could only face a long war with Germany. Although the sympathies of the US government and most Americans with an interest in foreign affairs were with the British,

French, and Poles against Hitler's Germany, the United States was not taking an active role in opposing Germany either.

Domestically, British rearmament measures were continuing, and plans were being made to reintroduce national conscription. Churchill, who had criticized Chamberlain's policies of appeasement, had been vindicated to some degree by the collapse of the Munich Agreement, but he remained outside the cabinet and political power.

Author Biography

The son of a British politician and an American mother, British statesman Winston Spencer Churchill was a lifelong believer in a close Anglo-American partnership. During World War I, he had served as first lord of the Admiralty, the British cabinet minister responsible for the Royal Navy, and in several other positions. In the 1930s, Churchill, although a member of Parliament from the ruling Conservative Party, was excluded from the cabinet of Prime Minister Neville Chamberlain. A "voice in the wilderness," he argued tirelessly for a more confrontational policy against the German dictator Adolf Hitler. Although frequently criticized as a warmonger, the failure of the Munich Agreement resulted in Churchill's views becoming increasingly mainstream. Churchill became prime minister in 1940 and served in that role for most of the war. He lost the premiership in the 1945 general election, but he remained active in politics as the leader of the opposition. He was re-elected prime minister in 1951 and served in that position until 1955. Churchill died at the age of ninety on January 24, 1965, in London. He remains one of the most popular British politicians in the United States.

HISTORICAL DOCUMENT

There is a hush over all Europe, nay, over all the world, broken only by the dull thud of Japanese bombs falling on Chinese cities, on Chinese universities or near British and American ships. But then, China is a long way off, so why worry? The Chinese are fighting for what the founders of the American Constitution in their stately language called: "Life, liberty and the pursuit of happiness." And they seem to be fighting very well. Many good judges think they are going to win. Anyhow, let's wish them luck! Let's give them a wave of encouragement—as your President did last week, when he gave notice about ending the commercial treaty. After all, the suffering Chinese are fighting our battle, the battle of democracy. They are defending the soil, the good earth, that has been theirs since the dawn of time against cruel and unprovoked aggression. Give them a cheer across the ocean—no one knows whose turn it may be next. If this habit of military dictatorships' breaking into other people's lands with bomb and shell and bullet, stealing the property and killing the proprietors, spreads too widely, we may none of us be able to think of summer holidays for quite a while.

But to come back to the hush I said was hanging over Europe. What kind of a hush is it? Alas! it is the hush of suspense, and in many lands it is the hush of fear. Listen! No, listen carefully; I think I hear something—yes, there it was quite clear. Don't you hear it? It is the tramp of armies crunching the gravel of the parade-grounds, splashing through rain-soaked fields, the tramp of two million German soldiers and more than a million Italians—"going on maneuvers"—yes, only on maneuvers! Of course it's only maneuvers just like last year. After all, the Dictators must train their soldiers. They could scarcely do less in common prudence, when the Danes, the Dutch, the Swiss, the Albanians and of course the Jews may leap out upon them at any moment and rob them of their living-space, and make them sign another paper to say who began it. Besides, these German and Italian armies may have another work of liberation to perform. It was only last year they liberated Austria from the horrors of self-government. It was only in March they freed the Czechoslovak Republic from the misery of independent existence. It is only two years ago that Signor Mussolini gave the ancient kingdom of Abyssinia its Magna Charta. It is only two months ago that little Albania got its writ of Habeas Corpus, and Mussolini sent in his Bill of Rights for King Zog to pay. Why, even at this moment, the mountaineers of the Tyrol, a German-speaking population who have dwelt in their beautiful valleys for a thousand years, are being liberated, that is to say, uprooted, from the land they love, from the soil which Andreas Hofer died to defend. No wonder the armies are tramping on when there is so much liberation to be done, and no wonder there is a hush among all the neighbors of Germany and Italy while they are wondering which one is going to be 'liberated' next.

The Nazis say that they are being encircled. They have encircled themselves with a ring of neighbors who have to keep on guessing who will be struck down next. This kind of guesswork is a very tiring game. Countries, especially small countries, have long ceased to find it amusing. Can you wonder that the neighbors of Germany, both great and small, have begun to think of stopping the game, by simply saying to the Nazis on the principle of the Covenant of the League of Nations: "He who attacks any, Attacks all. He who attacks the weakest will find he has attacked the strongest"? That is how we are spending our holiday over here, in poor weather, in a lot of clouds. We hope it is better with you.

One thing has struck me as very strange, and that is the resurgence of the one-man power after all these centuries of experience and progress. It is curious how the English-speaking peoples have always had this horror of one-man power. They are quite ready to follow a leader for a time, as long as he is serviceable to them; but the idea of handing themselves over, lock, stock and barrel, body and soul, to one man, and worshiping him as if he were an idol. That has always been odious to the whole theme and nature of our civilization. The architects of the American Constitution were as careful as those who shaped the British Constitution to guard against the whole life and fortunes, and all the laws and freedom of the nation, being placed in the hands of a tyrant. Checks and counter-checks in the body politic, large devolutions of State government, instruments and processes of free debate, frequent recurrence to first principles, the right of opposition to the most powerful governments, and, above all, ceaseless vigilance, have preserved, and will preserve, the broad characteristics of British and American institutions. But in Germany, on a mountain peak, there sits one man who in a single day can release the world from the fear which now oppresses it; or in a single day can plunge all that we have and are into a volcano of smoke and flame.

If Herr Hitler does not make war, there will be no war. No one else is going to make war. Britain and France are determined to shed no blood except in self-defense or in defense of their allies. No one has ever dreamed of attacking Germany. If Germany desires to be reassured against attack by her neighbors, she has only to say the word and we will give her the fullest guarantees in accordance with the principles of the Covenant of the League. We have said repeatedly we ask nothing for ourselves in the way of security that we are not willing freely to share with the German people. Therefore, if war should come there can be no doubt upon whose head the blood-guiltiness will fall. Thus lies the great issue at this moment, and none can tell how it will be settled.

It is not, believe me, my American friends, from any ignoble shrinking from pain and death that the British and French peoples pray for peace. It is not because we have any doubts how a struggle between Nazi Germany and the civilized world would ultimately end that we pray tonight and every night for peace. But whether it be peace or war—peace with its broadening and brightening prosperity, now within our reach, or war with its measureless carnage and destruction—we must strive to frame some system of human relations in the future which will bring to an end this prolonged hideous uncertainty, which will let the working and creative forces of the world get on with their job, and which will no longer leave the whole life of mankind dependent upon the virtues, the caprice, or the wickedness of a single man.

GLOSSARY

Covenant of the League: the charter of the League of Nations

devolution: a transfer of allocation of national authority to other bodies (e.g., provinces)

Hofer, Andreas: Tirolean leader of an 1809 rebellion against Napoleon's forces

King Zog: Zog I, King of the Albanians

writ of Habeas Corpus: an order requiring a person who has been arrested to be brought before a court (to determine the lawfulness of his or her detention)

Document Analysis

Churchill begins his radio address by acknowledging the ongoing Second Sino-Japanese War, in which he places himself firmly on the side of the Chinese and urges the American people to do the same. He describes the Chinese as "fighting for what the founders of the American Constitution in their stately language called: 'Life, liberty and the pursuit of happiness.'" Churchill then plunges into a description of a very tense moment in Europe. He enumerates the instances in which Hitler and Mussolini have taken over weaker regions and countries—describing the annexation of Austria and Czechoslovakia by Germany and the occupation of Abyssinia (now known as Ethiopia) and Albania by Italy, actions that Churchill compares to the aggression of Japanese militarists in China. However, Churchill avoids discussing the most imminent specific threat—the German aggression against Poland—in this address, perhaps fearing that Poland's authoritarian and anti-Semitic dictatorship would not seem very sympathetic to his American listeners.

The bonds of the "English-speaking" peoples are a theme frequently invoked in Churchill's writing and oratory. In "A Hush over Europe," he contrasts the safeguards against one-man rule found in the United States Constitution and the British Constitution with the absolute power of one man, Hitler, over Germany. As he often does, Churchill emphasizes the similarities of British and American political institutions and traditions rather than dwelling on their considerable differences.

Churchill sets the stage in Europe by vividly evoking the image of millions of German and Italian soldiers marching, suggesting that, though these soldiers are allegedly performing routine training maneuvers, war is imminent. Churchill mocks the claims of the Nazis to be acting for defensive purposes, pointing out that none of the smaller states surrounding Germany poses any conceivable threat to it, let alone the stateless Jewish people. He asserts that "if Herr Hitler does not make war, there will be no war." His evocation of the German peoples of the Italian region of the Tyrol and their persecution suggests that not even "Germanic" peoples themselves were safe from the menacing power of the new dictatorships.

Despite the grimness of the situation, Churchill still holds out hope for peace through the collaboration of the big and small powers threatened by Germany. He does not link the Soviet Union to Nazi Germany as an aggressive "totalitarian" power in this address, as he had in previous statements, perhaps because he had not yet abandoned hopes for an alliance to contain Germany between the Soviets and the Western powers.

Essential Themes

Just a few weeks after Churchill's address, Hitler's aggression culminated in a German invasion of Poland on September 1, 1939. The German attack was followed by British and French declarations of war on Germany and led to another Great War in Europe, which merged with the war in East Asia between Chinese and Japanese forces to become known as World War II. The Soviet Union divided Poland with Germany, but the Soviets later allied with Britain and France after being attacked by Germany in June 1941. Despite Churchill's urgings, the United States, while supportive of the anti-Nazi cause and cooperating with Britain in keeping the Atlantic shipping lanes clear, did not enter the war as a combatant until December 1941, following the Japanese attack on Pearl Harbor on December 7. Decades after World War II, the most common perception of its beginning in Europe remains shaped by Churchill's picture of a failed appeasement policy.

The idea Churchill put forth of an Anglo-American alliance based on a shared tradition of democratic and constitutional values, an idea with its roots in World War I, persisted for decades into World War II, the Cold War, and the War on Terror. Churchill in particular became an iconic figure for those who support closer relations between the United States and Britain and also for those supporting a muscular foreign policy.

—*William E. Burns, PhD*

Bibliography and Additional Reading

Gilbert, Martin. *Churchill and America*. New York: Free, 2005. Print.

―――――. *Winston Churchill: The Wilderness Years: Speaking Out against Hitler in the Prelude to War.* London: IB Tauris, 2011. Print.

Macdonald, C. A. *The United States, Britain and Appeasement, 1936–1939.* New York: St. Martins, 1981. Print.

Manchester, William. *The Last Lion: Winston Spencer Churchill: Alone, 1932–1940.* New York: Bantam, 1983. Print.

■ Charles Lindbergh: Neutrality and War

Date: October 13, 1939
Author: Charles Lindbergh
Genre: address; speech

Summary Overview

During the 1930s, Charles Lindbergh was one of the most visible American figures who argued that the United States should have nothing to do with conflicts in Europe, or anywhere outside the Western Hemisphere. As Europe descended once again into war in the fall of 1939, Lindbergh gave a number of speeches like the one he delivered on October 19, 1939, arguing that the United States should avoid getting involved again in a bloody struggle. This speech came early in the conflict, before the rapid German victories of 1940 and the initially successful German assault on Russia in 1941, and, therefore, the possibility of muddy, entrenched fronts was still very much alive in the minds of many Americans.

Indeed, Lindbergh—while his wishes were ultimately denied in December 1941, when the United States declared war on Japan—demonstrated the American public's ambivalence over the role the nation should play in the world and also showcased the very real popularity of neutrality during the 1930s. While Lindbergh thought the United States could allow no foreign incursion into the Western Hemisphere, he preferred for the nation to remain a symbol of democracy and freedom to other continents, rather than an active participant in the potentially bloody events in those places. Such thinking had largely been the dominant American mindset regarding foreign policy during the eighteenth and nineteenth century. Only in the 1910s had the ideas of President Woodrow Wilson—that events abroad mattered enormously for American security—begun to change such thinking. In addition, when combined with other trends of the 1930s such as the Nye Commission and the various Neutrality Acts, Lindbergh's prominence revealed that, at least for a while, many Americans were conflicted over whether or not the nation should get involved in the violent world events of the 1930s and 1940s.

Defining Moment

American entry into World War II was not a given when the war erupted in September of 1939. In fact, it took more than two years and a direct attack by Japan before the United States joined the conflict, and several events earlier in the 1930s seemed to indicate that the United States might refrain from fighting altogether. When Italy invaded Ethiopia in 1935 and the Spanish Civil War began in 1936, Americans had to decide how to react to an increasingly violent world. In 1935, 1936, and 1937, Congress passed various Neutrality Acts that both prohibited loans and the sale of American weapons to countries involved in a conflict and blocked US citizens from sailing on vessels owned by such nations. In addition, the American public was not eager to go back to the battlefields of France, especially after the Nye Committee, led by Senator Gerald Nye of North Dakota, held a series of hearings and investigations between 1934 and 1936 into the role of bankers and arms manufacturers in the country's participation in World War I. The committee's reports drew connections between corporate profits and the march to war, sparking public outrage and support for US neutrality going forward.

The more immediate context of Lindbergh's speech must also be noted. He was arguing his points at a time when Poland was just about to fall to Germany, but the rest of Europe remained untouched. He likely held the expectation that once again, German forces would get bogged down in an attack on France and the immovable fronts of World War I would return to grind up millions of men as before. He, and indeed most world leaders, could not predict the vast success of German

Blitzkrieg tactics in the spring and summer of 1940 that conquered the Low Countries, Norway, and France. So when the war began and President Roosevelt called for a revision to the earlier Neutrality Acts, which would result in the "cash and carry" policy, allowing countries at war to buy war material from the United States if they paid cash and carried the goods on their own ships, Lindbergh feared it would open the door to American participation.

Author Biography

Charles Lindbergh was one of America's most famous aviators, mostly because he made the first solo nonstop flight across the Atlantic Ocean in 1927, but also because of the kidnapping and murder of his young son in 1932. He was also an ardent proponent of American isolationism—that the United States should abstain from involvement in foreign conflicts. He, therefore, actively sought to convince Americans that only the Western Hemisphere mattered for US security and that the United States should avoid wasting its strength elsewhere in the world. After he opposed altering the Neutrality Acts, Lindbergh went on to help start the America First Committee, a group opposed to US involvement in World War II. He also supported President Roosevelt's Republican opponent in 1940, Wendell Willkie, who campaigned in part on the idea that it was only a matter of time until Roosevelt sent American troops to Europe. After the war, he was a writer and an environmentalist until his death in 1974.

HISTORICAL DOCUMENT

Tonight, I speak again to the people of this country who are opposed to the United States entering the war which is now going on in Europe. We are faced with the need of deciding on a policy of American neutrality. The future of our nation and of our civilization rests upon the wisdom and foresight we use. Much as peace is to be desired, we should realize that behind a successful policy of neutrality must stand a policy of war. It is essential to define clearly those principles and circumstances for which a nation will fight. Let us give no one the impression that America's love for peace means that she is afraid of war, or that we are not fully capable and willing to defend all that is vital to us. National life and influence depend upon national strength, both in character and in arms. A neutrality built on pacifism alone will eventually fail.

Before we can intelligently enact regulations for the control of our armaments, our credit, and our ships, we must draw a sharp dividing line between neutrality and war; there must be no gradual encroachment on the defenses of our nation. Up to this line we may adjust our affairs to gain the advantages of peace, but beyond it must lie all the armed might of America, coiled in readiness to spring if once this bond is cut. Let us make clear to all countries where this line lies. It must be both within our intent and our capabilities. There must be no question of trading or bluff in this hemisphere. Let us give no promises we cannot keep—make no meaningless assurances to an Ethiopia, a Czechoslovakia, or a Poland. The policy we decide upon should be clear cut as our shorelines, and as easily defended as our continent.

This western hemisphere is our domain. It is our right to trade freely within it. From Alaska to Labrador, for the Hawaiian Islands to Bermuda, from Canada to South America, we must allow no invading army to set foot. These are the outposts of the United States. They form the essential outline of our geographical defense. We must be ready to wage war with all the resources of our nation if they are ever seriously threatened. Their defense is the mission of our army, our navy, and our air corps—the minimum requirement of our military strength. Around these places should lie our line between neutrality and war. Let there be no compromise about our right to defend or trade within this area. If it is challenged by any nation, the answer must be war. Our policy of neutrality should have this as its foundation.

We must protect our sister American nations from foreign invasion, both for their welfare and our own. But, in turn, they have a duty to us. They should not place us in the position of having to defend them in America while they engage in wars abroad. Can we rightfully permit any country in America to give bases to foreign warships, or to send its army abroad to fight while it remains secure in our protection at home? We desire the utmost friendship with the people of Canada. If their country is ever attacked, our Navy will be defending their seas, our soldiers will fight on their battlefields, our fliers will die in their skies. But have they the right to draw this hemisphere into a European war simply because they prefer the Crown of England to American independence?

Sooner or later we must demand the freedom of this continent and its surrounding islands from the dictates of European power. America history clearly indicates this need. As long as European powers maintain their influence in our hemisphere, we are likely to find ourselves involved in their troubles. And they will lose no opportunity to involve us.

Our Congress is now assembled to decide upon the best policy for this country to maintain during the war which is going on in Europe. The legislation under discussion involves three major issues—the embargo of arms, the restriction of shipping, and the allowance of credit. The action we take in regard to these issues will be an important indication to ourselves, and to the nation of Europe, whether or not we are likely to enter the conflict eventually as we did in the last war. The entire world is watching us. The action we take in America may either stop or precipitate this war.

Let us take up these issues, one at a time, and examine them. First, the embargo of arms: It is argued that the repeal of this embargo would assist democracy in Europe, that it would let us make a profit for ourselves from the sale of munitions abroad, and, at the same time, help to build up our own arms industry.

Document Analysis

Lindbergh begins his address by assuring his listeners that he is not arguing for a pacifist stance. He believes that the United States can and should fight for certain objectives and defend certain territory. Further, he claims that if the United States adopts a policy of neutrality and non-involvement outside of the Western Hemisphere, that policy will only be taken seriously by other powers if the United States makes it readily apparent that it will fight with all its strength should outside armies and navies encroach on that hemisphere. At this time, Lindbergh was already worried that the actions of countries in the Western Hemisphere would bring foreign involvement or invasion: on September 10, 1939, Canada had declared war on Germany, only seven days after Britain and France. Thus, Lindbergh's desire to keep the Western Hemisphere entirely out of the European war had already been thwarted.

Lindbergh wants Americans to be clear about the point at which the nation should be willing to go to war, both for the sake of warning off foreign nations and for helping Americans avoid getting entangled in needless foreign wars. "The policy we decide upon should be clear cut as our shorelines, and as easily defended as our continent," he says, going on to explain that only a military threat within the Western Hemisphere should be cause for a military response from the United States. He says, "Let us give no promises we cannot keep—make no meaningless assurances to an Ethiopia, a Czechoslovakia, or a Poland." Between 1935 and the time Lindbergh is speaking, all three of those nations had fallen to fascist aggression, and Lindbergh does not want the United States to make hollow commitments to faraway places. With regard to the arms embargo and restrictions on shipping and credit to belligerent powers, he believes that the United States could still try to prevent the deepening of the conflict: "The action we take in America may either stop or precipitate this war." Overall, Lindbergh wants clear distinctions as to what American interests truly are, and he sees those interests as existing only within the Western Hemisphere.

Essential Themes

Lindbergh was trying to combat the growing Wilsonian world view that many US leaders had been adopting over the previous two decades, and which would become sacrosanct in US foreign policy after 1945. In the 1910s, President Wilson was the first US leader to make a compelling case that the structure of other governments around the world and the events that occurred in other nations had a direct bearing on the national security of the United States, especially because democracies tended not to fight each other. Lindbergh tried to convince Americans that, while he thought this was true about nations within the Western Hemisphere, such a view of the world at large was not accurate and that the United States was safe behind its oceans as long as foreign armies and navies did not enter the region. Therefore, he sought to return the United States to the dominant mindset of the eighteenth and nineteenth centuries, that the nation should be a beacon for democracy and freedom, but should not seek to actively protect or advance those concepts outside of the Western Hemisphere with armed force.

While Lindbergh's vision clearly lost out, it enjoyed wide popularity for many years, reflected in Roosevelt's hesitancy to involve the United States in the conflict, prior to the actual attack on American shores when the Japanese bombed Pearl Harbor in 1941. Lindbergh's efforts to preserve American neutrality indicate the internal tensions that democratic nations regularly experience over the massive use of armed force abroad.

—*Kevin E. Grimm, PhD*

Bibliography and Additional Reading

"1921–1940: September 4, 1934: 'Merchants of Death.'" *Senate.gov*. US Senate, n.d. Web. 11 June 2014.

"Charles A. Lindbergh—Biography." *Lindbergh Foundation*. Lindberg Foundation, 2012. Web. 11 June 2014.

Herring, George C. *From Colony to Superpower: US Foreign Relations since 1776*. New York: Oxford UP, 2008. Print.

Kennedy, David M. *Freedom from Fear: The American People in Depression and War, 1929–1945*. New York: Oxford UP, 2005. Print.

"Second World War (WWII)." *The Canadian Encyclopedia*. Historica Foundation, n.d. Web. 11 June 2014.

Culture, Crime, and More

In this section we look at noted cultural events and news stories of the 1930s, beginning with the establishment of "The Star-Spangled Banner" as the national anthem in 1931. It was a time of economic woes and worldly worries, and the idea of rallying the people behind a patriotic song was appealing to political leaders and the populace at large. The music was already used widely in military settings; by official decree, it was now to be the anthem of the nation.

Radio continued its rise in popularity throughout the 1930s. Besides musical programming and variety shows, there were now serial radio dramas, comedies, and a host of other entertainments. News "flashes" broke in occasionally to provide breaking information regarding the world outside of show business, and the president himself, Franklin Roosevelt, made good use of the medium in presenting his views on domestic and world affairs through semi-regular "fireside chats" broadcast over the radio. One newsworthy event was the crashing of the hydrogen-filled dirigible *Hindenburg* in 1937, which augured the end of the "balloon" era of commercial flight and the beginning of "live," or directly reported, radio news broadcasts. Another noted radio event was the "panic broadcast," as it was called, when writer-producer Orson Welles recreated *The War of the Worlds,* about a Martian invasion, over the air. Many people took it to be the real thing and hid themselves and their families—or scrambled—as a result. The power of radio seemed boundless.

The National Anthem Established: The Star-Spangled Banner

Date: March 3, 1931
Authors: Francis Scott Key; John Stafford Smith; US Congress
Genre: song; legislation

Summary Overview

The US national anthem is made up of two parts, lyrics based on the Francis Scott Key poem "Defence of Fort M'Henry" and music written by John Stafford Smith. The poem was written in 1812, after Key witnessed the Battle of Fort McHenry during the War of 1812, but it was not set to music and adopted for official use by the US Navy until 1889. Then, in 1916, President Woodrow Wilson, through an executive order, authorized its use in official state functions. Only in 1931 did Congress pass a resolution affirming Wilson's order and adopting the song as the nation's official anthem. President Herbert Hoover signed the measure into law the same year, making it part of the US Code (the statutes that control government actions). The law, reproduced below, describes the approved procedure for a proper "rendition of the national anthem." Also reproduced here are the four stanzas of the Francis Scott Key poem making up the anthem's lyrics. However, only the first stanza is commonly recited during public renditions of the anthem.

Defining Moment

Before this legislation was passed in 1931, the United States of America had been without a national anthem. While a simple song might not seem very important, it is an integral part of the national identity of many countries' inhabitants. Much like a university's fight song or creed, a national anthem is a rallying point around which a country's citizens can gather and feel a part of something larger than themselves. By the 1930s, the United States had been a county for over 150 years, and throughout much of the nineteenth century and early twentieth century, "The Star-Spangled Banner" had been popular and was played at military events, particularly during the raising of the American flag. Indeed, President Woodrow Wilson required its use at certain types of events in 1916; and in 1918, it played for the first time at a baseball game, during the World Series. Based on its wide use, its broad popularity, and its patriotic imagery, "The Star-Spangled Banner" was an obvious choice for the US national anthem.

The year 1931, then, was the first time that a set of rules had been written down and made part of the public record as to how and when to perform the official national anthem. The performing of the national anthem, especially in conjunction with the presentation of the American flag, was and is a symbol of the nation as a whole and all that that entails. Uniformed military personnel and civilian individuals were given separate actions to perform during the playing of the anthem, highlighting the differences between those two categories of citizens. Given that the song is based on a poem about a battle fought by soldiers, any military personnel present at the anthem's performance are, in effect, honoring their fellow soldiers before them and those who will come after. The War of 1812 was a chance for a young United States of America to prove its strength and enduring nature and a song from that period immortalized that nature and projected it forward for each successive generation.

Author Biography

Francis Scott Key was born in 1779 in Georgetown, Maryland, on his family's plantation. He studied law at St. John's College and eventually became a lawyer. He took on many high-profile cases, such as prosecuting President Andrew Jackson's would-be assassin, Richard

Lawrence, and was appointed a US District Attorney in 1833. He was also a slave-owner and very active in defending slavery, even prosecuting those who spoke out against the institution. (This is not an unusual position in light of his upbringing.) Key participated in the American Bible Society, the American Colonization Society. He married Mary Tayloe Lloyd in 1802 and the couple had two children. Key is best known for his amateur poetry. Most of his poems reflect his faith and have heavy religious overtones. While "The Star-Spangled Banner" calls upon God, its main theme is the enduring strength of the nation. Key died in 1843, almost ninety years before his poem was made into the national anthem.

John Stafford Smith (1750–1836) was a British composer and organist who is best known for writing the score that later was married with the Francis Scott Key poem to form "The Star-Spangled Banner." The original music is thought to have been written by Smith in the 1760s and was first published in 1778 as "The Anacreontic Song," the official song of a gentlemen's society made up of amateur musicians and students of music.

HISTORICAL DOCUMENT

36 U.S. Code § 301—National Anthem

(a) Designation.—The composition consisting of the words and music known as the Star-Spangled Banner is the national anthem.

(b) Conduct During Playing.— During a rendition of the national anthem—

(1) when the flag is displayed—

(A) individuals in uniform should give the military salute at the first note of the anthem and maintain that position until the last note;

(B) members of the Armed Forces and veterans who are present but not in uniform may render the military salute in the manner provided for individuals in uniform; and

(C) all other persons present should face the flag and stand at attention with their right hand over the heart, and men not in uniform, if applicable, should remove their headdress with their right hand and hold it at the left shoulder, the hand being over the heart; and

(2) when the flag is not displayed, all present should face toward the music and act in the same manner they would if the flag were displayed.

* * *

The Star-Spangled Banner

O say can you see by the dawn's early light,
What so proudly we hailed at the twilight's last gleaming,
Whose broad stripes and bright stars through the perilous fight,
O'er the ramparts we watched, were so gallantly streaming?
And the rockets red glare, the bombs bursting in air
Gave proof through the night that our flag was still there;
O say does that star-spangled banner yet wave,
O'er the land of the free and the home of the brave?

On the shore dimly seen through the mists of the deep,
Where the foe's haughty host in dread silence reposes,
What is that which the breeze, o'er the towering steep,
As it fitfully blows, half conceals, half discloses?
Now it catches the gleam of the morning's first beam,
In full glory reflected now shines in the stream:
'Tis the star-spangled banner, O! long may it wave

O'er the land of the free and the home of the brave.

And where is that band who so vauntingly swore
That the havoc of war and the battle's confusion,
A home and a country, should leave us no more?
Their blood has washed out their foul foot steps' pollution.
No refuge could save the hireling and slave
From the terror of flight, or the gloom of the grave:
And the star-spangled banner in triumph doth wave,
O'er the land of the free and the home of the brave.

O thus be it ever, when freemen shall stand
Between their loved home and the war's desolation.
Blest with vict'ry and peace, may the Heav'n rescued land
Praise the Power that hath made and preserved us a nation!
Then conquer we must, when our cause it is just,
And this be our motto: "In God is our trust."
And the star-spangled banner in triumph shall wave
O'er the land of the free and the home of the brave!

GLOSSARY

ramparts: a broad mound (of earth) created as a fortification around a place; usually topped with a parapet; anything used as a defensive blockade

vauntingly: in a boastful manner; vaingloriously

Document Analysis

The relevant portion of the US Code (36, section 301) addresses the military and civilian requirements when the national anthem is played, especially when the American flag is also present. While there is no specific penalty stated for breaking these rules (except, perhaps, for military personnel under the Uniform Code of Military Justice), the strictures noted here have become the norm for all public performances, creating a situation in which one is expected to conform to the guidelines under penalty of public disapproval. Also noted, again, are the different forms of conduct expected of military personnel, in and out of uniform, and civilians.

As for the lyrics, Key's poem touches on several ideals that remain relevant today and perhaps are timeless. While the language of the poem may be somewhat archaic for today's reader, the themes are still clear even 200 years after they were laid down. The spark of inspiration for the creation of the poem was the fact that Fort McHenry, in Baltimore, Maryland, managed to stay standing after being attacked by British forces. The poem opens the morning after the battle, with the speaker daring to hope that he might see the American flag waving over the fort. It is not until near the end of the second stanza, after describing the enemy who lurks outside the fort, that the speaker is able to state with certainty that, "'Tis the star-spangled banner, O! Long may it wave…." The third stanza begins more triumphantly, showing that even though the British, who were the dominant world-power at the time, may have boasted that they would destroy the young American country, they were unable to do so. Yet, the last four lines of stanza three show that terror and death were not absent; rather, they were the price paid for the continued liberty of "the free."

The final stanza is more typical of Key's other poems.

He shows the power of men who seek to protect their homeland, an act that gives them a strength and a purpose that cannot be overestimated. He also thanks God for his intervention in helping to preserve the lives of Key's countrymen. Key was devoutly religious, as were many others of his era, and he believed that the country should embrace the ideals of religion and freedom, in order to create the strongest nation possible.

Essential Themes
The central ideas of the national anthem are the strength and freedom of the United States of America, especially while it is under attack from outside forces. This is particularly relevant to the modern world, where threats seem to come from many sources, even if they are not as obvious or overt as the British sending their ships to engage US forces inside military forts. According to Key's poem, fighting for one's country, protecting it from outside threats, is one of the most important things a person can do. At the same time, he emphasizes the importance of being free. There is a delicate balance, in other words, that can too easily be upset during a crisis.

Key also forswears those who boast of their power, because it is that type of person who often comes before a fall. "The [British] band who so vauntingly swore" that they would destroy the Americans were defeated in battle (although for the war as a whole it is more difficult to identify a clear winner). In alluding to the defense of one's home and the reliance on a god, Key shows his belief that many obstacles can be overcome, even at great odds. Such faith in the power of religion and belief was a large part of the founding era of the country, even though the Constitution created an official separation of church and state.

Finally, the adoption of a national anthem created a formal rallying point for American citizens. Although, before "The Star-Spangled Banner," there was some debate about whether to choose and anthem and which one it should be, the Francis Scott Key poem seems to have touched on many of the ideals that were then and still are held dear by the widest possible swath of US citizenry. Not always the easiest piece to read or sing (with its somewhat antiquated language and its great musical range, from deep low notes to soaring high notes), still, "The Star-Spangled Banner" has, for two hundred years, given people solace and inspiration. Played at concerts, ball games, military events, Fourth of July ceremonies, flag raisings ("colors"), and many other events, the national anthem is a unifying symbol of the enduring quality of the American people and the nation they created.

—*Anna Accettola, MA*

Bibliography and Additional Reading
Cerulo, Karen. "Symbols and the World System: National Anthems and Flags." *Sociological Forum* 8.2 (1993): 243–71. Print.
Delaplaine, Edward Schley. *Francis Scott Key: Life and Times*. Biography Press, 1937. Print.
Silkett, John T. *Francis Scott Key and the History of the Star Spangled Banner*. Washington: Vintage America Pub., 1978. Print.
Muller, Joseph. *The Star Spangled Banner; Words and Music Issued between 1814–1864; an Annotated Bibliographical List with Notices of the Different Versions, Texts, Variants, Musical Arrangements, and Notes on Music Publishers in the United States*. New York: Da Capo, 1973. Print.

■ What I Knew About John Dillinger

Date: August 1934
Author: Evelyn "Billie" Frechette
Genre: memoir

Summary Overview

John Dillinger was the most notorious outlaw of the Great Depression. Declared "Public Enemy No. 1" by FBI director J. Edgar Hoover, Dillinger became a media sensation during the 1930s, as he and his gang robbed dozens of banks throughout the Midwest, repeatedly evading capture. Following a second highly publicized prison escape, the hunt for Dillinger became one of the most exhaustive in United States history, culminating in his death at the hands of federal agents outside a movie theater in Chicago. After the shooting public fascination with Dillinger only intensified, with much of the attention focused on his former girlfriend, Evelyn "Billie" Frechette, who at the time was serving a sentence on a federal work farm for having harbored and abetted a wanted fugitive. Hounded by offers of money for her story, Frechette put her memories to paper in a multi-part article for the *Chicago Herald and Examiner* in August 1934. In it, she recounts her time with Dillinger, painting a picture of a good man gone wrong, and the lonely girl who fell in love with him.

Defining Moment

In many ways John Dillinger was the perfect manifestation of his age. Following the booming, albeit fiscally lopsided, 1920s, the United States sank into economic turmoil after the stock market crash of 1929. Banks and factories closed, retirement and savings accounts were wiped out, and an increasing share of Americans found it ever harder to make ends meet. As the Great Depression intensified and popular resentment grew, several high-profile criminals gained wide attention in the nation's media. Baby Face Nelson, Pretty Boy Floyd, and Bonnie and Clyde became household names, functioning as both distraction and release for an American public frustrated by the failure of private and public institutions to offer any relief from economic hardship.

Among the celebrity outlaws of the 1930s, John Dillinger emerged as the most famous. Born in Indianapolis, Indiana at the turn of the century, Dillinger found himself in frequent trouble with the law. After a failed stint in the Navy, a failed marriage, and a string of short-term jobs, he and an accomplice robbed a grocery store of $50. Despite confessing to the crime and asking for leniency, Dillinger was sentenced to ten to twenty years in the Indiana state penitentiary system, where he quickly befriended other criminals who taught him how to become a successful bank robber.

Dillinger was paroled in 1933, at the height of the Great Depression. Resentful of society and unable to find work, he began robbing banks. Over the next several months, Dillinger and his gang stole tens of thousands of dollars. Newspapers covered the gang's escapades often exaggerating and inflating events to boost readership. It is even possible that some robberies were falsely attributed to Dillinger altogether. Partly due to the attention, FBI director J. Edgar Hoover declared Dillinger Public Enemy No. 1 in America's first-ever "war on crime." When, in early 1934, Dillinger was first captured and then escaped from what Indiana authorities had called an escape-proof jail, media coverage of the handsome and charming gangster only intensified.

Following the arrest of his girlfriend, Evelyn "Billie" Frechette, and a shootout with federal authorities at a lodge in Wisconsin, Dillinger went into hiding in Chicago. On July 22, tipped off by Anna Sage, a prostitute and Dillinger associate, that the bank robber would be attending a movie, federal agents were dispatched to the Biograph Theater. That evening, after the movie let out, Dillinger, accompanied by Anna Sage, dressed in an orange dress (though appearing red by the light of the street lamps), was shot dead by waiting agents.

The fact that the last movie Dillinger saw was the Clark Gable gangster film *Manhattan Melodrama*, along with the story of the "woman in red," all served to help expand John Dillinger's legend. Over 15,000 people went to see Dillinger's body at the Cook County morgue, and the outlaw became the subject of numerous books and articles. It was amid this frenzied atmosphere that "Billie" Frechette sold her stories of Dillinger, just a month after his death, to the *Chicago Herald and Examiner* and the magazines *True Confessions* and *True Romance*.

Author Biography
Evelyn "Billie" Frechette was born on the Menominee Indian Reservation in Neopit, Wisonsin in 1907. Part Native American and part French Canadian, Frechette grew up on reservations, and by all indications, she had a difficult childhood, living for a time in Milwaukee and eventually moving to Chicago. In 1932, she was married to Welton Walter Spark, a criminal who was sentenced to a fifteen-year federal prison term shortly before their marriage. Frechette became romantically involved with John Dillinger in October 1933. Over the course of their seven-month relationship, she accompanied him as he evaded local and federal authorities, though no evidence exists that she ever took part in any of his criminal activities, only once driving a getaway car after he had been shot. In April 1934, she was arrested by federal agents while Dillinger waited for her in a car several yards away. Frechette served two years on a federal work farm and, upon release, toured the United States with members of the Dillinger family in a show called *Crime Didn't Pay!* She eventually returned to Wisconsin and the reservation, where she died in 1969. Throughout her many years, her short relationship with John Dillinger defined her life.

HISTORICAL DOCUMENT

Part One – August 27, 1934

Crime does not pay!

By Evelyn Frechette

Only one big thing ever happened to me in my life. Nothing much happened before that, and I don't expect much from now on—except maybe a lot more grief. The one big thing that happened to me was that I fell in love with John Dillinger.

I'm in prison on account of that. The government people said that I "harbored a criminal." The criminal was John. I lived with him for several months, if that's what they mean. I loved him. I followed him around the country—from Chicago to Florida and then to Tucson, where we were caught. And then after we got out of the jail in Crown Point with the wooden gun he came to me again and we beat it to St. Paul, where we had the shooting scrape and nearly got killed.

Dillinger Waiting as Police Seized Evelyn.

So you see I was with John Dillinger from the time he came to Chicago after breaking out of the jail at Lima, O., until I got caught in Chicago last April—the time the police took me away while John was sitting in his car down the street waiting for me.

John was good to me. He looked after me and bought me all kinds of clothes and jewelry and cars and pets, and we went places and saw things, and he gave me everything a girl wants. He was in love with me.

If that's harboring him, all right then. I harbored him.

John's dead. I'm not sorry I loved him. That part I couldn't help. I'm sorry what happened to me and what it cost me after I was caught.

Only a Number Now in Federal Prison.

I'm a convict. Since the third of last June, when a federal judge in St. Paul sentenced me to two years. I've been in the United States detention farm at Milan, Mich. I'm not Billy Frechette any more, I'm a number, like Machine Gun Kelly's wife, who is here too, and like the rest of the girls on the farm.

I guess this is where they all end up. Maybe I've got it coming to me. I don't know. But I keep telling myself that I'm different. I'm in here because I fell in love with the wrong man—not wrong for me, you understand, but wrong if I wanted to keep it in the clear.

Falling in love with John was something that took care of itself. There are lots of reasons why. Some of the reasons are John's and some are mine.

Liked Dillinger for What He Was to Her.

I like John's kind. I don't mean because he was a criminal and carried guns around, and wasn't afraid of police or any one. There was something else. John might have been a soldier or something else besides what he was. He wasn't, of course, because something happened along the line.

I always figured that what he did was one thing and what he was was another. I was in love with what he was. Oh, maybe I was wrong, but you can't argue yourself out of falling in love! You just can't sit down and think it out.

I come from French-Indian stock. Maybe that has something to do with it. I'm proud of my Indian blood. My tribe is a good tribe and my people are good people. Maybe I'd better tell how I was brought up.

Born on Wisconsin Indian Reservation.

I was born on an Indian reservation at Neopit, Wis., sixty miles from Green Bay. I had two brothers and two sisters. My father died when I was 8 years old. He was French and pronounced his name without the "e," like Freshet.

My mother was half French and half Indian. Her tribe was the Menominees. They called them the wild-rice eaters. They used to have their hunting ground around Wisconsin and Michigan a long time ago, before the white man came and pushed them around.

Thinks of Indians Who Roamed Hills.

I think about that sometimes when I look out through the bars in the window at the hills and the trees here in Michigan. I get to thinking that my people use to roam around over those hills—long before the white man came along with his rules about harboring outlaws.

And I get to thinking that maybe the Indians had rules about things like that, too. Maybe if they caught a girl that was running around with an enemy chief they'd hold her and wait for him to come for her so they could kill him.

But I figure they would let her go after they killed him.

Recalls Working on Reservation as Child.

Nothing happened to me when I was a child. I don't remember anything that happened to me that was unusual. We had to work around the reservation with our Indian relatives and neighbors. My mother had a hard time bringing us up.

I remember I had an uncle that the government people thought a lot about. They sent him to Washington to do things for the Indians and he was a big man.

I got most of my schooling in a mission school on the reservation and then when I was 13 I went to government school at Flandreau, S.D. I stayed there for three years and then I went to live with my aunt in Milwaukee.

I worked as a nurse girl—when I could get work and that wasn't very often. I wanted to come to Chicago. I hadn't been any place in my life and Chicago was a big and wonderful place to me.

Sister an Actress in Amateur Plays.

I was 18 then. I worked when I could—nurse, and housework, and waitress. My sister, Frances, was there. She had a lot of Indian friends and they went around to churches and put on Indian plays. She was a good little actress.

They called themselves "The Indian Players" and I remembered they put on plays called "Little Fire Face" and "The Elm Tree." They got all dressed up in their feathers and beads and painted their faces and danced the way we used to on the Indian reservation.

It was a lot of fun and I used to go around with my sister to the church socials. I wasn't a very good actress. But I helped wash the dishes and helped cook parched corn and wild rice and other Indian dishes. And when they needed somebody I'd put on my costume and dance in the chorus.

Tells of Marriage to Welton Spark.

It was fun, as I said, but it seem that nothing exciting ever happened to me and I was all alone, you might say.

Then I met this man I married. I wasn't really in love

with him, but I was lonesome. His name was Welton Spark. Not long after we were married he was arrested and they sent him away to Leavenworth for fifteen years.

I don't even know what he did. It had something to do with the government mails. He never told me what he was up to. Being married to him didn't amount to much. I lost track of him right away.

Met Dillinger in North Side Cabaret.

I kept on working here and there and I got some girlfriends and we would date up often and go out cabareting. I liked going out where people were laughing and having a good time and cutting up. It was in a cabaret on the North Side where I met John Dillinger.

I'll never forget that. It happened the way things do in the movies. I was 25 years old and I wasn't any different from all the other girls that were 25 years old. Nothing that happened to me up to that time to amount to anything. Then I met John and everything was changed. I started a new kind of life.

It was in November, just about a year ago now, I remember. I was sitting at the table with some other girls and some fellows. We were having a good time.

Romance Begun in Glance and Smile.

I looked up and I saw a man at a table across the room looking at me. He didn't look away when I looked up. He just stared at me and smiled a little bit with the corner of his mouth. His eyes seemed to go all the way through me.

A thing like that happens to a girl often and doesn't seem to mean anything. This was different. I looked at him and maybe I smiled.

Anyway he knew one of the girls I was with and pretty soon he came over to our table and spoke to the girl and she said: "Billy, this is Jack Harris"

Didn't Know Then Who Dillinger Was.

He might just as well have said his name was John Dillinger then because I didn't know any different. I didn't read the newspapers. I didn't know for a long time after that what his real name was. I didn't know then he was the John Dillinger everybody under the sun was looking for.

But to me that night he was just Jack Harris—a good looking fellow that stood there looking down at me and smiling in a way that I could tell he liked me already more than a little bit. He said:

"Where have you been all my life?"

(In the next chapter of the story of her life with John Dillinger. Evelyn ("Billy") Frechette will tell how this casual meeting grew into a love affair with the nation's No. 1 criminal—an affair that was interrupted only briefly when Dillinger and his gang were captured.)

* * *

Part Five — August 30, 1934

St. Paul Shooting and Wounding of Desperado Is Described

I sit here in a jail cell that isn't any bigger than a pantry and wonder how I ever stood up during all those wild days when we had to sneak around like a lot of alley cats for fear we would get caught.

For instance, there was that day after the shooting with the police in St. Paul when Johnny sat there is the back seat of the car frowning and holding his leg and waiting for me to go and get help for him.

For a minute I thought I couldn't get up off the seat of the car. I felt sure that if I got out and started down the street I'd get a bullet in my back before I got two feet away.

But I went. I started to run down the alley and John shouted to me "Take it easy," and I slowed down. He didn't want to attract any attention in broad daylight.

Takes Ride While Green Gets Doctors.

I ran in the back way of the Eddie Green's apartment and brought him out to the car. Then Beth came down, and John asked her to take me for a ride while Eddie was getting a doctor. I guess he thought it was dangerous and he didn't want me to get caught, too, if there was going to be trouble.

We drove around for an hour or more and then came

back and waited a little before the doctor was brought up. He was Dr. Clayton May. Then we got in our cars and I rode with Eddie. We drove around and stopped at a place on Park Av., and they took John to get treated.

The doctor said he'd be all right. This doctor later went on trial with me for harboring Dillinger. He said on the witness stand that John and Eddie threatened him with machine guns and that Eddie followed him to see there wasn't any tip-off. Somebody else will have to tell that story.

Eddie Shot to Death by Police

This place was where the doctor's nurse lived. She was Mrs. Augusta Salt. We stayed there for three or four days waiting for John's knee to heal up. But it wasn't safe. We had to leave. I guess we got out just in time. They killed Eddie Green just after we left. The police shot him down in the street.

Where to? We couldn't go to another place in the Twin Cities. The police were looking in every house there for us. We couldn't go to Chicago. They knew the neighbor hood where John used to stay, and they were waiting for him there.

So John picked the one place where nobody would think of looking for him. He went home. He went back to his father's farm.

I argued with him about that. I didn't think it was safe. But he said: "Listen Billy. Who's smarter—me or the cops?"

It took us two or three days to get there because we had to drive around quite a lot. We didn't go places where we thought there might be danger. John couldn't get out and walk any place because he was limping pretty bad and that would be a dead give away.

Tells of Reunion at Family Home.

His dad was glad to see him when he got to Mooresville, and we had a real celebration. All his family came down to say hello. His half-brother, Hubert, was there, and his sister, Mrs. Hancock, came down from Maywood, Ind.

John's dad said he ought to keep out of trouble, but John just laughed. We took a lot of pictures. John had one taken with his wooden gun. He still thought it was a joke the way he got out. He gave the gun to his father as a present.

It wasn't safe to stay around the farm long. John was careless. He'd go out and sit in the yard with his sisters and play games where all the neighbors could see. I guess the only reason they didn't turn him in was they were afraid.

Anyway we left there on the 9th of April and drove to Chicago.

What were we going to do? Well we were going to settle down. We talked about it a lot on the way up. John thought he could do it now. He had plenty of money. He thought Chicago was as good a place as any.

John Gives Her Funds for Divorce.

We wanted to get married and John gave me the money for a divorce suit against my husband, Welton Spark, who was in Leavenworth. John and I had been in love with each other for a long time now—nearly seven months. And more than that, we got to know each other. John couldn't trust many people, but he could trust me.

That's what we were thinking about, but it sounds a little silly now. We couldn't settle down and keep out of trouble. They'd keep on looking for John. There was no use deceiving ourselves. We were going to get caught sooner or later. I got it sooner. We had just got into Chicago and I walked right into a trap.

Document Analysis

Partly a narrative of her time with John Dillinger and partly a defense of her life choices, Billie Frechette presents herself here as a good woman from difficult circumstances, who fell in love with a good man come from equally difficult circumstances. Dillinger, according to Frechette, although known to the American people as 'Public Enemy No. 1,' was someone else entirely. He was a victim of fate—a kind, loving, exciting man, whom she loved and who loved her in return. Her one and only regret is what happened to her because of him.

Frechette recounts her time growing up in the reservation system. She spends time telling about her childhood in Wisconsin and school in South Dakota. Her tribe was the Menominee, traditionally wild-rice eaters, who used to roam across Wisconsin and Michigan "before the white man came and pushed them around." Maybe if Indians still roamed the hills, she laments, Dillinger would still be dead, but she would be free.

Frechette tries to play on the reader's sympathies. She was a girl enchanted by the city, longing to break free from her poverty. Married to a criminal and struggling to make ends meet, she moved first to Milwaukee and then to Chicago. And it was there, in a cabaret, that she met Dillinger, although she did not know that he was John Dillinger. He stared at her, looking all the way through her, and in that moment she was entranced, love-struck. Perhaps this was a way out of what she thought was a life headed nowhere. Maybe, as she tries to impart again and again, she was just a silly girl who fell in love.

The couple's time together was brief. They were on the run, evading capture. Dillinger was wounded, but they found a doctor to fix him. A friend of theirs, Eddie Green, was killed by the police. The noose was tightening. Police and federal agents were everywhere. But through it all, Dillinger remained calm. They stayed with his father for a time and, from there, went back to Chicago. There is a palpable sadness in Frechette's story. The end fast approaching, the lovers doomed. When recounting Dillinger's family: "I guess the only reason they didn't turn him in was they were afraid." When recalling their plan to get married: "it sounds a little silly now." The end came with her capture, soon to be followed by his death.

Essential Themes
Billie Frechette, a poor girl from a Native American reservation in Wisconsin, knew John Dillinger for seven months. During those months they were lovers on the run, the most wanted outlaw in the United States and his willing accomplice. Although Frechette never fired a gun or robbed a bank, her mere association with Dillinger landed her in a federal penitentiary for two years. Just a month after his death at the hands of authorities, she sold her story to newspapers and magazines in the hopes of capitalizing on their relationship and rehabilitating her image. Despite never denying her love for Dillinger throughout her narrative, she clearly wants the audience to sympathize with her as a victim. She was hypnotized, in over her head, the product of a chain of events that stretched all the way back to the destruction of her people. It is telling that throughout the *Chicago Herald and Examiner* article, she never mourns Dillinger's death, but only her own circumstances. After her release, Frechette toured the country in a show called Crime Didn't Pay!, in which she retold her tale of victimhood and answered audience questions about Dillinger. In the end, Frechette was right, not much of note happened to her before she met Dillinger, and not much else would happen after. She became a footnote in his biography: whether victim, opportunist, or just a woman trying to survive, her life would forever be defined by 'Public Enemy No. 1.'

—KP Dawes, MA

Bibliography and Additional Reading
Burrough, Bryan. *Public Enemies: America's Greatest Crime Wave and the Birth of the FBI, 1933–34*. New York: Penguin, 2004. Print.

Matera, Dary. *John Dillinger: The Life and Death of America's First Celebrity Criminal*. New York: Carroll & Graff, 2004. Print.

Purvis, Alston. *The Vendetta: Special Agent Melvin Purvis, John Dillinger, and Hoover's FBI in the Age of Gangsters*. PublicAffairs, 2005. Print.

Toland, John. *The Dillinger Days*. Boston: Da Capo, 1995. Print.

■ The *Hindenburg* Disaster

Date: May 6, 1937
Author: Herbert Morrison
Genre: radio broadcast; report

Summary Overview
In 1937, the *Hindenburg*, a Zeppelin or cylindrical airship made with a rigid frame, was carrying passengers from Frankfurt, Germany, to Lakehurst Naval Air Station in Lakehurst, New Jersey. Unexpectedly, the Zeppelin caught fire and crashed onto the ground during its final descent, resulting in the deaths of thirty-five individuals, including one member of the ground crew. The document included here is a transcript of Herbert Morrison's eyewitness account of the tragedy, which would play on the radio the next day. As they did not yet have a complete understanding of the technology to broadcast previously recorded events, Morrison and his partner and engineer, Charles Nehlsen, were attempting to record the events and, for the first time, broadcast them later coast-to-coast. The change of Morrison's words and tempo conveys the shock and horror that the flaming ship inspired in every witness, knowing that there was nothing to be done.

Defining Moment
This radio report began as just another day for Herbert Morrison and Charles Nehlsen, but what they could not know was that, aside from the thirty-five lives lost, the crash of the *Hindenburg* would become the first-ever recording of a live event played as such on the radio. It was also essentially the death knell of the production and distribution of Zeppelins and dirigibles, which were now deemed too risky for commercial travel. On the day after the *Hindenburg* crash, May 7, 1937, Morrison was interviewed on national television, with clips from his three-hour recorded report being interspersed with the interview. This was the first time in broadcasting history that events that were recorded live were later aired for the general public. Morrison's recording further shows the difficulty inherent in seeing an event in progress and trying to describe it for others, especially through radio, which obviously has no visual component. Morrison had to describe what he was seeing, but also was personally affected by the tragedy; so his own emotions bled into the report. This was one of the first instances of "breaking news" ever recorded and showed that broadcasting styles would need to change in order to maintain a high standard of sharing information during a crisis, especially one that was happening live.

Possibly the most significant impact of this disaster, however, was the complete collapse of the airship industry. Although Zeppelins and dirigibles had been used with relative safety for over thirty years, considering the explosive nature of the gas which filled the balloon, both for German missions during World War I and later as commercial vehicles for trans-Atlantic flights, consumer confidence in these machines completely disappeared after this crash. This was not the first dirigible to catch fire, nor the most deadly (in 1933, seventy-three men were killed on the USS *Akron*). But it was the most spectacular, enhanced by the media coverage. Further, the cause of the disaster remains a mystery, although sabotage is highly suspected. Whatever the truth may be, dirigibles fell out of use almost entirely by 1940. It is possible that the end of dirigible era was owing in part to the public's hearing in the voice of Herbert Morrison the sheer panic and horror surrounding the event. Radio was and is a powerful tool for expressing emotion through the reporter's voice. It is as much for this reason as for its historical content that the *Hindenburg* broadcast is iconic in modern US history.

Author Biography
Herbert Morrison was born in 1905, grew up in Pennsylvania, and then moved to West Virginia. He married

a woman from Morgantown, West Virginia, named Mary Jane Kelly, and they remained childless. Many of the years of his life were dedicated to radio and, later, television broadcasting. He passed away in Morgantown at the age of 83 in 1989, survived by his wife, who passed in 2000.

Probably the most influential moment of Morrison's professional life occurred when he was thirty-two years old, as the *Hindenburg* disaster unfolded before his eyes. At the time he was working for WLS radio, an NBC affiliate out of Chicago. He continued to give interviews for most of the rest of his life, his memories of the event being sought after by professionals from all media, even decades later.

HISTORICAL DOCUMENT

It's practically standing still now. They've dropped ropes out of the nose of the ship, and they've been taken a hold of down on the field by a number of men. It's starting to rain again; it's—the rain has slacked up a little bit. The back motors of the ship are just holding it just, just enough to keep it from—It burst into flames!

Get this, Charlie! Get this, Charlie! It's fire—and it's crashing! It's crashing terrible! … It's burning and bursting into flames, and the—and it's falling on the mooring-mast and all the folks agree that this is terrible, this is one of the worst catastrophes in the world.

It's—it's—it's the flames, climbing[?], oh, four- or five-hundred feet into the sky and it … it's a terrific crash, ladies and gentlemen. It's smoke, and it's flames now … and the frame is crashing to the ground, not quite to the mooring-mast. Oh, the humanity—and all the passengers screaming around here. I told you, I can't even talk to people whose friends are on there. Ah! It's—it's—it's—it's … o–ohhh! I—I can't talk, ladies and gentlemen. Honest, it's just laying there, a mass of smoking wreckage. Ah! And everybody can hardly breathe and talk, and the screaming. … Honest: I—I can hardly breathe.

I—I'm going to step inside where I cannot see it. Charlie, that's terrible. Ah, ah—I can't. I, listen, folks, I—I'm gonna have to stop for a minute because I've lost my voice. This is the worst thing I've ever witnessed.

GLOSSARY

mooring-mast: the structure designed for the docking of any type of airship (Zeppelin, dirigible, etc.) outside of a hangar; also called a mooring tower

Document Analysis

This document—a transcript from the audio—contains two main themes that stem directly from the event. There is calm beforehand and shock and awe as the airship bursts into flames and goes down. While the portion reproduced here is only a segment of the complete radio broadcast, it is the most dramatic segment for it shows how quickly a routine flight can change into a disaster. The whole of the radio broadcast before the crash amounts to a basic recital of events as the Zeppelin comes in for a landing. The arrival of the *Hindenburg* was exciting because intercontinental travel was still quite new and because the *Hindenburg* was kicking off a new plan, in which ten trips would be made in a single year. Plus, a German vessel bringing passengers to the United States was newsworthy in the post-World War I, pre-World War II era. (Germany under Hitler was already generating controversy abroad.) Radiomen, journalists, and spectators all came out to witness the landing.

Yet it is the last part of the report that lives on, famous for its tragic recitation. Unlike the first part, the second part conveys the horror and helplessness that bystanders must have felt as the *Hindenburg* crashed, turning into a fiery wreck on the ground. Although reading the transcript does not produce the same intensity as hearing the broadcast on the radio, merely seeing the changing sentence structure and diction suggests the depth of the experience. First, Morrison breaks off mid-sentence to exclaim, "it burst into flames!" Then, he starts to direct his engineer, Charlie, to ensure that the crash is recorded. His repetitive use of words, such as "crashing" and "terrible," shows his astonishment at the affair. For a person whose livelihood depended on his way with words, he is here simply speaking what came to mind, reacting directly to events rather than carefully describing them. Then, in the third paragraph, Morrison states that he "can't even talk to people whose friends are on there." The whole event is just too devastating to exploit, and he respects that there is nothing he can do other than watch the tragedy unfold. By the end of the recording, Morrison states that he can't breathe, and he can't talk. A combination of the smoke from the crash and his own emotional turmoil has overwhelmed him and he must remove himself from the scene.

Finally, one line stands out in the transcript: Morrison's exclamation, "Oh, the humanity," is used to this day to express true horror (or, often enough, its sarcastic equivalent). Many television shows, books, and movies have used this expression with intentional and unintentional recall to the event that so impacted the world. Morrison's spontaneous interjection gained a life of its own and took its place among the pop culture canon, surviving long after the moment in which it was first uttered.

Essential Themes
Although fires and crashes were not unheard of in airships, overall these machines were a reasonably safe mode of transportation. They were used by several militaries, including that of the United States. The complete lack of customer confidence in airships after the *Hindenburg* crash, however, was not something that could be overcome. Little publicized fires and crashes aboard dirigibles used for military purposes were one thing; a highly publicized crash claiming civilian lives was another. As a result of the *Hindenburg* disaster, airplanes, a technology that was fast catching up with airships, emerged as the predominant mode of speedy transcontinental transport. While dirigibles, even now,

remain in production (at the Graf Zeppelin plant in Germany), they are used mainly as tourist attractions and are no longer the preferred transport of the elite.

Before the *Hindenburg* disaster, news reports were delayed affairs, the events being described having occurred a day or more earlier and then relayed through newspapers or (edited) radio announcements to the general public. Morrison's account of the *Hindenburg* was possibly the first, and definitely the most famous, firsthand account of a tragedy to be broadcast as such, rather than being reworked and retold by the reporter. It was paired with newsreels of the events, so that Morrison's voice was laid over images shot at the same time at the scene. There was no editing of Morrison's audio report, no script for him to read from. In later decades, this pairing, rather than the original radio broadcast, came to be iconic. And it was increasingly recognized, after the disaster, that reporters should be allowed to share immediately their reactions to important or tragic events. Even though "extra" editions of newspapers eventually permitted consumers of the news to learn of events more quickly, radio and, later, television pioneered in fast delivery of the news, ultimately producing live reports from the field.

—*Anna Accettola, MA*

Bibliography and Additional Reading
Jackson, Robert. *Airships: A Popular History of Dirigibles, Zeppelins, and Other Lighter-Than-Air Craft.* Garden City, N.Y.: Doubleday, 1973. Print.

Lehmann, Ernst A., & Howard Mingos. *The Zeppelins; the Development of the Airship, with the Story of the Zeppelin Air Raids in the World War.* New York: J.H. Sears & Co., 1927. Print.

National Geographic Television & Film. *Hindenburg.* New York: Films Media Group, 2012. Film.

"Herbert Morrison, 83, Hindenburg Reporter." *New York Times.* 10 Jan. 1989. Web. 23 Aug. 2014.

■ From the Federal Writers' Project: *Cape Cod Pilot*

Date: 1937
Author: Jeremiah Digges
Genre: book (excerpt)

Summary Overview

The Federal Writers' Project (FWP) was a New Deal program—part of the Works Progress Administration—that was designed to put unemployed writers to work. Through its American Guide Series, in particular, the project contributed significantly to Americans' understanding of themselves and the cultural and historical diversity they embodied. These guidebooks, covering the forty-eight states along with the major US regions, territories, cities, and other areas and topics, became a lasting legacy of the New Deal. One reason for launching the Guide Series was that the last useful guidebook to the United States was a 1909 Baedeker edition, addressed mainly to English travelers. The FWP's director, Henry Alsberg, stated that the Guide Series would give readers "information about the nation never before gathered together," allowing them to see "what is really happening to the American people" (qtd. in Mangione 48). The example offered here, an excerpt from *Cape Cod Pilot*, illustrates the kind of work that was being done inside the FWP.

Defining Moment

During the Great Depression nearly a third of the nation's workforce was unemployed or underemployed, and millions became homeless and hungry. Long lines formed in places where charities and relief organizations were giving out food, and shantytowns developed in public areas where struggling families and individuals strove to survive. Inside the homes of working families everywhere money was tight and food and other goods were not always plentiful.

Under the aegis of the Works Progress Administration (WPA), in 1935 the Roosevelt administration undertook to put 40,000 unemployed artists and writers to work in the Federal Arts Project. There were four separate divisions, one for visual artists, one for theater professionals, one for musicians, and one for writers. The visual arts featured mostly painters and sculptors. Many of the famed 1930s documentary photographers—Walker Evans, Dorothea Lange, Ben Shahn, Arthur Rothstein—worked separately under the Farm Security Administration (the idea being that photographers functioned primarily as capturers of images, not creators of them). Another group of visual artists, mainly muralists, worked under an allied program called the Public Works of Art Project. This program was responsible for most of the great murals that adorn US post offices and other government buildings across the nation. All of the various arts programs together were known as Federal One. The artists of Federal One produced posters, traveling art exhibitions, public art (and art restoration projects), community art demonstrations and workshops, concerts, recordings, plays, dance productions, photographs, and written works.

The Federal Writers' Project (FWP) involved a number of programs, but it is best known as the home of the American Guide Series, a collection of 400 guidebooks to states, regions, cities, towns, and villages across the United States. The FWP employed nonfiction writers, primarily, but also had on its roles selected fiction writers and poets as well as editors and technical writers. Besides the American Guide Series, FWP produced collections of folklore, autobiographical narratives by ex-slaves, and a number of histories, topical surveys, and reports on activity within the WPA. At its peak, in the spring of 1936, the writers' project employed nearly 6,700 men and women. Some of these writers were soon to become big names in the field: John Steinbeck, Ralph Ellison, Eudora Welty, Saul Bellow, John Cheever, and many more.

The guides encouraged Americans to take trips in automobiles, buses, and trains to see the country in which they lived. So popular did the guides become, in fact, and so well written were they, that they were reprinted often and later became collector's items. Even so, the project came under attack by critics who considered it either a waste of time and money or a left-leaning arm of the New Deal propaganda machine.

Chief among the program's critics was Texas Congressman Martin Dies, head of the House Committee on Un-American Activities (HUAC). Dies felt that the writers project (as well as the theater project) was infused with Communists or Communist-sympathizers, although the charge was mostly fabricated and aimed at bringing attention to Dies and his committee. The operation of HUAC was, in some ways, a test rehearsal for the more notorious persecutions that took place a decade later in the Senate under Joseph McCarthy. The evidence used against those accused of disloyalty was very flimsy and often presented by individuals who had been pressured to testify in order to save their own skins or who had personal or political axes to grind.

Among the FWP's chief supporters, on the other hand, was a group of forty-four US publishers. They maintained that the guides were free of any "Red" propaganda and, moreover, represented "a genuine, valuable and objective contribution to the understanding of American life" (qtd. in Mangione 15). The group also praised the series for operating efficiently and without financial waste. These same publishers, it should be noted, had a stake in the venture because the guides, though written under government auspices, were printed and marketed by independent presses. The arrangement was made in order to keep the government from competing with private industry, a concern that many New Dealers had already learned about through court actions against federal agencies, which were seen to be overstepping their bounds. *Cape Cod Pilot* came out amid these ongoing debates.

Author Biography

Jeremiah Digges, author of *Cape Cod Pilot*, is the penname of Joseph Berger. Berger was born in Denver, Colorado, in 1903 and graduated in journalism from the University of Missouri in 1924. He lived in New York City and worked as a reporter and juvenile book author until 1934, when he relocated with his wife and daughter to Provincetown, Massachusetts, at the tip of Cape Cod. Struggling as a writer, he befriended the local Portuguese fishermen who occasionally supplied him with free fish. Initially, he and two other experienced writers were turned down for the Federal Writers' Project, but the situation was soon corrected and Berger was contracted to write parts of the Massachusetts state guidebook, along with a work on Cape Cod. Although he continued to publish through most of the 1940s, Berger served as a government speechwriter in Washington, DC. From there, he became chief speechwriter of the March of Dimes. Berger died in 1971. With the collapse of the Soviet Union in 1991, once-secret records revealed that Berger had been approached by the KGB to serve as an agent after 1945, but apparently, the offer was rejected.

HISTORICAL DOCUMENT

CHAPTER I
Introduction

In the museum of the Old Dartmouth Historical Society in New Bedford there is a gilded mirror, and under it a card informing the open-mouthed visitor that here is a:

> Mirror in which General Grant AND Abraham Lincoln Both Looked

Invariably, the attendant at the museum says, the tourist looks up quickly into the glass—and is a little disappointed at seeing only himself there.

A guidebook should have better manners, I suppose, than to point back to the tourist as one of the "principal features of interest." But manners or no manners, a Cape Cod guidebook must single him out for this distinction; for within the past two decades, the tourist has stepped into the leading role; "summer business" has overshadowed all others; for most of the towns, it is now the mainstay.

There has been other commerce for the people of this sandy sliver of New England, industrial booms on which enduring fortunes were built. But the whaling, the foreign trade, the ship-building, the salt-making, all have passed; and the same evolution that wrote *finis* to each of these has brought the motor car and the hard-surfaced highway.

The Cape had no choice. It put its house in order for a new day, said farewell to the deep water and hung out a shingle, "Tourists Accommodated." Financially, it proved to be a happy way out of a lean era. As a magnet for tourists, Cape Cod was charged with so many historical currents, on the one side, and so many physical attractions on the other, that success was pretty well assured from the start.

A strange community evolved—"home" to a small, anciently settled population which carefully drew the line between "native Cape Codder" and "off-Cape furriner," took pride in its history and grimly tried to safeguard its traditions; and "resort" to an annual influx of four or five times as many people, some merely vacationing for a week or two, others buying homes and coming back each summer. In the 1936 season, the Cape Cod Chamber of Commerce estimated, 175,000 people visited the peninsula, a record to that time.

For the Yankees, these proud "natives," adjustment to the new order was neither simple nor wholly pleasant. It meant dropping the seclusion which their rugged little villages had cherished through ten generations. Time was when these towns could "warn out" residents of doubtful status; and even when the townsmen themselves began voyaging over the seven seas for their living, they were still most particular in having it understood that their homes were strictly their own.

When the Old Colony Railroad, now the down-Cape spur of the New Haven, was put through as far as Plymouth, and the company wanted to carry the line on to Provincetown, Cape Cod refused to accept the charter agreement. The old stagecoach scudded along fast enough — when the wind was fair — and the Lord only knew how many furriners would be stowing down in "the cars."

Editor Phinney of the *Barnstable Patriot* went through the towns, speechifying valiantly in favor of the railroad. Why, folks in other places, when they saw a chance like this, would sign on the dotted line and then run out to touch off fireworks!

But the folks of this place were "deaf as a haddock." Then, one day, the resourceful editor warned them that if the British should ever again attack the United States, the first place they would strike was Provincetown, and without a railroad, Provincetown and her neighbor villages would be cut off without escape. Editor Phinney knew his people. "The cars" came down-Cape.

While this controversy was raging, the Cape had no inkling, of course, of the use which furriners of a still later day were to make of this same old stage-coach route — which has been followed in the Cape Cod extension of U.S. Highway No. 6. A police check on a Sunday in the summer of 1936 showed that 55,000 motor cars passed over one of the canal bridges in twenty-four hours.

First an Indian trail, and then a wagon track, the route of U. S. Highway No. 6 had been known from Old Colony days as the "King's Road." By an act of the General Court in 1920, it was officially designated "The King's Highway," and markers were placed all down the line.

But the natives of Cape Cod didn't like that name. They never had liked it—at least not since the signing of the Declaration of Independence. The town of Orleans, especially, was in a stew over it, and after eight years of agitation, Orleans adopted a resolution in town meeting, "viewing with an interest that approaches grave concern this attempt, neither historically nor geographically correct, to rewrite American history."

Headlines began to appear in the Boston newspapers: "King's Highway Galls Cape Cod." Other towns began passing resolutions. They not only viewed it "with an interest that approaches grave concern;" they "considered it a deplorable situation," they even "contemplated it with growing alarm." And then, mysteriously, the "King's Highway" signposts began to disappear, one by one, first from the Orleans roadside, then through other towns. More years passed, more signposts vanished, and the name of the down-Cape road remained a highly debatable matter, until in February, 1937, the Governor of the Commonwealth signed a new law, which designated it "Grand Army of the Republic Highway."

It was a master stroke. Nobody bothered to pronounce the road's new name. Everybody was satisfied....

As the visitor from broad, inland America drives down the length of this sandy curlicue, and observes that it is taking him well out to sea, and that in spots it seems to be hanging as if by a thread, he may wonder at the durability of this land, its permanence as the living-place of people, the site of solid villages linked by old roads. On the map it looks as if it might carry away with the first good breeze, or go under before any big sea that should catch it broadside. There are points along the way whence both shores can be seen, and there is more than one spot where Father Neptune, congratulating himself on a particularly lively spree, has joined his hands, making a temporary channel.

But the inquiring visitor finds Cape people curiously indifferent to any prospect that the ocean might some day swallow their little peninsula in one gulp. "Narrow in the beam" though it is, the body of the Cape has proved seaworthy, its underpinnings have withstood all attacks within a period estimated by geologists at thirty thousand years. Battering surf and besieging tides are forever remodeling its coastlines; islands are on record which no longer exist; sand is washed from one corner to be deposited in another; windblown dunes bury whole forests. But all this mobility, plus earthquakes of which there were two in 1935, has failed to make Cape Cod "drag anchor"...

CHAPTER IV
Yarmouth

In recreating these old seafaring towns for an inland public of today, no honest reporter bears down too heavily on the "romance" of going to sea; which is to say—at the risk of getting an axe in my neck—that the majority of the literature on seafaring of old just hasn't been honest. Men went to sea for two rewards—first, bread and butter; and second, enough laid aside for future bread and butter to enable them to quit going to sea.

Certainly the calling was hazardous and exciting, and Cape Cod boys went down to the sea with their eyes shining. There were even a few hardy souls who actually felt enough "lure" and "fascination" to keep at it after their fortunes were made, and there was no further necessity; but to picture the old Cape Cod sea captain as a man drawn offshore by an adolescent craving for excitement or by a song-writer's nostalgia is simply bilge. As one Yarmouth skipper put it, "any man who would go to sea for pleasure would go to hell for pastime."

In his book *Shipmasters of Cape Cod*, Henry C. Kittredge gives a realistic and fairly unbiased account of the doings of these men of Yarmouth and the other towns. He tells of the coasting schooners (called by the foreign traders the "appletree fleet" because they were never out of sight of the orchards alongshore) which carried everything from sheep's wool from Nantucket to mahogany logs from Santo Domingo; of Ebenezer Sears, first American skipper to take a merchant vessel around the Cape of Good Hope; of Stephen Sears, too, who was seized by the Spanish in the Mediterranean while trying to sell a cargo of salt fish; of Elisha Howes, who, on making Boston with a load of figs from Smyrna, "improved his shore leave" by getting engaged to Hannah Crowell of Yarmouth; of the three celebrated Eldredge brothers, Captains John, Oliver and Asa, who skippered Liverpool packets and made great names and good fortunes; and of the races between such clipper drivers as Captain Frederick Howes of Yarmouth, in the *Climax*, and Captain Moses Howes, of Dennis, in the *Competitor*, who took exactly 115 days each, Boston to San Francisco, around the Horn, while the whole shipping world waited, with money placed on the one or the other. Before the race was over, it was said that the disappointed Boston waterfront was exclaiming, "A plague on both of your Howeses!"

There is no question but that these men loved a good ship, a fast ship. Among the thousand Cape Cod yarns that are variations on this theme is the one about Captain Eleazer, skipper of one of the trimmest schooners in the "Indies trade." His vessel, the *Bulldog*, was "built to split a drop of water into a halfmoon while she heeled," and he had let the town know he was proud of her. He married a girl named Abigail Bangs, and townsfolk began asking him if he planned to change the name of the vessel to the *Abigail* as a token of affection for his bride. His reply was, "No, I don't see fitten for to change the vessel's name. But if *Abigail* keeps on steady being a good girl like she is, I've been thinking I might have her rechristened *Bulldog*."

So go the yarns. There was actually precious little

of the hearts-and-flowers kind of sentiment in the love of these men for their ships. It was an affection based upon speed and seaworthiness, and upon nothing else. If a ship had these qualities, she was beautiful, she was loved. And they meant, in the order of their importance: first, money, for upon speed were based rates and other rewards, as well as the volume of business a ship-owner could attract to his vessels; second, safety of cargo, both from deterioration through a slow voyage and loss through a "broken" one; and third—and last—safety of life and limb.

Cape Cod owes its name to the good judgment of the English navigator, Captain Bartholomew Gosnold. Crossing the ocean in the *Concord*, he sighted land on May 15, 1602. At first he called it "Shoal Hope," but apparently realized that he could do better than that. "Near this cape," says his log, "we came to anchor in fifteen fathoms where we took great store of codfish, for which we altered the name to Cape Cod."

In a racier version of the incident, as given in an old poem by Benjamin Drew, the explorer is pictured as sitting on the deck of the *Concord*, contemplating the Cape and scratching his head for a name—finally deciding to call for a line and hook and name it for the first fish he caught.

> Old Neptune heard the promise made,
>
> Down dove the water-god —
>
> He drove the meaner fish away
>
> Arid hooked the mammoth cod.
>
> Quick Gosnold hauled. "Cape … Cape …
>
> Cape Cod!"
>
> "Cape Cod!" the crew cried louder;
>
> "Here, steward! take the fish along
>
> "And give the boys a chowder!"

An introduction to Cape Cod cannot properly close without a word about the weather. No greeting, no conversation is valid here until some reference has been made to it. Governor Bradford himself sets the fashion in his *History of Plimouth Plantation*. On August 15, 1635, revisiting the Cape when there arises:

> such a mighty storme of wind & raine as none living in these parts, either English or Indeans, ever saw…. It caused ye sea to swell up above 20 foote, right up & downe, and made many of the Indeans to clime into trees for their saftie.

And three hundred years later, to the day, Al Higgins, of Cape Cod, grants an interview to a reporter for the *New Bedford Standard-Times*:

> I got up early to see how the hens were making it. I no sooner got the henhouse door open when my best rooster hopped out into a gust of wind that stripped him to the pin-feathers and tossed him against the chopping-block with such a thump that the axe fell and cut off his head, slick as a whistle. There he was—killed, picked, and ready to clean. I don't believe there ever was such a gale.

They tell weather yarns and they use weather talk under oath in the courts. A Provincetown woman, testifying in a divorce suit against her husband, told the judge: "I came home one night, your honor, and Henry was snoring so hard you'd think the fog was coming in." And His Honor, having heard the Provincetown foghorns all his life, knew exactly what sort of noises Henry had made.

Their knowledge of the weather comes of lifelong study. There is the story, for instance, of old Cap'n Phineas Eldridge, retired skipper, who took to growing turnips on a farm in Eastham, but who had grown weatherwise through many years in command of a coasting schooner. One evening the Cap'n was late for supper, and his wife, glancing out the window, saw a light flitting about the turnip field. Then the Cap'n dashed in, spun the telephone crank and shouted, "Give me Chatham, quick! Hello, Chatham? I want Sam Paine, the postmaster. Hey, Sam! My hat's just blowed off and got clear of me, but she's scudding due south in this breeze, and allowing for the reef in the brim, I calculate she'll just about make in to your place in fourteen minutes more. Mail her back to me, will you, Sam?"

The hat, of course, fetched up on the specified doorstep in Chatham, in exactly fourteen minutes after the Cap'n hung up the receiver, and was sent back to him next morning by parcel post…

CHAPTER VII
Orleans

On U.S. 6, between Brewster and Eastham. One and one-half miles between Orleans town lines.

> Attention Visitors. I have the largest assortment of bric-a-brac, old books and other ancient articles to be found in the place. Also dories and small boats of the best makes at prices to suit.

Drawn in by the wording of the advertisement, I found the dories and small boats in the yard out back. They were priced "to suit" their condition, which, I found, did not suit me. So I went back in and bought books. One was a scrapbook. Then there were some charts and a couple of pilot books, and a great family bible. Inside the cover of the bible I read the name, J. Swift, and the date, 1844.

"Ah! Swift. A good old Cape name. Ought to be a birth and death log in the back, with perhaps some of those reverent or philosophical little asides that are somehow thought to befit such occasions." So I turned to the back. In fancy scrawl, across the columns reserved for the solemn record, was this:

> I like fried mackerel better than boiled.
> J. Swift.

I asked my Orleans dealer in bric-a-brac and small boats if he could tell me anything of interest about the old bible or its owner. (You are traditionally entitled to at least one good story from the best second-hand dealers. For myself, I set it down as axiomatic that if I don't get a story along with it, whatever I've bought, I probably am not getting my money's worth.) But this time my friend shook his head.

"You've got me there," he said. "I'm sorry I don't know the feller. If I did, I'd give you a whackin' good yarn about him!"…

CHAPTER XIII
Chatham

Return on U.S. 6 to Orleans. Left from U. S. 6 on State 28. Five miles to Chatham village.

"I don't care who put her there, she ain't set right! If that's magnetic north, I'll eat a sun-squall!"

Captain Noadiah Bearse called to him the eight other retired sea captains of Chatham who had been invited as dinner guests at the "launching" of the town's swankiest hotel. The nine old ship-masters had approved of everything, until Captain Noadiah discovered the compass set out front as a decoration. Gathering around it now, the others agreed she was out of line; the whole hotel was off her course; no good could come of it.

Captain Ezra Nickerson peered at it, snorted, turned away. "Mph! Wouldn't lay me a run for Vineyard Sound with that thing—for fear of hitting the Old Gray Lady!" The "Old Gray Lady," in case you haven't met her, is the island of Nantucket. "Why, anybody'd know magnetic north lays along here—a line with the peak of that shingled house!"

"What?" Captain Noadiah demanded. "Along there! Ezra, it's been a long time, all right, since you've navigated anything bigger than a cane-seat rocker, I can see that! Magnetic north lays directly by the stern sheets of the pungo alongside the house."

Seven other deepwater men raised an outraged chorus. They not only disagreed with Noadiah; Ezra was wrong too. And then as each pointed out magnetic north—somewhere between the pungo and the house—the others declared he'd lost his wits.

"Well, I've still got my compass," Captain Noadiah said. "She's pointed me to China six times. I'll just fetch her over tomorrow morning and prove I'm right." He looked about him contemptuously and added, "Just for myself. I may be old, but I hope to show I haven't gone clean adrift into second childhood yet!"

Next morning nine sea captains, bearing nine ancient compasses, appeared in front of the hotel. Each took his bearings, each gave a nod of satisfaction and tenderly closed the worn cover on the instrument, then turned and trudged home without a word to the others.

Nine old souls with nine battered, beloved relics of their seafaring days, had set the world to rights. And who are we, who have never trodden the quarterdeck of a square-rigger, to deny that from the Chatham Bars Inn magnetic north may lie on nine points of the compass?

GLOSSARY

beam: breadth

fetch up: to arrive at

furriner: "foreigner"

haddock: a type of flatfish

heel: to lean or list

pungo: a small sailboat

reef: the part of a sail gathered in under high winds (here applied to a hat brim)

square-rigger: a sailing vessel that uses a four-sided sail

stern sheets: sails at the back of a vessel

warn out: wear out

Document Analysis

It should be noted, first, that each state guide in the series followed a standard format and included information on the state's history, government, natural resources, industry and commerce, and principal cities and towns. Also included were selected tours through the state, accompanied by photographs. Facts and figures covering such topics as architecture, agriculture, education, arts and entertainment, recreation, and transportation were also presented. In most cases, the various components of a guidebook were prepared by different writers, the whole representing a team effort. There were exceptions, however, for non-state guides—as in this instance.

Cape Cod Pilot, that is, diverges from the form used in other books in the American Guide Series in that it attempts to present its subject in terms of personal experience. The writer and editors felt that the folklore and yarns that constitute the bulk of the book would be enhanced by use of the personal pronoun. As a member of the Federal Writers' Project, Berger/Digges is credited with the major writing, rewriting, and editing of the book. The book is also said to be the result of a team effort insofar as it came out as part of the series and benefited from nominal guidance and oversight provided by the central office in Washington, DC.

The author notes in the book's Preface (not shown here) that his intent is to obtain first-hand information and reminiscences of early days on the Cape from the men and women who lived there—particularly, "the skippers and crews of many vessels, trap-fishermen, surfmen, draggers and seiners." We see some examples of these "tales" and "yarns" here. We see, too, the author attempting to bring out the individuality of the persons he is interacting with while also striving for brevity. Thus, there is a kind of tension between the portraits of individuals and the illustrations of local "types."

There is an effort, too, to bring out what is unique about the place itself, without resorting to hyperbole or cliché. Project editors in Washington often complained about what they considered exaggeration or boosterism by writers as they tried to make each town or city different from the next one. Expressions such as "a quaint place," "the hardy settlers," "the famous so-and-so," "the brave warrior," and so on were common in the manuscripts supplied by the writers. In *Cape Cod Pilot*, the author avoids the most obvious clichés, partly by drawing on local expressions—many of them nautical in nature. In this way, he satisfies the requirements of the writing assignment and brings "local color" to the account.

Essential Themes

Cape Cod Pilot was well received by reviewers, *Time* magazine calling it "the boldest and best of the American Guide Series." It was also popular among readers, who bought out the first two printings (5,000 copies) almost immediately. This book and a few others that featured a single author or focused on interesting or unusual subjects brought greater attention to the FWP and may have helped assuage critics regarding the worth of the project. Many could now see that the FWP was providing a useful service to the country, allowing Americans to "discover" the nation and gain a better understanding of it and their place within it. The book also served Berger well personally, earning him a prestigious Guggenheim Fellowship and allowing him to write and publish on a healthy stipend for one year. (On the other hand, the Massachusetts state guide he contributed to ignited passions after an unfriendly reviewer noticed that more lines were given over to the recent Sacco-Vanzetti case than to the Boston Tea Party.)

One theme that comes through strongly in *Cape Cod Pilot* is that of "local color," depicted largely through the use of dialect speech and nautical expressions (colloquialisms). Although each guidebook sought to tell the story of a particular state or locality, there was also a tendency to gloss over social differences and political conflict in order to make a place appear safe and attractive for travelers. The editors in Washington, especially, worked to present a vision of the nation as one of progress and harmony. It seems that Berger's work generally reflected this outlook.

Despite the success of the WPA writers' project overall, Congress, in the face of ongoing political opposition and fiscal troubles, reduced the scope of the program in 1939 and urged individual states to continue it if they wished. By the time the program was closed completely in early 1943, it had employed nearly 10,000 writers and cost the government under $27 million—only a tiny fraction (less than one-quarter of 1 percent) of total WPA expenditures.

—*Michael Shally-Jensen, PhD*

Bibliography and Additional Reading

Bold, Christine. *The WPA Guides: Mapping America*. Jackson, MS: U of Mississippi P, 1999. Print.

Flynne, Kathryn A., with Richard Polese. *The New Deal: A 75th Anniversary Celebration*. Salt Lake City: Gibbs Smith, Pub., 2008. Print.

Mangione, Jerre. *The Dream and the Deal: The Federal Writers' Project, 1935–1943*. Boston: Little, Brown, 1972. Print.

Taylor, David A. *Soul of a People: The WPA Writers' Project Uncovers Depression America*. Hoboken, NJ: Wiley, 2009. Print.

On *The War of the Worlds* Radio Broadcast

Date: October 31, 1938
Author: George Dixon
Genre: article

Summary Overview

On the night of October 30, 1938, the twenty-three-year-old Orson Welles, a brilliant up-and-coming radio and theater producer, staged a live radio adaptation of H.G. Wells' *War of the Worlds*. Rewritten by Welles and his team to play as real-time news coverage of a Martian invasion of the United States, the radio play was taken to be true by thousands of Americans. Panic spread throughout the nation as concerned citizens crowded churches, jammed switchboards while seeking help from authorities, or packed up their belongings and raced for safety. Although historians debate the real extent of the panic and the motive of print journalists reporting on it, the incident quickly became one of the biggest news stories of the year and propelled the relatively unknown Orson Welles into the international spotlight.

Defining Moment

The 1930s were a traumatic period for the United States. Beginning with the stock market crash of 1929 and followed immediately by the Great Depression, things seemed only to get worse as the decade went on. The country was shocked when the son of famed aviator Charles Lindbergh was kidnapped and murdered and shocked again when the great airship *Hindenburg* exploded in a fireball over New Jersey. As unemployment rose and financial markets bottomed out, the Midwest was ravaged by the Dust Bowl along with a crime spree the likes of which had never been seen. While bad news seemed to prevail on the domestic front, the war machines of Germany and Japan pushed the world ever closer to armed conflict. Americans learned all of this by listening to their radios.

Although radio had been invented decades earlier, it wasn't until the 1930s that it emerged as a relevant medium for news and entertainment. President Franklin Roosevelt used the radio in his famous "fireside chats" to reassure a nervous American public, and serial shows, such as *The Shadow*, entertained millions. As networks began to adapt the technology to challenge the dominance of print, new innovations were developed to provide listeners with something that newspapers couldn't: immediate, live reporting of events. One of these innovations was the "flash," in which reporters would interrupt regular programming with breaking news. In September 1938, the use of the flash proved especially effective in coverage of what became known as the Munich Crisis, during which Adolf Hitler threatened war over territorial demands in Czechoslovakia.

Amid all this came Orson Welles. In 1938, Welles was a well-regarded, albeit relatively unknown, theater and radio producer out of New York, most famous for staging a production of *Macbeth* with an all black cast. Provocative, brilliant, and arrogant, Welles was signed by CBS to take over production of a weekly radio program, "The Mercury Theatre of the Air," set to adapt famous literary works as hour-long radio dramas. Running opposite the hugely popular "Chase and Sanborn Hour," the Mercury Theatre program suffered from low ratings and lacked an official commercial sponsor. Welles knew he had to do something big.

It is unclear whose idea it was to adapt H. G. Wells' classic *War of the Worlds* to radio, but there is little doubt that it was Orson Welles who masterminded the script. The dramatization was created to imitate news coverage, in real time, of a Martian invasion. Actors took on the role of reporters set to interrupt a music program with news flashes, providing field reports and on-air interviews with fictitious experts and government officials, some made to imitate real personalities, including the President of the United States. Welles also masterfully scheduled for the action to start five minutes after the hour, fully aware that an unpopular musical act on the "Chase and Sanborn Hour" might make listeners surf the dial to CBS.

Historians debate the number of listeners tuned in that night or how many of them actually believed the Martian invasion to be true, but it is certain that some portion of the public did believe what they heard—and panicked as a result. The following day, newspapers across the country ran banner headlines about what they called "The Panic Broadcast," reporting sensational stories of suicides, stress-related heart attacks, and an American public driven to the brink of madness. How much of this coverage was true and how much of it was the result of a concerted campaign against the print media's major new competitor, radio, is uncertain. In any case, the attention resulted in calls for investigations by Congress and the Federal Communications Commission (FCC) and lawsuits against Orson Welles and CBS. In the end, however, no punitive action was taken against any of those involved. After the brouhaha, Orson Welles went on to become an international celebrity, signing a three-movie deal with RKO and creating one of the greatest films in cinematic history, *Citizen Kane*.

Author Biography

The author of the account the "panic broadcast" reprinted here, George Dixon, was born in Toronto, Canada on July 22, 1900, where he worked as a reporter for various newspapers including the *Toronto Star* and the *Toronto Globe*. After immigrating to the United States, he went to work for the *Philadelphia Inquirer* and eventually the *New York Daily News*. On the day that Pearl Harbor was attacked by the Japanese, he was made a Washington correspondent; and in 1944, he began writing a syndicated column called the "Washington Scene." Throughout his career he reported on some of the biggest news stories of his day, eventually passing away of a heart attack in 1965.

HISTORICAL DOCUMENT

[New York Daily News, Oct. 31, 1938]

FAKE RADIO 'WAR' STIRS TERROR THROUGH U.S.

By GEORGE DIXON

A radio dramatization of H.G. Wells' "War of the Worlds"—which thousands of people misunderstood as a news broadcast of a current catastrophe in New Jersey—created almost unbelievable scenes of terror in New York, New Jersey, the South and as far west as San Francisco between 8 and 9 o'clock last night.

The panic started when an announcer suddenly interrupted the program of a dance orchestra—which was part of the dramatization—to "flash" an imaginary bulletin that a mysterious "meteor" had struck New Jersey, lighting the heavens for miles around.

A few seconds later, the announcer "flashed" the tidings that weird monsters were swarming out of the mass of metal—which was not a meteor but a tube-like car from Mars—and were destroying hundreds of people with death—ray guns.

Thousands flee

Without waiting for further details, thousands of listeners rushed from their homes in New York and New Jersey, many with towels across their faces to protect themselves from "gas" which the invader was supposed to be spewing forth.

Simultaneously, thousands more in states that stretched west to California and south to the Gulf of Mexico rushed to their telephones to inquire of newspapers, the police, switchboard operators, and electric companies what they should do to protect themselves.

The "space cartridge" was supposed to have struck at Grover's Mills, an actual town near Princeton. Names of well-known highways were used in describing the advance of the monsters. The voice had warned them to "pack up and move north because the machines are coming from Mars." The dramatization of Wells' novel had featured a fictitious speech from "The Governor of New Jersey," assuring the public that the National Guard has been mobilized to fight the "Martian monsters" and the Harlem residents had confused the mythical "Governor" with the President.

Churches in both New York and New Jersey were filled suddenly with persons seeking protection, and who found them, providentially as they thought, open.

At St. Michael's Hospital, in Newark, fifteen persons were treated for shock. In New York, police and fire departments and the newspapers were swamped with telephone calls from people, apparently frightened half out of their wits.

The telephone company also was deluged. The thing finally assumed such serious proportions that the Colombia Broadcasting System put bulletins on the air explaining that the "meteor" broadcast was part of a play and that nothing untoward had happened.

The broadcasting company added that the whole thing had been somewhat in the nature of a Halloween prank. The program, which came over station WABC from 8 to 9 P.M. was presented by Orson Welles' "Mercury Theatre of the Air."

"The War of the World's was a typical H.G. Wells shocker. It described the bombardments of England by huge "space capsules" carrying warriors from Mars. These inhuman gigantic warriors laid waste to England and killed hundreds of thousands of people. Finally, they were killed by germs and infections—because they came from a planet which had no disease, and thus were susceptible to every disease. In Wells' book there was no mention of the United States. In its dramatization last night the radio station changed the locale to America.

Within a couple of minutes of the first death and destruction bulletin the telephone calls began pouring in. Many of the callers seemed on the point of hysteria. One woman said she has relatives in the "stricken" section of New Jersey and wanted to know if their names were on the casualty lists.

Doctors offer help

The New York City Department of Health was among the first to call The News. The department wanted to know what assistance it could lend to the maimed and dying.

Hundreds of physicians and nurses were among the callers. Many of them said they were prepared to rush at once into the devastated area to aid in caring for victims.

Scores of motorists traveling through Jersey heard the broadcast and immediately detoured so as not to pass through the supposedly doomed region. Police in many small Jersey towns and villages called State Police Headquarters to offer assistance.

At Princeton University two members of the geology faculty, equipped with flashlights and hammers, started for Grover's Mills, two miles away, where the meteor supposedly fell. Dozens of cars were driven to the hamlet by curious motorists. A score of university students were phoned by their parent, and told to come home.

An anonymous and somewhat hysterical girl phoned the Princeton Press Club from Grover's Mills and said:

"You can't imagine the horror of it! It's hell!"

A man came into the club and said he saw the meteor strike the earth and witnessed animals jumping from the alien body.

In Watchung, N.J., an excited policeman on desk duty—notified by horrified citizens that a meteor struck somewhere nearby, sent squad cars out to look for injured.

Pleas of "What can we do?" Where can we go to save ourselves?" flooded New Jersey police switchboards from Hoboken to Cape May. In Newark alone two patrolmen handled more than 2,000 calls from hysterical persons terrified by the fake news bulletin.

Harassed Newark police, trying to reassure thousands of panicky citizens, received a call about a gas explosion in a six—family house at 145 Hedden Terrace. Emergency trucks raced to the scene to find that more than thirty people, occupants of the house, were on the street, holding their clothes and bedding.

Motorists warned

In Irvington, N. J. hundreds of motorists who hear the announcement of the meteor and the gas attack shouted warnings to each other in the streets.

"Drive like hell into the country; we're being bombed by enemies", drivers shouted to one another. Motorcycle police, astounded by the sudden bursts of speed by motorists, rushed to call boxes to inquire from headquarters about the supposed raids.

In the Sacred Heart Church in Elizabeth, priests were amazed by a sudden influx of panicky persons who rushed inside, fell on their knees and began to pray.

Meanwhile, City Manager Pail Morton of Trenton announced that he would ask an investigation of the program by the Federal Communication Commission.

State police at Morristown said that dozens of calls from irate radio listeners demanded that authorities obtain indictments against broadcast company officials.

The announcement that 7,000 National Guard members were being mobilized to defend New Jersey from the invaders, caused hundreds of guardsmen to swamp the 113th Regiment armory and the 102nd cavalry armory with calls and queries on where to report for duty.

A motorist parked near the Lodi Theatre in Orange, N. J. tuned in to the program, listened for a moment, and then ran breathlessly into the movie house.

"The state is being invaded," he screamed. "This place is going to be blown up!"

A minute later the theater was empty.

When Manuel Priola heard the broadcast in his bar at 433 Valley Road, Orange, he closed the cash register and announced to his customers:

"You folks can go where you like. I'm closing up this place and going home." And he did.

Evening services at the First Baptist Church in Caldwell, N. J., were well under way when a frantic parishioner dashed in and yelled that a meteor had fallen near by and the whole countryside was threatened. The Rev. Thomas Thomas calmed his flock and called them to pray for deliverance.

He's getting out

A terrified motorist asked Patrolman Lawrence Treger the way to Route 24.

"All creation's busted loose" he yelled, "and I'm getting out of Jersey."

Panic swept one apartment house in Greenwich Village, largely occupied by Italian families, after tenants caught scraps of the broadcast.

The super-realism of the drama sent Caroline Cantlon, an actress with a WPA Gilbert and Sullivan unit, to Polyclinic Hospital last night. Sitting in her room at the Markwell Hotel on 49th St. between Broadway and Eighth Ave., Miss Cantlon turned on her radio. She heard and announcement of smoke in Times Square.

She rushed out into the hallway and down the stairs. She stumbled and fell, fracturing her arm at the wrist

How it all began

The broadcast began with the usual announcement: "The Columbia Broadcasting System presents Orson Welles and his Mercury Theatre Players in a dramatization of H. G. Wells' novel, "The War of the Worlds."

Listeners heard a dance band playing languid Spanish numbers in the "Park Astoria Hotel." The music was interrupted suddenly by a flash. It was announced that a professor in a university observatory in the Southwest had noticed a series of gas explosions on the planet Mars.

The scene switched to Princeton where an astronomer was trying to explain the phenomenon in an interview.

There was another flash. A meteor had just struck Grover's Mills, near Princeton.

The professor and an announcer rushed out to inspect the meteor. On their arrival, they reported to the radio listeners that it wasn't a meteor at all—it was a giant tube of a metal that had no earthly origin.

Then the announcer cut in excitedly:

"Just a minute. Something's happening! Ladies and gentlemen, this is terrific! The end of this things' beginning to come off. The top is beginning to rotate like a screw! The thing must be hollow!"

Then voices could be heard as other fictitious spectators grew alarmed.

"Look! The darn thing's un-screwing!"
"Keep back there. Keep back, I tell you!"
"Maybe their's men in it, trying to escape?"
"It's red hot; they'll burn to a cinder!"
"Keep back there. Keep those idiots back!"

There was the clanking sound of falling metal and then more voices:

"She's off. The top's loose, Look out there! Stand back!"

Suddenly the monsters began crawling out—huge things impervious to bullets or any other missiles. It soon became apparent that they carried some sort of fire—arms which turned out to be death rat machines. These were trained on the crowd and 200 spectators died instantly.

Martial law was declared by the Governor of New Jersey and there were bulletins from State Militia headquarters in the vicinity of the spot where the Martians were in control.

Through the drone of airplane motors could be heard the radio reports of Army pilots to their headquarters:

"…One machine partially crippled. Believed hit by shell from Army gun in Watchung Mountains. Guns now appear silent. A heavy black fog hanging over the earth… of extreme density, nature unknown…"

"…Enemy now turns east, crossing Passaic River into Jersey marshes. One of the gigantic creatures is straddling the Pulaski Skyway. Evident objective is New York City. They're pushing down a high tension power station…."

"The machines are close together now and we're ready to attack. A thousands yards and we'll be over the first one!...Eight hundred…seven hundred…there they go! A giant arm is raised…there's a green flash…they're spraying us with flame! Two thousand feet. Engines are giving out. No chance to release bomb. Only one thing left to do…drop on them, plane and all. We're diving on the first one…mow the engine's gone…eight hundred feet"

Then "Operator N. 3" cut in form Newark with a warning:

"Poisonous black smoke pouring in from Jersey marshes. Gas masks useless. Urge population to move into open spaces. Automobiles use routes 7, 23, 24. Avoid congested areas…"

Then from "the roof of the broadcasting building in Madison Ave." came another bulletin:

"The bells you hear ringing are to warn the people to evacuate the city as the Martians approach.

It is estimated that in the last two hours 3,000,000 people have moved out along the roads to the north. The Hutchinson River Parkway is still kept open for motor traffic. Avoid bridges to Long Island—hopelessly jammed. All communication with Jersey shores closed ten minutes ago. Our army wiped out. This may be the last broadcast…we will stay here to the end…"

From the street below came the sound of voices rising in a hymn. The announcer continued:

"I've just been handed a bulletin. Cylinders from Mars are falling all over the country. One outside Buffalo—another in Chicago—St. Louis…"

The announcer kept on. One of the monsters was approaching, "his head even with the skyscrapers." People were dropping like flies as the poison gas spread. Now the monster was crossing Sixth Ave. Now Fifth Ave. Not it was only fifty feet away…"

Just as the whole world was toppling into oblivion, the real station announcer cut in with word that the gasping audience had been listening to a dramatization of H. G. Wells' book.

War's Over: How U.S. Met Mars

The radio's "end of the world" as some listeners understood it, produces repercussions through—out the United States. Samples, as reported by the Associated Press, follow:

- Woman Tries Suicide: Pittsburgh — A man returned home in the midst of the broadcast and found his wife a bottle of poison in her hand screaming: "I'd rather die this way than like that."
- Man Wants to Fight Mars: San Francisco—An offer to volunteer in stopping an invasion from Mars came among hundreds of telephone inquiries to police and newspapers during the radio dramatization of H. G. Wells' story. One excited man called Oakland police and shouted: "My God! Where can I volunteer my services? We've got to stop this awful thing!"
- Church Lets Out: Indianapolis—A woman ran into a church screaming: "New York destroyed; it's just the end of the world. You might as well go home to die. I just heard it on the radio." Services were dismissed immediately.
- College Boys Faint: Brevard, N.C.—Five Brevard College students fainted and panic gripped the campus for a half hour with many students fighting for telephones to inform their parents to come and get them.
- It's a Massacre: Providence, R. I.—Weeping and hysterical women swamped the switchboard of the *Providence Journal* for details of the "massacre." The electric company received scores of calls urging it to turn off all lights so that the city would be safe from the "enemy."
- She Sees "the Fire": Boston—One woman declared

she could "see the fire and told the *Boston Globe* she and many others in her neighborhood were "getting out of here"

- "Where is it Safe?": Kansas City—One telephone informant said he had loaded all his children into his car, had filled it with gasoline, and was goings somewhere. "Where is it safe?" he wanted to know. The Associated Press bureau received queries on the "meteors" from Los Angeles, Salt Lake City, Beaumont, Texas, and St. Joseph, Mo.
- Prayers in Richmond: Richmond, Va—The Times—Dispatch reported some of its telephone calls came from persons who said they were praying.

Senator Maps Bill to Censor Air Waves

Des Moines. Oct. 30 (AP) — Senator Clyde L. Herring (Dem', Iowa) said tonight he planned to introduce a bill in the next session of Congress "controlling just such abuses as was heard over the radio tonight." He said the bill would propose a censor—ship board to which all radio programs must be submitted.

Frank R. McNinch. Chairman of the Federal Communications Commission in Washington said that an investigation would be held at once by the FCC. He would not predict what action might be taken, but said a through probe would be made.

Wells…Welles

H. G. Wells, whose imagination has run riot for forty years, found it rather difficult to realize that anyone could have become alarmed over a broadcast of his "War of the World."

Reached by The News by trans—Atlantic telephone in London early this morning, the 72—year—old British author listened with interest to an account of what happened when his fantasy went on the air.

"How odd," he said. "I don't think I would care to comment until I hear more about it."

He wrote the "War of the Worlds" in 1898. It is often credited with inspiring most of the current craze for highly imaginative fiction.

The reaction of the public seemed almost as fantastic as the play itself to Orson Welles, the 23-year-old stage producer, who adapted the script from the Wells book and portrayed the principal character actor.

"We've been putting on all sorts of things from the most realistic situations to the wildest fantasy," Welles said, "but nobody ever bothered to get serious about them before. We just can't understand why this should have such an amazing reaction."

"It's too bad that so many people got excited, but after all, we kept reminding them, that is wasn't really true."

WABC explains

At 10 P.M., WABC sent out the following explanation of its "War of the Worlds" broadcast:

"For those listeners who tuned in to Orson Welles' Mercury Theatre on the Air broadcast from 8 to 9 PM tonight, and did not realize that the program was merely a radio adaptation of H.G. Wells' famous novel, 'War of the Worlds,' we are repeating the fact, which was made clear four times on the program, that the entire content of the play was entirely fictitious."

Britain Had a Radio Panic Back in '26

It's happened before.

In 1926 Father Ronald Knox broadcast from Edinburgh through British Broadcasting Company a burlesque called "Broadcasting the Barricades," in which he simulated the part if an announcer of news bulletins and gave out hair—raising and preposterous news.

Although the nature of the program was stated beforehand, newspapers and the broadcasting office were flooded with telephone calls asking: It is true the House of Commons is blown up? What has happened to Big Ben?"

Some listeners fainted, and it required announcements by the broadcasting company and reassurances in the press finally to quiet the nation's fears.

Document Analysis
George Dixon's report on the events of October 30, 1938 is fairly straightforward. He describes in detail the *War of the Worlds* broadcast and reports on the more shocking reactions to it. He does not hold CBS, "The Mercury Theatre of the Air," or Orson Welles responsible for the events, but he does repeatedly suggest, through his writing, radio's power to cause undue panic. Is this the fault of the listener or the medium? He does not say, but clearly this is a troubling development as far as the reporter is concerned.

According to Dixon's report, thousands of Americans fled their homes in search of safety. Motorists clogged streets. Hospitals were flooded by those suffering stress-induced ailments or with injuries resulting from panic over Martians invading New Jersey. Telephone lines were jammed at police and fire stations, at radio networks, and newspaper offices. Churches were overrun by the faithful. New York doctors and Princeton University geologists rushed to the scene of the action to offer assistance. College students called their parents to take them home. National Guardsmen reported to barracks for duty. Bar and restaurant owners closed their businesses. Emergency personnel went on high alert. Movie theaters emptied. Some people even committed suicide, or attempted to do so.

People did this because of the power of radio, because Orson Welles and his troupe used news flashes and simulated on-air reporting. Dixon recounts the highlights of the broadcast, the on-location reporting, the interviews with experts and government officials, the minute-by-minute destruction of the world, culminating in Orson Welles' announcement assuring audiences that what they were hearing was a dramatization of H. G. Wells' book. The same type of thing had happened before, Dixon points out. In 1926, a BBC broadcast sent thousands of people into a panic, convinced that the House of Commons had been blown up. Then, just as now, callers jammed phone lines. Orson Welles, reached for comment, said he was shocked by the event. "It's too bad that so many people got excited, but after all, we kept reminding them, that is wasn't really true." H. G. Wells couldn't understand how people could have reacted so strongly to a dramatization of his book. A Senator from Iowa promised action and the creation of a censorship board. The FCC would launch an investigation. Indictments were being handed down. Not any one person is to blame, according to Dixon: CBS did announce several times that the broadcast was a work of fiction, but, at the same time, radio did stir real terror. There were calls for action, reform, inquiry.

Essential Themes
George Dixon's article is typical of the reporting at the time. A lot of attention is focused on sensational reports of panic and injury. A gullible public went mad because of something fictional they had heard on radio. What is most interesting about Dixon's article is what is missing. There is a lack of investigation or any real analysis. Dixon is simply passing along the most attention-grabbing stories he can find, but at no point does he ask which of them might be true or not. How many people actually took to the streets? How many cases of suicide or injury could be tied to the *War of the Worlds* broadcast? What were the names of the doctors, academics, or emergency personnel who made their way to the supposed victims of the Martian attack? Dixon presents the reader with a lot of hyperbole, but very little in the way of corroborated facts.

We know today that many of the stories featured in this article and others were either grossly exaggerated or completely made up. In a sense, Dixon is responsible for the same kind of misrepresentation as Orson Welles. Today, historians estimate that only about 2 percent of the American public actually listened to the Mercury Theatre on October 30, and, out of those, only a small fraction actually believed that what they heard was true. It was only in the weeks after the broadcast, after weeks of articles like those by George Dixon, that people started coming forward with their own stories of madness attributed to the "panic broadcast." It was only months and years later that the entire event came to be mythologized as part of the American experience. Sensationalist reporting helped sell newspapers in a highly competitive market. This, along with a fear of radio by the print industry, may have contributed to the rush to publish astonishing tales. Ironically, the *War of the Worlds* broadcast and the reported reaction to it served to elevate Orson Welles to stardom and boosted radio to the position of most important medium of the time.

—KP Dawes, MA

Bibliography and Additional Reading
Gosling, John, & Howard Koch. *Waging The War of the Worlds: A History of the 1938 Radio Broadcast and Resulting Panic, Including the Original Script.* Jefferson, NC: McFarland, 2009.

Socolow, Michael J. "The Hyped Panic over 'War of the

Worlds.'" *Chronicle of Higher Education.* 55.9 (24 October 2008): 35.

"War of the Worlds." *American Experience.* Dir. Cathleen O'Connell. PBS, 29 Oct. 2013. Web. 17 Sept. 2014.

"War of the Worlds." *Radiolab.* NPR. WNYC, New York. 7 Mar. 2008. Radio.

Lou Gehrig: Farewell to Baseball

Date: July 4, 1939
Author: Lou Gehrig
Genre: address, speech

Summary Overview

On May 2, 1939, Lou Gehrig, the New York Yankees' first baseman, played his final game, removing himself from the lineup because of subpar play. A month later, he was diagnosed with amyotrophic lateral sclerosis (ALS), now commonly known as Lou Gehrig's disease—an illness that would take his life two years later. On July 4, 1939, the Yankees held Lou Gehrig Appreciation Day to commemorate his stellar career. His impromptu speech during the occasion remains one of the most revered in sports history.

Defining Moment

Known as the "Iron Horse," Gehrig set a record for consecutive games played, with 2,130, through seventeen seasons between 1923 and 1939; his streak remained unbeaten until 1995, when Baltimore Orioles shortstop Cal Ripken, Jr. surpassed it. His career statistics rank among the greatest in the game: His record of twenty-three grand slams was unbeaten until 2013, and he is fourth in runs batted in, with 1,993. His career batting average of .340 and home run total of 493 rank him near the top in both categories. However, to the great surprise of teammates, he began exhibiting trouble with his coordination during spring training before the 1939 season. Teammate Joe DiMaggio remembered Gehrig missing a significant number of fastballs and falling while dressing in the locker room.

On June 19, 1939, his thirty-sixth birthday, Gehrig learned from doctors at the Mayo Clinic in Minnesota that he had ALS, a neurodegenerative disease, effectively ending his career. After Gehrig's diagnosis, the Yankees announced his retirement, planning a Lou Gehrig Appreciation Day on July 4, 1939, to commemorate his life and career. Before a crowd of approximately 62,000 people, including New York mayor Fiorello H. La Guardia and teammate Babe Ruth, Gehrig delivered his famous speech. Though Gehrig had not planned to speak, the throng of well-wishers who chanted his name compelled him to step to the microphone.

Gehrig's career spanned both the heady days of the Roaring Twenties, symbolized in part by the great success of the Yankees during that decade, and the Great Depression. A little less than two months after Gehrig's speech, Adolf Hitler began the German invasion of Poland, thereby instigating World War II. Given the historical context, the men and women who heard Gehrig's speech, and the nation at large, faced their own forms of adversity. Gehrig stood on the precipice of death, yet he considered himself lucky to be surrounded by such support and love. Video footage of Gehrig during his speech shows an individual brimming with emotion, which only adds depth to his words. Though arguably one of the ten best players in the history of baseball, Gehrig's legend is built less on his on-field prowess than his farewell speech, during which he exhibited stoicism and gratitude in the face of mortality.

Author Biography

Henry Louis Gehrig was born on the Upper East Side of Manhattan, in New York City, on June 19, 1903. His parents, Heinrich and Christina, were German immigrants, who had three other children: two girls and a boy, who died in infancy. Gehrig had been studying at Columbia University for two years when he was spotted by a baseball scout for the New York Yankees; he began his career with the Yankees in 1923. Gehrig shared the early part of his career with Babe Ruth, and the two anchored the 1927 team, one that is widely regarded as the best ever. In his later career, he shared the spotlight with Joe DiMaggio. Two years after being diagnosed with ALS, Gehrig died, on June 2, 1941, with his wife

Eleanor by his side. She received flowers from President Franklin Roosevelt and more than 1,500 messages of sympathy.

HISTORICAL DOCUMENT

Fans, for the past two weeks you have been reading about the bad break I got. Yet today I consider myself the luckiest man on the face of the earth. I have been in ballparks for seventeen years and have never received anything but kindness and encouragement from you fans. Look at these grand men. Which of you wouldn't consider it the highlight of his career just to associate with them for even one day?

Sure I'm lucky.

Who wouldn't consider it an honor to have known Jacob Ruppert? Also, the builder of baseball's greatest empire, Ed Barrow? To have spent six years with that wonderful little fellow, Miller Huggins? Then to have spent the next nine years with that outstanding leader, that smart student of psychology, the best manager in baseball today, Joe McCarthy?

Sure I'm lucky.

When the New York Giants, a team you would give your right arm to beat, and vice versa, sends you a gift—that's something. When everybody down to the groundskeepers and those boys in white coats remember you with trophies—that's something.

When you have a wonderful mother-in-law who takes sides with you in squabbles with her own daughter—that's something.

When you have a father and a mother who work all their lives so you can have an education and build your body—it's a blessing. When you have a wife who has been a tower of strength and shown more courage than you dreamed existed—that's the finest I know. So, I close in saying that I might have been given a bad break, but I've got an awful lot to live for.

Document Analysis

Modern ballplayers are known as much for their market value as their skill in the game. Contracts worth millions of dollars make the headlines of the sports pages and websites. Few articles concentrate on the player's pure love of the game. Gehrig's speech, on the other hand, is filled with gratitude for those that joined him on his journey: "Look at these grand men. Which of you wouldn't consider it the highlight of his career just to associate with them for even one day?" He admits that he got "a bad break," but despite his mounting health problems, he describes himself as "the luckiest man on the face of the earth."

Within his short speech, Gehrig specifically mentions Jacob Ruppert, Miller Huggins, Ed Barrow, and Joe McCarthy. Formerly a congressman, Ruppert was the owner of the Yankees, helping to finance the construction of the original Yankee Stadium, which opened in 1923. Huggins played professionally for the Cincinnati Reds and the St. Louis Cardinals, before eventually becoming the Yankees manager during the 1920s. Barrow managed the Detroit Tigers and Boston Red Sox before handling the business operations of the Yankees. Lastly, McCarthy was the Yankees manager from 1931 to 1946, a period that included the last eight years of Gehrig's career. All these men facilitated Gehrig's baseball career in one way or another. His comments—such as, "Who wouldn't consider it an honor to have known Jacob Ruppert?"—attest to Gehrig's sincerity and his reputation as a thoughtful and intelligent person. He speaks of his gratefulness for having worked with managers Huggins and McCarthy, and does not forget to thank others in the Yankees hierarchy: "When everybody down to the groundskeepers and those boys in white coats remember you with a trophy—that's something."

Gehrig closes his speech by thanking his family—including his parents, who worked hard to provide an education for him, and his wife, who has stood by his side. He acknowledges that, though he has suffered a great misfortune, he still had "an awful lot to live for." Though he may not have planned to speak during the ceremony to commemorate his career, most agree that Gehrig could not have chosen a better way to demonstrate the man and ballplayer he was; essentially, his legacy is in this speech.

Essential Themes

Gehrig's genuine thankfulness for the outpouring of love and support from members of the Yankees to his fans, friends, and family is a theme that runs through his farewell speech. His speech reveals a man who did not take life's favors for granted. Given the historical context of his speech, toward the close of the Great Depression and on the cusp of World War II, his listeners were accustomed to uncertainty, and they could likely relate to the fact that Gehrig gave thanks not for material objects, but for the companionship of those around him. During the Great Depression, baseball afforded Americans a brief respite from thinking about their financial and familial struggles. They could be distracted by the game and its players. Gehrig, Ruth, and their teammates provided a diversion during troubled times.

For obvious reasons, Gehrig quickly became associated with ALS, and the condition is today still commonly known as Lou Gehrig's disease. This association put a face on ALS, increasing awareness of its effects upon the body. In this way, Gehrig has continued to bring hope and understanding to others, decades after he retired. ALS, which leads to paralysis, remains a fatal illness, and Gehrig's stoicism in the face of death, before a throng of more than 60,000 people, has become a legendary endeavor in sports. His proclamation that he considers himself "the luckiest man on the face of the earth," though tinged with irony, immediately became an inspiration to both fans and the general populace. For this, perhaps more than his on-field exploits, he became an American legend.

—*Jennifer Henderson Crane, PgDip*

Bibliography and Additional Reading

Brennan, Frank. "The Seventieth Anniversary of the Death of Lou Gehrig." *American Journal of Hospice and Palliative Medicine* 29.7 (2012): 512–14. AgeLine. Web. 10 June 2014.

Eig, Jonathan. *Luckiest Man: The Life and Death of Lou Gehrig*. New York: Simon, 2005. Print.

Viola, Kevin. *Lou Gehrig*. Minneapolis: LernerSports, 2005. eBook Collection (EBSCOhost). Web. 9 June 2014.

Appendixes

Chronological List

1931: Herbert Hoover to Reed Smoot Regarding the Bonus Loan Bill 201
1931: The National Anthem Established: The Star-Spangled Banner 265
1931: Bumming in California 83
1932: Henry Stimson to Senator Borah Regarding the Nine-Power Treaty 217
1932: Eleanor Roosevelt: What Ten Million Women Want 134
1932: President Roosevelt: Fireside Chat on "The Forgotten Man" 1
1932: Attack on the Bonus Army 205
1932: The Repatriation of Mexicans and Mexican Americans 146
1932: FDR on Government's Role in the Economy 5
1932: Herbert Hoover Speaks Against the New Deal 15
1932: Veterans March to Washington 209
1932: Women on the Breadlines 131
1933: Letter From Herbert Hoover to Franklin D. Roosevelt 27
1933: President Roosevelt: Fireside Chat Outlining the New Deal 31
1933: The Hurricane of 1932 in Puerto Rico 149
1933: John Maynard Keynes: An Open Letter to President Roosevelt 38
1933: Eleanor Roosevelt on Women and the Vote 140
1934: Letter-Report Concerning the Tennessee Valley 45
1934: Indians at Work 160
1934: United We Eat—The Phenomenon of Unemployed Leagues 88
1934: What I Knew About John Dillinger 269
1934: A New Deal for American Indians 156
1935: FDR on Social Security 51
1935: Letter from a Dust Bowl Survivor 97
1935: Criticism of the Neutrality Act 223
1935: Neutrality Act of 1935 227
1935: A Negro in the CCC 170
1935: Letter Regarding Assistance to the Poor 100
1935: Letter Regarding the Needs of Puerto Ricans in New York 176
1935: Defense of the Neutrality Act 233
1936-1937: Memories of the Flint Sit-Down Strike 104
1937: The *Hindenburg* Disaster 275
1937: Speech Against the President's "Court Packing" Plan 57
1937: Plea from a Scottsboro Boy 179
1937: It's a Great Life in the CCC 109
1937: From the Federal Writers' Project: *Cape Cod Pilot* 278
1938: Address Delivered by the Secretary of State 239

1938: President Roosevelt: Fireside Chat on the Current Recession 66
1938: Dear Mrs. Roosevelt 182
1938: Winston Churchill: "The Lights Are Going Out" in Europe 248
1938: On *The War of the Worlds* Radio Broadcast 286
1938: I'd Rather Not Be on Relief 113
1939: My Hopes for the CCC 121
1939: What REA Service Means to Our Farm Home 117
1939: Lou Gehrig: Farewell to Baseball 294
1939: The Hatch Act 75
1939: Winston Churchill: A Hush Over Europe 254
1939: Charles Lindbergh: Neutrality and War 259
1939: Our Jobless Youth: A Warning 186
1939: What Does American Democracy Mean to Me? 194

Web Resources

digitalhistory.uh.edu

Offers an online history textbook, Hypertext History, which chronicles the story of America, along with interactive timelines. This online source also contains handouts, lesson plans, e-lectures, movies, games, biographies, glossaries, maps, music, and much more.

docsouth.unc.edu

A digital publishing project that reflects the southern perspective of American history and culture. It offers a wide collection of titles that students, teachers, and researchers of all levels can utilize.

docsteach.org

Centered on teaching through the use of primary source documents. This online resource provides activities for many different historical eras dating to the American Revolution as well as thousands of primary source documents.

edsitement.neh.gov

An online resource for teachers, students, and parents seeking to further their understanding of the humanities. This site offers lesson plan searches, student resources, and interactive activities.

gilderlehrman.org

Offers many options in relation to the history of America. The History by Era section provides detailed explanations of specific time periods while the primary sources present firsthand accounts from a historical perspective.

havefunwithhistory.com

An online, interactive resource for students, teachers, and anybody who has an interest in American histor

history.com/topics/american-history

Tells the story of America through topics of interest, such as the Declaration of Independence, major wars, and notable Americans. Features videos from The History Channel and other resources.

historymatters.gmu.edu

An online resource from George Mason University that provides links, teaching materials, primary documents, and guides for evaluating historical records.

http://memory.loc.gov/ammem/index.html

Covers the various eras and ages of American history in detail, including resources such as readings, interactive activities, multimedia, and more.

http://millercenter.org/academic/dgs/primaryresources/new_deal

From the MIller Center at the University of Virginia, a great list of links for information and resources regarding the 1930s. Topics include FDR, New Deal Programs, oral histories from the era, cartoons, and more.

http://newdeal.feri.org/

New Deal Network is a great resource for students of the 1930s. It features original documents, photos, lesson plans, and more. Sponsored by the Franklin and Eleanor Roosevelt Institute and the Institute for Learning Technologies at Teacher's College/Columbia University.

http://ocp.hul.harvard.edu/immigration/

A Harvard University web-based collection, this site contains a large collection of primary sources on immigration to the United States, including 1,800 books and pamphlets, 13,000 pages from manuscripts and 9,000 photographs. Documents from the 1920s include Emergency Quota Act and the Oriental Exclusion Act.

http://www.fdrlibrary.marist.edu/education/resources/periodictable.html

This "Interactive Periodic Table of the New Deal," from the Franklin D. Roosevelt Presidential Library and Museum, offers brief summaries of the people and government agencies of the New Deal.

http://xroads.virginia.edu?~1930s/front.html

From the American Studies Program at the University of Virginia, a collection of resources pertaining to the culture of the 1930s as represented in art, architecture, film, print media, and more.

pbs.org/wgbh/americanexperience

Offers an array of source materials linked to topics featured in the award winning *American Experience* history series.

pbs.org/wgbh/americanexperience

From the award-winning PBS series "American Experience," a collection of films and other resources relating to the 1930s. Topics covered include the Dust Bowl, the Civilian Conservation Corps, and more.

si.edu/encyclopedia_si/nmah/timeline.htm

Details the course of American history chronologically. Important dates and significant events link to other pages within the Smithsonian site that offer more details.

smithsonianeducation.org

An online resource for educators, families, and students offering lesson plans, interactive activities, and more.

teachingamericanhistory.org

Allows visitors to learn more about American history through original source documents detailing the broad spectrum of American history. The site contains document libraries, audio lectures, lesson plans, and more.

teachinghistory.org

A project funded by the US Department of Education that aims to assist teachers of all levels to augment their efforts in teaching American history. It strives to amplify student achievement through improving the knowledge of teachers.

ushistory.org/us

Contains an outline that details the entire record of American history. This resource offers historical insight and stories that demonstrate what truly an American truly is from a historical perspective.

Bibliography

"1921–1940: September 4, 1934: 'Merchants of Death.'" *Senate.gov*. US Senate, n.d. Web. 11 June 2014.

"American President: Herbert Hoover (1874–1964)." *Miller Center*. U of Virginia, n.d. Web. 17 June 2014.

Aretha, David. *The Trial of the Scottsboro Boys*. Greensboro: Morgan Reynolds, 2007. Print.

Babb, Sanora. *On the Dirty Plate Trail: Remembering the Dust Bowl Refugee Camps*. Austin: U of Texas P, 2007. Print.

Beasley, Maurine, & Holly Shulman. *The Eleanor Roosevelt Encyclopedia*. Westport: Greenwood, 2001. Print.

"Bennett Champ Clark." *The Champ Clark House*. Champ Clark House, n.d. Web. 12 June 2014.

Bernstein, Irving. *The Turbulent Years: A History of the American Worker, 1933–1941*. Boston: Houghton-Mifflin, 1970. Print.

Bethune, Mary McLeod. *Building a Better World: Essays and Selected Documents*. Bloomington: Indiana UP, 1999. Print.

"Biography of Franklin D. Roosevelt." *Franklin D. Roosevelt Presidential Library and Museum*. National Archives and Records Administration, n.d. Web. 18 August 2014.

"Biography of Franklin D. Roosevelt." *Franklin D. Roosevelt Presidential Library and Museum*. National Archives, n.d. Web. 6 June 2014.

Blinder, Alan. "Alabama Pardons 3 'Scottsboro Boys' after 80 Years." *New York Times*. New York Times, 21 Nov. 2013. Web. 11 June 2014.

Bold, Christine. *The WPA Guides: Mapping America*. Jackson, MS: U of Mississippi P, 1999. Print.

Brennan, Frank. "The Seventieth Anniversary of the Death of Lou Gehrig." *American Journal of Hospice and Palliative Medicine* 29.7 (2012): 512–14. AgeLine. Web. 10 June 2014.

Brinkley, Alan. *Franklin Delano Roosevelt*. Oxford: Oxford University Press, 2009. Print.

Broner, E. M. "Meridel LeSueur, 1900–1996." *Nation* (17 Feb. 1997): 33–35. Print.

Buhle, Mari Jo, & Paul Buhle, eds. *The Concise History of Woman Suffrage: Selections from History of Woman Suffrage*. Urbana: U of Illinois P, 2005. Print.

Burrough, Bryan. *Public Enemies: America's Greatest Crime Wave and the Birth of the FBI, 1933–34*. New York: Penguin, 2004. Print.

Campbell, Dan. "When the Lights Came On." *Rural Cooperatives* 67.4 (2000): 6–9. Print.

Carroll, Sarah. "Causes of the Great Depression". *OK Economics*. Boston U, 2002. Web. 17 June 2014.

Cerulo, Karen. "Symbols and the World System: National Anthems and Flags." *Sociological Forum* 8.2 (1993): 243–71. Print.

"Charles A. Lindbergh—Biography." *Lindbergh Foundation*. Lindberg Foundation, 2012. Web. 11 June 2014.

Cohen, Robert. "Dear Mrs. Roosevelt: Cries for Help from Depression Youth." *Social Education* 60.5 (1996): 271–76. Print.

Cohen, Robert, ed. *Dear Mrs. Roosevelt: Letters from Children of the Great Depression*. Chapel Hill: U of North Carolina P, 2002. Print.

Cohen, Robert. *When the Old Left Was Young: Student Radicals and America's First Mass Student Movement, 1929–1941*. New York: Oxford UP, 1993. Print.

Cole, Olen, Jr. *The African-American Experience in the Civilian Conservation Corps*. Gainesville: UP of Florida, 1999. Print.

Collier, John. *From Every Zenith: A Memoir; and Some Essays on Life and Thought*. Denver: Sage, 1963. Print.

Collins, Sheila D., and Gertrude Schaffner Goldberg, eds. *When Government Helped: Learning from the Successes and Failures of the New Deal*. New York: Oxford UP, 2014.

Daniels, Roger. *The Bonus March: An Episode of the Great Depression*. Westport: Greenwood, 1971. Print.

"Dear Mrs. Roosevelt." *New Deal Network*. Franklin and Eleanor Roosevelt Inst., 2003. Web. 10 June 2014.

Deeben, John P. "Family Experiences and New Deal Relief: The Correspondence Files of the Federal Emergency Relief Administration, 1933–1936." *Prologue*. National Archives, 2012. Web. 25 June 2014.

Delaplaine, Edward Schley. *Francis Scott Key: Life and Times*. Biography Press, 1937. Print.

Deloria, Vine, Jr., & Clifford M. Lytle. *The Nations Within: The Past and Future of American Indian Sovereignty*. New York: Pantheon, 1984. Print.

DeWitt, Larry, Daniel Beland, & Edward D. Berkowitz. *Social Security: a Documentary History*. Washington, DC: CQ Press, 2007. Print.

Dickson, Paul, & Thomas B. Allen. *The Bonus Army: An*

American Epic. New York: Walker, 2004. Print.

Dickson, Paul, & Thomas B. Allen. *The Bonus Army: An American Epic*. New York: Walker, 2004. Print.

Dollinger, Sol, & Genora Dollinger. *Not Automatic: Women and the Left in the Forging of the Auto Workers' Union*. New York: Monthly Review P, 2000. Print.

Dray, Philip. *There Is Power in a Union: The Epic Story of Labor in America*. New York: Anchor Books, 2011. Print.

Duncan, Dayton, & Ken Burns. *The Dust Bowl: An Illustrated History*. San Francisco: Chronicle, 2012. Print.

Dunn, Susan. *Roosevelt's Purge: How FDR Fought to Change the Democratic Party*. Cambridge, MA: Belknap Press, 2010. Print.

"Dust Bowl Exodus: How Drought and the Depression Took Their Toll." *Bill of Rights in Action*. Constitutional Rights Foundation, 2005. Web. 24 June 2014.

Edsforth, Ronald. *The New Deal: America's Response to the Great Depression*. Hoboken, NJ: Wiley, 2000. Print.

Edsforth, Ronald. *The New Deal: America's Response to the Great Depression*. Malden: Blackwell, 2000. Print.

Egerton, John. *Speak Now against the Day: The Generation before the Civil Rights Movement in the South*. Chapel Hill: U of North Carolina P, 1994. Print.

Eig, Jonathan. *Luckiest Man: The Life and Death of Lou Gehrig*. New York: Simon, 2005. Print.

Fairbank, John K. *The United States and China*. 4th ed. Cambridge: Harvard UP, 1983. Print.

Fanslow, Robin A. "The Migrant Experience." *Library of Congress*. Library of Congress, 6 Apr. 1998. Web. 24 June 2014.

"Farm Labor in the 1930s." *Rural Migration News* 9.4 (October 2003). Web. 12 Sept. 2014.

"FDR's Greatest Hits." *Franklin D. Roosevelt Presidential Library and Museum*. National Archives and Records Administration, n.d. Web. 18 August 2014.

"Federal Emergency Relief Administration." *Gilder Lehrman Institute of American History*. Gilder Lehrman Institute, 2014. Web. 25 June 2014.

Ferraro, Vincent, comp. "Documents of the Interwar Period." *Resources for the Study of International Relations and Foreign Policy*. Mount Holyoke Coll., n.d. Web. 10 June 2014.

Flynne, Kathryn A., with Richard Polese. *The New Deal: A 75th Anniversary Celebration*. Salt Lake City: Gibbs Smith, Pub., 2008. Print.

Frame, Craig Steven. "History." *Mexican Repatriation: A Generation between Two Borders*. California State U San Marcos, 2009. Web. 6 June 2014.

Franklin, John Hope, & August Meier, eds. *Black Leaders of the Twentieth Century*. Urbana: U of Illinois, 1982. Print.

Freidel, Frank, & Hugh Sidey. "The Presidents of the United States of America: Franklin D. Roosevelt," *The Whitehouse: The Presidents*. The White House Historical Association, 2006. Web. 18 August 2014.

Fuller, Robert Lynn. *Phantom of Fear: The Banking Panic of 1933*. Jefferson: McFarland, 2012. Print.

Gates, Henry Louis, Jr., & Evelyn Brooks Higginbotham, eds. *African America Lives*. New York: Oxford UP. 2004. Print.

Gilbert, Martin. *Churchill and America*. New York: Free, 2005. Print.

Gosling, John, & Howard Koch. *Waging The War of the Worlds: A History of the 1938 Radio Broadcast and Resulting Panic, Including the Original Script*. Jefferson, NC: McFarland, 2009.

"Great Depression and World War II: The Dust Bowl." *Library of Congress*. Library of Congress, n.d. Web. 24 June 2014.

Guerin-Gonzales, Camille. *Mexican Workers and American Dreams: Immigration, Repatriation, and California Farm Labor, 1900–1939*. New Brunswick: Rutgers UP, 1994. Print.

Hamby, Alonzo L. *For the Survival of Democracy: Franklin Roosevelt and the World Crisis of the 1930s*. New York: Free, 2004. Print.

Hauptman, Lawrence M. "The Indian Reorganization Act." *The Aggressions of Civilization: Federal Indian Policy since the 1980s*. Ed. Sandra L. Cadwalader & Vine Deloria, Jr. Philadelphia: Temple UP, 1984. 131–48. Print.

Hedges, Elaine, ed. *Ripening: Selected Work*. 2nd ed. New York: Feminist, 1990. Print.

"Herbert Clark Hoover: A Biographical Sketch." *Herbert Hoover Presidential Library and Museum*. National Archives, n.d. Web. 17 June 2014.

"Herbert Morrison, 83, Hindenburg Reporter." *New York Times*. 10 Jan. 1989. Web. 23 Aug. 2014.

Herring, George C. *From Colony to Superpower: US Foreign Relations since 1776*. New York: Oxford UP, 2008. Print.

Hickok, Lorena A., Richard Lowitt, & Maurine Hoffman Beasley. *One Third of a Nation: Lorena Hickok Reports on the Great Depression*. Urbana: U of Illinois

P, 1981. Print.

Hodgson, Geoffrey. *The Colonel: The Life and Wars of Henry Stimson, 1867–1950*. New York: Knopf, 1990. Print.

Hoffman, Abraham. *Unwanted Mexican Americans in the Great Depression: Repatriation Pressures, 1929–1939*. Tucson: U of Arizona P, 1974. Print.

Holt, Daniel S. *Debates on the Federal Judiciary: A Documentary History, Volume II: 1875–1939*. Washington: Federal Judicial History Office, 2013. Print.

Hull, Cordell. *The Memoirs of Cordell Hull*. New York: Macmillan, 1948. Print.

Iverson, Peter. Diné: *A History of the Navajo*. Albuquerque: U of New Mexico P, 2002. Print.

Jackson, Carleton. *Child of the Sit-Downs: The Revolutionary Life of Genora Dollinger*. Kent, OH: Kent State UP, 2008. Print.

Jackson, Robert. *Airships: A Popular History of Dirigibles, Zeppelins, and Other Lighter-Than-Air Craft*. Garden City, N.Y.: Doubleday, 1973. Print.

Jaycox, Faith. *The Progressive Era*. New York: Facts on File, 2005. Print.

Jeansonne, Glen. *The Life of Herbert Hoover: Fighting Quaker, 1928–1933*. New York: Palgrave, 2012. Print.

Katznelson, Ira. *Fear Itself: The New Deal and the Origins of Our Time*. New York: Liveright, 2013. Print.

Kearney, James R. *Anna Eleanor Roosevelt: The Evolution of a Reformer*. Boston: Houghton, 1968. Print.

Kelly, Lawrence C. *The Assault on Assimilation: John Collier and the Origins of Indian Policy Reform*. Albuquerque: U of New Mexico P, 1983. Print.

Kennedy, David M. *Freedom from Fear: The American People in Depression and War, 1929–1945*. New York: Oxford UP, 2005. Print.

Kennedy, David M. "The Great Depression and World War II, 1929–1945." *Gilder Lehrman Institute of American History*. Gilder Lehrman Institute, n.d. Web. 10 June 2014.

Kirby, John B. *Black Americans in the Roosevelt Era: Liberalism and Race*. Chattanooga: U of Tennessee P, 1992. Print.

Lehmann, Ernst A., & Howard Mingos. *The Zeppelins; the Development of the Airship, with the Story of the Zeppelin Air Raids in the World War*. New York: J.H. Sears & Co., 1927. Print.

Leuchtenburg, William E. *Franklin D. Roosevelt and the New Deal, 1932-1940*. New York: Harper Perennial, 2009.

Liebovich, Louis. *Bylines in Despair: Herbert Hoover, the Great Depression, and the US News Media*. Westport: Greenwood, 1994. Print.

Lisio, Donald J. *The President and Protest: Hoover, Conspiracy, and the Bonus Riot*. 2nd ed. New York: Fordham UP, 1994. Print.

Lisio, Donald J. *The President and Protest: Hoover, Conspiracy, and the Bonus Riot*. Columbia: U of Missouri P, 1974. Print.

"Lorena Alice Hickok (1893–1968)." *The Eleanor Roosevelt Papers Project*. George Washington University, 2014. Web. 25 June 2014.

Macdonald, C. A. *The United States, Britain and Appeasement, 1936–1939*. New York: St. Martins, 1981. Print.

Maher, Neil M. *Nature's New Deal: The Civilian Conservation Corps and the Roots of the American Environmental Movement*. Oxford: Oxford UP, 2008. Print.

Manchester, William. *The Last Lion: Winston Spencer Churchill: Alone, 1932–1940*. New York: Bantam, 1983. Print.

Mangione, Jerre. *The Dream and the Deal: The Federal Writers' Project, 1935–1943*. Boston: Little, Brown, 1972. Print.

Matera, Dary. *John Dillinger: The Life and Death of America's First Celebrity Criminal*. New York: Carroll & Graff, 2004. Print.

McElhatton, Jim. "Hatch Act Probe Nets Hundreds; Few Penalized." *Federal Times*. Springfield, VA: Gannett Government Media Site, 2014. Web. 20 August 2014.

McElvaine, Robert S. *The Great Depression: America, 1929–1941*. 25th anniv. ed. New York: Three Rivers, 2009. Print.

McKay, Robert R. "Mexican Americans and Repatriation." *Texas State Historical Association*. Texas State Hist. Assn., 15 June 2010. Web. 6 June 2014.

McKenna, Marian Cecilia. *Franklin Roosevelt and the Great Constitutional War: The Court-Packing Crisis of 1937*. New York: Fordham UP, 2002. Print.

McPherson, Robert S. "Navajo Livestock Reduction in Southeastern Utah, 1933–46: History Repeats Itself." *American Indian Quarterly* 22.1/2 (1998): 1–18. Print.

Menaker, Richard G. "FDR's Court-Packing Plan: A Study in Irony." *Gilder Lehrman Institute of American History*. Gilder Lehrman Institute, 2014. Web. 23 June 2014.

"Milestones: 1921–1936." *Office of the Historian*. US Dept. of State, n.d. Web. 12 June 2014.

Modell, John. *Into One's Own: From Youth to Adulthood in the United States, 1920–1975*. Berkeley: U of California P, 1989. Print.

Morris, Bob. *Built in Detroit: A Story of the UAW, a Company and a Gangster*. Bloomington, IN: iUniverse, 2013. Print.

Muller, Joseph. *The Star Spangled Banner; Words and Music Issued between 1814–1864; an Annotated Bibliographical List with Notices of the Different Versions, Texts, Variants, Musical Arrangements, and Notes on Music Publishers in the United States*. New York: Da Capo, 1973. Print.

Mulvey, Deb, ed. *We Had Everything but Money*. Greendale: Reiman, 1992. Print.

National Geographic Television & Film. *Hindenburg*. New York: Films Media Group, 2012. Film.

Office of Special Counsel. "Overview." *Hatch Act*. Office of Special Counsel, n.d. Web. 20 August 2014.

Office of Special Counsel. *Political Activity and the Federal Employee*. Office of Special Counsel, 2005. Web. 20 August 2014.

Olson, James Stuart, ed. *Historical Dictionary of the Great Depression, 1929–1940*. Westport: Greenwood, 2001. Print.

Ortiz, Stephen R. "Rethinking the Bonus March: Federal Bonus Policy, the Veterans of Foreign Wars, and the Origins of a Protest Movement." *Journal of Policy History* 18.3 (2006): 275–303. Print.

Palm, Risa, & Michael E. Hodgson. "Natural Hazards in Puerto Rico." *Geographical Review* 83.3 (1993): 280–89. Print.

Parrish, Michael E. *Anxious Decades: America in Prosperity and Depression 1920–1941*. New York: Norton,

Philp, Kenneth R. *John Collier's Crusade for Indian Reform, 1920–1954*. Tucson: U of Arizona P, 1977. Print.

Pratt, Linda Ray. "Women Writers in the CP: The Case of Meridel LeSueur." *Women's Studies* 14.3 (1988): 247–64. Print.

"President Franklin Delano Roosevelt and the New Deal, 1933–1945." *American Memory Timeline: Great Depression/WWII, 1929–1945*. Lib. of Congress, n.d. Web. 13 June 2014.

"Puerto Rican New York during the Inter-War Years." *Hunter College: Center for Puerto Rican Studies*. City U of New York, 2010. Web. 12 June 2014.

Purvis, Alston. *The Vendetta: Special Agent Melvin Purvis, John Dillinger, and Hoover's FBI in the Age of Gangsters*. PublicAffairs, 2005. Print.

Raymond, Mary. "Reflections of Meridel Le Sueur." *Hurricane Alice* 5.3 (1988): 4. Print.

Reiman, Richard A. *The New Deal and American Youth: Ideas and Ideals in a Depression Decade*. Athens: U of Georgia P, 1992. Print.

Roach, Edward J. "Fechner, Robert." *American National Biography*. Ed. Mark C. Carnes. New York: Oxford UP, 2005. 166–77. Print.

Robles, Michelle. "Hardships in the Land of Enchantment: The Economic Effects of the Great Depression on the United States Territory of Puerto Rico." *University of South Florida Sarasota-Manatee*. Michelle Robles, 2010. PDF file.

Rodríguez, Havidán. "A Socioeconomic Analysis of Hurricanes in Puerto Rico: An Overview of Disaster Mitigation and Preparedness." *Hurricanes*. Ed. Henry F. Diaz & Roger Pulwarty. New York: Springer, 1997. 121–43. Print.

Roosevelt, Eleanor. *The Autobiography of Eleanor Roosevelt*. Cambridge: Da Capo, 2000. Print.

Roosevelt, Eleanor. *The Autobiography of Eleanor Roosevelt*. New York: Harper, 1961. Print.

Rose, Nancy Ellen. *Put to Work: Relief Programs in the Great Depression*. New York: Monthly Rev., 1994. Print.

Salmond, John A. *The Civilian Conservation Corps, 1933–1942: A New Deal Case Study*. Durham: Duke UP, 1967. Print.

Sanburn, Josh. "FDR vs. The Supreme Court." *Time*. Time, Inc., 2011. Web. 23 June 2014.

"Second World War (WWII)." *The Canadian Encyclopedia*. Historica Foundation, n.d. Web. 11 June 2014.

Shlaes, Amity. *The Forgotten Man: A New History of the Great Depression*. New York: Harper Perennial: 2008.

Silkett, John T. *Francis Scott Key and the History of the Star Spangled Banner*. Washington: Vintage America Pub., 1978. Print.

Sitkoff, Harvard. *A New Deal for Blacks: The Emergence of Civil Rights as a National Issue, Vol. 1: The Depression Decade*. New York: Oxford UP, 1978. Print.

Sleight, Kenneth. "America's Exodus: The 1930s and the Dust Bowl." *Bright Hub*. Bright Hub, 11 Mar. 2014. Web. 5 June 2014.

Smiley, Gene. "Great Depression." *Library of Economics and Liberty*. Liberty Fund, n.d. Web. 6 June 2014.

Smith, Jason Scott. *A Concise History of the New Deal*.

Cambridge: Cambridge University Press, 2014. Print.

Smith, Jean Edward. *FDR*. New York: Random, 2008. Print.

Socolow, Michael J. "The Hyped Panic over 'War of the Worlds.'" *Chronicle of Higher Education*. 55.9 (24 October 2008): 35.

Sommer, Barbara W. *Hard Work and a Good Deal: The Civilian Conservation Corps in Minnesota*. St. Paul: Minnesota Historical Society, 2008. Print.

Sterne, Joseph. *Combat Correspondents: The Baltimore Sun in World War II*. Annapolis: Maryland Hist. Soc., 2009. Print.

Sullivan, Patricia. *Days of Hope: Race and Democracy in the New Deal Era*. Chapel Hill: U of North Carolina P, 1996. Print.

"Surviving the Dust Bowl." *American Experience*. WGBH Educational Foundation, n.d. Web. 5 June 2014.

Taylor, David A. *Soul of a People: The WPA Writers' Project Uncovers Depression America*. Hoboken, NJ: Wiley, 2009. Print.

Terkel, Studs. *Hard Times: An Oral History of the Great Depression*. New York: The New Press, 2005.

"The Great Depression (1929–1939)." *Eleanor Roosevelt Papers Project*. George Washington U, n.d. Web. 6 June 2014.

"The Neutrality Acts, 1930s." *Milestones: 1921–1936*. US Department of State, Office of the Historian, n.d. Web. 11 June 2014.

"The Public Health Aspects of the Hurricane of San Ciprián, September 26–27, 1932." *Libraria*, n.d. Web. 16 June 2014. PDF file.

"Timeline of the Great Depression." *American Experience*. WGBH Educational Foundation, n.d. Web. 11 June 2014.

Toland, John. *The Dillinger Days*. Boston: Da Capo, 1995. Print.

United States. Dept. of State. *Office of the Historian*.

"Milestones: 1921–1936." Office of the Historian. US Dept. of State, n.d. Web. 10 June 2014.

United States. Rural Electrification Administration. Rural Lines, USA: The Story of the Rural Electrification Administration's First Twenty-Five Years. Washington: GPO, 1960. Print.

Viola, Kevin. *Lou Gehrig*. Minneapolis: LernerSports, 2005. eBook Collection (EBSCOhost). Web. 9 June 2014.

"War of the Worlds." *American Experience*. Dir. Cathleen O'Connell. PBS, 29 Oct. 2013. Web. 17 Sept. 2014.

"War of the Worlds." *Radiolab*. NPR. WNYC, New York. 7 Mar. 2008. Radio.

Weiss, Nancy Joan. *Farewell to the Party of Lincoln: Black Politics in the Age of FDR*. Princeton: Princeton UP, 1983.

"What Happened during the Repatriation of Mexicans from San Diego?" *San Diego Mexican & Chicano History*. San Diego State U, 7 Nov. 2011. Web. 6 June 2014.

Wheeler Azqueta, Robin. "Biography, Burton Kendall Wheeler." *Wheelercenter.org*. Burton K. Wheeler Center, 2013. Web. 23 June 2014.

Whisenhunt, Donald W. *President Herbert Hoover*. Hauppauge, NY: Nova, 2007. Print.

White, Richard. *The Roots of Dependency: Subsistence, Environment, and Social Change among the Choctaws, Pawnees, and Navajos*. Lincoln: U of Nebraska P, 1983. Print.

_____. *Winston Churchill: The Wilderness Years: Speaking Out against Hitler in the Prelude to War*. London: IB Tauris, 2011. Print.

Woolner, David. "African Americans and the New Deal: A Look Back in History." *Roosevelt Institute*. Roosevelt Institute, n.d. Web. 10 June 2013.

Worster, Donald. Dust Bowl: *The Southern Plains in the 1930s*. New York: Oxford UP, 2012. Print.

Index

A
Advisory Council on Economic Security 52
agin 49
Agricultural Adjustment Administration 191
A Hush over Europe 257
airship 275, 276, 286
Alabama Sharecroppers' Union 84
Alexander the Great 251
Allen, Florence 135
Allied forces 4, 237
Allied nations 225, 232
Alneeng, Nee 163
Alsberg, Henry 278
Amador, Armando C. 146, 147
America First Committee 260
American Bible Society 266
American Colonization Society 266
American Communist Party 210
American Communists 213
American Constitution 255, 256, 257
American Council on Education 189
American Expeditionary Force 205
American Expeditionary Forces 234
American Federation of Labor 94, 104
American Forestry Association 121, 126
American Forests 121, 127
American Guide Series 278, 284, 285
American Indian Defense Association 157, 161
American individualism 5
Americanism 91
American Legion 201, 203, 204, 207, 213, 234
American Newspaper Guild 187
American Relief Administration 202
American Revolution 7, 13, 301
American Student Union 186
American Workers' Party 89, 91
American Youth Commission 189, 190
American Youth Congress 186
America's Town Meeting of the Air 194
amyotrophic lateral sclerosis 294
Anacreontic Song, The 266
Anderson, Marian 195
Anglo-American alliance 249, 257
Anglo-Polish Alliance 254
annexation of Austria 239, 248, 257
Annexy, Jaime 151
An Open Letter to President Roosevelt v, 39, 299

Anthony, Susan B. 141
anti-Nazi 252, 254, 257
anti-Semitism 254
anti-trust laws 34
antitrust laws 9
appeasement 247, 248, 252, 254, 255, 257
Arkies 113, 115
Arlington Cemetery 211
Associated Press 46, 290, 291
Asti Butt Slim 84, 85, 86
Attucks, Crispus 195
authoritarianism 87

B
Baby Face Nelson 269
Baez, Alberto B. 176, 177
Bajo la marquesina 147
Baker, Jacob 91
Bakke, E. Wight 91
Baldwin, Stanley 249
Baltic States 222
Baltimore Evening Sun 206
Baltimore Orioles 294
Bangs, Abigail 281
Barnstable Patriot 280
Barron's 187
Barrow, Ed 295
barter 22, 91, 92, 94, 95
barter leagues 91
barter movement 91
Bates, Ruby 179, 180
Battle of Fort McHenry 265
Battle of Waterloo 2
beam 266, 281, 284
Bearse, Noadiah, Captain 283
Bellow, Saul 278
Beneath the Marquee 147
Berga, Pablo 151
Bethune, Mary McLeod 129, 194, 195, 196
Beverley, James Rumsey 149
Biograph Theater 269
Black Cabinet 195
Black Sunday 99
Black Thursday 15, 88
Black Tuesday 5, 131
Board of Indian Commissioners 158

body Brussells carpet 119
Boleg, Sie 86
bond 42
Bonet, Sancho 151
Bonnie and Clyde 269
Bonus Act 201
Bonus Army vi, xi, 199, 202, 204, 205, 206, 207, 208, 209, 213, 299, 303, 304
Bonus Expeditionary Force 204, 205, 209
Bonus Loan Bill vi, 203, 204, 299
bonus march 211
Bonus Marchers 210, 212
Borah, William, Senator vi, 217, 221, 299
Boston Globe 291
Boston Red Sox 295
Boston Tea Party 285
bottom up 1, 2, 3, 4
bourgeois 161, 167
Bradford, William 282
Braegger, Victor 151
Brains Trust 46, 49
Brandeis, Louis 61, 63
Branin, Carl 88
British Broadcasting Company 291
Broadcasting the Barricades 291
Brown v. Board of Education 196
Bruere, Martha Bensley 191
Brussels Conference 242
Buck, Pearl S. 218
Bulldog 281
bulls 83
bum 85, 86
Bureau of Immigration 146
Bureau of Indian Affairs 129, 156, 160
Butte, Woodfin L. 151
Byroade, George L. 151
Byron, George Gordon, Lord 250

C

Cairns, Joe 187, 192
Caldwell, William G. 151
Calimano, Enrique 151
callow fledglings 135, 138
Camp Dix 171, 172, 173
canalize 94
Candy Dodging Dayboy 85
Cantie Catchen 85, 86
Cantlon, Caroline 289
Cape Cod Chamber of Commerce 280

Cape Cod Pilot 278, 279, 281, 283, 284, 285, 299
capitalism 13, 38, 43, 108, 140, 188, 189, 192
capitalist 38, 213
Carlson, Eric 211
Carrión, Diego 151
Carver, George Washington 195
cash and carry 237, 260
Catlin, George 187
Catt, Carrie Chapman 141
CBS Broadcasting, Inc. 286, 287, 292
CCC Acts 125
Central Rank and File Committee 209, 211, 212
Chamberlain, John 186, 192
Chamberlain, Neville 248, 249, 254, 255
chattels 195, 196
Chautauqua 131
Cheever, John 278
Chicago Herald and Examiner 269, 270, 274
Chinese Bureau of Mines 28
Chinese Revolution of 1911 217
Chinese sovereignty 217, 221
Churchill, Winston vi, 215, 248, 249, 253, 254, 258, 300, 307
Cincinnati Reds 295
Citizen Kane 287
City man 39, 42
Civilian Conservation Corps 36, 45, 52, 66, 69, 75, 81, 109, 110, 112, 121, 122, 124, 126, 127, 129, 170, 171, 174, 191, 213, 302, 303, 305, 306, 307
civil rights xiii, 105, 107, 171, 179, 182, 194, 195, 196
Civil War 20, 62, 66, 98, 156, 168, 223, 239, 248, 259
Clark, Bennett Champ 233, 234, 238, 303
Clark, James Beauchamp 234
Clark, Joel Bennett 234
Clarkson, Louise 224
Cleveland Conference of the Rank and File Veterans 211
Cleveland, Grover 6
Climax 281
cloistrated 163, 167
code 49
Colcord, Joanna C. 91
Cold War 222, 247, 252, 253, 257
collectivization 104
Collier, John 129, 156, 157, 158, 159, 160, 161, 168, 169, 305, 306
Colombia Broadcasting System 288
Colón, Edmundo D. 152
Columbia Broadcasting System 36, 289

Comanche 164
Commission for Relief in Belgium 28, 202
Committee for Relief of Belgium 16
Committee on Economic Security 52, 53, 54, 55
communism xiii, 38, 43, 74, 89, 95, 192, 213, 252
Communist Party 78, 105, 107, 187, 191, 209, 210, 213
Competitor 281
Concord 282
Congress of Industrial Organizations 104, 115, 191
Connally, Tom 223, 225
constable 89, 90, 94
constabulary 94
Constitution 23, 58, 60, 62, 64, 75, 134, 140, 166, 255, 256, 257, 268
Coolidge, Calvin xi, 16, 28, 201, 202
Cooper, Fenimore E., Reverend 100
County Council of the Unemployed 90
Court of Indian Affairs 166
court packing v, 57, 299
court-packing bill 58
Covenant of the League 256
Cox, James M. 2, 6, 32, 67
Crime Didn't Pay! 270, 274
Crime does not pay! 270
crise des nerfs 188
Crisis, The 170
Crowell, Hannah 281
Cunfer, Geoff 97
Curtis, Charles 209
Cutting, Bronson M., Senator 17

D
Daily Worker 131
Dawes Commission 20
Daytona Educational and Industrial Training School for Negro Girls 195
Declaration of Independence 8, 11, 280, 301
Defence of Fort M'Henry 265
del Toro, Emilio, Chief Justice 151
deposit insurance 5
depreciate 42
Dern, George Henry 149, 154
Detroit Tigers 295
devolution 256
Didy Waw Didy 85, 86
Dies, Martin 279
Digges, Jeremiah 278, 279
Dillinger, John vi, 269, 270, 272, 273, 274, 299, 305, 306
DiMaggio, Joe 294
dirigibles 275, 277
dirt pneumonia 97, 99
Disabled American Veterans 213
Division of Negro Affairs 195
Doak, William N. 146
Dollinger, Genora Johnson 104, 105
Douglass, Frederick 196
down at heel 132
Drew, Benjamin 282
drouth 49
Dunbar, Paul Lawrence 195
Dust Bowl v, 45, 49, 50, 51, 58, 97, 98, 99, 113, 115, 116, 121, 126, 286, 299, 302, 303, 304, 306, 307
dust pneumonia 97
dusty pike 119

E
ejidos 163
élan vital 161, 167
Eldridge, Phineas 282
El Fantastico 84
Ellison, Ralph 278
Emergency Adjusted Compensation Bill 201, 202
Emergency Banking Act 27, 28
Emergency Conservation Work Act 109, 121, 126, 127
Emergency Relief Appropriation Act of 1935 66
Emergency Relief Construction Act 15
Englebrecht, H. C. 227
Esteves, Raúl, Colonel 151
Evans, Walker 278
Executive Order 8802 196
expansionism 239
expansionist 221, 247

F
Farley, James 64
Farm Relief Bill 33
Farm Security Administration 69, 113, 278
fascism 38, 43, 186, 188, 192
Fascist Italy 221, 239, 248
Fechner, Robert 109, 121, 122, 126, 127
Federal Arts Project xii, xiii, 81, 278
Federal Communications Commission 287, 291
Federal Council of Negro Affairs 195
Federal Deposit Insurance Corporation 81
Federal Emergency Relief Administration xi, xix, 45, 50, 88, 94, 191, 303, 304

federal Indian policy 156, 158, 168
federal livestock reduction program 160
Federal One 278
Federal Public Health Service 53
Federal Reserve 15, 18, 27, 28, 42, 70
Federal Reserve Board 70
Federal Writers' Project vi, 278, 279, 281, 283, 284, 285, 299, 305
feminist movements 105
Ferguson, William H. 151
fetch up 284
fireside chats xix, 28, 263, 286
First Amendment 78
Fisher Body Plant 2 105
Five Civilized Tribes 165
Five-Power Treaty 217
Five Tribes 165
Five Tribes Indians 165
Flint sit-down strike 104, 105, 107
floater 85
floaters 84, 85, 86
Flood Control Act of 1936 126
flop-house 84
Ford, James W. 209
Ford Motor Company 210
Fort McHenry 265, 267
Fort Meade 206
Fortune 187
Fort Washington 206
Franco, Francisco 84, 186, 239, 248
Frankfurter, Felix 38, 39
Frechette, Evelyn "Billie" 269, 270
free-market 1, 13, 27, 43
free-market capitalism 13, 43
French Revolution 252
Fruit Growers Cooperative Credit Association 152
furriner 280, 284

G
Gable, Clark 270
Gambs, John S. 88, 89, 95
Garner, John Nance 209
Gascoyne-Cecil, Robert Arthur Talbot 219
Gehrig, Lou vii, 294, 296, 300, 303, 304, 307
General Allotment Act 164, 168
General Allotment Act of 1887 168
General Motors 104, 105, 107
General Theory of Employment, Interest and Money, The 39

Georgia Skin 85
German Anschluss 239
GI Bill 234
Gilded Age 104
Glassford, Pelham 205
gold standard 34, 38, 39, 41, 83
González, Manuel 151
Good Earth, The 218
Goodrich, Carter 190
Gore, Robert Haynes 154
Gosnold, Bartholomew, Captain 282
Graf Zeppelin 277
Grand Army of the Republic Highway 280
Grant, Ulysses S. 279
Great Depression 1, 2, 4, 5, 6, 14, 15, 16, 25, 26, 27, 30, 31, 32, 36, 37, 38, 43, 45, 50, 51, 55, 57, 66, 73, 74, 75, 83, 86, 87, 88, 96, 97, 100, 103, 104, 109, 113, 115, 117, 120, 121, 127, 129, 131, 132, 133, 134, 138, 140, 141, 144, 145, 146, 148, 149, 155, 160, 170, 174, 176, 177, 178, 179, 181, 182, 185, 186, 187, 192, 193, 194, 201, 202, 203, 204, 205, 208, 209, 213, 217, 227, 233, 246, 269, 278, 286, 294, 296, 303, 304, 305, 306, 307
Great Emancipator 194
Great War 25, 61, 257
Green, Eddie 272, 273, 274
Grey, Edward, Sir 252
Guggenheim Fellowship 285

H
Habsburg Empire 248
haddock 280, 284
Hamilton, Alexander 13
Hanighen, F. C. 227
Harding, Warren 16, 28
Harding, Warren G. 6, 202
Harper's 187
Harris, William J. 146
Hastings, Edgar F. 146
Hatch Act 75, 76, 77, 78, 79, 300, 305, 306
Hatch, Carl 75, 76
Hawley-Smoot Tariff 3, 4
Hay, John 218
Hearst, William Randolph 17
heel 284
Henderson, Leon 189
Henry, Lou 202
Herndon, Angelo 62
Herring, Clyde L. 291

Hickok, Lorena 45, 46, 49, 50, 304
Higgins, Al 282
High Cap Swanginggate 85
Hillman, Sidney 188
Hindenburg 263, 275, 276, 277, 286, 299, 304, 306
Hiroshima 218
his 77
History of Plimouth Plantation 282
Hitler, Adolf 38, 248, 254, 255, 286, 294
hobo 84, 85, 188
Hofer, Andreas 256
Holmes, Fred. 151
Home Magazine 134
Home Relief 171, 177
Home Relief Bureau 171
Homestead Act 113
Hoover, Herbert 1, 4, 5, 15, 26, 27, 31, 36, 38, 83, 88, 96, 100, 134, 176, 201, 205, 208, 209, 217, 218, 222, 265, 299, 303, 304, 305, 307
Hoover, J. Edgar 269
Hoovervilles 83
Hopi 158
Hopkins, Harry 45, 46, 49
Hopkins, Harry L. 46, 89
House Committee on Un-American Activities 279
Howes, Elisha 281
Howes, Frederick, Captain 281
Howes, Moses, Captain 281
Hubert, B. Jay 84, 85, 86
Huggins, Miller 295
Hughes, Charles E. 219
Hull, Cordell 221, 239, 247, 305
Hunter, Lester 113, 115
hurricane of 1932 vi, 149, 299
Hurricane Relief and Rehabilitation Commission 151
Hurricane San Ciprián 155
Hushka, William J. 211

I
Ickes, Harold xii, 42, 158
I'd Rather Not Be on Relief v, 113, 114, 115, 300
Illuminating Engineering Society 118, 119
Immigration and Naturalization Service 146
imperialism 221, 239
Imperial Japan 83, 248
Indian civil service 166
Indian country 157, 158, 163, 164, 166
Indian Reorganization Act 129, 156, 158, 160, 168, 304

Indian Rights Association 167
Indian Service 157, 163, 165, 166
Indian Service administration 163
individualism 5, 8, 12, 13, 17, 27, 40, 189
Industrial Age 104
industrial capitalism 140
Industrial Revolution 8, 13, 134, 140
Industrial Workers of the World 94, 104
International Association of Machinists 122
internationalism xiii, 241, 246
International Labor Defense 180
International Workers of the World 95
intervention xiii, xix, 5, 13, 33, 36, 181, 233, 244, 250, 268
interventionist 5, 36, 45, 102
Iron Curtain 253
Iron Horse 294
isolationism xiii, 223, 225, 231, 232, 233, 241, 246, 260
isolationists 221, 245
Italianization 254
It's Up to the Women 140

J
Jackson, Andrew 265
James Crow 172
Jeffersonian principles 13
Jefferson, Thomas 13
Jim Crow 171, 194
Jim-crowing 212
Jiménez, Emilio S. 151
Judicial Procedures Reform Bill of 1937 57

K
Kanaga, Consuelo 84
karyokinesis 93, 94
Kellogg Briand Pact 220
Kellogg-Briand Pact 217, 220, 221
Kelly, Mary Jane 276
Kerr, Clark 93
Key, Francis Scott 265, 266, 268, 303, 306
Keynesian 43
Keynes, John Maynard v, xix, 38, 39, 44, 299
King, Frederick 151
King, Martin Luther, Jr., Dr. 196
King's Highway 280
King Zog I of Albania 255, 256
Kiowa 164
Kipling, Rudyard 250

Kittredge, Henry C. 281
Knights of Labor 104
Knox, Ronald 291
Kohn, Hans 190
Komitet gosudarstvennoy bezopasnosti 279
Komsomol 191
Kristallnacht 254
Ku Klux Klan 194, 196

L
Labor Action 89, 90
labor leaders xii, 48, 69
labor movement 104, 108
labor unions xiii, 104, 115, 189, 194
La Follette, Phil 188
La Follette, Robert M., Senator 17
La Guardia, Fiorello H. 294
laissez-faire 24, 38, 43, 88, 100, 176
Lakehurst Naval Air Station 275
Lange, Dorothea 278
Lansing, Robert 236
Lawrence, Richard 265
League of Nations 221, 222, 246, 256
League of Women Voters 142, 144
Legion of Youth 122
Lend-Lease Act 224
Le Sueur, Arthur 131
Le Sueur, Meridel 131, 133, 306
Lewis, John L. 105
Life 19, 108, 109, 113, 158, 168, 187, 222, 255, 257, 268, 274, 296, 299, 303, 304, 305
Lincoln, Abraham 194, 196, 279
Lindbergh, Charles vi, 259, 260, 286, 300
livestock reduction program 160, 168
Lloyd, Mary Tayloe 266
Long Broadway 85
Long Coat Lizy 85, 86
Long, Huey, Senator 17
Lou Gehrig Appreciation Day 294
Lou Gehrig's disease 294, 296
Loyalist 84

M
MacArthur, Douglas 199, 204, 205
Macbeth 286
MacDonald, Ramsay 144, 145
Machine Gun Kelly 270
Madison, James 242
Magna Carta 255

Manchukuo 218, 222
Manhattan Melodrama 270
March of Dimes 279
maturities 203
May, Claton, Dr. 273
McCardell, Lee 205, 206
McCarthy, Joe 295
McCarthy, Joseph 279
McCartney, Wilma 106
McDaniel, Eluard Luchell 83, 84, 86
McNinch, Frank R. 291
meliorism 188, 191
Mellon, Andrew 201
Memphis Commercial-Appeal 46
Mercury Theatre of the Air, The 286, 292
Mercury Theatre Players 289
Meriam Report 156, 157, 158, 161
Messrs 221
Mexican Revolution 146
Michelson, Charley 48
Michigan Women's Historical Center 105
migrant worker 113, 115
Miller, Robert L. 109, 112
Missouri Pacific Railroad 98
Mitchell, Wesley C. 89
monopolies 3, 34
Monroe, James 242
mooring-mast 276
Morales, Luis Sanchez 151
Morgan, J. P. 236
Morrison, Herbert 275, 277, 304
Morton, Pail 289
Mulligan Joe 84, 85, 86
Munich Agreement 248, 249, 254, 255
Munich Crisis 286
Munitions Investigation Committee 234, 235, 236, 237
Mussolini, Benito 57, 61, 186, 239, 248, 254, 255, 257
My Bonnie Lies Over the Ocean 90
My Day 182

N
Nagasaki 218
Napoleon 2, 256
Nation, The 179, 181
national anthem 263, 265, 266, 267, 268
National Association for the Advancement of Colored People 170, 179

Index • 315

National Broadcasting Company 36, 194
National Industrial Recovery Act 38, 104
National Labor Union 104
National Munitions Control Board 228, 231, 235
National Press Club 239, 240
National Recovery Program 92
National Socialists 248
National Woman's Party 144, 145
National Youth Administration xiii, 69, 184, 185, 186, 189, 191, 194, 195
Natural Development Association 91
Navajo 158, 160, 161, 162, 163, 168, 169, 305
Navajo Council 160
Navajo Tribal Council 168
Nazi Germany 83, 187, 221, 239, 248, 249, 254, 256, 257
Nazis 248, 250, 256, 257
Nazi-Soviet Nonaggression Pact 254
Nehlsen, Charles 275
neo-socialists 188
neutrality 215, 223, 224, 225, 227, 228, 231, 232, 233, 234, 235, 236, 237, 243, 244, 259, 260, 261, 262
Neutrality Act of 1935 215, 223, 225, 227, 231, 232, 233, 237, 299
Neutrality Act of 1936 223
Neutrality Act of 1937 223, 225
Neutrality Act of 1939 225
Neutrality Acts 223, 232, 233, 259, 260, 307
New Bedford Standard-Times 282
New Deal 6, 13, 15, 25, 26, 31, 32, 36, 37, 38, 43, 45, 48, 49, 50, 57, 64, 66, 74, 79, 81, 100, 103, 104, 109, 129, 135, 141, 174, 176, 177, 178, 187, 189, 197, 278, 279, 299, 301, 303, 305, 306, 307
New Dealers 46, 48, 279
New Masses 131
New York Daily News 287
New York Giants 295
New York Times 38, 39, 94, 181, 187, 277, 303, 304
New York Times Book Review 187
New York Yankees 294
Nicholson, Meredith 7
Nickerson, Ezra, Captain 283
Night of Broken Glass 254
Nine Power Treaty 218, 219, 220, 243
Nineteenth Amendment 134, 140, 141, 144, 145
Nobel Peace Prize 239, 247
noninterference 243
non-intervention 233, 244, 250
Norris, George W., Senator 17

North Atlantic Treaty Organization 225
Northern States Power Company 117
Nye Commission 259

O
offset 45, 53, 54, 118, 121
Okies 113, 115
Old Colony Railroad 280
Old Dartmouth Historical Society 279
Open Door 217, 218, 219, 221
Open Door policy 217, 218, 219, 221
Organization of American States 147
organized labor 6, 38, 57, 89, 104, 107, 115, 122
Owen, Ruth Bryan 136
Oxley, Howard 191

P
Pace, John T. 209, 210
pacifist 247, 261
packing the courts 57
Pact of Paris 220
Padín, Jose, Dr. 151
Paine, Sam 282
Panay 239
Panic Broadcast, The 287
Papagos 163
pari passu 167
parsimonious 136, 138
Patman, Wright 201, 205
patriotism 18, 142, 223, 227, 233
Patterson, Haywood 179
Patterson v. Alabama 180
pauper's oath 92
Pearl Harbor 215, 222, 225, 227, 232, 238, 247, 253, 257, 262, 287
Pendleton Act of 1883 75
Pennsylvania Unemployed League 89, 92
Pennsylvania Unemployed League at Pittsburgh 89
People's Institute 157, 161
Perkins, Frances 129, 135, 143, 145
pernicious 77
Philadelphia Inquirer 287
Pimas 163
Powell v. Alabama 180
Pretty Boy Floyd 269
Price, Victoria 179
Priola, Manuel 289
Problem of Indian Administration, The 156
pro-business 5, 27, 104

Producers' Exchanges 91
production-exchange association 91
Progressive Era 134, 135, 139, 140, 145, 305
Progressive Movement 104
prohibition 4, 60, 78, 137, 138, 223, 224, 225, 227, 228, 231, 232, 233, 235, 236, 237
Prohibition 6, 36, 149
Providence Journal 290
Public Enemy No. 1 269, 273, 274
Public Law 76-252 77
Public Works 71, 278
Public Works of Art Project 278
public-works program 94, 170
Pueblo 157, 161, 163
pungo 283, 284

Q
Qing dynasty 217
Quantity Theory of Money 41
Quiñones, Jose Ramón 151

R
Railroad Bill 33
ramparts 266, 267
Randolph, A. Philip 194, 196
Rank and File Committee 209, 210, 211, 212, 213
Reconstruction Corporation 21
Reconstruction Finance Corporation xi, 1, 9, 29, 211, 212
recrudescence 39, 42
Red Power movement 158
Red Scare 104
Red Wing Project 117, 120
reef 283, 284
referendum 138, 139, 162, 168, 244
relief fund 93
repatriados 146
repatriation 129, 146, 147, 148
reservation system 156, 273
Riggs, Bobby 189
Ríos, Antonio Vicens 151
Ripken, Cal, Jr. 294
RKO Pictures 287
Roaring Twenties 15, 88, 104, 109, 294
Rocking Chair Buddy 85
Roosevelt, Anna Rebecca Hall 135
Roosevelt, Eleanor v, 4, 26, 46, 50, 52, 74, 96, 103, 129, 134, 135, 139, 140, 141, 145, 182, 185, 194, 299, 301, 303, 305, 306, 307

Roosevelt, Elliot Bulloch 135
Roosevelt, Franklin D. v, xi, xiv, 1, 2, 4, 5, 27, 31, 37, 38, 39, 45, 49, 51, 54, 56, 57, 65, 66, 74, 79, 83, 87, 88, 100, 104, 107, 109, 117, 125, 156, 157, 161, 170, 176, 182, 186, 189, 194, 197, 208, 221, 223, 225, 227, 233, 299, 301, 303, 304, 305, 306, 307
Roosevelt-Ickes Indian policy 166
Roosevelt, Theodore 6, 9, 32, 34, 75, 134, 135, 141
Rosaly, P. J. 151
Rothstein, Arthur 278
Roy, Tekla 106
rule of reason 9, 241
Ruppert, Jacob 295
Rural Electrification Administration 117, 120, 307
Rural Electrification News 117, 119
Russian Revolution 252
Russo-Japanese War 217
Ruth, Babe 294

S
Sacco-Vanzetti case 285
Sage, Anna 269
Salt, Augusta 273
San Ciprián 149, 150, 153, 154, 155, 307
San Diego County Board of Supervisors 146
Scearce, Ralph 118
Scearce, Rose Dudley 117, 118, 119
Scottsboro Boys 179, 180, 181, 303
Scribner's 187
scrip 88, 91, 94, 95
Scripps-Howard 46, 48, 49
Seal Goodstuff 85
Sears, Ebenezer 281
Sears, Stephen 281
Seattle Labor College 88
seclusionist 245
Second Sino-Japanese War 257
securities 22, 29, 35, 69, 203
segregated 167, 170, 171, 173, 174
self-help leagues 91
self-help movement 93
Senate Munitions Investigation Committee 237
Senator Gerald Nye 259
Seventy-fourth United States Congress 223
Seventy-fourth US Congress 227
Seventy-sixth Congress 76
Shadow, The 286
Shafter Farm Labor Camp 113, 115
Shahn, Ben 278

Shandong Province 217
shantytowns 99, 278
Shaw, Anna, Dr. 141
Sheppard, Lucile Sanderson 224
Sheppard, Morris 224
Shipmasters of Cape Cod 281
Shoal Hope 282
Siaca, R. Arjona 151
sit-down v, 104, 299
Slicker Fastblack 85
Smith, John Stafford 265, 266
Smoot-Hawley Tariff Act 15, 225
Smoot, Reed 201, 202, 299
socialism 18, 74, 107, 118, 192
Socialist 5, 91, 105, 106, 107, 210
Socialist Workers Party 105
Social Security 51, 52, 54, 55, 56, 81, 129, 189, 228, 299, 303
Soil Erosion Service 162
sordid 195, 196
Souvestre, Marie 141
Soviet Union xiii, 38, 43, 93, 191, 247, 254, 257, 279
Spanish-American War 201, 224
Spanish Civil War 239, 248, 259
Spark, Welton Walter 270
square-rigger 284
Stanton, Elizabeth Cady 141
Star-Spangled Banner, The 263, 265, 266, 268, 299
Steinbeck, John 278
Stember, Samuel 209
Sterling, Margaret 187
stern sheets 283, 284
Stimson Doctrine 218, 222
Stimson, Henry L. 217
St. Louis Cardinals 295
stock market crash 1, 5, 15, 27, 51, 66, 81, 83, 104, 146, 178, 182, 269, 286
Stodelle, Ernestine 187
subsistence homestead 47, 48, 49, 165
Sudetenland 248, 254
suffrage 134, 144, 189, 195
Sugar Butt Sam 85, 86
Survey Associates 186
Survey Graphic 91, 93, 95, 160, 168, 186, 191
Survey Midmonthly 186
Sutherland, Alexander George 59, 63

T
Taft, William Howard 218
Tammany Hall 6
Taylor, Paul S. 93
Technical Board on Economic Security 52
technocratic 94
tenement 136
Tennessee Valley 3, 36, 45, 46, 49, 50, 299
Tennessee Valley Authority 47, 49
Thomas, Thomas, Reverend 289
Thompson, Malvina 185
Three Mexican Tales 147
Tierra mojada 147
Todd, R. H. 151
Toronto Globe 287
Toronto Star 287
totalitarianism 248, 250, 252, 253, 257
treasury issues 42
Treaty of Portsmouth 217
Treger, Lawrence 289
Tres cuentos mexicanos 147
tribal council 156, 160, 162, 163, 168
tribal council system 156, 160, 168
True Confessions 270
True Romance 270
Truman, Harry 16
trust busting 9
Tugwell, Rexford 48, 49
Turnabout Years, The 187
Twentieth Amendment 221
Twenty-One Demands 217

U
Unemployed Citizens' League 88
unemployed league 89
unemployed unions 93, 94
unemployment compensation 51, 53, 54, 55
unemployment insurance 5, 94
Uniform Code of Military Justice 267
union 84, 94, 104, 106, 107, 108, 137, 188, 191, 194, 196, 251
unionism 93, 94, 105
United Auto Workers 104, 105
United Brotherhood of Sleeping Car Porters 196
United Mine Workers 105, 107
United Nations 135, 141, 224, 225, 239, 247
United States Employment Service 184, 185
United States Food Administration 202
United States Housing Authority 70
United We Eat v, 88, 299
US Code (36, section 301) 267

US Food Administration 28
USS *Akron* 275
US War Labor Board 89
Utah League 91

V
Vandenberg, Arthur 201
Van Devanter, Willis 60
vauntingly 267, 268
Veblen-Commons Award 89
Versailles Treaty 254
Veterans Central Rank and File Committee 209, 212
Veterans of Foreign Wars 201, 204, 207, 214, 306
vicissitudes 52, 54
Vietnam War 105

W
Wall Street 121, 187, 211
Wall Street crash 121
Wall Street Journal 187
Walsh, Thomas J. 59
Wandall, Luther C. 170
warn out 280, 284
War of 1812 265
War of the Worlds, The 263, 286, 287, 289, 291, 292, 293, 300, 304
war on crime 269
War on Terror 252, 257
Washington, Booker T. 195
Washington Conference 219, 220, 221
Washington, George 4, 26, 50, 60, 74, 96, 103, 195, 234, 305, 307
Washington Naval Treaty 217, 221
Waters, Walter 213
Waters, Walter W. 205
welfare 7, 12, 21, 46, 52, 55, 67, 81, 92, 95, 122, 138, 150, 163, 182, 186, 203, 211, 220, 240, 241, 244, 260
Welfare Committee 147
Welles, Orson 263, 286, 287, 288, 289, 291, 292
Wells, H. G. 286, 289, 290, 291, 292
Wells, Ira K. 151
Welty, Eudora 278
Wet Soil 147
Wharton, Marian 131
Wharton, William 131

What does American democracy mean to me? 194, 195, 196
What Ten Million Women Want 134, 138, 139, 299
Wheeler, Burton K. 57, 64, 65, 307
Wheeler-Howard Act 156, 157, 158, 160, 168
Willkie, Wendell 260
Wilsonian world view 261
Wilson, Woodrow 2, 6, 9, 16, 28, 32, 67, 223, 227, 233, 237, 259, 265
Women of Courage 46
Women on the Breadlines v, 131, 132, 133, 299
Women's Auxiliary 105, 106, 107, 108
Women's Emergency Brigade 105
women's suffrage 144
Workers Ex-Servicemen's League 209
Work Relief 71
Works Progress Administration xii, xiii, 52, 66, 69, 75, 81, 113, 186, 191, 278
World Series 265
World War Adjusted Compensation Act 201, 205
World War I 1, 4, 16, 26, 28, 31, 109, 149, 199, 201, 202, 205, 209, 213, 217, 221, 223, 224, 225, 227, 233, 234, 237, 239, 246, 248, 249, 252, 254, 255, 257, 259, 275, 276
World War II 2, 4, 6, 16, 32, 37, 43, 52, 67, 74, 83, 95, 116, 148, 196, 202, 206, 208, 217, 218, 222, 225, 227, 232, 238, 239, 247, 249, 252, 254, 257, 259, 260, 276, 294, 296, 304, 305, 307
Worster, Donald 97
Wright, Andy 179, 180
Wright, Roy 179
writ of Habeas Corpus 255, 257

Y
Yale Record 187
Yankee Stadium 295
Young, Owen D. 20
Young Women's Christian Association 132
youth crisis 186
Youth Goes Round and Round 191
Youth Tell Their Story 189

Z
zeppelins 275, 277, 305